MEMORIES OF EMPIRE, VOLUME I

MEMORIES
OF
EMPIRE,
VOLUME I

THE WHITE MAN'S WORLD

BILL SCHWARZ

OXFORD
UNIVERSITY PRESS

OXFORD
UNIVERSITY PRESS

Great Clarendon Street, Oxford OX2 6DP

Oxford University Press is a department of the University of Oxford.
It furthers the University's objective of excellence in research, scholarship,
and education by publishing worldwide in

Oxford New York

Auckland Cape Town Dar es Salaam Hong Kong Karachi
Kuala Lumpur Madrid Melbourne Mexico City Nairobi
New Delhi Shanghai Taipei Toronto

With offices in

Argentina Austria Brazil Chile Czech Republic France Greece
Guatemala Hungary Italy Japan Poland Portugal Singapore
South Korea Switzerland Thailand Turkey Ukraine Vietnam

Oxford is a registered trade mark of Oxford University Press
in the UK and in certain other countries

Published in the United States
by Oxford University Press Inc., New York

British Library Cataloguing in Publication Data

Data available

Library of Congress Cataloguing in Publication Data

Data available

Typeset by SPI Publisher Services, Pondicherry, India
Printed in Great Britain
on acid-free paper by
MPG Books Group, Bodmin and King's Lynn

ISBN 978–0–19–929691–0

10 9 8 7 6 5 4 3 2 1

For
Sarah

Contents

Acknowledgements

For long it's been recognized that the printed book can function as an important medium in the formation of imagined communities. While this is true, books are also the outcome of specifically knowable communities and they are read, in part, by knowable communities. They are, amongst other things, testaments to friendships and to the very real—very knowable—relationships with others. In writing this first part of *Memories of Empire* I've all the while been conscious of the knowable community which has made the book possible. It's the product of scores of conversations without which it could have never have existed. Of the various pleasures I've experienced in writing it I suspect that the most significant have been the evolving friendships which have accompanied its production. Indeed I was frequently taken aback to discover that a number of people close to me seemed more concerned about the progress of these volumes than I was. Although I was always moved by the solicitous enquiries I received, I have never been convinced that the finished manuscript would warrant their level of concern. But about the generosity which prompted their enquiries I have no doubts.

My first encounters with history at university were with Gwyn A.Williams (or Gwyn Alf, as he came to be known in deference to mythic memories of Saxon democracy) and these will always stay with me. So too will the intellectual discoveries I experienced as a graduate student at the Centre for Contemporary Cultural Studies at Birmingham in the 1970s. Since then, I've had the good fortune to work in institutions in which I've learnt much from colleagues and students: in the Department of Sociology at Warwick University; in the Department of Cultural Studies at the University of East London; in the Department of Media and Communications at Goldsmiths College; and currently in the School of English and Drama at Queen Mary, University of London. It's been a pleasure to have visited regularly, and taught at, the Department of History at the University of Michigan, and I realize only now, as I come to the end of this project, just how many of these chapters I first explored publicly at Michigan. I recall everyone there with great affection. For more than twenty years I have had one kind of home in *History Workshop Journal* and, for a little more than half that time, another in *New Formations*. Each has provided me with incomparable intellectual stimulus. Many of the conceptual questions I explore in these volumes derive from my experiences of participating in these particular environments as much as they do from the discipline of history, narrowly conceived. That for the great bulk of my working life I've been located at some distance from professional historians is reflected in what I write, and how I write. There have been times when this has worried me, for it is a historical issue—the connections between the colonial past and the postcolonial present—which lies at the heart of these volumes. But there are many ways such a question can be approached, combining varying commitments to theoretical and empirical explanation. Inevitably, I have made certain methodological decisions. I've chosen to cover a lot of ground in a relatively little space, often at what I think of as an intermediate level of analysis between the abstract and the concrete. I think these decisions valid. Whether they are in fact convincing in conception, or in their execution, others will judge.

Chapter 4 originally appeared in Andrea Bosco and Alex May (eds.), *The Round Table: The Empire/Commonwealth and British Foreign Policy* (London: Lothian Foundation Press, 1997). A revised version is reproduced here with thanks to the Lothian Foundation and, particularly, to Alex May. Extracts from Chapter 5 appeared in different form in Becky Conekin, Frank Mort, and Chris Waters (eds.), *Moments of Modernity: Reconstructing Britain, 1945–1964* (London: Rivers Oram Press, 1999), and are reproduced here with permission from the publisher.

Many years ago Lord Amery, Sir John Biggs-Davison, Cedric Gunnery of the Monday Club, Lord Home, Lord Molson, Enoch Powell, and Sir Peregrine Worsthorne, amongst others, made time to talk with me about the history of British Conservatism and I thank them. My interests then were less about empire, though readers will see how one or two of these exchanges, in particular, came to shape the conceptual questions I address here.

I thank, too, friends and colleagues who have influenced my writing of the manuscript more than any of them will ever know: David Albury, Claudia Alvares, Charlotte Brunsdon, Chris Campbell, Mary Chamberlain, Phil Cohen, Graham Dawson, Andrew Gamble, Christine Geraghty, Simon

Gikandi, Rachael Gilmour, Julian Henriques, Barnor Hesse, Kali Israel, Richard Johnson, Cora Kaplan, David Killingray, Mary Langan, Javed Majeed, John Marriott, Frank Mort, Mica Nava, Sean Nixon, Heather Nunn, Pete Osborne, Catalina Palma, Alice Ritscherle, Jacqueline Rose, Michael Rustin, Camilla Schofield, Gareth Stanton, Stuart Ward, Carol Watts, Helen Williams, and Sally Wyatt. Richard Smith gave great help in searching out many leads, and in numerous other ways too.

Much of my thinking about postcolonial history has been shaped by the controversies which in recent years have gripped public life in Australia. In fact I'm surprised, as things have turned out, that readers will see relatively little evidence of this in any of the three volumes. Paul Pickering commented on the portion that does appear, to great effect. Long ago Gillian Swanson arranged a short fellowship for me in the School of Cultural and Historical Studies at Griffith University, for which I shall be eternally grateful; she and Colin Mercer provided a wonderful initial welcome to Australia. Subsequently I have spent many hours in conversation with Bain Attwood, Judy Brett, Paula Hamilton, and Marilyn Lake, from whom I have begun to learn about the complex politics of historical debate in Australia, as well as about history more generally. Due to the intervention of Kate Darian-Smith, Director of the Australian Studies Centre at the University of Melbourne, I was able to attend the fourth in the series of the British World conferences held at the university and to spend a period in the Centre, which proved a rich experience.

The British World conferences, beginning in London in 1998, came at a good time for me, allowing me immediate access to the current findings of the imperial historians. I am grateful to the conference organizers, and to the British Academy who funded my journey to Cape Town in 2002, for the second in the ongoing series. On that occasion Bill Nasson proved a sterling host. I would like to thank Saul Dubow and the late Stanley Trapido, each of whom encouraged my first excursions into the history of Southern Africa.

I have incurred many debts to specialists in Caribbean history. These will be acknowledged in the second volume, where I address West Indian perspectives on the colonial situation.

Donal Lowry and Philip Murphy offered extensive observations on my chapters on the Central African Federation and on Rhodesia, and I am grateful to them both, as I am to Mark Garnett. As I was preparing the manuscript for publication Geoff Eley, in an act of selfless Stakhanovism, read almost the entire draft of this first part at breakneck speed, marshalling a response which allowed me to see how most effectively to complete the book. Catherine Hall and Wendy Webster also provided last-minute commentaries which proved extraordinarily helpful. Ruth Parr, late of Oxford University Press, commissioned the volumes and the enthusiasm she displayed was what every author wishes. I am saddened that she left the Press before the books were published. At OUP Christopher Wheeler, Rupert Cousens, Seth Cayley, and Stephanie Ireland all demonstrated consistent good grace and efficiency editorially, and I thank them all, as I do Jane Robson, Hayley Buckley, and Emma Barber as regards production.

I am particularly indebted to two scholars whose investigations into the continuing domestic consequences of the end of the British empire have for long overlapped with my own: Stephen Howe and Wendy Webster. Although we have only seldom worked together, I think of them—mostly from afar—as close collaborators. Sonya Rose over the years has read much of the volume and has proved a warm and thoughtful interlocutor. Susannah Radstone, with whom I've been working on an allied project, guided me through the ever-more labyrinthine debates on memory. Lynne Segal has been a vital and happily close neighbourly presence. Neil Belton and Dave Morley gave encouragement and true friendship over a long period. The influence of Stuart Hall, who slips into these volumes as a historical actor in his own right, is present on every page. Although he is no historian of empire, his capacities to understand the impact of the historical past—particularly the colonial past—on the political present have been of incomparable importance to me. Until recently I had spent nearly all my professional life working with, or adjacent to, Sally Alexander: when this proximity came to an end I experienced a great loss. For many years we had, in the interstices of institutional life, talked about friends and families and, with equal passion, about history. I'm sure that many of her insights appear here without my even realizing that they are hers. I've worked for almost as long with, and known for longer, Catherine Hall, who has read many drafts, and whose understanding of the workings of empire has been decisive for me. She is a generous intellectual and, above all, an inspiration. I owe her much.

When I was writing the manuscript I most often had in mind two of my oldest friends, James and Gregor, each an exemplar of good faith in hard times. I doubt that people who know them, or they themselves, would be able to detect their influence in the arguments which I present in this or in the succeeding volumes. But therein, perhaps, lies the virtue and mystery of friendship.

My gratitude to Sarah, Hannah, Henry, and Jamie runs deepest of all. This needs to be acknowledged here, although there is always so much more to say. In the meantime this first instalment—notwithstanding the fact that a rumination on the properties of the white man will do little to cheer her—is for Sarah.

He explained it at length. There was a shadow king who did whatever a king should do. It was the shadow king who went to parades, took the salute and did those things with which we associated the king. The shadow king was part of the English tradition. The English, the boy said, were fond of shadows. They never did anything in the open. Everything was done in the shadow, and even the king, the greatest of them, worked through his shadow. Somebody asked if you were ever talking to a real man or a shadow when you talked to an Englishman, and the boy said yes. Some of them were the man and the shadow at the same time, but more shadow than man. But you had to be careful when you had anything to do with English people. It was always difficult to distinguish between the man and the shadow, and sometimes it was all shadow. The man got lost somehow and nothing remained but the shadow.

(George Lamming, *In the Castle of my Skin*, 1953)

Introduction

'The Thing'

Some impression of the event must have been left inside me. Where is it now?

(Freud to Wilhelm Fleiss, 15 October 1897[1])

'Yes, that's what strikes me,' he said, rousing himself to help her, 'how you've spoilt England while I've been away.'

(Virginia Woolf, *The Years*, 1937[2])

Long ago, on a spring evening in 1988, I found myself walking along the smart streets of Belgravia in London's West End heading toward South Eaton Place in order to interview Enoch Powell. My purpose was to put to him certain questions about the history of British Conservatism. It was almost exactly twenty years since his savage Birmingham speech denouncing black immigration, and he and his prophecies about race in Britain had recently been much in the news. I can't recollect with any clarity my thoughts at the time. Certainly, I was anxious. I had, by this time, conducted a number of interviews with Tories of Powell's generation. For the most part these had gone fine. Some were revealing, some not. In the first instance—until I tired of them—they were always of ethnographic interest. With one exception (a man of a marxisant past, long since disavowed), the figures I interviewed were consistently courteous. Yet even before a word was spoken they knew, to borrow the formulation of the times, that I was not 'one of them'. I wrote to each of them from my institutional location, the Polytechnic of East London, an establishment not intimately known to the apostles of high Toryism. My suit, for which I'd developed an inexplicable fondness, I had bought expressly for the purpose of the meetings; it was the cheapest I could find on the rails of Oxford Street's Mr Byrite, imported from Portugal. I suspect its sartorial shortcomings were conspicuous. None of this appeared to disturb the susceptibilities of those whom I interviewed. My own political positions remained uninterrogated, and differences between them and me hedged around. In a peculiarly English manner, rules of engagement were observed on both sides. The closest I came to being quizzed about my own commitments was when an affable William Whitelaw enquired whether I was a voter. When I assured him that I was he gave every impression that he was as pleased as Punch, remaining far too respectful of the ethic of British constitutionalism to pry further. I chose not to disclose the fact that the last vote I'd cast, in a local election, had been for our neighbourhood *halal* butcher—a man who subsequently turned out to be, I fear, far to the right of Viscount Whitelaw.

The Powell occasion was different. I had invested in new footwear, a pair of brogues which proved so ill-fitting that little droplets of blood seeped through the leather. I took with me an ancient, cumbersome, reel-to-reel tape-recorder which I knew was going to tax my ingenuity. But most of all Powell had engendered in an entire political generation fierce, unremitting enmity. As I approached his home I couldn't help but question the wisdom of what I was about to do.

In the event all seemed to pass smoothly. I had done a serious amount of work, and the more Powell appreciated this the readier he was to talk. Most of what we discussed has little bearing on the pages which follow. A number of his answers helped clarify for me specific puzzles I had about Conservatism in its domestic, British modes. He was helpful in a number of ways, and offered me a copy of a talk he had recently given. There were, though, surprises. When I asked him about the political dimensions of the ending of his friendship with Iain Macleod he paused for a long while, admitted that Macleod had been the only person in politics to have hurt him, and then ventured the idea that such issues turned not only on the interaction between personality and politics, but encompassed too the question of 'men's bodies'.[3] This opened a line of enquiry I hadn't anticipated, and I found myself having to draw breath and muster alternative questions at short notice. I had no intention of pressing him about his Birmingham speech, as I was sure nothing new would be revealed. He had, in any case, recently made his own position clear, seeing no cause for retraction. 'Re-read after twenty years', he had stated, 'I am struck by its sobriety.'[4] But I was keen to know more about the circumstances of the occasion in Northfield, in June 1970, when he had dilated on the dangers deriving from varied enemies within, announcing to his audience that they were witnessing the end of the nation.

He explained that at the end of the 1960s he had opened a file which he called 'The Thing'. In it he had recorded all the examples of subversion that he encountered, prompted in the first instance by the vision of student unrest. The drama of the universities he believed to be part of a wider and deeper disorder, evident in many different guises. What had panicked Powell, impelling him to make a start on the file, was the amorphous nature of this subversion. These were acts which occurred within civil society more often than they did in political society, conventionally understood, and they were generally cultural or symbolic in form. In themselves they were likely to be of rather minor significance: instances of disrespect, perhaps, or insolence, to use a favoured word, indicating that inherited social hierarchies had slipped out of place. He explained that as a high Tory he had come to be mesmerized by the confrontation with what he perceived to be an elemental anarchy. 'I was fascinated', he confessed, 'by this engine for the destruction of authority.' Cumulatively, Powell believed, these everyday acts of insubordination threatened the very existence of civilized life and, at home, the very existence of the nation. Yet he was disturbed by the fact that what he understood to be the unravelling of England proved, in practice, to be a curiously low-key affair. The very ephemera of its dramas, Powell implied, produced a strange invisibility, such that the deepest consequences of each moment of subversion—of each rupture in the social fabric—could not be divined for what it truly was. These perplexed musings took him back to Edmund Burke, and to Burke's famous call for unceasing political vigilance. From these years, especially, Powell took it upon himself to speak out, enlisted by the ghost of Burke. The forces of subversion gathered in close, multiplying at every turn.[5]

During the years of his prominence it was commonplace to hear everyday observers—callers to radio phone-ins, partisans in pub discussions or in exchanges on public transport, students in class: what might be called the non-professional participants in the public sphere—insist on Mr Powell's intelligence. From this derived his aura, an aura that made him a very unusual sort of celebrity and which was part and parcel of the deference accorded to him. On the question of Powell's intelligence, once a matter of unending disputation, I'm happy to remain agnostic. As I see it, there is no reason to suppose him any more or any less intelligent than the bulk of his political colleagues. But I'm sure, whatever else he was, that he was also an intellectual. He was interested in ideas, in where they came from and how they came alive and shaped the public life of a nation. In talking of his own life he would frequently reconstruct his past as an intellectual history, alighting upon dramatic moments when new ideas possessed him. This way of thinking separated him from many of the politicians with whom he worked. And in contrast to the other Conservatives I'd interviewed Powell, it transpired, proved curious about my own motivations. At the end of the interview, as I was laboriously packing up my tape-recorder, he asked me about my political allegiances. I could have dissembled, and maybe I should have. In the event, though, I didn't. With perhaps a shade too much brio I informed him that my sympathies were close to those of the subversives whom he had been monitoring. I was to be numbered amongst 'The Thing'. At that point, notwithstanding the fact that—on the face of it at least—I'd simply answered the question he had put to me, the terms of our encounter instantly shifted, leaving my own position exposed. Right at the last minute too much had been spoken. Powell's countenance turned dark, formalities ceased, and I was speedily bundled out onto the street.

My ejection I could understand. But in the intervening years I came to wonder why Powell had been unable to name the disorder he saw all about him. Signs of it were evident everywhere he looked, but it remained impossible for him to identify or to name what he could feel. It was a crisis, for all its potency, marked by its invisibility. There seemed something uncanny about this disorder, as if it were simultaneously present and absent, real and unreal. Neither its namelessness nor its invisibility prevented him, and others like him, from speaking out about it at every opportunity. Indeed this crisis so affected those caught in its spell that it generated great torrents of excitable speech. But in Powell's case, certainly, no amount of reflection appeared to bring him nearer a resolution. The exact form of the crisis remained an enigma. Why should this be so? What was 'The Thing', and what did it represent?

One of my aims in these volumes is to do what Powell, and many others, found themselves incapable of doing: to identify and name the disorder they perceived but could not grasp. My own view is that in this disorder, or in this perception of disorder, we can discern the political-cultural effects of the end of empire 'at home', in the domestic society itself. The same phenomenon registers too in the startling, highly charged manifestations of popular support for Powell in the aftermath of his Birmingham speech of 1968. Empire was never an entirely external process to Britain, and nor was decolonization.[6]

Yet it must be clear that the relations between the many-faceted processes of decolonization, on the one hand, and the domestic popular movement of Powellism, on the other, are, as we would expect, complex. Each operated according to different historical times, and even now each seems (at first glance) to occupy distinct cognitive worlds. There was no one-to-one correspondence between them, and many displacements occurred. Part of the difficulty in thinking this through, however, derives from the assumption that decolonization couldn't really possess a life that significantly shaped the domestic culture. If we conceive of decolonization to comprise principally the comings and goings of assorted mandarins at Lancaster House, bargaining with colonial leaders about the details involved in the transfer of power, then this must have some validity. But if decolonization is understood in more expansive terms, as representing the closing of a very long history of imperial relations in which all domestic Britons were situated, then the question looks strikingly different. Following the epigraph from Freud above, I am inclined to think that 'some impression' of this long history must have been present in the body politic when the empire came to an end. But how these traces can be located, and how we will know them when we see them, create many difficulties.

If it is hard to get a perspective on this problem, even indeed to know where to look, it is not only because of the complexities involved but also because it is a history we're still living. Its power to organize the present is not yet finished. It is this complex set of issues, I suggest, that analysis of the Powellite moment illuminates.

By the time of Powell's speech in Birmingham in 1968 the formal empire of the British had, bar a few vestiges, come to an end. It had become, far more rapidly than anyone had anticipated, the past. Henceforth it could only exist in memory. Few caught up in the Powellite turmoil of 1968 could have had a contemporaneous experience of empire. If their experiences were at all shaped by empire, this could only have happened through the medium of memory. That this poses many challenges for historical method is undeniable. Yet this is the crux of my argument. Memories of the colonial past in this period are of great significance. They constituted an active, combustible element in the Powellite moment. If we can grasp how these memories worked we may also be able to explain the ferocity of emotion that was unleashed at the height of the crisis, in 1968 and after. We need, so far as this is possible, to enter this mental world.

Powell himself, in his earlier life, had been militant in his enthusiasm for the British empire. By 1968 he had long jettisoned these early affiliations, having arrived at the conclusion that the empire had represented nothing more than a detour from the essentials of what constituted the true national history. Decolonization, from this perspective, afforded the opportunity for a more profound, revivified patriotism to emerge. Yet at the same time he continued to imagine postcolonial England (if that is what it was) from the vantage of a man for whom the precepts of colonial order remained the natural order of things. Despite the faith he held in the powers of his own intellect, this for Powell was a conviction he never chose to question. Indeed, for him it was the kind of conviction, residing deep in the self, which *couldn't* be questioned. This I take to be an instance of his acting out the reflexes of times past. In a real—psychic—sense he was inhabiting the present as if it were the colonial past. Even with the empire gone and with his own insistence that this was so, the sensibilities of colonial life continued to exert their power over him. There were occasions when he admitted as much. But for the most part, in his later political career, he saw no reason to talk about empire. It was for him an event better forgotten. In this respect Powell was representative of a generation which, as the empire neared its end, found that they encountered many inhibitions in speaking about the imperial past. This wasn't a personal idiosyncrasy, or not only that, but a recurring feature of the larger public culture. It was better to forget.

Yet this highlights the conceptual problems which memory itself, as an object of study, presents. It might look as if I am proposing two contrary arguments. On the one hand I'm suggesting that there was an element of the public culture in which the imperial past could not be spoken, and where the imperative to forget predominated. On the other, I'm emphasizing the simultaneous salience of memories of empire in the mentalities of Powellism. The contradiction, however, is only apparent. Memory and forgetting are not separate practices, but are interlinked, the one a function of the other. There is never one without the other. But we also need to distinguish, in this case, between *a desire* to forget and *an inability* to forget.

To say that there were aspects of the past which could not be spoken refers as much to a social prohibition as to what we conventionally think of as forgetfulness. The speed of social transformation from, say, 1955 (the time

of Winston Churchill and Sir Anthony Eden) to 1965 (Harold Wilson) was
staggering. In 1955 the values of empire could still be justified by national
figures in public life as they were, unadorned, without qualification, embarrassment, or anxiety. Ten years later after decolonization itself had gathered
pace, and after the intervention of pop culture, rock music, angry young
men, satire, such explicit paeans to empire were considerably harder to hold
in place. Generation was a decisive factor, the generation born during or
after the war possessing a markedly different relation to empire from their
parents and grandparents. When, for example, the Beatles were awarded
their MBEs in 1965, this formally marked an imperial-state occasion, for the
group were officially recognized as Members of the British Empire. This
caused predictable outrage amongst correspondents to the conservative
press, with much spleen vented and ink spilled. On 14 June Hector Dupuis,
a former Liberal MP in the Canadian parliament, announced that he was
returning his OBE, followed by C.V. Hearn of Egham, Captain David Evan
Rees of Cardiff, George Read of North Devon, and James Berg of Bagshot.
But the significance of the event lies in the fact that from June, when the
news was announced, until October, when the Queen conferred the honours at Buckingham Palace, the Beatles played the entire theatrics of the
occasion for high farce, and did so with flair. The government, the bulk of
the media, and maybe even the monarch herself were all complicit in this.
The laughter only stopped four years later when John Lennon returned his
medal to the Palace, motivated in part by conventional anti-colonial commitments.[7] By the time the award occurred, or thereabouts, those who
identified with the imperial past could no longer rely upon their cultural
dominance in the public life of the nation. Their words no longer carried a
natural authority and increasingly they found themselves facing derision,
their espousal of imperial values regarded as anachronistic or eccentric. With
great speed, the empire had become the past, not only chronologically but
politically and socially.

This isn't to suppose, though, that the empire simply disappeared from
view, and ceased to have any role in the iconography of the national community. The rituals surrounding the monarchy, for example, continued to
be significant, though the focus was shifting from the imperial aura of the
crown to the private lives of the royal family. The funeral of Sir Winston
Churchill, in the same year that the Beatles were honoured, was projected
as an epic event in the history of the nation-empire, although it might also
be understood as the final occasion when remembrance of this kind proved

possible. The power of such ceremony was waning, and the generational divide widening. As the Labour cabinet minister, Richard Crossman, observed of Churchill's funeral, 'It felt like the end of an epoch, possibly even the end of a nation.'[8] Symbols of the imperial past increasingly appeared as a matter for satire or comedy, or they became subject to a jokey commercialization. Public manifestations of empire were conspicuous. But by the time of Powell, in the late 1960s, they were most frequently articulated *as if they were of no consequence* for contemporary metropolitan life. There are many examples, but we can continue the theme. On Peter Blake's inspirational cover for the Beatles's *Sgt Pepper* album, released in June 1967, the four Beatles themselves were dressed to look like day-glo reincarnations of old-time colonial governors, sporting various imperial insignia including, in the case of Paul and George, their MBEs. The legends of empire, T. E. Lawrence and David Livingstone, joined them, as did Sir Robert Peel, who appeared just below Mae West.[9] This was popular art as politics as well as humour, for in intermixing the esteemed with the profane it championed a demotic, vernacular sensibility against the forces of inherited social hierarchy. But this wasn't a politics, in the 1960s, which could countenance a history of imperial times as if it mattered to those living in the present. On the contrary it depicted the empire as a past to run from.

This represents a historical moment driven not by oblivion, in which nothing could be recalled, but rather by a partial, selective forgetfulness. It marked a denial about the efficacy of the past. While recognizing the fact of empire, it allowed no way of imagining the means by which the imperial past might ever infiltrate the present. Those—in more cerebral manner—who believed that the time had come when the empire was better forgotten lived by the same prescriptions. They themselves had not *forgotten* the imperial past. They too wished that they might forget, but the memory remained.

It is not easy for historians to chart these subtle, shifting conjunctions of remembering-forgetting—'forms of remembrance,' as Jacqueline Rose writes, 'which hover in the space between social and psychic history'—or to get the full measure of what is not, or cannot, be spoken.[10] But if it is the case that there were in the national culture certain inhibitions about engaging with the imperial past, then there is the possibility that what couldn't be spoken in one sphere of the society would appear elsewhere in the social landscape, transformed, elliptical, perhaps not even fully conscious, but none the less meaningful, and attesting to the pasts which couldn't otherwise be spoken.[11] Here we confront not the wish to forget, but the impossibility of forgetting. This is what occurs in the popular eruption of Powellism.

Ideologues of the emergent New Right of the late 1960s and the 1970s, Powell included, spent their time telling themselves and others that the nation had journeyed from a state of order to a state of disorder.[12] In this lay their *raison d'être*. To rectify this disorder they became evangelicals for the new creed of law and order, which they imagined would put right the various dysfunctions which were stalking the nation. If we take them at their word we encounter a historical sequence composed of three movements. We begin with an initial situation of social—colonial—order, move through the disturbances brought about by practitioners of subversion, and close with the endeavour to impose, in heavily accentuated form, a new system of law and order. But this does not conform to any determinate historical reality. To think in these terms conceals the fact that neither order nor disorder is a category open to final empirical verification. In their New Right usage these categorizations were products of a specific political investment, predicated on extravagant fears of social collapse, in which judgement was wayward. Order and disorder were as much fantasies as they were given realities. Order, in this sense, is always a quality peculiar to the past, to life 'a generation ago', rather than to the present.[13] More particularly, for Powell and others order was inextricably tied to the colonial past. Order in other words is crucially part memory, a phenomenon necessarily prompted by the exigencies of the present. With this in mind we need to amend the given sequence of events, as proposed by Powell and the New Right. During these years, all originates with the perception of disorder. The idea of order *follows* from this perception, and is governed by it. Memories of the ordered past are thus the consequence of the experience of disorder. And like all memories they are organized in the present.

These memories of an ordered past, in the 1960s and 1970s, I argue, were driven by a powerful, if displaced, recollection of forms of authority which had been deeply shaped by the experience of empire. But why was this so? Why should memories of *this* past have become pressing just as the empire was ending?

As we might expect with Powell, much turns on race. In race lies the link between the end of empire and Powellism for, as I hope to show, to remember the colonial past was to remember race through its peculiarly British idioms. Colonial societies work through race. The conception of civilization which was diffused by the British throughout the many lands of their empire—dominions, colonies, mandates, protectorates—was, for all its liberality, one that was racialized. Yet if the colonies worked through race then, by extension, so did the metropole. There were, as I describe in this volume, many opportunities for Britons in the metropole to imagine themselves as white. Racial whiteness, I argue, played a critical role in empire, both in colony and metropole. The traffic between Britain and its overseas territories was always heavy. People, goods, and stories constantly circulated between the imperial centre and its peripheries. The imagined geographies of empire, particularly of the white settler societies, operated close to home. From the late nineteenth century especially a plethora of organizations encouraged domestic Britons to become participants of empire, such that they would learn to narrate their own lives as imperial men, women, and children. Identifying oneself as white functioned as the precondition for these narrative acts. This needs to be emphasized. It was something that Powell himself came to learn early on in his life. Yet having said this, whiteness in the metropole was most often a relatively mediated, understated identification, much to the consternation of those of proconsular disposition, aggrieved that the Britons who lived at the centre never sought the racial prowess of their British cousins on the frontier. Natives, generally, were a long way away. Nearly everyone—friends, neighbours—looked much the same. For the most part whiteness rarely needed to be made explicit. Its modes of transmission went largely unnoticed, as white was the norm. It was perhaps most effective in informing Britons who they were not.

With the coming of numbers of non-white migrants into Britain, what previously had principally been mediated and understated came—in circumstances of perceived crisis—to be experienced as more real, more urgent. Whiteness became a more intensely immediate phenomenon, sustained and given life by a strange brew of memories of the colonial past. As decolonization progressed, black migration to the metropole functioned as the trigger which released and organized new memories of empire.

In 1968 the influential anthropologist, W. E. H. Stanner, delivered the annual Boyer lectures for the Australian Broadcasting Corporation, Australia's equivalent of Britain's Reith lectures. He set out to imagine what 'a less ethnocentric social history' of Australia would look like. In the course of his argument he addressed the question of what he called 'The great Australian silence', by which he meant white forgetfulness about the role of the Aboriginal peoples in the continent's history. He believed this forgetfulness to have been systematic, and—through unspoken agreement—to have been socially sanctioned. But he was not convinced that a silence of this sort, however systematic, was immune to change. What once was unspeakable, he claimed, could under new conditions again enter the speech of the nation. 'Like many another fact overlooked, or forgotten, or reduced to an anachronism', Stanner observed, 'and thus consigned to the supposedly inconsequential past, it requires only a suitable set of conditions to come to the surface, and to be very consequential indeed.'[14] In Britain of the 1960s public memories of empire were largely inconsequential in the sense that they severed *that* past from *this* present. However, the proximity of black migrants worked to activate memories of the imperial past—memories of white authority, in particular—which were indeed more consequent, bringing the empire's past back into the field of contemporary vision. These darker, more pronounced racialized memories of empire coexisted, in time, with the jokey and the inconsequential. In the first instance they had little purchase on public life. For the most part they were articulated on the anxious margins of the public domain: in letters to MPs and to the local press, in cyclostyled statements put out by neighbourhood anti-immigration groups and so on. The shock of Peter Griffiths's electoral win in Smethwick in 1964, on an explicitly racial platform, served as a portent. But the decisive public breakthrough was represented by Powell in Birmingham in 1968. As a result of the speech race became speakable in new ways, given life by new memories of old times. As a local workman shouted out to Powell on the day after the speech: 'It needed to be said.'[15] What publicly had been unspeakable had now been spoken, and the contours of memory realigned.

Much of what Powell and his varied followers perceived to be orderly and disorderly was either in itself emphatically racial or, if nor directly pertaining to race, none the less read through a racial optic. The racial encodings of order, as whiteness, and disorder, as blackness, were endlessly repeated. The presence in Britain of non-white Commonwealth migrants, arriving to settle in the metropole, was viewed by Powellites, and by their various outriders, as bringing into the nation a new sort of metropolitan native. I'll argue that they became, in effect, a new type of native *after* their arrival in Britain.[16] Much as with the traditional, colonial native of imperial times, there emerged an overriding current of opinion persuaded that the new migrants were inescapably bearers of disorder. The language and instincts of the colonial past were never far away. At the same time, indigenous white Britons more easily began to imagine themselves explicitly as white men

and as white women. Significant numbers came to discover themselves to
be a species of white settler, confronted by forces which they believed were
usurping what providence long ago had bestowed upon them. Blackness
seemed to infiltrate the domestic, the intimate, and the sexual, endangering
the domains of life which were cherished as most feminine and private.[17] At
the very moment of decolonization, a language of racial whiteness assumed
a new prominence *at home*. A nominally archaic, colonial vocabulary was
called upon to make sense of a peculiarly contemporary domestic situation:
the impact of extensive non-white immigration.[18]

Those who found themselves embracing a racial whiteness in these years,
however, did not do so, like their colonial forebears, as heroic makers of history. On the contrary, they did so as representatives of a defeated people,
betrayed by those charged to lead them. A minority spoke explicitly in
terms of an empire destroyed by its multifarious foes. Many more evoked
the idea of the once victorious nation now defeated by unseen forces, by
the enemies within and without whom Powell vowed to expose. Others
still imagined their street or neighbourhood as an island of whiteness, as
isolated as once were the homesteads on the *veld* or in the bush, prey to
racial assault, but located *here*, the familiarity of what was once homely
transmuting into an unnerving spectre of unhomeliness. At the height of the
empire the dominating story of whiteness had been heroic, told in the masculine mode, in which the settler made history by conquering native and
nature alike. By the empire's end starkly contrasting stories of whiteness
came to be narrated: of vulnerable, aged white women, living in the mean
streets of collapsing English cities, subjected to incessant indignities by the
natives who were now inexplicably in their midst; or of little white girls
alone in a class of coloured immigrants. Conqueror, it seemed, had become
conquered. Those who yearned to be white had nowhere to go but inward,
living out the impossible reveries of a past colonial order.

Un-nameable, forgotten, invisible, unspeakable: these are themes that
keep recurring. In part they arise from the peculiarities of modern, contemporary renderings of racial difference in England where the common languages of race have been deeply encrypted. Even the most apparently
unambiguous statements can teem with the nuance of unuttered meanings.
Despite the great volubility around race much remained, as I'll show,
unspoken.

These themes also arise as we deal with memory. The past is irretrievably
absent. Even so the past still exercises its power over the present, in ways

which to us—as historical actors—are not just un-nameable, but largely invisible. This exercise of the power of the past on the present is itself uncanny, a perception which we might understand to be the predominating property of memory itself. Memory brings the past into the present, but does so under its own terms. If the events of the past are experienced as peculiarly difficult, silence and unspeakability may continue long into the future and, as we know from the current literature on trauma, they may only come to be recognized for what they are much later in time.[19] At the moment of Powell, I'm suggesting, the imperial past, recent though it was, was subject to many proscriptions. Its consequence went unheard, and was rendered invisible, perceptible only through a number of displacements. A wager which underwrites the promise of history, as an imaginative practice, is that it can free us from mere 'pastness' and make speakable what was once unspeakable.

★★★★★★

These silences entered the formal historiography. Until recently, it was rare to come across accounts of the empire which acknowledged that the connections between the imperial past and the metropolitan present signalled a matter of historiographical importance, and that this was a question worth exploring further. Now this is an issue that has come to life, and it is currently a cause of controversy amongst historians.[20] There are two predominating, substantive areas of contention. First, opinion is divided about the degree to which the domestic British nation can be considered to have been imperial or, more specifically, the degree to which its population was affected by the empire. Second is the question of race. On the one side are those who believe that a study of empire will reveal much about the evolutions of race in its modern, British forms, contributing to our knowledge of the racial thinking which characterizes our own, putatively postcolonial, times. On the other are those who contend that this attention to race has been exaggerated, and that it results in historical procedures which extrapolate from the present and produce a distorted view of the past. Race, they argue, was never the decisive issue in colonial rule; that it was certainly never so in the metropole; and that attempts to link together contemporary racial issues with the imperial past are ill-judged.

Readers will have guessed my own views. I am persuaded that the empire did in fact significantly shape the lives of those living in the metropole; and I am equally persuaded that the empire has much to tell us about race.[21] Thus when I say that 'Colonial societies work through race' and that 'by extension, so did the metropole' these are both contentious claims, which make evident my position in these arguments.[22] I am conscious that, as I have presented the two sides in the debate, there is reason for much qualification. That is necessary. But as things stand, on the essentials I see little room for compromise. The controversy, in this sense, is a real one.

Apart from the substantive issues of contention there are also equally significant problems about historical method, and these have yet to be addressed explicitly. Questions of mentalities, of identities, and of memory are crucial, though not easily resolved.[23] More particular is the question of racial identity. How these are variously defined will, in part, organize the resulting conclusions. My own conviction is that a method which is exclusively empirical cannot reveal those many elements of the story which are hidden from the naked eye. By temperament and training, like many brought up in English intellectual traditions, I'm more at ease arguing empirically than I am abstractly. But an empirical approach alone cannot open up what has been made silent, or invisible. It cannot explain, for example, either what 'The Thing' is or what it represents as a historical phenomenon. Nor, as I indicate at greater length in Chapter 3 of this first volume, can it track what is dynamic in the shifting complexities of racial identification, and of the accompanying erotics.[24]

We can see how these methodological issues are played out by looking at Bernard Porter's *The Absent-Minded Imperialists*.[25] In the debate on empire and metropole Porter is an advocate of the sceptical viewpoint, and his book is the most comprehensive, most completely researched, defence of this position. He doesn't think that domestic Britons were ever seriously touched by empire and he is not convinced, so far as the metropole is concerned, that there is much to be gained from linking race to empire. He offers an intransigently literal reading of the evidence. He admits to a certain blokeishness when it comes to historical interpretation which, he chooses to tell his readers, doesn't always find favour with his partner who harbours more feminist and postmodernist inclinations. Ambiguity and ambivalence do not enter his historical imagination. His portrayal is straightforward. He depicts, on the one hand, the dyed-in-the-wool imperialists, the enthusiasts for empire; and on the other, the vast bulk of the population who express a natural indifference to anything as remote and as faraway as empire. He spends many pages searching for those he can identify as imperialists. If he can't spot them he assumes he has no option but to discount the imperial influence. As most of the time such figures cannot be found his

hypothesis is easily validated. When they do insist on intruding, as sometimes they must, he can find reasons why they should be explained away, or
why they were only of marginal significance. Thus his case is proven and the
case closed.

Undoubtedly there is some truth in this approach, insofar as the lived
forms of popular ideologies seldom mirror the ideas to be found in the
tracts and blueprints produced by accredited social intellectuals. At the
beginning of the twentieth century there were precious few people outside the power centres of the imperial state who spoke about empire in the
philosophical terms adopted by, say, Lord Milner. This isn't to claim, however, that through a compacted process of transformation and translation
these ideas couldn't take on life in popular culture. I hope to show, in this
opening volume, that this occurred. The problem with Porter's method of
proceeding is that it begs the question of how we conceive what an imperial
identity is. He supposes that to prove the efficacy of empire it is necessary
to find evidence of willing cohorts of metropolitans whose identifications
with empire were complete, fully part of themselves, who admitted as much,
were happy that it was so, and who meant what they said. The tone we hear
resembles that of a member of the bench as much it does that of a historian.
Enthusiasm or indifference, sheep or goats. These are the polarizations that
structure his argument, resulting in a sense of the past so knowing and rectilinear that it is divested of all complexity and mystery.

British historians have been challenging positions such as Porter's for half
a century.[26] It is unlikely that identities are ever as transparent, conscious, or
as finished as this.[27] My own emphasis, to the contrary, falls on a conceptualization in which narrative plays a defining role. Of great consequence are
the stories we tell about ourselves, especially those which address the seemingly innocent question of 'Where are you from?', as too are the stories
which are told about us. Identifications, from this point of view, come to be
understood as more fragile, fleeting processes, with many potential outcomes, including perhaps a measure of necessary failure or impossibility.
I doubt that many readers will find this controversial, though I'll argue at
the end of the final volume that it was in part the breaking of the colonial
empires which enabled such theorizations to happen. To think in this way
requires sharper specification than that offered by the categorizations of
enthusiasm (rigid and exclusive) and indifference (capacious and concealing
too much). To begin to narrate one's own life in the language of empire did
not necessarily require obeisance to the full paraphernalia of high imperial

jingoism. A quiet, restrained patriotism was not always distinguishable from an underlying faith in the rightness of the British overseas. More especially, to imagine oneself as white—or to recognize that others were imagining one to be white—was to enter a symbolic domain of racial classification and of gender difference in which the influence of empire impinged at every point.

Porter, as a historian, gives no credence to the efficacy of narrative, or to the power of the symbolic world.[28] For him, the stories which circulate through a society—in families and schools, in neighbourhoods and workplaces, in the official operations of the state—appear to have no bearing on the making of a life. Only that which is directly experienced can count. The consequences of this are bizarre, as we can discern from his discussion of race. Race does not appear much in the book. Every so often he introduces what he deems to be the abnormal figure of the 'racist', whose prejudices should not be confused, he insists, with the—unspecified—racial attitudes of the majority of the British people. (In much the same way he relies upon the terms 'sexist' and 'macho' to describe historical periods: thus his contention that Britain was more 'sexist' in the past, but not necessarily 'racist'.) But the overall absence of race derives from his belief that it didn't much matter. He claims that until the period of mass non-white migration in the postwar years racial issues could only have appeared as an irrelevance to domestic Britons. Because he believes that British people in the metropole knew of non-whites predominantly through images and stories their views of race and ethnicity, he states, 'are likely to have been superficial and unimportant in any practical way...The whole issue did not matter to them.'[29] This assumes that knowledge gleaned from stories must only be regarded as 'superficial'. It assumes that race can only be operative when different ethnic groups are in immediate proximity. It assumes that when this does not pertain then—somehow—racial thought cannot happen. It assumes that whiteness cannot be considered to represent a racial positioning. And it assumes, finally, that when the first West Indian migrant disembarked from the *Windrush* at Tilbury in June 1948 he was walking into a historical void untouched by the imperial past, in which English minds were yet to be made up. Assumptions such as these mark the moment when supposedly methodological strategies reveal themselves to be more deeply ideological, for—unannounced and unnoticed—they reproduce in the historiography the mentalities of the imperial past, as if they are the last word in historical truth.

Distinctive though Porter's historical method is, he is not alone in this regard. To insist on the inconsequentiality of empire can reproduce unwittingly much older perceptions, infusing the silences of the past into the historiography of the present.[30] Much depends on perspective. From its inception imperial history was little more than an arena in which competing strategies for various forms of colonial authority could be rehearsed, but in which the defining project of empire could itself never come under scrutiny. Though these days are long gone, the determination to open up the story of empire to new voices—colonized as well as colonizers, black as well as white, women and children as well as men, queer as well as straight—has met continuing resistances. A tone of easy omnipotence still pervades the literature, as if intellectual authority remains the necessary preserve of those situated at the centre. Above all a more pluralist, complete picture of empire needs to interrogate that most naturalized of phenomena, whiteness itself. On occasion methodological choices in the historiography appear to be little more than exercises in fending off a certain discomfort about confronting questions of race. When the fact of racial power is acknowledged such admissions are too easily accompanied—in an instant—by explanations insisting why no more need be said, performing what Roland Barthes has typified as 'the staging of an appearance-as-disappearance'.[31] What is presented as urgent can be postponed for a more leisurely future.[32] That the historiography can be inflected in this way, transforming the consequential into something apparently inconsequential, is—arguably—testament to the continuing effectivity of the imperial past which histories of this type seek to deny.

Many years back the distinguished historian, J. G. A. Pocock, delivered in his native New Zealand a lecture which has since become renowned. His purpose was to emphasize that Britain has for long been composed of different nations, and that for much of the modern period there existed a 'greater' Britain overseas. In a dazzling, elegant challenge to historians he endeavoured to counter a provincialism which continued to presume that all that was significant was to be located in the heartlands of the imperial centre. In the intervening period what was once a provocation has now become an orthodoxy, at least formally so. Yet what is less well remembered is that Pocock was at the same time questioning conventional opinion about the authority of the historian, touching on issues concerning the very nature of the historical imagination. He pondered what he identified as 'the paradigmatic command of self', suggesting that such centring of the

self on the part of the historian was *also* responsible for generating a parochialism of the intellect. To command the self in the manner he describes is
to ensure that only what is already known or familiar can enter the imagination—only that which is *the same*—reproducing rather than transforming
the givens of historical knowledge, an insight which has underwritten many
of the recent feminist histories of empire.[33] With due courtesies Pocock
quietly implied that this was a predicament most sharply evident at the
centre, for the perspective of the centre imposes necessary limits on how the
historical past, and the historical present, can be charted.[34] Historians, he
indicated, much like anthropologists of old, need to discover how they
might learn to integrate into their practice a recognition and espousal of
difference, relativizing their own sense of self, and adopting what he called
'a tangential sense of identity' or, in more telling terms, 'a twofold consciousness'.[35] This would require, for instance, grasping not only how the
British saw themselves, but also how they were seen by those they ruled.

The notion of a 'twofold' or double consciousness has a long history in
theorizations of race and racial oppression. To think in these terms in relation to whiteness opens new and necessary questions. To explore the issue
of racial whiteness offers a means—a privileged means, in my view—for
understanding the empire and the forms of its demise, as well as for drawing
out some of the silences in the current historiography. However, the centrality I give to race in these volumes cannot conclude the argument, as if
no more need be said. It is where the argument begins.

★ ★ ★ ★ ★

Memories of Empire is composed of three parts of which this is the first; it is
to be followed by *The Caribbean Comes to England*, and then finally by
Postcolonial England? I need to explain the themes of this first volume and
to indicate, more briefly, the shape of my overall argument across the work
as a whole, highlighting the concerns of the two succeeding volumes.
Enoch Powell—eccentric, heretical, often crazed—appears at the very
beginning of the opening volume and at the end of the final one. The
structure of my narrative works back historically from the moment of
Powell in Birmingham in April 1968. In the Prologue I recapitulate this
episode and set out to demonstrate both the extent of popular mobilization for Powell and the intensity of the political emotions of those who
identified with him. The populist backing he commanded was critical.
Powellism, I suggest, created Powell.

The significance I assign to Powellism is based on the conviction, against a fair bulk of received opinion, that the racial antipathies unleashed under the banner of Enoch Powell shouldn't be understood as a temporary or marginal aberration in the otherwise harmonious evolution of a multicultural society, or as the expression of a deranged minority. The Powellite intervention, from 1968 to the mid-1970s, moved to the centre of national life, and recast the public culture. For sure, there is plenty of evidence to show that Powell himself had many opponents, and that prominent public figures went on record to confirm their hostility to his ideas and, on occasion, to the man himself. Yet even so Powell became the touchstone for speaking about race and nation, and still continues to be so many years after his death. Just when you think that he has finally been dispatched, back he comes. Like a traumatic memory he always returns. In 1968 his authority determined what the debate was about. As a result, white fears of black, and an inchoate jumble of racial bigotry, crossed the threshold from private reverie to public wisdom.

To return to the Powell of 1968–70, or to read the letters from those who believed in him, is a disquieting experience. Many of them, perhaps the majority, were women, creating from below a new type of politics. In recovering these writings we hear the voices of people who felt, deep in their souls, that their familiar world had been shattered. Yet it is apparent that those who were won by Powell were seeking to resurrect what they came to remember, in a slow, painful epiphany, as a lost time of whiteness. They imagined that there had once been an age—in the past, a generation ago, in metropole or colony, somewhere, some time—where white authority had prevailed. Memories of the figures of the white man and of the white woman, of the frontier and of the settler colony, of the white dominions, of the white man's country or, more elusively, of an abstract 'overseas' where white folk could go about their business unmolested: all served as a resource for making sense of the collapse that they felt ate into their lives. The disorder of the present worked to project back into the past memories of a lost, fantasized racial utopia.

This opening volume examines the dominating elements of the imperial past from which these memories drew, for I accept (against more radical theorists of memory) that these were memories that did indeed possess *some* grounding in the realities of the historical past. I set out to highlight a specific, evolving sensibility in which the co-ordinates of racial whiteness cohered. My overriding concern is with the metropole and then, secondarily, with the transactions between it and the white settler societies of the empire. The story encompasses a long duration, beginning in the middle of the nineteenth century and closing with the end of white Rhodesia in 1979–80. It moves back and forth, between past and present, between history and memory, and between metropole and colony. In this sense, it works as an experiment in the recounting of differing historical times. Parts are necessarily synoptic, particularly the first two chapters where I set the scene for more focused explorations which come later. In some respects I remain close to the essentials of an old-fashioned imperial historiography. The icon of the white man is of primary interest to me. So too, methodologically, is a biographical approach: the lives of prominent public men occupy much of my attention. 'Men's bodies' are never far away.

I hope, though, to convey something of the trajectory of the figure of the white man, and of the correlate idea of the white man's country, in the shifting cultures of Britain's empire. The white man may seem to be an uncontentious entity, obvious enough, and not in any need of conceptual investigation. But I don't think that this is right. The idea of the white man has less to do with empirical beings—men with pale skins—than with an entire fantasized, discursive complex which underwrites its creation. What appears to be straightforward turns out to be very complex. The old colonial pioneer-legends tell of the heroic deeds of the white man, whose repute derives from his independence: battling against nature and the native, he is a man confident in his capacity to transform the world in his image. All seems to radiate from him.[36] My own purpose is to put a contrary view. The white man of the late nineteenth century, I suggest, was the product of an entire discursive apparatus. Both the state and powerful institutions in civil society were active in his making. His body, his sexual practices, his family arrangements, his contact with racial others: all were regulated.[37] On occasion, his socialization was articulated explicitly in terms of the duties of the white man; more often, though, particularly in the metropole, the injunctions to racial whiteness were understated, or silent. However, the multiple direct public and private interventions designed to fashion young boys into the mystical figure of the white man, with all his prowess, only tells part of the story. Of equal significance were the indirect, or negative, initiatives which appeared not to concern him at all, but which sought to regulate the lives of the white man's others. For the white man could only be a white man in relation to his others: his whiteness and his masculinity acquired meaning only in relation to those who had no claims, or lesser claims, to whiteness or to masculinity. In the *first* instance, his persona as a white man derived from the elaborate system of symbolic classification—of race and gender, class and sexuality, and so on—which prevailed. Thus when new social figures entered the late Victorian social landscape—the contagious prostitute, the destitute alien, the homosexual man, the hooligan, and the ever-expanding spectrum of those deemed unfit—they appeared far removed from the world of the respectable white man. These putatively dissolute beings came to experience directly the coercive, administrative attention of the state. But the discursive naming and organization of these recidivist characters, together with the consequent moves towards their incarceration and surveillance, served to quarantine the white man from the social contagions of the day, leaving him pristine and the object (in Gramsci's terms) of the gentler, educative, or 'prize-giving' activities of the state. *Their* presence did much to shape *his* world. The luminous presence of the white man, I suggest, was predicated on the organization of darker social forces, not only overseas but at home as well.

This configuration of the white man at the end of the nineteenth and the beginning of the twentieth centuries was, as Marilyn Lake and Henry Reynolds demonstrate, a global phenomenon. It was at this moment, they argue, that the strict binary of white and non-white first became current, evident not only in the settler territories of the British empire but so too in the United States of Theodore Roosevelt. Indeed, in this emergent white world—with the idea of the white Pacific functioning as its core—Britain itself barely featured, for Britain was only ever ambiguously a white man's country, and there emerged in these years significant voices in the metropole articulating the fear that Britain's leadership of the English-speaking world was on the point of being usurped by the USA.[38] Taking a longer view, but one which is equally ambitious geographically, James Belich places these same developments in the process which he names as the 'settler revolution', a profound economic, demographic, and social transformation which created the white man's countries as white.[39] These global perspectives add a new dimension to the historiography. My own concerns, as I have explained, are more limited: my principal focus is the metropole, and how such notions—the white man, the white man's country—touched the home society.

Yet while my emphasis falls on the presence of empire in the metropole—on the connections between the two—this can only form part of the argument. For, paradoxically, in order to grasp the connections between the metropole and the overseas empire we need to be alert to the ideological or cognitive *disconnections* which were also operative. Knowledge of imperial lives overseas was always heavily mediated for those at home, and particularly so in the popular media, and the mediations are critical. The great majority of those who inhabited the metropole knew little about the mechanics of imperial governance. Indeed, the stories of empire which circulated most readily in the metropole were often those which were most mediated, and most partial, but at the same time most charged and open to human investment. In official terms such stories were of dubious pedagogic value, despite their narrative power. Thus popular knowledge of empire, I argue, worked as a strange compound of knowledge and ignorance, having the effect simultaneously of connecting and of disconnecting the peoples at the centre with the peoples overseas.

At the beginning of the twentieth century Australia and South Africa, particularly, were deemed by their founders to be determinedly vanguard nations of the white race, inaugurating a new global epoch in which the fruits of modernity would be brought to the southern hemisphere. Such were the passions invested in the idea of the white man's country. The aspirations were grandiose, the new-world future just a step away. But just as race (as whiteness) was the means by which this future civilization could be imagined so race (as non-whiteness) proved the greatest obstacle to the realization of these dreams. The management of the non-white peoples of the new nations could never properly conform to the ideas propounded in the founding national myths. Well before the century's end these dreams for the future had become unhinged.

The settler societies produced many a dedicated tribune of white civilization. My aim is to reveal the degree to which these tribunes, or some of them, learnt to speak not only for their respective colonial nations but for the larger world of what many chose to call Greater Britain. They pursued a range of matters which affected the future of all Britons, in the metropole as well as overseas. Much of their authority derived from their incessant boast that they alone knew the native. From this single perception derived an entire politics. For to know the native was to know oneself, and to recognize one's obligations as a white man. Those who did not know the native—Westminster politicians compromised by the requirements of political calculation, the effete pen-pushers of Whitehall—could within this scheme of things neither properly know themselves nor the true consequences of their own actions. For all their cultivation, their ignorance of the racial realities endangered the future of the British people. Such a situation, it could seem, required those at the centre to be tutored in the essentials of Britishness by the colonials who, by force of circumstance, had fully learnt what it entailed to be British. Knowing the native generated a conception of imperial civilization which, against expectations, at critical moments came to inform domestic British politics itself. To speak in such terms was to imagine a world in which the figure of the white man was properly at the centre of things, working not only to propound the stated virtues of whiteness and masculinity but also (as I argue in Chapter 3) functioning as a means to hold in place the given hierarchies of social difference, *tout court*.

This manner of thinking was evident when the colonial tribunes of the British race turned their attention to the predicament of the mother country. It was evident too in the public pronouncements of the returning proconsuls. Having served the empire overseas—where the fate of Britain appeared to be less a fact of life than a matter of sheer human will—a generation of proconsuls returned home to be confronted by a society where, they reckoned, slackness prevailed and where civilization itself induced a pathological unmanliness. White men, it seemed, were rarely to be found at home. The great proconsuls of the modern empire were classically represented in the years before the First World War in the figures of Lords Curzon, Cromer, and Milner. When these grandees of empire re-entered the domestic scene each found himself naturally gravitating to the zealous extremities of political life. Questions of state—defence of the realm, Unionism, the battle against women's suffrage—assumed for them an urgency, for they carried within themselves a peculiarly colonial apprehension of the extinction of Britain's civilization. For them, and for many like them, maintenance of Britain's imperial ascendancy required that the domestic population should be as resolute in their public and private affairs as the ethnic Britons on the colonial frontier. To the returning proconsuls politics operated according to uncompromising, masculine imperatives. Parliamentary niceties could only ever be secondary, while race, nation, and empire intervened at every point as immediate issues of absolute, unyielding principle. So high were the stakes that those who saw things in a different light discovered that they were not merely political opponents, but branded as treacherous, their very irresolution condemned as abetting the destruction of the race.

A hard proconsular imperialism however met many obstacles. Curzon, Cromer, and Milner incited fierce controversies. For all their attempts to organize populist movements overcoming what they took to be mere party factionalism, their immediate political successes were short-lived. Notwithstanding their urbanity the political managers with whom they jostled for power—now as allies, now as antagonists, depending on the conjunctural fluctuations of the moment—proved quite as ruthless as any proconsul. Popular support, too, was at best wayward. The larger populace proved stubbornly attached to the putatively feminine diversions that the domestic civilization offered them: a modicum of material comfort, a few snatched hours for leisure devoted to various respectable or unrespectable pastimes, the pleasures afforded by the emergent institutions of mass culture. All turned out to be more alluring than advocacy of a frontier ethic. Ideologically, the proconsular instinct for authority challenged a significant spectrum of liberal opinion, whose roots ran deep. Although we cannot assume, a priori, that the frustrations experienced on national-imperial matters by Milner, say, or by Cromer, were a necessary function of the immutable liberalism of the metropole, the struggle between contrasting definitions of the nation—authoritarian versus liberal—was real enough. Time and again the returning proconsuls of the Edwardian years were exasperated by the resistance they encountered, fearing for much of their later lives that they had travailled in vain.

It was this conflict between contrasting conceptions of empire which led me to Jan Smuts. From the end of the South African War, in 1902, for the next half century Smuts was the incomparable political ideologue of British South Africa. He was no proconsul, though he was a colonial who came to be an ubiquitous presence in the political and intellectual life of the metropole, and who came to stand as a supreme tribune of Greater Britain. Philosophically, his inherited aspirations were genuinely liberal. Britain, or England, meant for him the traditions of John Bright, an iconoclastic feminism, and the essentially social-democratic ethos espoused by the New Liberals of the early twentieth century. Yet Smuts himself was never shy in informing the imperial government that he knew the native, that he was committed to all that white supremacy entailed, and that when authority needed to be exercised he was the man for the job. The claim that one knew the native necessarily generated a politics of a markedly authoritarian temper. Such a contrary, Faustian figure deserves attention. My purpose in engaging with Smuts is to demonstrate that he spent his life attempting to reconcile two irreconcilable philosophies. At war within him were, on the one hand, the ethical hopes of the New Liberals and, on the other, a racially driven, proconsular conception of empire. Though the latter consistently triumphed, his troubled evasions about race and liberty were received by the public men of the metropole as the product of a wise and mighty intellect. In part, I suggest, this can be explained by the fact that the dilemmas he confronted were not his alone. Just as his liberal aspirations were turned inside out by empire, so they were for many of his generation. For many a liberal and radical, particularly in the slipstream of Joseph Chamberlain, made the same political journey as Smuts.

In my penultimate chapter—on Sir Roy Welensky and the Central African Federation—the register of my argument shifts, and the focus moves to Westminster politics, more narrowly conceived. My purpose here is to track the political lines of connection between white colonies in crisis, confronting their destruction, and the metropolitan right of the Conservative party and its various outriders. I suggest that the political crises in the white settler nations generated the beginnings of a protracted ideological crisis at home, in which the elements of a New Right politics can first be discerned.

Through the twentieth century the various tribunes, proconsuls, and imperial political figures whom I describe in this volume shared the conviction that the purity of the frontier worked to illuminate the decay and degradation of Britain. This was a structure of thought, however, which had wide currency and which was not restricted to the daydreams of the occasional grandee. There were, of course, many anticipations. As I explain, this way of seeing things perhaps first cohered, in its modern, colonial-racial form, in the writings of James Froude in the 1880s. By the turn of the century it formed something like the common sense of the more self-conscious, radical imperial mentalities. It was central to Kipling, the laureate of proconsular imperialism. It ran through the juvenile genre of popular colonial literature. It underwrote Baden-Powell's vision of the scouting movement. It had, in sum, a long if uneven life. Cumulatively, though, it bequeathed a paradoxical legacy. Devotees of empire spoke for England or (variously) for Britain. Yet those who subscribed to this frontier vision of empire came to imagine the home nation increasingly to be the source of all manner of pathologies, and to be essentially corrupt. By the time of the Rhodesian crisis, in 1965, both Ian Smith, the prime minister of Rhodesia, and his supporters in the metropole took this dichotomy to be self-evident. Thus on the one hand Rhodesia represented a land where the fundamentals of ethical life were laid out for all to see, transparent and uncomplicated, given sustenance by the careful, benevolent racial management imposed by the white settler. On the other hand England appeared to be complicit in its own colonial and internal defeats, ethically compromised, beset by racial and sexual laxness, and the very fount of disorder. The paradox was this. Those devoted to England not only repudiated what they purported to love. They also concluded that what they most cherished had become, through some inexplicable misfortune, an impossibility. The end of empire had produced, it seemed, not merely (to adapt J. R. Seeley's terms) the contraction of England, but its destruction.

★★★★★

In the second part, *The Caribbean Comes to England*, I step outside the phantasmagoric world of the white man, shifting the angle of vision in order that we can see the British through the eyes of the colonized. More particularly, I aim to reconstruct the Caribbean experience (or strictly, the English-speaking Caribbean experience) of Britain's imperial civilization in the middle decades of the twentieth century.

The Caribbean is important for my purposes for two principal reasons. First, in the decades following slave emancipation the formal institutions of Victorian culture came to be deeply embedded in the social life of the Caribbean. In language, gender relations, religion, sport, literature, and schooling the West Indian nations were (excluding the settler societies themselves) formally closer to the mother country than any other colony. The fact of emancipation had instilled in generations of Caribbean peoples a regard for Queen Victoria and for the values of liberality which, as monarch, she was believed to personify. This is not to say that society in the Caribbean conformed to the ideals of the mother country, for this was far from so. It is to claim, however, that all that was most urgent—sovereignty, nationhood, conceptions of the self, freedom—was comprehended within the syntax of Britishness. What the West Indians were able to do, as both British and non-white, within this cognitive system does much to reveal the inner structures of Britishness itself. Whether conservative or radical, for the empire or against, West Indians of the middle years of the last century knew the curriculum of the British from the inside, for the British world was their world. While their formal culture pulled them deep into Britishness, though, their racial dispositions worked to place them outside the orbit of the home civilization, and as such the West Indian migrants came to be the object of much morbid curiosity for those who inhabited the metropole. These ambiguous, shifting locations generated an anti-colonial politics of complexity and great imaginative reach, from which we can learn much—in general—about the end of the colonial epoch.

Second, a great deal of the intellectual work of Caribbean decolonization was conducted, not in the Caribbean, but in the metropole. Location, in this respect, mattered. The diasporic thinkers of West Indian independence were not only engaging with the formal artefacts of British civilization, from afar, in tropical locales where colonial propriety carried with it an edge of unreality, but also with the lived realities of the metropole as it was: in the street, in the shops, at the workplace. This offered a generation of West Indians the means for elaborating a peculiarly charged, comprehensive interpretation of imperial Britain. Moreover this was a critique—from the inside and intimate, and simultaneously from the outside, perplexed and often hostile—which necessarily put race at the centre of the analysis. Given the reticence with which race was addressed elsewhere in the public life of the nation, this migrant reading of the metropole opened many new questions. Indeed, it was of strategic significance politically, for it linked together as one the racial question with the wider politics of decolonization.

I have been impressed by this Caribbean tradition of anti-colonial thought and it provides a conceptual framework for much of what occurs in these volumes. Going back to the work of C. L. R. James, George Padmore, Amy Ashwood Garvey, George Lamming, and Claudia Jones, and to others less familiar, has been important for me. I find it curious, though, that outside the field of Caribbean studies their influence is not better known. Enthusiasts for postcolonial theory, for example, while well-versed in the writings of the francophone West Indian Frantz Fanon, may know little about his anglophone counterparts. In part, this may be explained by the fact that C. L. R. James and those who followed in his wake fashioned their anti-colonialism in a peculiarly English idiom: while Fanon thought in terms of Descartes or Hegel or Bergson, those from the British West Indies were as likely to work through *their* critique in terms of cricket and the Victorian novel. This produces many difficulties for a later generation of readers, for whom these ways of thinking carry a diminishing resonance. This was a generation which articulated its critiques of the empire through the categories, not merely of Englishness, but of a Victorian Englishness, a Victorianism which was often most evident in matters of gender and sexuality.[40] The legacy is contradictory. Yet even so, part of my purpose in this second volume is to argue that this anglophone tradition of Caribbean thought has the potential to tell us much about Britain's empire in its final years, and about the continuing reproduction of colonial habits long after the empire has gone.

These are intellectual issues, which touch on some of the founding theoretical positions which have shaped *Memories of Empire*. But in the broader panorama the Caribbean presence did much to alter the experiences and possibilities of indigenous white Britons, and how Britishness itself might be lived. Alongside the story of the racial injustices meted out to the migrant there is its counter-point, telling of the creation of new contact-zones—both public and private—between black and white, and of white lives transformed. This is not a story of unalloyed triumph, bearing testament to the irresistible rise of multicultural Britain. But it does attest to the slow, uneven, and continuing Creolization of the British. And looking back at the earliest monochrome newsreels depicting the arrival of the first West Indian migrants, over half a century ago, one can glimpse the extent of this transformation and wonder that it ever happened at all.

★★★★★

To adopt this Caribbean perspective offers, then, a number of possibilities. It allows us both to locate metropole and colony in 'a single analytical frame' and also, more specifically, it enables us to see with greater precision the domestic, metropolitan consequences of decolonization.[41] It is a perspective which unites the racial dimensions of decolonization (overseas) and the colonial dimensions of race (at home). But to demonstrate this it is neces-sary, I believe, to return to the question of racial whiteness. In the closing part, *Postcolonial England?*, I set out to reconstruct the conflicting registers of whiteness in the metropole during the age of decolonization.

To varying degrees the anti-colonial movements of the middle decades of the twentieth century determined not only to dismantle the identifiable institutions of colonial rule, but also to break the often less tangible powers of the white man. Since at least the latter half of the nineteenth century, to be colonized was to *become* a native. Learning to recognize oneself as a native, as John Comaroff and Jean Comaroff have noted, was the common experience of the colonized.[42] Consequently, for the destruction of colo-nialism to be effective the native had to cease to be a native, and had to imagine his or her selfhood anew, an argument which Fanon, amongst oth-ers, deployed with fierce passion. The violence of decolonization—not, we might add, the special preserve of the French, the Belgian, the Portuguese, or the Dutch situations, to the exclusion of the British—was overdetermined

by the racialization of the principal antagonism: of colonized versus colonizer, of natives versus whites. Racial whiteness was an active element in
the process of decolonization shaped, for us who have followed after, by the
history of decolonization itself. For when the colonial power resisted independence, it did so in the name of white authority. The presentiment of
disorder that decolonization incubated was above all about race, driven by
the fear that white ascendancy was about to be turned upside-down and
that, in the final reckoning, the natives were to have their day.

The imaginings of racial whiteness in the metropole—the means by
which men and women came to recognize themselves as white, and came
to articulate their fears and desires explicitly as white men and women—
were not immune to the influence of these distant events. The transactions
between the imperial centre and the overseas possessions were as intense,
perhaps more intense, in the dying days of empire as they had been at the
height of Britain's imperial rule. The apprehension that a racial-colonial
order was coming to an end was not confined to the colonies. As we shall
see in a moment, when Powell reported that a constituent had informed
him that 'In this country in fifteen to twenty years' time the black man will
have the whip-hand over the white man', the location was Wolverhampton
and the country was England. But the sentiment itself directly echoes the
febrile common sense of the final moments of colonial authority. What had
occurred in the colonies now appeared to be happening in England: the
extinction of white authority, and thereby—as a consequence, it seemed—
the extinction of the nation itself.

This gets us close, I think, to what Powell understood—or, more accu-
rately, failed to understand, and could not properly name—as 'The Thing'.
End of empire, I shall suggest, was one of the subterranean components of
Powellism and, more generally, of the Powell–Thatcher years.

Reading Powell imposes its costs. There have been countless occasions
when I have returned to his writings unsure about my own investments,
wishing I could turn to something more congenial. In a curious way he
chose to live his life as if dislocated from the contemporary world. It wasn't
only his studied, fetishistic obeisance to the customs of times past, in speech,
dress, and manner. He carried into the postwar years the political instincts
of proconsular imperialism. Milner's conception of race patriotism, in its
essentials, was not far removed from Powell's philosophy of nationhood.
Powell's admiration for Curzon, discovered when he was serving as an
officer in the Raj, was uncompromising. And while his regard for the nation

of his birth was endlessly repeated, as much as any proconsul he increasingly found it a constant source of disappointment. Messy, boring, everyday England—the England of anonymous high roads and fast-food joints—could never live up to his professions of love. Within every rank there appeared to be bred traitors whose defining purpose was to destroy the nation. In his imagination he lived the old imperial ethic of the frontier; the true qualities of the nation, he believed, were to be found at its extremities, where danger was most proximate. But confronted by the end of empire, and by the contraction of England, the frontiers which called to him were not the fantasized locations of the high colonial period, separated from home by continents and oceans. On the contrary, these were frontiers which had opened up inside the home territory. In the first instance these were relocated in his mind to the mundane urban spaces to be found in Northfield, Birmingham, replete with childhood memories, and in Wolverhampton, locales where the frontier was defined exclusively by the opposition between black and white. And later, as even these frontiers gave way, and as the collapse of England (it seemed) continued apace, he alighted upon County Down, in Northern Ireland, simultaneously home and colony, where the Protestant population were, he persuaded himself, fighting the last rearguard action to maintain the integrity of the nation. If Powell's instincts were proconsular, the political arena in which he fought—we can see—was postcolonial. By the 1970s the only 'overseas' available to him was the province of Northern Ireland.

Powell knew well enough the realities of the United Kingdom after empire. From the middle of the 1950s his understanding of politics was based on the realization that the empire could be no more, a fact he came eventually to welcome. In him there occurred a peculiar amalgam of the colonial and the postcolonial. It is for this reason that I argue Powell can be understood by way of the paradoxical designation, postcolonial proconsul.[43]

Powell was a singular character. On occasion he was representative of nothing more than his own narcissistic peculiarities. But this should not disguise those other moments when, as I have indicated here, his politics assumed great significance. He was the principal political-philosophical precursor of Thatcherism: indeed, as Anna Marie Smith has noted, the most significant continuities between Powellism and Thatcherism 'lie in their articulation of … post-colonial nationalism'.[44] From 1968 to the early 1970s, at the height of his popularity, many called themselves Powellites, or identified with what he believed. They didn't do so because of his views on the Book of Common Prayer or on the crown, nor even as a result of his early espousal of monetarism. They did so because he was able to speak to them unashamedly as fellow whites, mesmerized by the twin spectres of national decline and coloured immigration. Yet empire itself was not the primary means by which these assertions of white subjectivity were first made manifest, either for Powell or for his followers. Only a minority spoke their fears in an explicit language of empire. The overall tone was often more feminine and domestic. Those who did commit themselves to a ritualized mourning for the loss of empire were among the blimpish, crankish few. For the great majority of Powellites, or for his various fellow-travellers to be found amongst the emergent cadres of the New Right, empire represented little more than a lost dream, counterpoising the depredations of the present to the memories of a more welcoming past.

In Bernard Porter's terms that would be the end of the matter. If no one admitted to the influence of empire, then there could have been no such thing. My aim, in the closing volume, is to put the contrary case. And I do so by arguing for the efficacy of memory. When supporters of Powell declared themselves to be white men and women; when they wrote to him complaining that black people had secreted themselves under the eaves of their own homes, invading a space which did not belong to them; when they urged that blacks should be 'sent back'; when they professed to know the ways of the migrant, and decried his or her insolence; when they dreamt of sunlit lands overseas where white rule prevailed; when they imagined their nation to have been defeated, or no longer what it once was, or no longer existing—all drew upon memories of the imperial past. Inside the nation's forgetfulness about empire, the memory-traces remained. Empire may not have been spoken for what it was. It was, however, present.

This reracialization of the old metropole produced a politics of great emotional charge. However it was also hugely divisive, contested at every point. Powellism acted as a powerful agent in breaking up the old political system, and in anticipating Thatcherism, but it was never hegemonic. Many countervailing forces arose, not least from the non-white migrants—and from their sons and daughters—who had journeyed to the erstwhile mother country. Blackness itself came to function as a resource from which to understand the political predicament of the English. Contrary currents coexisted in the same historical moment, the reracialization of the nation coexisting with its incipient Creolization. In a strange conjunction, the histories of the white colonizers and the histories of the non-white colonized both came home to the metropole simultaneously, converged, and were played out—belatedly—during the time of Powell and Thatcher. Underwriting the disorder of these years were the unappeased memories of the imperial past.

★★★★★

One final note is necessary. Readers will have observed that I have referred variously to England, Britain, Greater Britain, as well as to the empire itself. I have at times shifted from one to the other, without explanation. Many of the imperial figures I discuss barely noticed the systematic imprecision in their various formulations. When they were required to spell out where exactly their identifications lay, they encountered all kinds of difficulty. Powell, for example, once an enthusiast for the ideal of Greater Britain, in his later life claimed allegiance, at differing times and with differing emphases, to England, to Britain, and to the United Kingdom. His idea of 'the nation' slipped easily, as circumstance demanded, between any one of them. Renowned as an English nationalist, his political journey to County Down was conducted in the name of Unionism. Symptomatic of the same lack of discrimination were the terms employed by the Caribbean migrants, who endeavoured to understand for themselves the civilization of the mother country. For many, England and Britain were interchangeable categories. Sometimes it is clear which nation the author—imperialist or critic—had in mind. When this is so I use what I take to be the appropriate term. On many occasions, however, no such precision is possible, and the ambiguities remain.

My own focus, I should make clear, is on England, as the core nation of the imperial civilization. But inevitably this requires my engaging with different Englands, at different phases in its history: during the expansion of England, as well as during its contraction. In this sense, *Memories of Empire* explores the fate of England as Greater Britain rose and fell.[45]

Prologue

Reveries of race, April 1968

The Midland Hotel in the centre of Birmingham was big and unin-spired, once posh but never plush. In the new Birmingham of today, in its refurbished guise of the Macdonald Burlington Hotel, the shell of the old building now houses a vast atrium in which are located an all-too-familiar standardized bookshop and an all-too-familiar standardized coffee-shop. During the week the old Midland Hotel used to cater for the commercial representatives of Middle England and—on Friday and Saturday evenings—served as a useful locale for people to meet for their first few drinks, before moving somewhere else more enticing. When I first knew it, in the 1970s, it was still a hotel of the railway age rather than of the airport age, though soon finding itself having to compete with the intercontinental US and Japanese hotel chains. Unlike many provincial hotels of its period, it wore its history lightly. In fact, it wore its history so lightly that it in its final years it seemed devoid of memory altogether, one of those non-places of con-temporary times, functioning only as a space through which hapless tran-sients moved in order to reach somewhere else.[1] Yet the Midland Hotel lies in the heartland of Joseph Chamberlain's civic-imperial, Venetian-Gothic Birmingham of the 1870s and 1880s—Corporation Street, the High Street, New Street. It was a block or so away from the great public palaces of the town hall, art gallery, and library, in Victoria Square, monuments simultane-ously to a radical civic pride and to the splendours of empire. It was in the town hall, in May 1903, that Joseph Chamberlain himself—just returned as colonial secretary from his triumphant tour of the recently conquered Boer republics in South Africa—launched his campaign for the economic and racial unification of the empire, imagining a time when the future populations of the white colonies would be peopled by the sons and daughters of that inestimable, universal figure of the coming century, 'Birmingham man'.[2]

Two generations after Chamberlain's dramatic speech—when the empire, bar an occasional remnant or two, had vanished—Enoch Powell, a self-declared son of Chamberlain's imperial Birmingham and the Tory MP for the neighbouring constituency of Wolverhampton South-West, prepared to speak in the Midland Hotel.[3] It was the afternoon of Saturday 20 April 1968 and he was to address the annual general meeting of the West Midlands Area Political Centre. The historian could (if in Joycean mood) safely assume that Mr Powell's bladder was full, for such was his custom in delivering his major speeches: the consequent discomfort, he confessed, concentrated the mind.[4] On this occasion, he needed all the concentration he could summon. His speech, he confided to a friend beforehand, would 'go up like a rocket' and 'it's going to stay up'.[5] His concern was race and immigration and he determined, as he saw things, to speak the truth of race—to confront what other politicians had dared not speak. Weaving together a lurid brew of rumour, anecdote, and myth, he unleashed a ferocious attack on the black immigrant in Britain. What he had to say assumed the virtues of racial segregation, and assumed too that the only future for Britain lay in tougher policies of racial exclusion. In this he challenged the traditional rhetoric of the British state, and the predilection of its personnel for framing policies and aspirations in the language of racial inclusion. In closing, Powell memorably declared, quoting Virgil's *Aeneid*: 'Like the Roman, I seem to see "the river Tiber foaming with much blood"', suggesting in prophetic mode the imminence of a race war in local streets. Joseph Chamberlain's 'Birmingham man'—or, in this instance, his close neighbour, Wolverhampton man ('a middle-aged, quite ordinary working man employed in one of our nationalised industries')—acquired, in this later-century Powellite scenario, a more immediately belligerent racial disposition.[6] The effect of this one speech was cataclysmic. 'Rivers of blood' instantly entered the popular imagination, and Powell's destiny was henceforth inescapably tied to this moment. But so, in more complex ways, was the destiny of the peoples inhabiting these islands.

I won't say much in detail about the speech itself. It is worth noting, though, that Powell regretted he hadn't quoted from the *Aeneid* in the original Latin. In all the turbulence which followed, he was worried too that he might have misquoted. Given his lifetime of scholarly dedication to exegetical readings of the classics, this would have been particularly galling for him. And it so happens that he had. It was not the Roman but the Sybil—the most famous of the prophetesses of antiquity—who issued the warning of imminent bloodshed. And Virgil describes her, the Sybil, storming wildly in her cave before chanting 'her dreadful enigmas' and 'shrouding the truth in dark phrases'.[7]

Of the immediate consequences the most alarming, though also the most predictable, was the intensification of racial fear of those living in Britain who were not white. 'I remember', recalls Stuart Hall, a Jamaican recently arrived in Birmingham, 'the sudden, shared feeling of fear, the sense of hostility, the huddling together against the impending violence, the unspoken aggression in the streets as little groups of black men and women came together to discuss how to respond to the violence it seemed calculated to unleash.'[8] Or for another manifestation:

> As Powell's speeches appeared in the papers, graffiti in support of him appeared in the London streets. Racists gained confidence. People insulted me in the street. Someone in a café refused to eat at the same table with me. The parents of a girl I was in love with told her she'd get a bad reputation by going out with darkies. Parents of my friends, both lower-middle-class and working-class, often told me they were Powellite supporters. Sometimes I heard them talking, heatedly, violently, about race, about 'the Pakis'. I was desperately embarrassed and afraid of being identified with those loathed aliens. I found it was almost impossible to answer questions about where I came from. The word 'Pakistan' had been made into an insult. It was a word I didn't want to use about myself. I couldn't tolerate being myself.[9]

These experiences were not unique. They were, amongst the non-white population of Britain, the norm.[10]

On the day which followed Powell went to his local church in Wolverhampton, the Collegiate Church of St Peter where, later in the day, the rector was to hold a memorial service for Martin Luther King who had been assassinated a fortnight before. On leaving the church, a local plasterer, Sidney Miller, called out: 'Well done, sir! It needed to be said'—the first recorded popular voice in the impending crisis.[11] That evening, Edward Heath, the leader of the Conservative opposition, having consulted with colleagues through the day, telephoned Powell's agent in Wolverhampton. Powell's own phone, only recently installed, had been blocked by the Post Office at his own request. Heath arranged to speak with Powell, and duly informed him that he had found the speech 'to have been racialist in tone and liable to exacerbate racial tensions', and that he was duly sacked from the shadow cabinet.[12] Mrs Thatcher, we might note, having joined the shadow cabinet the previous year, urged Heath to be cautious, and thought it wiser, at least in the short term, for Powell to retain his position, expressing 'strong' sympathy for 'the gravamen of his argument'. She did concede however that the speech was 'strong meat'.[13]

But Westminster was outflanked by Fleet Street, and Fleet Street in turn by the spontaneity of the popular response. According to the survey conducted by Douglas Schoen, seven national papers were initially unfavourable to Powell, and only two favourable. Those favouring Powell were the *Express* and the *News of the World*, with a combined circulation of 10 million, compared to the 11.3 million of its various rivals.[14] *The Times*, still in 1968 influential, respectable, and perceived to be the principal organ of political society, was unequivocal in its denunciation, naming its leading editorial 'An evil speech', and pointing to the irresponsibility of uttering such words so recently after the murder of Martin Luther King.[15] The *Telegraph*—undoubtedly still the house paper of the Tory party—was a deal more equivocal. Its editorial conceded that Powell had expressed genuine popular anxieties, as well as those of many Conservative MPs. It criticized Heath for sacking him, suggesting that he (Heath) had capitulated to pressure from his party's 'left wing' confirmed, the *Telegraph* believed, by Heath's 'use of the favourite left-wing catchword, "racialist"'. And it concluded that Powell was more truly representative of the Conservative 'middle ground' than his shadow-cabinet antagonist, Edward Boyle.[16] As it turned out, equivocal responses of this type to Powell—deploring his tone or style, while surreptitiously conceding on fundamentals—were to prove significant, and not only within the Conservative camp.

In the immediate aftermath of 20 April, the eruption of popular feeling drove the political crisis. As the drama progressed, Powell's critics were placed on the defensive as a popular voice—white, embattled, and for all its deferential incantation of the customs of English liberty and neighbourliness, menacing—became increasingly organized and effective. It was not simply that Edward Heath, as leader of the Conservative opposition, was embarrassed, or the government challenged. This was more properly a crisis of the state, in which the political arena itself came to be recast. April 1968 represented a decisive moment in the protracted shattering of the postwar social-democratic settlement, a crisis, moreover, which turned on race. We can see now that a certain manner of political conduct, still described at the time as the circumscribed culture of 'the establishment', was coming to an end.[17] Here too the events of April 1968 played a role. In these weeks historical change worked at breakneck speed, and even when the immediate crisis quietened, the authority of the pre-existing order was never quite restored.

One index of the conjunctural crisis lies in the humdrum activity of letter-writing. In the days that followed Powell's speech, letter-writing and petition-signing became volcanic, equal in scale to the great campaigns of the disenfranchised in the nineteenth century. In the 1960s, letter-writing and all its attendant customs—buying stamps at the post office; catching the post—still composed the routines of domestic communication not yet dominated by the telephone. The same is true of the transactions of political life: the very recent absence of a phone in the Powell household in Wolverhampton may have been quirky for a politician, though still conceivable. But the speed and tempo of the crisis were driven by the electronic media. The predominance of letter-writing notwithstanding, this was the television age, in which the temporal and spatial structures of political life were compressed, creating ever more potential for the distant events of the public arena to carry a new urgency and proximity. We can reasonably suppose that one incentive for writing a letter would have been the knowledge gleaned from the news bulletins that, hour by hour, thousands of others, friends and neighbours, were doing the same.

Letters to local councillors, to MPs and other public figures, to the local and national press, even to the government, provided one means by which those who believed themselves to be unrepresented by official society could seek representation. Letter-writing in this mode functioned as a bridge between public and private, giving what were perceived as essentially private worries a public form. Letters gave voice, as putatively private and personal media, to what otherwise was unspeakable in public. They were a medium which organized, in Benedict Anderson's terms, a community which indeed could be imagined, and that carried a political authority which transcended the private, individual, domestic conditions in which these letters were first thought and written. The letters created a new affective nation, for whom Powell was spokesman and for which the neighbourhood worked as principal axis. In so doing they devised a peculiarly homely racism.[18] The discovery by one of these multitude of letter-writers that his or hers was a voice which needed to be heard; making the time and the space in the domestic routine to write; buying the stamp and catching the post...these unseen individual acts, in this moment, acquired dramatic, collective significance. Although we cannot be sure, it is likely that a huge majority of the letter-writers were women, writing from their kitchens and front-rooms, an issue I shall explore more fully in the final volume. This was a politics which required no induction into the mysteries of constitution, organization, or principles. For the price of a stamp anyone could join.

But the discovery of this subjective voice could only mean, in the wake of Powell, that others, down the street or around the corner, were compelled to confront a commensurate subjective dislocation—of being dispossessed, for example, of the capacity to 'tolerate being myself' (in the instance quoted above). For the politics of letter-writing in postwar Britain was not only a matter of domestic custom or general public outrage. Letter-writing was also an activity in which those whites who believed themselves to be victims of racial oppression learnt a public language in which their anxieties could be articulated. It is instructive that, in his speech, Powell used the letter as a powerful rhetorical device: quoting one at length (notoriously), and in addition telling of 'the hundreds upon hundreds' he had recently received.[19] By nominally speaking on behalf of his unknown correspondents, he spoke what hitherto had been politically unspeakable. He said as much himself: 'How dare I say such a…thing?'[20] The authority of his voice, publicly reading out anonymous letters expressing private fears, licensed others to speak out in public too. It marked the creation of charged circuit of political rhetoric, with amplification occurring at every point. But clearly these were not popular sentiments which had been formed in a day, prompted merely by the sight of Powell speaking on the television, or reading about him in the press. They had an existence prior to Powell, though not one easily accommodated in the pre-existing political landscape. They had a longer, complex, subterranean history, imbricated deep inside the social experiences of the modernization of British society in the period since the end of the Second World War. Part of the difficulty, in looking back, is to see how these structures of feeling first cohered and acquired a social existence, and to understand the historical memories which gave them life. The formation of this repertoire of mentalities was structured on the movement from the informalities of gossip or chat to a politics of race, with its appointed philosophy; from private to public; and from the unspeakable to the speakable. But when these mentalities became speakable this was not simply, or not only, a case of them assuming a new authority in the public sphere, as if public life were merely enlarged. The very idea of what was properly public altered too.

The Wolverhampton *Express and Star*, deploring Powell's 'extravagant' language while appreciating the power of his argument, changed its traditional format in order to air the views of its readers. Of the letters received, some 5,000 supported Powell, a mere 300 were reckoned to be critical. In the paper's subsequent postcard poll, 35,000 readers thought Heath was wrong to have sacked Powell, while only 372 believed otherwise.[21] Clem Jones, the paper's editor and the friend to whom Powell had confided that his speech would go up 'like a rocket', broke his friendship with Powell the day the speech was given. He later recalled the aftermath:

> We gave over a couple of pages to readers' letters. I only used letters that I was one hundred per cent sure of where they came from. The proportion was, I suppose, ninety to ninety-five per cent pro-Enoch. We had to scrape, every day, to try and find a few balancing letters, some of the letters that I had were pretty abusive of me, containing excrement and that sort of thing, half a dozen sheets of used toilet paper. I had people ringing me at home, all sorts of hours, and saying, 'Oh, is that the bloody nigger lover?' Just like that. But that was inspired sort of stuff. I had a couple of windows broken at home, and a lot of abusive telephone calls.[22]

Every national newspaper was inundated with letters on the issue, as were Tory MPs and Conservative Central Office. Heath himself was the recipient of copious quantities. 'They didn't arrive just in bundles but by the sackful', according to his parliamentary private secretary, Jim Prior. One memory of Prior's is that 'Ninety-five per cent of them or more were obscene', whereas on another occasion he suggested: 'ninety-nine per cent of it backed Powell. But I wonder if Powell really knows or understands to this day the filth he collected to his side. A number of letters were so vilely written that it was offensive for the girls in Ted's [i.e. Heath's] office to read them: others carried their message by including excrement.'[23]

The most daunting aspect of all this, though, is the post directed to Powell himself—Mr Powell's postbag, as it has become mythologized. There can be no doubt that the quantity of mail Powell received in the aftermath of his Birmingham speech was spectacular. There is consensus too that the vast majority of these letters supported him. There is less certainty about the precise figures involved. Part of the difficulty derives from the fact that there were simply so many of them. The great bulk of them still remain unread and undocumented. Most of them are lodged with Powell's constituency papers at Stafford Records Office, where they are housed under conditions of confidentiality. According to the first authoritative accounts, on Tuesday 23 April some 23,000 letters arrived for Powell; the following day, 50,000, when the Post Office had to commandeer a special van solely for his mail. Within the fortnight, it seems, he had received approximately 100,000 letters, excluding telegrams, of which only 800 took issue with him.[24] The most recent and careful biographer offers a rather different view, though agreeing with the figure given for those letters expressing dissent. 'By early May more than 43,000 letters and 700 telegrams had been sent to Powell, four of the telegrams and 800 of the letters disagreeing with him.'[25] Even this suggests that he had been receiving between two and three thousand letters a day and maybe, in the slightly longer run of things, one hundred thousand is not too far off the mark. When, eight years later, Powell deposited his papers at Stafford, he listed (amongst other things) 'A collection of about half a million letters received by me from the general public since April 1968 classified by subject and in the order of date or of the events to which they refer.'[26] These clearly were not all written in the aftermath of Powell's Birmingham speech, although very many of them would have been. He continued to receive huge amounts of mail throughout 1968, his postbag increasing precipitously when he returned to the question of race in a speech in Eastbourne on 16 November. For the present, all we can do is safely to assume that in the twelve months after April 1968, the absolute minimum number of letters Powell received from constituents and from the public would have been upwards of 50,000, and in all likelihood very many more; the maximum figure, however, was probably double this, or perhaps even higher.[27] Whatever the true extent of this postbag, this represents an archive of popular writing on a colossal scale, of the same order as Mass Observation in the late 1930s and 1940s. People wrote to Powell, determined to tell him their life-stories.

Many of the letters written in support carried more than one signature. Some came from households, signed by husbands on behalf of their families; some from factories and workplaces: 359 postal workers from one town, for example, or thirty members of staff at a single branch of a bank.[28] All the immigration officers at Heathrow Airport (including, according to the *Telegraph*, three who were black) signed a round robin expressing their gratitude, and inviting Powell to visit them at their work.[29] Television footage showed ladies bearing little Union Jack pennants delivering a petition direct to Powell at his South Eaton Place home, with one woman announcing that 'eighty-eight per cent of Slough' was behind him.[30]

Less than three weeks after the speech, *New Society* published an analysis of approximately three and a half thousand of these letters, researched and authored by Diana Spearman, who was a close personal friend of the Powells and who had worked for the Conservative Research Department for many years. She was to turn up later in the 1980s as a founding spirit of the Salisbury Group, a coterie of intellectuals who shared an admiration for the philosophies propounded by Mrs Thatcher. It was apparent to Spearman that the letter-writers 'came from every social class and from every part of the country'. In attempting to categorize the contents of the letters, though, she was faced with a problem. Initially defining 'racialism' in terms of belief in the inherent inferiority of coloured people, she discovered that only 0.3 per cent of her sample could thus be designated. (Six of these, she noted, 'expressed a strong faith in the virtues of Saxon or Norman blood'.) Given the furious views on race which were then crossing the airwaves, breaking into and recasting public discussion at every point, this didn't seem to make much sense. She therefore extended her definition of racism 'to cover general accusations against the immigrants, the use of words generally considered offensive to them, such as nigger or coon'. But in a bizarre twist, she continued the sentence by adding the following qualification: 'unless they occur in letters in which a specific complaint is made'. She thus determined to exclude all letters from the 'racialist' category which, for example, advocated 'Send[ing] them back'. By using this tactic, she managed to move the percentage of those deemed 'racialist' from the unlikely 0.3 to the more convincing, but still reassuringly manageable, figure of 2 per cent. 'Some of the letters described as racialist', she explained, 'might be unskilful attempts to express concern about the future of the country.' There was a gamut of complaints about the behaviour of immigrants; some about 'black power utterances' and the spectre of the United States; and two about the student leader Tariq Ali. Driving these complaints was the conviction that the letter-writers knew the immigrant. 'I have read your speech and you are a 100 per cent right. People who don't *live* in the areas don't know.' The largest single category (about a third) articulated their anxieties in terms of nation rather than of race. 'No Briton wants to see his traditional way of living, the country he has loved and fought for, lose its identity, and particular character through the over great acceptance of too many peoples of quite different cultures and ways of life.' Or again: 'To change the name of our great country to no man's land [sic]'.[31] For a particular generation, memories of the Second World

War and of the danger of military defeat were mapped onto a new danger of racial defeat: 'Thank God I've found someone that has spoken for the white people of England. Did we go through the day and night terror of doodlebugs, incendiary bombs and bombing so that these hoards of black locusts might come here and buy the homes we've known for years and make our lives unbearable.'[32] Ex-colonial civil servants and missionaries wrote to confirm that Hindus, or Africans, had neither the will nor the capacity 'to integrate'. A dominant theme underlying many of the letters was gratitude to Powell for having the courage to speak out, in contrast to the timidity of the mainstream politicians who had ceased to represent the interests of their constituents. 'If it weren't for people like you, important issues wouldn't even be discussed. Thank you sir.'[33] Or again: 'Good luck sir, in your efforts to save our country'.[34]

These letter-writers were instrumental in creating a public community which imagined a shared ethnic predicament. They created the possibility for the unseen or subterranean reveries of race to be explored in the public domain. Epistolary reveries have a long history. In his discussion of anonymous, threatening letters of the late eighteenth and early nineteenth centuries, E. P. Thompson refers to the historical research of Richard Cobb. 'It would now seem, Richard Cobb tells us, that half the valets of pre-Revolutionary Paris, who followed the nobility servilely through the suave *salons* were nourishing in their reveries anticipations of the guillotine falling upon the white and powdered necks about them.' Thompson continues: 'But, if the guillotine had never been set up, the reveries of these valets would remain unknown. And historians would be able to write of the deference, or even consensus of the *ancien régime*. The deference of eighteenth-century England may have been something like that, and these letters its reveries.'[35] Of course, this is not to construct exact parallels. The historical circumstances were radically different; and the letters addressed to Powell were far from threatening—on the contrary. But there is an echo in the way in which, at moments of crisis, private reveries take public form and become politics. Many of these letters to Enoch Powell, posted from white communities which now believed themselves to be living on the vertiginous edge of the nation, carried an intrinsic populism. Not only did their authors know the blacks; they knew them to a degree that the guardians of official society, sheltered and patrician, could not. In this lay the authority of the letter-writer, an authority possessed by those otherwise powerless, and with which established public figures could not compete. They were writing as if from the colonial frontier. To present themselves in this way, as distant but properly militant tribunes of white civilization, was to activate memories of more formal colonial situations. They represent less an investment in historical time, and more a shared, collective dream-time, driven by the fantasy of restoring an imaginary lost past. In the climacteric of race in April 1968, the threshold between private reverie and public wisdom changed drastically and long-forgotten, or repressed, memories of the colonial past assumed a new resonance.

Although Powell's postbag was certainly gargantuan in April 1968, the phenomenon had been anticipated before. The tempo of letter-writing to Conservative MPs appears to have first quickened in the period 1960–1, when coloured immigration, especially from India and Pakistan, rose steeply and when public discussion about imposing restrictions on coloured immigrants was at its height.[36] This was a concern of constituents not only in the big cities but of those in more unexpected locations too: Bedford, Esher, Abingdon, Stratford, Harrogate. In May 1961 the Tory MP William Straubenzee, who represented Wokingham, noted the increase of letters on the issue:

> for the first time I am starting to receive from my constituency letters revealing anxiety about coloured immigration into the United Kingdom. I realise that this is an exceptionally thorny problem but undoubtedly it is becoming one in which the general public are getting increasingly restive.

The vast majority of the letters were hostile to the continuation of unrestricted immigration. Representative is a letter sent to John Profumo in July 1960, in which it seemed as if England itself were on the point of being decolonized:

> What *is* the matter with the Conservatives they don't face up to this matter [sic]. I woul'nt [sic] have voted, nor worked for the Conservatives had I known they would allow things to drift as they are. 'Wind of Change' indeed. It is a wind of change for England + unless something is done England will not remain England for long…There is the utmost danger of this country being so swamped we shall not be masters in our own land.[37]

The passions unleashed in April 1968 had been slowly building up for perhaps a decade or more before.

And the phenomenon continued, although on a smaller scale, after April 1968 as well. During the 1970 election, for example, Powell received between five and six thousand letters: considerably less than in the earlier moment, but still significant. The displacement of race to nation remained a continuing theme. An enthusiast from Anglesey wrote:

> I admire and trust Mr. Heath, but believe that he won largely because your philosophy and brave stand in the face of abuse and ridicule struck a note which inspired a majority of voters with a sense of confidence and courage they have not felt for years. I belong to that majority—the silent majority, hidden and forgotten, largely ignored—I mean the English, white, protestant. We have had no spokesman for decades, no organisation, no party, we do not organise, we have no popular folklore, and our sense of nationalism is muted to a degree that its voice can hardly be heard. But we are a vast majority and we have responded to your voice.

It is significant to note, here, the speed with which the idea of 'the silent majority'—coined only days before by Richard Nixon—became domesticated for the British. Another correspondent, from Falmouth, informed the chairman of the Conservative party on the eve of the election that 'the true leader of England' was Enoch Powell, 'the guardian of its virtue'.[38]

In discussing Powell's letters of 1968 and 1970, Diana Spearman is at pains to emphasize the respectability of their authors. Organizing this reading, and making it possible, is the slide in the letters themselves between race and nation. From Spearman's perspective, if race were a potentially awkward term, always in sight of disreputable passions, the idea of nation was essentially wholesome and above board, incapable of connoting anything more than a gentle and thoroughly justified patriotism. She thus sees these correspondents as honest, concerned, and above all, democratic, keen as citizens to be included in the public discussion about the fate of their nation. They become, in her view, the true descendants of a stalwart, liberty-loving English yeomanry. In her comment on the 1968 post she noted: 'Most of these complaints come from people living among immigrants and obviously not very used to putting their ideas on paper. The expressions used are sometimes vivid, though never obscene. The most extreme word in the whole range of letters is "bloody".'[39] Good sense prevailed. Present in the letters themselves, and in Spearman's reading, is an implicit sense of national history, in which nation and liberty are one.

But the fantasized, mythic Powell addressed in these letters—'the true leader of England' and 'the guardian of its virtue'—has got to *do* something, just as King Richard had to return to scourge evil barons and St George had dragons to slay. Myths like this, which placed Powell at the heart of the nation, called upon him to be active, commensurate with his positioning as a leader of white men. In some popular representations Powell was literally placed at the centre of the nation: photographs show demonstrators carrying the Union Jack with Powell's name emblazoned at its centre.[40] He had to act for the people, and for those too powerless or vulnerable to fight for themselves. It was at this point, however, that respectability and liberty necessarily became compromised, for explicitly or implicitly the aspirations projected onto Powell demanded of him that he cleanse the land—for him, in other words, to contain or expel the black immigrant. 'Send them back.' These are the reveries which underpin Powell's postbag. An alternative quote from the *Aeneid* comes to mind: 'If I cannot bend the Higher Powers, I will move the Infernal Regions'.[41]

Critically these letters to Powell don't tell the full story. In a literal sense, perhaps, Spearman is right. In their writing we do see a kind of crabbed, populist respectability or, to put it another way, deference, a deference both to Powell and to the weight of the traditions of English history. Yet as much as in the case of Cobb's Parisian valets, or of the authors of the threatening letters unearthed by Thompson, deference is a stance which can breed its own violent passions and dreams of recompense. Thus while Powell may be addressed in a spirit of breathless deference—'Well done, sir!'; 'Thank you, sir!'—*Heath* receives envelopes stuffed full of shit. The pertinent reveries of race, we can see, are enacted out in more than one arena; only to look at the formally deferential (at the letters to Powell) is to miss too much. Deference to Powell and hatred of Heath are not so much separate manifestations, as part and parcel of the same reverie. They represent a splitting of a single psychic object: on the one hand, the guardian of all virtue; on the other, all that is base and vile. Part of the interior psychic work of these letters is embodied in the endeavour to stake out the frontiers between the two—the good and the bad—desperate in their attempts to segregate virtue from all that which defiles.

Even in the most moderate, apparently most well-meaning letters, this antagonism is racialized—white, or England, as virtue, black as defilement. Sometimes this is clearly stated, sometimes not. But where such a view is consistently explicit is in the anonymous, threatening letters of our own times: the abusive letter to black neighbours, or to those blacks temporarily caught in the media spotlight.

On the evening of 5 November 1972, Robert Keenan was walking home from a pub in the Villa Road area of Handsworth, Birmingham, when he was seriously assaulted by three teenagers, Paul Storey (of mixed race) and two of his friends. They were arrested; Storey was identified in court as 'the ringleader', and sentenced to twenty years' imprisonment. His mother received a bundle of abusive letters. In these, she and her son were urged to 'Go back to Jamaica'. (She is white and her son was born in the UK.) An indiscriminate assortment of racial epithets was directed to her. One letter included reference to 'niggers', 'R.C.', 'Southern Ireland' and 'Pakis', at which point the mythic Powell was invoked who, the rhetorical logic of the letter implied, would make everything again as once it had been: 'Oh for Enoch Powell to clear the lot of you, back to your own land'. Another letter-writer called upon a more violent fantasy:

> So you are going to appeal against the sentence you shameless ...; his conduct is a tribute to the bringing up you gave him. I hope he never comes out alive: it's men like Mr Justice Croom Johnstone [sic] we need in this country, God bless him. We can do without your half cast [sic] bastard with his evil eyes and murderer's forehead. I am a good judge of character, he was born to kill. If I was in prison I would consider it a great insult to live cheek by jowl with the likes of him. I hope they will bring back the hanging [sic]. In America a mob would surround the jail and lynch him. Don't worry about your bastard, but the victim, poor man.[42]

Like its eighteenth-century counterparts, this is a vengeful call for blood. It holds together deference ('God bless him') and the incitement of the lynch-mob—an instance when the United States is imagined not as the spectre of the terrors yet to come to Britain, but as the homeland of white supremacy where popular justice can be carried out with impunity. Powell is not invoked, in this letter, as avenging angel—and, in the mind, one can hear him distancing himself from such brutality, as on other occasions he felt compelled to do. And yet, the yearning for an inviolate white nation—for an impossible England of the imagination—necessarily worked from its antithesis. Quite how the danger to the nation was to be extirpated, symbolically or in reality, was a pressing question for Powellites, and not just Powellites, of all stripes. In addressing it, all masquerades of decency fell away.

It is difficult to comprehend what motivates the violence in such utterances. All I can do here is to indicate one point, which I shall return to later. In the speeches of Powell and in the letters of those sympathetic to him, there occurs the suggestion that the destruction of the nation brings about not just the end of national identity, but the end of identity *itself*. The fear that England might lose its identity, that it might become a 'no man's land', ran deep, with powerful subjective consequences. There were two dimensions to this. One was the perception that the simple social presence of blacks in Britain would bring to an end the civilized attributes of England as 'a white man's country'. In this scenario, the smells emanating from unknown dishes—or any one of a thousand random irritants of modern urban living—could speedily become racialized. Acquiring metaphysical potency, such manifestations of alien living substantiated the belief that England's preternaturally long, providential history was about to be undone. The other was the erotic dimension, in which love-making between black men and white women would (it was feared) produce *identity-less* children—'half-castes', 'neither one thing nor the other'—destroying England from within, unseen, from within the bedroom, and in the process jeopardizing white mastery itself.

The domestic setting of these letter-writers is important. In postwar Britain, white anxieties about racial others have been peculiarly located in letters like these. From the early 1950s, they were received by public figures, and in the right circumstances could carry much weight. They were at their most powerful when they appeared as letters to the press, especially in the local press in those urban areas with a black migrant presence. To look at these letter-columns is to catch sight of the social processes by which men and women slowly began to imagine themselves anew as a 'white man' or a 'white woman'.[43] They suggest the degree to which black immigration was perceived to impinge on the very essentials of home, in all its complex variables. We do not need to imagine the location of these fears, for they are there in the letters themselves. As their authors sit in their front-rooms, or in their kitchens, pens held above the paper, the perceived outrages are proximate and sensuous: they can be smelt, heard, seen. Letters, Carolyn Steedman suggests, are 'pieces of text that are most intimately connected to biological bodies'.[44] The alien body is close by. We can witness the configurations of whiteness intensifying.

In the days immediately following 20 April, despite the stand taken by the political leaders of each party and by the editors of the heavyweight press, popular support for Powell seemed to mobilize in every quarter. Some of those opposing him, in Westminster or in Fleet Street, conceded plenty to his cause, and invariably discovered they were using the language and terms defined by Powell himself. It is impossible, in all this, to distinguish the degree to which the upsurge of active support for Powell was orchestrated by the media or was a genuine outburst 'from below', for each continuously spurred the other. The postcard poll undertaken by the Wolverhampton *Express and Star*, for example, could perhaps be seen as a perfectly proper journalistic enquiry, organized to assess the mood of local opinion—although maybe in the circumstances the outcome was only too predictable, given that the poll was conducted entirely within the terms defined by Powell. But there can be little doubt that the result, demonstrating the astonishing extent of sympathy for Powell, would have strengthened his political hand and encouraged Powellites, or Powellite waverers, elsewhere to press their case. What all this palpably wasn't, though, was merely a media event, got up in a few newsrooms, hitting the headlines, and then forgotten in the next tabloid flurry. So far as these can tell us anything, the opinion polls following the speech provide an indication of the scale of popular support. Gallup recorded 74 per cent, ORC 82 per cent, NOP 67 per cent, and the *Express* 79 per cent in favour of what Powell had proposed in Birmingham. The corresponding figures against were 15, 12, 19, and 17 per cent. On the matter of his dismissal, Heath won approval from 20 per cent (Gallup), 18 per cent (ORC), and 25 per cent (NOP), and disapproval from 69, 73, and 61 per cent respectively.[45] Five years later, in February 1973, a quarter of all MORI respondents claimed that Powell was the MP who best represented their views. There is evidence, too, that Powell's popularity reached beyond those touched by the conventional institutions of political society. In May 1969 the readers of *Honey* voted him the man they would most like to see as prime minister.[46]

These figures, in their broad lineaments, need to be taken seriously. In his diary Richard Crossman observed that Enoch Powell 'has changed the whole shape of politics overnight'; looking back on the episode, the Conservative thinker and politician Ian Gilmour believed that Powell had become 'the most popular politician in England'.[47] From April 1968 to February 1974 Powell effectively functioned as an alternative, third political party. In the run-up to the 1970 general election every daily newspaper, with the exception of the *Guardian*, gave more coverage to Powell than to the whole of the Liberal Party.[48] In Gramscian terms, Powell became a political party in his own right: he constructed a new political terrain, in which his own conception of civilization, unadorned, could be spoken; he challenged the prevailing political consensus and recast public opinion, such that what he had to say became politically speakable; and he won a steady bedrock of popular support. What other prominent Conservative could have triggered such shock when, on the eve of the 1970 general election, he urged the country to vote Conservative?[49] The most careful analysis suggests that Powell's was the decisive influence in the Conservative victory in 1970 and that, when his allegiances had shifted, he was a considerable factor, too, in the Labour victory of February 1974.[50] Politically, these were Powell's years; they were his because of the sustained popular support he could call on; and the popular coalition he created was united on one thing only—race.

In the United States in the 1960s one of the dominant forces driving the white backlash was the belief that civil rights legislation had positioned the federal government on the side of blacks, and that whites consequently were becoming victims of malign bureaucratic forces against which they were powerless. Such projections jammed together quite separate antago-nists—Washington politicians, and civil rights activists—into an enemy of startling capacities, and fired the genuine populism of white militancy. A similar logic was at work in the United Kingdom. Race relations legisla-tion, lacklustre as it was, became the object of hatred as a result of the belief that it curbed the liberties of ordinary white citizens, confirming the fact (so the argument went) that the establishment—the Labour government, Heath, the toffs at *The Times*—were 'all for the blacks'. (On Monday 22 April the *Telegraph* reported on its front page that North Wolverhampton Working Men's Club had voted unanimously to retain its colour bar. This was legal as the club was private. Maybe lacklustre is too generous a read-ing.) Powell had timed his Birmingham speech to intervene, outside Westminster, in the debate on the Race Relations Bill, which was to receive its second reading on 23 April; the intervention occurred at a strategic moment, for the Conservatives were split on the matter. This constitutional occasion—the reading of the bill—became the focus for a rather different form of popular activity: more traditional for some than letter-writing, but in the cause of what was increasingly coming to be articulated as the politics of a white backlash.

On Monday 22, Tuesday 23, and Wednesday 24 April a number of strikes were organized to demonstrate sympathy for Powell. These were political strikes, with no parallels in the postwar period (outside Northern Ireland). They occurred throughout the country, including Powell's West Midlands; they were spontaneous and angry. The most significant, politically, were those which centred on Westminster. Between 800 and 2,300 dockers (the estimates vary, paper by paper, the *Express* producing the highest figure) marched to parliament on the Tuesday.[51] The second reading of the Race Relations Bill was in progress (watched from the gallery by the Trinidadian, Learie Constantine, in his capacity as a member of the Race Relations Board).[52] The strike had begun in the West India Docks, and in all some 4,000 dockers stopped work. There was no great job instability at this time in the docks—this did not occur for another couple of years—and many of them had a strong Communist party presence. The divisions ran deep.[53] But those who supported Powell marched to Westminster in order publicize their feelings and to petition their MPs. They had a lot of waiting to do, and while they were waiting many of them drank substantial quantities of liquor. They sang 'Bye, bye blackbird' and 'I'm dreaming of a white Christmas'— taunts which had been heard ten years earlier on the streets of Notting Hill during the white riots of 1958.[54] According to the *Express*, parliament was 'besieged', claiming with absolutely no justification that 'never before' had such a thing happened.[55] The Labour MP for the dockland constituency of Stepney, Peter Shore, was denounced by the demonstrators as a 'traitor' and Ian Mikardo, Labour MP for Poplar, another constituency in the docks, was identified as a 'Japanese Jew', and roughly handled.[56] As the *Telegraph* delicately opined, 'The demonstration included some good-humoured jostling with the police'.[57] There were suggestions that old-time members of far-right groups had been active in getting the strikes and demonstration going, though dockers were not renowned for being ordered around politically. Indeed, Barbara Castle, the secretary of state for employment, said as much at the time to Frank Cousins, the leader of the dockers' union, the Transport and General Workers' Union: 'This is the first time in recent history that anyone has been able to get them out on the streets on a political matter.'[58] One of the leaders of the demonstration, Harry Pearman, spent half an hour with Powell in the House of Commons. On emerging from the meeting he declared that it had 'made me feel the English blood was not dead. He made me feel proud to be British.'[59]

The following day it was the turn of the Smithfield meat-market porters. Like the dockers, they too had arrived in Parliament Square in their work-clothes, a sign of their independence and their separation from the normal business of Westminster. The overalls of some of the marchers were streaked in blood. Again, there is some evidence of a far-right presence. Big Dan

Harmston, an Oswald Mosley enthusiast and thus, in adhering to Mosley's own inclinations, mildly hostile to Powell, said this: 'There was a mood about the place. If that day I'd said, "Pick up your cleavers and knives and decapitate Heath and Wilson", they'd have done it. They really would—but they wouldn't have done it the next week. It was just that mood of the moment—like storming the Bastille, I suppose.'[60] The song they sang was 'When the whites go marching in'. They carried with them a petition signed by 2,026 of their 'comrades'.[61]

Demonstrations are good for television, certainly more so than letter-writing. One television-film extract shows the dockers congregating in Parliament Square on the Tuesday, the bronze figure of Jan Smuts—the long-time prime minister of South Africa—gazing down on the scene just off camera. A journalist approaches a knot of demonstrators and asks them if they support Powell. They are vociferous in their affirmation. The camera moves in on one man in the centre of the scene. He points to the Palace of Westminster and proclaims, direct to camera and nation: 'He is the only white man in there', to which there is noisy, possibly inebriated, assent from his friends.[62]

To be sure, this is a fleeting moment. We cannot even be certain that the clip was ever shown at the time on television, itself a peculiarly impermanent medium. But the words are none the less important. In spirit, they exemplify the sentiments of many of the demonstrators, strikers, letter-writers, petition-signers, and those who voted for Powell in the various polls. The 'he' in the declaration doesn't need to be further identified: a mythic quality is already cohering. Factually, of course, Powell was far from being 'the only white man in there'. Amongst MPs alone, there were at least six hundred or so, not to mention peers, assorted police, and flunkies. But *their* whiteness, and their white masculinity, had been compromised. Heath, Wilson, and the rest were not truly white men at all. They were, at least potentially, 'traitors' to race and nation, or more inventively perhaps, 'Japanese Jews'. In the ethnic drama being played out in this scene, whiteness becomes an attribute, to be earned or lost. Ethnicity, it seems, is pre-eminently a matter of the imagination.

In its modest way this is as significant a moment of ethnic discovery as many of the more well-known episodes associated with the 1960s.[63] It is important for its role in contemporary British history, and for its place in the processes by which Britain has become postcolonial, if that is indeed

what has occurred. In many different registers, with many different consequences, sizeable numbers of those white Britons caught up in the turmoil
of Powellism discovered themselves, anew, to be white.

These ethnic discoveries were imaginative acts. But to work they needed
historical memories in order that they might live in the imagination, for
memory is not only the past recollected, but a means of becoming. What
were these memories?

I

Ethnic populism

In his Birmingham speech Enoch Powell recalled what has now become a legendary encounter: 'A week or two ago I fell into conversation with a constituent'. In the symbolic structure of the speech, this 'quite ordinary man' turned into a figure of allegorical force. Aside from any other responsibilities, he—or more properly, this rhetorical figure—comes to stand for ordinary, decent, white folk, calmly going about their business. If he can be understood, strictly, as Wolverhampton man, he was also close cousin to the more familiar, mythic figure of Birmingham man. Powell continued:

> After a sentence or two about the weather, he suddenly said: 'If I had the money to go, I wouldn't stay in this country'. I made some deprecatory reply, to the effect that even this government wouldn't last for ever; but he took no notice, and continued: 'I have three children, all of them been through grammar school and two of them married now, with family. I shan't be satisfied till I have seen them all settled overseas. In this country in fifteen or twenty years' time the black man will have the whip-hand over the white man.'

The stark appearance of the figure of 'the white man'; the Manichaean antagonism between black and white; the recovered memory of the terror of the plantation: this is shocking. But this disturbing sentence overshadows the one which precedes it. 'I shan't be satisfied till I have seen them all settled overseas.'[1]

It might seem in this context as if 'overseas' has a rather general, abstract quality to it. I shall argue, to the contrary, that this is deceptive and that it works, at least in part, as a synonym for empire. In colloquial terms 'overseas' could often mean not just *any place* overseas but, specifically, Britain's imperial possessions.[2] In the 1950s Sir Anthony Eden, for example, in explaining his own commitments to empire, was keen that this should be acknowledged. According to his close confidante, Evelyn Shuckbrugh, Eden used to say to me that if you were to open the personal mail arriving from overseas in any post office in England you would find that 90 per cent of it came from beyond Europe, from Australia, Canada, India, Africa, anywhere, indeed, where British soldiers and administrators had served or British families settled. How could we ignore all that? That was what he meant by 'feeling it in his bones'.[3]

This is a peculiarly homely notion of empire, in which 'any post office in England' serves to unify English people wherever they are, in the home-nation or in far-flung colonies. It is a vision of empire which is less the product of the mind than of sensation and feeling, a knowledge of ethnic inheritance lodged deep in the body.[4] And as Eden's rhetorical question makes clear—'How could we ignore all that?'—it carries too a necessary politics. These intonations may be lost to a contemporary ear. Thus it is revealing that in the many, extensive textual readings of the Powell speech this echo of empire has warranted no attention. To emphasize its pertinence is simply to read with the grain of the speech, restoring a meaning recognized more readily at the time than in subsequent years.

In his novel, *The Satanic Verses*, Salman Rushdie has famously taken the British to task for failing to understand that much of their history has taken place 'overseas'. It is a failure which he sees as intrinsic to Britishness, resulting from a kind of collective, contemporary amnesia about the empire and about Britain's history of violent colonial conquest. This is an interpretation I find persuasive. But Rushdie's formulation may not be sufficiently precise. Forgetfulness might seem to suggest that memories of empire have been forever obliterated, nowhere to be heard or seen. Yet as I suggest later, if an entire historical experience has disappeared from contemporary memory, or by some means has been repressed so that it has little or no purchase on current public discussion, traces of this history may enter popular consciousness through more surreptitious means. Memories of that history may be displaced, appearing in unlikely forms or in locations where they may not seem to belong. These memories do not simply vanish from the social landscape, but appear—unasked—at unexpected moments. They can be discerned too in other stories, which on the surface might seem to have little to do with the imperial past. That such things happen, turning on the prohibitions on speaking about or recalling specific events from the past, is recognized well enough in popular humour—as we know from Basil Fawlty's frenzied injunctions not to mention the war. Such moments allude to a past which is not yet closed, and which continues to live in the present.

Or as Rushdie points out elsewhere in *The Satanic Verses*, 'What's a ghost? Unfinished business, is what...'[5] The notion of overseas employed by Powell's interlocutor, I'll suggest, works as a memory trace in this way. More particularly, it functions as a displaced memory of empire, one which remains 'unfinished business'.

Powell's unnamed constituent, assuming that such a person existed, declared himself to be a white man. This invocation of whiteness I take also to be a memory of empire. It catches the idea that, as an imagined England disintegrated and, it seemed, could no longer serve as home to its indigenous white peoples, there was a place overseas where the proper protocols of whiteness prevailed, where white mastery could be restored, and in which a true homeliness might be revived. This was less a literal location than a place of the imagination, remembered through many displacements. The very amorphousness of the idea of overseas is telling. The colonial overseas may indeed signal a place where terrible things happened, as Rushdie implies; but also, from the contrary perspective, it represented a site of utopian possibility where white authority could be most completely fulfilled. Indeed one of the ways by which empire—'overseas'—has been remembered, and continues into the present, is through acting out, in later generations, the inheritance of being a white man or a white woman. From the late nineteenth century an entire archive of stories circulated through the metropole, counterpoising the decay of the metropole to the vitality of the frontier, where white lives could be more fully realized than at home. Whiteness in the metropole was, for good reason, generally unconsciously inhabited, unspoken, muted, often only ever articulated in moments of anxiety and felt danger. In the normal run of things, though present, it remained invisible. Whiteness, as I argue later, is only comprehensible in relation to the variety of forms which are deemed to be 'not white'. One of the peculiarities of metropolitan whiteness, which explains its apparent intangibility, is the degree to which non-white peoples colonized by the British were geographically distant, such that it could appear as if the white lives of the metropole had no real, living connection to those who had been colonized. Whiteness on the margins of empire, on the other hand, was called upon to do different things, and to work at a higher intensity. Yet the traffic between frontier and metropole, in both people and stories, was always extensive such that neither was ever sealed off, one from the other. It is with this traffic, in so far as it touches on the dispositions of whiteness, that I am most concerned in this volume.

More especially, to imagine *settling* overseas, which for Powell's constituent represented the only possible salvation, brings to mind a particular historical experience. There were many parts of the empire where British men
and women were posted but rarely chose to settle. More favoured to settle
were those colonies which could be construed as being white, or as having
the capacity—to use a term common at the turn of the nineteenth and
twentieth centuries—to become a 'white man's country'.[6] By the end of
the nineteenth century Canada, Australia, and New Zealand, for all the
complexities of their racial compositions, were generally viewed from the
perspective of the metropole to have made this transition to white countries
with most success. Well into the twentieth century, South Africa and
Southern Rhodesia, with their much greater non-white populations, were—
to say the least—more problematic in this regard. The emergence of these
colonies *as* white colonies is itself of historical significance. Yet I am suggesting that, whatever their racial realities, for whites in the metropole they
could serve as the idyll of fantasized white homes, uncompromised by the
complexities and chaos of modern life. In this way the white colonies,
dominions to be, had a privileged position in giving form to white lives in
the metropole. 'The new country is never simply a geographical location',
writes Paul Carter, it is also 'a historical and poetic destiny'.[7] For later generations, this constituted a colonial past which could still be felt 'in the
bones' or which, in moments of perceived danger, could come alive again,
more immediately, in the imagination.

Overseas: the settler colonies

So when we are told of Enoch Powell meeting a constituent who expressed,
in 1968, a desire that his children be 'settled overseas' the most plausible
interpretation is that this is a reference to the old dominions of white settlement. Continental Europe in the 1960s still represented a relatively
restricted option. If racial fear were the chief anxiety, the United States
would have been an unlikely choice for Britons beginning a new life, for in
the more febrile white imaginings of the time the US was already well on
its way to fully fledged Black Power. Rhodesia might have been attractive,
though tricky to manage legally. Perhaps South Africa would have been
judged acceptable in its exercise of white power, under the leadership of
John Vorster's National Party? But if not Rhodesia or South Africa, there

was always Canada, New Zealand, or Australia—as indeed, in the case of Australia, there had been for Powell himself, in earlier years. For an 'ordinary' working-class man of his generation—in his forties or fifties we could assume, born not much after Powell himself—the likelihood is that he had in mind, or was remembering, the historical experience of the white colonies. When the fictional Tony Hancock, a few years earlier, had felt compelled to emigrate from his East Cheam residence, convinced his liberties as an Englishman were jeopardized by the imposition of an iniquitous sixpenny increase in his rates, it was naturally Australia, New Zealand, and Canada that he first considered. This being popular comedy, he ended up elsewhere—in Baffin Land.[8]

Between 1948 and 1975, some 30–40 per cent of respondents to Gallup polls in Britain regularly expressed a wish to settle overseas. In March 1948, of the 42 per cent of respondents who declared such an interest, 9 per cent selected Australia, 9 per cent South Africa, 8 per cent New Zealand, 6 per cent Canada, and only 4 per cent specified the USA.[9] Thus in 1948 approximately *one in seven* of the UK adults surveyed stated a desire to settle in the traditional white colonies. The only significant change in later years, in the 1970s, was a fall in those expressing a wish to migrate to South Africa.[10] In all, in the period from 1945 to 1960, over one and a half million Britons—or 80 per cent of the total of UK emigrants—set off for Australia, Canada, New Zealand, South Africa, or Rhodesia.[11] When, in March 1946, the Australian Assisted Passage Scheme was announced 96,000 applications, representing 240,000 people, were lodged within the first two months. Within six months this had almost doubled to 400,000. In the first three months of 1957—a time relatively free from sharp privation, or conspicuous social crisis—Australia House received 35,000 letters of application, while in January 1957 Canada House was conducting 6,000 medical examinations each week.[12] The generic attraction of the old white dominions, however, has not entirely vanished in the intervening years. Emigration to Australia peaked in 1969, with a total of almost 80,000.[13] At the start of the new century, in 2001, Australia, Canada, and New Zealand remained, in the view of Britons, among the most desirable alternatives to living in the UK.[14] Though one must suppose that this has little consciously to do with empire, it does demonstrate a degree of continuity between the colonial past and the postcolonial present.

In the postwar years the decision to emigrate came about as the result of an entire complex of private, domestic judgements which now remain largely hidden from sight of the historian.[15] Alongside the sense of adventure and expectation of those departing, one can only imagine the thousands of domestic dramas which such decisions must have impelled. While most emigration was voluntary, a numerically relatively small exception, though an important one socially, was comprised of those children for whom the decision to migrate was imposed upon them by outside agencies. These included orphans (New Zealand offered to take any British child orphaned by the war) and children in the care of private welfare societies, particularly those with religious affiliations. By the end of the 1950s, however, the emigration of children had virtually ceased altogether.

Yet while the great bulk of the migrants saw their decision to leave as a private matter, to be judged solely in terms of their own personal futures, the imperial state intervened actively to encourage a new generation of dominion migration. In a series of agreements with the separate dominions, the British government invested heavily in empire emigration. The old Empire Settlement Act of 1922 was renewed in 1952, in 1957, and again in 1962. While it was evident that the immediate economic benefits went to those societies in which the migrants chose to settle, representing an immediate economic loss to Britain, support for emigration derived from high imperial reasoning. Politicians from both parties advocated the peopling of Britain's erstwhile possessions with British newcomers of the right type, or the right 'stock'. (This proved to be Tony Hancock's downfall. Despite his much vaunted, if doubtful, blue-blooded ancestry he was not deemed of suitable stock for the usual destinations. Hence his arrival in Baffin Land.) The long-term political purpose was to strengthen the ties between the mother country and the—white—Commonwealth. This was an imperial policy in which the gradations of Britishness were finely etched. As Kathleen Paul has demonstrated, the idea of 'British stock', on which these policy debates were grounded, signalled Britons of a particular type: white, with the capacity to 'assimilate' to their respective host nations.[16] Striking is the degree to which an older language of imperial affinity continued into the postwar period. The reasoning of Lord Cranborne (the future Lord Salisbury, who appears later in these pages) was entirely characteristic. In May 1944 he had advocated imperial migration on the grounds that 'the interchange of blood between one part of the Commonwealth and another must tend to strengthen the whole and to multiply the links that hold it all together'.[17] Eight years later, as secretary of state for Commonwealth Relations, he spoke in similar terms, proclaiming that 'a transfusion of blood...strengthens the whole'.[18] In 1958, on a visit to Australia, the prime minister, Harold Macmillan, announced his commitment to ensuring that Australia 'remain British in blood and tradition'.[19] 'Stock', 'blood', 'family': these were the categories in which the old white settler colonies were construed after the Second World War. If the individual migrants themselves had their own private reasons for deciding to leave their home nation, as they departed they necessarily positioned themselves in an institutional nexus in which the imperatives of an older colonial order still prevailed.[20] As Arthur Calwell, the first minister of Australia's Department of Immigration, announced in 1946: 'Australia hopes that for every foreign migrant there will be ten people from the United Kingdom.'[21]

There is evidence that at least some postwar British migrants sought to flee Britain because of their belief that black immigrants, West Indians in particular, were becoming too numerous. At the end of the 1950s the *Observer*'s correspondent in the Rhodesias noted that 'Latterly, some new arrivals have gratified reporters from the local newspapers by saying that they have left Britain because it is being overrun by West Indians and that they wish to live in a land where the black man is kept in his place.'[22] 'With coloured people in a country', one migrant to Australia declared, 'you lower the standard of living. In Australia you're keeping it a "White Australia" for Europeans.' Anxieties about national decline, commonly expressed by migrants, could too be racially—or eugenically—inflected.[23] There is also evidence, which may be the more significant, of the essentials of white identifications intensifying in the moment of migration itself.[24] Most of the Britons who migrated to Australia, for example, took the four-week sea-voyage. A portion of them kept journals and diaries, some of which have been examined by James Hammerton and Alistair Thomson, who have also conducted interviews with a number of the surviving settlers. According to their findings, on the voyage out memories of Britain's imperial past—the tales learnt as schoolchildren; 'the ghosts of Francis Drake and Captain Cook'—informed the ways in which the migrants made sense of their own experiences. 'Memory followed memory', in the words of Elizabeth Jolley, who had sailed to Perth with her family in 1959. But perhaps the greatest impact derived from the experiences of disembarking en route, and visiting briefly the seaports of the Mediterranean, the Indian Ocean, and the Pacific. The immediate impression of these habour areas was of inefficiency, dirt, and disorder. First impressions of Australia, commensurately, were of a land both 'clean' and 'homely', or in the words of the migrant Graham Little,

Australia appeared 'very clean and very like England'. The stories of these journeys characteristically come to be framed by the antagonism between cleanliness and dirt, order and disorder, and implicitly between white and non-white. 'A British imperial identity', writes Thomson, '—though sometimes challenged within the ship along the fracture line of social class and ethnicity—was reinforced by the migrants' confrontation with "the natives" as they traversed the ports and harbours.' He indicates too his suspicion that, when he interviewed the migrants late in their lives, the racial stereotyping which the contemporary written accounts exhibit was modified, or indeed 'censored', by the interviewees themselves. 'Empire', he concludes, 'is a thread which runs through the migrant stories, and it is usually an empire which brought order, cleanliness and efficiency to lands which are now reverting to their previous squalid and corrupt state.'[25] The fact of migration itself could thus recast the syntax of whiteness, such that its sentiments could be more intensely felt, and the authority it carried be more sharply spoken.[26]

The numbers of those emigrating from the United Kingdom to the 'white empire' in the postwar period were significant. We know, in addition, that many more wished to emigrate, or at least said that they did. The presence of migration to the white colonies, both actual or desired, marks an important dimension of the postwar experience in metropolitan Britain, suggesting the continuing pull of empire even in the age of decolonization. This postwar migration was, as we know, part of a longer history. From 1880 to almost the beginning of the First World War, about a quarter of a million people left the United Kingdom to travel to non-European destinations each year. From 1910 this number rose steeply, almost doubling. In the 1880s and 1890s only a third of emigrants from Britain had journeyed to the empire, the majority choosing to travel to the USA. In the early part of the twentieth century the balance shifted. In the first decade, about half of British emigrants sailed to Canada, Australia, New Zealand, and South Africa; thereafter, from about 1911 until the end of the 1920s, the figure rose to some two-thirds.[27] Demographically, these distant settler societies flourished. In 1831 the European population of New Zealand was a mere one thousand; fifty years later it had risen to half a million.[28] In the half century after 1815, more than a million British immigrants arrived in Canada, whose population increased seven-fold in these years.[29] Later in the century, the white population of South Africa doubled in little more than a decade, from 1891 to 1904, with perhaps 70 per cent of this increase coming from British emigration.[30] In Eric Richards's words, 'The British became a global people in the late nineteenth century.'[31]

This vast movement of people, peaking in the late nineteenth century but stretching back to the late eighteenth century and forward to the mid-twentieth century, is described by James Belich, in his important book *Replenishing the Earth*, as constituting the 'settler revolution' which created the 'Anglo-world'. Belich recounts the social and economic features of this great transformation. He also attends, if more briefly, to its cultural conditions of existence. Ideologically, what he calls 'settlerism', he claims, 'ranked in historical importance with the other great Anglophone "isms" of the day, such as socialism, evangelism, and racism'; while 'settler populism' represented 'a political creed that proved to be a brake on, or sometimes rival of, elite social rule throughout the Anglo-world and throughout the nineteenth century, from Andrew Jackson in the 1820s to the radical Australasian governments of a century later'.[32] To consider 'settler populism'—or ethnic populism, the term I use here from the metropolitan vantage—an equivalent to socialism, or to racism, may be conflating too much. But I think that Belich is right to emphasize the significance of this collective settler experience as an identifiable mentality. It certainly possessed a long duration and, as his narrative demonstrates, it was sanctified by a profound commitment to the protocols of racial whiteness: by what W. E. B. DuBois in 1903 understood to be 'this new religion of whiteness'.[33]

Persuading potential migrants to pack their bags, leave their homes, and journey to the other side of the globe was not an issue which was left to chance. Religious and philanthropic organizations were active in promoting emigration, motivated in part by fears of the impending 'over-population' of Britain. Agents from the colonial nations, posted in Britain, were tireless in their projection of life overseas. In a time when mass advertising was beginning to develop, the bid to persuade potential recruits was systematic, particularly in Scotland. Agents from Canada, Australia, and New Zealand had to compete with each other, as well as with representatives from the American Midwest. In the 1840s the New Zealand Company had fifteen staff in its London headquarters in Broad Street, at a time when the entire Colonial Office employed only twenty-five people. In the 1870s the New Zealand government had seventy-three agents in Scotland alone, and advertised in 288 Scottish newspapers.[34] Colonial agents organized advertising campaigns to saturate towns and villages with bills and placards, displayed in libraries, post offices, railway stations, hotels, and farmers' clubs.

Wall-maps and promotional literature were given to schools, and atlases to the pupils.[35] This was one means by which an amorphous 'overseas' began to take shape, and become more concrete; in distributing atlases to school-children, in which Britain and its white colonies were given due promi-nence, new mental maps became possible; and the emigration of neighbours and family created intimate connections between home and a discernible overseas, generating a peculiarly homely rendering of 'overseas', which Eden would have appreciated.[36]

In May 1907, the Scottish imperialist and author, John Buchan, whose memories at this time were still fired by his experiences in South Africa a little while earlier, reflected on these changes occurring in the empire. The recent Imperial Conference, he believed, marked

> a complete departure from the view common fifty years ago which conceived of the Empire as made up of Britain plus a string of poor dependants. It rec-ognizes the fact that the Mother Country is *prima inter pares*, and that the Empire is an alliance into which all the members enter on equal terms. But it is more than a mere alliance—it is a family partnership, and a working part-nership. There is the bond of blood and a common ideal between the mem-bers, and, since they work for a common purpose, there must be some machinery for joint deliberation and joint action.[37]

These were, by the time Buchan was writing, representative views. They regularly punctuated imperial thinking, from the mid-nineteenth to the early twentieth century. 'Mother country'—'family'—'the bond of blood'. This set of interconnected terms, although signifying the possibility of inclusion, did not apply to all nations of the empire equally. The metropole—the 'mother country'—was located at the centre. 'Bonds of blood' applied exclusively to the white colonies. And 'family' indicated a variety of possi-bilities—encompassing both the idea of siblings, for those deemed to be of the same race, and the notion of offspring, for those more backward races in need of the firm hand of authority. The defining, master-sign of blood alerts us to the irrepressibility of a deeply positioned racial connection. Even, in similar encomia, when the emphasis appeared to fall exclusively on matters of language, culture, or civilization, the image of blood was never far away. As the Earl of Meath, the originator of the Empire Day Movement, declared at the Delhi Durbar celebration in London in 1912, there existed in the case of the dominions, he believed, the triple bond of blood, religion, and language: 'the three great ties which served as a strong chain binding white man with white man'.[38] The interlocking of nation and blood, and nation and race, appeared as an indistinguishable set of relations in the dominant conceptions of empire in the late nineteenth century.[39] In a later epoch, when these imaginative connections were less easily spoken and when the formal relations of colonialism had diminished, the old themes still recurred. Thus in the Powellite aftermath blood functioned as a central symbol: rivers of blood, Saxon blood, Norman blood, blood-stained overalls, 'the English blood...not dead', even Mrs Thatcher's 'strong meat'. This manner of thinking—'thinking with the blood'—has registered as a powerful symbolism in the making of modern nations.[40] So too it did in the making of an expanded, Greater Britain.

Yet there is also an ambiguity in Buchan's optimism. On its own, 'the bond of blood' he believed to be insufficient to ensure harmony in the field of actual politics. Joint action, in order to work, required machinery: a machinery which needed to be centralized, to have its administrative and representative councils, and to win consensus equally from the various different parts of the empire. Yet one of the inescapable themes of imperial history at the opening of the century was the reluctance of the colonies to subsume their own new-found nationalisms to a larger system of unification or federation, which (colonials feared) would simply re-enact the power of British rule. The complex affiliations of a greater ethnic loyalty were always in potential conflict with the contending affiliations of nation, or of a local patriotism, even within the imagination of single individuals. This was a fact that the most enthusiastic promoters of empire in the metropole were not always willing, or able, to fathom.

Buchan's passing reference to the empire of 'fifty years ago', which he contrasted to the empire of the Edwardian period, is acute, for it draws attention to the fact that those parts of the empire which were bound to the mother country by the 'bond of blood' were, politically, products of the latter decades of the nineteenth century. The belief that Britain might stand as the mother country, both first among, and equal to, its white colonial descendants, was an invention of the second half of the century, gathering pace as the century progressed. In the case of Australia, for example, transportation of convicts to New South Wales had been abolished in 1840, and in the years that followed the migration of free colonizers was encouraged by the state, for the first time ensuring that whites outnumbered the Aboriginal population. The ending of transportation, in the words of Catherine Hall, had turned Australia 'from a prison to a land of promise'.[41] It was in this period that an idea—not of democracy, but of inclusion—first cohered, in which the white overseas subjects of the crown were recognized as constituents in the larger entity of a single Greater British people, a vision which was driven by a profound conception of shared ethnic patrimony.

Retrospective accounts by imperial ideologues, written when the dominions were an established feature of the British Commonwealth, sought to emphasize the inevitability of their evolution, as if the external dimensions of the British matched the providential progression of their internal history, bringing peace and civilization to all alike. Winston Churchill's speeches from May 1940, for example, resonate with such convictions.[42] Or when Queen Elizabeth sailed into Sydney harbour in 1954 at the start of her tour of the dominion and saw for the first time the Australian nation, she made much of the fact that it confirmed for her the virtues of British civilization.[43] The emergence of the white settler colonies, as white, was—to the contrary—a protracted, never-ending, and violent process. The historiography is complex. Much turns on the nature of the so-called second British empire, that is, on the colonial system which coalesced in the late eighteenth century in the aftermath of the American War of Independence.[44]

British colonial strategy in the early decades of the nineteenth century was—both in rhetoric and in actual policy, and with barely no exceptions— despotic, far removed from anything which might resemble a liberal ethos. A comprehensive account is provided by Christopher Bayly. He offers two overriding arguments. First, the colonial period from the 1780s to the 1830s (the conventional periodization of Britain's second empire) represented a moment of incomparable imperial dynamism. In the 1770s and 1780s Britain was in retreat against France in America, Asia, the eastern Mediterranean, and the Caribbean; by 1820 its empire ruled over 26 per cent of the world's population, and by the 1830s it accounted for a third of world trade. This was a recovery without prior historical parallel, equalled at the time of writing, Bayly reckons, only by Prussia in the middle of the nineteenth century and by the US after 1942. Second, the motor driving this colonial expansion Bayly identifies as a resurgent state, organizing a revivified system of aristocratic and Creole power drawing in, he says, 'the hard men from the peripheries'.[45] This was an authentically conservative regime, but one active in intervening in new social arenas both at home and in the colonies. It marked a modernizing conservatism, dedicated to the business of creating a new polity, and committed to the watchwords of church, crown, law, and trade. From this perspective the second British empire of the early nineteenth century can be seen to have represented 'a series of attempts to establish overseas despotisms which mirrored in many ways the politics of neo-absolutism and the Holy Alliance of contemporary Europe', or 'a series of loosely linked aristocratic fiefdoms'.[46] The dynamism of this recharged colonial state also served to generate new patterns of ethnic belonging—not least for the British themselves—and new divisions between ethnic groups in the colonial sphere. In the metropole, the continuation of the long war with France and the reaction against domestic variants of Jacobinism saw the culmination of the historic processes in which a British patriotism was formed—an 'internal' history which was inseparable from the intensifying tempo of colonial expansion.[47] In the colonies themselves Bayly notes a number of developments: the codification of ideas of racial hierarchy; the increased disciplining of colonized populations; and the spread of new systems of unfree or indentured labour. The outcome resulted in the organization of modern landed elites, composed almost exclusively of white Anglo-Saxon Protestants, ruling over local peasantries, and held together by a variety of officially sanctioned 'tributary patriotisms', which in turn were subject to the overarching authority of the crown.

As Bayly describes this imperial system, there was no marked distinction in policy that radically differentiated the future white colonies, as a whole, from the rest of Britain's overseas possessions. This only occurred as a result of later transformations. The abolition of slavery in 1833 formally marked the British empire as an empire of free labour. According to Frederick Cooper, the ideal of free labour was crucial in framing the mentalities, for more than a century, of decision-makers in London; it also provided a potent element to the complex meanings of Britishness, which in later years were drawn upon, not only by imperial administrators, but by settlers, 'natives', and domestic critics of empire alike.[48] Yet it was in the two or three decades after emancipation that popular opinion in the metropole turned against former slaves, and that racial perceptions hardened. In the middle years of the nineteenth century imperial rulers in London were confronted by a series of far-reaching crises: the Indian uprising in 1857–8; the massacre in Jamaica in 1865; and the revival of the Maori wars in the 1860s. The prose of racial fear was relayed not only in the public media of the respective colonies, but in the organs of opinion at home as well. In the aftermath of this violence, the distinctions between the 'white' empire, identified in terms of a (near) ethnic equivalence, and what Buchan depicted in the putatively racially neutral terms of 'poor dependants' became more heavily pronounced. In the 1830s and 1840s, as Thomas Holt demonstrates, Canada had been 'discussed in much the same terms as the mixed societies to the south', as (in other words) the colonies in the Caribbean. By mid-century, the distinctions were sharper and they turned on race.[49] Canada could no longer be comprehended as comparable to the Caribbean.[50] It might seem as if the Whig, free-trade, free-labour arrangements broke with the despotic imperialism of the earlier period, but there were continuities as well as discontinuities. The 'peripheries' continued to produce their 'hard men' and, as ever, their influence on the public life of Greater Britain—as some were beginning to understand the settler lands—was far from negligible. Racial hierarchies were more deeply entrenched. The emergence of the white empire needs, then, to be situated in relation to the development of the specifically non-white, dependent empire. While some providentially crossed the threshold and joined the family of Greater Britain, many more were destined to live their lives as 'natives'. But the whites were deemed to be constituents of Greater Britain precisely because they were not natives. The liberality of the one, based on an imagined kinship, was a function of the illiberality of the other, based on an equally imaginary conception of inherent racial authority.

The idea of a Greater Britain necessarily brought into question the predicament of Britain itself.[51] The question of the relation between the two—Britain and Greater Britain—was, at the turn of the nineteenth and twentieth centuries, a matter of unending controversy, with tracts and pamphlets rolling off the presses advocating a thousand and one different solutions for formalizing, or extending, their union. But above all, the consolidation of the white colonies in the last part of the nineteenth century deepened the possibilities for imagining colonialism to be a liberal, inclusive, popular arrangement, as opposed to something despotic or absolutist. Critically, the inclusion of overseas Britons in an imagined Greater Britain coincided with the protracted organization of the institutions of mass democracy at home.[52] Indeed, as we shall see, there were significant figures who believed that the white colonies offered a privileged arena for radical intervention. In this view, the settler communities were perceived to be more receptive to the reforming impetus than the hidebound traditions of an effete England at home. There existed imagined Englands of unbounded conservatism and tradition represented, for example, in the writings of Anthony Trollope. But there were too alternative imagined Englands driven by the spirit of historic radicalisms which, on occasion, sought even to retrieve the broken traditions of the seventeenth century, *restoring* overseas what had been usurped at

home. Empire could assume, in the hearts of some of its most zealous protagonists, a popular, radical provenance, in which the white man functioned
as the key agent of progress, pitted against the traditions of aristocratic privilege.[53] The hopes underwriting emigration turned on 'an intense but qualified egalitarianism', in which freehold property rights, independence from
masters, hostility to domestic service, and material abundance shaped the
dreams of the future.[54] That these were aspirations tied all but exclusively to
the evolving white colonies is true. And as such, their radical spirit was
compromised in its very fundamentals, for the settler colonies were not
white by fortune alone; they had to be rendered white, and the mechanisms
of white authority had daily to be reproduced and maintained. Yet the
increasingly numerous initiatives to popularize the appeal of empire at
home addressed indigenous Britons as *participants* in the adventure of empire,
as if the empire were truly theirs.

Those won to the cause of empire in Britain were conscious of their
political obligation to make it a popular issue. From the 1880s to the beginning of the First World War an entire network of civic-imperial organizations
was created which aimed to recruit members, generate popular support, and
influence national opinion, all with the objective of pressing home the cause
of Britain's imperial standing: the Imperial Federation League, the Imperial
Maritime League, the Imperial South Africa Association, the Navy League,
the Primrose League, the Tariff Reform League, the Empire Day Movement,
not to mention the varied youth movements, and many more.[55] There is
much debate within the historiography about the forms of popular knowledge which these organizations generated. I shall come back to the more
particular questions in later chapters. Here we can note the sheer scale of this
mobilization, which drew in not merely the manly citizen well briefed in the
protocols of constitutionalism, but the recently enfranchised and also—comprising many poorer men, and all the women and children caught up in this
groundswell of popular activity—the unenfranchised. Some of these organizations were more obviously political than others. Paid-up cadres in the
Navy League or the Tariff Reform League—both of which had their wom-
en's sections—were intervening directly in matters of immediate importance
for Westminster. Dressing up to attend the local Primrose habitation for an
evening's entertainment supplied by pierrots, jugglers, and ventriloquists;
contributing to a subscription for a local memorial to a neighbour killed in
the war in South Africa; or practising *veld*-craft in the local copse in improvised khakis: these clearly represented activities of a different order. Yet they

all worked to produce a particular kind of subject, and a particular kind of relationship between the private self and the public polity, and they were educative in apprising the participants what the greater imperial polity was. The émigré political theorist, Moisei Ostrogorski, understood at the time that the Primrose League, for example, represented 'a machinery which manufactures sentiments' and which worked as 'the greatest promoter of the "socialization of politics" '.[56] In 'socializing' politics and in manufacturing 'sentiments', these imperialist organizations needed, at the most rudimentary level, to tell their stories of empire. To make any impact, they needed to address the private person in a manner which was meaningful to her or to him; and if the home-citizen truly were to become a participant in empire, the empire needed to be made homely. There were occasions when the various attempts to mobilize the home population, and to create a new type of imperial citizen, were effective, and occasions when they weren't. But in their sum, the accumulation of stories of empire which were orchestrated for the people at home in this period recast the terms in which Britain itself could be imagined as a community. In this, the projection of Britons overseas—kith and kin, of the same blood—was pivotal for their shared whiteness, spoken or not, made them equivalents. To begin to narrate one's own life in these terms was to begin to 'think with the blood'.

Yet the stories told in the metropole, emphasizing adventure and heroism, rarely conformed to the brute realities of daily life in the distant lands of the empire. From the earliest times of settlement, right through to the late nineteenth and early twentieth century, the life of the vast majority of migrants was one of unrelieved toil. Some went as convicts, others under various forms of duress. Even those who went voluntarily, with a measure of enthusiasm, faced enormous odds. Sailing to New Zealand in the nineteenth century, for example, was a perilous experience. Children were particularly prone to die from disease on the journey, even before they had to face the hazards of their new lives. Sixty-five children died on *Lloyds* in 1842, thirty-one on *Brother's Pride* in 1863, twenty-five on the *Scimitar* in 1874. 'Even in the 1870s, there was a strong chance that a family with six children, en route to New Zealand to give them a better future, would lose one of them.'[57] Such was the grim calculus of emigration. The psychic costs involved were formidable.[58] Ford Maddox Brown's painting, *The Last of England*, captures something of these anxieties. On arrival, the newcomer confronted the need to create a means of subsistence, labouring hour by hour, interrupted only by memories of life back home, both men and women dependent on their own muscular power.[59] Precariousness pressed in from every quarter. Bernard Bailyn's comments on pre-revolutionary America would have held true for many parts of the white settler colonies of later times. 'It was a world of constant risk, its gentility preyed upon not only by natives culturally disorientated and dispossessed of their land, but by marauding "crackers" and other "banditti"—creoles gone savage—no better, it was said, than bloodthirsty aborigines.'[60] Colonial life was not only hard and violent. It was essentially disorderly, conforming barely at all to the visionary ideals of the advocates of empire in the metropole.[61]

A fine reconstruction of colonial life 'on the edge of empire' is presented in Adele Perry's discussion of British Columbia in the 1850s and 1860s.[62] British Columbia, in these years, was a three- to six-month voyage away from Britain. First Nation peoples outnumbered white settlers dramatically, and men outnumbered women. In 1855 the white population was just 774; fifteen years later it had risen to 8,576. The incoming settlers included Europeans, white Americans, and migrants from east of the Rockies; they encompassed as well Chinese, Afro-Americans, and other non-white peoples. Outside the towns the population was overwhelmingly male, involved in fur-trapping and, after 1858, in the search for gold. Even as moral reformers dwelt upon the dangers of white men having sexual relations with First Nation women, the practice was common, both in the towns and outside. So too were all-male households, signalling the possibilities for what was perceived to be another sort of vice. Drink, gambling, and violence were common pastimes, and prostitution served as an alternative means of employment for both white settler and First Nation women. Far from the colony representing all that was deemed best about the values of Victorian civilization, it more resembled its grotesque parody. Political and civic leaders, clerics, and respectable families of substance pressed to eradicate this colonial disorder. In 1861 the YMCA opened a branch in Victoria; temperance societies, literary institutes, and libraries were founded. Anglican and Methodist missionaries sought to instil the virtues of monogamy. Policemen were discouraged from living with First Nation women. Urban areas became more rigidly segregated racially, with dance-houses and brothels coming under stricter controls. Under the pretext of the smallpox epidemics in the early 1860s, curfews were imposed on the indigenous inhabitants of the towns, forced removals took place, and a pass system was introduced, not merely intensifying the division between settler and native, but doing much actually to assemble the personality of 'the native'.

While, on the one hand, the colonial state devised sharper, more punitive systems of regulation for First Nation women, on the other it did much—through its proxy, the Hudson Bay Company—to encourage white emigration from Britain. Local politicians were convinced that it was not only necessary to increase the white population, in general, but more especially to ensure that greater numbers of white women arrived in order that conventional family and sexual practices could be more broadly introduced. When the *Tynemouth* arrived in Victoria on 19 September 1862 it carried sixty young English women whose journey had been organized by the Female Middle Class Emigration Society. Arriving in a land in which whites were in a conspicuous minority, and in which women constituted perhaps a third of the white minority, it is little surprise that what in the metropole had been unremarkable was now, on 'the edge of empire', the cause of unceasing comment. The cargo of white women caused a sensation. Huge crowds amassed, all wanting a glimpse (as the press put it) of 'the rosy-cheeked English beauties'.[63] As these emigrants arrived in the colony their whiteness—in the eyes of others, and very probably in their own sense of themselves—intensified. But in a self-confirming logic, the increasing presence of white women, feminizing and domesticating what previously had been the domain of a masculine unruliness, created further pretexts for the segregation of the First Nation peoples from the settlers. In January 1859 the colonial press had already argued that the very appearance of indigenous peoples 'in the midst of civilised society' was 'little short of an insult to female modesty'.[64] To transform British Columbia into the semblance of a white man's country required dutiful white women to play their part, for without white women there could be no white man's country.[65] It required too a particular system of discipline which touched every aspect of colonial life, in which racial logic predominated and in which the segregation between settler and native was codified, in all its many manifestations. Indeed whiteness served as the defining optic through which the imposition of colonial order in the settler societies was imagined.

When Enoch Powell's anonymous constituent invoked the idea of an 'overseas' where the sovereignty of the white man predominated, he would not have been recalling the disorderly realities of the early settler societies. On the contrary, memories such as these fastened on the outcomes, not on the mechanics, of colonization: on the homely virtues of what colonialism had achieved, which could still be felt 'in the bones'. His was a reverie—indeed, as I will go on to show, a popular reverie—in which these inchoate memories of the imperial past provided a means by which he could articulate the predicament of his own and his children's lives. The racial disorder of his own times could make him, and countless other enthusiasts for Powell, speak as if they themselves were living on the old racial frontier, and as if they were another, if ill-served, generation of settlers. And they knew, for this they *had* learnt, that it was the settler, and not the native, who had made history.[66]

Ideological frameworks: Dilke, Seeley, and Froude

Many different histories converged to produce the possibilities for understanding the settler societies to be specifically white and, simultaneously, to belong intimately to the people of Britain. I am concerned here with just one part of this larger history. In the latter decades of the nineteenth century there appeared in England a literature which both heralded the new situation and sought to further the cause of unifying the Anglo-British spirit, at home and abroad. It was a literature as much concerned about ethnicity as about sovereignty, and it contained a powerful populist impulse. It charted what I understand to be the elements of a new sort of ethnic populism, whose inspiration came from the white colonies, but which was in many ways a metropolitan phenomenon, responding to metropolitan issues. I have in mind three defining books, published between 1868 and 1886: Charles Dilke's *Greater Britain* (1868); J. R. Seeley's *Expansion of England* (1883); and J. A. Froude's *Oceana, or England and her Colonies* (1886).[67] These were books representative of a period when faith in the capacities of the white race—evoked as English or British, Anglo-Irish (as Froude puts it), Caucasian, Teuton, or Anglo-Saxon—was moving to the very centre of intellectual life.[68] Race was becoming an ever more common, and ever more explicit, arbiter of civilization. There had been, before, occasions when prominent imperial ideologues had expressed the hope that the civilization of the English would be implanted in colonies overseas. This has a long history, leading back at least to Elizabethan England.[69] But Dilke, Seeley, and Froude were addressing a popular readership at a time of burgeoning mass democracy, with the purpose of reconceptualizing the very nature of (variously) the English or the British people. They set out to demonstrate that the people of the metropole could indeed participate in the making of a Greater Britain. And they endeavoured to

explore the racial or ethnic union of any future global British polity.
Froude's biographer, writing about his subject, expressed himself in terms
characteristic of the genre as a whole: 'His object…was to kindle in the
public mind at home that imaginative enthusiasm for the colonial idea of
which his own heart was full.'[70]

I will discuss Dilke and Froude first; and then I shall come to Seeley. The
earliest of these texts, Dilke's *Greater Britain*, is in some respects the most
interesting, as one can see in it the symbolic structure of an entire genre of
writing beginning to take shape. Contrary positions jostle, one with the
other. It is essentially a travel-book, though with bits of cookery and philosophy thrown in. After completing his studies at Cambridge, Dilke sailed
to the United States, and then journeyed on to Canada, New Zealand,
Australia, and India. 'In 1866 and 1887, I followed England round the world:
everywhere I was in English-speaking, or in English-governed lands. If
I remarked that climate, soil, manners of life, that mixture with other peoples had modified the blood, I saw, too, that in essentials the race was always
one.' Axiomatic was his conception of 'the grandeur of our race', manifest
in what he identified as 'Alfred's laws and Chaucer's tongue', and which
continued the essentials of 'Saxondom'.[71]

This concocted, mythic notion of 'Saxondom', attesting to the democratic qualities of the Anglo-Saxon nation before the imposition of the
Norman yoke in 1066, was coming to the end of its (very long) useful life.[72]
But it signifies, even in its attenuated mid-Victorian form, Dilke's radical
credentials. He wrote as a self-professed radical, whose sense of the potential
unity of the English overseas depended more on his concept of race than it
did on his regard for the traditional practices of English constitutionalism.
In fact *Greater Britain* grew out of an earlier plan to write a *History of
Radicalism*. In the imagination of the author the two projects merged into
one. 'When I first came to Radicalism of the time present I discussed it
under various heads, of which the first was Great Britain, the second the
British colonies, & the third the United States, showing…the predominance which colonial questions were already assuming in my mind.'[73] The
History of Radicalism never got to be written, as *Greater Britain* took its place.
It is clear, though, the degree to which radicalism and the imaginative properties of the new colonies worked as one. The patrimony of Tom Paine—
arriving in Philadelphia in 1775, indicting the mother country for all manner
of corruption and looking to settler America as the spiritual home of the
radical cause—remained powerful.

Details of sovereignty were not, for Dilke, the chief issue. He didn't much care whether Canada remained part of Britain or not, though on balance he thought it would be better off independent and a republic. (Enthusiasm for Canada in Britain of the 1860s seems to have been meagre in every quarter.) He concluded that the connection with Australia should be maintained, as there was no equivalent to the United States—as in the situation with Canada—to complicate matters, realizing that this both differed from the bulk of enlightened opinion in Britain, and might undermine what would 'perhaps be morally beneficial to Australia'.[74] These were pragmatic choices, not questions of principle. Thus Dilke was happy to consider the United States as part of the Saxon inheritance, overlooking the secondary issue of its sovereign independence. This disregard for the scope of British sovereignty, and consequent agnosticism about the crown was, at the time Dilke was writing, one position amongst many. Not much later it would be a scandal.

Race was what mattered. The English were the most civilized. By good fortune this was a fact confirmed by nature. Supremacy over inferior races was thus England's destiny. By '1970' (Dilke seemed very exact about this: by the moment of Powell, in fact) the destiny of 'the English race' would be assured.[75] Yet this faith in the supremacy of white England carried with it sentiments which imperialists by the early twentieth century found difficult to comprehend. The degradation of the blacks in the southern states of the USA Dilke attributed to the historic legacy of slavery and to the prolonged moral collapse of the planter class (an 'aristocracy' able to fire the anger of any authentic radical), and not to a function of their blackness. Dilke was able publicly to *consider* the virtues of miscegenation, at one point admiring the 'half-breeds' of British and Maori parentage—a shocking notion only a few years later.[76] He dealt with the Sepoy Rebellion in India in 1857 in an uncharacteristically dispassionate manner, concluding it represented, not an inferno unleashed, but a civil war between two legitimate parties, and was caustic in his observations on the humiliations inflicted on the colonized population and in his views on the contemptuous philosophy of the officers' mess. He was peculiarly attuned to the catastrophic consequences of colonialism. In India, and in the east generally, he believed that colonialism had destroyed the traditional elites. As a consequence:

> There remains the slave class, and little else. We may select a few of these to
> be our policemen and torturers-in-chief, we may pick another handful to
> wear red coats, and be our guards and the executioners of their countrymen;

we may teach a few to chatter some words of English, and then, calling them great scoundrels, may set them in our railway stations and offices; but virtually, in annexing any Eastern country, we destroy their ruling class, and reduce the government to a mere imperialism, where one man rules and the rest are slaves.[77]

This was not to be the usual voice of imperial enthusiasm. It is too shockingly amoral, too little concerned with the distinctive civilization of the English. But in a curious way Dilke, because of his faith in race over nation, didn't regard himself as an imperialist at all: 'mere imperialism'—by which he meant territorial conquest of a weaker nation by a stronger—he assumed did not rate in the higher scheme of things.

This lack of imperial fervour derived from Dilke's conviction in racial destiny. The scenario was simple enough. The English were destined to flourish, the aboriginal peoples inhabiting the new colonies of the white man destined to die. Dilke's radicalism was imbricated in a bizarrely vernacular Darwinism. 'The English fly is the best possible fly of the whole world, and will naturally beat down and exterminate, or else starve out, the merely provincial fly.'[78] This is where the hard, supremacist convictions of Dilke's faith in 'Saxondom' are evident. Alfred and Chaucer may have been constituent features of the mythic Saxon legacy, but so too was the dynamic of the racial struggle, between the English and the 'inferior' races, and between the dearer and 'the cheaper' races.[79] 'The Anglo-Saxon is the only extirpating race on earth…Up to the commencement of the now inevitable destruction of the Red Indians of Central North America, of the Maories, and of the Australians by the English colonists, no numerous race had ever been blotted out by an invader.'[80]

And this was also where Dilke was at his most ambiguous. He was convinced, for example, that 'the white man' and 'Red Indians' couldn't exist on the same soil. He was convinced too that the dominion of white over red was not only assured, but that it would prove beneficial: 'After all, if the Indian is mentally, morally, and physically inferior to the white man, it is in every way for the advantage of the world that the next generation that inhabits Colorado should consist of whites instead of reds…The gradual extinction of the inferior races is not only a law of nature, but a blessing to mankind.' Yet racial domination of the white man was to be achieved without 'cruelty or fraud'.[81] Dilke knew much about both. His was a narrative of colonialism which was not shy about cataloguing the violence of the frontier. 'We live in an age of mild humanity, we are often told; but, whatever the polish of manners and of minds in the old country, in outlying portions of the empire there is no lack of the old savagery of our race.'[82] The planter class of the southern states in the USA, the free-booting pioneers of the Midwest, and colonials in Canada, New Zealand, and Australia: all were indicted. There are moments, though, when outrage is absent and when the colonial violence of the white man appears simply as the inevitable function of the expansion of 'Saxondom'. He compared the destruction of the Aboriginal population in Tasmania to the white pogroms on the natives in the western United States—a matter of pride to their boastful perpetrators—commenting only that: 'There is in these matters less hypocrisy among the Americans than with ourselves.'[83] It is not always clear what he thought about the practicalities of 'extirpation'.[84] At times it seems as if miscegenation would, avoiding all 'cruelty or fraud', provide the solution— though there is evidence that his anxieties about miscegenation accelerate through the book. At other, more abstract, moments it looks simply as if native peoples were to wither away when confronted by superior civilizations. This was Dilke's view of the situation in New Zealand. 'In America, in Australia, the white man shoots or poisons his red or black fellow, and exterminates him through the workings of his superior knowledge; but in New Zealand it is peacefully, and without extraordinary advantages, that the Pakeha beats his Maori brother.'[85] This central ambiguity of how extirpation was to occur runs through the text. It may seem a paradox, given Dilke's belief in the inevitability that indigenous peoples were destined to become extinct, that in later life he committed himself to the Aborigines' Protection Society. While convinced that the fate of primitive peoples was sealed, he was still able, it seems, to mourn their loss. But mourning of this sort carries with it too a kind of forgetfulness about the sins of human commission and omission.[86]

The expansion of England he believed would impinge on different races in different ways. He certainly believed that competing white races could be absorbed into the English, by their acquiring the English language and the English law. 'Celts' overseas, though decidedly un-Saxon in Dilke's perception, provided the most uncomplicated case. 'The son of Fenian Pat and bright-eyed Biddy is the normal gaunt American, quick of thought, but slow of speech, whom we have begun to recognise as the latest product of the Saxon race, when housed upon the Western prairies, or in the pine-woods of New England.'[87] Norwegians in the USA, on the other hand, though unequivocally white, presented 'the appearance of a tough morsel

for the English to digest'.[88] Equally, Chinese or Asiatics more generally in
the Pacific regions colonized by the white man, needed to be segregated.
But most of all, the destiny of native peoples was to be duly extirpated.
Thus Dilke described the English in America 'absorbing the Germans and
the Celts, destroying the Red Indians and, checking the advance of the
Chinese'—the last a chilling euphemism.[89]

By the twentieth century, metropolitan views of the white dominions
barely took into account the aboriginal inhabitants of these colonies. In the
public mind, their transformation into white men's countries had effectively
become complete. Early in the century 'Red Indians', Maoris, and Aborigines were accorded a minor role in the spectacle of Greater Britain. They
appeared in theatrical extravaganzas or as living *tableaux* in imperial exhibitions, confirming for metropolitan audiences the truths of ethnic evolution.
A little later they played a more significant symbolic role in the set-piece
dramatizations of the British crown, in coronations most especially. But
they had ceased to be definitive, and in a profound sense they remained out
of view, subordinate to the presence of the white colonial 'kith and kin'.
This invisibility induced an amnesia too, as if all the white settlers had done
had been to settle. Dilke's *Greater Britain* was written at an earlier moment
when the violent conquest of native peoples was still in progress, and when
native attack and colonial retribution presented themselves as an unavoida-
ble experience for colonial and traveller alike. Dilke's is a text in which the
raw mechanics of extirpation were still visible, whatever the views one ultimately attributes to the author himself. But it is also a text which first put
together the elements of a peculiarly English justification for the racial
supremacy of the English—a justification which had as one of its deepest
resources Dilke's radicalism. It was a justification which in turn was to be
validated by the simplest of tautologies. The mere existence of the English
overseas in the white dominions—civilized, liberal, pacific—attested to the
rightness of the history which had made it happen. Destiny, indeed.

Greater Britain was a public success. It quickly went through four editions
and was well reviewed. It remained widely read for some half century. Its
publication in 1868 established Dilke as a young man of influence. At the
same time he was enjoying his literary success, he was elected to parliament
on a platform of 'moderate radicalism' (in the words of an early biographer,
Roy Jenkins, who knew a thing or two about moderation), beating two
Tories, one of whom was W. H. Russell, who had been the celebrated *Times*
correspondent in the Crimea.[90] Most of all, for Dilke himself, the book

brought him into close collaboration and friendship with John Stuart Mill—even though Mill himself entertained doubts about the centrality accorded by Dilke to the influence of race on national character.[91]

Froude and Seeley were of different political temperaments from Dilke. Froude was a distinguished historian—indeed, regius professor of modern history at Oxford University—and had carried out various inquiries into colonial issues for the government. He was an intimate of Thomas Carlyle, becoming his biographer and the editor of his writings. Seeley was also a regius professor of history, though he was at Cambridge. He had found himself appointed to the professorship in 1869 on the basis of credentials which contemporary professional historians may find a trifle bewildering, as his only substantial publication had been an anonymous life of Christ. He soon came to be influential in the professionalization of historical study both in the university—the historical tripos was introduced four years after his appointment—and more widely through the medium of working men's colleges. In 1881 he began to work systematically on colonial history, most likely, it seems, lecturing in the first instance to future members of the Indian Civil Service. Initially keen that his lectures should remain unpublished, he was persuaded otherwise by Florence Nightingale in May 1882. The book came out, with the title *The Expansion of England*, and by 1885 some 80,000 copies had been sold. Its first publication closely followed the British occupation of Egypt; thereafter it remained in print, its reputation as an imperial primer established, until 1956, when the British were once more bombarding Egypt, though on this occasion to less effect.[92]

While Dilke wrote as a radical, Froude allied himself to the cause of Carlyle, and thus was always ready to berate any radical nostrum he spied on the horizon.

> I am no believer in Democracy as a form of government which can long be of continuance. It proceeds on the hypothesis that every individual citizen is entitled to an equal voice in the management of his country; and individuals being infinitely unequal—bad and good, wise and unwise—and as rights depend on fitness to make use of them, the assumption is untrue, and no institutions can endure which rest upon illusions.[93]

And yet it is striking that when Froude came to consider the problem of white settler colonialism, he felt compelled to place at the heart of his investigations the question of liberty and popular government. He opened his account by comparing the situation of his own day with the hopes—'the dream' as he describes it—of James Harrington two and a half centuries before.

> Harrington would have been himself incredulous had he been told that, within a period so brief in the life of nations, more than fifty million Anglo-Saxons would be spread over the vast continent of North America, carrying with them their religion, their laws, their language, and their manners; that the globe would be circled with their fleets; that in the Southern Hemisphere they would be in possession of territories larger than Europe, and more fertile than the richest parts of it; that wherever they went they would carry with them the genius of English freedom.

Indeed, so momentous had been these developments that the colonial English, amongst whom Froude continued to count the citizens of the USA, some of whom may never have known the realities of territorial England, had come to outnumber the domestic English: 'the number of our kindred in these new countries is already double that which remains in the mother country'.[94]

Yet Froude was astute in seeing that what Harrington imagined to be the solution—popular representation—had turned out to be the problem.

> The element on which he calculated to ensure the combination—the popular form of government—has been itself the cause which has prevented it. One free people cannot govern another free people. The inhabitants of a province retain the instincts which they brought with them. They can ill bear that their kindred at home shall have rights and liberties from which they are excluded. The mother country struggles to retain its authority, while it is jealous of extending its privileges of citizenship. Being itself self-governed, its elected rulers consider the interests and the wishes of the electors whom they represent, and those only. The provincial, or the colonist, being unrepresented, suffers some actual injustice and imagines more. He conceives that he is deprived of his birthright. He cannot submit to an inferior position, and the alternative arises whether the mother country shall part with its empire or part with its own liberties.[95]

This resistance to colonial representation occurred, according to Froude, in the official rather than in the popular mind. Governments, he believed, had ignored the call for colonial self-government. Governments aided, admittedly, by an ill-informed section of the people had interceded between colonials and natives to the detriment of the former. 'The colonists being on the spot, desired, and desire, to keep the natives under control; to form them into habits of industry, to compel them by fear to respect property and observe laws.' Ignorant intervention from London resulted only in 'irritating

the whites by accusations either wholly false or beyond the truth, and mis-
leading the coloured races into acts of aggression, or disobedience'.[96] And it
had been governments (including that of 'the greatest, or at least the most
famous, of modern English statesman', whom Froude had questioned on
the matter—and whom I take to be Disraeli) which had been keen to jettison the settler colonies on account of their demands on the exchequer.[97]
The people, on the other hand, were a different matter.

> The people of England have made the colonies. The people at home and the
> people in the colonies are one people…We and the colonists have lived apart
> and have misunderstood one another. They require to be convinced that the
> people of England have never shared in the views of their leaders. We have
> been indifferent, and occupied with our own affairs; but we, the people, always
> regarded them as our kindred, bone of our bone, flesh of our flesh.

For the men of the colonies are 'men of our own blood and race'.[98]

'We, the people.' Dilke's radicalism, Froude's anti-democratic conservatism: both were bent to create a populism, or more specifically, an ethnic or
colonial populism. If the government was ignorant of, or just plain uninter-
ested in, the larger issues of the race, then the people—as the nation—
needed to be addressed directly, and it was they (or 'we') who needed to
make the issue one of public import. To think in these terms implied that
the government was insufficiently attuned to the racial instincts of the people, for it was in the authentic English people at home and overseas—in
England and in the 'other Englands', as Froude called them—that the true
racial compact was to be found.[99]

There is, however, a further layer to the argument. If the people were
more truly English than their governors, then the settlers in the white colonies had the potential, at the very least, to be more English, and by extension
more white, than their counterparts at home. This could work in a number
of ways. Froude perceived the American rebels of 1776 as 'too English',
meaning that they were more committed to the principles of a manly liberty than their rulers in London.[100] It could work in terms of specifics, as in
Froude's comments on the English language spoken in Australia.[101] But
more profoundly, the white colonies were imagined by Froude as the pure
counterpoint to the decay, degradation, and dirt of domestic England. The
power of English civilization, unsullied and pure, idealized to its fullest
extent, was most intensely imagined as located—not in territorial England—
but on the distant frontier of those 'other Englands'. These 'other Englands'
are as England *was*: before the imposition of the Norman yoke; before

factories and the effluence of industrialization; before, in fact, history. Thus he could speak of the colonies as locales where 'children grow who seem once more to understand what was meant by "merry England"'.[102] This process of splitting England into its good and bad components, and projecting the good nation onto far-flung, unknown lands, gave these reveries their power.[103]

Froude's argument was, in part, ecological. Urbanization was bringing squalor and decay, affecting the race itself.

> What England would become was to be seen already in the enormously extended suburbs of London and our great manufacturing cities: miles upon miles of squalid lanes, each house the duplicate of its neighbour; the dirty street in front, the dirty yard behind, the fetid smell from the ill-made sewers, the public house at the street corners.[104]

On the one hand the excrement, the sewers, and the mean streets; on the other the utopian spaces of the frontier. In mid-Victorian Britain, internal disruptions to the social order could take on the disposition of racialized tribes—the savages of the rookeries, the Irish when out of place, and so on, all darkness and chaos—while those living their lives on the frontier could assume a kind of hyper-whiteness, a shadowless space of burning sunlight which served as permanent counterpoint to the perceived decay corroding the imperial centre, mired in shit and darkness.[105]

Dilke and Froude wrote from their own experiences as global travellers, bringing the truths of the frontier to the reading public of the metropole. Seeley's contribution to the genre is at first sight more detached, analytical, and historical, but the spirit which impelled him was similar. Seeley does not simply recount the story of the empire. *The Expansion of England* enacts it, symbolically and theoretically. His lectures were delivered at a moment when it appeared as if the colonial frontiers could expand no further—or more accurately, when indigenous peoples were finally being quelled as a military force. In this respect Seeley should be read alongside Frederick Jackson Turner whose more memorable lecture, 'The Significance of the Frontier in American History', was delivered to the American Historical Association in July 1893. In the American north it was only in 1890 that the native armies were finally defeated, in North Dakota; while at the other end of the continent, the Europeans of Buenos Aires and Santiago—living in those 'honorary' white British dominions of Argentina, and Chile, as Hobsbawm has called them—had put an end to regular indigenous attacks only as late as the 1880s, due largely to the arrival of the Remington rifle.[106] Global frontiers were closing in.

The expansion of the United States westwards, consolidating its power over the Pacific coastline, and the commensurate drive of Russia to the east, to its Pacific coast, posed the greatest threat, in Seeley's view, to the British empire. The political question was simple. England, as he saw it, had lost its first empire in the 1770s. A century later he identified four great groupings of territories: the Dominion of Canada; the West Indian islands; the South African possessions; and the antipodean colonies. To these he added India, 'subject to the Crown', 'ruled by English officials', but 'inhabited by a completely foreign race...and bound to us only by the tie of conquest'. Most telling of all between England and India there existed 'no community of blood'. Before long, he surmised, the white colonial population would be greater than that of the domestic population of England. Was this empire to be lost too? Or was it possible to unify the empire sufficiently to compete with the USA and Russia? Unlike Dilke, Seeley was not overly swayed by a belief in an inherent national or racial destiny, in which the outcome was already assured. For him this was a matter of contingency and politics: in sum, of history.[107]

Seeley organized his account of the nation in terms of its external dynamics. Or more emphatically, he sought to dismantle the dualism of 'internal' and 'external' altogether by insisting on the necessary unity of the two. 'It seems to be assumed that affairs which are remote from England cannot deserve a leading place in a history of England', he noted, complaining of a historiography 'much too exclusively European'. He believed the central issue of early colonial Europe had been the presence of the New World which 'does not lie outside Europe but exists inside it as a principle of unlimited political change'. In the eighteenth century, he concluded, anticipating Salman Rushdie's conception of 'overseas', 'the history of England is not in England but in America and Asia'.[108]

Seeley's is a history of England which pays scant attention to its monarchs, its parliaments, or the peculiar grace of its people. Unthinking evangelicals of empire, who perceived something 'intrinsically glorious in an Empire "upon which the sun never sets"', he derided as the 'bombastic' school. Indeed, Seeley was singular in his rejection of creeds of racial superiority.[109] It is rather the authority of the English state which functions as the prime mover (much as it does in Bayly's more recent account), an authority active as much in the colonies as in the metropole. His own hopes were clear: that metropolitan rule would prove sufficiently benign, and colonials sufficiently accommodating, for there to emerge throughout the empire a consensual unity founded upon a shared recognition of English ethnicity. 'If Greater Britain in the full sense of the phrase really existed, Canada and Australia would be to us as Kent and Cornwall.'[110]

To the degree that this had already occurred, it confirmed in Seeley's mind the conviction that England, strictly, possessed no empire, for the colonies merely operated as an organic extension of the home nation. Thus imperial England differed from all previous empires in that it had avoided conquering subservient lands, and was singular too in exhibiting an absence of 'violent military character'.[111] In this scenario, India presented some complications—just as it did, eighty years later, when Enoch Powell arrived at the same conclusion, alighting upon his idea that England had never had an empire.[112] This approach entailed a scepticism about the eternities of England which imperialists of a less cerebral cast of mind were not generally keen to pursue. Seeley deplored an 'unhistorical way of thinking' which assumed England always to have been the same. 'That we might have been other than we are, nay that we were once other, is to us so inconceivable that we try and explain *why* we were always the same before ascertaining by any inquiry whether the fact is so.' 'The expansion of England', he continued, 'involves its transformation'.[113]

This was a historical argument about the organization of England and its empire; it was also a national-imperial argument about the organization of historical truth. There is much in both these arguments which is convincing. But when Seeley thundered against Walter Scott, Lord Macaulay, and William Thackeray for coquetting with a feminized poetics of history, and when he delivered his own injunction to historians ('Make it true and trustworthy'), he positioned himself not simply as the innocent defender, or discoverer, of historical truth. He was too in the business of 'conquering' it unilaterally, to use Joseph Conrad's term, and recruiting a monologic politics of history for his own purposes.[114] For in Seeley, the intellectual co-ordinates of an expansive Englishness received philosophical accreditation. An empire which wasn't really an empire, conquests which weren't really conquests, dominions overseas ethnically identical to the mother country: these represented powerful reconceptualizations of imperial England, and they were to become recurring components in the story of empire which dominated metropolitan perspectives for the next two or three generations.

It might seem as if Seeley's emphasis on the imperial state checked the kind of populism espoused first, in this context, by Dilke, and then later by Froude. But his was still essentially an inclusive, even a liberal argument, addressed to an imperial people. It was one based on understanding the centrality of the ethnic ties binding England to its white colonies.[115] The tragedy of the 1770s, for Seeley, had been the fact that the government in London had claimed brotherhood with the British in North America 'and yet it had ruled them as if they were conquered Indians'. The lesson was obvious enough. White settlers ought not be treated as 'conquered Indians'. Given Seeley's insistence on the great importance of the authority of the metropolitan state, his ability to adopt as his own the image of the metropole as the 'mother country', and of colonial subjects as 'sons' and 'daughters' in the process of becoming 'grown-up', marks a significant moment in the evolution of imperial thinking.[116] This vocabulary sits strangely with the more analytical passages on the structures of the colonial state or on the contingencies of historical process. For all the sophistication of his historical understanding, this was a vocabulary which allowed back into his analysis categories of nature: blood, family, and organic connections tying parent to child. Paradoxically, this produced a history which was more feminine in its assumptions (the mother country with her offspring), and which—ideally, in Seeley's mind—would serve to justify a relaxation of political authority between centre and white colony. But even in this least excitable of imperial treatises, which scoffed at dogmas of racial superiority and sought to expand the inclusive structures of nation and empire, bonds of blood constituted the principal issue. As much as Dilke before him, or Froude after him, Seeley was 'thinking with the blood'.

Dilke, Froude, and Seeley had very different professional lives, different—even antagonistic—politics and different intellectual temperaments. While Dilke and Froude reported back to the metropole from the colonial frontiers, Seeley was a man happily settled in Cambridge. Dilke thought in terms of Britain, or Greater Britain. Seeley's concern was England, though he was not averse to thinking England the core of a future Greater British global nation-state. Froude liked to contemplate the future of England in terms of the various 'other Englands' which were emerging across the seas. Yet they all made the conceptual case, based on their readings of a global Anglo-British ethnic compact, for appreciating the specificity of the settler colonies. In their various presentations of the racial complexion of the future dominions they worked to establish that these were not societies composed of conquered natives but of peoples equivalent to themselves. In their multiple encodings of what it was that bound these distant peoples to those of Anglo-Britain, they sought to establish the settler colonies as white. And in so doing, they established too the whiteness of their metropolitan readers.

Froude's conservative, anti-radical populism went furthest in expressing an anxiety about the state of the metropolitan civilization. In his view, industrialization had blighted the inheritance of old England, and the ancient virtues of the English had migrated, he implied, to those 'other Englands' across the globe. In this Froude provided a measure of conceptual coherence to those reveries of race which located the true England overseas. James Belich, writing about New Zealand, argues that a crucial impetus in the act of migration to the settler colonies was the idea of 'restoration'. 'For the decent, this meant implementing a populist paradise or folk Utopia. New Zealand was to be England as it should be, and allegedly had been—steady jobs and good living conditions, together with mutual respect between master and man, were to be restored. For the respectable and genteel, restoration consisted in the moral regeneration of the "simple life".' 'These unauthorised motives for migration', he goes on, 'were semi-tangible but strong, and they helped create a powerful and enduring colonial populism…Colonial populism existed outside Britain, yet was not peculiar to any particular neo-Britain. It was a feature of the ethos of expansion, drawing people out and changing them as it did so, such that migrants going from different fragments to different frontiers developed similar characteristics.'[117] But this was not only an outward expansion. Froude, and to a lesser extent Dilke and Seeley, elaborated the essentials of a new national-popular civilization that determined to demonstrate the wisdom of reshaping the domestic nation in terms of its overseas colonies. As Seeley emphasized, were this to happen the idea of England and of its people would itself necessarily be transformed.

In the 1860s the violence of the frontier was palpable, deeply impressed in the writing of Dilke. By the 1880s it was as if violence and 'extirpation' had never occurred, and the expansion of the English could proceed unimpeded, for the well-being not only of the far-off colonists but so too for the people at home.

Carlyle and Mill

There is one last point about these imperial primers. It concerns the intellectual patrons of Froude and Dilke: respectively, Thomas Carlyle and John Stuart Mill. In 1849 Carlyle had published his notorious 'Occasional Discourse on the Negro Question' in *Fraser's Magazine*—an article retitled by Carlyle, four years later, 'Occasional Discourse on the Nigger Question'.[118] In his toxic prose Carlyle had retrospectively condemned the emancipation of slavery in the West Indies; he had articulated anew faith in racial hierarchy, reaffirming the virtues of white supremacy over black, and the virtues, too, of the 'beneficent whip'; and he had unleashed an uncompromising attack on white philanthropists, in Britain and the West Indies, who had endeavoured to represent black interests. The article was intended by Carlyle as the first instalment of his 'declaration of war against modern Radicalism', in the words of his chosen biographer, the self-same J.A. Froude, and it is indeed significant that Carlyle made relations between black and white the object of his opening salvo.[119] According to Froude, this was the moment when Carlyle's own claims to radicalism finally ceased, remarking too, with little exaggeration, that the 'Occasional Discourse' had generated 'universal offence'.[120] Mill replied to Carlyle, spelling out the liberal justification for understanding relations between black and white as a social or circumstantial matter, and not as a phenomenon preordained by nature. For Mill, blacks possessed the potential to rise to the same level of civilization as whites.[121]

Carlyle's denigration of emancipated blacks carried with it a commensurate elevation of the ideals of the white man. Moreover, for Carlyle masculinity, as much as the ethnic responsibilities bequeathed by the white Anglo-Saxon heritage, also carried absolute duties and privileges. In his idealized vision, white men were *more masculine*—more active, more independent, more able to make both themselves and the social world in their own image—than their black counterparts. In actual fact, however, Carlyle was often horrified at how unmanly public men in London turned out to be—they were not 'red-blooded *men*'—indicating, perhaps, a theme which later was to become more prominent: that masculinity on the frontier, not the metropole, was where true English manhood was most completely realized.[122] Nevertheless, at the end of 1865 he discovered his imperial hero:

Governor Eyre of Jamaica. After a riot occurred outside the courthouse in
Morant Bay, Eyre had proclaimed martial law and inflicted terrible retribution on the colonized population. The London press reported the initial
riot as if it were driven by a frenzy of blood-letting, as if the blacks of
Jamaica had set out literally to consume their oppressors, a view confirmed
by the eventual publication in the press of Eyre's own testament.[123] Public
opinion divided. On the one hand, the Eyre Defence Committee was
launched, whose principal spokesman was Carlyle; opposing him, and
speaking for the Jamaica Committee, was Mill. The dispute dominated
public life for some two years. If anything, in the years since the publication of his 'Occasional Discourse', Carlyle had become even more outspoken and reckless in his denunciation of the blacks of the West Indies, and
more eager to speak the unspeakable. Yet, from having been the cause of
'universal offence' in 1849, by the 1860s these same sentiments ensured he
was in prestigious company, with a considerable body of public support
behind him.[124]

The events in India in 1857 certainly marked one turning point in these
intervening years—this was the moment, too, when the term 'nigger' entered
common currency.[125] Mill himself was convinced that the Civil War in the
United States had been a critical factor in weakening the earlier consensus
in Britain on the emancipation of black slaves and in contributing to a hard-
ening of white antipathy. He was unflinching in his condemnation of the
white plantocracy of the Confederacy, believing that 'Their success...would
be a victory of the powers of evil'. And he noted too the consequences in
Britain, aghast at

> the rush of nearly all the whole upper and middle classes of my own country,
> even those who passed for Liberals, into a furious pro-Southern partisan-
> ship...the generation which had extorted negro emancipation from our West
> Indian planters had passed away; another had succeeded which had not learnt
> by many years of discussion and exposure to feel strongly the enormities of
> slavery...[126]

By the time of the Eyre controversy, Mill's sense of a deepening racial
hatred within Britain toward the blacks of the colonies was profound.
Perhaps this too was the occasion when racial reveries in Britain were first
manifest in systematic letter-writing. 'As a matter of curiosity', Mill
recorded, 'I kept some specimens of the abusive letters, almost all of them
anonymous, which I received while these proceedings were going on.
They are evidence of the sympathy felt with the brutalities in Jamaica by

the brutal part of the population at home. They graduated from coarse jokes, verbal and pictorial, up to threats of assassination.'[127] Dilke, in *Greater Britain*, recognized the same developments. Confronted with the degradation of blacks in the southern states of the US, just one year after the end of the Civil War and with the Eyre debate still raging, his comment was this: 'We ourselves are not guiltless of wrong-doing in this matter: if it is still impossible openly to advocate slavery in England, it has at least become a habit persistently to write down freedom. We are no longer told that God made the blacks to be slaves, but we are bade remember that they cannot prosper under emancipation.' Referring specifically to the aftermath of Morant Bay, he continued: 'All mention of Barbadoes [sic] is suppressed, but we have daily homilies on the condition of Jamaica', implying that such homilies worked to fuel white fears of inevitable black insurgency.[128]

Mill and Dilke certainly considered that white antipathies toward blacks were intensifying in British opinion in the 1850s and 1860s. As Catherine Hall has shown in her study of Birmingham, the manly citizen of 1867 was no longer, as he had been in the 1830s, a self-declared friend to the Negro. He was, on the contrary, 'convinced of the need for authoritative rule in the empire, and of the fundamental distinctions between Anglo-Saxons and others'.[129] An issue of significance arises from these episodes, though, which is more closely connected to my argument here. In the 1850s and 1860s Carlyle and Mill occupied contrary, polarized positions on the responsibilities of the British toward colonized blacks. But in the subsequent period, from the late 1860s to the mid-1880s, their respective followers, Froude and Dilke—on the issue of what might be called a specifically white colonialism—converged. There are complexities in this. Mill, as we have already seen, was doubtful about some of Dilke's enthusiasm for race, though for long he had been a supporter of colonialism. On questions of the non-white populations in the colonies, there was room for divergence between the two. But even so, on the fundamental question of the expansion of England, Froude and Dilke, the direct inheritors of Carlyle and Mill, held common ground. If the issue of non-white peoples continued to divide them, in their shared affirmation of the role of Greater Britain they were at one. Indeed the emerging appeal of these distant 'other Englands' was able to reconcile what for the prior generation had been irreconcilable. As Seeley had emphasized, the invention of the white empire had transformed England at home.

The metropolitan state

These ideas, I argue, did not remain merely bookish, or abstract. They, or their derivatives, reshaped the political and ethical arenas of public debate, and gave life to new conceptions of England as an imperial civilization. In the various imperial organizations invented in the Edwardian period we can witness their entry into popular life. But it is also the case that these ideas were transmitted to the heart of the state. This can be followed by looking briefly at the two figures of Joseph Chamberlain and Lord Milner.

Chamberlain's politics took him from radical republican to high zealot of British imperialism. Chamberlain and Dilke were close political allies, bound together (until Dilke's political downfall in July 1885) by their shared allegiance to the radical cause and by their common task of devising a strategy for advancing radicalism inside the Liberal party. Chamberlain read and was persuaded by Seeley's lectures.[130] Before embarking for the Cape in December 1884, Froude had contacted Chamberlain to ask if he had any message for the people of the colony. To this Chamberlain replied: 'Tell them in my name that they will find the Radical Party more sternly Imperial than the most bigoted Tory.'[131] In his earlier political days, however, Chamberlain had always been perplexed by the popular appeal of empire. In 1876 he had urged his fellow Liberal MPs not to bother to vote against the legislation proclaiming Victoria empress of India, 'as if it mattered a straw to anyone'.[132] Two years later he was bemused by the jingoism activated by Disraeli's determination to defend Constantinople. Clearly, as time went on, his imperial sympathies grew. In 1882, for example, he felt ambivalent about, rather than hostile to, the occupation of Egypt; by the time of the Sudan crisis of 1885 he was thinking in terms of 'a Dictator' to secure victory.[133] But ultimately it was the fact of the white settler societies which fired Chamberlain's imagination and made him an imperialist. Neither the Raj nor the Ottoman empire, both of which were dear to Disraeli, provided scope for the exercise of Chamberlain's radicalism. The white empire, on the other hand, did just that.

Late in 1887, having been outmanoeuvred by Gladstone on Irish Home Rule, having cut himself adrift from the prevailing party alignments, and with his political career in the doldrums, Chamberlain joined an official delegation to travel to Washington in order to resolve the question of disputed fishing rights in the Gulf of St Lawrence—hardly an assignment designed to buck him up. Nor did first impressions of the USA cheer him. With his local loyalties as fierce as ever, he found New York a poor comparison to his native Birmingham.[134] A passionate romance with the daughter of the US secretary of the army, however, put him in a better frame of mind. And so did his trip to Canada. Toronto he liked as (of course) he thought it resembled Birmingham. There, at the end of December, he delivered a speech on Anglo-Saxon nationality, noting

> the greatness and importance of the distinction reserved for the Anglo-Saxon race, that proud, persistent, self-asserting and resolute stock which no change of climate or condition can alter, and which is infallibly bound to be the predominant force in the future history and civilization of the world.

'The interest of true democracy', he continued, 'is not towards anarchy or the disintegration of empire, but rather the uniting together [of] kindred races with similar objects.' He believed the English in particular had a gift for realizing such ambitions, adding 'the working out of the great problem of federal government…seems to have been left in charge of the English people'.[135] This was Chamberlain's own gloss on the Anglo-Saxon theme, pressed—in terms of immediate politics—in order to persuade the Canadians of the inadvisability of signing a commercial treaty with the US, and airing ideas about federation which had been germinating in his mind since the Home Rule crisis of the previous couple of years. To the contemporary reader it may look like no more than the usual racial sentiment of the time. To his Canadian listeners, unaccustomed to hearing anything positive coming from Westminster statesmen, it was cataclysmic. Chamberlain's recent biographer describes the aftermath: 'He swept his audience away with enthusiasm. Some wept. Others climbed up on tables, waved dinner napkins, and shouted themselves hoarse.'[136] Shortly after, in his own mind, he connected this argument about Canada to his ideas about the future development of South Africa.[137] Early in his career as an MP Chamberlain had been virtually alone in voting from the outset against the British annexation of the Transvaal. By 1899, as colonial secretary, he was the decisive figure in the home government determined to defeat the Afrikaner republic and bring it under British rule.[138]

We can return here to the moment with which I opened the prologue: Chamberlain's speech on 15 May 1903 in Birmingham town hall to his Unionist constituents, following his official visit, as colonial secretary, to the defeated Boer republics. The speech marked one of the great interventions

in twentieth-century British politics; it launched a concerted bid to integrate
economically the white colonies, through a system of imperial preference or
tariff reform; and at the same time—in appealing directly to the people, over
the heads of the established political leaders—Chamberlain attempted to
create, by means of the Tariff Reform League, a popular extra-parliamentary
political movement.[139] There is good reason to see this as a popular movement of the right, even though Chamberlain's politics did much to redraw
conventional boundaries between conservatism and progressivism. Certainly,
at this point in 1903, and in the immediate aftermath, this was a politics with
a high populist charge. But it was also in large measure consciously a colonial
white populism, constructing as a single entity white working men of the
empire, irrespective of the particular 'England' each inhabited. In this sense,
ethnicity overrode nation and it marked another, more directly political, version of the white populisms initially theorized by Dilke, Froude, and Seeley.
In Chamberlain's rendition, though, the idea of England was articulated
through his local identification with Birmingham, drawing upon the mythologized figure of 'Birmingham man'. The means by which radical working
people could overcome their political and social exclusion, and truly become
an active and leading spirit in the nation was, in Chamberlain's view, for
them to participate in the business of empire. He determined to universalize
'Birmingham man' as the model for the true imperial citizen of the future.
'Birmingham man', and the empire he represented, Chamberlain believed,
were the future.

   'I could come to no great city in South Africa, hardly to any village or
wayside station, in any of the colonies, but always, it seemed to me, I was
cheered by the presence and enthusiasm of Birmingham men, proud to
recall their connection with our city, and anxious to prove that neither time
nor distance had lessened their affection for their old home.' For Chamberlain,
Birmingham lay at the heart of the empire, a beacon of the radical tradition.
(And indeed, long before Chamberlain himself entered the political scene,
by the middle of the nineteenth century many 'other' Birminghams had
been transplanted to the white colonies: three in New Zealand, five in
Australia, and ten in Canada.[140]) Loyalty to Birmingham, however deep it
ran, represented according to Chamberlain only one 'local patriotism'
amongst many: Scots, Boers, and the new-found national identities of
Canadians, Australians, and New Zealanders were all instances of local-
patriotic sentiment. The means by which these local patriots could 'become
more and more one people' lay in the capacity of the citizens of empire to

foster a 'feeling of Imperial patriotism'. Specifically excluding the case of India (much as Seeley had done), Chamberlain explained that this ambition to create imperial loyalties was the task of 'our own kinsfolk...that white British population that constitutes the majority in the great self-governing colonies of the Empire'. The black or indigenous populations of the white colonies went unmentioned, as did the West Indies. Everyone else he designated as 'foreigners'.[141]

Chamberlain believed (as did John Buchan) that his generation had revived the spirit of empire. Empire, he thought, 'has had a hard life of it. This feeling of Imperial patriotism was checked for a generation by the apathy and the indifference which were the characteristics of our former relations with our colonies.'[142] The South African War had convinced him of the depth of colonial regard for Britain, persuading him that this period of indifference had come to an end. Like Buchan, he believed too that some mechanism was required to ensure that imperial loyalty converged with the self-interest of the mother country and of each of the self-governing colonies. This provided Chamberlain's ethical or political justification for his campaign for tariff reform. Symptomatic of his increasing rapprochement with the Unionists was his singular imagining of the old and the new as one. 'We', the English, he described as 'an old country', 'the result of centuries of constitutional progress and freedom'. The empire—specifically the nascent white dominions—represented, however, not the past but the future: 'But the Empire is not old. The Empire is new. The Empire is in its infancy. Now is the time when we can mould that Empire, and we and those who live with us can decide its future destinies.'[143] For Chamberlain, the empire was the means by which domestic England could properly become a modern nation, simultaneously realizing the historic radical programme. Empire represented not the negation but the apotheosis of his radicalism.

Chamberlain's was a powerful conception of the modernizing impetus of empire. The white colonies were not only home to migrant Britons, but also the means by which 'the old' would continue to be renewed. The condition on which he imagined the entry of working men into the life of the nation was that the nation itself would be enlarged, not only internally through the expansion of the franchise but externally through the making of a Greater Britain. This is what the figure of 'Birmingham man' was to portend. 'He' was the source for all that was vital for 'the white British population' of the colonies, while at the same time the force of Chamberlain's argument suggested that 'his' aspirations could be most fully realized in the Britain overseas rather than in the Britain at home. Having brought progress and order to Birmingham, the vision of distant lands beckoned.

To move from Chamberlain to Milner is to move from the profane to the mystical. Despite Chamberlain's transition from radical to Unionist, he himself remained tied to the political institutions of the home nation. He had cut his teeth on organizing political caucuses; his base in his local constituency required the incessant orchestration of mass meetings and the making of improvised public rituals; Westminster became his political home. His determination to launch the Tariff Reform League was conceived not as a bid to create a new political movement, *per se*, but more as a means to revitalize the old traditions of Unionism. Milner, by contrast, never had this grasp of the realities of domestic constitutional politics. He was a man of the state who dreamt of a popular following, and a man of the empire who despaired of the metropolitan nation. Having served the empire overseas, the return to actually existing England continued for Milner to be a never-ending disappointment. For all his declarations of love for country, it was the idea of the settler colonies—whiter, more manly, more homely—which possessed him.

By those who allied themselves to him, and by his epigones, Milner was revered, just as he was hated by a multitude of others. He exuded a sense of empire which was comparable to the passion of religious faith, and often spoke in such terms himself. When high commissioner in South Africa he created around him his so-called Kindergarten of young enthusiasts of empire (of whom John Buchan was on the outer fringes); returning to Britain at the end of the first decade of the century—enthralled by the excitement of fashioning South Africa into both a nation and into a white man's country—they organized themselves into the Round Table, a high-minded political lobby devoted to the objectives of imperial federation.[144] There was always something eccentric about the Round Table. Despite the public men they attracted, and despite their influence on imperial thinking, their leading figures (Lionel Curtis and Philip Kerr, the future Lord Lothian, pre-eminently) could never quite square the excitement of their early manhood in South Africa with the requisite political realities of Whitehall and Westminster. Working as cadres of militant imperialism in the domestic polity, they met frustration as often they did success. This is instructive, perhaps, in reminding us of the fluctuating appeal of high imperial policies in ruling circles (especially amongst the old Toryism of the countryside), even at a moment conventionally seen as one of powerful colonial instincts. Even so, in the larger ethical or intellectual domain the group did much to consolidate the religion of empire espoused by Milner.

Milner himself represents a strange conjunction. For all his zeal, he devoted the greater part of his life to the minutiae of making colonial rule work. He was an administrator for many years before he became a politician. His first post overseas was as director-general of accounts in the Ministry of Finance in Cairo, a job he left to become chairman of the Board of Inland Revenue. In 1897 Chamberlain, as colonial secretary, invited him to become high commissioner in South Africa. Proconsular authority was what he yearned for, though he would have preferred Egypt to South Africa: 'the sober joys of a well-rendered estimate are tame compared with Empire building'.[145] As one of the leading figures responsible for precipitating the war with the Transvaal, he kept his nerve steady, and steadied those around him, including Chamberlain. When victory had been secured, he preoccupied himself with the business of reconstruction, absorbing himself in matters to do with land settlement, afforestation, railway amalgamation, and much else. Unlike the younger men around him, he didn't particularly relish his time in South Africa—though he still refused the post of colonial secretary when it was offered him after Chamberlain's resignation in 1903, just as he was to refuse the viceregal position in India two years later.

He was a collectivist who thought of himself as a socialist and whose early formal political allegiances were to the Liberals; eventually he gravitated to the new Unionist coalition, though he liked to style himself 'a free lance, a sort of political Ishmaelite'.[146] His disdain for democracy was deep, though he endeavoured to secure independent representation for working men, but not through the Labour party.[147] His attitudes were as intransigently proconsular at home as in the colonies. Domestic political arrangements never held much meaning for him. Politics for Milner was defined, above all else, by race and empire.

He was not alone in these views. (He used to meet with Rudyard Kipling each Empire Day, in a bid to ensure the event was marked by appropriately principled company.) When in March 1897 he was due to sail to the Cape to take up his post of high commissioner, his admirers organized a farewell dinner at the Café Monico. H. H. Asquith, Joseph Chamberlain, A. J. Balfour, G. J. Goschen, John Morley, and George Curzon—the cream of the political elite—were all present, with some 130 others. In his speech of thanks Milner took the opportunity to reflect on his imperial faith. He recalled his time at Oxford University more than twenty years before when many of those present—there were twelve former presidents of the Oxford Union in the assembly—had first come to imperial affairs.

> But there were some half-dozen of us who hammered away—I dare say we bored our audience—at these ideas: that the growth of the Colonies into self-governing communities was no reason why they should drop away from the Mother Country or from one another; that the complete political separation of the two greatest sections of the English-speaking race was a dire disaster, not only in the manner in which it came about, but for coming about at all; that there was no political object comparable in importance with that of preventing a repetition of such a disaster, the severance of another link in the great Imperial chain.

He went on:

> the opinions which I then feebly attempted to support have only grown stronger...I have a fatal habit of seeing that there is a great deal to be said on both sides of a case...But there is one question upon which I have never been able to see the other side, and that is precisely the question of Imperial unity. My mind is not so constructed that I am capable of understanding the arguments of those who question its desirability or possibility.

His 'most audacious' dream was to render service to the 'world-wide State' of the British empire, and to be 'a civilian soldier of the Empire', in a cause in which he held absolute belief. Chamberlain, in being called upon to respond, made a speech which—*to Milner*—appeared 'very political and rather bellicose'.[148]

By the end of his posting, in 1905, his pessimism about particulars was as strong as his optimism about the general: however dismal were the day-to-day practicalities of colonial administration, his faith in the larger project intensified.

> My wishes for myself are summed up in the desire to get out of this...I am under no illusions about 'finishing my job' here. It is like the heads of the hydra...Since I got back a year ago we have simply saved the Colonies economically. It was an awful fight but the result is that the financial outlook is completely altered. Fresh follies might of course spoil it. They might spoil anything.

Milner, always profoundly sceptical in political life of the will of the people, was not to be swayed by liberal sentiments, especially when they

arose from a milieu with no first-hand experience of colonial conditions. Thus he continued: 'The next cause of anxiety is the foolish haste
to get "representative" or "responsible" government. Let others deal
with that.'[149]

These were views expressed in private. In public, about local conditions
he said much the same, though in a rather different voice. About imperial
civilization itself, however, there was no sign of equivocation. As Milner
described himself, he was 'from head to foot, one mass of glowing conviction in the rightness of our cause'.

> What I pray for hardest is that those in South Africa with whom my words
> may carry weight should remain faithful, faithful above all in times of reaction,
> to the great idea of Imperial unity. The goal of all our hopes, the solution of
> all our difficulties is there…This question, as I see it—the future of the
> British Empire—is a race, a close race, between the numerous influences so
> manifestly making for disruption, and the growth of a great, but still very
> imperfectly realised, political conception. The word Empire, the word
> Imperial, are, in some respects, unfortunate. They suggest domination, ascend-
> ancy, the rule of a superior state over vassal states. But as they are the only
> words available, all we can do is to make the best of them, and to raise them
> in the scale of language by a new significance. When we call ourselves
> Imperialists, talk of the British Empire, we think of a group of states, inde-
> pendent of one another in their local affairs, but bound together for the
> defence of their common interests, and the development of a common civili-
> sation, and so bound, not in an alliance—for alliances can be made and
> unmade, and are never more than nominally lasting,—but in a permanent
> organic union. Of such a union, we fully admit, the dominions of our sover-
> eign, as they exist to-day, are only the raw material. Our ideal is still distant,
> but we are firmly convinced that it is not visionary nor unobtainable.[150]

This was from Milner's farewell speech in South Africa, delivered in
Johannesburg on 31 March 1905.[151] It took him an hour and twenty minutes to deliver and, in his words, it was phrased 'quite mercilessly' and 'without adornment or relief'.[152] He took his (mainly British) audience to task
over their illusions about the benefits of self-government; over their hasti-
ness to effect reconciliation with the defeated Boers; and over what he took
to be the indiscriminate exclusion of blacks from political society, Milner
himself favouring a continuation of the strategy described by Cecil Rhodes
as 'equal rights for all civilised men'. Critical, though, was his belief that 'the
true Imperialist is also the best South African'. This encouraged his audience, and the larger white society in South Africa, to refuse to subsume their

national instincts, as *South Africans*, to the authority of Britain, but instead to create a unity of the two, in which each functioned as an expression of the other. Soon after his arrival in South Africa he became an advocate of 'local patriotism' (in much the same manner as Chamberlain himself), of which this idea represented an elaboration.[153] Milner knew better than most that this unity of colonial nation and empire would require its 'machinery' in order to be fully realized. But at the deepest level, this had its mystical or poetic conditions. The organic connection between the population of the mother country and the white population of the colony existed only as a consequence of race, and of the purported relations of blood between the two.

The idea of 'the Mother Country' and Dilke's term 'Greater Britain' recur in his speeches and articles. The empire itself functioned merely as the expression of what Milner himself defined as 'the racial bond'. 'From my point of view this is fundamental. It is the British race which built the Empire, and it is the undivided British race which alone can uphold it.' These racial connections, he declared, were 'more primordial' than mere material ties, for the race comprised 'the bond of common blood, a common language, common history and traditions'. Indeed, in attempting to prevail upon the white dominions to assume the burdens of imperial responsibility, he was hoping that this would serve to staunch the flow of Britain's 'best blood and sinew' from the mother country to the colonies, and thereby help avert the threat of the degradation of the metropole.[154] These ties of blood were not, though, evenly distributed across the empire. The emergence of the white colonies as potential dominions indicated the need to distinguish between the component parts of the empire—especially between those where British 'blood' predominated, and those where it was largely absent.

By the first decade of the new century such analytical distinctions were becoming easier to voice. In June 1908 Milner contributed his own views in a speech entitled 'The Two Empires' to the Royal Colonial Institute.

> I often wish that, when speaking of the British Empire—that is to say, of all the countries of which His Majesty is sovereign, *plus* the protectorates, we could have two generally recognised appellations by which to distinguish the two widely different and indeed contrasted types of state of which that Empire is composed. Contrasted, I mean, from the point of view of their political constitution, though the contrast, no doubt, as a general rule, has its foundation in racial, or, what comes to the same thing, climatic, conditions. I am thinking of the contrast between the self-governing communities of European

blood, such as the United Kingdom, Canada, Australia and New Zealand, and the communities of coloured race, Asiatic, African, West Indian, or Melanesian, which, though often enjoying some measure of autonomy, are in the main subject to the Government of the United Kingdom.[155]

Much of Milner's public life was spent urging those who possessed 'European blood' to subscribe to the overarching dictates of imperial citizenship, regarding their variant 'local patriotisms' merely as distinctive forms of the larger entity—for English or Welsh as much as for the Afrikaners in South Africa or for the French in Canada. It is probable that this conception of plural allegiance—not a common occurrence in English thought—derived from his upbringing in Germany, where Milner identified two sorts of patriotic affiliation: that to 'the "narrower" and the "wider" Fatherland'. In his own manner, he thus understood his own allegiances to be both to the wider 'Fatherland' of empire and to the narrower 'Fatherland' of the United Kingdom.[156] And in this plural conception of citizenship, he believed, lay the only hope for the future destiny of South Africa.

For those imperialists drawn to the white empire rather than to India, as both Milner and Chamberlain were, South Africa presented itself as the decisive issue on which the future of the empire hinged. Could a nation be forged from a country composed of defeated white Afrikaners and a major-ity black population, not to mention a substantial number of Indian settlers, which would accord to the fundamentals of a white man's country *and* whose citizens would choose freely to live as subjects within the British empire? In New Zealand and Australia the principal inhibition initially fac-ing British settlers had been the aboriginal populations. In Canada First Nation resistance had been compounded by the presence of French inhab-itants. But in South Africa the black population was significantly larger than the white population, and white society itself was split ethnically. In this lay the supreme test for the destiny of empire and the civilization of the white man. Milner, and those around him, believed themselves to be in the cruci-ble of history—'a mass of glowing conviction'.

Three days after Chamberlain's Birmingham speech of May 1903, Milner put these issues to an audience in Johannesburg:

What is the good…of perpetually going on shouting that this is a white man's country? Does it mean that it is a country only inhabited by white men? That, of course, is an obvious absurdity, as the blacks outnumber us by five to one. Does it mean a country which ought only to be inhabited by white men?

Well, as an ideal that would possibly be all very well, but as a practical statement it surely is perfectly useless. If it means anything, it means that we ought
to expel the black population, thereby instantly ruining all the industries of
the country. What it does mean, I suppose, if any sane meaning can be applied
to it, is that the white man should rule. Well, if that is its meaning, there is
nobody more absolutely agreed with it than I; but then let us say that plainly,
and do not let us only say it, but let us justify it. There is only one ground on
which we can justify it, and that is the ground of superior civilization.

   The white man must rule, because he is elevated by many, many steps
above the black man; steps which it will take the latter centuries to climb, and
which it is quite possible that the vast bulk of the black population may never
be able to climb at all.[157]

Never resolved, however, was the matter of who, or what, exactly the white
man was. In Kipling's poetry can be found a mystical, and highly abstract,
projection of the ideals of white civilization which lauded (for example) US
expansion at the expense of the Spanish: 'Take up the White Man's burden—
Send forth the best ye breed'.[158] But when things were closer to home, it
could never be decided whether Britain's European rivals for colonial power
were white or not, just as the position of the Afrikaners remained structurally
ambiguous. Sometimes these rivals were white, sometimes not: it all depended
on whether they were contrasted to the native (in which case they were
white) or to the British (in which case they weren't, as the British fortui-
tously rated rather higher in the hierarchy of whiteness than anyone else).
But it is also the case that the South African experience required the figure
of the white man to be imagined according to imperatives which differed
from the archetype early pioneer of Australia or New Zealand. For in South
Africa white settlers confronted a situation in which there was colossal mineral wealth and a huge pre-existing native population. To make South Africa
into a white man's country it was necessary to transform the mineral deposits
into working mines and the natives into working miners. Carlyle's injunctions—the authentic white man works, and creates the conditions for the
native to work—were not far away. In this respect, for all Milner's mysticism,
the idea of the white man, as a cognitive structure, became a means for imagining the transforming power of capital. And in the way of such myths the
reverse was true as well: the spectacular capacities of capital confirmed, day
by day, the supernatural powers of the white man.[159]

   Milner was aware of the empirical problems in determining who was
who ethnically. Rather than employing the idea of 'Saxondom', or one of its

correlates, he chose to use an expansive conception of the nation. Thus 'the nation' included 'all the peoples of the United Kingdom and their descendants in other countries under the British flag'. He recognized that 'the inhabitants of England, Scotland and Ireland are of various stocks', and that these variations persisted

> even when they are not, as in the case of the Irish, emphasised and nourished by political dissidence. And yet to speak of them collectively as the British race is not only convenient, but it is in accordance with broad political facts. Community of language and institutions, and centuries of life together under one sovereignty, have not indeed obliterated differences, but have superadded bonds, which are more than artificial, which make them in the eyes of the world, if not always in their own, a single nation, and which it will prove impossible to destroy.

He was happy to concede though that this idea of the nation may not have been 'ethnologically accurate'—which was just as well, given his own German birth, upbringing, and education.[160] Empirical exactitude was not the issue.

Giving shape to Milner's thought was the increasing fusion of the three dominating categories: race, nation, and empire. One could not be imagined without the other: indeed, Milner strove to turn them into equivalents. His final 'Credo', published posthumously by *The Times*, represented an appropriate summation of his thinking:

> I am a British (indeed primarily an English) Nationalist.
> If I am also an Imperialist, it is because the destiny of the English race, owing to its insular position and long supremacy at sea, has been to strike fresh roots in distant parts of the world. My patriotism knows no geographical but only racial limits. I am an Imperialist and not a Little Englander, because I am a British Race Patriot. It seems unnatural to me...to lose interest in an attachment to my fellow-countrymen because they settle across the sea. It is not the soil of England, dear as it is to me, which is essential to arouse my patriotism, but the speech, the tradition, the spiritual heritage, the principles, the aspirations of the British race. They do not cease to be *mine* because they are transplanted. My horizon must widen, that is all.
> I feel myself a citizen of the Empire. I feel that Canada is my country, Australia my country, New Zealand my country, South Africa my country, just as much as Surrey or Yorkshire.

His generation, he believed, had maintained the empire ('held the fort') against sceptics and critics; in his youth the end of empire had been regarded

'as an inevitable, almost a desirable eventuality'. Partly because 'so much of
our best blood' had gone to the colonies it was imperative to subject oneself
to 'the first great principle—follow the race'. Soon, he declared, all will be
'Imperialists', both in the 'Motherland' and overseas.[161]

English nationalist, British race patriot, imperialist, sentiments as strong
for Surrey as for South Africa: the terms have no conceptual cohesion, for
they have become interchangeable. From the publication of Dilke's *Greater
Britain* to Milner's 'Credo' there occurs an increasing fusion of the ideas of
race, nation, and empire, in which the charged figure of the white man is
called upon to exemplify the unfolding drama. Milner himself represented
a single, if prominent, strand in this deeper transformation. By the early
decades of the twentieth century one didn't have to be a Milnerite to speak
in these terms. In many different registers and idioms, race and empire
moved to the centre of the imagining of the domestic nation, and in this the
invention of the white empire proved critical.

For all the turmoil and disappointments Milner confronted, and for all
his deep authoritarianism and political zealotry, he could none the less alight
upon an idea of empire which transcended discord and heralded the realization of a state of being which was fully human. In this, perhaps, we can see
evidence of his schooling in German idealism. Clearly, this conception of
history was steeped in ideas of racial destiny. But it was this prospect of a
harmonious end of history that made the strife of daily political struggle
bearable, and gave it meaning.

> For the British race has become responsible for the peace and order and the
> just and humane government of three or four hundred millions of people,
> who, differing as widely as possible from one another in other respects, are all
> alike in this, that, from whatever causes, they do not possess the gift of main-
> taining peace and order for themselves. Without our control their political
> condition would be one of chaos, as it was for centuries before that control
> was established. The *Pax Britannica* is essential to the maintenance of civilised
> conditions of existence among one-fifth of the human race.[162]

Even in Milner, this could be given a homely or domestic rendering.
Adumbrating his 'Imperialist creed' at the end of 1906, he put it this
way:

> Just think what it means, for at least every white man of British birth, that he
> can be at home in every state of the Empire from the moment he sets foot in
> it, though his whole previous life may have been passed at the other end of

the earth. He hears men speaking his own language, he breathes a social and moral atmosphere which is familiar to him—not the same, no doubt, as that of his old home, but yet a kindred atmosphere.[163]

To conceptualize the empire in these terms was to conceptualize imperialism, not as a rapacious force embodying the will to power, but as a means to make a potentially hostile world homely, at least for white Britons.

This domestic articulation of empire was to have, in the metropole, an important purchase on the ways in which imperial rule was imagined. A significant reading in this vein—strikingly different in tone from Milner's characteristically more full-blooded assertions—can be seen in the patriotic reveries of Stanley Baldwin, in which the fusion of race, nation, and empire appears not only effortless, but part of the natural way of things. One need only look to his most celebrated speech—his hymn to the nature of England—addressed to the Royal Society of St George in May 1924, and delivered almost exactly a year before Milner died. It carries Baldwin's typical emphasis on the domestic, pastoral lives of the English and works, in his usual manner, by understatement and sentiment. Here we can see how the myth of constitutional England converged with the myth of pacific settlement in the dominions, such that each came to be imagined in terms of the other, and ultimately as a single, indivisible history.

> These are the things that make England, and I grieve for it that they are not the childish inheritance of the majority of the people to-day in our country. They ought to be the inheritance of every child born into this country, but nothing can be more touching than to see how the working man and woman after generations in the towns will have their tiny bit of garden if they can, will go to gardens if they can, to look at something they have never seen as children, but which their ancestors knew and loved. The love of these things is innate and inherent in our people. It makes for that love of home, one of the strongest features of our race, and it is that that makes our race seek its new home in the Dominions overseas, where they have room to see things like this that they can no more see at home. It is that power of making homes, almost peculiar to our people, and it is one of the sources of their greatness. They go overseas, and they take with them what they have learned at home: love of justice, love of truth and the broad humanity that are so characteristic of English people.[164]

Baldwin's Conservatism was always tinged by an apprehension of lost time, a loss brought about by the forces of modernity. The power of his rhetoric lay in its capacity to remind his listeners of those sites of contemporary life where emotional plenitude could still be experienced: in the countryside, in family and home, in gardens, in imaginative literature, in the language of the people. For these were forms, he believed, in which the impulse and values of the past (those things 'which their ancestors knew and loved') were still alive in the present. He was indeed a master of the pastoral translating, in Empson's terms, the complex into the simple. But crucially he suggests here, as did Froude, that the nation's past was peculiarly alive in the settler colonies. Those who chose to settle overseas 'have the room to see things . . . that they can no more see at home'. Memories of the English past transmute into memories of empire. In turn these memories of empire create, in Baldwin's evocation of England, the tangible desire for an England overseas where the idylls of the past are still present. As Baldwin himself might well have asked, 'How could we ignore all that?'

Nation against state

Chamberlain and Milner shared a distrust of the traditions of statecraft bequeathed by Whig and Tory custom, and each strove to devise a politics which addressed the expanding electorate by conceptualizing citizenship as simultaneously active and imperial. Froude's invocation of 'we the people'—the people of both nation and empire—was one which they made their own.

But any such populism was founded on the tensions between the nation-people and the state. In times of crisis, when the politicians were perceived to be pursuing the interests of the state rather than of the nation, the ethnic populism which had been cast ideologically in the later decades of the nineteenth century could be mobilized *against* the state, when the people sought to claim back the nation, in its racial essence, from the depredations of the politicians.[165] The idea of a single imperial citizenship, moreover, was always fraught, generating simultaneously centripetal identifications—affiliation with the metropolitan nation-state—as well as the old centrifugal forces of empire, evident in the drive to pull away from the centre and in the mounting confidence of particular colonial nationalisms. I explore this contradictory dynamic of colonial nationalism in the chapters to come, looking at the cases of Australia and South Africa. The centrifugal elements of this imperial story came to a head in central and southern Africa in the 1960s, as I show in the last two chapters, when settler 'loyalists' denounced the *British state* by proclaiming their ethnic rights as a branch of the con-stituent *British people*.

However, this contradictory dynamic—allegiance to the politics of the state and allegiance to a populist politics decreed by the imperatives of ethnicity—was also present in the statecraft of the great Edwardian procon-suls, who were forever extolling the idea of the white man of the colonies in contrast to his putatively emaciated siblings in the cities and suburbs of England. Lords Milner, Curzon, and Cromer returned from their overseas postings—Curzon from India and Milner from South Africa in 1905, Cromer from Egypt two years later—to confront what they believed to be a nation in precipitous decline, presided over (from 1906) by a government that was complicit in the destruction of empire and nation. In seeking to reproduce the frontier ethos—the ethos of the white man—in the metropole they found they were required to counter every sign of disorder across the nation as a whole. Empire, for them, functioned as the antidote to the col-lapse of the centre, of England itself. The fear was endlessly repeated, though Cromer's 'The Government of Subject Races', published in 1908, rehearsed the argument with maximal clarity.[166] As the title makes evident, his pur-pose was to elaborate his conviction that racial domination lay at the heart of the colonial endeavour, assuming that the authority of the colonizer derived from his knowledge of the native. At the same time Cromer insisted that as much as the races overseas needed to be taught their racial position-ing as natives, so the home peoples of the empire needed to recognize *their* racial responsibilities—notwithstanding the fact that their 'subject races' were separated from the metropole by oceans and continents, existing beyond the immediate line of vision of the home population.[167] For Cromer and the proconsuls, the battle for nation and empire took place on every front, the merest inkling of an abdication of will on the part of the nation's rulers signalling a danger to the entire social and racial order. The state they believed was weak, while representative democracy they saw as a principal cause of the nation's decline, advocating it be put 'in its proper place'.[168] In 1905 Curzon had lost the confidence of the Conservative administration and arrived in London in ignominy.[169] In the autumn of the same year the Liberals opened their campaign to censure Milner for his role in the 'Chinese slavery' scandal in South Africa. In his final days in Cairo, Cromer found he was unable to garner the support of the home government, and experi-enced his departure from office as a brutal defeat. When he returned to England he couldn't abide the ridicule he was subjected to by his political opponents.[170] Their return to domestic politics proved disorientating. These were figures, by training and repute, who were 'public men', accustomed to speaking with the authority of the state behind them. But when they returned to England they were excluded from office, and only precariously located in the institutions of the state.[171] Through these years their hostility to the state deepened, certain that they were living through a political emergency—Milner always considered himself 'an emergency man'—which required extraordinary measures.[172] Central to their politics was the apprehension that ethnic enemies had now come to operate *inside* the ruling bloc. On the significant issues of the day they manœuvred themselves to take up battle against the state, and did so in the name of the Greater British people.

For Cromer the decisive sites of danger were to be found in German militarism, in women's suffrage, and in Home Rule for Ireland. He was presiding spirit of the National League for Opposition to Women's Suffrage, and active in opposing Home Rule. Curzon was incensed by Lloyd George's budget of 1909, and was drawn to the brink in defence of the House of Lords in August 1911. Since 1907 Milner had been exercised by the idea of creating an effective anti-socialist politics by recruiting the organized working class to the full national-imperial programme of Unionism, built upon specifically labour institutions. The budget of 1909 he condemned as 'evil'.[173] And from the end of 1913 he too was active in the struggle to resist Irish Home Rule, both by organizing the British Covenant in support of radical Unionism in the Protestant north, as well as by fomenting mutiny amongst the King's forces in a desperate bid to break the military power of the Liberal government in Ireland, creating in the process a proconsular or Caesarist populism 'from above'.[174] Common to all three was the fear that corruption was located at the summit of the state.

Ireland served as a touchstone. In the Unionist rebellions before the First World War in the Protestant north of Ireland, and in the actions of their sympathizers in mainland England, we can discern the meeting of opposites—centripetal and centrifugal, loyalty and treachery—which underpin many manifestations of a colonial populism directed against the state.[175] To close this chapter, I shall look briefly at Kipling, and highlight the connections between the Orange populist politics of Protestant Ireland and the idea of a specifically English popular politics on the mainland.[176]

In May 1914 Kipling delivered what a recent biographer describes as 'the most fanatical speech of his life'.[177] The scene was Tunbridge Wells—not known for its fanaticism—where he addressed a crowd of 10,000, imploring his listeners to support the cause of radical Unionism in the Protestant north of Ireland by joining the League of British Covenanters. Like his contemporaries, Cromer and Milner, Kipling was categorical in his belief that the Liberals' acquiescence to Home Rule demonstrated the loss of political will on the part of the governing class and that, as a consequence, the Protestants of the north had become—by default—the saviours of England. And like Enoch Powell after him, he imagined Irish Unionism to be the vehicle which would redeem England. Kipling was much cheered by the gathering agitation in Ulster in 1913, sure that it represented 'the first move in the revolt of the English' and the 'beginning of the counter-revolution against the radicals in the Liberal Party'.[178]

At Tunbridge Wells Kipling derided members of the government as 'outlaws' and as 'conspirators'. 'The Home Rule Bill broke the pledged faith of generations', he claimed, bringing into the realm 'officially recognised sedition . . . conspiracy and rebellion'. He went on:

> A province and a people of Great Britain are to be sold to their and our enemies. We are forbidden to have any voice in this sale of our own flesh and blood; we have no tribunal under Heaven to appeal to except the corrupt parties to that sale and their paid followers . . . Ulster, and as much of Ireland as dares express itself, wishes to remain within the Union and under the flag of the Union. The Cabinet . . . intends to drive them out. The electors of Great Britain have never sanctioned this . . . Civil War is inevitable unless our rulers can be brought to realise that, even now, they must submit these grave matters to the judgement of a free people. If they do not, all the history of our island shows that there is but one end—destruction from within and without.[179]

In these words we confront the moment when 'the people' is mobilized against the state. On the one side Kipling positions the 'faith of generations', the 'people of Great Britain', 'a free people': in sum, 'our own flesh and blood'. On the other are the 'outlaws' and 'conspirators', 'enemies', 'corrupt parties', and 'paid followers': in sum, 'our rulers'. In this perspective Britain's statesmen are identified as ethnic traitors, betrayers of race and nation. Ethnicity—'our own flesh and blood'—bequeaths a higher law than that sanctioned by mere institutions of the state, and one which is absolute in its remit. If the politicians fail to recognize the power of this ethnic compact then destruction will follow, 'from within and without'.

Kipling articulated this argument in the midst of a profound domestic-imperial crisis. The peculiarities of Ireland's location in the empire are evident. Ulster's Protestant population simultaneously constituted for Kipling a 'province' and a component element of ethnic 'Great Britain'. Yet it is also clear that he was content to live with the conflation—shifting though it was—between the core domestic nation and the notion of Great Britain. *England's* redemption was, he insisted, to be achieved by means of the overseas province–colony. More particularly, radicalism at home was to be defeated by calling upon a 'counter-revolution' arising from the colony. In this instance the 'Great British' people overseas were the upholders of purity, counterpoised to vacillation and corruption in high places at home. In Kipling we can see how a crisis in the imperial state was conceived also to be an ethnic crisis. His speech was driven by accusations that his putative compatriots were, in truth, insufficiently national, or racial. In turn this led him, as it must lead any who employ such thinking, to fervid imaginings of treachery. And where else does treachery happen than at home?

2

Colony and metropole

I was confronted by a young Aboriginal man who stopped me in the street. He was very drunk; his glance was unguarded. He put a hand on my shoulder, staring intently at me. He didn't say a word; nor did he need to. The brown eyes were riveting, brimming with overpowering emotion...[i]t wasn't particularly personal. It was ancestral and awful. It was also a history lesson of the most powerful kind.

(Henry Reynolds, 1999[1])

Towards the end of the preceding chapter I invoked the words of Stanley Baldwin, revealing his colonial reveries. Baldwin rarely gave the impression he was ever excited about anything. Empire never enthused him—in the way it did a figure such as his fellow Tory, Leo Amery, for example. It was simply there, like God or Shakespeare, testament to the civilization of the English, a matter not of passion but of faith. Seeley's ideas proved a direct and lasting influence on him.[2] But he never demonstrated a burning desire to see the colonies, despite entertaining the vague notion that, once he'd retired from politics, a tour of the dominions was something to be considered. For all the contrivance of his rural provincialism he usually chose to holiday in the more fashionable resorts of Europe, Aix-les-Bains in the summer, skiing in St Moritz in the winter. When he first became prime minister in 1923 he confessed in a letter to his mother that he knew 'little of the Dominions', though there can be no doubt he knew even less about the rest of the empire.[3] And when, in the following year, he was reflecting on the wonder of colonial life, he had still only once travelled to the empire overseas; as a young businessman at the end of the previous century he had visited Montreal, even then a modern conurbation of nearly a quarter of a million. Thereafter, in 1927, forsaking with some reluctance his usual August in the south of France, he accompanied the Prince of Wales to Canada, thereby becoming the first serving prime minister to visit an overseas dominion. (In his speeches on the tour Baldwin was keen—as he put it to the King on his return—to counter ideas planted in the US press by Lloyd George that the English 'are played out, idle, hopeless and so on'.[4]) Five years later he returned to Ottawa for the Imperial Economic Conference, an experience he found burdensome, the cantankerous behaviour of the dominion premiers, as he saw it, leaving little scope for the various representatives to confirm the ideals of empire. And that was the extent of Baldwin's immediate experience of colonial life. Neither Africa nor India was for him, and Australasia too distant. His paean to the affiliations of England overseas was expressed in projections startling in their simplicity, informed as much by fictionalized romance as by political realities, and evident of a life insulated from anything other than a deep, if abstract, metropolitan profession of faith. In this he was, I think, representative of many domestic Britons of his milieu who didn't know, first-hand, the empire—one of the 'Kiplingized Englishmen' whom those who believed themselves true colonials were always ready to denounce.[5]

The idea, which Baldwin took as self-evident, that the white colonies had simply become settled, home to England overseas, systematically screened from view the hysteria about race which underwrote their foundation. It obliterated all that was unsettling and unhomely about these new nations. The attribution of whiteness—for men, women, and children, and for the imagined nation itself—was not just a virtue to be propagated. It was, rather, an inner dynamic of unremitting fervour in which all the forces which conspired to abet the unhomely needed to be extirpated—even when this required deeds which in their savagery were themselves decidedly unhomely. (When Governor Eyre was first able to thank his supporters in England, he emphasized his delight that there to welcome him were 'so many of the fair, the gentle, and the good—those who render homes happy'.[6]) Nature untamed; racial others; femininity out of place; anxieties about one's inner self: all could be perceived as conspiring to unsettle. Whiteness provided the syntax in which these dramas could be thought. In this larger story of the evolution of the settler colonies this dynamic is always overdetermining. Fanon's attempt to place what he called the 'delirium' of race at the heart of the colonial endeavour is appropriate.[7] Yet far from providing a given resolution to ethnic yearning, whiteness remained necessarily, tantalizingly incomplete and unobtainable. How else can we explain its repetitious ubiquity?

In the second half of the nineteenth century the emergence of the white colonies as functioning, modern nation-states created structures of racial exclusion which were Manichaean in inspiration, alive with all manner of psychic anxiety and controversial politically. One source of political controversy derived from the differing imperatives of metropole and colony. Despite the organization of legally sanctioned racial segregation in the colonies in the late nineteenth and early twentieth centuries, official pronouncements from London continued to profess the ideals of racial inclusion. In the metropole, determination to exclude invariably also worked with a commitment to include, resulting in a complicated, contingent, and ultimately irresolvable dialectic of exclusion and inclusion. But to white colonials who believed themselves to be in the vortex of racial struggle, public men in London could all too easily appear as exemplars of bad faith, their homilies on racial inclusion defying the hard lessons learnt by the colonial. The colonials knew the native—as they repeated often enough—in a manner which those removed from the racial struggle could never hope to emulate. In this scenario, metropolitan politicians condemned themselves as either ignorant, duplicitous, or both. The division between those at the centre, and those who either were, or who imagined themselves to be, on the frontier, constituted a powerful cause for dissension in the seemingly harmonious family romance of the mother country and her offspring.

Yet the cross-currents between metropole and colonies never resulted in simple dichotomies in which the mentalities generated in the one locale remained insulated from those in the other. As I hope to show, the shifting imaginings of the figure of the white man depended on the transactions between centre and periphery. We cannot pinpoint either the time or the place when the idea of the white man—in its received, imperial form—first arose. But from the late nineteenth century, we can track the movements which occurred in the symbolic organization of its particular variants. In this, the movement from the colonial frontier to the metropolitan centre is decisive.[8]

The ideological tensions between imperial rulers at the centre and white leaders in the colonies, while never absolute, constitute an important dimension in the conflicting repertoires of white identities which emerged at the end of the nineteenth century. In 1897, on the occasion of Queen Victoria's Diamond Jubilee, Joseph Chamberlain expressed his own views on the matter. In his role as colonial secretary he addressed the premiers of the self-governing colonies. He understood, he said, the threat to their nations represented by 'Asiatics', and he believed the colonies were justified in protecting 'the legitimate rights of the existing labouring population'. But he was also sure that the premiers needed 'to bear in mind the traditions of the Empire, which makes no distinction in favour of, or against race or colour; and to exclude, by reason of their colour or by reason of their race, all her Majesty's Indian subjects, or even all Asiatics, would be an act so offensive to those people, that it would be most painful, I am certain, to Her Majesty to have to sanction it'.[9]

Or we can see similar thoughts uttered by Milner. As he testified on the eve of his departure from South Africa, he was prepared to contemplate limited political and social rights for those blacks who possessed demonstrably civilized capacities—sentiments which he predicted would not find favour with his Johannesburg audience. He returned to the theme three years later when he distinguished between Britain's 'two empires': the white descendants of the mother country, on the one hand and, on the other, the racially more backward dependencies. He understood, he claimed, the 'terrors' which 'not unnaturally' occurred when whites found themselves confronting other races in close proximity. But for Milner the presence of the 'second', dependent, empire also created overriding imperial obligations, which a simple race politics was in danger of discounting. 'If there were more interdependence', he suggested, 'there would be less misunderstanding.' He was troubled by 'the most unfortunate conflict which has arisen between the people of the self-governing states of the Empire and its coloured subject races over the question of immigration'. He went on:

> As regards this particular question of free immigration of Indian or other coloured people, being British subjects, into the self-governing states, I think that there are considerable faults on both sides. I hold that we in this country are to blame for failing to appreciate the many sound and reputable reasons (though I do not deny that there are also bad and despicable ones) which make the people of the Colonies so opposed to the permanent settlement of alien coloured races, even if they be British subjects, among them. They are threatened with a danger of which we have no experience, and they are in my opinion quite right to guard against it. No one who has lived among them will fail to appreciate the causes of their anxiety. On the other hand they are, no doubt, often to blame for the harsh, unjust and unreasonable form which their anxiety, however just and reasonable in itself, often takes. If it were not too serious, one would be tempted to smile at the crude ignorance which makes so many of them confound all men of coloured race, from the high-class and cultured Asiatic gentleman or noble, to the humble coolie, in the

common category of 'niggers'. But I do not know that home Britons would
be much better if they had not had for many years the education which
responsibility for the dependent Empire gives, and especially if they had not
so many men living among them who have had lifelong experience of the
coloured races of the Empire. Our colonial fellow-citizens, devoid of all sense
of responsibility in the matter, and without that expert guidance which we
enjoy, are largely at the mercy of the primitive and untutored instinct of aver-
sion from alien races.[10]

What for Milner might appear as 'primitive and untutored' instincts could
appear to those living on the colonial frontier to be the very essence of
racial truth. This antagonism went to the heart of the colonial rendering of
whiteness.

   In this chapter I address a number of interconnected issues. I begin with
some short general, conceptual reflections on the idea of the frontier, as a
racialized boundary, which is a theme that runs through this and the subsequent volumes. I indicate too the discrepancy between highly idealized metropolitan projections of what the frontier represented, and its more chaotic,
anxious lived forms. Next, I locate these general reflections empirically in
terms of evidence drawn from Australia. First, drawing principally from the
findings of Henry Reynolds, I continue my discussion of the significance of
the racial frontier.[11] Second, I introduce briefly the issue of the colonial
nation. And third, I look in more detail at the public career of the veteran
Chartist and Birmingham man Henry Parkes, who became premier of New
South Wales later in the nineteenth century. In the latter part of the chapter,
I suggest how these distant colonial realities—the notion of the racial frontier; 'Asiatics'; whiteness itself, manifest in the figures of the white man and
white woman—found their echoes in the life of the metropole.

The idea of the frontier

In these transactions between metropolitan Britain and its colonies, the idea
of the frontier was potent.[12] The frontier marked the boundary between
civilized settlement and untamed nature, and between the colonial settlers
and the various non-white, mainly but not exclusively indigenous, peoples.
Although the single term often signified both meanings, my emphasis here
falls on the idea of the racial frontier. Frontiers, as a function of their very
purpose, are always invested with powerful symbolic properties. Writing in

1909, Sir Alfred Lyall—who had been active in putting down the rebellion in India in 1857—thought that to breach a frontier was to induce, strictly understood, a trauma: 'Among compact and civilised nationalities an exterior frontier, thus carefully defined, remains, like the human skin, the most sensitive and irritable part of their corporate constitution…to break through it violently is to be inflicting a wound which may draw blood'.[13]

Frontiers serve to demarcate one cultural system from another. That is what they are designed to do: to unify and to homogenize. But the dynamic of human difference has a marked tendency to smuggle itself across given boundaries and frontiers, subverting the geometries of power which these selfsame frontiers seek to hold in place. In the late nineteenth century, as nations and empires were built, we can witness the determination to police the chaotic, kaleidoscopic patterns of everyday life such that each national or racial culture was clearly demarcated from its neighbour. In these circumstances the imaginative elements of a civilization came to be peculiarly vital at its finite, liminal points. Thus for the most part these were dramas which were associated—from within the purview of the metropole—with far-off colonies, particularly with the settler colonies. Yet a central argument of these volumes is that the imagined manifestations of the racial frontier possessed an impressive mobility. In nineteenth-century British Columbia, as I noted in the last chapter, as colonial order progressed the racial frontier came ever more present in the lives of the settlers, touching not only the outlying regions, but also moving into the towns, neighbourhoods, and streets which lay at the heart of colonial life. Nor was this only a colonial matter, narrowly conceived. Although metropolitan conceptions were inspired by colonial realities, frontiers could assume other guises as well, in other locales. As I suggest in this chapter, and later on in these volumes, the language of the racial frontier, steeped in the syntax of the colony, could also be heard at home, in the metropole.

At the end of the nineteenth century and at the beginning of the twentieth the racial frontiers of the colonial empire were a source of endless fascination for the people of the metropole. Ideas of the frontier carried a range of conflicting meanings. They condensed emotions both about the imminent possibilities of human self-realization, and about the inescapable presence of human vulnerability, highlighting an intensity of experience which signals a militantly modern structure of feeling. And necessarily, if only by implication, they narrated a series of stories telling the British people who they were—or more accurately, perhaps, who they weren't.

Migrant Britons were drawn to colonial life for manifold different reasons. Alongside the proselytizers of colonial order we should not forget, as well, that the pleasures of disorder had their enthusiasts, who determined to distance themselves from what they experienced as an overly intrusive, overly disciplining, home civilization. Yet the plurality and complexity of the varied life-stories of the settler Britons rarely reached back, in public form, to the metropole. Many short-circuits occurred in the narrations of frontier life. Metropolitan views of the colonies came to be heavily mediated, the brute facts of distance inviting the simplification of perceptual categories. The settler—in the masculine form as the figure who made history—assumed a privileged position in the public narratives of the metropole. It was as if all radiated *from him*, concealing the power of capital and the power of the imperial state. Epic transformations, it seemed, were the consequence of the white man himself. Indeed it was first and foremost on the frontier that whiteness happened.

In 1907 Lord Curzon delivered what was to become a renowned lecture at Oxford University devoted to the theme of the frontier. Curzon had been viceroy of India for seven years and a Tory MP for twelve, a public man amongst public men. He was a high-minded product of Eton and Balliol, who in adult life kept a replica of his Eton room at Kedleston. As a younger man he had travelled widely through the remote frontiers of the Middle and Far East, writing authoritative books on the diplomatic and strategic issues which confronted him. Yet by the time he addressed his Oxford audience he was bitter and frustrated, seriously depressed by opposition to his policies in India and emotionally broken by the death of his wife. To return to Oxford, where he had recently been installed as chancellor of the university, was to inhabit a welcoming masculine world of reassurance and like-mindedness, where matters of intellect could transcend private grief.

For Curzon, frontiers were not created by those Europeans who settled in the outer reaches of the colonies. Rather they were the product of the specialized knowledges organized by a rare breed of men who possessed mastery of both periphery and centre. The 'formulae' of the frontier, he believed,

> are hidden in the arcana of diplomatic chancellories; its documents are embedded in vast and forbidding collections of treaties; its incidents and what I may describe as its incomparable drama are the possession of a few silent men, who may be found in the clubs of London, or Paris, or Berlin, when they are not engaged in tracing lines upon the unknown areas of the earth.

Curzon, clearly, was enamoured by the romance of these unknown 'silent men', the disinterested embodiment of imperial power and knowledge, whose intellects determined the destinies of faraway peoples. These figures, moving effortlessly from the hostile terrains of the frontier to the best of London clubs, were to characterize much popular fiction of the period. But it was not only a matter of the intellect. Curzon imbued the frontier with idealized projections which conformed to the dreams bred within his own social caste and gender:

> Outside of the English Universities no school of character exists to compare with the Frontier...I am one of those who hold that in this larger atmosphere on the outskirts of Empire, where the machine is relatively impotent and the individual strong, is to be found an ennobling and invigorating stimulus for our youth, saving them alike from the corroding ease and morbid excitements of Western civilization. To our ancient Universities, revivified and reinspired, I look to play their part in this national service. Still from the cloistered alleys and the hallowed groves of Oxford, true to her old traditions, but widened in her activities and scope, let there come forth the invincible spirit and the unexhausted moral fibre of our race. Let the advanced guard of Empire march forth, strong in the faith of their ancestors, imbued with a sober virtue, and above all, on fire with a definite purpose. The Empire calls, as loudly as it ever did, for serious instruments of serious work. The Frontiers of Empire continue to beckon. May this venerable and glorious institution, the nursery of character and the home of loyal deeds, never fail honouring that august summons.

The romance and purity of the frontier worked in his imagination as a counter to the internal decay of the imperial nation. On the frontier, wondrous things could happen, and England itself be resurrected.[14]

Yet if the aspirations and apprehensions of imperial Britain assumed both a visceral and a moral intensity on the edges of empire, the colonial frontier was also a place where known realities were peculiarly in flux, and where contrary senses of the self could meet.

As I shall show in more detail in Chapter 4, at the beginning of the twentieth century the metropolitan idea of the frontier was encoded in masculine terms. The settler was the agent not only of his own history, but of the history of others too, and as a mythic figure conceived in a commensurately masculine mode. In the plethora of boys' colonial romances which were published in Britain in the opening years of the century, the frontier featured as the location which promised young manhood its most testing, most spectacular rites of passage. What appeared in the imperial treatises as an abstraction—the dying out of weaker races, the making of a Greater Britain—reappears in this literature as forcefully embodied. The frontier called for extreme feats of masculine bravado. But masculine bravado can be as vicious as it is virtuous. As Marilyn Lake has argued in the context of the Australian bush, the unconstrained, perverse, and violent eroticism of mobile, marauding white men never conformed to the urbane ideals of the white man, whose very purpose was to protect and uplift both his womenfolk and those natives with whom he came in contact.[15]

A prime illustration of the contradictions underpinning frontier masculinity is provided in Elspeth Huxley's account of Lord Delamere. Delamere, born into the blue-blooded English aristocracy in 1870, was a man of volatile character, for whom the increasingly bourgeois conventions of his home country—particularly matters of financial solvency—proved unwelcome. Like a number of his class he alighted upon the idea of settling in eastern Africa. Though it cannot be said that he ever exactly prospered, he became an energetic, pioneering settler in the highlands of what later was formally established as Kenya. Elspeth Huxley, younger than Delamere, was brought up in Kenya and recalls meeting him as a child. She proved a great admirer. In 1935 she published a two-volume history which took for its title *White Man's Country: Lord Delamere and the Making of Kenya*. This is settler history in heroic mode.

> Delamere cast himself for this rôle of capitalist-experimenter. He would be the first to show that in East Africa England had possessed herself of a miniature new dominion, a little New Zealand tucked away between deserts and tropics and lakes, where yet another cutting from the British parent stock could be planted and would grow and flourish.
>
> This was the ultimate ideal—this and nothing else. He wanted to prove to the world that East Africa was a white man's country. He wanted it to become a true British colony in the sense that Australia and Natal had been colonies— places where people settled for good and tried to build a replica of England that would endure so long as the British race itself persisted, places that modelled for themselves an independent economic life and evolved a tradition of their own, and eventually won the award for which they had been contending, the privilege of self-government. He wanted to see East Africa travelling this path, and to be one of those who would guide its destinies.

Delamere, in this incarnation, is the paragon of colonial order, the personification of the idea of the white man's country, and the esteemed maker of history. Yet, without a blink, she also represents another picture, drawing from his adventures when he was living in Nakuru around the year 1908:

One night he knocked up an Indian store-keeper and insisted on buying all the oranges in the shop. He returned to the hotel carrying two full baskets and distributed the oranges to all the guests. Then he marshalled them outside and led a storming party who pelted all the windows with the oranges until every pane of glass was smashed. The French manager, unable to call in the one policeman to arrest his employer, thought it very odd...

One of his most spectacular exploits occurred in Nairobi. He had had a hilarious evening in the old Nairobi club. It was shortly after street lighting, a great innovation, had been introduced...Delamere was never without his revolver, and the street lights were too tempting a target to be resisted. He shot out the lamps in Government Road, one after the other, with a remarkable aim considering the circumstances, and finished up the evening by despatching the lights just outside the provincial Commissioner's house.

Delamere, Huxley tells us, 'always retained a schoolboy delight in destruction. He liked to see things broken up.'[16] Delamere's may well have been an extreme character. But early settlement placed a premium on masculine prowess, an attribute which could take many contrary forms. Here we can see the very imperative of colonial order—the construction of a 'white man's country'—generating its own infantile, masculine disorder.

However, although masculinity was privileged in accounts of frontier-life, there were many instances when pioneering white men found themselves embarking upon conventionally feminine tasks, especially in the earlier years of the settler colonies. The homosocial households of British Columbia in the middle decades of the nineteenth century required men, amongst other things, to cook and launder, and to nurse each other.[17] When in the early 1830s Edward Eyre, the future Governor Eyre of Jamaica, began life as a sheep-farmer in New South Wales he had many new skills to learn.

Brought up amidst the comforts of a Yorkshire vicarage, accustomed to having his food prepared, his washing miraculously done, his fires laid, Eyre learned not only how to care for stock, build and carpenter, and grow food supplies, but also how to sew on buttons and care for his clothes, cook, often after catching the fish or fowl first, render down fat, make candles, salt beef and bread, twist up tobacco, make his own wool bags for the wool from the first shearing... This was English masculinity with a difference.[18]

Conversely, the codes of femininity operated according to different norms: the conventions concerning appropriate feminine behaviour in the metropole could not function in the circumstances of colonial life. Mary Procida's analysis of the gender and racial organization of the Raj holds true,

at a general level, for other colonial situations as well. The force of her argument lies in her insistence that colonial life, in itself, was inimical to the
feminine: feminine women, like effeminate men, were not suited to imperial endeavour. Yet this is not to say that women were excluded from the
enterprise of empire, for as she claims in a neat formulation: 'The empire
may have been masculine, but it was certainly not exclusively male.'[19] In
Australia, for example, many women found themselves chopping trees, digging water-holes, whitewashing walls, embarking on kangaroo hunts, while
those who had been used to relying on servants at home had to learn an
array of new skills. More generally matters of female propriety necessarily
took on new dimensions in the bush.[20]

Certainly, in much of the frontier literature produced in the metropole
there is evidence enough of resourceful girls and women taking on, especially in moments of danger, active, determining roles and, when necessary, being as manful as any man. If Baden-Powell, for example, cherished
the vision of the manful qualities of the frontier winning adherents
amongst the pampered urban population of the metropole, he saw no
reason why girls should be excluded simply because of their gender.
Refusing to be flummoxed when girls started joining his scout troops in
1908, the following year he set up a separate organization for them, headed
by his sister, and together they later co-wrote a handbook addressed specifically to the new generation of aspiring girl guides. Not really believing
that girls should be girlish, the Baden-Powells adopted a rather enlightened position, exhorting their young recruits to be comrades in arms
rather than to think of themselves as conventional, subordinate dependants of their brothers. Various tasks were outlined ('Hem a handkerchief
or duster') appropriate for girls of the time, but these look dutiful rather
than representing the deepest energies of the new movement. In the
chapter on 'Frontierswomen' Baden-Powell, clearly the author at this
point, perks up and relates a number of heroic tales of girls in the bush
who take it upon themselves, when the militia is down, to repel 'native'
attacks with hand-grenades and service revolvers—all evidence of 'what a
London girl can do'.[21] The naturalized presence of native incursions, as a
component of the larger playfulness of the movement, is itself revealing.
So too, however, is the movement from the feminine to the masculine.
Women may have been accorded a special role in making barren lands
homely, as Stanley Baldwin implied in his wistfully domestic renditions of
empire. But projections such as these assumed not only that colonial order

had triumphed with good grace, but that at the same time it had come unerringly to mirror the most elevated customs of the English at home. The realities of colonial life belied such pieties.

Even the figure of the settler, seemingly as white as could be, turns out to be a more complex construct than his or her whiteness would seem to suggest. Settlers may have been British, even close relatives of Birmingham man. But they were also colonials, with their own ways and with their own distrust of the metropolitan centre. The old settler boast of knowing the native could only work because in that very act the settler became, in part, the native.[22] To master the natives, and know their ways, required a measure of identification. As we know from the fiction, mythic frontiers-people learnt native languages and skills, adapting them for their own purposes, in order to learn how to survive in a strange and hostile land. An unspoken intimacy underwrote the contact-zones of the frontiers, in which the imperatives of the settler civilization were necessarily compromised. Cooperation between settler and native was as much a feature of the frontier as violence and conflict. The costs of this intimacy were articulated in the common-sense colonial injunction concerning the perils of 'going native'. Both native and settler were separated from the polite cultures of capital city and metropole; this too shaped the populist ethic of whites on the frontier. For all their stark differences, both shared—in metropolitan eyes—an accumulation of strangeness. These identifications informed, perhaps, the virulence of the racial convictions of the settler. Repudiation of the non-white native was simultaneously repudiation of part of the white self too, that hybrid dimension which had indeed learnt to know the native. Whiteness itself was thus always necessarily in jeopardy. The frontier, for these reasons, represented incessant internal as well as external danger, where the prescriptive ideal of the figure of the white man was simultaneously both absolute *and* the location where it was most likely to collapse. It marked the moment where race was both most actively played out and where it was at its most ambivalent. The frontier was the theatre in which fantasies of racial terror flowed most freely.

Baden-Powell's *Scouting for Boys* appeared within a matter of weeks of Curzon's Oxford lecture on the frontier. The two tracts occupied quite different mental worlds. They shared, however, the belief that it was on the frontier that the virtues of the imperial civilization of the British were most fully realized. How, though, were such ideas formulated in the colonial situation?

The Australia colonies

Fear was not an emotion much discussed in the lecture halls of Oxford, yet early on in the history of Australia principally it was fear which ate into the soul of whites living on the frontier. Even in the latter part of the nineteenth century a shepherd on an isolated north Queensland station left the following account of his first night out alone:

> I turned my attention to going to bed. I arranged my blankets in a corner of the hut, and lay down (as I thought) to sleep. But sleep would not come. First of all, I began to think what a long way off I was from my fellow-men, at least from men of my own colour, cut off entirely from all assistance, should I require it. Supposing I was taken ill, suppose the blacks attacked me, I might shout for help, no one could hear me. Then I began to argue that this was all nonsense, I was well and strong, and there were probably no blacks anywhere near. It was foolish to annoy myself with such idle speculations, I had better go to sleep, but it was no use; all the horrible stories that I had ever heard thronged to my recollection: of men attacked by savages and murdered, of ghastly corpses subjected to frightful mutilations, of dead men lying unregarded and found days after in lonely huts. Then I began to picture to myself the dreary bush outside, and the forms that might even then be creeping up in silence, shortly to be broken by unearthly yells. I lay now broad awake, and the perspiration streamed from every pore. My hearing seemed unnaturally sharpened, and the Bush seemed so noisy as it had before been silent: all around the hut I fancied I heard the cracking of dry sticks, and the rustling of grass.[23]

Fear was endemic: if not universal, it was systematic. It was a fear which was both localized—a response to particular acts by particular people in particular places—and amorphously ubiquitous, activated by collective memories of a community in the telling and retelling of 'horrible stories'. In the diary of one young settler, 'the dreaded danger' was believed to consist 'in blacks keeping in the background, out of sight, pouncing upon you at night unawares, the fearful Myall tribes do this, and are never to be seen to approach the white man's camp unless to murder or burn'.[24] Or as a letter-writer to a Brisbane newspaper observed: 'there are thousands, that can be spent on Defence Forces, to protect the inhabitants of this country from the invisible, perhaps imaginary, but for certain distant enemies; but we cannot afford to keep an efficient body of police to keep in check the enemy we have at our door, the enemy of every day, the one that slowly but surely robs and impoverishes us'.[25]

The pioneer white settlers in Australia were both colonizers and colonials, both heroic agents of their own history, and subject to the rule of others.
While epic tales of their exploits were related by admirers of empire in distant Britain there were, alongside the heroism, other stories to be told. The
presence of fear generated a strain of self-consciousness amongst the settlers
themselves that, whatever else they might have been, they were also victims.
For life on the frontier was prey to circumstance beyond the human control
of the settlers themselves. The forces of climate and of nature, criminal or
violent incursion, the laws decreed in the urban capital of the colony and in
the metropole, the effects of a collapse in commodity prices, or in banking
institutions: all impacted from outside the given community, making failure
a critical component in the experience of the settler.[26] Settlers could feel
that there existed many enemies, 'robbing and impoverishing' them, all too
easily breaking up the fragile, hard-won structures of 'every day'. About
many of these perceived enemies there was little that could be done. But
where they could impose their will, or attempt to impose their will, was on
the local indigenous peoples. In the insightful words of James Stephen,
under-secretary at the Colonial Office, writing in 1841, critical was the

> hatred with which the white man regards the Black which resulted from
> fear—from the strong physical contrasts which intercept the sympathy which
> subsists between men of the same Race—from the consciousness of having
> done them great wrongs and from the desire to escape this painful reproach
> by laying the blame on the injured party.[27]

Fear carried with it enmities and violence. In Britain, those expressing the
truths of white civilization could do so and maintain a degree of gentility, the
matter of extirpation of other races presenting itself as a distant abstraction.
In Australia, as in the other white colonies, becoming white entailed the
immediate activity of rendering others—generic 'natives'—subordinate: not
on occasion, but incessantly, in repeated assertions of white authority.[28] The
means by which this racial system was reproduced included the deployment
of a sophisticated theatre of symbolic violence, in which white authority
worked through the very texture of every aspect of civil society, compelling
those deemed to be natives through fear, as Froude insisted, 'to respect property and observe laws'.[29] The reproduction of this order involved too repeated,
systematic acts of cruelty—murder, torture, rape, abductions, poisonings,
beatings of men and women, adults and children. A state of war between
black and white defined the first hundred, or hundred and fifty, years of the

Australian territory. As one ethnographic study of 1880 described the situation, 'the advance of settlement has, upon the frontier at least, been marked by a line of blood'.[30] Sometimes this was a war of frontal assault, sometimes it operated at a lower intensity. Some districts were pulled into its vortex while others remained relatively free: violence was 'ragged, sporadic and uneven'.[31] Yet at a low estimate, tens of thousands of Aborigines were killed; and perhaps some three thousand whites.[32] During these years, for much of which Australia can properly be understood to have been a frontier nation, it was common practice for whites themselves to believe that they were at war with the country's indigenous inhabitants. Migrant Britons in Australia thought themselves to be much like whites in any other colonial society: the events in India in 1857, or in Jamaica in 1865, could be seen to address their own predicament. British soldiers, surmised one settler, were commended for shooting 'Kaffirs, Zulus, Abyssinians or any other inferior race': why not white Australians in *their* war?[33]

Imposition of civilization and its laws demanded acts which were uncivilized and illegal, a paradox which was justified by the barbarism of the wild native. In such circumstances an *excess* of violence, sanctioned by a free-wheeling white populism, was commonly accepted as morally appropriate. The unleashing of racial terror in Australia and the infliction of retribution and reprisals on those Aborigines innocent before the law, were necessary to hold the ground of white settlement and to teach the blacks 'a lesson'. An efficient 'pounding', 'customary chastisement', 'a dressing down', 'a thumping', 'a shaking up': all testified euphemistically to the need for revenge.[34] The advantages and disadvantages of extermination were publicly discussed in tones of cool reasonableness, posing a technical as much as a moral question. Colonists in the late 1830s and early 1840s in New South Wales openly talked of extermination of the Aborigines, as their Tasmanian counterparts had ten years earlier.[35] Even later in the century Sir Arthur Gordon, the erstwhile high commissioner in the Western Pacific, attempted to explain to his friend, William Gladstone, the prime minister, not only that such sentiments prevailed, but that in the colonial situation they were still properly speakable. He noted that he had 'heard men of culture and refinement, of the greatest humanity and kindness to their fellow whites, and who when you meet them at home you would pronounce to be incapable of such deeds, talk, not only of the *wholesale* butchery ...but of the *individual* murder of natives, exactly as they would talk of a days sport, or of having had to kill some troubling animal'.[36]

Yet, in the words of Henry Reynolds, 'Australia was a colony of settlement not of conquest. The common law arrived with the First Fleet; the Aborigines became instant subjects of the King, amenable to, and in theory protected by, that law.'[37] The imperial government in London, and its representatives in the colony, did intervene to ensure that the rule of law was upheld and that Aborigines would receive, in practice, their due rights. Through the 1830s the Colonial Office reiterated the fact that Aborigines were British subjects. And just as Chamberlain and Milner later recoiled against the effects of 'primitive and untutored' racial hatred in the British colonies, so in Britain and in Australia there were many who advocated protection for the Aborigines. In the early days of settlement, political leaders were able, on occasion, to excuse the blood-letting between whites and Aborigines as the consequence of the confrontation between the savagery of the native and the savagery of the convict, neither of whom could claim to be civilized.[38] Later, as evidence of frontier violence amassed, staff at the Colonial Office in Whitehall legitimately complained of the weakness of the imperial state, frequently finding it impossible to intervene on the ground to prevent frontier skirmishes. But formal declarations of legal principle or of philanthropic aspiration, or even recognition of the limited powers of London itself, had to contend with the overriding imperatives of asserting colonial order.[39]

Servants of the state, in both colony and metropole, shared an investment in white authority and conviction of the justice of British overseas settlement. If in the early decades of settlement a steady stream of memoranda arrived from London urging that goodwill and reconciliation be shown to the Aborigines, on the defining issue—the question of land rights—support was for the settler, and on this matter the settlers could call upon the full authority of the imperial state.[40] When it proved necessary to protect land, the Colonial Office sanctioned war against those whom the settler had dispossessed. Equivocation of this sort went to the heart of the colonial project. (This can be observed as well even in the syntax of Milner's apparent admonition of colonial intemperance, quoted above, a revealing example of the coexistence in a single utterance of the forthright and the equivocal.) It also underwrote the very conception of Greater Britain. As Westminster conceded increasing measures of self-government to the Britons overseas, so in the case of Australia it surrendered responsibility for the Aborigines to those very settlers it had previously condemned for their involvement in racial violence. Responsibility for all Aborigines north of the Tweed River, for example, passed from London to Sydney in 1856 and then, three years later, from Sydney to Brisbane.[41] This not only inaugurated a renewed phase of frontal assault, but—as a result of legislation passed in the Queensland parliament, in 1861 and again in 1880—deprived the Queensland Aborigines of their status as British subjects.

In terms of the distinctive mentalities of centre and periphery, however, there is much evidence to demonstrate that the expected norms of civilized behaviour could bend, or break, when confronted by the exigencies of a proximate, perceived barbarism. This is demonstrated with great clarity, for example, in the diary of J. B. Jukes, a scientist aboard the survey ship, HMS *Fly*, which worked the Australian waters in the 1840s. Skirting the Queensland coast, the ship's crew came into contact with many groups of Aborigines. On one occasion a fight broke out and a member of the crew was speared. It was, wrote Jukes, 'the first time in my life in which I had seen wounds (and, as it turned out, death) inflicted in open field, or in any other kind of strife. A burning feeling of mixed rage and grief, and a kind of animal craving for revenge, seemed to take possession of the heart, and a reluctance to leave the spot till some kind of amends had been obtained.' He examined further what these emotions had meant to him:

I have always joined in reprobating the causeless injuries sometimes inflicted by civilized, or quasi-civilized man, upon the wild tribes of savage life; and many atrocities have doubtless been committed in mere wantonness, and from brutality or indifference. I have always looked, too, with a favourable eye on what are called savages, and held a kind of preconceived sentimental affection for them, that I believe is not uncommon. I had been inclined to suppose that they were rarely the aggressors, and were always more sinned against than sinning. One such practical example as this, however, wrought a great change in my feelings on these points; and though far, I hope, from abetting cruelty, I could make great allowances for any one who, under such circumstances as I have detailed, took a larger revenge than the strict justice of the case demanded. I felt that the life of one of my own shipmates, whatever his rank might be, was far dearer to me than that of a wilderness of savages, and that to preserve his life or avenge his death I would willingly shoot a dozen of these black fellows; and I could read the same feelings in the eyes of those around me. Nor was this feeling very transient; for many days or weeks after, it would have been felt as a relief by all those who saw Bayley's fall, to have come into collision with any party of black fellows they could have been justified in firing on.[42]

Jukes was perhaps unusually reflective. But there is no reason to think that the feelings he described were unique. We know for example of the public career of Edward Eyre. As a young man in Australia and New Zealand, Eyre's views of the indigenous peoples were relatively benevolent; thirty years later, in Jamaica, and in a different historical moment, racial fear consumed him.[43] Circumstance predominates. The issue is not one, it follows, of the civilized centre counterpoised to the barbarism of the peripheries. It is rather a question of the complexities of the civilizing impulse itself, in which barbarism and civilization functioned not only as polar opposites but also—on occasion—as expressions of each other. The division between the civilization of the British, and the need to quell or to extirpate in the name of colonial order, was often located by a fine and sometimes invisible line, in which many imponderables presented themselves.

By the latter part of the nineteenth century, with white settlements increasingly secure, fear of Aboriginal violence decreasing, and the need for labour intensifying, white communities found themselves having to decide the degree to which blacks should be 'admitted', and the inherited frontiers recast. A number of Aboriginal men and women made their own decisions to 'go in', and to seek residence and work in white settlements.[44] Conflicting views appeared in the press. In June 1869 the editor of the *Port Denison Times* took stock, as he saw it, of the debate in his own locality:

> ...it is far better to see them [Aborigines] coming thus fearlessly amongst us than to know that they are skulking in the scrubs cowering from fear of the white man's bullet, their hand against every [white] man and every [white] man's hand against them. But on the other hand it becomes us as invaders to enforce submission to our laws on the part of the conquered. We have hitherto done this by the strong hand, that is to say, to unhesitating recourse to powder and ball. Against this system all right feeling men have thoroughly revolted and it has lately been hoped that the time had come when, with regard to our own safety, a milder system might be inaugurated and more friendly relations established between us and those whom we have supplanted.

This, however, was a situation which required even greater vigilance:

> ...we must not cease to be firm and must take especial care to show our black neighbours that whilst we are willing, nay anxious, to hold our hands from slaughter, we are at the same time determined to enforce at all hazards and by any means submission to our laws that any infraction of them will be met by retribution prompt and severe. If we do not we will be failing in our duty alike to them and to ourselves. For we shall not only endanger the safety of our own citizens, which after all should be our first care, but we shall render inevitable a return to the bloody system, the possible termination of which we have all regarded with so much hope and pleasure.

This was a conception which needed to be worked out in its particulars:

> ...we hold that the action taken by the sergeant of police as described in our
> last issue, we mean the flogging of the gin [an Aboriginal woman] who had
> stolen the child's petticoat, was, though perhaps not strictly legal, quite the
> right thing to do in the circumstances. We should not perhaps have alluded
> to this but that during the past week there have been under our notice several
> instances of offences committed by the blackfellow which though not of
> themselves of a very heinous nature are just such that as if allowed to pass
> unchecked will embolden the savages and lead to more serious outrages...The
> moral of all this is that we should not allow ourselves to be thrown off guard
> in our dealings with them.[45]

This is an argument conducted in terms of citizenship and the law, and at
odds with those advocating a continuation of a strategy of frontal assault or
extermination. It is written in a tone of civility ('quite the right thing to
do') and is self-consciously modern, recognizing the degree to which settler
societies had become sufficiently rooted that they could allow a measure of
coexistence with their racial antagonists. It marks the first step away from
Milner's 'primitive' conception of race, and anticipates the invention of an
entire battery of institutions devoted to the discursive management of a
new and dangerous racial situation. It is also an argument whose conception of citizenship and the law is particularistic. Citizens (those entitled,
whatever the costs, to 'our first care') are exclusively white, and the law is
parcelled out in such a way that the rights of citizens—whites—cannot be
compromised. If this entails flogging blacks for infractions, and 'retribution
prompt and severe' for more 'heinous' crimes, its greater purpose is to ensure
'submission to our laws'.

This is not, though, an abstract argument. It opens with the recognition—'first and foremost'—that 'we see daily in the midst of us numbers of
the former lords and ladies of the soil in almost their native costume marching about with that lordly air that so distinguishes them'. It is driven by a
sense of dislocation: that people and things ('in *almost* their native costume')
have slipped out of place. *They*, with their airs, are 'in the midst of us', the
frontier no longer functioning as a means to separate 'them' from 'us'. (Ten
years earlier, in British Columbia, the same perception was articulated in
almost exactly the same terms: what should be done when indigenous peoples appear 'in the midst of civilised society'?[46]) Anxiety turns on the mundane, the everyday, and the homely: a child's petticoat is pilfered from a
settler's home, or (a little later on) the reader hears of the damage done to

Mr Muller's peach tree.[47] These represent the micro-dispositions of power, in which command over *place* is contested. It is not about blacks in the abstract, nor even about their numbers, in the abstract. It is about the presence of blacks in a specific location which increasingly is coming to be defined as white. At issue is the territorial imperative, by which the local community asserts its right to be white, and by which the nation is transformed into a white man's nation. A vast multitude of these contested, parochial, micro incidents—petticoats and peach trees—are but local acts in the invention of the white man's country: 'the scraps, patches and rags of daily life' which, as Homi Bhabha observes, 'must be repeatedly turned into the signs of a national culture'.[48] For all the evident presence of ideas of race and empire in this historic transformation, decisive—in giving this transformation, literally, form—was the idea of the nation.

The making of the colonial nation

The Commonwealth of Australia was founded on 1 January 1901. For those in the metropole won to the ideas of Dilke, Seeley, and Froude, it must have seemed a providential moment. The creation of the Australian nation was historic proof of the benevolence of the British empire and of its fundamental dedication to the values of liberality and consensus. Whatever the difficulties which lay unresolved in the emergence of colonial nationalism—politically and strategically, as well as culturally—the overriding conclusion imperially minded Britons could draw was that it reflected well on themselves. That the birth of the Commonwealth coincided with the war in South Africa, where the same ends were being sought by considerably more belligerent means, was further proof of the essential rightness of the colonial relation with Australia. If within the prevailing imperial mentality in London Australia were a side-show in comparison to South Africa, it was a rather reassuring one to have—and augured well for when it came to negotiating with the defeated Boers, demonstrating what they in turn could aspire to. In Australia, the pacific, organic expansion of England and of its civilization was there for all to see: a new white nation had evolved, testament to all that was most homely about the empire. Thus in the metropole the birth of Australia was a matter for self-congratulation, though not, it has to be said, a cause for wild rejoicing. The event seems not to have touched the sensibilities of Lord Salisbury, the prime minister, despite the fact that, as a much younger man, some half century before, he had travelled to New South Wales.[49] Joseph Chamberlain, as colonial secretary, telegraphed his greetings. In Australia itself the Queen's representative, the Earl of Hopetoun, a man of dubious celebrity, excused himself from the festive banquet on 2 January on grounds of fatigue. The Times was glad that all passed with welcome good taste, implying that worse had been anticipated. In London the event barely received any public recognition. The lord mayor raised the Commonwealth flag above the Mansion House and, curiously perhaps, the bells of Bow Church were rung.[50] But no more. Even so, it was achievements of this sort which were remembered by Baldwin in 1924, or by Churchill and the Australian prime minister, Robert Menzies, during the Second World War.[51] Maybe these memories, or ones derived from them, were present in the mind of Enoch Powell's constituent in 1968, when he too dreamt of a country homely and properly the possession of the white man, a nation where white rule prevailed but where the profane, grisly mechanics of white supremacy—by a strange alchemy—were not so readily recalled.

The organization of the new nation, in this classic age of nation-building, had many dimensions. As the motley mass of white immigrants from Europe arrived in Australia, they were possessed by the imperatives of their own individual, or familial, destinies. In the first instance, larger affective solidarities were projected back, in memory, to whence they came rather than forward to the abstraction of new colonial collectivities. Home, in this context, might mean neighbourhood or village as much as a more general idea of the old country. 'Home'—the old home—was an idea which permeated every sentence of emigrant letters.[52] These letters home, in themselves, are testimony to the power of 'old' ethnic identifications, of the local, the known, and the remembered. The discovery of new arenas of collective life, of which a shared whiteness could be one, marked the moment of dislocation in which the idea of home moved from the longing for a known past to the longing for a stake in the future, in the new country, for sons, daughters, grandsons, and granddaughters. When the idea of home could be projected forward, into the future, the possibilities for a new affective relation—that of the nation—came into being.[53]

Alongside the homely, and making its future possible, was the heroic. Visionary tyros had set out to conquer the vastness of time and space which confronted them, creating a modern nation out of (it was supposed) the wilderness. Railroad construction, telegraph cables, elaborate postal systems—all constituted the infrastructure of future nationhood, and all were built against colossal odds. Between 1860 and 1890 railways comprised the fastest growing industry in Australia. By 1854 Melbourne had its own permanent telegraph, followed in 1857 by Adelaide, in 1858 by Sydney, in 1861 by Brisbane, and in 1877 by Perth, while telegraph links to Britain were established in 1872. The huge city post offices, great monuments to nationhood and still present in the postmodern cityscapes of our own times, were also products of this period: Melbourne in 1867, Adelaide and Brisbane in 1872, and Sydney in 1874. Telephone exchanges were opened in Melbourne in 1878, Brisbane in 1880, Sydney in 1881, Adelaide and Hobart in 1883, and Perth in 1887.[54] Before the First World War, commercial shipping lines carried mail from the United Kingdom to the empire for a flat-rate penny charge, a material substructure for imagining the collectivity of Greater Britain. These new productive and human forces were indeed harbingers of the modern. They served to unify the national territory, creating the means by which a citizen at any single geographical point would have the technical means to communicate with and—in theory—know his fellow citizens. The chaos of diversity was to be transformed into a nation marked by homogeneous structures of space and time.[55]

All but invisible from the purview of the metropole were those occupants of the national territory who had no claims to be nationals, no claim—as some would have it—to be there at all. Aborigines were excluded from the political nation, and excluded even from the census until 1967. This was an exclusion frequently justified by the common belief, aside from more brutal hatreds, that they were destined to die out and thus could play no part in the future: the birth of the new nation signified nothing if not the future. Despite earlier debates, legal segregation grew tighter in the period leading up to nationhood, beginning in Queensland in 1897. In government reserves Aborigines could not marry, consume alcohol, accept employment, manage their own assets, or leave without permission of white officials.[56] Their exclusion from national life was thus underwritten and made palpable by geographical segregation. It was both a legal and cultural fact. In the symbolic enactments which inaugurated the new nation, it was made clear, for example, that 'this great country should not be peopled by a mongrel or piebald race' but that it should be unequivocally the 'white man's Australia'.[57] With the nation achieved, and the settler triumphant, the slaughters of the indigenous peoples 'gradually faded from public consciousness, written histories, and school texts', only to resurface at a later date, in the words of Ann Curthoys, as 'the return of the repressed'.[58]

If it were expected that the Aboriginal population would die out, other ethnic groups required different solutions.[59] In the first year of the Commonwealth the Immigration Restriction Act sought various means to exclude new non-white migrants from entering. More radically in the same year, under the provisions of the Pacific Islands Labourers Act, the Pacific Islanders, or Kanakas, who had been brought to northern Queensland to work in the sugar-cane fields, were expelled from the new nation. Such were the requirements for making Australia home for kith and kin.

Yet these seemingly contrary impulses—the innocent, homely, heroic, and even democratic aspects of nationhood, on the one hand, and the savage imperatives of racial segregation and deportation on the other—were not unconnected.[60] The will to homogenize the national space had its racial conditions of existence as well: it wasn't only the territory which needed to be made indivisible, but the people too. In a revealing speech, one of the dominating figures in the movement to federate Australia, Sir Henry Parkes, moved effortlessly from railways to race. As an authentic tyro of the modern, he welcomed railways as a necessary condition for full nationhood. In part, he averred, they served a military purpose, allowing the speedy dispatch of troops. But there was too a deeper civic function: 'It might not be known that a man could take his seat in a carriage at Charleville, in Queensland, and travel right through to Williams' Spring in South Australia, a distance of 2,636 miles. [Applause].' This imagined, railway-travelling citizen of the future, however, was a man of specific ethnic disposition. Parkes immediately followed his thoughts on railways, without any visible break, by calling for 'a uniform law regulating the introduction of aliens of inferior races [Hear, Hear]'.[61] In this epoch the only means by which a modern nation could be imagined was as a white nation. The homeliness of integration necessarily coalesced with the violent, unhomely business of segregation. Both were functions of the same drive for nationhood—for the yearning for a white man's country—in which the circumstance of race was overdetermining. The homely vernacular of the British settler, of kith and kin, and of the virtuous pioneer, carried too the freight of those denied this racial providence. In the imaginings of the nation the cross-currents between the homely and the unhomely were always complex, shifting back and forth in unpredictable ways. The interior life of the nation itself was incessantly split between those elements worthy of integration, and those dangerous or debased manifestations which needed to be named and managed. Race—the truths of whiteness—provided a rich means by which the internal boundaries of the nation, in all their fluidity, could be mapped and held in place.

Henry Parkes

To think these issues through in more detail I can review the career of Parkes himself. He was a Birmingham man, a radical, who made the journey to Australia, and for whom the reverie that the new colony would become the exclusive possession of the white man became an act of faith—a dream so obviously desirable it could hardly bear the weight of rational explanation, and simultaneously so impossible to achieve that it became a source of unrelenting anxiety. He became premier of New South Wales on five occasions between 1872 and 1891.[62] In Australia this is a story so well-known it is hard to distinguish from myth. In Britain, it is barely known at all. Many years back the pre-eminent nationalist historian of Australia, Manning Clark, complained to Elspeth Huxley—as we have seen, an indefatigable ideologue of British colonialism—that although Parkes had been a local man no one teaching history at Birmingham University had ever heard of him, and that the university library possessed but a single speech.[63] It is worth recording that Parkes represented an episode in a distinctly British, as well as an Australian, past.

Parkes was born in 1815 in Stoneleigh in Warwickshire, in a rural community close to social collapse, a location he later described as 'the heart of Old England'.[64] In the early 1820s his family moved to Birmingham where he worked as a child in a local rope-works, and where subsequently he became apprenticed to an ivory-turner. As a young man in Birmingham he joined the Mechanics' Institute; he became a member of the Carr's Lane Chapel, a forcing-ground for radical Nonconformity; he subscribed to Thomas Attwood's General Political Union for parliamentary reform; and he was passionate in his denunciations of West Indian slavery. 'I felt myself moulded like wax in the heat of the splendid declamations of George Thompson, the anti-slavery orator.'[65] He immersed himself in self-education, and took regularly to writing poetry. By 1837 he was active in the Chartist movement. In all particulars, this conformed to the classic formation of a provincial radical man—Birmingham man—of the period.

Two years later, in March 1839, he emigrated to Australia with his pregnant wife, Clarinda, a decision prompted by the failure of a commercial venture he had launched at home. Before embarking he wrote a final letter to his family, which reads as if he were poised on the very edge of the valley of death. Though desperate to escape Birmingham and the penury he felt it condemned him to, the wrench of leaving ran deep.

> The very name of Birmingham will no longer meet my eye, except when I unconsciously write it on some part of the ship that bears me over the beaming waters, or in some gloomy tree in the wilderness of Australia. I shall hear no more of Birmingham except from my own tongue, or from my weeping wife's, when we think of those dear friends who live there, and of those angel-infants of our own, who sleep there in their little graves. And when I do hear from you again, will it be of death? Alas! My forebodings are very painful.[66]

So terrible were his experiences of emigration that he didn't feel able to write again for almost another year. His daughter, Annie, who edited his *Emigrant's Home Letters* after his death, thought that Australia at that time 'must indeed have appeared a veritable land of convicts and blackfellows'.[67] Parkes's own first feelings for Australia indicate the doubts that assailed him. 'I have been disappointed', he wrote home, 'in all my expectations of Australia, except as to its wickedness.' Or somewhat later, in September 1840: 'we cling to the hope of returning to Old England'.[68]

In Sydney he found work as a skilled artisan. He made contact with journalists who began to his publish his poems, some of which from early on were explicit in extolling the virtues of 'the white man'.[69] In 1850 the Australian Colonies Government Act separated Victoria from New South Wales, granted limited self-government to both colonies and halved the qualification for the franchise, bringing it into line with the £10 level that prevailed in Britain. In this situation, from 1851, he shaped his inherited Birmingham radicalism to colonial circumstances, entering a nascent political culture in which an indigenous populism pitted itself against both convict and cheap foreign labour (on the one hand) and (on the other) the oligarchy composed of the colony's landowning and pastoral elite. This was a populism, too, which identified 'the repressive powers of Downing Street' as a further enemy.[70] Tutored in politics by Robert Lowe, he was elected to the legislative council of New South Wales in 1854. (Lowe, at this time, was undergoing a momentary and entirely uncharacteristic spell of demagoguery, before returning to Britain to settle into his self-appointed role as Cassandra during the Reform crisis of 1866–7.) From that time on, Parkes combined politics and journalism. In 1850 he was the presiding figure at a new weekly, *Empire*, which declared in its first issue: 'COLONIAL RADICALISM—OUR OWN CREED'. Every man, the paper announced, should 'stand erect, as a freeman should', knowing 'that the glorious sun over his head, and the fruitful soil beneath his feet, were made for him'. The people in the colony, he believed, could never be conservative, for there was nothing to conserve 'save the smile of the blue heavens'.[71] A variety of radical causes he made his own. He was active in campaigning against transportation. He denounced Sydney University for modelling itself on Oxford and Cambridge, rather than on London University, a fact which struck Charles Dilke as well.[72] He and the pages of the *Empire* were vociferous in welcoming railways, as confirmation of colonial modernity. When gold was discovered near Bathurst he condemned both the presence of the Chinese labourers, whom the gold attracted, and the oligarchs for their cruelty towards the new labour force. From early on until its demise in 1858, the *Empire* was increasingly drawn to fanning anti-Chinese hatreds.[73]

His was a histrionic temper, which made public life a ceaseless torment. Neither sexual nor financial continence came easily. As premier he was forced to beg bank managers, on his knees according to legend, to honour his personal cheques. Manning Clark has presented the following portrait:

> He was driven on by passions that were outside the ken of men who had been brought up in Melbourne provincial bourgeois rectitude. Parkes twice suffered the humiliation of bankruptcy in a society all too prone to judge a man by his solvency. His second wife had been snubbed at Government House in Sydney. He himself was often derided for his lower-class way of speaking. His passion for women was insatiable, and he was not relieved of the ravages or the pleasures of that 'fierce and savage monster' till he sank into the grave just before his eightieth birthday. Everything about the man was on a grand scale. His figure was huge, his eyes bulbous, his eyebrows bushy and ample; his white hair was carefully brushed back and across a commanding brow.[74]

Later, after he had died, a Devonshire man launched a public vendetta against Joseph Chamberlain who, in the eyes of the disgruntled creditor, had been unduly laudatory about Parkes's memory in the House of Commons. Russell Endean, the aggrieved party, was sure that in his personal affairs Parkes was nothing more than a villain, and he was keen that the world should know.[75]

Because the costs of these various indiscretions were cumulatively high, Parkes's political career had many unforeseen interruptions. In 1861 he returned to England as an emigration agent, to encourage others to follow the journey he himself had made as a younger man. He addressed crowds of 5,000 in Birmingham town hall, and similar numbers in other towns in the Midlands, the great numbers confirming the appeal of the white colonies. To his Birmingham audience he boasted that in New South Wales the old Chartist demand of manhood suffrage had become a reality, although he was perplexed that this produced not a single cheer from an audience he found to be worryingly quiescent when it came to matters of constitutional politics. As the press reported, he closed his speech to the tightly packed ranks of Birmingham men—men very much like he had been—by saying:

> If people liked to stay in England, all he had to say was God bless them in the dear old country. He was as much an Englishman as any man present. The people in Australia were as thoroughly English as the people of the mother-country; they had forfeited nothing by going to a distance of fourteen thousand miles. Shakespeare and Milton belonged as much to them as to the people of England; they possessed by right of inheritance an equal share in the grand traditions, the old military renown, the splendour of scientific discovery, and the wealth of literature, which had made England the great civilising power of the world.[76]

This claim to the civilization of England was characteristic, just as it was to be in later years for Menzies. Time and again his speeches and poems look back to the great figures of English constitutionalism as a shared inheritance for Australians. Freedom came 'sealed with Hampden's blood', as he wrote in an early poem.[77] Milton, Cromwell, Pym, Hampden, Shakespeare, Wentworth, Latimer: these compose his intellectual patrimony, drawn directly from 'The Good Old Cause' of English radicalism and of English Protestantism. In one critical respect the history of Australia repeated, in Parkes's mind, that of England: its birth was marked by an absence of strife and blood-letting. In the poem he called 'The Flag' he indicated that

> In other lands the patriot boasts
> His standard borne through
> Slaughter's blood...[78]

Though neither in England, nor in Australia. In both nations, he claimed, there existed 'no remembered sores/Of once-distempered blood'.[79]

Like many of the native-born English Parkes allowed himself a certain latitude when it came to distinguishing between the English and the British. That as a young Chartist he appropriated for himself the language of the free-born Englishman is apparent. It was this that he deployed, many years later, when he addressed his audience in Birmingham town hall. But to a

greater extent, as a colonial radical, he embraced the idea of the free-born
Briton. In this was encapsulated a political idea of constitutional rights—
appropriate for all 'Greater Britons'—which necessarily was more inclusive
than the merely English emphasis. In Parkes's trajectory, however, we can
witness the incremental racialization of this founding category of political
rights.

It was on the occasion of his return to Birmingham that he first met
Thomas Carlyle. Much to his delight he was invited for tea and oatcakes
with the great man, and discussed public affairs and literature. In the future,
he was always to regard Carlyle as a good friend, sending him, in 1867, a
possum-rug which (Parkes confessed) 'I not a little admire', though whether
this enthusiasm was reciprocated we do not know.[80] On a later trip to
London he met with Froude, whom he was able to escort around Sydney
when the latter was on his travels researching *Oceana*.[81] Florence Nightingale
was a friend, and soon he became close to Tennyson, dedicating to the latter
a late volume of his own verse.[82] Respect for the traditions of the old
Chartists, combined with a new regard for Carlyle and Froude, may not
seem the most likely of evolutions. But nor was it eccentric, a function
merely of Parkes's penchant for gambling with his public reputation, or for
London high-life. Carlyle, as we saw in the last chapter, deliberately exploited
hostility to the Negro in order to undermine the radical commitments of
his opponents. And just as Joseph Chamberlain's radicalism found its apotheosis in the empire, so too did Parkes's in the populist attractions of colonial
nationalism based on the precepts of a white man's country.

Parkes would not have thought himself a man of the frontier, possum-
rugs notwithstanding. He was a man of the city, and commensurately urbane
in his preoccupations. The Aboriginal presence neither impinged much on
his everyday life in Sydney, nor concerned him excessively as a politician,
despite the public prominence of the issue in the city in the 1870s and
1880s.[83] One cannot imagine him, over oatcakes in Cheyne Walk, boasting
to the esteemed man of letters about his prowess as a man of the bush. On
the contrary, he would have been at pains to stress his own intellectual
sophistication. His sense of cultivation he believed to reside in the ethnic
inheritance of the English, even as he espoused a conception of colonial
nationalism which could differ forcefully from the requirements of political
authority emanating from London.

The kernel of the Parkes myth has him, in June 1889, travelling from
Brisbane to Sydney and stopping off at his old constituency of Tenterfield,

where—in the school of art—he announces his programme for unifying the Australian colonies into a single nation. Like many such originary stories, it works better as myth than as historiography. In an instant (we hear) Parkes became the founding father of the modern nation, and the motel which now stands near the spot where he made the speech, and which bears his name, is there to prove it.[84]

Hyperbole aside, it is the case that in the following February a federal conference met in Melbourne, whose delegates agreed to draft a new federal constitution. Federation was still a long way off; many impediments arose, not least in New South Wales. Even so, Parkes undoubtedly was an inspirational figure in making the conference happen and in determining its outcome. In replying to the opening toast to 'A united Australasia' he expressed the following sentiments:

> The crimson thread of kinship runs through us all. Even the native-born Australians are Britons, as much as the men born within the cities of London and Glasgow. We know the value of their British origin. We know that we represent a race…for the purposes of settling new colonies, which never had its equal on the face of this earth.[85]

These were fast becoming conventional opinions: the providential capacity of Britons, wherever their place of birth, to settle new lands was clearly at a premium. In his own accent, and with his own idiosyncrasies undisguised, Parkes was imagining a particular version of the future white Australian nation. It was a future made possible by the fact that in Australia, more so 'than the people of any other country, especially of any other new country', there existed a common racial stock: 'We knew each other', he stated; we are 'one people'.[86] This had allowed British emigrants to create 'a new England under these sunny skies'.[87] In so doing, Australians had brought into being the possibilities for a nation which other white colonials, in Canada and in South Africa, would, Parkes felt sure, be wise to emulate.[88] But this was not *only* to be a repetition of England. It was to carry as well a distinctively colonial imprint. When Australia would finally be born as a nation, Parkes claimed, 'the dream of going "home" would die away. We should create an Australian home… We should have "home" within our own shores'.[89]

In the old country such sentiment warmed many hearts, radicals and conservatives alike, evident of the truth of an ever more confident racial destiny. The published *Official Record of the Proceedings* of the federal conference in Melbourne included extensive reports from the national and provincial press in Britain and Ireland, amounting to almost two hundred closely printed pages, covering all political viewpoints. The tone was unanimously celebratory, the *Pall Mall Gazette* predicting that 'the crimson thread' speech was sure to be 'a classic', and *The Times* identifying Parkes not only as 'the most commanding figure in Australian politics' but, too, 'the heart and soul of the federal movement'. At this time Parkes was a hero *in Britain*.[90]

The British race, for Parkes, possessed the capacity to settle new colonies. Those descendants of Britain inhabiting Australia were, he believed, 'unequalled in all the whole range of the human race, in nation-creating properties'.[91] Clearly, other races could not claim this quality, or could not claim it in equal measure. Race and nation operated as one in his imagination. That the ethnic realities he confronted did not conform to his imaginings meant that a great measure of his undoubted political energies needed to be devoted to putting the matter right: to ensuring, in other words, that the new nation would be a white man's nation.

But as I discuss in the next chapter, white is more a fantasy than an empirically verifiable social reality. It never functions as a stable, fixed sign, and it carries no necessary connection to the observable dispositions of skin coloration. What, in the late nineteenth-century Australian colonies, white meant cannot be self-evident. The vast majority of the settlers came to agree on the requirement that Australia be established as a white man's country. But in the Parkesian scheme of things this also required the careful management of Irish Catholics. Parkes's dedication to the traditions of British Protestantism, in which 1688 served as the spiritual incarnation of the new political dispensation, led him to be deeply suspicious of Fenianism of all stripes. Unlike some of his contemporaries Parkes never implied that the Irish were close, in the racial hierarchy, to black, condemned to some racial penumbra, between black and white; but nor, given Catholic exclusion from the given traditions of his native radicalism, were the Irish white in the same way that he was. Whiteness functioned in this context as the guarantor of an independent spirit, free from ancient idolatries. To enter the realm of whiteness was a means, for Parkes, of championing liberty, even at the same moment as affiliation to the codes of whiteness resulted in the creation of new structures of exclusion.

In his own account of the making of Australia, and of his own part in it, published in 1892, he looked back to his role in this period and emphasized the degree to which, from the outset, he had insisted that the Australian colonies should receive only the best sort of immigrant from the mother country, noting especially the required 'care and discrimination in the selection of suitable persons and precautionary steps against exceeding the means of absorption in the industrial pursuits of the colony'.[92] He was continually at odds with the Catholic bishops over the issue of secular education. After the attempted assassination of the Duke of Edinburgh in Sydney in 1868, by a suspected Fenian, his anti-Irish attacks became more strident and more public. In the following year he informed the electors in East Sydney about the Irish that 'I am opposed to their coming here in excessive numbers', as this would transform 'the social character of the country'.[93] Despite his attempts to engineer a tactical truce through the period of high party factionalism in the 1870s, the curtailing of Irish immigration remained a constant theme. He found it difficult to suppress the momentary outburst, such as the occasion in November 1880 when, in the Masonic Hall in Sydney, he could not resist counterpoising Irish vice to 'Anglo-Saxon' virtue.[94] A few months later, as the colony's premier, he set out to explain to the legislative assembly the crux of the problem. He was happy, he said, for the English, Scots, and Irish to come to Australia. (He made no mention of the Welsh.) But he would not countenance a majority of immigrants from Ireland. 'I say that I want to preserve a majority of Englishmen and the descendants of Englishmen in this country.' This was a matter of Protestantism and 'the character of the country'. Immigration of the wrong sort, he maintained, would unbalance the country.[95]

We might suppose that Parkes would have been a deal happier if no Irish at all had ever emigrated to Australia. In themselves he did not consider the Irish to be an intrinsically destructive force, but rather one whose overall numbers needed to be managed. They were not from his perspective unspeakably, categorically other, in the manner of the Aboriginal population. Nor were they racially as other as the Chinese, who incurred considerably more of Parkes's condemnation than the Irish, and for whom he deemed exclusion the appropriate solution. Irish Catholics, having been denied the proper ethnic inheritance of Protestantism, should—he believed—never be allowed to determine the future of the nation; but nor, on the other hand, would properly regulated minorities of Irish be in a position to upset the nation's 'character'. It might seem, then, as if Parkes represented an ambivalent hostility towards the Irish and unambivalent hatred towards the Chinese. But even though his attacks on the Chinese were unremitting, and even though he clearly hoped for an Australia free from 'Asiatics' of all sorts, this is not quite right. For while he could hardly bring himself to utter compliments toward the Irish, to the Chinese he was, in the earlier years at least, *able* to be complimentary. In some respects the Irish proved more troublesome than the Chinese to him precisely because of their proximity.[96]

Parkes's antagonism to Chinese migrants in New South Wales had been apparent since the beginnings of his political career in 1851. This coincided with the discovery of gold in New South Wales, which—it seemed—would bring vast riches, establishing its dominance over its colonial rival, Victoria, and strengthening the case for securing from Britain a greater measure of self-government. This was undoubtedly Parkes's view, believing that gold would not only bring material prosperity for the people, but a new political order as well, in which the influence of the oligarchic squatters in the colony would be overcome. As it happened only very small deposits of gold were found in New South Wales, whereas substantial fields were discovered in Victoria, where the wealth poured in, the effects of which are still evident in the civic centre of Melbourne today. The short-lived goldrush in New South Wales, however, exacerbated the labour crisis. Two solutions presented themselves. One would have been to reintroduce transportation; the other would have been to import indentured Chinese workers. Parkes was committed deeply to the ideals of free labour, as the precondition for effective manhood. Yet his opposition to the arrival of Chinese bond labourers was principally based, not on any philanthropic position, but on race alone. Those who proposed such a solution, he wrote in the *Empire* in February 1852, were seeking to 'shovel in upon us an abhorrent mass of foreign Paganism, festering with all incestuous and murderous crimes'. Compared to the Chinese, he believed, even convict labour would be preferable.[97]

Yet as he was prone to reiterate, it wasn't the Chinese, in general, whom he feared. It was rather the Chinese who were 'out of place'—that is, those who insinuated themselves inside the territory of the newly evolving nation. If we take him at his word, it was regard for the nation, as much as it was his racial animosity, which drove him to pursue his campaign of exclusion against the Chinese. To allow numbers of Asiatics to populate the colony, or the future nation, would create a new class of 'coolie', or unfree labour, which on his radical criteria Parkes found repugnant.

The need to coordinate the anti-Chinese legislation of the different Australian colonies provided the initial and principal impetus for colonial representatives to convene. The first inter-colonial conference had taken place in 1867, devoted—not insignificantly—to the question of postal communication. This had also been the occasion when Parkes himself had first publicly raised the matter of federation.[98] The second, more influential, inter-colonial conference, which met in Melbourne in November 1880 and in Sydney in January 1881, was called at Parkes's instigation specifically to discuss the problem of Chinese immigrants. This was followed, in 1883, by a fractious meeting on collective defence, and on allied matters which impinged on the race question, such as quarantine from infectious diseases and safeguards against the influx of criminals. From these evolved the embryonic structures of the inter-colonial conference of 1890–1 which met to explore the idea of federation, and which was finally authorized to draft an appropriate constitution. Ironically, it was New South Wales which rejected the proposals that eventually emerged. Rivalries between the colonies still remained active, and in the event they were only overcome as a result of the collective fear of non-white migrants. Faith in the power of white labour proved decisive in the making of the Australian nation.

Just as in the metropole attachment to the protocols of the free-born Englishman could beget a consequent xenophobic disdain for those deemed to have been born in servitude, so in the Australian colonies the same myths transplanted worked in similar fashion, though directed less to the continent's original inhabitants than to those, 'Asiatics' of all types, who competed in the labour market.[99] From his *Empire* days, we can see evidence of such spontaneous, untutored racial thinking in Parkes's political pronouncements, and in his verse as well. In these views he was representative. He did not create the racial issue in New South Wales, nor could he have. But his significance lies in the fact that he was a prime mover in establishing race in the colony as a public and political matter.

At the end of 1878 members of the Seamen's Union walked off the ships of the Australian Steamship Navigation Company at Circular Quay in Sydney, in protest at the numbers of Chinese the company was employing. By the beginning of the following year the seamen won their victory and greater restrictions on the future employment of Chinese workers were agreed. The scale and determination of the strike were noteworthy. But in other respects it marked just another episode in everyday racial strife. It was precisely this issue that Parkes alighted upon. That same year, 1879, he piloted through the New South Wales assembly a bill to regulate Chinese immigration. The council set it aside, and there the matter rested until the following May. Further unrest in the interim prompted Parkes to propose the inter-colonial conference, devoted specifically to the question of the Chinese presence in Australia, in a more audacious bid to resolve the issue.

In Sydney in January 1881 the conference, with Henry Parkes in the chair, resolved 'that the introduction of Chinese in large numbers in any part of the Colonies is highly undesirable, and recommends uniform legislation on the part of all Colonies to restrict the influence of Chinese into these colonies'.[100] He, and two other representatives, were called upon to travel to London in order to petition the secretary of state and to demonstrate the strength of colonial feeling. This they did, but to no avail. Not only were officials in the Colonial Office worried about the diplomatic consequences with China and other Pacific powers, they were also concerned about the effect such legislation would have on those Chinese who were British colonial subjects. In this, imperial interests diverged from those expressed by the colonial politicians.

On his return from London Parkes was informed by his inspector-general of police that Chinese immigrants were embarking in greater numbers for New South Wales as conditions in California were making America an increasingly hostile prospect.[101] This state of affairs perturbed him and spurred him into more urgent action. In June, using the pretext of a small-pox scare, his government ordered all vessels arriving from Hong Kong to be quarantined, the supposed contagion of the alien proving a powerful card to play in the popular politics of the colony.

Speaking in the New South Wales legislature in July 1881, he announced that he had no sympathy for those whites who condemned the Chinese as immoral or depraved. 'On the contrary, I have at all times maintained that so far as I could judge, they were an industrious, a thrifty and a law-abiding people.' Yet despite these views, and despite too the admitted undesirability of imposing restrictive legislation, he was persuaded by the need to press ahead. The Chinese may have been industrious, thrifty, and law-abiding. But that represented only part of the story.

> I object to them, in the first place, because they do not assist in the permanent settlement of the country. I object to them, in the second place, because they are a class of persons who cannot possibly have any real sympathy with British progress, and with the development of those principles at which we all aim in promoting the progress of a British population. I object to them also on account of the vast numbers of the nation to which they belong.

As a democrat, he insisted it was improper for the colony to have within its borders a subservient or inferior class of people, and *thus* the entry of Chinese had to be curbed. He concluded: 'Is it part of our duty to encourage or to throw open the gates of the country to the inundation of persons who in no sense come to assist us in founding an empire, but who come here to better as far as they can their own condition, intending to return to the country?'[102] This plea for the restriction of Chinese immigration thus took an intriguing turn. It was not the Chinese *as such*, which lay at the source of the problem; it was, rather, their incapacity to 'settle' and 'to assist' in empire-building. In exhibiting this flaw, he implied, they existed at the furthest end of the racial spectrum from the most assiduous and elevated settlers, the British.

That same month, in defiance of the wishes of London, New South Wales enacted a bill 'To restrict the Influx of Chinese into New South Wales'. Within a few years all the Australasian colonies had imposed similar legal restrictions.

This, though, was not the end of the matter. In his own account of his role in Australian public life Parkes provides only fleeting mention of the events of 1881. 'A few years later', he wrote in what effectively were his political memoirs, 'as we shall see, the trouble had to be faced again and dealt with in a far more drastic manner.'[103] The issue came to a head again in 1888, when once more Parkes attempted to persuade both the New South Wales legislature and the Colonial Office to resolve the problem once and for all. By this time in his career, his earlier belief in his own racial generosity had given every indication of having diminished; yet at the same time his populist, nationalist, and democratic convictions appeared, correlatively, to have gained in assurance. Indeed, his own narrative demonstrates the extent to which the fundamentals of his colonial nationalism were forged in his struggle to exclude the Chinese. Colonial nationalism in the Parkesian mould was populist in two distinct registers. First, it was inseparable from belief in the providential history of the free-born Englishman, certain that the fruits of liberty were won by the people rather than by their rulers. Second it was a populism driven by the conviction that the white colonials in Australia knew about the local racial realities, as they perceived them, in a manner no functionary in London could possibly comprehend. This in turn provided a compelling rationale for those settlers who were coming to imagine themselves as a distinctive nation, separate from the metropole. In this sense, for those who proclaimed themselves to be radicals, the new Australian nation held the promise of embodying all that was best in the old popular traditions of dissident England. Far from Australia being understood merely as a 'repetition' of England, it could be imagined as much more than that: as *an* England in which the truer, more authentic spirit of English civilization prevailed.

It is clear from his reflections of 1888 that a predominant factor in his hostility to the Chinese in Australia derived from his worries about competition in the labour market, fearful that the wages of the white man were being undercut by cheaper immigrant labour. He was at pains to add, though, that this affected not merely the dignity and well-being of the white worker, but did much to damage the life of the white family. 'Every mother of a working-man's family is an uncompromising opponent and every child imbibes the feeling of resistance and denunciation from its parents.' It was precisely amongst the most respectable working-class families, he felt sure, that antagonism would burn most fiercely. His own views were rather more abstract, turning on the dangers of 'loosening the consanguineous ties which bind a state together'. By this stage he spoke more easily of the Chinese as 'a servile race' and an 'inferior nationality'. In writing to the secretary of state for the colonies, at the end of March 1888, he presented unequivocally the dilemma which confronted the colony. 'My colleagues concurred with me', he explained, 'that the wisest course was to get rid of the trouble altogether'. To propose such a thing, he realized, would leave him open to the charge of tyranny. But such measures were necessary in order 'to preserve the British type in the population'.[104]

When the issue came before the New South Wales legislature once more, Parkes's earlier restraint simply capsized. By this time the Chinese signified nothing but disorder. Those in the colony were 'a gangrene in the body politic', a 'poison...running through the veins of society, poisoning the very health of our social life'. This was a toxin 'all the more deadly for its being so subtle, so unseen, and so little demonstrable to the ordinary observer'. The Chinese presence was now a 'plague', soon to 'ripen into the dismemberment of society'. 'Mothers'—white mothers—were peculiarly vulnerable to this threat, positioned on the frontline of family and home, of the homely.[105] But the—white—working man suffered too. And if their will were broken, then the future of the nation, of 'British progress' itself, would be placed in jeopardy. 'They are really the blood, the bone, the sinew, the mind, and the spirit of the social fabric.'[106]

Parkes was aware that these opinions would not be well received by the prime minister, Lord Salisbury, in London. The more vehement the views about race and immigration in the colony, the more persuasive became the argument about separation from the mother country. Or as Parkes put this: 'we must be loyal to ourselves'. Ratification by London over a matter of such consequence for the colony would be merely legalistic or 'technical'. Moral power resided with the colonials, for they were preoccupied, not with mere legalisms, but with the greater 'law' on which depended 'the preservation of society in New South Wales'. In making such a judgement, Parkes was asserting the fundamentals of a newly emergent colonial nationalism in which, paradoxically, only separation from Britain could properly maintain the ethnic inheritance of a British offspring overseas.[107] Indeed this paradox, where an apparently ultra-loyalism to the codes of Britain could tip into sedition against the imperial government, had been present in Parkes's politics from the very beginnings of his activities in New South Wales. In the agitation of 1849–51, organized to resist the reintroduction of transportation, his attachment to the constitutional traditions of the British took him, according to a contemporary historian, 'to the point of open rebellion' and 'to the edge of sedition'.[108] This too he had conceived to be a matter concerning the very survival of the colony. In these commitments he expressed what would become a powerful refrain in future conceptions of race politics, in which the imperatives of racial preservation overrode mere matters of law, and in which the instincts of the colony took precedence over the policies of the metropole.

In such views the divide between race and nation barely held. Imagining the new nation as a white man's country made each a synonym for the other. The British inheritance could work, in part, because it was white. It came to signify, for Parkes, a racial concept: Britishness, once invoking a set of liberties, came through the course of his political career to be overlaid by faith in the singular race patriotism of its bearers. In the colony whiteness mattered; it needed to be voiced. It provided a resource in which the popular aspirations of the new nation could be articulated. In Parkes's mind this was at the same time essentially a democratic argument. His was a single voice, with its own particular inflections which were truly his. But there is very little distance, either in time or in political language, between Parkes of the 1880s and the collective inscriptions which later resulted in the legal invention of White Australia. Indeed, White Australia, both as doctrine and policy, was already well established before federation itself had been

accomplished.[109] As one of the Commonwealth's most dispassionate historians wrote over a generation ago of the new nation, 'The first thing which
was demanded from its first parliament was a permanent guarantee that the
country would remain for ever "white".'[110] This represented, as Arthur
Deakin—the first prominent native-born politician, another prominent
federalist, and great admirer of Milner—claimed,

> the profoundest instinct of individual or nation—the instinct of self-preserva-
> tion—for it is nothing less than the national manhood, the national character,
> and the national future that are at stake...No motive power operated more
> universally...and more powerfully in dissolving the technical and arbitrary
> political divisions which previously separated us than did the desire that we
> should be one people and remain one people without the admixture of other
> races.[111]

White Australia, as Deakin suggested, was an idea with which no other
instinct could compete in its capacity to generate 'universal' accord. In this
guise the nation appeared, to borrow from Stuart Hall, as 'an engine of
modernity', working to draw 'people away from particularistic attachments'—away from the social relations of custom and obligation—at the
very same moment it created new ('delirious') ethnic structures of inclusion
and exclusion. To become modern was to become white.[112] In this lay the
defining paradox and extraordinary appeal of the nation, impossibly universal and particular at the same moment. By the time of federation, faith in
the essentials of White Australia functioned as the common sense of settler
life—no more, no less, for white represented what a nation *was*. Robert
Huttenback describes the 'slow evolution of a policy that started out as
nothing more than a set of laws basically designed to keep Chinese off the
Australian goldfields into a racial philosophy that enjoyed many of the trappings of a state religion'.[113] In Parkes we can observe the beginnings of this
evolution.

Like all 'state religions' faith in the transcendent virtues of white consan-
guinity could take many puzzling, heterodox forms, not all of which received
the same degree of official imprimatur. As Milner was to discover, espousal
of the doctrines of whiteness invited 'ethnological' confusion, opening up
labyrinthine discussion of who was white and who was not and who,
amongst those accorded whiteness, was the whitest. The ethnic identities of
the white settlers in the new nation were riven by competing claims and
projections. The patrimony of England was as divisive an inheritance as

much as it was a factor of cohesion, as many Irish migrants to Australia knew well enough. Even so these competing, conflicting claims ran through a discursive field in which the absolutes of whiteness prevailed. The ideas of Dilke, Seeley, and Froude constituted one part of this.[114] And as Parkes himself hinted, the colonials understood themselves to possess a greater capacity to be white than their metropolitan cousins, and their men to be more manful. Being a white man in Australia was not only a matter of bearing and judgement—though it was that—but also, pre-eminently, it was a matter of physique. In the colonies the white man ceased to be an abstraction and became embodied. The particular fetishization of the white colonial body, female as well as male, begins at this symbolic moment.[115]

Debate in Australia during the South African War provided the occasion for many such boasts. The white man in Australia, it seemed, was more fully white than 'the Britisher himself'; he was not only 'technically' but 'morally' white, and stood in the 'vanguard' of the white race.[116] Confronted by alien peoples and by an alien landscape, the white man in the colony could more fully realize himself than his counterpart in the metropole. It had only been the 'weaklings', according to the future prime minister, Billy Hughes, who had remained at home, tied to the apron-strings of the mother country.[117] At the very moment of the foundation of the new Australia the masculine ideals of the nation were to be tested in the realities of war, in South Africa. Sixteen thousand Australian men volunteered to fight. In their own imaginings, and it seems in the minds of many of those who waved them off, these spirited colonial men, touched by the sunlight of a true democracy, were quite different from the stunted, undernourished Tommies who were emerging from a dark and decaying urban England and heading for the same destination as their colonial cousins.[118] This was a point which certainly impressed Kipling who was sure, when first seeing the Australian volunteers in South Africa, that he had never come across a 'cleaner, simpler, saner, more adequate gang of men'.[119] In the blood spilt in South Africa, Australians found an appropriate myth in which the ideals of 'national manhood' could be fixed in collective memory. For a moment it could indeed seem as if Australia, geographically and culturally distant from the compromised civilization of old Europe, stood at the vanguard of what the white race might yet become.[120]

The founders of the new nation determined that Australia would be a white man's country. In 1900 Edmund Barton, shortly to be the first prime minister, had announced that 'We have decided to make a legislative declaration of our racial identity.'[121] The inspiration for this 'declaration' derived from many sources, both domestic and global. The influence of racial thought from the United States, in the wake of Reconstruction, was significant, as Marilyn Lake's and Henry Reynolds's investigations have shown.[122] They also emphasize the degree to which, more broadly, the idea of a white man's country was particularly a construct of the New World. In this reading, white fears which had been generated by the accelerating demographics of non-white peoples—especially in the Pacific world and in the western hemisphere—lay at the heart of the making of White Australia. Thus while the Commonwealth of Australia was heralded by much predictable rhetoric which was both heroic and epic, dilating on the idea of Australia as the racial vanguard of the future, this was also a sensibility which concealed a deep and widely shared anxiety that the white race was already declining—in relative terms, at least—and which carried too the apprehension that the globe was already becoming, in racial terms, postcolonial. The construct of the white man's country, they observe, represented an essentially defensive strategy to respond to these shifting global, demographic circumstances. In a wonderful, evocative phrase, they conclude that 'whiteness was born in the apprehension of imminent loss'.[123]

In tracing a transnational network of racial theorists who brought notions of the coming decline of the white race to public prominence, Lake and Reynolds pay most attention to Charles Pearson, who in 1893 published *National Life and Character: A Forecast.* Pearson was an Englishman who had taught history at London University and who, in 1869, emigrated to the Australian colonies. The book, when it was published, was lauded by Theodore Roosevelt in the United States, by Gladstone in Britain, and by many of the political figures who brought into being the new Australian nation, including the leading proponents of the White Australia policy, Deakin, Barton, and H. B. Higgins. Indeed when in 1901 Barton spoke in parliament in support of the measures designed to inaugurate White Australia, he held Pearson's book in his hand and quoted from it at length. The book, as Lake and Reynolds demonstrate, is chock-full of anxious predictions about the fate of the white man, on the verge of being 'elbowed and hustled, and perhaps even thrust aside'.[124] They argue that what was at stake in the founding of White Australia was, above all else, white manhood itself. In the light of Pearson's diatribes Marilyn Lake identifies what she calls the new figure of 'the white man under siege', proposing that the racial fears he articulated represented 'a drama of white masculine humiliation'.[125]

She thus offers the intriguing paradox that the founding fathers of the Australian Commonwealth believed that, just at the moment they entered nationhood, external forces were conspiring to rob them of what they most treasured: their whiteness and their manhood.

These are important reflections, which offer much insight into the particular conjunction, at the turn of the nineteenth and twentieth centuries, of whiteness and masculinity, and of the ways in which the intoxicating figure of the white man provided a model to think of the nation.[126] The very notion of the settler, I have suggested, was for long understood as simultaneously agent and victim of history. In Parkes the anxieties which attended his incantation of the values of white civilization were palpable. The ideals signified in the notion of the white man represented a yearning for a particular sort of colonial order; that these reveries also produced their own pathologies should not surprise us. They alert us, I think, to the impossibilities of whiteness, an issue I explore in the next chapter.

As policy, White Australia remained operative until 1966, and was finally only abandoned formally six years after that, in 1972. Not 'for ever "white"', but still an extraordinary run. Despite embarrassed disclaimers towards the end, it boasted a long life.[127] The thousands of British migrants who travelled to Australia during this period, willingly or not, were journeying to a nation fashioned as a white man's country.

My discussion of colonial nationalism has turned on the role of Sir Henry Parkes in New South Wales. Stories could be told of similar developments in these years in Queensland or in British Columbia, in Natal or in New Zealand. In each locale there emerged an energetic white populism, emanating from white men in the labour market fearful of proximate 'Asiatics', and defining itself against distant rulers in London, and—in the case of British Columbia—against the government across the Rockies in the east, perceived to be equally remote. There were, of course, many variations; Asians arriving as indentured labourers created a different situation from their arrival as sovereign individuals in the free market, legally entitled to compete with white workers on equal terms. Even so, a common dynamic can be identified. An influx of non-white labourers would be attracted to the goldfields, plantations, or railways; white settlers, confronted, as they saw it, by racial antagonists on *their* territory, would recreate themselves in the image of white Anglo-Saxons, with an inventive array of virtues peculiarly theirs; the Chinese, or Indians, would be discovered to possess none of the defining characteristics of a settler population; white tribunes on the ground—Noah Shakespeare in British Columbia, Timothy Wobblechops in New South Wales, and their like—would compose letters and petitions to bring the matter to the attention of the local, colonial public; after many tussles with London, restrictive legislation was enacted.[128] This was the pattern of events. In the final years of the nineteenth century, a systematically racialized language of contagion evolved in these colonies, which perpetually invoked the dangers of swamping, disease, sexual misconduct, and dirt, and which worked its way into the norms of public speech. No arena of daily life seemed immune from the dangers of racial contagion. The twelfth item of legislation passed by the federal parliament of the Commonwealth of Australia, for example, stipulated that the new nation would subscribe to mail contracts which had guaranteed that vessels carrying the mail employed only white labour. In the course of these ethnic struggles a collective colonial identity was cast. Deakin's notion of 'national manhood' was appropriate. 'He', the white man, made the nation in his own image; he made it, in other words, safe, ready to be made homely. And in a bizarre twist, this homeliness represented a system of values which increasingly came to be deemed universal in its reach, just at the very moment when new racial exclusions, Manichaean in intent, were proliferating.[129] The white man had transformed himself into the custodian of human destiny.

From colony to metropole

The creation of the Commonwealth of Australia produced amongst the British no great fanfare of celebration. But it did much, certainly in retrospect if not at the time, to affirm the sense of the liberality of the British empire, in which in due course all Britain's offspring would undergo the business of separation, whilst still holding dear the foundational civilization in which they had been nurtured. It did much to affirm, in the metropole, the often unspoken faith in the essential rightness of a white man's country, as an index of a modern, ordered way of life. In the early years of the twentieth century, in the time of Chamberlain and Milner, few in Britain would have perceived any difficulty in this ideal. Not much later, by the end of the First World War, the possibilities that the reasoning in this putatively self-evident truth might contain some flaw registered more forcefully. Especially this was so in response to the pressures of Indian nationalism, for within the prevailing order of things India could not as readily be regarded as a modern nation. How these conflicting ideals—between colonial nationhood and white order—were to be reconciled became a matter of the deepest contention when, through the 1920s and 1930s, India pressed for the privileges accorded to the existing white dominions. For a period in the early 1930s this issue preoccupied the British government more than any other single matter.[130]

How such notions entered the popular common sense of the metropole, and came through various displacements to be remembered again in the aftermath of formal empire, is a theme which runs through the following chapters. There isn't the opportunity to continue this discussion of Australia, nor to take account of the histories of New Zealand or Canada. In consequence there are many important developments which I cannot address directly. The growing imperial significance of the crown is one such point. Another, not unrelated, is the development of new technologies of communication, in particular the wireless and the cinema. A third is the resolutely vernacular cultural terrain in which many of these memories lived, in the pulp and schlock of a commodified mass culture which even now tend to resist the scholarly endeavours of imperial historians. The vision of the Prince of Wales, sculpted life-size entirely in butter, to be found at the Canadian stand at the 1924 British Empire Exhibition at Wembley, may only throw an oblique light on the matter of imperial governance. But it still stays in the contemporary mind, working as a medium by which all manner of adjacent memories can come to life.[131]

It might none the less seem as if the issues which exercised Henry Parkes in New South Wales, or which preoccupied other assorted tribunes of the British race in colonies closer to hand, were remote from the lives of the inhabitants of late Victorian and Edwardian England. The 'native' question did not directly impinge on the English. Outside Limehouse, and one or two other tiny neighbourhoods in the seaports, the Chinese did not figure largely in the social landscape. According to the 1911 census the total number of Chinese seamen residing in Britain totalled a mere 480, and seamen formed the largest single occupational group. This minuscule number of Chinese actually living in Britain, though, did nothing, to curtail the extravagant imaginings of Sir Arthur Conan Doyle and of other like-minded pioneers of popular sensationalism.[132] Despite the oft repeated plea that race is all about numbers, in the case of the Chinese in Britain this could not have been further from the truth. Race was about race.

Yet the legal as well as the imaginative frontiers of the domestic nation, circumscribing the heartland of Greater Britain, were recast in this period in a manner which is at least analogous to the experiences in the white colonies. If in Britain the bulk of agitation was directed to sealing the nation against the arrival of undesirable, orientalized Jews from central Europe, the will to establish the homogeneity of national life was in all respects similar. The protracted and ultimately effective campaign to impose anti-alien legislation, in the 1905 Aliens Act, marked a decisive redefinition of nationhood, and resulted in a more vigilant policing of the frontiers between the 'us' who composed the nation and the 'them' whose fortunes were destined to remain outside.[133] That this coincided with a more tightly administered system of frontier controls requiring travellers to bear passports was entirely logical.[134] At the same time that the imagined community of the English was at its most expansive overseas, at every point—internally and externally—the frontiers of the nation were drawn tighter.

We know from the analytical insights of Seeley that there is no given division between the 'internal' and the 'external' properties of expansionist England. Expansion, the existence of imperial England, confounded this dichotomy. For just as some of 'them' were located in the domestic nation, so there were many of 'us'—kith and kin in blood and bone—who lived in far-flung points around the globe. At every moment, internal discussion about who was, and who was not, entitled to participate in the public life of the nation—the ever-contentious issue of the franchise—connected with the evolving gradations and hierarchies established in the colonies. Between 1867 and 1883, at the earliest point when the white colonies were coming into being as white, the domestic electorate in Britain multiplied four-fold. Just as the legislators at Westminster allocated appropriate degrees of self-government to those colonial whites overseas who shared the ethnic inheritance of the British, while imposing stricter, centralized authority on the 'less developed' darker races, so the attributes of ethnicity, class, and gender were called upon to determine the nature of the new domestic electorate. In the mind of those creating the legislation these represented not separate functions but the undifferentiated project of creating the imperial nation, with all the proper social hierarchies in place, and with the relations between the internal and external dimensions of the nation properly regulated from the centre.[135]

When Joseph Chamberlain addressed 'Birmingham man' in May 1903, he was speaking exactly to that constituency of independent working men

who had been enfranchised by the constitutional advances of the Reform
Act of 1867 and by its successors. Just as Parkes could imagine the working
man of New South Wales to be the 'blood, bone, sinew, mind and spirit'
of the emergent Australian nation, so Chamberlain believed the radical
working man of Birmingham to be the foremost agent in the making of a
revivified, energetic England. But the figure of Birmingham man was simultaneously also positioned in the vanguard of empire, as the principal creator
of England overseas. In the passion of the moment, high from his triumphal
tour of South Africa, in Chamberlain's imagination there was no distinction
between the radical spirit of Birmingham man in the metropole and the
radicalism of the Birmingham men who populated the white colonies, 'our
kinsfolk' who comprise the 'white British population that constitutes the
majority in the great self-governing colonies of the Empire'. They had both
become expressions of the same universal desire for building white civilization under the banner of English liberties, such that 'this great Empire of
ours' was on the point of becoming 'one free nation', founded on the 'union
of the British race throughout the world'.[136]

Even so, one must still wonder. Speeches by politicians are renowned
neither for their veracity, nor for the accuracy with which they represent
popular sentiment. Impassioned appeals to 'the British race' or to the 'white
British population' clearly made sense to Chamberlain, in the Cape or in
the Transvaal, but what of those in his audience in Birmingham town hall,
whose local communicative world of the tram and the *Birmingham Daily
Post* would seem to be considerably more circumscribed? Forty years before
Chamberlain's speech, Parkes himself had addressed Birmingham men in
the same town hall, and was perturbed to be confronted by a palpable lack
of enthusiasm for the democratic aspirations he held most dear, and which
he believed to be the common inheritance of all who hailed from
Birmingham. Was the same incomprehension, or scepticism, evident in the
responses to those public invocations of white civilization which, on the
colonial frontier, had proved so compelling?

As ever, the evidence is fragmentary. All the usual difficulties in attempting to determine popular attitudes to race come into play. But current
historiography provides some clues. Two issues present themselves. First,
the spectre of the 'Asiatic', the Chinese in particular, was, against expectation perhaps, close to the very centre of public life in late Victorian and
Edwardian Britain. Second, and in part in consequence, the figure of the
white man did carry a determinate popular resonance through these years,

at least in some arenas of social life. In each case, the organization of the labour market proved decisive. This tells us part of the story. We can look at each of these in turn, summarizing recent findings.

From the turn of the century British seamen were notable in contriving to protect the value of their own labour by restricting the opportunities of Chinese and Asian co-workers, and in doing so relied upon the power of class militancy, as Laura Tabili has shown.[137] Historically, British naval and merchant shipping had been manned by a heterogeneous ethnic mix of sailors.[138] But after the shipping companies' attacks on the unions in the 1890s, the slow recovery of union organization took place on the back of attempts to exclude non-white labour: in shipping, certainly, the syndicalist moment of 1910–14 turned on a collective belief in the specific privileges due to the white man. The language of the 'yellow peril', so much a feature of the imaginative landscape of populist labourism in British Columbia or New South Wales, became part of the common sense of white British seamen struggling to re-establish the value of their labour power in the market.[139]

A language test, devised specifically to exclude Chinese competition, was instituted by the employers, under union pressure, in 1908. The paper of the National Sailors' and Firemen's Union of Great Britain and Ireland, *The Seaman*, made the running, declaring that racial exclusion was not a matter of 'prejudice' but rather 'an economic and Trade Union question pure and simple'. Yet the full panoply of anti-Chinese anxiety appeared issue by issue. Tom King, for example, the MP for Lowestoft, addressed a mass meeting at Great Yarmouth in the spring of 1914 in the following terms, as reported by *The Seaman* on 1 May:

> The Chinaman ate rice with a knitting needle, while a Britisher wanted meat and a knife and fork, he clothed himself with a loin cloth while the Britisher wanted a suit of clothes; and he lived in a nest, while a Britisher wanted a house. The Chinese and Lascars were not to be brought up to our standard, but an effort was being made to bring our standard down to theirs.

That same year, Havelock Wilson, the president of the NSFU, fought a parliamentary by-election solely on the Chinese issue. For Wilson, at least, the trade-union question 'pure and simple' took on quite other dimensions, compelling him to reflect on 'white girls [with] half-caste children...sufficient to make any Britisher's blood boil with indignation'. By the following decades, according to Laura Tabili, within the shipping industry 'imperial racial categories and racial subordination were reconstituted on British soil'.[140]

The proximity of white and non-white labour in merchant shipping, and the degree of racial antagonism which followed, were clearly distinctive. Indigenous white seamen were, in terms of their occupation, British in a very particular way, untouched by the expectations of localized working and domestic cultures. One might reasonably expect the influence of colonial thinking to have registered more deeply on seamen than on those involved in more insular occupations. To NSFU militants in these years, whiteness mattered. It effectively became an attribute which itself was commodified, as a function of a wider popular struggle which, on occasion, was simultaneously explicitly anti-capitalist.[141] But despite the distinctive mobility of seamen, echoes of similar racial assumptions could be heard elsewhere.

Just before the full momentum of the anti-Chinese campaign gathered pace in the seaports, the spectre of the Chinese presence had entered national debate. The issue derived from Milner's decision to allow the importation of indentured Chinese labourers to work in the mines in the Transvaal. Milner, convinced that maximizing mineral output was the first requirement in ensuring that South Africa constituted itself as a white man's country, pressed the issue from early on. Chamberlain, as colonial secretary, equivocated, won—as he had been before—by the logic of Milner's arguments but fearful, as he noted in his diary, that 'such action would be extremely unpopular and would raise a storm at home'.[142] In the event, after a succession of complex negotiations in London and in Johannesburg, and with a new colonial secretary appointed, the first shipload of 600 Chinese labourers arrived at Durban from Hong Kong on 18 June 1904, and began working on the Rand on 2 July. Gold output soared—though so too did the number of white and black miners newly recruited. In Britain, opponents of the government famously charged the Unionists with introducing 'Chinese slavery'. Just as Havelock Wilson was to win a by-election due to the vigilance of his opposition to the 'yellow peril', so a mining constituency in Cornwall voted for a radical who opposed the introduction of Chinese labour some four years *before* the first Chinaman had disembarked in Durban, and (in the same election) John Burns in Battersea could stand on a platform dedicated to curb an influx of Chinese labour, affirming 'Equal rights for all white men in the world over'. On occasion, then, elections for Westminster were won or lost on the question of Chinese labour.[143] In the general election which opened in December 1905, the Liberal party took the cause of 'Chinese slavery' to the very heart of its political campaign, abetted by the knowledge that Milner himself had sanctioned the imposition of summary corporal punishment on Chinese labourers whom employers regarded as fractious. 'I feel', declared Winston Churchill in October 1905, newly arrived on the Liberal benches, 'that this question of Chinese labour must be the great moral issue at the general election.'[144] And so it came to be. By confronting Milner on his advocacy of Chinese labour, and Chamberlain on tariff reform, the Liberals found conspicuous issues which allowed them to traduce the entire colonial record of the Unionists as *dirigiste* and illiberal. And in drawing on the language of anti-slavery, Liberalism was also presented as the historic inheritor of an old progressive, philanthropic tradition.

But the issue of Chinese labour was a complex matter, double-edged in its deepest motivations. It could indeed serve to mobilize an older radicalism, in which pro-Boer sentiments converged with a powerful condemnation of the Randlord titans. Yet this revival of the essentials of a radically inspired England could simultaneously tip into a racial logic which had precious little to do with emancipation. We can see this double movement in Churchill's October speech. He spoke in the name of his new-found radical Liberalism, keen to denounce the authoritarianism which Milner, Chamberlain, and their South African allies represented. But the image of the contagious alien presence was brought home too. Inviting his Manchester audience to imagine the situation in the Transvaal, Churchill described the following scene:

> Outside the cordon of police are the deserters, the men whom even the luxuries of a Johannesburg compound could not keep in content, roaming about over those vast plains, crouching among the rocks, hunted like wild beasts, shot at sight, living by murder and rapine, the terror of the world, half the world between them and their own sunny China.

The problem lay, Churchill implied, not simply in racial exploitation as much as in racial mixing.

> But I think experience has shown that the instinct which prompted the working men of this country and of the great colonies of Australia and New Zealand to protest so passionately, so vehemently, against the introduction of Chinese labour was a true instinct, founded on real reason and a great perception of the underlying causes and forces which were at work. [Hear, hear.] Dangers which were utterly unforeseen, even by those who were most implacable opponents of this labour, have arisen. Ugly and vicious consequences which they had never predicted have actually come upon us.[145]

Churchill's subsequent appointment as a junior minister at the Colonial Office required him to tread more carefully in the future, for the new Liberal government could not countenance the immediate repatriation of the Chinese labourers from the Rand, despite the rhetorical passion with which the party had attacked the old Unionist administration not so long before. Even so, Churchill was still content to proclaim that the presence of Chinese miners jeopardized 'the true interests of the white man in South Africa [cheers]'.[146]

Some of these same complexities had appeared a few years earlier in the manifestations of Edward Carpenter's pro-Boer radicalism. In a newspaper article in January 1900 he conceded that the Boers had 'their faults', including a barbarous attitude toward black Africans, though he thought their cruelty was less 'systematic' than that of the British. Their mythically simple way of life appealed to Carpenter. Their right to sovereignty, he believed, was equal to that of the British if Liverpool had been overrun by 100,000 Chinese, 'smothering our civilization and introducing their hated customs and ways'.[147]

It is not easy to judge how the various currents in the 'Chinese slavery' agitation were manifest in popular life, though its rendering as an ethical issue, as much as one which was narrowly party-political, might suggest that it drew into its orbit a wider section of the population, including those without the franchise, than merely the dedicated Liberal voter. Its significance as a national issue should not be underestimated. Radicals, Liberals, and philanthropists: all in their various guises stretched out the hand of sympathy to the racially exploited Chinese labourer, forced to endure an existence of severe privation. In the case of Churchill these humanitarian instincts inextricably carried with them fears of racial mixing—his 'ugly and vicious consequences'. How representative Churchill was in thinking in these terms, we do not know. But there are indications, at least, that through these years popular hostility to the idea of racial mixing was becoming more easily voiced. And that these anxieties should be articulated in terms of the Chinese, whose social presence for most domestic Britons was barely measurable, does much to suggest that the sociological realities of 'race' (numbers, proximity) are only ever part of the issue.

From the perceived presence of the Chinese within the putatively white nation there derived an inventory which affirmed the capabilities, specifically, of the white man—in Great Yarmouth as much as in Sydney. But popular conceptions of the white man, and of his privileged position within the labour market, had other sources too. Here, too, recent research provides a glimpse of these emerging realities.

On 1 March 1914 a monster demonstration of trade unionists made its way in a seven-mile column to Hyde Park in London, comprising some half a million workers. In a rare moment of consensus, *The Times* and the *Daily Herald* agreed that the demonstration marked one of the largest which the capital had ever witnessed. In the view of the official publication of the engineering union, the event represented 'the greatest and most impressive of its kind that has ever taken place in the heart of the Empire'.[148] The purpose was to demonstrate solidarity with nine trade-union leaders, seven of whom were British-born, who had been summarily deported from the Transvaal by Louis Botha's deputy, Jan Smuts. On first appearance this too might have seemed a trade-union matter, 'pure and simple'. But the unions to which the deported workers belonged insisted on the exclusion of black and Asian workers. For skilled white workers in South Africa, defence of workplace privilege against de-skilling, on the one hand, and against the introduction of coloured labour, on the other, fused into a single struggle. From 1907 militancy on the Rand had been organized around this overriding issue. These exclusionary practices were not, for British workers, a contingent issue. As much as Havelock Wilson in the NSFU, Ben Tillett, the leader of the dock-workers, and others could be heard in the pages of the *Herald* extolling the virtues, explicitly, of the white worker and alerting their readers to the dangers of the cheapening of white—'British'—labour by the employment of non-whites. Expressing solidarity with fellow workers in the white dominions inevitably meant endorsing given racial hierarchies, for that in part was what colonial industrial disputes were about, and valorizing if only from afar the ideals of white labourism. Even though for British workers competition by non-whites represented a distant anxiety, whiteness itself became a means by which the self-identity of the male worker, and the disposition of his liberties, could be thought and organized.

But to those workers demonstrating in London, this was not a matter merely of sentiment, or of an abstract solidarity. The degree to which sections of the English working class lived as a mobile workforce, crossing back and forth across the Atlantic, or travelling between Australia and South Africa, itself is of significance, just as there was sustained traffic between the colonies themselves.[149] Syndicalism itself, largely North American in inspiration, was an expression of Australian and South African realities as much as merely British.[150] These were worlds of labour which overlapped, one with another. The Australian labour movement served as a model, though in fact many Australian labour leaders had been born in Britain.[151] Australian unions had been active in their support of the great London dock strike of 1889.[152] There were, in 1904, some 5,000 Australian miners and artisans in the Johannesburg area, drawn there as a result of their experience in the mining industry. Robert Burns Waterston, secretary of the South African Labour Party and one of those deported by Smuts, had been born in Bendigo in Victoria; Peter Whiteside, the president of the Witwatersrand Trades and Labour Council, originated from Ballarat. (The South African Labour Party was the first political party in the Union to advocate the separation of races in the labour market: it was an organization, one might add, predominantly made up of English-speakers, not Afrikaners.) Indeed, Australian labour activists played a critical role in bringing to South Africa the essentials of a successful, state-sanctioned white-labour policy, a situation recognized at the time by the labour leaders on the Rand.

Australia provided one dimension, Britain another. Since the discovery of gold on the Witwatersrand, miners from Britain had travelled to the Transvaal in a steady stream, especially from Cornwall, where labour was skilled but the mines exhausted. As Jonathan Hyslop notes, in 1905 *nearly half* of the 16,000 white miners on the Rand originated from Cornwall. The Miners' Association was founded by a Cornishman, Tom Matthews. On one mine on the Rand, Ferreira Deep, the entire white workforce came from a single Cornish pit, Dolcoath. In the late Victorian and Edwardian period, the economy of Cornwall was intricately tied to the economic rhythms of the Rand. A. L. Rowse, reminiscing in the 1940s about his childhood, recalled: 'At home people knew what was going on in South Africa often rather better than what was happening "up the country": the journey across the seas to another continent was more familiar to them than going very far "up the country," say as far as London.'[153]

Yet it wasn't only miners who composed this international traffic in labour. The British Amalgamated Society of Engineers had branches in South Africa, Australia, and New Zealand claiming, in 1913, some 3,000 members in South Africa and 11,000 in Australia and New Zealand. Three thousand ASE members from the London branches alone participated in the March 1914 demonstration in Hyde Park.[154] These geographical realities, complicating the obviousness of the frontiers of the core imperial nation, served to bring home the injunctions of a white labourism which had been cast, first of all, in the colonies. The predicament of white workers in South Africa could seem, to Cornish miners or London engineers or sea-men based at Lowestoft or Great Yarmouth, to be their predicament as well.

The extent of the solidarity of organized workers in Britain for their South African brothers was comprehensive. The Labour party, the unions, the working-class press, and prominent public labour leaders all lent sup-port.[155] The opposition to the transportation of indentured Chinese work-ers to the Transvaal had anticipated much of the popular outrage of 1914. In some unions the matter had been a constant source of anxiety for a number of years. In the 1914 campaign the fate of whiteness was interpreted with differing degrees of intensity. At one end of the spectrum J. O'Connor Kessack, in the Glasgow paper *Forward*, saw things like this:

> The coloured man's life is low, his food simple and inexpensive, and his cloth-ing so scanty as to be financially negligible. He costs the Capitalist a mere fraction compared with the white man. He is squeezing the white man out. That is the real Yellow Peril. The standard of life is in danger, and *the white man must either fight the evil influence or go under and carry white civilization with him.*

The struggles on the Rand, Kessack believed, were simply 'the preliminary skirmishes of the great battle which will determine whether African and Asiatic shall displace White'.[156] Others were less inclined to draw directly on the vocabulary of whiteness, and they thereby established a rather different set of priorities. At the Labour party conference in January 1914, for exam-ple, Ramsay MacDonald, who had toured South Africa in 1902, offered a different reading. He moved an emergency resolution which attacked the actions of the South African government for 'violating the most elementary rights of *British* citizenship'.[157] And yet, even from within this perspective, white workers in the Transvaal, South African or Australian, were essentially positioned as part of 'us', representing the same interests, the claim to a rec-ognizable, shared ethnic inheritance, and with the same hopes for civiliza-tion. Many of these attributes may have been condensed in the aspirations of whiteness; but it wasn't always necessary to speak them explicitly. Profound ethnic affiliations, and their consequent structures of exclusion, could be affirmed more silently.

These comments on the mentalities of white labourism cover much time and space very quickly, and can do no more than suggest that the racial preoccupations of Henry Parkes, say, or of the instigators of the White Australia policies, were not so remote from the realities of metropolitan

Britain as one might at first suppose. In fact, where the perception of even distant competition from 'Asiatics' in the labour market arose, rather similar structures of feeling occurred; and there were moments too when anxieties about Chinese workers, and all they represented, moved close to the centre of national, electoral politics in Britain. Conversely, notions about the specific virtues of the white man could be heard in Britain as well as in its overseas possessions which in these years were coming to be defined as white. The idea of Australia, especially, as a white man's nation, ethnically and territorially homogeneous, had discernible echoes in England too.

This, then, comprises part of the story: England learning from its frontier societies how to become a properly white man's country. But the social experiences were uneven, and qualification is called for. While it may indeed be the case that we can hear more insistently in these years calls for the white man to receive his due, as often we can hear other voices which berated England for its incapacities to be properly white or properly manful. After all, Englishmen did not have to contend with the rigours of the bush; they lived in a society which encouraged (so the complaints went) easy-living and softness, indeed, a kind of femininity. Notwithstanding all the public successes in his life, and despite his conviction that he had turned opinion on colonialism around in his lifetime, Milner was still more likely to despair about imperial England than to be persuaded by its triumphs. For all the difference in their intellects, Curzon and Baden-Powell were at one in their belief that the excitements offered by modern, urban civilization bred unmanly desires and a degenerate population. Curzon, on returning from his viceregal duties in India, was disturbed by the triviality of the new craze for bridge amongst his friends. It marked for him a symptomatic moment of decline, evidence that the metropole fell far short of the ideals of order and discipline required by life in the colonies.[158]

Even the metaphors favoured by imperialist thinkers reflect this underlying ambiguity. Milner, as we have seen, was dedicated to all that was subsumed within the idea of the white man's country. But he was also fond of thinking of England as the mother country. How could the mother country function as a white man's country? What gender was England to be?[159]

Those who aspired to the ideals of the white man's country assumed a certain symmetry between the prerogatives of whiteness and the prerogatives of manliness. But this was more wish than reality. The will to create the nation in the image of the white man represented a powerful, dynamic component in the imaginings of empire at the turn of the

century. The force of this thinking, however, derived from its impossibilities—its dislocations—as much as its effective, realized settlement. On
the frontier the vision of the white man's country encountered many
inhibitions: in its various migrations back to the metropole, these inhibitions redoubled. It was an enduring paradox, for example, that the
medium which perhaps did most to instil the ideals of the white man of
the colonial frontier for the domestic population of the metropole—the
sensationalist novel, or 'the shocker'—was itself regarded as a medium of
dubious integrity. The colonial romance elevated the values of independent, manly physical action whilst working at one remove, through
reading, and thereby abetting the more feminine qualities of romance
and fancy, abetting too (for some) the sin of slothfulness. Conforming a
proper manliness to the prerequisites of a specifically metropolitan civilization was not easily achieved.

This suggests, more generally, the difficulties in harnessing metropolitan
popular life to the formal programme of empire, for the popular, as a cultural force-field, does not readily comply with the cerebral requirements of
high-minded political thinkers. In particular, if we shift our vision away
from the masculine redoubts of organized labour, we can see these discrepancies accumulating. Popular life itself, I am suggesting, activates specific
dislocations, creating a culture organized by its own maxims which rarely
sits easily with those which are externally imposed. These various forces
bringing about dislocation do not obliterate the remembering of an imperial 'overseas' and the concomitant encodings of whiteness. But they serve
to make these memories more complex, more unstable, and more difficult
to reach. To close this chapter, we can look at one last instance.

On 8 May 1899 a popular extravaganza opened at the Empress Theatre,
Earl's Court, which took for its title 'Savage South Africa'. It was a spectacular, commodified performance addressed to the people of the metropole,
playing upon any number of fantasized notions of the racial frontier, and
comprising part of a larger 'Greater Britain Exhibition'.[160] The show had
recruited some 200 participants from a variety of native ethnic groups in
South Africa; some Malays (confirming Milner's doubts about ethnological
exactitude); and a handful of Cape and Transvaal Boers. Its impresario was
a Londoner, Frank Fillis, who had set up a network of circuses and theatres
in South Africa and who, for 'Savage South Africa', had secured financial
backing from many powerful friends of Cecil Rhodes. (Chamberlain, as
colonial secretary, had not been at all enamoured of the prospect of this reti-

nue arriving in the imperial capital, though he discovered he had no legal means to halt it.) The show itself represented a hybrid spectacle, drawing on the traditions of the circus, ethnographic exhibitions, and historical melo-drama. The first part

> re-enacted incidents from the 1896 uprising in Matabeleland—a running bat-tle between a stagecoach and Ndebele warriors and an attack on a white homestead, ending with 'the eldest daughter plung[ing] over cliff and river rather than be taken alive'. Then, in the second part, came the scenes from 1893: Lobengula 'reviewing his troops and perform[ing] the ceremony of throwing the assegai in the direction they are to go to annihilate the white man'; and, as the climax of the evening, a re-enactment of the Shangani Patrol, a central episode in imperial and white Rhodesian mythology when Major Allan Wilson and twelve British troopers were separated from the main body and—singing 'God Save the Queen'—cut down by Ndebele.[161]

There is much here that continued to underwrite the mythic making of Rhodesia, well into the second half of the twentieth century. I shall return to these themes in the final chapter.

We can see that many of the ideas which composed the imperial treatises of Dilke, Froude, and Seeley reappear here in the vernacular, transported from the steady prose of elevated public men to the more volatile impera-tives of spectacular sensationalism. This shift represents not just a change in genre, or a symbolic transformation of merely technical significance, but a deepening of the potentialities for such ideas to enter and live in popular experience.[162]

The popular press warmed to 'Savage South Africa', despite some hesita-tion about the spectacle's 'gimcrack' staging. The masses flocked to it. The star of the show, Peter Lobengula, who claimed to be both the eldest son of King Lobengula of Matabeleland and a true veteran of the campaigns of 1893 and 1896, became a metropolitan media celebrity. By July, however, the press was seeking out another angle. Rumour had it that Prince Lobengula was about to marry a young white woman who went by the appropriate name of Florence, or Kitty, Jewell. She was, according to the cumulative reports in the press, pretty, vivacious, respectable, and—through-out the various episodes of public scrutiny she and her lover endured—composed. She was the daughter, as one might have predicted, of a Cornish mining engineer who had emigrated to South Africa. The couple had met in Bloemfontein, and when Lobengula left with the Fillis troupe Kitty Jewell followed him to London, where the romance flourished.

Confronted with the imminence of inter-racial matrimony the tone of the press at once hardened. Harmsworth's *Evening News* was quick to stake out the terms of the debate, but all the same was representative of wider opinion: 'There is something inexpressibly disgusting about the mating of a white girl with a dusky savage.'[163] Higher-brow publications dwelt with equal outrage on the dangers of miscegenation. The public panic gathered pace. The *Evening News* duly campaigned to have the impending marriage stopped. For three days in succession the couple attempted to have their union legally sanctioned, but they were obstructed in turn by the management of 'Savage South Africa', by the local vicar, by the Chancellor of the Diocese of London (an unexpected source of authority, one must assume), and by Kitty's mother—a troubling fiasco which, in all its details, anticipated by some half century another London scene when, again, a black South African of royal parentage would attempt to marry a young white English woman.[164]

From this point on, journalistic anxiety encompassed not merely Peter Lobengula and Kitty Jewell, but the issue of miscegenation itself which meant, essentially, the fear of love-making between black men and white women. The expressions of these fears in the press were graphic, and worked with a ferocity which, even thirty years before, would have surprised the emergent tribunes of white imperial civilization. The mere presence of black men, inhabiting their 'Kaffir Kraal' in full view of the paying public, at sixpence a look, was itself construed as an incitement, encouraging a potentially wayward white femininity to indulge in unspeakable temptations. Harmsworth's *Daily Mail*—itself at a critical juncture of its recasting of public life—was (we are informed) shocked to discover that 'Women, apparently of gentle birth, crowd round the nearly-naked blacks, give them money, shake hands with them, and even go down on their hands and knees in order that they may investigate further the interior of the overcrowded huts.' The view of *Vanity Fair* was this: 'The modern woman—superior as she is—affects to adore the highest in man, not the lowest. Yet here is a specimen of her sex most eager to tie herself to a savage. We should like to regard her as an exception but why do so many women take pleasure in touching and patting and even stroking these black persons?' These perceptions were endorsed by the *Morning Leader*:

> The outcry was at first against the danger that these natives would run in a huge city and in a strange land. It looks as though, by the strange irony of fate, some of the 'conquering race' require to be saved from themselves. For some

time the monstrous record of drunken orgies, of wild escapes and escapades
in the streets went on, and all that was bad enough. But since then it has
become notorious that English women have petted and pampered these specimens of a lower race in a manner which must sicken those who know the
facts.

The *Mail*, especially, provided the imperial dimension, drawing directly
from the common sense of the settler:

> All of her race take care that in Africa an English woman shall be
> respected... English people having female relatives in South Africa might well
> feel some anxiety for the women who live in close proximity to natives who
> are worse than brutes when their passions are aroused. Colonists know how
> to keep these passions in subjection by a wholesale dread of the white man's
> power and that dread is being dissipated by familiar intercourses at Earl's
> Court.[165]

Through August—the heat, supposedly, inflaming normally dormant
English passions—the *Mail* conducted a relentless campaign against the
show, which was duly closed. Kitty Jewell and Peter Lobengula drifted apart.
She dropped out of the press limelight, while he ended up as a miner at the
Agecroft Colliery in Salford. When the South African War came to its close,
Frank Fillis turned his hand to transporting Boer generals to St Louis,
Missouri, where they refought their battles for enthusiastic audiences.

The press response to 'Savage South Africa' marked a crisis which
occurred within whiteness. It was, first, impelled by the ambiguous positioning of femininity within the larger domain of whiteness. The panic, as
articulated by the press, was due precisely to the fact that Kitty Jewell—a
decidedly modern woman, according to the stories which circulated—was
taken to be not an exception to, but on the contrary representative of, her
gender. Peter Lobengula received not one offer of marriage from a single
white woman in London, but many. For all the energies invested in organizing the proper racial protocols of the nation, here was evidence of white
women of cultivation transgressing public injunctions with impunity: which
in turn provided further pretexts for redoubled moral intervention from the
self-appointed guardians of the race. It was, secondly, experienced specifically as a metropolitan crisis. In the colonies, the press insisted, an equally
lax approach to the erotics of race could not conceivably have happened.
(Though of course, as we know, it happened all the time.) Here indeed the
metropole was understood to be working to dissipate 'the white man's
power', with grave consequences for those whites, 'our sisters', who were

confronted by a more precarious racial existence on the frontier. And third, it was a crisis which took place within the domain of popular life. On the one hand there came to the fore the ventriloquist populism of the *Mail*, which effectively engineered the crisis and pushed it to its conclusion. On the other, various putatively unruly elements—women, the poor and uneducated, the inebriated, Peter Lobengula himself—continued to write themselves into the script, insistently conflating the boundaries of social difference which upholders of the ideals of the white man's country sought assiduously to keep in place. We can catch this condensed, in all its deep ambivalence, in one press report of the attempted nuptials: '"Oh Lor, I wish I was a nigger," said an enthusiastic admirer of the bride who stood leaning over the churchyard wall.'[166]

The locations of whiteness became, I have suggested, more pressing in the metropole in these years. In trying to demonstrate how this happened there is good reason to emphasize the constituitive power of the colonial connection. The historical outcomes were of great significance. But they were never predictable.

★★★★★

I have been concerned in these two opening, synoptic chapters to present a degree of historical structure for the idea—fleetingly expressed much later in the twentieth century—of an 'overseas' which carried in it the promise of a life of fulfilment, of emotional plenitude, which England could no longer offer. That conception of overseas was an idea which evoked an imagined or a lost time, and which articulated this desire through the categories of racial whiteness. This was not a contingent factor in my view, but systematic. For all the complexities and displacements, the moment this desire took form and was uttered, it represented what I am most concerned with in this book: a memory of empire.

3
Remembering race

[A] grand year for the White Man.

(Rudyard Kipling, August 1898[1])

Our veins run warm with English blood.

(Louise Mack, *An Australian Girl in London*, 1902[2])

In the emerging Greater Britain of the late nineteenth century, as I suggested in the previous chapters, competing signs of whiteness—the white
man, the white woman, the white man's country, white blood—assumed a
new prominence in public speech. Whiteness served as one index for imagining what the values of the imperial civilization of the British represented.
It seems that, although this is harder to demonstrate, the subjective power of
whiteness could, in particular circumstances, intensify too: that the occasions when people made sense of their individual predicaments, both public
and private, by actively thinking of themselves as white, multiplied. Essentially colonial idioms came to be amplified in Britain itself, incubated in the
plethora of imperialist organizations which sprang up in the late Victorian
and Edwardian period. This is not to say that there emerged a single language of racial whiteness; nor that the new articulations of whiteness were
uncontested; nor that the experiences were uniform for men and women,
adults and children, metropolitans and colonials; nor even that it touched
the inhabitants of the metropole universally: identifications with the imperatives of whiteness operated with different degrees of gravity, according to
circumstance. Nor should this dictate a hard chronology: the antecedents
for such thinking may well indeed mark a longer *durée* than I have indicated.[3] When any such imaginings come to be centred in prevailing symbolic systems, complexity, contradiction, and the interplay of multiple

historical times are definitive, not closure or singularity. The following chapters bear this out. People's ethnic identifications are as diverse, as infinite, and as unpredictable as the ways they live their femininity or their masculinity. Even as its symbols were increasingly present, the meanings of whiteness remained fraught, riven by contradictory desires.

But it is not only a question of contingency. Over time patterns and interconnections can be discerned. The proliferation of ideas of whiteness at the turn of the nineteenth and twentieth centuries, and the intensity they assumed within imperial cultures, have cohered (for us, who have followed historically) into a discernible inheritance, with its own dynamics and structures. England, as an imaginable community, still carries the imprint of this past. We can still hear its echoes and feel the emotional rhythms of its memories. Indeed I doubt whether England can be imagined without this past impinging.

This in turn raises the question about the ways in which the imperial past has been remembered, and brought into the present. There is a danger that this is taken too literally. Historians may be peculiarly prone to wishing that the past is remembered with a resonant clarity. It is an occupational hazard. Not very many people think like historians, including, for many dimensions of their own lives, historians themselves. Huge swathes of the past, especially the comings and goings of high politics, which seem so important in the immediate, quickly become confused in memory or enter oblivion. It is not only Henry Parkes who remains forgotten in the public cultures of Britain today, but the more influential, domestic figures of Chamberlain and Milner as well. Nor would it be right to assume, even for the period when an imperial culture was at its most confident, that educated citizens in the metropole knew very much about the detailed workings of the colonies, of Canada, say, or of New Zealand. In much the same way, educated Britons today, for the most part, can pass through life knowing precious little about the internal political complexion of Italy, or of the Ukraine, or even of Éire. People cannot recall such details if they never knew them in the first place. In one of the earliest titles of the celebrated series, 'Studies in Imperialism', John MacKenzie—for all his evident enthusiasm to demonstrate the importance of empire in shaping what he called 'the home societies of Europe'— retrieved the following salutary information. Colonial Office surveys conducted between 1948 and 1951 revealed that 59 per cent of domestic Britons were unable to name a single colony, while one inspired respondent offered the example of Lincolnshire. Three per cent thought that the United

States was still part of the empire, and this in the time of Marshall Aid.[4] If in our own times memories of empire exist, in some form, as social facts, findings such as these assure us that they certainly do not work by the mechanics of technical factual recall, in the manner of *Wisden* or pub-quizzes. We need to know what of the imperial past has been remembered, how it has been remembered, and how these memories of the past have been generated by the imperatives of the present, requiring us to disinter the complex, shifting workings of collective mentalities.

This chapter discusses, first, the matter of racial whiteness; and second how, so far as the themes of these volumes are concerned, we might address the question of memory itself. As I argue throughout, Britain's empire, in the period of high imperialism from the middle of the nineteenth century through to the middle of the twentieth century, worked through race. Remembering race, I suggest, worked as a privileged means by which the imperial past entered the postcolonial present.

Codifying the white man

When the twentieth century dawned such celebrations as occurred took place on 1 January 1901, in contrast to the frenzied impatience of the millennial partying which brought things forward to 1 January 2000. As we have seen, 1901 coincided with the founding of the new Commonwealth of Australia. *The Times* thought it proper to consider the significance of the birth of the new nation, as well as offering some typically sedate reflections on the prospects which lay ahead for Britain and its empire. 'This day', *The Times* intoned, 'a daughter-nation sprung from our loins is celebrating in the distant Pacific her birth as a great federated State.' Prosperity marked the progress of New Zealand and Canada and though there were 'difficulties' in South Africa—the paper's columns listing the quick and the dead of the imperial army were testament to these 'difficulties'—even there 'our colonists have shown, like their brothers from Australasia and Canada, that they possess in full measure the qualities that have made England great'. A 'manly' imperial people was in the making in the self-governing colonies, the consequence of nations which had come into being 'without any of those violent breaks with the past which in less happy lands than ours have robbed the victories of freedom of the blessings and advances they naturally produce'. Above all, against those detractors who were sceptical of a true, manly patriotism, *The Times* reaffirmed 'the innate devotion men feel to those of their own blood'.[5] It chose not to dwell upon the manner in which a 'manly' people inhabited 'a daughter-nation'.

In the same issue an entire column was devoted to an advertisement for Clarke's Blood Mixture, 'The World-Famous Blood Purifier'. This claimed that the remedy could 'cleanse the blood of all impurities' by banishing 'bad blood'. Because 'Blood Is The Life' it 'should be kept pure'. Lengthy endorsements were carried from happy purchasers, giving an everyday, ordinary feel to the prose. From the sample of opinion quoted, the medicine seemed most efficacious in responding to skin disorders. A fireman who worked at Scotland Yard recounted how two of his children suffered from eczema so severe that they were compelled to leave their school in order not to disturb the susceptibilities of their classmates. On a tram to Tottenham a stranger noticed the children's affliction, identified the problem, and recommended Clarke's. Thence all was well.[6]

In a modest, homely way Clarke's Blood Mixture functioned, in this instance at least, to heal the disfigurements of the skin and restored a proper whiteness to the children, so once more they became effective social beings. The consequences of bad blood had been righted.

A fireman on the tram to Tottenham, turning his thoughts to patented elixirs, demonstrates a very different mentality from the easy omnipotence of a *Times* leader. But the imaginative invocation of the purity of blood and its converse—bad blood—joins them. In the view of *The Times* communities which generate authentic devotion amongst men are, by definition, consanguineous. By extension 'our' blood transmutes into 'good' blood, and 'bad' blood into the blood of others.

In imperial Britain at the start of the twentieth century, thinking with the blood was a natural feature of the social landscape. It provided a means to affirm nation and whiteness. In societies in which white and non-white lived in more immediate proximity, and where there was a higher degree of racial intermixing, more elaborate linguistic refinements emerged to pinpoint those moments when white blood and white bodies became compromised: in the Caribbean, for example, in the calibration of 'mixed-bloods', from those deemed half black to those who were one-sixty-fourth, with precise terms, too, indicating maternal and paternal lineages (sambo, mulatto, quadroon, mustee, and so on, in an ever-more dizzying spiral of classification); in the USA, where 'the single drop' of non-white blood could determine the finality of racial exclusion, many states carrying the legal stipulation

that a child with a single great-grandparent of African-American descent
was black; or in South Africa, where the apartheid regime sought to codify
the racial provenance of every individual within the nation. In Britain, these
specifications were largely absent; but the symbolism of blood, and its associated erotics, still played a role, as they did in Europe's other colonial
empires.[7]

In the pressing situation of apartheid South Africa, the novelist
J. M. Coetzee explored these issues by drawing on Gaston Bachelard's conception of a 'poetics of blood', and alighted upon Bachelard's contention
that this is 'a poetics of tragedy and pain, for blood is never happy'. Coetzee
employed this insight to explore the fiction of Sarah Gertrude Millin—after
Olive Schreiner, commonly taken to be white South Africa's most prominent early novelist—and in doing so made the following distinction: 'It is
through the poetics of blood rather than the politics of race that Millin's
imagination works.' In many respects this is an odd formulation, for 'a poetics of blood' inevitably has to be 'a politics of race'. Nevertheless to think in
these terms can be valuable. In the imaginative world of Millin, Coetzee
argued, the perception of the racial flaw, carried unseen in the blood from
mother or father to child was axiomatic. Pain and tragedy thus function as
inheritance—as the effect of blood lines—about which the individual can
do nothing save tragically live out the consequences of his or her inherited
racial flaw. As Coetzee observed, blood functions here as 'a form of unconscious memory, passed down through the generations'. In Millin's terrifying
aesthetic, this invisible inheritance, carried in the body, marked a collapse
signifying 'a fall from the grace of whiteness'.[8]

To the ideologues of Greater Britain blood signified the unbreachable
bonding of the imperial community, and also a certain grandeur. The attribution of whiteness was a valuable commodity to possess, although such a
perception was often screened from view. That good blood could turn to
bad signalled, exactly, a fall from whiteness. By employing this language it
could seem as if the blood in the veins of the white man and the white
woman (the mysterious concoction of white blood) was what guaranteed
his and her place in the civilized world. Whereas it was, of course, the
reverse. Their place in the colonial hierarchy was determined by the fact
that they were the bearers of the forces of modernity. Imperialists might
have believed that modernity was a product of their whiteness; but it was
whiteness which was the sign of their being modern, and of their role as
self-appointed makers of history.

One of the themes which I follow in this volume is the transition from a racial politics organized by a conception of blood—in which race properly is a matter of destiny—to one which is informed more profoundly by notions of civilization or culture.[9] Like all epistemic paradigm-shifts, this has been an uneven process, with much evidence that the old still coexists within the new. Indeed, by the time the empire was breaking up, in the years of Enoch Powell, the symbolics of blood took on a new life. It became a means to remember the lost time of a greater past, when racial order prevailed. Enthusiasts for Powell were not averse to thinking with the blood. Blood became a means to imagine a purer past, in order to speak to the present. Blood signified the inner, bodily connection to the remembered times of the past, in which history had been passed from generation to generation *in the same blood*. Thus the epigrammatic, hallucinogenic insistence in the midst of the Powellite crisis that 'The English blood was not dead' or, as evocatively from a London boy twenty years later, the boast that 'I've got Saxon blood in me', or even the popular apprehension of 'rivers of blood'.[10] In this way, the demise of the imperial past, we can see, was in part experienced through a poetics of blood, in which a fall from whiteness entered the lived experience of those who believed themselves dispossessed in the present. Locked into the deference which can be identified in the responses to Powell was an entire epic of pain which dramatized the tumultuousness of 'unhappy blood'. English blood, Anglo-Saxon blood, unhappy blood: such were the registers of whiteness, indicating too the degree to which antique modes of remembrance were carried into the postcolonial present.

From the researches of an earlier generation of social historians, much of whose work was Foucauldian in inspiration, we have become acquainted with the late Victorian predisposition for inventing an entire galaxy of new refractory and dissident social subjectivities: the contagious prostitute, the destitute alien, the male homosexual, the incorrigible loafer, the hooligan, and many more.[11] To these we should add, encompassing a larger time and conspectus, the native, the coolie, the lascar, the ayah, and those other types whose personas were exclusively determined by their colonial or subordinate racial locations. Indeed, the common racialization of pathological metropolitan figures marks the importance of the symbolic transactions between the idea of the residuum and its like at home, and of the native overseas.[12] These discursive constructs are now familiar figures in the late nineteenth-century social landscape, and we know too about the administrative measures deployed to manage or rectify those identified as the human carriers of a range of such recidivisms. More silent, though, is the norm against which such refractory individuals were tested. The mobilization of the figure of the white man, as we can observe with greater clarity from the colonial perspective, works as a component of this larger historical transformation: or more specifically, critical in this historical moment was a proconsular delineation of the idea of the white man—the idealized 'manly Englishman' of the period—whose advocates could be found not only overseas but in the metropole as well.[13] Yet the white man in these years, I suggest, was not the obvious, empirical phenomenon we might suppose. We need to uncover the discursive or epistemic networks which enabled this fantasized figure, with all its extraordinary powers, to come into being. In this I follow Ann Laura Stoler's observation that the principal historiographical task is not to determine 'who was the colonizer and who was the colonized, nor to ask what the difference between metropolitan and colonial policy was; rather, it is to ask what political rationalities have made these distinctions and categories viable, enduring, and relevant'.[14]

This idea of the white man can be understood as the symbolic (positive) counterpoint to the range of symbolic (negative) contagious figures who populated the late Victorian imagination, each dependent on the other. To think in these terms requires us to grasp the centrality of the conjunctions binding the normative with the perverse or the primitive: of the structural, relational connections between the masculine and the feminine, manly and unmanly, white and non-white, rational and irrational, the fit and the unfit. Some years ago Partha Chatterjee introduced the idea of what he called 'the rule of difference' to describe how the social organization of difference— the workings of gender and sexuality, race and class, nationality and religion, to name the most prominent determinations—moved to the fore in the epoch of European colonialism.[15] This or cognate conceptions have informed a number of powerful feminist readings of empire. These emphasize not only the prevailing social hierarchies, but also the intersections which occur between different subject-positions. Colonial masculinity, for example, as Mrinalini Sinha points out, 'had as much to do with racial, class, religious, and national differences as with sex difference', and the same applies to the ordering of different femininities.[16] To think in these terms is to recognize the variant configurations of power, which coalesce along multiple axes. While whiteness signifies power, the power it bestows is not uniformly distributed.

The whiteness—or the 'white blood'—which accrued to the white man was necessarily the function of white womanhood. As we saw in the opening chapter, drawing from Adele Perry's discussion of nineteenth-century British Columbia, the reproduction of the white man, and of white men's countries, depended on the sexual, and hence too on the moral, purity of white women. For British Columbia to become recognized as a white colony the segregation of white and First Nation women had to be installed and its protocols reproduced day by day. In doing so, the whiteness of white women acquired a new luminosity: the more deeply the migrant 'rosy-cheeked English beauties' were positioned in the colonial situation, the whiter they became.[17] And commensurately, while whiteness flourished on one side of the racial border, on the other the First Nation women, sexually and racially dissolute in comparison, came face to face with the harder administrative agencies of the state. A white man's country without white women was prey to all manner of dangers: to inter-racial or same-sex liaisons, to the birth of mixed-race children, and to the absence of feminine virtue in the private sphere.[18] At every point, the organization of whiteness was inseparable from the imperative to discipline sexual desire, and to hold in place the complex hierarchies which were generated by the social rules of difference.[19]

If the absence of white women in the empire overseas caused alarm to those who had established themselves as the moral custodians of Greater Britain, their presence proved equally problematic. Prodigious energies were devoted to the regulation of female sexuality in order to ensure that white purity was maintained. Most of all, the social—and often legal—prohibitions against inter-racial sex represented the core dynamic of the operations of 'the rule of difference' in the high colonial period. Though commonly transgressed in practice, in the collective imagination of the colonizers the taboo itself worked as something akin to the truth of settler societies. There were occasions, too, when this putative truth entered the life of the metropole. As I indicated in the last chapter, the respectable female visitors to the 'Savage South Africa' extravaganza in 1899 who—as a consequence of their perceived prurience—caused dismay in the popular press were significant on two grounds: the episode reveals the degree to which white femininity functioned as a defining sign of civilization, while at the same time it confirms the fact that the desires of actual white women never easily conformed to the ideals propagated in the public life of the nation.[20] Some years later, in the aftermath of white riots in the British dock areas in the summer of 1919, the radical *Reynold's Newspaper*, in a dictum of extraordinary economy, pronounced that: 'A foolish woman and a Negro may easily cause a serious riot, for the white man will not put up with it'— in which the white man's prohibition ('not putting up with it'), directed against the potential unreason of both white femininity and black masculinity, proved absolute.[21] Yet for all the certainty on which such reasoning was based the symbolic systems from which the foundational categories arose— masculine and feminine, white and black—were, paradoxically, conspicuous for their uncertainties. Indeed, it was precisely because of the prevalence of uncertainty, and a fearful, unspeakable apprehension of the unconscious projections in play, that the proscriptions needed to be rehearsed incessantly and at such high pitch. I shall return to this point in the next chapter, when I discuss the fiction of John Buchan, an author who was exemplary in his commitments to proconsular manhood.

There are various ways in which the question of the conjunctions between the white man and his various others can be approached. Mrinalini Sinha has investigated the connections between the figurations of the 'manly Englishman' and the 'effeminate' Bengali men of the late nineteenth century, although her emphasis falls more on the latter than on the former. Whiteness is a more explicit theme in Philippa Levine's studies of white female prostitution in colonial life, which also enables us to understand the structuring of white masculinities. She takes Hong Kong, India, Queensland, and the Straits Settlement as her case-studies, focusing on the years 1857–70 when, in Britain, the Contagious Diseases Acts were implemented, ostensibly as a means to save the nation's imperial forces from the ravages of syphilis. The rationale for the passing of the Acts, both in the metropole and overseas, lay in the perception that venereal disease represented a specifically racial poison, and that the principal conduits of the disease were women. Although there were relatively only very few white prostitutes in the colonies they were, as Levine demonstrates, of enormous symbolic significance, out of all proportion to their numbers, for they confirmed the existence of what otherwise could not be spoken: the fact of white degradation. Their presence, it was feared, would lead the native to confuse the distinction between loose and respectable white women, as well as creating a new stratum of unfit white men in the person of the pimp and the procurer. By selling their white bodies to non-white men they were held to be guilty of abetting what Levine identifies as the 'failed masculinity' of the native population.[22] And as they did so they could be

perceived to be commodifying what otherwise was deemed to be providential—whiteness itself.

Levine argues that white prostitutes in the colonies were 'female but not
feminine'.[23] Just as their femininity was compromised by their trade, so too
was their racial positioning. They occupied, according to Levine, 'a racial
borderland' on the very extremities of the domain of whiteness, compelling the authorities to adjudicate on what, in other quarters, might have
seemed self-evident: the possession, or not, of whiteness.[24] There occurred
a perpetual slippage between the designations English and European, with
the former boasting a privileged claim to the benefits of being white,
though this claim was vitiated in the case of white working-class women.
The provisions of the European Vagrancy Act, passed in India in 1874, left
considerable doubt about who should be classified as white, or as European.
Throughout the empire the presence of Jewish women confounded the
categorizations both of white and of European. In the settler colonies,
most notably in Queensland, legislation, as in Britain, was specifically
directed against the practices of working-class women—legislation which,
in the case of Queensland, continued well into the twentieth century.
Yet whatever the impossibilities involved in demarcating the borders
between white and non-white women the task itself could never be abandoned. While prostitution was commonly believed to be the natural function of the low level of civilization of the native, those whites who did
become prostitutes—troubling though they were—might still, it was
hoped, have had within them some means to redeem themselves such that
they might return to proper white conduct. Unlike their native sisters,
European women were recognized as possessing powers of reason, while
English women could additionally claim a legitimate home which, once
reform had been accomplished, might once again become theirs. This
potential for redemption derived from the last vestiges of whiteness in possession of the 'fallen woman'. In sum Levine's account demonstrates the
degree to which the sexual disposition of the white prostitutes determined
their ethnic positioning.

A connected figure, closer to home, whose racial location was similarly
disrupted as a consequence of his sexual disposition can be highlighted in
the emergent persona of the male homosexual, whose place in the social
system came to be more strictly demarcated by the provisions of the 1885
Criminal Law Amendment Act. This development came to be dramatically
evident ten years later during the trial of Oscar Wilde, and in the years

which followed the pressures to locate homosexual men outside the given national community intensified.[25]

We need further research on where the imperial determinations of these domestic transformations might lie. But there may be some clues. As I have been suggesting, the idealized figure of the white man, the progenitor of white men's countries, and the guardian of all human destiny, cohered in these particularities in Britain in the last third of the nineteenth century, notwithstanding the existence of many antecedents. One impulse for this derived from the experiences of returning proconsuls—public men of great influence like Milner, less exalted functionaries such as John Buchan, and a host of more anonymous characters who made the return from the colonies to the metropolitan realities of an industrialized, urban society—keen to transplant the energies and ethical rectitude of the white man of the frontier to the home society. But as I have attempted to show, this interaction between colony and metropole, based on the conviction that the frontier was the site of moral and bodily purity while England itself was in some measure degraded and dissolute, had a much broader resonance in national life: it was never solely the preserve of those who could claim commanding positions in the state, or who made the move from overseas back home. This is true, too, of the intoxicating fantasy of the peculiar prowess of the white man. Indeed, this variant of an incorruptible, white imperial masculinity crystallized in the same historical moment as that of the modern idea of the homosexual man. While these were no doubt experienced at the time as radically separate departments of social life, with no conceivable connection between them, from our historical vantage we can understand them as manifestations of an integrated social system of symbolic classification. Each worked as a function of the other; without the one, the other could not exist. The systematic repudiation of effeminacy was prominent in many dimensions of colonial thought, and the split in masculine life between the manly man and the effeminate or homosexual man did much to make the normative thinkable.[26] The *juridical* presence of an identifiable male homosexual, by demarcating a pathological masculinity from a properly civilized, manly masculinity, made it possible to construe the figure of the white man in all its purity, unsullied by base or degrading erotic desires.[27] In form at least, this symbolic divide was total.

When Lord Curzon addressed Oxford students, dilating on the sublime qualities of the frontier, or when Lord Milner was enthusing about the future of South Africa, or when Joseph Chamberlain rhapsodized about the virtues of Birmingham man overseas, they were explicitly imagining the imperial world to be masculine.[28] And just as an anonymous docker in 1968 could claim that Enoch Powell was 'the only white man in there', making reference to Powell's position in the Palace of Westminster, so two generations earlier Rudyard Kipling could declare, in a letter to his cousin Stanley Baldwin, that Chamberlain was 'the only man in the Cabinet'.[29] The idealized white man, in these renditions, was the predominant, imagined agent of imperial endeavour. He was properly white in body, mind, and spirit, and he was properly masculine, in which no hint of effeminacy—nor of its correlate, homosexuality—could be discerned. His masculinity required him to be protective towards white women, for in their bodies lay the future of the race. But notwithstanding his socially sanctioned desire for the feminine, he could not, within the terms of the prevailing codes, in any respect *become* feminine, or become contaminated by femininity. The white man, as an imaginative construct, was formed not only by 'his' strict separation from femininity, but more categorically by its insistent repudiation. This was a repudiation which occurred not only in the inner life, nor only as an external requirement of social propriety. The proconsular men of late Victorian and Edwardian Britain lived at a time of unprecedented female and feminist agitation, which dominated public life from the demonstrations against the Contagious Diseases Acts in the 1860s through to the suffragette campaigns before the First World War. Significant numbers were not only hostile in private to this spirit of rebellious femininity; they organized in public to break its political power. The returning proconsuls, Lords Curzon and Cromer, for example, expended colossal energy in launching and mobilizing the Anti-Suffrage League to this end. 'The German man is manly, and the German woman is womanly', Cromer told an anti-suffrage meeting in Manchester in October 1910. 'Can we hope to compete with such a nation if we war against nature, and endeavour to invert the natural role of the sexes? We cannot do so.'[30] Kipling, that proconsul of the literary imagination, was convinced that even limited female suffrage in Britain would destroy India, Egypt, and 'all the East'.[31] Both would have concurred with Curzon's conclusion that 'For the discharge of great responsibilities in the dependencies of the Empire in distant parts you want the qualities not of the feminine but of the masculine mind.'[32] Where, one wonders, was femininity's pervasive subversion to be located?

Such statements hardly stand as unadorned empirical observation. Deeper subterranean psychic currents prevailed. The overriding conceptual picture which emerges from recent studies allows us to grasp racial whiteness, with its attendant articulations of gender and sexuality, as a complex symbolic formation which is perpetually in movement and into which communities or individuals enter, navigate their way through, and (on occasion) exit. Thinking of whiteness in this way has the virtue of recognizing the mobility of the processes by which ethnic identities work. In different historical periods and in different locations, particular communities, observably white according to the conventional criterion of skin coloration, have possessed structurally ambiguous relations to the hierarchical cultural fields in which whiteness has been sanctioned. Sometimes peoples are white; sometimes not. Entire social groups—prostitutes, convicts, the inhabitants of the urban rookeries—were at times divested of their whiteness, partly on grounds of their perceived delinquency, but also partly as a function of social class itself.[33] The Irish through much of the nineteenth century (and sometimes since) have occupied a peculiarly contingent positioning as white, especially in contrast to the more deeply centred cultures of the English.[34] Thomas Carlyle noted, with characteristic distemper, that Irish whiteness was an inconvenience for, 'having a white skin and European features', the Irish 'cannot be prevented from circulating among us at discretion, and to all manner of lengths and breadths'.[35] As I explain in the next chapter, much the same was true of the Afrikaners in the period of the South African War of 1899–1902. But this was not only due to the prerequisites of white authority shifting over time. It was also a function of who else was active in the field of vision at the same moment. Compared to the British, Afrikaners could be deemed (by a British observer) not really white; compared to black Africans, they could be perceived (by that same observer) necessarily white. Ethnic identity, in other words, is in its innermost forms relational, and even such seemingly obvious categories as black and white can move freely according to circumstance.

Up to a point it is useful to think of these discursive hierarchies of whiteness in terms of margins and centres. But these distinctions are always in motion, the imagined spatial locations constantly dissolving one into the other. One could plausibly assume that the symbolic power of a culture would reside at its centre, not its margins. Yet as we saw in the last chapter, the idea of the white man was largely fashioned on the frontier, where the loss of whiteness was perceived to be a constant possibility.[36] At the same time, however, given the all-encompassing, protean properties which underwrote identifications with racial whiteness, the divide between the white

man and his others was not one which operated solely in the overseas colonies. The racial frontier was not 'out there' at all—or not only there—but
traversed the interior spaces of home as well, in need of constant policing.
The unhomely, and all that conspired to unhinge whiteness, were not peculiar to the colonial frontier. To emphasize the dynamism of whiteness is to
indicate something of its pathologies: wherever white was, even where it
was most centred, there too precariousness impinged. Homi Bhabha, turning his attention to the colonial past, is right to emphasize the fact that what
he calls the white imperial subject 'is itself involved in the drama of its own
disjunction, its own displacement in the structure of identification'; it has,
he continues, 'to enter into a discourse of whiter-than-whiteness, a form of
excessive or over-identification that turns the imperial subject around upon
itself to face the *impossibility* of its own desire'.[37] The more it resolved the
greater the anxieties it seemed to bring. Blood, after all, is never still.

In the metropole the language of the white man was perhaps most audi-
ble across the vast range of late nineteenth-century juvenile literature, as
I discuss in the next chapter. Here was a public arena in which the codes of
the white man, in all their contested divergences, were dramatized. Popular
novels for boys emerged which sought to adumbrate the duties of the white
man. This composed a body of writing which was explicitly based on the
repudiation of the feminine, both in the content of the stories, and in the
generic form of their writing. Most unsettling about this literature and
what, in a later age, came so easily to be parodied, was how all-embracing—
how militantly normative—this centring of the category of the white man
came to be. 'He' becomes a figure whose very rationale was based on his
capacity to repudiate anything which differed from what he himself was.
The otherness of ethnicity and gender was absolute, as the very term 'the
white man' commands us to accept.[38] In the most arresting of these narratives, however, the reader is presented with the young hero learning to
overcome his own internalized transgressions, to curb his own tantalizing,
infantile desires to identify with anything other than the rectilinear white
man. When his journey through the story is complete, the protagonist
becomes a strange, abstracted, pathological creature, striving to embody all
that otherness is not.

These systems of white masculinity were, in this period, organized
through the imposition of fierce hierarchies of difference, distinguishing the
white man from 'his' many others. Indeed, the figure of the white man
came to represent an interior being with the capacity to repudiate, within

'his' own being, otherness *itself.* In this, in this historical moment, lies one of the most startling impossibilities of whiteness. On the one hand, the conditions of existence for the white man depended on the elaboration of highly charged systems of social difference. Yet, on the other hand, in imagining the terms of 'his' own life, no whisper of the other was permitted to cross the threshold and enter '*him*'. This simultaneous drive both to reproduce others as others, and to repudiate difference within the self, opens up important if difficult questions about the dynamics of racial whiteness. It allows us to perceive whiteness as the medium through which the colonial order was thought and lived. And it requires us to reflect on the necessary impossibilities of whiteness: on the impossibilities of ever extirpating the imperatives of human difference, of otherness, from the self. Marilyn Lake writes of the white man imagining himself to be 'under siege', even when he appeared to be omnipotent. As I shall argue in later chapters, white men—historical white men—were puzzled by their vulnerabilities, bewildered even, unable to comprehend the extent to which their anxieties were a function of the social prohibition against recognizing and accommodating the others which they themselves had created.

Yet if the protocols of racial whiteness proved an impossibility, so too did the larger social imaginary which evolved from the founding category of the white man.[39] Human desire, we know, cannot be as obsessively managed as the advocates of imperial discipline dreamt. Those accredited with the deepest capacities to reason were, often enough, brought low by the dark desires residing deep within their selves. The dysfunctions predominated.

Nor was this a system without its paradoxes. For white men or women to desire the native was a matter which posed the gravest danger. For the white man to desire the white woman was, of course, stipulated, assuming the circumstances were appropriate—and so long, that is, as he maintained in his domestic life the proper bounds of his masculine self. But the injunctions to the white man to expunge from himself all signs of social difference left him, in daily life, peculiarly dependent on the social intercourse of men like himself. Indeed, many institutions were invented to accommodate this masculine culture. The deep homosocial, maybe even the homoerotic, dispositions of the world of the white man in late Victorian and Edwardian Britain cannot, I think, be understood as contingent.[40] We are back with Enoch Powell's notion that male friendship turns on the question of 'men's bodies'.

The study of racial whiteness in this period not only brings into focus the increasing capacity of particular social individuals to view themselves as white; nor is it simply about the phantasmagoric theatre in which English men and women lived in relation to the native. In the end whiteness itself may turn out to be a secondary matter. The crucial issue was the drive simultaneously to produce and to repudiate difference, to which—in lived experience—whiteness, and the idea of the white man more particularly, offered a solution, or to which it offered an imaginary solution.[41] The systematic, persistent desire both to elevate difference as an absolute, and to declare oneself untouched by the various others created by this process, cannot occur—either in a culture generally or in an individual human life—without the intervention of all manner of repressions and displacements, threatening at every moment that which is most sought.

When at the beginning of the twentieth century enthusiasts for empire pondered the source of Britain's imperial power, they were accustomed to conclude that it was to be found in the attributes of the civilization to which the people of Greater Britain could lay claim. The power of the empire resided in the activities of the white man, in the particular civilizing capacities of white femininity, in white brains and in white blood. In this view, whiteness was a possession. But we could suggest, to the contrary, that those who held such views were possessed, in the older supernatural meaning of the word, by whiteness. The forces of capitalism, colonialism, and modernity generated the wealth of the British world. To suppose that this was a function of whiteness was indeed to create a vision of the world in which historical realities were turned on their head. Whiteness was the consequence of capitalism, colonialism, and modernity. This is what W. E. B. DuBois was proposing when he argued, in 1903, that what he termed 'the discovery of…whiteness' was 'a very modern thing', 'a nineteenth and twentieth century matter, indeed'. He believed that this discovery—that the world 'is white and by that token wonderful'—had occurred 'in a sudden emotional conversion'.[42]

This idea of 'a sudden emotional conversion' is a beguiling thought, but it begs many historical questions. It reminds us, against earlier generations of imperial ideologues, that whiteness has a history, and that it is closely connected to the history of modernity. Yet DuBois's formulation, frequently quoted by students of whiteness, needs greater historical specification. In the previous chapters I have sought to outline a particular, conjunctural mentality. Its intellectual lineaments stretch from Carlyle and Froude; its political representatives can be seen in Chamberlain, Milner, and those around them, and its cultural representatives in Kipling, or John Buchan, or Baden-Powell. It was driven, I suggest, by an acute sense of the magical determinants of colonial life overseas, and it had a significant if uneven reach into the domains of popular life. The imperialists of this and later generations whom we see at closer range in succeeding chapters were not just weakly, or indifferently, colonialists. They were zealots in the cause of the white man, propounding a heavily accentuated insistence on the virtues of white masculinity. In this specific ideological constellation we can catch sight of the fantasized figure of the white man at the point of his greatest drama.

This tells us much, conceptually. It also works, I believe, as a privileged moment in the longer duration. But whiteness did not, in these years, always cohere in this particular symbolic formation, nor did it in later times.[43] These plural and conjunctural formations, in the larger history of white ethnicity, prove decisive.

The abolition of whiteness

My reading of the dynamics of racial whiteness in the period of high imperialism draws from a corpus of work located within the overarching network of the black Atlantic, in which the cross-currents between the histories of the European colonial empires and the histories of African-America prevail. A short analytical detour may be helpful, even if this seems to take us some way from Britain's imperial past. Partly this is to clarify some of my observations about whiteness, and partly also to address the current political question concerning the 'abolition' of whiteness.

Whiteness has for long been an object of sustained critical attention, although until recently not much amongst white people themselves. bell hooks has written about perceptions of whiteness as a 'way of knowing' for black people, which has entered a folk culture, which has existed as a means for blacks to survive, but which has bequeathed a relatively small written, theoretical record.[44] The transition from this folk culture to the academy is recent. The academic field of studies devoted to analysis of whiteness is composed of a familiar clutch of titles, a product of the 1990s and of the period since.[45] Their significance lies in the fact that these are often studies of whiteness written by whites themselves. Like all such handy accounts of origins, though, a statement like this conceals as well as reveals. I shall say something about this work in a moment. But first there is a case for extending the historical perspective, and thinking back to the published accounts by black thinkers which considered these 'ways of knowing'—the ways blacks knew whites—and which, concomitantly, demanded reflection on what whiteness was. This takes us back to the period of decolonization in the postwar period.

A defining shift occurred in the 1950s. In April 1955 the Bandung Conference was convened with representatives from across Africa and Asia marking, in the words of one its inspirational figures, President Sukarno of Indonesia, 'the first inter-continental conference of coloured peoples in the history of mankind', dedicated to advancing the end of the colonial epoch.[46] At this critical moment in the history of decolonization, the Bandung Conference served to highlight the idea of opposition to the rule of the white man as an integral part of the anti-colonial struggle. The conviction that the epoch of the white man was drawing to a close, although certainly not without precedent, assumed in this period a new urgency.[47] It did so amongst anti-imperialists of all stripes. And, conversely, it did so too amongst the old colonial elites in the metropolitan heartlands. In March 1957, for example, the British prime minister Harold Macmillan, in preparing notes for his opening address at the forthcoming Bermuda Conference with President Eisenhower, claimed that 'For about 2,500 years Whites have had their way. Now revolution: Asia/Africa.' Reminiscing about his own Victorian childhood, he expressed his fears that the colonial, Christian civilization of the West, in which he had been reared, was nearing its end— though Macmillan, a man of more determination than he let on, was keen to establish a rearguard skirmish against its foes.[48] The end of the colonial empires could, with good reason, be experienced in the metropole as the demise of a civilization whose deepest values had been encoded and lived as essentially white.[49]

Much of the mechanics of anti-colonialism in the 1950s was principally preoccupied with the transfer of power, and with race inasmuch as it affected these larger strategic objectives. But these transformations generated other voices which worked to open up the connections between an anti-colonial politics, on the one hand, and, on the other, the subjective requirements of breaking with the conditions of white rule. We might think, for example, of Frantz Fanon, Richard Wright, or James Baldwin, whose work represented a paradigm shift in the conceptualization of race, and which drew into the line of vision the imperatives of whiteness.[50] These were all New World intellectuals, who witnessed the end of European colonialism at close quarters.[51] In each of these writers we can hear the dispositions of racial power turning. Here I shall say a little about Baldwin—a black radical whose radicalism derived as much from his experience of being a sexual dissident in America as from his blackness—for many of the formulations I have used in this chapter up to now derive, indirectly on occasion, from him.

'The world is white no longer, and it will never be white again.'[52] These words, written by Baldwin in Europe and deriving from his experience of Europe, close his final essay, 'Stranger in the Village' in his collection *Notes of a Native Son*, which was first published in 1953. The prophetic tone is significant. When he announced that 'the world is white no longer' this was less an empirical observation than a statement of political intent. It signified the historical perception that the world was on the point of a momentous transformation and that the end of the inherited racial order, if not present, was at least thinkable.

However it is not always clear where Baldwin thought that whiteness was to be situated, nor how it was to be understood. As we shall see in a moment, he veered between different explanations. There were occasions, in the heat of the struggle confronting the billy-sticks, the hoses, and the dogs when such a question—he knew well enough—had no purchase. More often, though, he worked from the realization that race functioned as a kind of fabrication or fantasy and that too strict a focus on visible epidermal characteristics—on pale skin—was never going to unlock the secrets of the white world. The power of his writings derive from his capacity to hold together, sometimes in a single sentence, the lived experience of race, subjective and internal to the human individual, and its larger public, even global, configurations. His are rich reflections. Yet for my purposes it is possible to extrapolate from Baldwin's writings three distinct interpretations of whiteness, each of which operates at a different level of abstraction.

First, at the most concrete level of analysis, Baldwin was concerned with how whiteness operates in the psychic and emotional organization of the inner life. His thinking on race is founded on his belief that whites *created* blacks: whites did so, he argued, by seeking to preserve in themselves an impossible purity by projecting onto the black other all that was deemed abject and unspeakable within themselves.[53] This syndrome, he suggests, we witness when we confront the battery of racial epithets (and, by extension, sexual epithets too) which prevail in modern life. Racial difference, for

Baldwin, is constituted by this projection of the self—of those parts of the self experienced as troubling—onto racialized others. The consequences of this founding conviction are profound. If such a splitting of the self underwrites the practices of race, then black and white are inevitably reciprocal entities. Neither can exist without the other, for each is already in the other. For Baldwin the salient point, as well as the most contentious, resides in the conjunction: white *and* black. Any conception of white purity, or of whiteness alone, or of a society dreaming of white exclusivity untouched by its black other is, in these terms, doomed from the beginning, for whiteness without blackness is an impossibility. To forsake blackness is to forsake part of the white self.

But this marks only the first stage of his argument. Of equal significance was his conviction that this projection in turn generated an unconscious denial, or forgetfulness.[54] At the very moment projection occurred, the fact that anything of the sort ever took place was systematically disavowed by whites—although never entirely banished from white consciousness— making racial difference appear simply a part of the natural order of things. The power of this denial, and its systematization in American life, Baldwin insisted, could result only in the imprisonment and crippling of the white self, and in the consequent corruption of the larger body politic. This white disavowal of the dynamics of racial difference preoccupied Baldwin. Drawing from competing conceptual vocabularies this incapacity to acknowledge the realities of racial power could be interpreted in terms of psychic repression, or of ideological mystification, or of bad faith. Baldwin, in his American idiom, preferred to call it, simply, innocence—not the innocence of William Blake, but a deadly, self-destructive pathology which fed the racial traumas of his nation.[55] Those whom Baldwin accused most for their innocence were the whites of the United States, responsible for their conscious–unconscious commitment to being a white man, or to being a white woman: from this, he claimed, was activated the racial crisis from which his nation's historic violence flowed.

Second, as these propositions imply, whiteness also functions as a set of social relations. Baldwin was always careful to track the connections between the psychic realities of race, often drawing from his own biography, and the workings of the polity. The constituents of white and black were never only a question of psychic and emotional forces: they were organized and reproduced by the state and by powerful institutions in civil society. Innocence, for example, was not merely, as Baldwin conceived it, the favoured mental state of white Americans. It was a way of being, fostered by an entire civilization: by the movies its people saw, the food they ate, the cars they drove.[56] 'People are trapped in history', he wrote in 'Stranger in the Village', 'and history is trapped in them'.[57] Even in the most intimate, private moments—maybe especially in the most intimate, private moments—whiteness was socially driven, he argued, determined from without as well as from within the individual psyche.

And third, Baldwin considered whiteness to be a historical event. By announcing that the world will be white 'no longer' he assumed that at some point in history the world had once been made white. Most often he attributed this 'whitening' of the world to the onset of European colonialism.

Baldwin's explorations arose principally from his own life in what he insisted on calling his native land. Yet while they emphatically carry an American particularity, they are not restricted to the American experience. His conceptualization of the double process of projection and disavowal, and of the consequent amnesia about racial difference, offers a fruitful way to understand more generally how racial whiteness works in the modern world.[58] These perspectives on whiteness, working at different levels of abstraction, are useful methodologically: whiteness as a manifestation of the inner life; whiteness as a complex of social relations which order the external world; and the idea that we might also think of whiteness as a historical event.

The study of whiteness is important insofar as it makes visible what too frequently remains persistently invisible. 'Eddy is white,' writes Toni Morrison in a path-breaking study of whiteness, 'and we know he is because nobody says so.'[59] Or as Kobena Mercer has argued: 'the real challenge in the new cultural politics of difference is to make whiteness visible for the first time, as a culturally constructed ethnic identity historically contingent upon the violent denial and disavowal of "difference"'.[60] To suggest that white people have an ethnic identity just like anyone else, modest though this must seem as a proposal, is still something which needs to be stated. BBC news bulletins, for example, still routinely refer to representatives of 'the ethnic community', by which they mean a particular sort of citizen marked by the fact he or she possesses a racial identity, in contrast to the majority white population. There can, though, be something disturbing in the way in that a previously dominant intellectual and social system gets reinvented as an object of special academic enquiry, as if it had only ever been

marginalized before. Men's studies, straight studies, white studies: it is hard
to be convinced that such initiatives represent more than guilty special
pleading on the part of the socially privileged. Richard Dyer, the author of
one of the most stimulating books in the field, has expressed similar anxieties. In doing so he employs a perhaps not altogether innocent image: 'My
blood runs cold at the thought that talking about whiteness could lead to
the development of something called "White Studies"'.[61] Some discrimination is called for.

  For David Roediger, an early maestro in the investigations of racial whiteness, essentially whiteness signifies the negation of all that is human. He draws
from a late, short essay of Baldwin's, 'On Being "White" and Other Lies', in
order to develop this notion. Partly recapitulating Baldwin's argument, and
partly providing his own gloss, Roediger makes these observations:

> It is not merely that whiteness is oppressive and false; it is that whiteness is
> *nothing but* oppressive and false. We speak of African American culture and
> community, and rightly so…In her passionate attacks on both the concept of
> an African American race and that of a white race, Barbara Fields character-
> izes African Americans as a 'nation'. Whites are clearly not that. There is an
> American culture, but it is thoroughly 'mulatto'…If there is a Southern cul-
> ture, it is still more thoroughly mulatto than the broader American one. There
> are Irish American songs, Italian American neighborhoods, Slavic American
> traditions, German American villages, and so on. But such specific ethnic
> cultures always stand in danger of being swallowed up by the lie of whiteness.
> Whiteness describes, from Little Big Horn to Simi Valley, not a culture but
> precisely the absence of a culture. It is the empty and therefore terrifying
> attempt to build an identity based on what one isn't and on whom one can
> hold back.[62]

I suggested above that the simultaneous production and repudiation of otherness, which I take to lie at the heart of the dynamic of racial whiteness,
can only occur by generating a degree of destruction of the white self as
well as the destruction of the other. Roediger may be alluding to something
of the sort when he claims that whiteness is 'based on what one isn't'. But
the terms in which he conducts his argument are significantly different. For
him whiteness is false, a lie, and signals the absence of a culture. Whiteness,
in this scenario, seems capable of only being subsumed within the logic of
genocide. Yet to my mind this creates more questions than answers. How is
whiteness a lie, or false? How is this falsity to be ascertained? Does it suggest
that those oppressed by white supremacy embody truth? What would an

absence of culture mean? Even—or especially—genocides require their imaginings, their symbolic systems, which give meaning to their ferocious enmities and allow their realization in deliberate, calculated acts of cruelty and destruction. It is not an absence of culture which is the problem, but its presence.

The key problem turns on the disputed, difficult question of what whiteness is, or how we understand it to operate. For Roediger, in this statement if less in his substantive historiographies, it appears to be little more than a lie or, in a different conceptual idiom, false consciousness, counterpoised to which there is some manifest truth. This is a thin abstraction, which ultimately has the effect of removing the problem of whiteness from history, and construing it only as a moral issue. My own emphasis, as I have explained, falls on the relational or reciprocal properties of whiteness, in which psychically white and black are already in each other. Fanon's comment is apposite: 'For not only must the black man be black; he must be black in relation to the white man.'[63] Whiteness alone is indeed a psychic impossibility.

Yet Roediger is obviously right to say that historically racial whiteness is a form of being which is predicated on the will to subordinate others. Its dynamic turns on the repudiation of non-white, and indeed of otherness more generally. This is, though, an ambivalent process in two ways. It is ambivalent because, to refer to Toni Morrison again, it exhibits 'all the self-contradictory features of the self', desire as well as antipathy.[64] And it is ambivalent too because repudiation of non-white, or black, has a compulsive drive which is not restricted to whites: black identities, too, have been founded on the repudiation of the black self, as Fanon, Baldwin, and many others have repeated, interrogating the pains of self-hatred. The imaginative forces which generate racial polarization between black and white do not parcel out vice and virtue in neatly colour-coded dualities.

The historiographical project of explaining how white ethnicities have been formed and transformed is important. Deriving a politics from such investigations, however, with preappointed friends and foes, too often short-circuits critical issues. In its received, insistently radical variants, in particular, it fails to be convincing. One of the unspoken emotions running through this political endeavour is—not so much shame—as guilt. The question of the moral responsibility of white people for what has been done in our/their name in history, and for what is still being done now, cannot so easily be resolved.

Desire for reparation is a motivation, consciously or unconsciously, for many different sorts of writing. It also works as a vital impulse in the historical imagination. But there are many facets to this. As studies of whiteness have become more established one strand in particular stands out: that which is devoted to 'the abolition of whiteness', the strategy advocated by Roediger, and closely connected to that which favours 'treachery' to the white race, which is the line adopted by the journal that carried the insurrectionary title, *Race Traitor*, edited some years back by Noel Ignatiev and John Garvey.[65] 'Abolition' and 'treachery' are both absolute terms, with no place for ambivalence, the idea of treason to one's race being a staple of racist militancy, not least in Britain during the Powellite moment of 1968. These terms suggest a politics in which everything is known: lines are drawn, argument mobilized, merely the details need to be resolved. One can see something of the tenor of this in *Race Traitor*. It is hip, voluble in its self-assuredness, and high on its own voluntarism. Its logic is apparent. It might seem, at first sight, as if this is a politics which breaks an easy essentialism. White is uncoupled from skin colour or from any other biological determinant: it is repositioned, in the suitably pithy formulation of Malcolm X, as 'a state of mind'. White race traitors can cross the line and enter a new habitus: that of blackness. Yet if this is conducted in the name of hybridity, or a mulatto culture as Roediger suggests, and if whiteness is *nothing*, then what is it that whiteness brings to this new hybrid? In fact, blackness itself remains uninterrogated, the site effectively of a new essentialism. If whiteness is posited as the negation of the human, then blackness does indeed come to represent the truth of human life. 'Blackness', observes Noel Ignatiev, 'means total, implacable, and relentless opposition to that system [of race privilege]'.[66] Intervention is reduced to the question of where the political boundary is to fall. Contributors to the journal, for example, found they couldn't decide on the politics of *The Blues Brothers*: on whether it represents, on the one hand, a politically exemplary white indebtedness to black culture (whites becoming the repudiated self) or, on the other, whether it marks a familiar white appropriation of black (blacking up). The formalism of the positions adopted in the debate, assuming that the movie represents, inscribed deep in the text, either one thing or the other, is indicative of a wider way of thinking.

Revolutionary etiquette, too, remains contentious. In one interview Ignatiev was asked: 'Is it appropriate to tell a person of color that you have abandoned your whiteness?', to which he replied, with a measure of circumspection: 'I would never say that, although I might say that I was working on it.'[67]

This argument derives from a simple social constructionism which runs in the following way. In human reality there are no white people. Certain groups chose to become white when conquering ethnic others, as part of the business of creating a colonial order. Whiteness, then, stands as the mark of this racial domination: that is what it is. It then becomes possible for us, today, to see this for the moral flaw it is, and to choose to cease being white. For the race traitors, this involves some move to blackness, which signifies all that the system of racial privilege is not. For the James Baldwin of the 1984 article (different, to my mind, from his more usual—and more complex—reflections), because 'there *are* no white people' whiteness becomes a matter exclusively of an absolute 'moral choice'.[68]

One can agree that the emergence of a perceived white race was indeed connected to the history of colonialism and racial subjugation. One can agree too that whiteness—the fantasy of whiteness—is associated with many terrors, a recognition which enters the white imagination, dramatically, with Herman Melville. This would indeed suggest the desirability of, or necessity for, abolishing whiteness as a precondition for living with difference.

Much however revolves around terminology. If whiteness is only 'a state of mind', with no presence in unconscious desire and no place in the larger network of external social relations, then we could leave the matter there. But what if it is more than that? This is where it is important, especially, to identify distinct levels of abstraction.

Ethnic identity, as much as any other identity, generally entails a degree of agency or choice. (The extremity of extreme situations derives in part from the refusal of a racial oppressor to allow such choices to be made.) It may well be that these are choices framed by everyday pressures, such that they do not seem to be choices about identity at all: they are just a means of getting from one daily situation, of no apparent consequence, to another. But out of such seemingly inconsequential practices of everyday life identities are spun. We might recall the racial meanings invested in Mr Muller's peach-tree, for example, discussed in the last chapter.

Alternatively, in other historical situations, race is a more formidably conscious political act, in which deliberate decisions can be made to recast the self. An example of such conscious intervention comes from the South African novelist Nadine Gordimer, writing after the collapse of apartheid, in 1999:

Five years into freedom. What kind of fossil should I be, unearthed from the cave of bones that was apartheid, if my essential sense of self were to be as white?

There are some who still have this sense—suffer it, I would say. I don't posit this in any assertion of smug superiority; I would just wish to prod them into freedom from confinement. And there is also the other—unadmitted— side of feeling superior as white: being ashamed of being white.

We South Africans are going as best we can about the business of living together. Being white as a state of determining my existence is simply not operative.[69]

A sensibility such as this is relatively new in historical terms, for it breaks categorically with a received notion, as dramatized for example by Gordimer's literary forebear, Sarah Gertrude Millin, that race is destiny.

Yet at the same time, as Gordimer herself shows in her fiction, ethnicity exerts pressures and determines. Ethnicity as unrelenting confinement is certainly a common preoccupation in black sensibilities. It is a theme which burns through James Baldwin's prose. Or as Fanon puts it: 'I am overdetermined from without'.[70] Agency, clearly, is circumscribed. Ethnic identities are not just willed into or out of existence. Roediger and those affiliated to the tenets of *Race Traitor* make it sound as if individuals can leave the domain of whiteness simply by voluntary action, as a result of a moral choice on behalf of the individual. Many courageous instances do indeed come to mind. Nadine Gordimer's categorical decision, for instance, is exemplary: 'Being white as a state of determining my existence is simply not operative.' Yet as we know from South Africa's Truth and Reconciliation Commission, decisions such as these, on the part of individual whites, do not resolve the problem of white accountability either for injustices in the past, economic and social as well as more immediately violent, or for their continuation into the present. Leaving behind the privileges bequeathed by whiteness may not be so easily achieved. Social relations and the complexities of the psychic life, as much as individual conscience, come to bear. Whiteness is determined from without as well as from within. We do not have to imagine situations in which, for white people, being-for-others (to employ a Fanonian formulation) is a matter of life as opposed to death, for they are all too common. One can understand James Baldwin choosing to assert that 'there *are* no white people', for it brought to the fore his inimitable commitment to moral responsibility, and registers his characteristic impatience with the category of identity itself. Whether it is persuasive, however, depends on one's definitions. I am suggesting that whiteness is not only 'a state of mind'; it is also an external, determining social relation which is lived historically in all its human, emotional complexities. Neither is it false consciousness, nor simply a discourse. Ethnic identifications, whiteness included, are complex subjective processes which bring into play all the contradictory forces of the inner life, as well as the impress—for good or ill—of prior histories.

The problem, exactly, is working on it. To talk of abolition and treachery prescribes a politics in which the white self comes to be considered only as an object to be made ready for destruction. This may be seen as reparation. But it is, in Melanic Klein's terms, an instance of manic reparation, in which reparation to the past can only be made in the present by annihilating the self.[71] This is a mode of restitution in which no place is opened for ambivalence or for subjective complexity. It is exclusively a matter of responding to external events in preordained, correct terms. Nor does it allow historical discrimination. White is always the same old story, from Little Big Horn to My Lai, from Governor Eyre to Stephen Lawrence. In its omnipotent, Jacobin urge to free the present from the past, this manner of conceptualizing whiteness cuts out a vital step in the processes of remembrance and reparation. It omits those processes in which past travails are brought into consciousness, in which the connections between past and present come to be known, worked through, and experienced in new ways and from which, consequently, discriminating moral and historical judgements can be made.

This brings us to the question of memory.

Memories

We can return for a moment to James Baldwin. In 1963 he published, to huge acclaim, *The Fire Next Time* which, insofar as it considers the matter of whiteness, seems to be closer to 'Stranger in the Village'—in which whiteness works in a reciprocal relation to blackness—than to his 1984 projection of whiteness as mendacity. The short volume opens with a letter to his nephew, James. In it, he says this about white people:

> They are, in effect, still trapped in a history which they do not understand; and until they understand it, they cannot be released from it. They have had to believe for many years, and for innumerable reasons, that black men are

inferior to white men. Many of them, indeed, know better, but, as you will discover, people find it very difficult to act on what they know. To act is to be committed, and to be committed is to be in danger. In this case, the danger, in the minds of most white Americans, is the loss of their identity. Try to imagine how you would feel if you woke up one morning to find the sun shining and all the stars aflame. You would be frightened because it is out of the order of nature. Any upheaval in the universe is terrifying because it so profoundly attacks one's sense of one's own reality. Well, the black man has functioned in the white man's world as a fixed star, as an immovable pillar; and as he moves out of his place, heaven and earth are shaken to their foundations.[72]

This, in fact, exemplifies a way of thinking committed to bringing the past to consciousness, to work at the past in order that it becomes amenable to conscious reflection and intervention. In part it is what Baldwin himself sets out to do in *The Fire Next Time* when he confronts the subjective consequences of race. He is particularly clear, in this passage, about the ambiguities of 'knowing', highlighting the capacity of whites simultaneously to know and not to know about race. There is, though, a shift in perception from his writing of a decade earlier. For all his characteristic perception of race as confinement, he accords a greater role to the intervention of human agency. *The Fire Next Time* is a memoir, recreating episodes from his childhood. This allows him to review the transformations he has witnessed in his own lifetime, and to contrast his own life to that of his father.[73] The critical difference which separates the two biographies is that, in the lifetime of the son, the black man (to use Baldwin's words) was moving 'out of his place'. Civil rights, and the more distant echoes of Bandung, had intervened. This dimension of his argument is historical, recognizing the profound transformations brought about by the dismantling of the colonial epoch. The larger social structures in which black and white operated had changed, and had done so as the result of the self-activity of non-white peoples. Baldwin implies that, thereafter, the force-field of white no longer exerted the same power. There occurred, in consequence, a myriad of particular, local instances of whites believing that they were falling out of their privileged ethnic domain. The frontiers of whiteness seemed to be contracting and its internal powers diminishing. As whites stood still (so it might seem) the ground was moving from beneath their feet. White people could feel that they were losing their whiteness—losing, indeed, their identity and their 'sense of their own reality'.

Baldwin explained that he was principally concerned with the United States, though it is clear that he had in mind other arenas of racial conflict as well. To depict whiteness in this way, as he does, perceiving it to be transmuting into a kind of vertiginous lived experience, patently can only stand as an abstract, general observation. Yet these vicissitudes in white experience do comprise one element in the larger story of decolonization. In many different locations, the experience of a beleaguered whiteness came to be more insistent, a phenomenon illuminated by Richard Wright in his identification of 'the white man...at bay'.[74] For some whites, these larger historical changes were to be welcomed, or impinged only marginally on their lives; others they terrified, inducing them to confront the prospect of the loss of white identity by becoming partisans of the white race. Yet for this transformation to be experienced as a fall from whiteness, whiteness itself needed to be invested with a prelapsarian past. In these circumstances the idea of a lost time of whiteness had much interior work to do, creating new ways by which the past could be remembered.

Ethnicity works by remembering. Despite common-sense appearances, ethnic identities are not given by natal circumstance, from which all else follows. They are organized and rearranged through narratives of becoming, such that throughout a life new selves can be fashioned from old stories.[75] This is a theme which underpins the substantive chapters of these volumes. Here, though, it is appropriate to say something about the formal properties of memory itself.

Memory is a term which is becoming ever more capacious, encompassing radically different facets of individual and collective life. There are many different sorts of memories, from internal, subjective dream-like recollections of times past to the public commemorations which symbolically organize a community, society, or nation. Different kinds of memory pertain to different kinds of mnemonic activity. The pasts which shape themselves on the analyst's couch are not generally like the ones we tell a new lover, or which we summon to explain to enquiring children where they are from, or which we tell about ourselves in public situations. And none of these resembles the collective form of public commemoration which exists all around us. That memory covers an entire spectrum of mental and social operations is clear. In this study I am chiefly concerned with the passages from the subjective inner world to the public-political stage.[76] Perhaps the best way of describing my object of analysis would be as a memorial consciousness, in which both individual and public memories play their part. I have indicated something of this in my attempt to suggest the significance of such condensed mnemonic symbols as 'overseas', or 'the white man', in the larger practices of remembering empire. This is not the past with which psychoanalysis concerns itself, for I place greater stress on the conscious movements of the mind. But as I have acknowledged, there *are* unconscious dimensions to this sort of memory activity, which present serious methodological difficulties. These are also, necessarily, memories constituted in the present, created in response to the imperatives of the present. Memory works in the present, and brings the past into the present. Which pasts it brings into the present, and on what terms, must always remain an open question. But memories are not histories. If an idea of a lost time of whiteness was brought into consciousness in the moment of decolonization, as I believe it was, this was far from representing any given historical past. Similarly, to claim that one is the bearer of the same blood as one's ancestors evidently evokes a psychic, not a historical, reality. Such modes of memory, I argue, illuminate important dimensions of the wider, social history of the end of empire during the Powell years.[77]

It might seem as if memories rate amongst the least substantial forms of historical evidence, the hardest to reach empirically, comprised of mere fleeting sensations in some recess of the mind which continue to defy existing human knowledge. While this may be true up to a point, at the same time we can only grasp memories in their mediated manifestations. As memories enter consciousness, and in the act of their being communicated, they begin to take shape, to assume a discernible form, and come to be articulated in particular generic patterns. Memories of empire do not exist in an amorphous, insubstantial arena of some notional collective memory. They arise in concrete situations: in conversations with an MP, in memoirs, in political speeches, in letters, in trade-union newspapers, in dreams recorded in diaries, in responses to academic ethnographers, in a host of public commemorative acts. In each instance the mediations necessarily intervene, and social and generic rules govern the ways in which particular memories enter consciousness and, in turn, how they organize the public world. It is less their presence which causes problems than their mediations and displacements. As Maurice Halbwachs argued at the beginning of the twentieth century, memory may be a property of the individual mind, but memories themselves are also stored in, and recollected through, social institutions.[78]

How memory operates in contemporary modern societies is an issue about which scholarly opinion is polarized. On the one hand it is common to be told that our own modern, or postmodern, times are characterized most of all by a shared social amnesia. The past is no longer known, it is merely commodified or spectacularized, and lived as style, pastiche, nostalgia, simulacrum, or, more straightforwardly in the English situation, heritage. This is a reading propounded with admirable sophistication by Fredric Jameson, though its immediate theoretical antecedents go back to Theodor Adorno.[79] For Jameson, the issue is how we can emancipate ourselves from the tyranny of a perpetual present:

> The problem is…how to locate radical difference; how to jumpstart the sense of history so that it begins again to transmit feeble signals of time, of otherness, of change, of Utopia. The problem to be solved is that of breaking out of the windless present of the postmodern back into real historical time, and a history made by human beings.[80]

In less philosophical guise, this pertains directly to the questions raised in this book. One resolution to the problem of memories of empire is to suggest that the dominating memories are those which reach us in commodified form, through the cinema, television, or advertisements, in which the imperial past works most effectively as a manifestation of period *couture*, interwoven with a little erotic display of non-white bodies and moist pudenda, writhing in an imagined tropics of times past.[81] In this view, empire is turned into its costumes and heritage acts to depoliticize the past. There is substance to this critique. To this day there is a repertoire of such images of empire around about us, always ready for recycling at a moment's notice. Their very familiarity ensures their longevity. They evoke not a historical past, but a past already fabricated by other commodified media. There is good reason to think that the relentless circulation of such signs does indeed carry deep within itself a kind of amnesia, in which the historical past moves out of reach of the present and where, in the words of Luisa Passerini, 'memory can turn into a form of oblivion, between nostalgia and consumerism'.[82]

Similar convictions have come to underpin the ambitious project overseen by Pierre Nora, which sought to reconstruct nothing less than the history of memory in modern France.[83] As Nora himself explains in his conclusion to his final volume, an enterprise which had originally set out to be 'a counter-commemorative type of history' came to be overtaken by the very phenomenon it had determined to expose: commemoration itself.[84] Memory, he believes, has come to exercise what he calls a 'commemorative bulimia' in all contemporary societies which see themselves (or once saw themselves) as 'historical', that is, 'as based on human freedom, rather than governed by divine will'.[85] In France he concludes that this affliction has been peculiarly severe, the unintended consequence, in his view, of the unreason unleashed by the events of May '68, which served to destroy the national memory which had been created by the Revolution of 1789 and consolidated in the Third Republic. In the wake of this collapse of the springs of national memory all that remain are the amorphous, decentred forms of commemoration driven by the market, by the media, by tourism and entertainment, and by advertising. The discontinuity of memory has supplanted the continuity of history to such a degree that even his own practice as a historian, as Nora has it, has come to be compromised.

On the other hand, the counter-argument proposes exactly the opposite. In this view of things, the archives in which memories are held have never been so extensive in human history. By virtue of the electronic media we can see still and moving images of past events of more than a century ago, composed at the time of the events themselves, and hear the voices of people who died long before we were born, such that historical time itself is stretched. In February 2001, to take an example close to my theme, the British Library released online a sound-recording of Nelson Mandela's speech from the dock delivered in Pretoria's Palace of Justice on 20 April 1964, during the Rivonia trial when he was on trial for his life—and when, in the words of Neal Ascherson, 'he spoke to his apartheid judges as Danton and Wolfe Tone had spoken to their accusers'.[86] For many years the recordings had been forgotten and, when they were rediscovered, they existed on such antiquated systems that only great labour and ingenuity enabled them to be retrieved in a form compatible with modern technologies. It is truly a new historical experience to *hear*, nearly half a century on, Mandela declare that 'the ideal of a free and democratic society in which all persons will live together in harmony and with equal opportunities…is an ideal for which I am prepared to die', and to hear too the gasps uttered by others in the court. Here the past is immediately, sensuously active in the present and works at a qualitatively new pitch.

This is one aspect. A connected, if analytically separate, argument suggests that as a consequence of the plethora of representations of the past existing in contemporary societies, popular desire to know about the past—

to read about it, watch it, 'live' it—increases in potential too. Memories, in this scenario, are not only everywhere, but they allow new democratic possibilities for the excavation of historical knowledge. If there exists a crisis in the inherited authority of the professional historian, as Raphael Samuel for one argued, then the scope for new forms of popular, unofficial historical knowledge is already all around us.[87]

For all their contrasting conclusions, these viewpoints describe the same phenomenon. They suggest that there is something specific to the structures of memory which are produced in a society dominated by a commodified mass media. Whether optimistic or pessimistic, both sides in this debate share the acknowledgement that modern life has broken attachments to the past and that new ways need to be invented to revivify what has been lost. How this basic theme is played out in theoretical discussion can be confusing. The same presentiment can be ascribed to there being too much memory, or too little; to there being too much history, or too little; to there being memory rather than history; or history rather than memory.[88] Whatever the take, though, the problem has a common provenance: the difficulties which prevent modern subjects from connecting with their pasts in such a way that 'life' itself (in Nietzsche's terms) is enhanced rather than diminished.

Here too a sharper historical contextualization is necessary. Too often academic discussion of these issues is framed in terms of the overbearing abstraction of postmodernity, assuming a cataclysmic shift has occurred, generating a new epoch in which all the rules of the game—epistemological, ontological—have assumed radically new configurations. A more nuanced reading would offer a more complex picture, in which we could see that many of today's transformations, which appear so novel, have a deeper history. Perhaps this is particularly so of memory, about which such extravagant claims have been made.

A theme which runs through these pages concerns the role of the new and electronic media. From the time of the telegraph and telephone in the latter part of the nineteenth century, through to the arrival of the cinema and radio, and then later of television, the means by which people learnt to understand themselves as historical individuals changed profoundly, although to a large degree this has been a historical transformation barely visible to the naked eye. This was not simply a result of the range of information supplied by the emerging new media, though this was important. It had as much to do with the new ways in which knowledge was ordered, and with the greater mediations by which the external world came to be perceived.[89]

On the one hand the resources for remembrance increased, the development of photography and the telegraph, for example, providing memory 'a sort of jailbreak from the body'.[90] On the other, the deepening mediations by which older times were recalled seemed to render the lived experience of the past more remote and ever harder to access, creating the peculiarly modern syndrome in which memory appears simultaneously to be everywhere and nowhere.[91] In a study such as this, concerned as it is with memories of empire, it might seem as if, while the fortunes of empire moved back and forth, memory itself remained relatively constant. This though is an illusion. Mnemonic activity itself was subject to historical transformation. Indeed—although I am conscious that I do not explicitly address this issue—empire was constitutive of modern modes of memory.[92] There is now a growing literature which demonstrates the close ties between the development of new media forms and the establishment of colonial authority, especially in the field of photography.[93] We know too about the emphatically imperial determinations in the emergent memorial practices of the nation in the aftermath of the First World War.[94] The cultures of colonial populism which came to be organized in late Victorian Britain, in which the domestic subjects of the crown were called upon to become participants of empire, represented not simply the potential for new memories, but for new means for remembering as well. In the schoolroom and lecture-hall, with magic-lantern and phonograph, in the various youth movements, the relations between past and present became more tightly administered by both the state and by private agencies.[95]

The power of a polity to shape its national past, and to invent its requisite traditions, accumulated in these years. Dilke, Froude, and Seeley dedicated themselves to mobilizing a national past in which empire predominated. Other less respectable media (such as the spectacular dramatization of 'Savage South Africa') exploited a new vision of the past, extolling the heroism of the white man overseas. Memory, in this sense, was a matter of power.

Memory and forgetting

Part of the difficulty of the debates about memory arises from the polarization of viewpoints, as if forgetfulness and memory are separate faculties, and as if modern societies are characterized by either the one or the other.

Remembering and forgetting are not separate mental processes; they work together, as moments of the same imaginative act.[96] That this is so also brings us to the difficult question, raised at the start of the chapter by J. M. Coetzee, concerning the existence of 'unconscious memory'. James Baldwin gave this a practical rendering when he suggested that whites simultaneously acknowledged and denied race, knowing but not knowing, an exemplification of negation in the psychoanalytical vocabulary. This reading of the racial situation, though, has more general application, turning on the capacity simultaneously both to remember and to forget.

I can take an example from one of the 'other Englands': not, in this instance, one of the white colonies, but the black colony of Barbados, popularly known by its inhabitants as 'Little England'. It concerns the memory of slavery, and comes from a famous passage in George Lamming's *In the Castle of my Skin*, a novel written at the same time as Baldwin's 'Stranger in the Village'. In a fine reconstruction, we can witness the *articulation* of memory and amnesia. It depicts the celebration of Empire Day in a school in the middle of the 1930s, and opens with memories of Queen Victoria, 'a good queen because she freed them'—'them' being the slaves.

> An old woman said that once there were slaves, but now they were free. The small boy was puzzled. He had seen prisoners several times. They passed in chain gangs early in the morning on their way to work. And he knew what that meant. They were being punished. After they had served their sentence they would be free again. But the old woman wasn't talking about that. She was talking about something different. Something bigger. He asked the teacher what was the meaning of slave, and the teacher explained. But it didn't make sense...He told the teacher what the old woman had said. She was a slave. And the teacher said she was getting dotish. It was a long, long, long time ago...It had nothing to do with the old lady. She wouldn't be old enough. And moreover it had nothing to do with people in Barbados. No one there was ever a slave, the teacher said. It was in another part of the world that those things happened. Not in Little England. The little boy didn't like the sound of it. He had dismissed the talk about slaves, but he was very anxious for the old woman. Who put it into her head that she was a slave, she or her mother or her father before her? He was sure the old woman couldn't read. She couldn't have read it in a book. Someone told her. Moreover she said she was one. One of these things. Slave. The little boy had heard the word for the first time and when the teacher explained the meaning, he had a strange feeling...Thank God, he wasn't ever a slave. He or his father or his father's father. Thank God nobody in Barbados was ever a slave. It didn't sound cruel. It was simply unreal...They would forget all about it since it all

happened too long ago...They had read about the Battle of Hastings and William the Conqueror. That had happened so many hundred years ago. And slavery was thousands of years before that. It was too far back for anyone to worry about teaching it as history. That's really why it wasn't taught. It was too far back. History had to begin somewhere, but not so far back. And nobody knew where this slavery business took place...Probably it had never happened at all. The old woman, poor fool!...She must have had a dream. A bad dream! They laughed quietly. The whistle was blown. Silence, silence! It came up like a ghost and soon faded again.[97]

The old woman's folk memory of slavery provides the boy with one perspective. But this unwanted, disturbing memory is subsumed by other perspectives and by other stories, such that he comes to perceive slavery, in Barbados, as unbelievable and 'unreal'. One story—'this slavery business'—is pushed out of his psyche by another (the Battle of Hastings, William the Conqueror and all it represents). Stories of the past gleaned from official authorities (schooling, book-learning) gain greater credibility, allowing the boy to mock the ignorance of the old woman. But there is the hint, as well, that the boy's initial puzzlement does not vanish completely. In the laughter of the boy and of his companions; in their consequent silence; and in the 'ghost' which comes and fades: anxious traces of the memory of slavery—or in Coetzee's terms, 'unconscious memories'—remain, present but unspoken or unspeakable. This is so in the psyche of the boy himself. But, as Lamming indicates in the novel, this forgetfulness or unspeakability comes as well to recast the public cultures of Barbadian society.

This captures, in fiction, something of the movements between the interior world of the psyche and the larger external, social—and in this instance, colonial—world. It raises crucial issues about the ways in which, in our own times, race and colonialism are remembered. Forgetfulness does not imply complete oblivion. A totally forgotten world would be nothing. Forgetfulness leaves traces which may not be present in the conscious mind of an individual at all, or which may be displaced. So far as a collective culture is concerned, forgetfulness is closely connected to the social proscriptions of unspeakability, as Lamming shows in In the Castle of my Skin. This suggests not that some disturbing past event is invisible in public life, but that it cannot be spoken in a way which allows it to have purchase in the present.

If we turn to another West Indian novel we can see this at work. At the beginning of the second part of Jean Rhys's Wide Sargasso Sea (first published in 1966), Antoinette and her new husband from Europe travel to the

Caribbean island of Dominica. They arrive at a village called Massacre. Antoinette is asked by her husband: ' "And who was massacred here? Slaves?" 'To which she replies:' "Oh no." She sounded shocked. "Not slaves. Something must have happened a long time ago. Nobody remembers now." '[98] This is indeed a reference, as Peter Hulme points out, not to black slaves but to the indigenous Caribs. As he indicates, it is not that nobody *knows* what happens: it is that nobody *remembers*. Or rather, as he continues, that nobody *cares* to remember. Nobody is prepared to make the effort to remember, to make this past speakable, and to bring it into public consciousness.[99] This is not a forgetfulness which wipes away all traces of the past, and induces oblivion. It is, on the contrary, a forgetfulness organized by a continuing, if unspoken, disturbance.

In the previous chapters I suggested that the originary violence of the white settler societies faded over time from public memories, both in the colonial societies themselves and in the metropole. The violence of conquest appeared in subsequent narratives (such as the passage I quoted from Stanley Baldwin) as a vanishing mediator, invisible on the surface of the text but the precondition for its existence. Ann Curthoys has explored the ways in which the slaughter of the indigenous peoples in Australia 'gradually faded from public consciousness, written histories, and school texts'; moreover this was, she argues, a transformation which coincided with the formation of the Commonwealth as a modern nation-state, and indeed was a function, she contends, of a foundational white Australian nationalism.[100] It is not that nobody knew what had happened; it is that, in an act of disavowal, nobody cared to remember.

In the Introduction I referred to the 1968 Boyer Lectures of W. E. H. Stanner. His purpose was to imagine what he called 'a less ethnocentric social history'. In exploring the idea of 'The great Australian silence', which he believed underwrote the mentality of white Australians in their relations to the Aborigines, he emphasized that this was not 'a total silence on all matters aboriginal'. It was rather a matter of things which white Australians 'unconsciously resolved not to discuss with them or treat with them about'. This was not a state of affairs, he explained, which could be ascribed to an 'absentmindedness', but was a properly 'structural' feature of the society itself. He conceded that this might have 'begun as a simple forgetting', but it had 'turned under habit and over time into something like a cult of forgetfulness practised on a national scale. We have been able for long to dis-remember the aborigines that we are now hard put to keep them in mind when we most want to do so.'[101] As an anthropologist, Stanner's depiction of 'a cult of forgetting' was employed to describe primarily the workings of a society, not the inner life of an individual. He was critical of professional historians whom, he claimed, were largely to blame for the silence inscribed in the white mentalities. But as contemporary historians have demonstrated, there did in fact exist, at least from the 1940s, a body of literature which addressed just those questions that Stanner had declared to be unspoken. To the plaintive questions 'Why didn't we know?' and 'Why were we never told?' should be added the more intractable questions: 'Why didn't we ask?', 'Why didn't we listen?', and 'Why weren't we able to hear?'[102]

Even so, Stanner's anthropological approach highlights the social dimensions of forgetfulness, or in his terms, 'a cult' of forgetting. As he pointed out, 'Mythologizing and disremembering are part and parcel of each other.'[103] Forgetting registers not in an absence of stories, but in their multiplicity, where one story—'mythologizing'—silently displaces its neighbour.[104]

A more mainstream sociological-psychological account of such national 'cults' of forgetfulness is provided by Michael Billig, who propounds the idea that the familiarity of a home culture ensures that its everyday symbolic transactions for the most part only weakly register in the conscious mind. This is close to Gramscian theorizations about common sense: though common sense represents a stratum of knowledge in which many popular notions receive legitimation, it is also a form of knowing which passes by largely unnoticed *as knowledge*. Billig bases his argument on Ernest Renan's well-known lecture of 1882, in which he declared that 'forgetting…is a crucial factor in the creation of a nation'.[105] The ways nations are remembered, Billig suggests, involve 'a complex dialectic of remembering and forgetting'. He distinguishes between 'waved' and 'unwaved' flags, or—not resisting the pun—flags 'flagged' and 'unflagged'. The latter he depicts as 'mindless' flags, those which are consistently present in daily life but which refuse to draw attention to themselves. These flags, or other such totems of the nation, 'are providing banal reminders of nationhood: they are "flagging" it "unflaggingly". The reminding, involved in the routine business of flagging, is not a conscious activity; it differs from the collective rememberings of a commemoration. The remembering is mindless, occurring as other activities are being consciously engaged in.' He continues: 'Psychologically, conscious remembering and forgetting are not polar opposites which exclude all middle ground. Similarly, traditions are not either consciously remembered (or co-memorated) in flag-waving collective activity, or consigned to a collective amnesia. They can be simultaneously present and absent, in actions which preserve collective memory without the conscious activity of individuals remembering.'[106] Billig uses Pierre Bourdieu's concept of habitus in order to explain the structuring of these cultural relations, and he emphasizes the fact that Bourdieu defines habitus as '*embodied history*, internalized as second nature and so forgotten as history'.[107]

Billig's concept of banal nationalism supposes that much on the surface of social life passes by unnoticed, and helpfully brings together into a single frame remembering and forgetting. He doesn't have much to say about the operations of the subjective mental world which allow this to occur, nor about the unconscious—as opposed to the 'unnoticed'—determinations in acts of forgetfulness. In my view, forgetfulness is not as innocent as this assumes. When something is forgotten from an individual consciousness, or is pushed aside in the stories a society tells about itself, then chances are that something important is happening. To follow this line of enquiry takes us to the field of psychoanalysis. As I have indicated earlier I do not think it appropriate to conceptualize my object of study in strict psychoanalytical terms: the memory worlds I am interested in are distinct from those which preoccupy the psychoanalyst. But I am conscious too that some of my own formulations have been influenced, at a degree of intellectual distance, by friends and colleagues whose understanding of memory has been shaped by psychoanalytical traditions. The emphasis I have given to the concept of displacement, for example, comes directly from this approach. Other instances I shall come to in a moment. Yet in a larger sense, the fact that I find myself drawn to questions of amnesia, silence, and unspeakability, to the guilty facets of forgetfulness, to phenomena out of place and out of time, to the impossibilities and pathologies of whiteness, or to the imperatives of those mesmerized by a lost time of whiteness: to think in terms of these (normalized) dysfunctions expresses, I suspect, a debt to a psychoanalytical manner of thinking about which I have not always myself been fully aware. They attest to the darker side of memory, as something foreign within us.[108]

Much of the psychoanalytical endeavour, in its many variants, is indeed about the conjunction of memory and forgetting. It has the virtue of demonstrating that what is consciously remembered may well be shaped by memories which lie below the surface of consciousness, omitted from the fully conscious mind. Psychoanalysis presents a dynamic understanding

of memory, in which the articulation of memory and forgetting is constituted as an active, interconnected, and determinate relation. Forgetting
does not occur in a different department of the mind: it is part of what
memory is. What appears to be most clearly remembered—that which is
most prominent in conscious thought—may, moreover, provide clues as to
the nature of adjacent memories which have been omitted or repressed.
Underwriting such conceptions is a theory of repression, turning on the
idea that some memories are driven from the conscious mind, most forcefully when they are associated with degrees of pain or anxiety. Some
things *cannot* be remembered, or *cannot* have purchase in the present, and
other memories serve to conceal them. George Lamming suggests something of this sort in the passage cited from *In the Castle of my Skin*.
Memories of slavery were concealed, or screened to use Freud's term,
by less disturbing memories—for the aspiring Little Englanders of
Barbados—of the Battle of Hastings. 'What is important is suppressed and
what is indifferent retained', as Freud put it.[109] Here too we can see that a
forgetfulness (crucially, of 'what is important') does not disappear, but is
invested in other—displaced—stories.

Psychoanalysis is rich in distinguishing the different means by which
memory functions. Of particular relevance to the discussion of whiteness is
the question of repetition. There are occasions when, according to Freud,
an individual 'does not *remember* anything of what he has forgotten and
repressed, but *acts* it out. He reproduces it not as a memory but as an action;
he *repeats* it, without, of course, knowing that he is repeating it.' In this
Freud identified 'the compulsion to repeat'. From this observation he drew
the critical distinction between 'acting out' and 'working through'. The
former represents the unconscious repetition of a mental state, a kind of
neurotic form of remembering.[110] The latter represents the process in which
what is unconscious slowly becomes conscious, and comes to be recognized
for what it is: that is, a form of remembrance which works to bring the past
into a determinate relation to the present. The processes of working through
are organized by overcoming resistances so that memory—as opposed to
unthinking repetition—can occur. Or as Adam Phillips glosses this, to 'act
out' is to live in the present 'as if it were the past'.[111] This provides a valuable
way of thinking about the inheritances of ethnic systems, and in particular
the inheritances of colonial whiteness and of what I have indicated to be
the lost time of whiteness. One way of understanding memories of empire,
for example, is to recognize that they are carried into the post-imperial

epoch by an acting out or unconscious repetition of prior racial assumptions and practices which themselves had been formed in the interstices of empire, in the metropole and on the colonial frontiers.[112] In our own times the compulsion still remains to live out, in new ways, these old ethnic forms.

A lost time of whiteness

I am aware there is more to say on all these points. All I've attempted here is to navigate a path through the current debates in order to offer the reader an idea of my own usages.[113] But to conclude this chapter, I'll bring the argument back to an earlier theme.

I am most concerned with the transactions between the interior world of the individual and the public stage of politics. Private memories of public events take many heterogeneous forms. In Halbwachs's terms, historical facts become 'transported' into 'symbols'.[114] This is an important insight, which I stick to in my own investigations which follow. Yet early in his professional life Halbwachs broke from his youthful enthusiasm for the philosophy of Henri Bergson, his intellectual commitments gravitating to Durkheimian analysis of cultural systems composed of socially organized symbols and rituals. It was these interests, in the 1920s and 1930s, which brought him into collaboration with the *Annales* historians, Lucien Febvre and Marc Bloch, whose own studies of *mentalités* proved inspiring for an entire generation of historians. It was, too, this Durkheimian tradition which was formative in the emergence of the structural anthropology associated with Claude Lévi-Strauss.[115] In sociology, history, and anthropology, this Durkheimian reading emphasized culture as a determinate social system and this signalled a productive theoretical advance. But it did so at the cost of grasping the rhythms of lived experience and interior life. The 'transportation' of fact to symbol has its psychic and emotional dimensions. The 'involuntary' aspects of this transformation occurs, in the words of Marcel Proust, 'beyond the reach of the intellect', in sensation and emotion as much as in cognition.[116] As Proust sought to demonstrate in one idiom, Freud in another, memory is most active, most transformative, when emotions and psychic energies are most highly charged: it is in these moments that 'memory crystallizes and secretes itself'.[117]

This returns us to the intensities of emotions, visible on the stage of public life, during the Powellite crisis of 1968. Memories of a lost time of whiteness—and of lost sites of whiteness—were articulated with raw passions. These were not memories which could easily register in Colonial Office surveys, quizzing the domestic populace about their knowledge of colonial governance. They worked according to other rules: they were fleeting, composed from fictions and reveries rather than from information gleaned from the leaders of *The Times* or the *Telegraph*. I noted in the previous chapters James Belich's idea that the poetics of the colonial frontier was formed by a fantasy of 'restoration': by the belief that old times could be restored in new lands. This belief in restoration, rather like the earlier conviction that a Saxon utopia had been undone in 1066 by the imposition of Norman exploitation, ran deep in popular sentiment. Freedoms lost at home could yet be realized in the lands once designated as Greater Britain. And these reveries of restoration were underscored by the shifting, complex, conceptions of whiteness which gave life to many impossible dreams.

My interrogation of these issues was prompted by the words of Enoch Powell's anonymous constituent in 1968. I have suggested some ways in which his memories might be located historically. To what extent my own suggestions conform to the realities of his historical existence we will probably never know. We cannot even be sure if he *had* a historical existence. All I can do is offer what I take to be a plausible reading of his imputed representativeness.

But we do know about Enoch Powell. Invited late in his life to comment on a historical analysis of mid-twentieth-century Britain, which inevitably raised the issue of national decline, Powell identified 'a factor which the historian chronically neglects: the emotional factor'. He went on:

> One, of course, understands why the historian neglects it, it is unquantifiable, it is rather shameful, and it is difficult to handle, but without the emotional factor I do not think one can understand the turn-around which occurred in this country or some of the most surprising things which this country did in the second half of the twentieth century. When I resigned my chair in Australia in 1939 in order to come home to enlist, had I been asked 'What is the state whose uniform you wish to wear and in whose service you expect to perish?' I would have said 'The British Empire'. I would have had no doubt in giving that reply.

He proceeded to refer to this reverence for the empire as a 'delusion', a fall for the allure of 'gigantism' which, he explained, had afflicted the British throughout much of their history. In subscribing to this view, he was doing little more than advocating a common historiographical assumption that in the postwar world the British governing classes continued to be haunted by the belief that they were representing a great power whose greatness was to stretch long into the future. But it is less this conventional historical interpretation which is of interest than the manner in which Powell's memories were presented. 'So our whole behaviour was coloured and characterised by this world into which we had been born, the world in which we were a "great power".' Then he said this:

> I know it is not so; but I also know that on my deathbed I shall still be believing with one part of my brain that somewhere on every ocean of the world there is a great grey ship with three funnels and 16-inch guns which can blow out of the water any other navy which is likely to face it. I know it is not so; indeed I realised at a relatively early stage that it is not so. But that factor, that emotional factor, that gigantism, will not die until I, the carrier of it, am actually dead.

He closed these thoughts by invoking Nietzsche, and reflecting on death.[118]

Powell was an old soldier who did not perish in the service of the empire, a fact, he liked it to be known, he regretted for the rest of his life.[119] We do not know whether, on his death, he was still entertaining reveries about the might of the imperial navy. We do know, however, that he was buried in the brigadier's uniform of his old regiment, the Royal Warwickshire.

These memories of Enoch Powell are particular. He represented a strange conjunction. While he gave every impression of working through memories of race, he ended up acting out their deepest forms with great assiduity to detail, living in the present as if it were the past. Powell also reveals how ethnic memory in England interweaves race with nation, nation with empire. Rarely did he choose to speak explicitly in terms of whiteness, though the essential encodings are clear, and the displacements active. In Powell's memories we can hear the echoes of an observation made by Henry James, living in England at the time when the various other Englands overseas came into being. In a homely phrase, what impressed James most about the English was their 'quiet and comfortable sense of the absolute'.[120] It was not only 16-inch guns that entered memory, but less tangible characteristics too.

4

The romance of the *veld*

[In South Africa] civilisation will march with barbarism...A man would have but to walk northward...to reach the country of the oldest earth-dwellers, the untameable heart of the continent. It is much for a civilisation to have its background—the Egyptian against the Ethiopian, Greek against Thracian, Rome against Gaul. It is also much for a race to have an outlook, a far horizon to which its fancy can turn. Even so strong men are knit and is art preserved from domesticity.

(John Buchan, 1902[1])

In the autumn of 1986, when I was working on the metropolitan rather than on the imperial co-ordinates of British Conservatism, I needed to interview a representative of the Monday Club. The Monday Club, as I shall explain later, was a pressure group which teetered on the far right-wing edge of the Conservative party and which has at various times been an important ideological influence. Through the 1960s it worked hard to turn back black immigration, and it did much to find a means by which race and immigration could become speakable in the mainstream of political life. More particularly, after Ian Smith proclaimed Rhodesia's unilateral independence from Britain in 1965, it took Smith's cause as its own. The Monday Club did much to bring these two issues together and to present them as one, concocting the idea of whites as a newly vulnerable section of the population, be it on the farmlands of Rhodesia or in the collapsing inner-city spaces of the metropole.

Unable to discover the Monday Club address in the phone-book, I wrote to Conservative Central Office. Eventually I received a response, was given a phone number, and invited to make contact. I was informed that the address I needed, Orlando Road, was in Clapham, South London. A little while later, having fixed an appointment, I set off. It transpired that Orlando

Road was at the Brixton end of Clapham. Given the extent to which Brixton had established itself as the heart of black London, it was not hard to imagine that those who staffed the Club's headquarters could believe they were bordering enemy territory. My destination turned out to be a dilapidated, crumbling Victorian redbrick house, in evident disrepair. The door was answered by a well-scrubbed, middle-aged white Englishman, in three-piece pinstripe suit and gold watch-chain; an Oxford man, a figure of impeccable courtesy who—I am sure I haven't imagined this retrospectively—periodically took snuff as we talked. He went by the name of Cedric Gunnery, and he was director and treasurer of the Monday Club. His air of prosperity and well-being was at odds with his physical surroundings, for dilapidation and disrepair were more evident on the inside of the house than the outside: it resembled nothing more than the kind of student tip one recalls from younger, less exacting days. The only other person who appeared to be there was a young man, black, responsible for manual labour—mainly, by the look of it, shifting bundles of pamphlets devoted to the cause of racial separation—to whom I was not introduced. He quietly got on with his work, eyes downcast.

I was shown into a ramshackle office, piled high with cyclostyled papers amid a debris of unwashed crockery and milk-bottles. Our conversation began, tentativeness evident on both sides. After a while I asked him about Mrs Thatcher, who—as all the pundits concurred—was poised to win the next election (her third), and whose victories (it seemed at the time) stretched out endlessly into the future. On the whole he was pretty pleased, indicating that so long as she remained in charge the best policy for the Monday Club was to keep out of the way, for here was a prime minister intent on doing their work for them. Only on two issues did he express reservations. First, he thought Mrs Thatcher was soft on capital punishment. And secondly he was worried about South Africa. He feared that anarchy and chaos were about to be unleashed, and that the British government had failed to support its natural allies, the minority white government. He came out with a phrase whose meaning I had some problem in getting straight. 'The red carpet', he said, 'is rolling over South Africa'. Later, I arrived at the conclusion that this invocation signified not anxiety about visiting dignitaries (my immediate, bewildered thought) but instead a highly strung conception of a remorseless, unrolling communism enveloping the wide-open spaces of the *veld*. Then, as I remembered it, he spoke in impassioned, lyrical terms about South Africa, about its beauties and possibilities. And as he talked, sitting in front of a window partly open to let in a draught of sharp autumnal air, the grimy, greasy net curtains, once white, flapped lazily about him.

I found it unnerving, sitting in a house on the edge of Brixton in the 1980s, listening to this man extol the virtues of South Africa as a white man's country. The experience seemed to confirm abstract theories of dissonant historical times. But it was a dislocating moment none the less. Over the course of time, in formal presentations and in private conversations, I took to retelling my experience of this encounter and, as I did, the story became increasingly embellished. His enthusiasm for the *veld* became more intense, the curtains grubbier, and my own incomprehension greater. I no longer needed to check my notes, for I knew the story and knew how to pace it for maximal effect. Until, as one eventually does, I was rereading the relevant file and came across my notes. And then I slowly came to realize what I might have known all along. Gunnery was lyrical about South Africa and, though not using the exact terminology, he did affirm the virtues of it as a white man's country. Here was a man sitting on one frontier, imagining another. That much was true. But the embellishments, and the significance I read into them, were as much mine as his. The boundaries between his voice and mine were, I realized, more fluid than I had cared to notice. I left that interview not so much with his memories faithfully transcribed in my note-book, but with my own memories of empire brought into consciousness. This I had not expected.

I still do not fully understand what occurred. I had had no connections to colonial Africa, barely any to Africa at all. I was not conscious of the fact that I had any memories of South Africa, at least not of the lyrical sort. How could I have remembered a place I never knew? Surely twenty or so years of conventional anti-apartheid commitments would have generated sufficiently powerful counter-narratives to have erased any lingering, ideological traces of imperial recidivism? Apparently not, for these memories came from *somewhere*.

This is a brief ethnographic excursion. In retrospect I can see that the encounter with Gunnery, and my place within it, triggered a number of things. It would be possible, as others have done—historians and novelists— to continue these explorations in autobiographical mode, conducting a kind of historiographical self-analysis. In theory I have no resistance to this, at any rate not consciously; and given that we possess some wonderful models for such writing, I have no doubts about the intellectual integrity of narrative strategies which work in this way. But for reasons which need not detain readers, I have not chosen this route. I am more concerned here, and in the explorations which follow, to see if there is a plausible argument for showing where these memories might have come from, and how they worked.

Within the colonial sensibilities of the English, South Africa has at critical times functioned as both the fantasized frontier of the nation and as the utopian image of what actually-existing England, destroyed by the mundane forces of an unforgiving modernity, is not. The imperialists of the early twentieth century, and a handful of tribunes of the radical right later in the century, perceived the precarious future of English civilization to be as much at stake in South Africa as on Dover beach. The drama of South Africa as a frontier nation—representing one extremity of English conquest, in immediate proximity to both Boers and blacks—generated a culture in which political truth assumed the uncompromising clarity, and hard beauty, of sunlight on the *veld*. Time and again travellers from the British Isles to southern Africa attested to the capacity of the landscape to overwhelm them, inducing for many a lifelong passion.

Falling in love with the new territories, however, could prove disorientating, for the experience of the frontier could call into question the polite verities of the old country. Early adventurers, whose quests had been conducted in the name of English civilization, could find themselves increasingly at odds with the lived culture of England itself, and with its concomitant political imperatives. In the early part of the twentieth century the denunciation of the metropolitan population by those who had experienced at first-hand the colonies was a common and powerful motif in the political culture, demonstrated above all by the obsessions of the returning proconsuls, convinced that the traditional rulers had lost the will to govern. The English at home—domesticated, grown soft, and given, it might seem, to a life of wild luxury—could all too often confirm the fears of the colonials that racial degeneration was sapping the strength of the empire from its centre. English civilization in England itself could be suspect. In October 1901 Rudyard Kipling wrote to Cecil Rhodes from Cape Town: 'England is a stuffy little place, mentally, morally and physically', while Baden-Powell, brisk as ever, declared: 'It beats me why any Briton continues to live in say, Wigan, when South Africa is open to him.'[2]

In part, this was a stance about ethics, setting up a dichotomy in which the dissolute life of the metropole, succumbing to any number of inconsequential fashions, was pitted against the simplicities of the colonies. In this view of things life in South Africa itself actualized a kind of moral truth. But this argument about ethics was never far removed from parallel arguments about race and ethnicity. The immediacy of the racial question in southern Africa forced the upholders of English civilization to be vigilant about fundamentals in a manner which the metropolitan English were not called upon to emulate. Whether this was encoded in terms of a hard concept of race and racial degeneration (as it was early in the century), or in terms of ethnic loyalties and dispositions in which the overseas English declared themselves more truly English than those at home (as occurred in Southern Rhodesia in the 1950s and 1960s), the axis of the argument remained the same. Those on the frontier, by virtue of knowing the native, knew themselves more deeply; and thus they inhabited at greater pitch the true protocols of England.

The paradox, though, was that those who fell head over heels in love with colonial life, even if only briefly, could open themselves to a perplexing array of psychic displacements from what might still powerfully be imagined as home.[3] The experience of settling could prove profoundly unsettling.

The difficulties in determining what counted as a white man's country redoubled when it came to South Africa. South Africa represented a test-case for assessing the future of white civilization. Every department of social life, from the most intimate to the most public, was explicitly perceived—constantly, pathologically—in terms of race and racial supremacy. This was no last-minute imposition, smuggled into the polity by illiberal, unscrupulous Afrikaners, but the founding principle on which the Union of South Africa, as a nation, was created, and sanctified by Westminster.

In the imaginative transactions between the metropole and the South African colony we can learn much about the prescriptions of English civilization. I am principally concerned with those grouped on the political right, sympathetic to empire, rather than with the critics of colonialism. I concentrate on the period of the Anglo-Boer War of 1899–1902 and on its aftermath, suggesting that in these years the home-nation came actively to be reimagined through the lens of South Africa, and that these archival memories were to have a long history. More particularly I am interested in John Buchan, whom I introduce briefly here but discuss more fully later in the chapter.

Readers may think John Buchan too easy a figure to confront, too predictable, a man so completely won by the imperial conventions of his time that he could not possibly have any resonance in a later epoch.

I hope to show that this is wrong. Buchan is interesting because for most of his adult life he operated at the heart of the imperial state; and at the same time he was also an intellectual of empire in a wider sense, capable of producing both learned tracts and sensationalist novels.[4] He was regularly perceived by friends and colleagues as the incarnation of civilized values. He determinedly occupied the radical or liberal wing of Unionism, finding chauvinistic self-aggrandizement to be vulgar and self-destructive. He was a Scot who came to articulate his deepest ethical feelings in the ethnic codes of England. And after his death, in the age of decolonization, when one might have thought the time had come for him to be forgotten, his personal and literary reputation were accorded an unexpected, generously uncritical, and continuing afterlife. Most people I talk to assume him to be entirely discredited. But this is not so. For thirty or forty years now hardly a hostile word about him has appeared in print. The accolades are still his. Contemporary public intellectuals can still be found who, in all appearances completely untouched by the conventional milieu of English colonialism, can none the less identify in Buchan all that was good about England and its civilization. Such a figure needs to be understood.

He was, moreover, one of the pre-eminent philosophers of the white man's country. He was a thinker in the traditional sense (penning treatises for the initiated elites), but also in the wider, Gramscian meaning of giving these ideas life in popular institutions and in popular mentalities. I have indicated earlier that in the generation of ethnic memories, and of memories of empire more broadly, juvenile literature was of great significance. In this, Buchan proved himself to be a modern master. Through this medium he sought to universalize the values he believed to be the especial preserve of the white man. It was entirely appropriate, too, that he should end his days, if not exactly as a philosopher-king, then perhaps more accurately as a kind of proconsular-intellectual, as governor-general of one of the lands in which the aspirations of the white man ran deep, in Canada.

Yet it is also the case that Buchan's life and career dramatize the impossibilities of all that he held most dear: what I have summarized earlier as the impossibilities of whiteness. There are indications, in his writings and in the various personal collapses he suffered, that his mind was not entirely closed to these apprehensions, which marked what he feared most.

South Africa formed him. As a young man he sailed out on the Union Castle line in September 1901 and remained until July 1903, just under two

years in total. In his later life he was never to return and much of his subsequent writing can be seen as a way of managing this loss. In South Africa,
he later wrote,

> I recovered an experience which I had not known since my childhood,
> moments, even hours, of intense exhilaration, where one seemed to be a
> happy part of a friendly universe. The cause, no doubt, was largely physical,
> for my long treks made me very fit in body; but not wholly, for I have had the
> same experiences much later in life when my health was far from perfect.
> They came usually in the early morning or sunset. I seemed to acquire a
> wonderful clearness of mind and to find harmony in discords and unity in
> diversity, but to find these things not as conclusions of thought, but in a sud-
> den revelation, as in poetry or music.

These sentiments echo Stanley Baldwin's, quoted earlier, in which the colonies represent sensations associated with childhood and emotional fulfilment, and which modern life in the metropole could only ever intermittently
provide. This experience of the colonial sublime shaped Buchan's politics,
transforming him, in his own words, into 'a citizen' and bestowing upon
him 'a political faith'.[5]

Writing in 1940, however, he reflected on the shifting fortunes of his
faith:

> Those were the days when a vision of what the Empire might be made
> dawned upon certain minds with almost the force of a revelation. To-day the
> word is sadly tarnished. Its mislikers have managed to identify it with ugliness
> like corrugated iron-roofs and raw townships, or, worse still, with a callous
> racial arrogance. Its dreams, once so bright, have been so pawed by unctuous
> hands that their glory has departed... Something like the sober, merchandis-
> ing Jacobean colonial policy has replaced the high Elizabethan dreams...
>   I dreamed of a world-wide brotherhood with the background of a com-
> mon race and creed, consecrated to the service of peace; Britain enriching
> the rest out of her culture and traditions, and the spirit of the Dominions
> like a strong wind freshening the stuffiness of the old lands. I saw in the
> Empire a means of giving to the congested masses at home open country
> instead of a blind alley. I saw hope for a new afflatus in art and literature and
> thought. Our creed was not based on antagonism to any other people. It was
> humanitarian and international; we believed that we were laying the basis of
> a federation of the world. As for the native races under our rule, we had a
> high conscientiousness: Milner and Rhodes had a far-sighted native policy.
> The 'white man's burden' is now an almost meaningless phrase; then it
> involved a new philosophy of politics, and an ethical standard, serious and
> surely not ignoble.[6]

Buchan was close to death when he made these reflections on his youthful dreams. They are thoughts which, to the modern eye, reverberate with ambiguity, as he himself half feared. The historical world which made such words possible was much more cruel than he ever allowed himself to imagine. That the fundamentals of this faith should have cohered in South Africa, at the very moment when the conditions for the country's own tormented history were being put in place by its new conquerors, provides a properly profane counterpoint. But the fact remains: what drove Buchan's imagination was his experience in South Africa.

On returning to Britain in 1903 he hoped immediately to set off for Egypt, where Lord Cromer had planned to appoint him to an administrative post. But no vacancy arose, and his hopes were thwarted. With 'much restlessness and distaste' he went back to the bar. There followed a period of ennui, in which the humdrum domestic realities of the metropole could not compare for him to the sublime excitements of the colonial frontier. The political parties, he wrote later, proved 'blind to the true meaning of empire'; 'London had ceased to have its old glamour'; money and vulgarity ruled. He felt as if he were imprisoned in Plato's cave, 'conversant not with mankind but with their shadows'. 'I began to have an ugly fear', he concluded, 'that the Empire may decay at the heart.'[7] The adventure stories he wrote in England during this period were, in part, attempts by him to recover the intensity of the colonial moment. One need only think of the opening paragraphs of *The Thirty-Nine Steps*, drafted by Buchan in Broadstairs, in which Richard Hannay—only 'three months in the Old Country' after a long sojourn in Rhodesia—was 'pretty well disgusted with life'.[8] Home, in this colonial drama, produced not an affective location, but disgust, self-loathing even. Or as he recalled in his autobiography: 'South Africa had completely unsettled me.'[9]

Buchan's decision to travel to South Africa had been determined by the war. For all his high-mindedness and horror of 'raw townships', the first job assigned to him was the administration, as he described it later, of 'the concentration camps for women and children established by the army'.[10] His Oxford friend, the ubiquitous Leo Amery, had put him in touch with Lord Milner, the British high commissioner in South Africa, and Milner agreed to Buchan's appointment. Amery and the Oxford connection were important. The romantic passions of these young men, which could fuse the common room of All Souls and the *veld* into a single psychic reality, were organized by a high-voltage conception of masculine friendship and duty, and found philosophical purpose under the tutelage of Milner.[11] After the muscular exertions conducted in carrying out their imperial duties during the day, they duly dressed for dinner and good conversation in the evening.[12] When they returned from the colonial frontier, these intellectuals truly did set out to inaugurate 'a new philosophy of politics', attempting to transport the ethics of the frontier to the imperial centre at home. Westminster, Whitehall, *The Times*, Oxford University: this was the political milieu they addressed, in their despatches and treatises, a male world of familiarity and easy patronage.[13] Amery, still undergoing his apprenticeship as a potential editor of *The Times*, was the paper's chief correspondent in South Africa during the war, and the editor and principal author of the seven-volume *The Times History of the War in South Africa*.[14] As A. J. P. Taylor put it of Amery, 'His most decisive weapon has always been a letter to *The Times*.'[15] Quintessentially, Amery sought to influence through the medium of public opinion those who mattered, the strategists of high politics.[16] Buchan's significance, on the contrary, is that he attempted to reach the popular mind.

South Africa in the popular imagination

But the idea of South Africa carried other resonances too, touching a wider reading public and activating the popular imagination.[17]

Determining the affiliations of a popular culture, in all its lived complexities at any single historical moment, represents a recurring problem within historiography. There is none the less a large historiographical literature devoted to uncovering the connections between the South African War and popular feeling, in which the object is to discover which sections of the population subscribed to, or did not subscribe to, the sentiments of nationalism and imperialism. This, though, has met many inhibitions. The difficulties in holding all the complex determinations together, and saying something of more than particular significance, has encouraged some historians—in this field as in others—to give up, and to subscribe to the fashionable view that not much happened anyway, so the least said the better. My own view is rather different.

It is too easy for historians of high politics or of empire to assume that popular culture exists as a neutral field, through which preassigned ideas move back and forth. This loses sight of the dynamism of vernacular cultures, and of their transformative capacities. This is particularly relevant for the period of the South African War, for we should recognize the degree to which the war itself *produced* a new popular culture in which the relations between high politics and low culture became more proximate and more mobile. The very resources of popular culture expanded. In an evolving interchange between producers and consumers the range of cultural commodities available increased exponentially—movies, still photographic images in all their guises, spectacular shows, exhibitions, songs, popular print of many different varieties. After the siege of Mafeking was lifted, for example, urban markets in the metropole were flooded with a vast new array of kitschy knick-knacks which had been manufactured so that the mass of the people could celebrate the empire's victory. The combination of determined propaganda, entrepreneurship, and a genuine popular desire to know what was going on, or at least in more elusive form to participate in some manner in the general excitement of the times, resulted in a new expansion of popular forms in the metropole itself. In such a world mass politics itself took on new meanings and possibilities.

More especially the war coincided with a new moment in technological advances in the mass media.[18] Most notably the birth and speedy advance of the cinema, allied to new forms of the popular press (the *Daily Mail* most of all), created new possibilities for systems of images to intervene and recast popular life. For many, the first moving images of their lives would have shown them scenes from South Africa.[19] At the end of Chapter 2, when I described the crisis produced by the extravaganza 'Savage South Africa', I alluded to the influence of the *Daily Mail* in this new public sphere, in framing and driving forward popular stories about 'us' and about those others 'in our midst'. At this moment the *velocity* of popular culture increased. This is not only to observe that the number of images of faraway places increased and arrived in the metropole with greater speed, though this is important. It is rather to suggest that the resources for collective memories deepened, became more complex, and perhaps simultaneously more fragmentary, with the mass media creating new possibilities for a new regime of popular memory. As Bill Nasson has noted, the Boer War 'was a war waged on the very edge of modern memory'.[20]

These technological advances were never 'merely' technological. We need to remember, for example, that when Alfred Harmsworth founded the *Daily Mail* in 1896, he expended great effort in *training* his journalists into the mysteries of the vernacular.[21] In so doing he invented as he went along a new ventriloquist vernacular in which popular sentiments were created in corporate institutions, and then paraded as if they represented the authentic voice of the people—carnivalesque, humorous, shocked, outraged, delighted, and chauvinistic.

As a result, in popular journalism, and in the cinema as well, the lines dividing truth from fiction became more fluid and more difficult to track. As Benedict Anderson indicated in his study of modern nationalism, fictions incrementally 'seeped into' the real.[22] Fictionalized representations increasingly fixed the memory of real historical events. Or to put this in other terms, unknown locations and events could be 'remembered' by a domestic population which had never experienced them first-hand.

To think in this way is to emphasize the significance of the structures of the popular media, rather than the actual content (pro- or anti-jingo) of the opinions they relayed. Decisive is the fact that the channels of popular communication were themselves amplified, such that 'the popular' assumed a new salience and social centrality. Mass culture was coming to be more profoundly mediated. This in turn has consequences for understanding the emergent relations of ethnic, or national, or imperial affiliation.

If we turn to the great social theorists of the period, whom we now recognize as the creators of the intellectual discipline of sociology, we are reminded that modernity itself was theorized as a dynamic process which drew individuals away from particularistic identifications, and relocated them in more atomistic, or anomic, and certainly more administered, social environments. But new collectivities, imagined or mediated, developed in conjunction with these modern dynamics of individualization. I have already touched on this in Chapter 2. There I referred to nineteenth-century emigrants to Australia, from rural Ireland, writing home. Drawing from the work of David Fitzpatrick, I suggested that relations of affective affiliation were composed almost entirely in terms of locality: home, family, neighbourhood. Arriving in Australia these affective ties initially remained in place, as the surviving letters confirm.[23] Gradually, however, in the colony new and more expansive ways of imagining home emerged, not least of which (eventually) was the possibility of imagining oneself to be an 'Australian'. But this, as Benedict Anderson and others have pointed out, was a more mediated, and necessarily a more deeply 'imagined', collectivity than the one which they had left behind in Ireland, where everyone in village, street, or neighbourhood was known to them, face to face. By extension, we can think of the same processes at work in Britain at the turn of the twentieth century. Not only did the expansion and new centrality of the popular media invite their audiences to imagine themselves as participating in new communities, beyond those of immediate locality, but these were communities—as in the very concept of Greater Britain, for example—which were themselves more heavily mediated than those of known neighbourhoods.

This was the terrain on which were fought out, with varying degrees of deliberation, competing identifications, including those of nation and empire. Also, less consciously perhaps, it was in this arena that participants could negotiate an understanding of themselves as British, or as an enthusiast of empire, or as white. Ernest Gellner has this to say about the relationship between the mass media and nationalism:

> The media do not transmit an idea which happens to be fed into them. It matters precious little what has been fed into them: it is the media themselves, the pervasiveness and importance of abstract, centralized, one to many communication, which itself automatically engenders the core idea of nationalism quite irrespective of what in particular is being put into the specific messages transmitted.[24]

The intensification of mediated imaginings, I am arguing, intensified too the possibilities for thinking ethnically.

Thus the key question turns on what could, or could not be, imagined. Concentrating only on the content of media messages tends to encourage too rationalist, or too reductively cognitive, a conclusion, as if the popular media functioned only as neutral channels through which information was imparted. The example of Harmsworth, inventing a vernacular language appropriate for his own medium, is instructive. It demonstrates the fact that as they enter popular life signs and symbols are not merely imported from one part of the social world to another, but—as they move—they are transformed. Vernacular encodings of imperial affiliation rarely resembled the higher orders of imperial discourse, with which, for example, Leo Amery felt at home They worked according to different syntactical rules—more imagistic, perhaps, or more caricatured and carnivalesque—in which signification itself was less reliably fixed. (Again we could think back to the different vernacular voices in play in the Lobengula crisis which shadowed the showing of 'Savage South Africa' in London.) These are still complex modes of communication, even if they are often more fleeting and allusive. But they are, in Roland Barthes's terms, mythic, working by a symbolic logic rather than one elaborated by the full authority of socially sanctioned reason.[25]

This, too, is of significance for understanding the communicative circuits through which ethnic identifications move. What concerns me here is the way in which South Africa came to be imagined in the metropole by those who knew it only from fictional and journalistic accounts. It is the mode in which South Africa came to be narrated that is important, for it is the form of narration which is as influential as the more obvious, or manifest, moral of the tale. For these modes of narration of white adventurers 'out there' could inform the fictions those at home told about their own interior lives, particularly, in this age of empire, the stories about ethnic identifications and the often unnoticed registers of whiteness. Popular fiction, yellow journalism, and instant history have a privileged role in an explanation of this kind, for these were the genres in which one can trace the domestication of the colonial imperative, in which the fictions of the frontier came home and organized the common-sense philosophies of the metropolitan civilization.

The South African War represented a pivotal moment in the making of this new mediated culture, which was to continue long into the twentieth century. Looking back we can see how sustained was this shift.

While Leo Amery was working the corridors of power, others equally dedicated in their imperial sentiments found the distinctions between high politics and low culture, and indeed between fact and fiction, harder to maintain. Significant, for example, was Edgar Wallace, who in the 1910s and 1920s determined to write bad novels at high speed for the mass market, in order to reap with maximal ostentation a dizzying fortune. His ambition was realized and he did indeed become the most successful commercial writer of the 1920s. Posted to South Africa in 1896 as a diminutive and undernourished squaddie, it was there that his effective writing career began, and where he was inspired, and subsequently encouraged, by Rudyard Kipling. In 1899 he bought himself out of the army, found employment with Reuters, and thence was hired by the *Daily Mail* as a war correspondent, his capacity to master the intricacies of vernacular prose a requisite skill. Years later, Jan Smuts, by then prime minister of South Africa—although he made it clear that he found Edgar Wallace 'a hopeless character'—none the less felt compelled to admit the 'elemental power' of his writing.[26] In Wallace's subsequent career as an author, amidst the eighty-eight crime novels, the Hollywood screenplays, and the works on military history, he was responsible for two of the great twentieth-century popular myths of Africa to work their way into the domestic imagination: *Sanders of the River* and

King Kong, both of which are mythic invocations of the magical properties of whiteness. His ability to move between different cultural industries, and his skill in writing in different popular genres, indicate the easy transactions between fiction-writing and popular journalism in the early part of the century. In fact, these transactions included politics as well, for the author-as-celebrity cashed his status as an early media star in order to launch a political career.[27]

Edgar Wallace's mentor, Kipling, was also a powerful influence in evoking the idea of Africa for those who never knew it, and represented too an important conjunction between popular literature, journalism, and politics. In South Africa, he briefly edited a paper for serving soldiers, an activity which took him to the haphazard frontlines of the war as much as any accredited military correspondent and, back in England, he raised a volunteer company in Rottingdean. For the duration of the war he submitted his verse free of charge to *The Times*, effectively establishing himself as the nation's official chronicler of the conflict. In the full compendium of his work can be found eulogies to Rhodes, Milner, Chamberlain, and Lord Roberts, the overall military commander in South Africa. At the opening of hostilities he offered his poem, 'The Absent-Minded Beggar', to the *Daily Mail*, insisting only that those who reproduced it should contribute to a fund to buy tobacco and other small comforts for the troops. Kipling recounted it thus: 'Sir Arthur Sullivan wedded the words to a tune guaranteed to pull teeth out of barrel-organs. Anybody could do what they chose with the result, recite, sing, intone or reprint etc., on condition that they returned all fees and profits to the main account…which closed at about a quarter of a million.'[28] Through routes such as these his most famous poems became embedded in the lived culture of the imperial nation, extending the conventions of high literary production. As George Orwell observed some forty years later, his words travelled 'far beyond the bounds of the reading public, beyond the world of school prize-days, Boy Scout sing-songs, limp leather editions, poker-work and calendars, and out into the yet vaster world of the music-halls'.[29]

In this lies the extraordinary quality of Kipling as a figure in the twentieth-century literary canon. He was a writer who could cross both high and low, and who was genuinely able to translate the ethos of the frontier into a vernacular idiom. As such the sentiments of his poems became an unassuming, unconscious presence in the national culture. His relentless determination to commemorate the dead of the national community, the anonymous footsoldier on the *veld* as much as the colossi of empire, marks a critical moment in the production of an imagination which was both imperial and popular, the creation of an imaginary past serving to encourage metropolitans to become participants of empire. These were memories of the nation, drawn from the frontiers of India and South Africa, which Kipling's populist rhetoric was able to speak *as if* they truly were the memories of the people. In this lie the properly mythological dimensions of his work.[30]

Another war correspondent, in this instance in the person of Winston Churchill, can also be credited with fashioning a potent South Africa of the imagination, a myth which he was happy to rewrite and adorn as his life proceeded. For a handsome salary Churchill was employed by the respectable and energetically Conservative *Morning Post*, sailing to South Africa as the paper's accredited correspondent within three days of war having been declared. His hopes of taking with him a movie camera and cameraman, however, were not fulfilled. But his ambition was confined neither to journalism nor to politics. In 1900 his first novel, *Savrola*, was published. Years later, in the 1930s when he was hard up financially and politically, he took to boiling down the classics of English literature for the readership of the *News of the World*. But more than anything the epic quality of his politics derived from his capacity to live his public life through the imaginative categories of fiction. When called upon to invent yet again his autobiography for the drafting of *My Early Life*, the positioning of his early self as a hero straight out of Robert Louis Stevenson was explicit, as was his tendency to see his life as 'An endless moving picture in which one was an actor'. (Audiences confronted many years later with the execrable *The Young Winston* were thus watching the return to film of a story which had originally been imagined cinematically.[31]) The same year his novel came out he rewrote his *Morning Post* reports in more ebullient prose and had them published as *London to Ladysmith* and *Ian Hamilton's March*, in which his own exploits were not modest and in which the distinction between straight journalism and autobiographical adventure was slight. In the genre of the *Bildungsroman*, South Africa became the backdrop for adventure and the site where true masculine maturity could be fulfilled. It was fitting too that, on 18 February 1901, he devoted his maiden speech in the Commons to a vindication of imperial intervention in South Africa. But these youthful texts were also critical in organizing Churchill's *own* memories of empire. He never set foot in India again after departing in 1897, nor in South Africa after 1900. His last sight of a British colony in Africa occurred in 1908. Thus when as prime minister he vowed in his Mansion House speech of November 1942 that he would never 'preside over the liquidation of the British Empire', it was the empire of the Victorian epoch, vivid from his own youthful memories, that he knew most intimately.[32]

To take some further instances: Arthur Conan Doyle, on Christmas Eve 1899, aged 40, announced to his wife that he had decided to volunteer for service in South Africa. His age stood against him, and he was placed on the reserve list. Undeterred, he joined a hospital unit and sailed to Cape Town, remaining in South Africa until Pretoria was captured in July. This fleeting visit, interspersed between his activities supporting the Boys' Empire League and his decision to stand as a Unionist candidate in the 1900 election, provided the material for an instant four-volume history of the war, which he completed that same year. His purpose in writing the history was to defend the reputation of the British soldiers serving in South Africa, pitting himself against their liberal critics at home. He was knighted for these public services during the war, not for his literary endeavours.[33] Yet another war correspondent, who in this case had also served in the Crimea, the children's writer G. A. Henty, felt compelled to rush off a couple of yarns though, mainly because of his advancing years, he had no inclination actually to make the journey to South Africa. These stories carried what were to become formulaic titles, the very staple of future school-histories: *With Buller in Natal* and *With Roberts to Pretoria*.[34] Two of the later volumes of Amery's *Times History* were edited by Erskine Childers, who had also served in South Africa and who has some claim as the inventor of the thriller, before embarking upon a political life which brought him into confrontation with the British state.[35] More anonymous contributions could be found in the cheap-format, serialized histories published by Harmsworths and Cassells. *Chums* boasted a regular column, 'Flashes from the Front', and similar copy could be found in George Newnes's *Captain*, and in the specialist *Boy's War News*, many of which magazines also championed the myriad imperial youth organizations, or those devoted to national defence, which in the modern argot were effective and influential gun lobbies.[36]

What is probably the most widely read English-language tract of the twentieth century, *Scouting for Boys*, was rooted in the experience of the *veld* and, thanks to the astute commercial sense of the *Daily Express*'s proprietor, Arthur Pearson, very quickly became integrated into the mass culture of the metropole. After the war Pearson's *The Scout* was selling 110,000 copies a week. During the siege of Mafeking, Baden-Powell elevated himself into something closely resembling a media star, his presence dominating the reports in the commercial press at home (thanks particularly to Lady Sarah Wilson's reports published in the *Daily Mail*) and his image sanctified in a mass of cheap novelties, a curious moment when kitsch and the ideals of imperial manhood were one. In the youth movements which mushroomed in the wake of the war, even young people largely excluded from the reading public could still have the opportunity to transcend the known habitat of the neighbourhood, and imagine for themselves the ethos of the frontier.[37]

Or to turn to visual media: photojournalism became a constituent part of news reporting, especially after the arrival of Lord Roberts as commander-in-chief, who cultivated a close relationship between the armed forces and the press corps. At the height of popular enthusiasm for the war, a single company in Britain was producing each day 25,000 stereoscopic pictures of the events in South Africa. Episodes of the military campaign were frequently filmed—though the distance of the enemy, and their predilection for concealing themselves, meant that many of the more dramatic encounters had to be restaged for the cameras, most often close to the front but on occasion, it transpires, on Hampstead Heath and in Bolton. (Lord Kitchener, placed in command of the final destruction of the Boer armies, thought it unfair that the Boers employed these tactics, commenting that they were not 'like the Sudanese who stood up to a fair fight. They are always running away on their little ponies.'[38]) The humdrum business of soldiering received more attention from film-makers and photographers than in any previous war, expanding the expectations demanded of the cinema. Newsreels and filmed commentaries created a new audience at home, with the capacity to *see* the landscapes of the much-vaunted imperial community of which, at every turn, the home populace were invited to imagine themselves a part. The war was, as well, narrated in many different kinds of theatrical spectacle, at Madame Tussaud's, for example; it became a theme in the language of advertising; board-games were devised on the theme of 'Boer or Britain?'; it dominated the burgeoning picture-postcard industry; and at the war's end, the building of memorials was greater than anything seen since Trafalgar and Waterloo.[39]

This brief inventory could be extended. But the point should be clear. Rudyard Kipling, Arthur Conan Doyle, Winston Churchill, Baden-Powell, Edgar Wallace, let alone Lord Milner, Joseph Chamberlain, or Leo Amery: these were not negligible public figures. Amongst them are two of the small clutch of British writers who have won the Nobel prize for literature. In their different ways each was projecting an idealized image of South Africa, and each constructed his own public. Fact and fiction mingled, especially where these publics crossed. Fiction-writing, journalism, and politics could operate within the same imaginative, or mythic, space. In addition, the sheer volume of images was impressive. Most of the stories which circulated were underwritten by a conviction of the moral intensity of the frontier, and of the empire at home. But even when this was not the case, there can be no doubt of the degree to which South Africa was powerfully positioned *within* the imagined community of the British nation. Nor of the degree to which popular journalism, fiction, and politics sustained each other.

This shift was necessarily uneven. There are many examples of those who went on public record to declare the shame they felt toward their nation, including Kipling's Aunt Georgie—Georgina Burne-Jones, once muse to the Pre-Raphaelites—in Rottingdean.[40] This plethora of images and stories could not possibly create a new unitary British identity, their very variety generating the conditions for a plurality of identifications. As with many such wars, enthusiasm at home ebbed and flowed, victories instilling a certain enthusiasm, defeats a measure of disillusionment, but the sheer length of the conflict serving in the longer term to curb spontaneous expressions of unguarded jingoism. Allegiances were riven. Condemnation of the war, for example, did not necessarily imply the adoption of a pro-Boer stance. Alongside the cultures of imperial Britain there existed a counter-public, drawn from the Nonconformist provinces, from the liberal and the feminist intelligentsia, and from sections of the labour movement, which was as vehement in its support of the Boers as the imperialists were in their denunciation. Far from there falling into place a unitary national culture, imperialist from top to toe, there were contending publics—two nations, or more—each of which judged the moral worth of its own dispositions from its respective stance on South Africa. As much as in the 1960s and 1970s, South Africa became a defining issue dividing conservatives from progressives.[41] Thus although the rhetoric of empire appears to be everywhere—for good reason, for it *was* everywhere—it cannot always be taken on its own terms. Juveniles or adults reading literature proclaiming the virtues of empire, for example, did not automatically subscribe to the exhortations with which they were presented. Enoch Powell talks of his father, a pro-Boer Lloyd George Liberal, reading Carlyle—the spiritual ancestor to the radical imperialists of the period—not for his views but for his prose.[42] Such examples of dissonant readings must be numerous, though always difficult to reconstruct.

There can be little doubt, though, that the pro-Boer public was a subordinate public, its reflexes curtailed by the growing power of the institutions of commercial culture which, in the name of a *modern* patriotism as much as in the name of conventional party politics, tended to be drawn to the adventures of the colonizers. The inhibitions in proclaiming a pro-Boer position in public are illustrated by the most influential of the boy's magazines of the period, *The Boy's Own Paper.* The magazine's owners and senior staff were largely Baptist, largely pro-Boer, and thus hostile to the jingoism of its rival publications. Yet the editors felt unable to speak this in the pages of the paper. All they could do, in relation to South Africa, was to fall silent. Given the prevailing noise in *The Boy's Own*'s companion papers, this effectively was to disengage from the public debate, and leave the running to the imperialists.[43]

Clearly, the situation was fluid. John Buchan, as we shall see, offers a complicated picture, discovering on his treks through the *veld* 'harmony in discords'. Conan Doyle, for all his determination to involve himself in fighting for the empire, retained a sympathy for the Boers: his first act on arriving in Cape Town was to visit Boer prisoners, distributing money he had collected in Britain.[44] Or after hostilities stopped, we can witness in Jan Smuts, the strangest reconciliations between the traditions of John Bright and Quaker rectitude, on the one hand, and Milnerism, on the other.

Even so the overall dominating position of the pro-war, pro-empire stories circulating through the body-politic counts for much. Although we can never be sure how these were read and internalized, certain clues about the conditions of popular life serve as helpful guides. To learn for example that on the eve of the war over 20 per cent of the male population of the United Kingdom, aged 17 to 40, had had previous military experience might minimally suggest a degree of sympathy for those fighting overseas, and even perhaps for the cause for which they were fighting.[45] But categories like pro-empire, or jingo, need to be refined. We need to be able to reach more intangible, elusive identifications. I have been arguing that the evolution of new media created the conditions in which identification with mediated, more 'imagined', collectivities moved to the fore. In effect, these new cultural formations produced new possibilities for national or ethnic allegiances. After all, cultures produce nations, not nations cultures. Hovering behind the controversy concerning the measure of popular support for the war is the larger, difficult question of what sort of (imagined) communities people believed they belonged to. This concerned not only the issue of national allegiance, but so too that of race and ethnicity. Where were the lines to be drawn between 'us', in its multiple guises, and the equally manifold varieties of 'them'?

For imperialists of the stamp of Milner and Chamberlain, the war in South Africa represented a decisive struggle to create the Greater Britain of which they dreamt. White troops from the overseas dominions were heralded as brothers-in-arms. (But not troops from India.[46]) Yet recognition of whiteness could register in a less programmatic manner, touching deep within the self.

The South African War was an imperial war not only due to the fact that it was conducted for the purpose of territorial annexation, but also because other colonial nations were drawn into the conflict as allies of the British. Some 49,000 colonial troops served in South Africa—from Australia, Canada, and New Zealand.[47] Protestant Ireland was vociferous in its loyalty: on the outbreak of war, orange lodges in all parts of Ulster offered their services. There is evidence of deep imperial patriotism amongst the Irish in the Cape.[48] Imperial instincts overrode old Calvinist allegiances in Scotland.[49] Nonconformist Wales showed every enthusiasm for the cause of empire.[50] And yet, in strictly nationalist terms, outside England the consequences were contradictory. One of the means by which Australians, for example, came to see their new nation as standing in the vanguard of white civilization was as a consequence of their involvement in the fighting in South Africa. Yet at the same time, this affiliation to the ideals of the white man, and to the ethnic codes of empire, could also work to encourage a greater commitment to the essentials of a specifically colonial nationalism and to a loyalty to Australia as an entity separate from the metropole. This ambiguity runs deep. Ethnicity generally worked as a centripetal force within the empire, encoding the ideas of ancestral liberties, kith and kin, the crown, and white civilization. That this could, on occasion, be described as 'British', or even 'English', was confusing, though this confusion attests to the determining location of the core imperial nation. The ambivalent placing of the subaltern imperial nations, though, in relation to the larger British nation-state was emphatic. On 5 June 1900 the Union Jack was raised above Pretoria. It had been made by Lady Roberts—we can see where her sense of imperial duty lay—and carried by her husband on his campaign. In the corner of the flag she had stitched an unobtrusive shamrock.[51]

Thus if ethnic attachment—encoded in terms either of whiteness or of some notion of a Greater Britain—exerted a centripetal influence, national identity tended to work in the opposite direction, exerting a centrifugal force, and serving to divide those in service of the empire. Nationalism, for new peoples or for putatively unhistoric peoples, was in this period still of relatively recent invention, the category itself labile. Indeed as we have seen, for the future white dominions the war itself proved a critical moment in creating *the possibility* for nationhood and in elaborating a conception of what a new nation, apart from the mother country, might entail.[52] In this way the syntax of ethnic belonging was itself transformed, at the moment when politics in the metropole was in the protracted process of being universalized and the masses drawn into the political nation. If national affiliation turned out to be divisive, then much came to rest on the repertoire of ideas which across the empire invoked a shared ancestry, especially on notions such as kith and kin and its various cognates.[53] In South Africa these ideas were fired by a primal allegiance to the inheritance of a specifically white civilization.

The black presence

The narratives which told the story of South Africa that appeared in Britain during the war of 1899–1902 were, as one might expect, superimposed on other memories of prior colonial encounters. As in all such remembering, this was a process which blurred specificities of time and place, disrupting historical coherence. Yet a connective logic was at work—one more symbolic, or emotive, than reasoned, and one which was marked by its stark simplicity. In the imagining of South Africa the structure of racial fear—more specifically, a fear of blackness—became one means by which South Africa could most easily be understood by the domestic British who did not know the region. This didn't operate at a constant pitch, nor was it present all the time. I argue below that when the Boers were defeated the imaginings of the black presence moved nearer to the centre of things. But this should not conceal the coded projections of blackness, and concomitantly of whiteness, which shadowed the narrative constructions, in Britain, of the war itself. Racial fear of non-white peoples was, from the latter part of the nineteenth century, a pronounced feature of the colonial story. Its very simplicity in mythic terms enabled it to reactivate collective memories from older episodes: from the rebellion in India in 1857 pre-eminently, but also from the Zulu wars, the campaign in the Sudan, and from the Ndebele and Shona uprisings of the 1890s. It was a way of imagining colonialism which stripped history of its complexities, which elevated the imperatives of racial truth, and which delivered a ready-made cognitive grid by which a distant world could be grasped. It worked as myth, transforming what otherwise seemed unknowable into the known.

There is, though, an obvious paradox. The principal enemy, the Afrkaners, were white. Many British writers of different political complexions devoted great energy in order to make sense of the Boers, and to understand where they belonged in the ethnic scheme of things. Many different solutions cohered which depended, in part, on political perspective, though positions shifted markedly over the course of the war. The Boers could be scrupulous or unscrupulous, manly or weak, childlike or advanced, civilized or uncivilized. W. F. Monypenny, on leave from *The Times* and five days into his editorship of the *Johannesburg Star*, was happy to conclude that the Boers 'are very Oriental, treacherous and cunning in a small way, but with no backbone and no real cleverness'.[54] The oddity of the Boers derived from a mentality which found it impossible to imagine white Africans. If Boers were not black, they had to be European. But these were Europeans who for four hundred years had been cut off from the engine of civilization— from Europe itself—by both geography and language.[55] The fact that within this view Afrikaners shared a common if distant European heritage, and that they were white, signified a measure of existential recognition denied the blacks. Yet when accorded this recognition, they were conventionally deemed less civilized, or less white, than the British. Lord Kitchener, for example, was convinced that the 'Boers were uncivilized Africander savages with only a thin white veneer'.[56] Colonial whiteness remained the normative category by which all others were to be judged. Boers could occupy a place in the ethnic scheme on the outer edges of whiteness oscillating, according to the author's predilections, between a sturdy if enclosed strain of European identity and an ascription which barely qualified as white at all. There could be much movement within this spectrum, but the language of whiteness, upon which all discussion of the anomalous Boers turned, constituted the critical organizing principle. The common identity of white and British was self-evident: for others it was contingent.

British whiteness carried with it a set of responsibilities and political prescriptions. Leo Amery made this clear when he laid out the governing principles for *The Times History* of the war. Significantly, he opened his account by insisting on the historical contrast between the contemporary situation in South Africa and the events in India in 1857:

> The struggle [in South Africa] has not been to uphold the rule of Englishmen over Asiatics, but to secure political equality for Englishmen in a country where the English composed more than one half of the whole population. We have fought, not to maintain the white man's burden, but to vindicate the white man's birthright—the right of all white men that come into a new country, and join the work of developing and making it, to claim their share of its political privileges. Our endeavour has been not to preserve our hold over an alien dependency, but to prevent a vast region inhabited by men of English blood or that of those stubborn Low-German stock that is so nearly akin to our own—a region susceptible of indefinite development and destined some day to play an important part in the world—from being lost to the community of liberty-loving and progressive nations that make up Britain.[57]

This statement is imprinted with all the high imperial instincts one associates with Amery. As Lionel Curtis, one of Milner's young protégés in South Africa, observed in a letter home: 'Read Amery's Preface to his *History of the War* and you will learn something of the sanity of Jingo opinion out here'.[58] But Amery's words may be more revealing than at first they appear. They imply that the whiteness attributed to the Afrikaners rose to the degree that blacks entered the field of vision. It is clear from this passage that the rights of white men were seen to compete with the interests of others who remain unmentioned: the indigenous inhabitants of the 'new' country. In the British imagination Afrikaner claims on whiteness were acceptable when viewed in relation to the blacks, but more precarious when compared to the British themselves.

Either way, affirmations or denials of whiteness were premised on a repudiation of blackness and of its perceived perils. To adopt John Barrell's pithy formulation, it is a matter of 'this, that and the other'. While Briton and Boer oscillated between the poles of 'this and that', a third term—the black other—both made possible the linkage of the two principal terms and at the same time was repressed by it. This third element, the other, is according to Barrell 'equally threatening to both'.[59] Even in the militantly pro-Boer, anti-imperial sensibilities of Emily Hobhouse, for example, the cognitive imperatives of whiteness subsumed an authentic radicalism. Britain may have divided between pro-Boer and anti-Boer factions, with a powerful political line separating the two. But there were unspoken affinities as well as division, indicating what could and could not be imagined within the governing mentalities of Britishness itself.[60]

In the imaginative projections of South Africa much of this was implicit, or occurred below the surface of the text. It did not need to be spoken incessantly, for to affirm whiteness was in its very affirmation a repudiation of blackness. It is this which accounts for the paradox. Racial fear of blacks was a theme which occurred not everywhere, but anywhere, any time. The meanings of South Africa, within the white purview, were overdetermined by it. Yet it was a structure which appeared most frequently in minor key, by means of displacement, from the margins.

This internal textual argument can be illustrated. Arthur Conan Doyle, whom as we have seen carried some sympathy for the Afrikaners, opens his account of *The Great Boer War* by attempting to straighten out the enigma of the Boers as an ethnic group:

> Take a community of Dutchmen of the type of those who defended them-
> selves for fifty years against all the power of Spain at a time when Spain was
> the greatest power of the world. Intermix them with a strain of those inflex-
> ible French Huguenots who gave up home and fortune and left their country
> for ever at the time of the revocation of the Edict of Nantes. The product
> must obviously be one of the most rugged, virile, unconquerable races ever
> seen upon earth. Take this formidable people and train them for seven genera-
> tions in constant warfare against savage men and ferocious beasts, in circum-
> stances under which no weakling could survive, place them so that they
> acquire exceptional skill with weapons and in horsemanship, give them a
> country which is eminently suited to the tactics of the huntsman, the marks-
> man and the rider. Then, finally, put a fine temper upon their military qualities
> by a dour fatalistic Old Testament religion and an ardent and consuming
> patriotism. Combine all these qualities and all these impulses in one individ-
> ual, and you have the modern Boer—the most formidable antagonist who-
> ever crossed the path of Imperial Britain.[61]

The passing reference to 'savage men and ferocious beasts' provides a signifi-cant insight, serving to frame the virtues of the Boers as a race, whilst divid-ing them from those who have no place in the spectrum of white civilization.[62]

In the body of the text, however, blacks barely make an appearance. 'At the same instant every Boer along the line of the donga sprang up and emp-tied his magazine into the mass of rushing, shouting soldiers, plunging horses, and screaming Kaffirs'; 'The British concealed themselves by the path, but Blackburn's foot was seen by a keen-eyed Kaffir who pointed it out to his masters'; 'The Kaffir drivers were already afoot and strolling out for their horses, or lighting their fires for their masters' coffee'; or most eloquently, describing an encirclement during the battle of Ladysmith, 'A Kaffir was despatched with promises of a heavy bribe, but he passed out of history'. In four volumes and some 700 pages, a handful of references such as these appears to say all that has to be said about the role of the blacks in the conflict, a matter of no manifest import. Yet this is not quite all. On three occasions the Boers—the respected white antagonists—are taken to task for uncivilized treatment of blacks, confirming that in the hierarchy of the white nations the Boers, in comparison to the British, fall short. Civilized regard for the 'kaffir', however, is shot through with the deepest ambivalence. On one occasion this is made explicit. While Conan Doyle expects from the British an enlightened—un-Boer—governance for the blacks he also *knows* the dangers this holds. For the 'Kaffirs' are 'warlike': 'once the assegais were reddened no man could say how far the mischief might go'.[63] Such truth requires no elaboration.

This textual argument, however, requires historical contextualization. When war first broke out, both Afrikaner and British leaders went to great lengths to assure their white populations that blacks would not be mobilized. A. J. Balfour and Joseph Chamberlain, both senior figures in the Unionist government, were adamant on this, though characteristically it was Jan Smuts, the Boer general, who was most explicit. The prohibition on black mobilization he believed 'essential to the continued existence of the white community as the ruling class in South Africa'.[64] The reality, however, proved very different. In the event vast numbers were called upon. The British recruited at least 10,000 black people, perhaps as many as 30,000, some of whom served as armed combatants.[65] On the ground, as one would expect, the range of relations between blacks and whites was as varied as any other set of human relations, spanning intimacy and camaraderie to mutual hostility and violence. In some circumstances, the idea of England could prove a potent resource for blacks intent on breaking free from local Afrikaner regimes, or from Afrikaner occupation, an imaginary Englishness providing a mental space free from Boer authority and the *sjambok*. This was especially so in the Cape, as Bill Nasson shows in his magnificent history, in which he discusses the fate of Abraham Esau—'a kind of budding Emiliano Zapata', whose life as a primitive rebel was given ideological shape by the unlikely influence of Tennyson's *Locksley Hall* (which carries its own vivid racial assumptions and whose author, we should recall, was active in the defence of Governor Eyre). As in many wars of the modern period black mobilization could provide a degree of emancipation.[66]

At first sight these historical realities might not appear to fit with an idea of South Africa, fuelled by fantasies of racial fear, projected back to the metropolitan British population. In part, this is a question of how myths function. They work by flattening out the chaos of lived realities into elemental stories which are able to move freely from circumstance to circumstance. The lack of fit between historical realities and the imaginary offers one way of thinking what myths are about. But it may also be a question of historical timing. Only after the war, when accommodation between Briton and Boer was in process, did the third element—the black other—again move into dominance in colonial narratives of South Africa.[67]

At the Vereeniging peace negotiations in 1902 the native franchise was an issue deliberately fudged by the British. Unadorned, visceral racial fear, however, entered the official proceedings. On 31 May Smuts and his Afrikaner ally, J. B. Hertzog, drew up a memorandum in which, amongst other things, they stated that they

> specially observe . . . that the Kaffir tribes within and without the frontiers of the two Republics, are mostly armed and taking part in the war against us, and through the committing of murders and all sorts of cruelties have caused an unbearable condition of affairs in many districts of both Republics. An instance of this happened not long ago in the district of Vryheid, where fifty-six burghers on one occasion were murdered and mutilated in a fearful manner.[68]

Here one can see the popular anxieties which drove racial fears—amplified through rumour—entering public life and receiving official sanction. For Smuts and Hertzog there was every reason why accommodation with the British needed to be accomplished speedily.

In a symbolic moment of great importance, when hostilities ceased, the victorious Joseph Chamberlain travelled to the Transvaal where, on 8 January 1903, he was petitioned (in Dutch) by Smuts. The aspirations in Smuts's petition were significant. 'We can now look one another in the face', he declared, 'like *white men* [emphasis in the original] and that already is a big step forward in the history of South Africa.'[69] Smuts himself was to be bitterly disappointed when, as it turned out, Chamberlain proved unforthcoming, resisting to the end Afrikaner entreaties. Even so, Smuts was right. The future alliance of Briton and Boer was predicated on mutual recognition of shared whiteness, which henceforth—its protagonists hoped—would override merely local ethnic differences between those of European descent. Or as Nasson argues, after the turmoil of the war, in which many numbers of black Africans determined to fight for their own emancipation, the new white alliance required that the advances blacks had made be turned back.

> The postwar 'reconquest' of Africans—both economic and political—was as urgent as, and indeed inseparable from, the politics of national state formation and the reconstitution of South Africa as an imperialist enclave...various forms of sustained, bitter resistance to that unfolding second 'conquest' stretched into decades.[70]

When the war between Afrikaner and Briton was settled, both could turn their attention to the urgent matter of 'reconquest'.

For advocates of empire in Britain such sentiments redramatized older memories of colonial conquest. Both before and after the South African War those endeavouring to establish British colonial rule carried in their minds earlier precedents. Historical traces of the Sepoy Rebellion, particularly, recurred.[71] Indeed, this was an event which still reverberated in living memory. Fifty years after the revolt itself, in 1907, a gathering of survivors took place at the Albert Hall. Naturally, it fell to Kipling to write the official verse, commemorating

> The remnant of that desperate host
> Which cleansed our East with steel.[72]

Leo Amery, as we have seen, thought it the most natural thing in the world to open the *Times History* with a discussion of the comparative historical significance for the empire of 1857 and the war in South Africa.

Baden-Powell can serve as another example. He had been posted to India in 1876. He recounted his experiences there some four decades later, in 1915, in which—in a complicated reconstruction—he recalled memories of his memories:

> Twenty years had elapsed since the Mutiny, but our knowledge of India was chiefly derived from reading accounts of that episode, and therefore when left alone for the night in this empty-looking house, with doors and windows open to the night, we naturally imagined the possibility of having our throats cut at any moment, and therefore we slept with our pistols handy, when, as a matter of fact, we were as safe as if we had been in a hotel in London, but it added a touch of romance to our journey, and every minor experience was to us of great moment at that time.

The buildings of Lucknow, still marked by the fighting, were of 'intense interest to us as visible reminders of the struggle which had taken place for the maintenance of British supremacy in India'.[73] And there were indeed plenty of stories of 1857 in circulation. According to an article published in *Blackwood's* in 1887, there were more accounts of the Mutiny in popular fiction than of any other nineteenth-century event.[74] Some thirty years after this, when Baden-Powell came to contemplate appropriate historical pageants for his newly formed scout troops, there was an inevitability about his choice falling upon the capture of Delhi and the defeat of the insurgents.[75]

In early 1896 Baden-Powell was posted to Matabeleland, where he was brought face to face with the dynamics of racial terror. The uprising of the Ndebele and Shona in March had resulted in attacks on whites in isolated homesteads. Baden-Powell, second in command, was ordered to regain control of the area, and left to determine for himself the appropriate means. In an exercise of systematic retribution his forces broke the power of the rebels. All the mechanics of a counter-guerrilla operation were set in place: the burning of villages, symbolic and real terror manifest in the rooting out of putative spies, exemplary executions. His personal fascination with the details of executions is well documented. From the heart of the campaign he sent back his dispatches to the *Graphic* in London, illustrated with photographs taken with his Eastman camera, creating a public narrative of his own deeds as he went along. These reports formed the basis for his subsequent history of the reconquest, which first appeared in 1897. It was here too that Baden-Powell first developed his ideas on scouting, 'the best of all arts, sciences, or sports'. In effect, he translated the 'adventure' of racialized counter-insurgency into the practice of scouting appropriate for imperial children back home.[76] This was a view of the world which, with understated but incontrovertible authority, runs through the prose of *Scouting for Boys* and *Scouting for Girls*. 'When the militia was down' urban boys and girls from the metropole would know the responsibilities bequeathed them by their race.

The campaign in Matabeleland established white-settler power in Rhodesia. It was to have historic consequences throughout the twentieth century, and into the century which followed; it represented as well a critical moment in which narratives of racial fear cohered in the white imagination. According to Terence Ranger, 'The sudden unsuspected risings in which the houseservants, the customers in the stores, the respectful old men, suddenly turned into killers, burnt themselves deep into the white Rhodesian consciousness.'[77] Echoes of these colonial fears, turning on the perpetual savagery of 'the native', could be heard in the metropole too: in its literature, its pastimes, its politics.

Or maybe, if Baden-Powell is deemed too eccentric, we could look to Winston Churchill. On joining the 4th Hussars in 1895 he noted that although the veterans of 1857 had, by this date retired from the army, the memory of the Rebellion was still alive. His old commander at the military college at Sandhurst had been badly wounded in the campaign, while Lord Roberts, the commander in chief of the imperial forces in South Africa, had won his Victoria Cross in putting down the rebels.[78]

For Churchill, race and racial fear always loomed large. 'My earliest memories', he declared in *My Early Life*, 'are Ireland'. More specifically, the danger of Fenian outrages impressed themselves as his first coherent perception of the public world. But this quickly became imbricated with perceptions of more distant foes, drawing in the most parochial corners of a tranquil English community.

> My next foothold of memory is Ventnor. I loved Ventnor…When I first stayed at Ventnor we were fighting a war with the Zulus. There were pictures in the papers of these Zulus. They were black and naked, with spears called assegais which they threw very cleverly. They killed a great many of our soldiers, but judging from the pictures, not nearly so many as our soldiers killed of them. I was very angry with the Zulus, and glad to hear they were being killed.[79]

As a young soldier on the North-East frontier, at the battle of Omdurman, and as a derring-do correspondent in the South African War, Churchill's views on race no doubt differed little from those of the other officers with whom he served. The early infantile anxieties (recorded, it should be noted, when he was in his fifties) can easily be discerned. His reports take as axiomatic the barbarism of non-white races, the frenzied irrational brew of 'Mohammedanism' with its 'mad mullahs' and 'mad fakirs', the delusions of the 'negroid races' and so on. Speaking in the voice of civilized reason, an attraction for cathartic bloodshed is never far away—evident most of all in his exultant description of the massacre of the Mahdi's army at Omdurman (where 'the Sudanese' had, it seems, decided in good conscience to fight fairly). His experiences in South Africa conformed to his earlier experiences of race.[80] Civilization and racial fear were proximate in his mind. When the question of the native races was debated in the House of Commons in February 1906, when Churchill himself was at the very start of his ministerial career in the Colonial Office, the issue for him was clearcut. All turned on the possession of civilized capacities. But underlying this was the fear of 'native risings' and of the 'black peril': the irreducible, palpable fear that those other races who had been allowed to cross the threshold and claim for themselves the designation 'civilized' might—in an instant and obeying nothing more than mere whim—turn upon those who previously had welcomed them. 'And let us not once forget', Churchill warned, 'that all native risings begin with massacre of a few lonely whites and end in the butchery of many blacks.'[81]

There is no doubt that Churchill himself was prey to wild anxieties about non-whites which touched him to the end of his life. But his sense of disorder wasn't only racial. Forty years on, in his first administration, he and his secretary of state for India, his old schoolfriend Leo Amery, found themselves locked into a fierce struggle in determining the appropriate response to colonial resistance in India. Amery, diehard imperialist and a dedicated tribune of the white race who, like Churchill, had cut his teeth in South Africa, could not comprehend the intensity of Churchill's reaction, at times believing he had taken leave of his senses. In his diary of 16 June 1944 he wrote of him:

> Winston again delivered a tirade against de Gaulle and, his eyes flashing with fury, warned us all against this enemy of England as he had warned us against Hitler. I doubt whether outside Brendan [Bracken] and [Lord] Cherwell any of the Cabinet really agree with him. This, like India or any form of self-government for coloured people, raises in him a wholly uncontrollable complex.[82]

Ten years later, he could still be found (whilst admitting he was 'a laggard' on such matters) writing to his old friend Dwight Eisenhower announcing he was 'sceptical about universal suffrage for the Hottentots'.[83] While this particular position might (or might not) have been perceived as perverse, more generally his 'uncontrollable complex' is of historical significance, and not a mere quirk which historians, in proper deference to a genuinely colossal figure, should courteously pass by. It is, amongst other things, too intimately connected to childish fantasies of assegais and to a social experience of empire, and indeed to a larger conception of English civilization, for it to be ignored.

But Churchill was as volatile on these matters as on all else, and there were moments during his time at the Colonial Office when he spoke in quite different tones. Military engagement against an insurgent army of 'fakirs' was one thing, conforming to an inherited, aristocratic martial spirit and, as Churchill saw things, necessary for the defence of the crown. In other circumstances, indiscriminate 'butchery of natives' could prove an outrage to him, exhibiting a wanton savagery which was inimical to the codes of Christian civilization. Yet as we have seen, timing is relevant, for Churchill uttered his warnings about the perils of black uprisings in the aftermath of the South African War itself, when white fears in South Africa seem to have been at their most febrile, and when these fears appear to have touched more deeply the colonial mentality in Britain as well.

There are two particular episodes which have entered the historiography: the events of June and July 1904 in the Transvaal, and the more significant occasion in Natal in 1906. The first of these can be understood as *une grande peur* of classically Lefebvrian dimensions. According to the historian of the episode, Jeremy Krikler, 'a considerable fear of impending black revolt swept through the Transvaal', though any verifiable incidents of black rebellion proved to be non-existent. These realities notwithstanding, the forces of the state were mobilized to counter the perceived uprising. What is relevant here is Krikler's explanation for the panic. The key element for him is the prior activities of blacks. He identifies an authentic 'peasant war' having erupted in the Transvaal during the war, which came close, he argues, to shattering the Boer states and bringing Afrikaner landlords as a class 'to the edge of utter destruction'. This experience, he suggests, proved so deeply traumatic that the collective memory of it remained repressed, subsequently breaking out in unexpected forms, in 'irrational, seemingly impenetrable, phenomena such as the panic of 1904'.[84] This manner of explanation is not without its critics. But it is important in suggesting the intensity of racial fear in the aftermath of war.

The second episode was triggered by the imposition of a poll tax on all adult males in Natal. In February 1906 officials at the Colonial Office learnt that two white policemen had been killed in disturbances arising from protests against the new taxes. The consequences took on horrific proportions. Between February and August some three and a half thousand to four thousand black people were killed, as were some twenty-four white men, though no white women and children were harmed, and white property went largely unscathed. By the end of March, one official at the Colonial Office was comparing the scope of the Natal crisis to that of Morant Bay in Jamaica forty years earlier.[85] It was while confronted with this crisis that Churchill issued his warnings quoted above, and in condemning the 'disgusting butchery of natives' he was directly attacking the Natal government. Nevertheless, it is clear that the anxieties which were burning through the white mentalities of Natal and the Transvaal also registered in the thinking of the Colonial Office and the metropolitan government. It was true as much of the secretary of state, Lord Elgin, as it was of Churchill. Indeed, writing of the Colonial Office in this period, Ronald Hyam concludes: 'One of the most remarkable facts about the treatment of the native problem is that it was consistently discussed within the context of apprehended native risings against Europeans.'[86]

The moment of the Transvaal and Natal panics was a time when racial fears were quickly amplified through the institutions of public opinion. F. E. Colenso, writing from Natal at the height of the crisis, published a short booklet in London attacking the 'lucubrations of English journalists' who, 'under the head of the "Black Peril"', propagated the view that 'the outlying districts of Natal are as dangerous as the Sioux-infested backwoods of Fenimore Cooper's novels'. 'The actual experience of the Natal colonist is uniformly fatal to that theory of peril to the Whites, which has proved in the past to be so fatal to the Blacks.' Colenso went on to condemn 'the para-lysing effect of an atmosphere of panic' in the mind of the white authori-ties.[87] But such interventions carried little purchase.

One such 'lucubration' had come a little while earlier from Roderick Jones in *The Nineteenth Century and After*. Roderick Jones had been a Reuters correspondent in South Africa, and was a close friend to both John Buchan and Jan Smuts. Titled simply 'The Black Peril in South Africa' it dwelt on the problem of the black voter in the Cape. The argument was unswerving. The 'Kafir', according to Jones, had become a decisive electoral force in the Cape, and the white parties, dictated by short-term opportunism, were doing all they could to accommodate black demands in order to win black votes; unprincipled practices of this sort on the part of white politicians encouraged the 'deficient behaviour of the natives of the Cape', in which they compared unfavourably to the black inhabitants of the Transvaal. In the longer term, the black peril turned on demographics. When the black elec-torate increased it would, by sheer force of numbers, bring with it 'the edi-fying spectacle of black men ruling whites—surely a weird conceit of fortune'. 'The solitary ray of sunshine', suggested Jones, lay in the emerging alliance between 'the Englishman and the Dutchman', while the only pos-sible solution required 'the white man rigorously excluding the native from political power, and strenuously discountenancing anything like social equality between the two races'. 'At present', he concluded, 'the white man is nursing a snake in his bosom'.[88]

In the aftermath of the war public debate in South Africa and in London became preoccupied with the means by which the new nation could properly become 'a white man's country'. And this may account, in part, for the greater visibility of non-white peoples in postwar public debate, at least in Britain. With the arrival of the first batch of indentured Chinese labourers in Durban in June 1904, the ethnic mix became yet more complex. The Indian population was large, skilfully organized in Natal by Gandhi. Black Africans, Chinese, Indians: South Africa gave every indication of resisting all endeavour to transform it into a properly white nation. Churchill, in pondering the future of the white populations of east Africa, viewed South Africa as a model at all costs to be avoided: 'A vast army of African labourers, officered by educated Indians or Chinese, and directed by a few individuals of diverse nationalities employing cosmopolitan capital—that is the nightmare which haunts the white population of South Africa.'[89] Elgin, Churchill's senior at the Colonial Office, saw 'the risk of multiplying what we call white men's countries, where there are a very small number of whites in the midst of an overwhelming number of blacks'.[90] Roderick Jones quoted Balfour and Lord Grey to the same effect.[91] And one can legitimately assume that he knew Milner's Watch Tower speech of 18 May 1903, in which Milner himself attempted to resolve the nature of a 'white man's country' and think through the logistics of a programme of 'white supremacy'.[92] This question—of what constituted a white man's country—lay close to the heart of the British colonial imagination in the first decade of the century. And as a result, as we have seen in previous chapters when confronting the predicament of the white man 'under siege', projections of South Africa became locked into wider fears. Within the white imagination, 'the black peril' had a tendency to acquire a momentum greater than itself, to slip out of its given habitat and to join hands with myriad other spectres. At a point on the distant horizon it released the greatest fear of all: that the epochal dominance of the white races was drawing to a close. In the volume of *The Nineteenth Century* in which Roderick Jones's polemic was published, there occurred within just six months two articles on 'The Yellow Peril', one on 'A White Australia' and another, by Sir Harry Johnston, on 'The White Man's Place in Africa'. Debate about the historic denouement of 'the Caucasian' was further heightened the following year, when the Japanese forces secured victory over Russia. In a highly fantasized scenario Johnston concluded: 'The news of the Japanese success was discussed in the souks of Morocco, the mosques of Egypt and the coffee-houses of Turkey, in Indian bazaars and African mud-houses. It was the first set-back of the Caucasian since the Neolithic period.'[93]

The racial logic which generated such perspectives, as in Australia, also created the ideal of an ethnically homogeneous nation. Whiteness, too, became the sign of what a new nation should be. When Australia's prime minister Andrew Fisher travelled to the new state of South Africa at the end of 1910 he noted that the Union 'could never become in the Australian sense, a white man's country. It must always be a black man's country, ruled over by an aristocracy of white labour.'[94] This was a partisan view, exhibiting the chauvinism of a devotee of White Australia. Yet fundamentally South Africa was abnormal only to the degree that it was there that this ethnic predicament was at its most dramatic and at its most irresolvable.[95] And for this reason the question of whiteness came characteristically to be mediated through the racial optic of South Africa.

English memories

At this point I can draw the threads of the argument together and reflect on some of the more prominent shifts in perception. There is a specific generational memory, principally of those who served in the South African War, but also—less intensely—of those who witnessed the campaign through the domestic media, either as adults or children. Churchill the young journalist, though playing fast and loose with the formalities demanded by the War Office, could be taken as representative of the former. As an example of the latter one might think of Clement Attlee, a decade younger than Churchill. Attlee's personal ties to South Africa were never immediate, but his loyalty to the imperatives of empire was unassailable, and in this the war of 1899–1902 played a part. According to his enthusiastic biographer, 'At home, at Haileybury and at Oxford, Attlee breathed the ...welcome air of loyalty to, and pride in, Queen and Country. It was in his lungs, from the days of his first memory of the outside world...' At school during the war he and his jingoistic peers felt cheated that their pro-Boer headmaster denied the pupils a holiday to celebrate the relief of Ladysmith. The boys took matters into their own hands, skipped classes, and paraded through Hertford and Ware in support of the empire. For this they were thrashed, an outcome which Attlee himself believed (as one would expect of him) to be 'without doubt the proper thing to do'.[96] To look at things from this perspective, one can see how the later alliance between Churchill and Attlee in 1940 was, on essentials, cemented by a long history. Party politics may have divided them but a shared recognition of ethnic loyalties created a deeper affiliation.

Churchill could not accept Attlee as 'a man with whom it is agreeable to dine'.[97] However on nation and empire he was sound.

But these direct memories and sensibilities, and the way they worked themselves into the larger culture, appear to have been relatively circumscribed. The South African War has only recently moved out of living memory. What is believed to have been the last surviving white combatant died only in 1993, on the eve of Nelson Mandela's inauguration as president, while a Channel 4 film made six years later interviewed a woman who had been interned by the British, and a number of others who recalled the impact of the war on their childhoods.[98] Yet it is notable that Churchill himself, in his final years, rarely seems to have reminisced about his early adventures in South Africa. In a life in which every last detail has been recorded with fetishistic brio, it is revealing that there are no recorded allusions to South Africa in his last ten or fifteen years. His deep regard for Smuts, who died in 1950, provided his last emotional link. One of the last of his memories was recorded in September 1940, during the Battle of Britain, when (by comparison with contemporary events) he could recall his time in South Africa as a romance: 'Towards bedtime the P.M. very animated, reminisced about the South African War (the last enjoyable war, he called it) and the beauties of the Veld.'[99] This reticence, I think, was common.[100] The reason is clear enough, and it was noted by Churchill in the memoirs he penned in the 1930s. The majority of those who served in South Africa, and who survived, were to die in the war of 1914–18. 'The South African War accounted for a large proportion not only of my friends but of my company; and the Great War killed almost all the others.'[101] Memories of the Boer War in the imagined community of the British came to be overshadowed by the nightmare of the First World War. The imperial glories of the opening year of the war in South Africa barely survived nearly two years of relentless counter-insurgency, in which set-piece battles gave way to blockhouses, barbed wire, and the public scandal of the internment camps for Afrikaner women and children, in which many thousands died; they certainly could not be embraced with the same innocence after the slaughters of the Western Front.[102] As in the aftermath of many other wars, those who survived were forced to remember in silence.

But other transactions were at work. In 1915 D. H. Lawrence published *The Rainbow*. In telling the story of the Brangwens, Lawrence created an imaginative world in the middle of provincial England, a verdant, redbrick

landscape hemmed in by coal-pits and small farms. At a critical moment in
the novel Anton Skrebensky returns from active service in the South African
War, on leave before being posted to India. He travels to Nottingham to
meet again with Ursula Brangwen. They take a tram to the outer limits of
the town, and in the darkness walk along the River Trent.

> Then in a low, vibrating voice he told her about Africa, the strange darkness,
> the strange, blood fear.
>
> 'I am not afraid of the darkness in England,' he said. 'It is soft, and natural
> to me, it is my medium, especially when you are here. But in Africa it seems
> massive and fluid with terror—not fear of anything—just fear. One breathes
> it, really, like the smell of blood. The blacks know it. They worship it, really, the
> darkness. One almost likes it—the fear—something sensual.'
>
> She thrilled again to him. He was to her a voice out of the darkness. He
> talked to her all the while, in low tones, about Africa, conveying something
> strange and sensual to her: the negro, with his loose, soft passion that could
> envelop one like a bath. Gradually he transferred to her the hot, fecund dark-
> ness that possessed his own blood.[103]

It is tempting, perhaps, to move quickly on from this passage, for it fulfils all
the expectations which a contemporary reader is likely to have of Lawrence's
prose. But the abruptness of the entry of Africa and of Negro masculinity—
so heavily overdetermined that the syntax strains—into Ursula's life, and
into the middle of England itself, is genuinely shocking. The passage draws
from a conventional symbolic repertoire, which is familiar enough; it drives
these themes forward. What it also suggests, however, is the manner in which
Lawrence himself had come to remember the South African War: not as a
confrontation between two white peoples, but as blackness unleashed, signifying passion, terror, and blood.

Or from the same moment, we can see a similar manifestation of the
same phenomenon:

> I dreamed that I was in a sub-tropical country, separated from my friends,
> standing alone in a small shack or shed which was open on one side so that
> I looked out on a wide open space surrounded by bush or scrub. In the edge
> of the bush I could see a number of savages armed with spears and the long
> pointed shields used by some South African native tribes. They occupied the
> whole extent of the bush-edge abutting on the open space, but they showed
> no sign of active hostility. I myself had a loaded rifle, but realized that I was
> quite unable to escape in face of the number of armed savages who blocked
> the way.

Then my wife appeared in the open space, dressed entirely in white, and advanced towards me quite unhindered by the savages, of whom she seemed unaware. Before she reached me the dream, which up to then had been singularly clear and vivid, became confused, and though there was some suggestion that I fired the rifle, but with no knowledge of who or what I fired at, I awoke.

These are the memories of Arthur Tansley, then working at the Ministry of Munitions, who, inspired by the impact of this dream, subsequently devoted his professional life to psychoanalysis.[104]

These modes of remembering South Africa were particular. They did not always pertain. But they represented also, patently, a way of forgetting. Within the culture of domestic Britain public testaments to the war have become ever-more random, manifestations of broken memories which carry only the merest echo of former historical realities: the Kop at Anfield Road; street-names resonating with the aura of distant places— Bloemfontein, Mafeking, Pretoria—or honouring the ghosts of once-famous generals; snatches of popular songs or of Kipling; arcane rituals in the dwindling bands of organized youth movements.[105] Of the great number of memorials erected throughout Britain to the fallen soldiers of the war—of which there were over 900—many or most have since been destroyed or vandalized, or fallen into disrepair.[106] Or as a sharp-eyed observer commented in 1959: 'A street here, and old second-hand book there, and vague memories are sometimes kindled by a name.'[107] This is a process of forgetting which has been institutionalized. One vignette provides a clue. In 1941, thirty-nine years after the end of the South African War and twenty-seven years after his death, Madame Tussaud's decided the time had come to remove the waxwork figure of Lord Roberts from its exhibition.[108] Was this a matter of any concern? Who now notices the life-size statue of him astride his horse which still dominates Glasgow's Kelvingrove? Who now remembers him?

To what degree these memory-traces have organized the cultural force-field for later generations, who witnessed nothing of these early dramas of South Africa, must remain an open question. The range of experience is too variable for a consistent answer. But in one respect, for all his manifold singularities, Lawrence was symptomatic, for the narratives emanating from southern Africa did become charged by the idea of blackness. We can look, for example, at one image which recurs: that of the assegai, and its associated symbolism.

As we have seen Conan Doyle could claim in passing that 'once the assegais were reddened no man could say how far the mischief might go'. In this single image an inchoate set of racial fears became condensed. It appeared, as we have seen, in Winston Churchill's earliest memories. It appeared too in the unhappy denouement of the relationship of Kitty Jewell and Peter Lobengula. In January 1902, when Kitty Jewell found herself in the probate court seeking a divorce on grounds of cruelty and adultery, she was asked by Sir Francis Jeune, the president of the divorce division: 'Did he stab you with an assegai?' To which Kitty responded: 'He did.'[109]

The term itself, significantly, seems to have been a colonial invention, stemming from Berber origins. When fighting flared between British and Zulu in Natal in 1879, *The Times* referred on 29 March to 'the dreaded assegai', a moment in British history reconstituted for later generations by Stanley Baker and Michael Caine in the 1964 movie, *Zulu*. A year later, in F. E. Colenso's history of the war, a Zulu combatant was quoted as reporting that a number of British soldiers 'were nearly all assegaied'.[110] The image recurs again in the 1890s. The illustrated press in the metropole—*The Graphic* and *The Illustrated London News*—turned these images into something of a convention.[111] A churchman assured the world that 'the gradual substitution of the rifle for the stabbing assegai will directly diminish bloodshed'.[112] Bertram Mitford's popular novel of 1894—*The King's Assegai: A Matabili Story*—is, as the title suggests, devoted to the 'romance' of the king's 'splendid specimen of an assegai'. In Baden-Powell's account of his campaign in Matabeleland the themes of war-dances and assegais run through the narrative. The frontispiece, directly echoing Stanley Wood's illustrations to Mitford's novel, shows, according to Baden-Powell, 'A Matabele warrior making disparaging remarks', armed with an assegai. He explains further, 'The enemy would come out on the rocks before a fight, and dance and work themselves into a frenzy, shouting all sorts of epithets and insults at the troops.' A decade later, after the crisis in Natal, the image is to be seen again. The indefatigable Mitford published two novels on the theme—*Forging the Blades: A Tale of the Zulu Rebellion*, in which one chapter concerns the making of assegais; and *The White Hand and the Black*.[113] Much later, in 1933, Noel Coward's movie *Cavalcade* fused together, with no apparent need for comment and as if from nowhere, memories of the South African War with the image of the assegai.

We might think too of the manner in which this image of black warfare comes, through a process of transculturation or cultural transference, to inhabit a different position within white cultures. White South African soldiers at Delville Wood on the Somme in the First World War blacked up, and mimicked Zulu war-cries and dances, relishing their reputation as *les zulus blancs*.[114] Until its final days in 1979–80 the British South African Police in Rhodesia carried as its insignia an image of a lion rampant with an assegai lodged in its chest.[115] Or it can occur in more domestic mode. Maybe something of the sort can be discerned in the boy scout movement.[116] Smuts kept a collection of assegais in his library on his farmstead.[117] One oral source from England recounts an assegai hanging above the mantelpiece in the front room as he was growing up in the 1950s and 1960s as a child in the West Midlands—a curious, menacing object, disconnected from any known historical realities, but nevertheless signifying an unsettling idea of racial difference.[118] In 1964 a social historian could look back to the Festival of Britain of 1951 and claim that it marked the end 'of the stifling weight of Victorian grandeur, a clearing out of the last of the Wolseley helmets, Zulu assegais, and the faded Edwardian plush from the national attic'.[119] This may suggest too stark a periodization, though there can be little doubt that that the power of these memories diminished in the postwar world. By 1960 Tony Hancock, contemplating where to emigrate, was put off by the idea of South Africa as he 'didn't fancy being chased down the Mall' by irate natives armed with assegais.[120] Like other formalities of empire, the recollection was becoming less a conscious memory than a memory-trace, its disturbance screened as a joke.[121]

As memories of the South African War attenuated, or dissolved, in the metropole, other memories—prior memories of blackness—intervened. For a population in the metropole who did not know South Africa, a set of meanings about race became attached to very particular images. These were images which could echo, in quite different circumstances, in the future. The idea of the assegai provides one example of a process which short-circuited historical realities, connecting different historical times and geographies, and thus unifying distinct historical episodes. To recognize such images was to know the African, which in turn confirmed the truth of a history which *already* was known in its essentials. It represents a mental procedure which is entirely self-confirming. In mythic terms, the image of the assegai became good to think with. It generated its own stories, creating the means by which a colonial imagination could hold in place the anxieties arising from the passions of racial difference.

John Buchan

'You ask me if I never long for Africa. Indeed I do. I have never got Africa out of my bones.'[122] Thus John Buchan in a letter to his son in 1935, more than thirty years after he had left South Africa. Buchan loved South Africa. To the end of his life it shaped the ways in which he imagined himself. But it was also a psychic projection imbued with loss, longing, and disappointment.

Buchan was a man of many talents, able, it seemed, to turn his hand to anything. He wrote over a hundred books—novels, histories, biographies, screenplays, a published author who had entered *Who's Who* before he had even arrived at Oxford. G. M. Trevelyan believed his biography of Walter Scott to be the 'best one-volume biography in the language', while his 24-volume history of the First World War *The Edinburgh Review* ranked with the histories of Lord Macaulay.[123] From relatively humble origins, he quickly came to move amongst those who were at the very apex of the imperial state, on terms of relaxed intimacy with the most powerful and influential figures in the land. His father was a Free Church minister who, in 1886, moved to Unionism in response to Home Rule and to the death of General Gordon. He married into the mainstream of the aristocracy, Henry James, it seems, persuading the family of the bride-to-be that Buchan was a good catch.[124] He was a respected politician and administrator, the personification of the great and the good which proved so integral to the organization of the British state in this period. He was adept at all manner of country activities. He had, by all accounts, a gift for friendship. And he ended his days as governor-general of Canada, drafting in the final moments of his life a book on angling which remained unfinished.

He was a Tory but, like many of his generation, not a party man. An older radicalism, inherited from his father's Liberalism and commitment to the Free Church, was still evident through his political life. Like all good Tories boasting a heretical daring, he befriended the socialist Clydesider MPs. He held views on the socialization of the economy which later generations in his party (and not only in his party) would regard as unspeakably revolutionary. He thought democracy 'an attitude of mind' and found J. B. Priestley's 'political creed very much the same as mine'.[125] He didn't much like the culture which accompanied the advance of material prosperity for the masses, but resisted the temptation to damn all progress. He attempted some rather enlightened forays into the aesthetics of modernism, though he was the first to admit that more often than not he retreated, baffled by all he had confronted—an encounter in which he was not helped by a long correspondence with Ezra Pound, which puzzled him yet more. He was a man of learning, whose genuine intellectual curiosity instilled in him a rather attractive degree of modesty.

However, underpinning all was an immovable commitment to empire, 'the data of our politics', whose 'well-being is, like the monarchy, an axiom of all sane political creeds'.[126] On this he was implacable. The line dividing virtue from vice was not determined, for him, by party politics but by the perceived requirements of the British state and, closely interconnected, by the complex of lived experience and affiliations encoded in the dynamics of ethnic belonging.

Buchan was simultaneously Scottish-national and British-imperial in a manner not easily understood a century later. He never forgot his Scottishness, especially its literature and landscape, which nourished his allegiance long after he had ceased to live in Scotland. Scotland, imagined most of all through Sir Walter Scott, had just enough of the frontier about it to resonate with his adult experiences of South Africa and Canada, memories of each enfolding one into the other. Scotland instilled in this Tory Unionist his residual radicalism; it mitigated a narrow parochialism which dominated the lives of many of his English Tory colleagues, allowing him to override divisions which to him appeared merely of secondary significance; and it created in him sympathy for the emergent colonial nationalism of the new dominions, connected to the metropole through ties of ethnicity rather than by shared national identity.

But the move south to England got to him. (Or as Tom Nairn might put this, Buchan was party to his own self-colonization.) It was Oxford which 'enabled me to discover Scotland', a discovery which occurred, more specifically, at Brasenose College, of which he wrote: 'There is nothing in the land more English than Brasenose.'[127] His sense of the past, as 'the matrix of present and future', increasingly took on an English hue.[128] At Oxford and in its surrounding landscape he unearthed 'the drama of England'.[129] In a moment of despair during the First World War he tramped through the Cotswolds, returning 'with the conviction that the essential England could not perish. This field had sent bowmen to Agincourt; down the hill Rupert's men, swaying in their saddles, had fled after Naseby; this village had given Wellington a general; and from another a parson's son had helped to turn the tide in the Indian Mutiny.'[130] After the war, still dogged by despair, he purchased 'the little manor house' of Elsfield, four miles north of Oxford, in a bid to imbibe the historical truths of the nation which he saw inscribed in the landscape, a history which would bring with it, he believed, 'the dignity of repose'. 'England is full of patches which the tides of modernity have somehow missed, and Elsfield was such an one.'[131] Increasingly, Buchan's use of the first-person plural loses precision, the narrative of the British sliding into that of the English.

Yet the closer he came to the power-centres of the state, the more disturbed and anxious he appeared to be. This is apparent in both his public and private writings. In the photographs of him, in all the extravagant finery he was required to wear as a symbol of his great offices, we see a man ill at ease with himself. Those born to such heights cultivate a habit of quietly ridiculing the vulgar masquerades required of them, power and irony inextricably one; Buchan, an arriviste in this sense, strove to take them seriously.[132]

There are a number of possible explanations for this unease. For all the reflex references to a blissfully happy marriage, and to the pleasure he took in bringing up his children, there are too many silences, too many references to long periods of unexplained confinements, and too many hints of swathes of private unhappiness. On this it is not possible to say more, for the published autobiographical and biographical details remain too circumspect.

An alternative explanation is that his final post in Ottawa represented a kind of exile from the real centres of power, and that he died an isolated figure.[133] There is some truth in this, even though there is evidence of an underlying unease in his life from long before the Ottawa posting. Whatever the regiments of Buchan apologists may claim, it is blindingly clear that the man himself craved public honours. Nor could proconsular duties in Canada compare for him to South Africa or India, where his ambitions pointed. Yet during his time in Canada he was in close contact with successive sovereigns; he had the ear of the most senior of British and Canadian politicians; he struck up an intimacy with Franklin D. Roosevelt—listening to 'negro spirituals and plantation songs' in the White House after dinner; he became the first British citizen to address Congress; and in the realm of letters, he was honoured by Yale University in the company of Walt Disney, albeit with Thomas Mann in tow. This is a strange marginalization.[134]

A slightly different inflection, however, would provide a different sort of answer. It may be nearer the truth to suppose that worldly preferment could not offer him the consolation he desired. It is not that he never reached the centre of things. On the contrary, he got there fast only to find that the privileges it bestowed of little consequence. To say this is to take account of the Calvinism in which he was reared. Here indeed was a man who strove hard for fame and fortune, driven to acquire such things. But the more these came his way the less enchanting each became, bequeathing to him both public splendour and inner loneliness. The civilization which formed him ethically, and which he served so assiduously, he also found at a profound level to be wanting, even at times disturbing.

There are two issues here. First, South Africa and the idea of the frontier stayed with him. As he claimed, it was there that he had first become a citizen and first discovered a politics. On this matter his proconsular sentiments were entirely conventional: decay at the centre, vitality on the frontier. On the frontier, imperial ideals could be lived in their truest form, the civilizing potential of the white race bringing order to chaos, unencumbered by self-interest. The incompleteness of civilization on the frontier was its virtue. Conversely, loss of direction in the heartlands of empire left the metropole exposed to new and sinister internal enemies, the edifice of civilized life continuously threatening to tip into chaos. On the frontier the duty of the white man was clear, determined by the proximity of barbarism. In urban Britain, although there were manifold dangers, they could not as easily be *seen*: the duties required to maintain this urban civilization of the British always appeared to Buchan to be more complex, to be muddied or compromised. Agitators could go about their business mingling with 'the ordinary people', while intellectuals, given to all manner of abstraction, reaped confusion. The invisibility of these dangers invited an authoritarianism powerful enough to seek them out and ensure their extirpation, a theme which impresses itself in Buchan's prose. But at the same time, his liberal instincts balked. As a counterpoint, he projected onto an imaginary frontier, and back into his own young manhood, the simplicities of a life which he believed to be vanishing.

Second, as for his entire generation, the experience of total war called into question Europe itself. A younger brother died in the first war ('He was one of those people who seemed to have been born especially for the Great War'), as did a number of close friends.[135] He was sure that as a result of the First World War 'the pillars of civilization were cracking and tilting'.[136] In his fiction, he offered two different interpretations of this failure of Europe—though neither could quite (in Conradian mode) make the link with colonialism. His novel, *The Three Hostages*, published in 1924, marked his first attempt to think through in public—in fictional form—the catastrophe of total war. Its speculations were not analytically sophisticated. Its tone was close to the cosy bonhomie of the speeches of his friend, Stanley Baldwin, which resembled not so much the sentiments of the saloon bar as those of the Savoy Grill.[137] The characters in the novel seemed sure enough that civilization (as they perceived it) was on the point of becoming unhinged. The key insights derived from the character of Dr Greenslade, whose monologic perceptions of the world about him, given credence by his professional accreditation, were so accomplished that he deserves to be better known.

> Original sin [he claimed] is always there, but the meaning of civilization was that we had got it battened down under the hatches, whereas now it's getting its head up. But it isn't only sin. It's dislocation of the mechanisms of human reasoning, a general loosening of the screws.

Or again:

> The barriers between the conscious and the subconscious have always been pretty stiff in the average man. But now with the general loosening of the screws they are growing shaky and the two worlds are getting mixed...That is why I say you can't any longer take the clear psychology of most civilized beings for granted. Something is welling up from the primeval deeps to muddy it.

This peroration was concluded with the observation that 'all the contemporary anarchisms' are connected.[138] Echoes of such thinking, in which 'the average man' seems to have things screwed up pretty tightly, are not unheard in our own times. But this is an intriguing position. This voice of John Buchan's—he spoke on other occasions in other idioms—was the voice of an unbridled anti-modernity. It represented the mirror-image of a cultural leftism of the period which did indeed try to connect, as he might have seen it, all the 'contemporary anarchisms' of the time—Bolshevism and the aesthetic avant-garde, psychoanalysis and primitivism—in order, exactly, to lift the lid and loosen the screws. The devastating effect of the war gave these 'anarchisms', Buchan believed, intellectual credence. In consequence, his was a conception of civilization beset by foes at every turn, even at its very centre.

Later, though, he offered a less colloquial, less breezy view of these issues. In 1941 his final novel was published, *Sick Heart River*, drafted in Canada, but written with an eye to the catastrophes taking place in Europe. It offers, for those who care to read it in this way, a redemptive denouement. But this, as I see it, is not entirely convincing. An altogether bleaker imaginative construct lies at the centre of the narrative. In it, Buchan portrayed an aged hero who underwent an authentic collapse, losing all faith in his 'philosophy'. In a moment of feverish despair, 'Memories of the war in which he had fought raced before him like a cinema show'. Europe he saw as a 'carnage pit'. 'The effluence of death seemed to be wafted to his nostrils over the many thousand miles of land and sea. He smelt the stench of incinerators and muddy trenches and bloody clothing.' The action of the novel takes place in the arctic wastelands of Canada, which—distance notwithstanding—seemed compromised by the extent of the barbarism dominating far-off Europe. Indeed, it was only an odyssey to the far north of the country—'a part of the globe which had no care for human life'—that permitted a new faith to be constituted.[139] By the time Buchan came to write the novel the frontier could only retain its purity by repudiating all that was human. Civilization and social organization seem inevitably to reproduce death and disorder. Yet the uninterrupted whiteness of the frozen landscape offers a strange comment on the ethical imperatives of the frontier, as if this absolute whiteness simultaneously signified absolution and annihilation. This not only hints at the impossibility of whiteness, but of civilization itself.

These have not exactly been the issues around which contemporary controversies about Buchan have turned. Current opinion seems less concerned about the paradoxes and impossibilities of his faith in colonial civilization, and more about the degree to which (in contemporary terms) he was, or was not, a democratic being. The debate is simple enough. In 1953 Richard Usborne published a study of the fictional adventurers of early twentieth-century Britain, *Clubland Heroes*. In it he condemned Buchan for anti-Semitism, and for purveying all the prejudices of the British upper class of the period.[140] This was followed, in 1960, by an article by Gertrude Himmelfarb in *Encounter* who also took issue with his anti-Semitism.[141] A counter-attack then occurred, against these authors in particular, and against what was perceived to be a growing groundswell of popular hostility to Buchan and to his books. This was led by David Daniell, who published an article in order to demonstrate that Buchan was not 'a fascist shit'.[142] It runs through the meticulous biography written by Andrew

Lownie which, for all its desperation to remain even-handed, is peppered with apologies and, amongst other things, is at pains to show that Buchan's heroes are properly heterosexual.[143] And it can be seen in a more unexpected quarter where we find David Cannadine, not known for his courtesy to Westminster toffs, insisting that Buchan, Baldwin and Sir Edward Grey were three of the most 'significant exemplars of inter-war decency'.[144] The odd thing about this chronology is not that Buchan's defenders have moved into the fray, but rather the fact that for the past forty or fifty years barely a hostile word has been published about him.[145] Indeed, he has been recuperated as the rational, civilized gentleman, secure in the grip of his own inner life, while chaotic irrationalisms and bigotries stalked the world around him.

It is the dualism of this debate which is most unconvincing. The key term, and the most problematic, is civilization. Buchan did indeed personify the urbane civilization of his caste—scholarly and gentlemanly, hostile to fascism when he saw what it entailed and, for the many who admired him, far from being a shit. Within the terms of this social code, Cannadine is right to emphasize Buchan's decency, just as he is right about Baldwin. But here we need to be reminded of the ways in which cultured, civilized norms, at the same time as being cultured and civilized, reproduce modes of authority and structures of exclusion and inclusion, which compose the essentials of what Fanon identified as a peculiarly Manichaean 'delirium'. We need to ask, simply, how the norms of British imperial culture worked when confronted by alternative conceptions of civilization, in which what was 'essentially British' was perceived as offering a view of human conduct which was less than universally benign? For the ethnic absolutism inscribed in the very heart of British imperial culture—an absolutism which reproduced with understated ease confirmation of the *rightness* of the British—carried heavy costs, and jeopardized the civilizing project itself. It is not as if the decent folk, the Buchans and the Baldwins, stood on one side, and the cads and bigots on the other. That is to remain too fixed within the prescriptions of the culture itself. On the contrary, the exertions necessary to realize a civilization appropriate for the white man ensured that decency became impossibly imbricated in the pathological drive to exclude and subordinate. In this Buchan, for all the seemingly contradictory interpretations of his life, is representative of his larger culture. And so too is Churchill. His 'uncontrollable complex' was not his alone.

The totem of the white man

In his novels John Buchan revealingly describes the idealized fiction of the white man as a 'totem'. Or as I argued this in the last chapter, the white man was an identification which could only work in the imagination, as a fantasy. But these fictions, or imaginative acts, were played out in historical reality. The truth of these fictions—imagined but real—had demonstrable, determinate consequences.

Buchan's popular novels, I argue, were devoted to exploring the protocols of the white man. To a contemporary reader it might seem as if these explorations were only of minor historical significance, removed from the domain of 'real' politics, that is, from the workings of the state. Their resolutely vernacular dispositions might encourage us to pass them by with some dispatch. But as I indicated earlier, there is no reason to assume that the rhetorics of high politics and the imaginative structures of popular fiction were unconnected. On the contrary one of the novelties of the popular culture which emerged at the time of the South African War was precisely its capacity to transform the sphere of politics itself. For this reason I emphasized the interconnections between literary fiction, popular as much as highbrow, commercial journalism, and political treatise, suggesting that they could all share the same imaginative space and, on occasion, the same authors. Indeed, the kind of fictions we encounter in the popular novels can be found operating in the 'real' world of politics. This can be illustrated.

If we turn to accounts of the recruitment of colonial officers, for example, from the beginning of the twentieth century we can see that there existed highly elaborate, highly codified expectations about the manner in which the potential recruit, about to be transmogrified into a white man on the imperial frontier, should conduct himself.[146] The clearest expression occurs in the memoirs of Sir Ralph Furse, who virtually single-handedly organized overseas colonial recruitment from 1910 to 1948. By the time he retired, it was likely that every senior administrator in every British colony had been recruited by him. His recollections were published in 1962, and they represent an extraordinary distillation of the temper of colonial civilization of these years, and of the masculine institutions which endeavoured to ensure its reproduction. Whiteness, as such, is not spoken; nor, in the heartlands of Whitehall, would one expect it to be. We know all the characters are white, as Toni Morrison might have put it, because no one tells us.

But without the centring of whiteness the memoir could not work as it does. The very obviousness of whiteness as truth precludes its articulation, its silence a condition of its operation. Furse's reminiscences carry a fore-word by Lord Salisbury ('Bobbety', whom we shall meet again in a later chapter, in less tranquil posture, as an agitator on the outer reaches of a Conservative party confronted by precipitate decolonization, and as found-ing spirit of the Monday Club). Salisbury informs the reader that he was Furse's fag at Eton, and that never a kindlier soul existed. Furse himself recounts the influence of the histories of J. R. Seeley on his childhood, and his growing reverence for Lord Milner and Leo Amery. He reconstructs with undisguised passion a world (he called it England) which revolved around the male public schools (Eton pre-eminently), Oxford and Cambridge (though Oxford more than Cambridge), the military, and the civil service. In this there occurs an astonishingly sensual evocation of All Souls of Oxford University which represented, as Furse saw it, the undis-puted apogee of masculine thought and refinement. This was a world supremely at one with itself. Difference barely impinges. Ethnicity is affirmed only in its silences, for those who cross the magic threshold and enter the colonial civil service, destined to manage ethnic others, inevitably, necessarily, conform to the unspoken imperatives of race. The feminine is duly circumscribed, though an anxiety registers that maybe *not enough*. Complaining of the predominance of female intellectuals of empire in the 1930s and 1940s (he cites Margery Perham, Elspeth Huxley, and Rita Hinden), Furse allows himself to record the opinion that 'It is no disparage-ment to the ladies to regard this abstention of the masculine intellect as unhealthy'.[147]

Through his professional life, Furse was obliged to discriminate between those candidates who made the grade, and those who did not; and amongst those who did, to ensure that the most able were placed in the most chal-lenging situations. He prided himself on the thoroughness, open-minded-ness, and lack of preferment with which he went about his business. He liked to think of himself as something of a specialist in the matter of the human personality. And one way of understanding what his business *was* is to see it as assessing the claims of various applicants to be a white man. In the fiction of the time, straightness of character and an open countenance were registered in the physiognomy and, for those with the power to tell, the value of a man could be surmised in an instant, merely 'by the look of him'.[148] Furse worked by such principles though, scrupulous to the last, he was always careful to guard against his own first impressions. He offers the following account:

> Then there was a very intelligent and able young man who on coming in gave me the tips of his fingers in a languid handshake. The interview revealed nothing against him, but those limp fingers worried me. We were considering him for Palestine where intelligence was certainly needed but so was toughness. When he hung out his fingers to say good-bye I slipped my hand forward and gripped his whole hand. His palm was hard as nails. I put him in and he proved a success.[149]

Of a further applicant he wrote: 'A really admirable man, strong, looks one straight in the face'. Of another, less convincing candidate, he noted this:

> Tall, light-haired, slim but well-built...a good open face with a good deal of grit in it...a very good athlete...brains I expect fair...a fourth [i.e., a fourth class degree]...but had influenza just before. He had a slightly affected way of shaking hands...but made a good impression and is I think really up to [the] East African standard.[150]

Many such stories are told, all alluding to the author's professional perspicacity. In telling these tales, the imaginative ideals of what a white man is begin to take shape, and a certain familiarity is invoked—a certain shared sense of where 'we', the author and his imagined reader, belong. We can also grasp here the fictions of whiteness, in which the truths incubated in the genre of imperial romance crossed over to the practices of the state. Many of those who joined the colonial civil service in the 1930s did so, by their own accounts, because of the influence of the cinema (*Sanders of the River* was particularly cited) and of the novels by such authors as G. A. Henty.[151]

These, clearly, are specific modes of imagining the configurations of white masculinity, exuding an air of class superiority which is entirely absent from the anxious appeals to the rights of the white male worker which I discussed at the end of Chapter 2. Yet echoes of this voice can still be heard in the literature today. Andrew Lownie, in the most recent biography of John Buchan, gives this account, with no hint that he is describing anything unusual:

> Each of Buchan's sons would go up to different colleges at Oxford. Johnnie had never been particularly academic at school and had obtained poor results in his School Certificate. It was only at his second attempt that he became a member of his father's old college, where he took up rowing, founded the

Falconry Club and in 1934 came down with a Fourth class degree. He then joined the Colonial Administrative Service and was posted to Uganda as an Assistant District Commissioner.[152]

This was a masculine culture which prized firm handshakes and straight speaking. It was not one which encouraged reflection on its own inner dynamics. To grasp these deeper historical realities we need to turn to the fiction.

Buchan's heroes, all are male and white, inhabit this same imaginative world. They possess a pre-eminent magical property. They have the capacity to disguise themselves as people of any race, regardless of colour, language, or any other conceivable feature. This is a power which derives from the fact that the white man knows the native. It is not a knack which can be reciprocated, for in this imaginative schema the native cannot possibly know the white man. 'We call ourselves insular, but the truth is that we are the only race on earth that can produce men capable of getting inside the skin of remote peoples.'[153] Whiteness is power, and power is whiteness.

In the formal narrative structure of these novels there is one dominating countervailing force which can take this power away and temporarily dispossess the white man of his capacity to reason and command: narcotics, administered to the hero without his knowledge by one of the principal wrong-doers. Hypnotism comes close, but never quite serves, for to contend with manly psyches as indomitable as Table Mountain itself (as the psychology of one of Buchan's heroes is described) requires something greater than the mere inducement of a state of suggestibility. These stratagems of dispossessing the white man of his reason depend on classically oriental wiles; as narrative devices, they were to have a long history in the future of the spy novel and thriller. Struggling against the power of the drugs administered to him, the hero of *The Three Hostages* does his utmost to retain hold of his identity by reasserting, in his own mind, his patriarchal authority and position in society. In order to survive, the mantra needs constant repetition: 'Something deep down in me was insisting that I was Sir Richard Hannay, K.C.B., who had commanded a division in France, and was the squire of Fosse Manor, the husband of Mary, and the father of Peter John.'[154] Identity for the white man, it would seem, merely needs to be spoken in order to become realized.

But for all this grit, there is evidence in the novels that there may be other forces that have the capacity to immobilize the hero, though these are disturbing forces which operate inside his mind. When confronted by a variety of antagonistic others, the bemused hero finds himself experiencing unpredictable sensations. There is always the moment when he discovers, inexplicably, his own attraction to that which is most threatening and foul. The erotics of ambivalence are clearly present. When Richard Hannay encounters the evil Medina, 'He fascinated me as a man is fascinated by a pretty woman', to such a degree that his co-adventurer, Sandy Arbuthnot 'was jealous of this man who was putting a spell on everybody'. Or on facing Medina's mother, Richard Hannay 'realized it was the most wonderful face of a woman I had ever looked on. And I realized in the same moment that I hated it, that the beauty was devilish, and the soul within was on fire with all the hatred of Hell.'[155] In *Greenmantle*, this same confusion of fascination and repulsion occurs when Hannay encounters the Prussian pederast, von Stumm. But he is paralysed most of all by the erotic power of the overriding antagonist, the beautiful Hilda von Einem. 'Women had never come much my way, and I knew about as much of their ways as I knew about the Chinese language.' Being watched by her inverted the conventions of sexual power: 'I felt that I was under the scrutiny of one who is a connoisseur in human nature', a perversion which proved 'an offence to my manhood'. 'I see that I have written that I knew nothing about women. But every man has in his bones a consciousness of sex. I was shy and perturbed, but horribly fascinated...[she] had the glamour of a wild dream.' She was like 'a cyclone or an earthquake'. Breaking from her presence, he returns to his hotel and does what any man in his predicament would do: 'I had a rub down and then got into my pyjamas for some dumb bell exercise.' Sandy Arbuthnot falls for her too, and consequently loses his powers of reason, 'fired by her madness'. For the narrative to close, and for the protagonists to be sure they can recover their manhood, the destruction of Hilda von Einem is required. A stray Russian shell does the job, and the dangers stirred by an eroticized femininity are averted.[156]

These are not complex modes of writing. But they are unexpected, for they highlight the instabilities which underwrite the seemingly invulnerable character of the white man. In his public life, Buchan was an unashamed protagonist of the white race, believing that the men who administered the empire were the standard-bearers of civilized reason. This was a culture which was explicit about deeming whiteness an attribute to be earned.[157] Yet the novels, written in the same spirit, were systematically about the confusions between masculine and feminine, straight and queer, and as we shall see, between black and white. The psychic work required to elevate the figure of the white man, and all the time to differentiate him from his others, produced its own ambivalence. Those deemed to be other, repressed in one moment, had the habit of reappearing the next in magisterially grotesque or hybrid form, as objects of fascination and attraction. This was a construction of self and other which was both eroticized and racialized, producing an entire spectrum of pathological antagonists in bewildering numbers and manifestations. The founding, centred figure from which these procedures worked—the white man—clearly did not emerge unscathed, for these others were barely 'out there' at all, but were interior to the very imaginative acts which made the white man what he was. Not only this. The Richard Hannays, with their KCBs and their public standing were, the fictions suggest, riven with the desire to transgress. The theme of illicit identification with the dangerous and the grotesque, with everything that the white hero *is not*, is as prominent a feature of these stories as the clean-cut jaw and the capacity to reason.

These pathological projections refused to remain in place. They were essentially mobile. We have seen this in relation to Winston Churchill, in whose mind antagonists proliferated. From his writings it is evident that these manifold others—Fenians and Zulus, mad mullahs and Charles de Gaulle, it doesn't much seem to matter—all possess the same disposition. They are all fanatic and irrational.[158] On each occasion the self was reconstituted, the boundaries shifted once more, confusions multiplied, and new fanatics could be spotted on the horizon. Where we might expect propriety we find confusion. Consistently in Buchan's adventure novels, the male heroes are feminized and, so far as they ever make an appearance, spunky British women turn out to be 'thorough sportsmen'.[159] In this sense too, the frontier itself proliferates. It functions not only as the imaginative projection of the line dividing white from black, existing on the distant reaches of the empire. It has a more frenzied, interior psychic existence. Frontiers are everywhere, always in need of being redrawn and properly policed. They make the nation safe, making it possible to *be* a national. Yet disorders are proximate: between a masculinity which knows its place and a femininity which doesn't; between heterosexual and homosexual; between the English and the alien; between gentile and Jew; between the citizen and his invisible enemies. All require demarcations, calling upon a known repertoire of images—assegais and the like—to enable a measure of psychic order to be imposed. In *The Three Hostages* a frontier is projected between Berkeley Square (the civilization of the known West End) and Gospel Oak (the unknown racialized), while 'London itself is like the tropical bush—if you don't exercise constant care the jungle, in the shape of the slums, will break in.'[160] In prose of this temper we can see the figure of the white man cohering in all its essentials, predicated on the desire to repudiate anything and everything different from himself.

It is little surprise that Buchan, in identifying what he understood to be the singular virtue of the British empire, believed it lay in the skill of the colonists in 'domesticating the strange and the terrible and making portents homely'.[161]

Many commentators on Buchan have suggested that he was a writer deeply placed in the philosophical traditions of British Conservatism, and that the prevailing theme of his fiction, and indeed his politics, is of the fragility of the divide between civilization and chaos.[162] This is true, but it ignores the subjective dimensions. Buchan was preoccupied with the struggle between civilization and anarchy, and—in its imperial idiom—with the question of what constituted a white man's country. But his fiction also compels its readers to ask the question: what of the white man himself?

Proconsular reckoning

On his appointment as high commissioner in 1897 Milner declared that 'S Af [sic] is just now the weakest link in the imperial chain'.[163] The final destruction of the two Afrikaner republics was, for Milner, the precondition for overcoming this weakness. The new alliance between Briton and Boer, reconstruction, and eventual union in 1910 created a new nation which transformed South Africa into what many hoped would make it the strongest link in the empire.

Buchan played a minuscule role in this public drama, a single reference in Amery's 7-volume *Times History* getting it about right.[164] On arrival, as I have noted, he had responsibility for the internment camps for Afrikaner women and children; although it would be misjudged to conflate this experience with later developments in Europe, the conjunction which brought together the first experiment in mass internment of enemy civilians with an intensification of the dynamics of race and ethnicity is a disturbing one.[165] He spent a deal of time with Joseph Chamberlain on the latter's triumphal tour early in 1903, complaining of him that he lacked 'vision and daemonic power', an estimation which seems entirely wrong.[166] He briefly involved himself in the resettlement of Boer farmers in the months which followed the war. And he tried his hand at writing a proconsular treatise, which he published in 1903 under the title: *The African Colony: Studies in the Reconstruction*, which won high praise, particularly from Lord Cromer, and which has more recently been described as 'a comprehensive defence of Milner's programme for reconstruction'.[167]

The future of South Africa, Buchan declared, was 'far-reaching and vital to the future of the English race'.[168] His purpose in the book was to understand what that future would be. For the most part, in contrast to the fiction the dominant tone is a no-nonsense objectivism, though as in many such treatises of the period it mixes in a good quotient of memoir and travelogue. Three themes stand out: the ethnic status of the Boers; landscape and the longing for national form; and the organization of the black proletariat. Yet all are linked by the desire to create out of the heterogeneous elements of the land a nation properly homogeneous. Buchan, having internalized well enough the proconsular mentality of his times, was attempting to discover what determined the constituents of the white man's country in South Africa.

With marked brevity, he acknowledged that Southern Africa did possess a history prior to conquest, identifying the civilization of the bushmen with that of the neolithic era. But from the fifteenth century 'the history of South Africa becomes almost exclusively the history of its white masters'. This allowed him to move straight into a discussion of the Boers. Adopting the tone of one of his fictional characters he claimed: 'It is a fair working rule of life that the behaviour of a man in his sports is a good index to his character in graver matters', which happened to be fortuitous for the British but unlucky for the Boers, for it was here that the Boer could be seen 'at his worst'. 'Without a tradition of fair play, soured and harassed by want and disaster, his sport became a matter of commerce, and he held no device unworthy in the game.' The Boer he found a simple, unimaginative character. 'The old sluggish Batavian stock (not of the best quality, for the first settlers were as a rule of the poorest and least reputable class) was leavened with a finer French strain, and tinctured with a little native blood.' But though destined to 'mental sluggishness', the Boers had their virtues, and needed to be won over by the British. 'We can ask for no better dwellers upon a frontier.' Indeed, they shared with the British a certain skill for domesticating the wilderness. 'Other races send forth casual pioneers, who return and report and then go elsewhere; but the Boer takes his wife and family and all his belongings, and in a decade is part of the soil. In the midst of any savagery he will plant his rude domesticity, and the land is won. With all her colonizing activity, Britain can ill afford to lose from her flag a force so masterful, persistent and sure.'[169] These abstract reflections on the nature of Afrikaner life had a clear political purpose. They may not have been diplomatically put, incubating in D. F. Malan, the first prime minister of the apartheid era, for example, a lasting enmity.[170] But even so, from them Buchan hoped to determine the fundamentals of the future alliance between Boer and Briton, and thus the internal configurations of the white domination of South Africa.

Travel-writing and depictions of the landscape constitute the second part of the book, opening with an account of 'Evening on the high *veld*'. Many lyrical passages follow. This is not merely a flowery interlude: it is a vigorous attempt to imagine the nation, and to *locate* it in its given landscapes.[171] In a bold if daunting leap of the imagination, Buchan announced the *veld* to be 'full of memories for the English race', claiming that it was only through England that South Africa as a nation could be realized. It was not difficult, he continued, even for a 'London shopboy' to get a mental picture of the *veld*, and would become even more so 'when South Africa gets herself a literature'. The *veld* 'has entered into patriotic jingles, and has given a *mise-en-scène* to crude melodrama'. 'No landscape', he concluded, 'is so masterful as the *veld*'.[172] Thus the purpose of a colonial literature, he implied, was to allow the new nation of South Africa to be imagined *in the metropole*.[173]

The final section moved away from the historical and geographical dimensions of the nation in order to discuss the overriding practical issue: the relations between capital, labour, and race in the mines. 'The cardinal economic fact is the existence of gold.' 'Without capital the Transvaal is a piece of bare *veld*; with capital wrongly applied it is a hunting-ground for the adventurer and bogus-promoter.' For Buchan the crux of the matter was labour, just as it was, he explained, on the West Indian plantations. The mines needed plenty of cheap labour. It was possible, he contended, to attract black labour from central Africa. A second solution he proposed was to stratify labour in the mines according to race, sending 'the Kaffir' into the deepest, most perilous sections and allowing white miners to work in the less exposed areas. A third possibility was to import 'under rigorous supervision' Chinese labour on a system of short contracts. Buchan was adamant that temporary contracts were essential in preventing a situation arising in South Africa which had already occurred in Australia and in the USA. 'The Chinese are the born interlopers of the world'; he feared their coming to South Africa would bring with it a certain 'leakage'. This solution he believed to be most dangerous.[174]

Yet proximity between black and white brought its own troubles. 'A coloured race living side by side with a white people furnishes one of the gravest of moral cruces', for it tended to trigger a 'deterioration in moral and mental vigour' of 'the masters'. The 'kernel' of the problem was this: 'how to keep the white man from deterioration without spoiling the Kaffir'. Buchan did not wish the black population to be in a state of 'perpetual tutelage'. He even hoped for eventual equality, though he was sceptical that this would ever be achieved. He was not prepared to countenance the continuation of the native franchise, though 'we can grant rights which are substantive and educative and capable of judicious extension'. The ultimate issue, however, turned on the connection between manhood and work. Natives had to work. On this there could be no contention. 'The Kaffir owes his existence to the white man; in return he should be compelled to labour for hire and take his proper place in a world which has no room for his vegetating habits.' But the public regulation of labour threatened to upset the requirements of white masculine duty, curtailing the male citizen's capacity freely to sell his capacity to labour. 'We need not concern ourselves with the so-called degradation of Kaffir manhood implied in compulsory labour, for such self-conscious manhood does not exist; but we are very deeply concerned with the degradation of white manhood, which will inevitably follow any of the facile solutions which are tried in the market-place.'[175]

This was a dilemma which recurred time and again in the literature. The idea of a white man's country was no mere fancy, the idea of both ethnicity and gender going to the heart of the matter. To pose the problem in this way was already to accept the logic of segregation, a segregation to be effected along lines determined by the imperatives of the white man. When it came to South Africa, even the most constitutionalist, or liberal, expressions of English civilization proved virtually incapable of imagining the nation without the imposition of segregation. To think in any other way would, necessarily, compromise the essentials of the white man's country, which would in turn be to compromise civilization itself.

In expressing these anxieties, Buchan was also rehearsing convictions about the independence of manhood which stretched back to older radical traditions of the early nineteenth century. But in denying the essential manhood of black masculinity, the diktats of a newer racial logic also intervened.

In this, the influence of Thomas Carlyle was not far away. Buchan's was a complex articulation of what once were contending traditions, constituting a language ostensibly liberal or radical in its fundamentals, but one entirely subsumed by an unbending acceptance of the evident truths of racial supremacy. In recasting and fusing these traditions, Buchan was neither the first nor was he alone. These were common assumptions amongst the British in the founding moment of the South African nation. But that this happened affected also the trajectory of these older radical traditions in Britain itself. When, from the late 1880s, Unionism could become the apotheosis of radicalism, it did so because an exclusive ethnicity came to define those properly of the nation. Stories from the frontier provided the imaginative resources for this to happen. Even London shopboys who had never left their native city could remember the *veld*.

Shockers

Buchan called his adventure stories shockers, his air of disparagement indicating that their chief aim was to while away some leisure hours snatched from the higher things of life. It is ironic that this Calvinist Tory, puzzled by and fearful of the onset of mass culture, should be remembered for his popular fiction while his contemplative scholarly reflections are no longer read. It is ironic too that he wrote for the mass market in order to underwrite the costs of his country manor and to finance his sons through Eton and Oxford. *The African Colony* represented an intervention in high politics of the type which Leo Amery would have appreciated, its very form testament to the continued willingness of men of learning to lend their weight to the administration of the empire. It was read within a small elite—some 500 copies were sold—whose job it was to mould public opinion, and then it virtually disappeared from view. *Prester John*, on the other hand, Buchan's pulp novel about a black uprising in South Africa, published in 1910, the same year the Union was founded, had much deeper reverberations. Its success, ironically, was testament to the tendency of high and low to get confused, a fact which so disturbed Buchan himself. To use his own term, alongside his other stories it entered the popular memory of the nation.[176]

During his lifetime his fiction was widely read. By 1960, more than a dozen of his novels could boast hardback sales in excess of 100,000.[177] He was read throughout the empire—by C. L. R. James and V. S. Naipaul in their different generations at Queen's Royal College in Port of Spain, by Chinua

Achebe in Nigeria, and by Ngũgĩ wa Thiong'o in Kenya.[178] But it is surprising that his reputation barely faltered as the empire fell away. Pan published his novels in paperback in 1952; Penguin, to celebrate the company's twenty-first anniversary in 1956, brought out ten of the novels simultaneously, a privilege accorded only to Buchan himself, to H. G. Wells, and to Bernard Shaw. A vast new readership was generated by this paperback revolution. Mrs Thatcher was to be found reading him on the eve of the 1959 election, just before she entered parliament for the first time.[179] The most notorious she-been in Sophiatown—according to Bloke Modisane, and he would have known—took the name 'The Thirty Nine Steps', around the corner from Milner Road.[180] The BBC, through various dramatizations, kept the Buchan industry turning over, and took to designating the Scottish Borders as 'Hannay Country'.[181] The remakes of the movies continue to be shown, and in 1988 Thames Television—in the era of *Dallas* and *Dynasty*—reinvented his hero Hannay for the small screen.[182] For those of more *recherché* inclination, the John Buchan Society was founded in 1979, with its own journal devoted to such topics as Richard Hannay's train-rides, or to the various makes of car featured in the novels. This is not to be confused with the John Buchan Club, a later sect devoted to the minority pursuit of Scottish Thatcherism, and calling upon the pantomime bombast of Teddy Taylor and Sir Nicholas Fairburn.[183] As late as 1994, 100,000 copies of John Buchan novels were borrowed annually from public libraries, establishing him in the same league as Charlotte Brontë, Arthur Conan Doyle, George Eliot, and Virginia Woolf.[184] In July 2005, when the director-general of the BBC was called upon to report to the appropriate parliamentary committee on broadcasting policy, one could hear an audibly miffed Lord Fowler complaining to him that— owing to emergency programme rescheduling in the wake of the bomb attacks on London—he had missed on his wireless the second episode of *Greenmantle*.[185]

In her denunciation of Buchan published in 1960 Gertrude Himmelfarb observed that as a consequence of the racial attitudes represented in *Prester John* it would, at the time, have proved impossible to have reissued the novel in the United States. Himmelfarb, a woman of intransigently conservative instincts, does not have a reputation as a frontline activist on such matters. But she was writing when civil rights were prominent in the public mind.[186] In Britain, on the other hand, at this same moment, from the early 1950s until the mid-1960s—at the time of decolonization itself—nearly a quarter of a million paperback copies of the novel were sold.[187] It has been in print ever since and reissued regularly; between 2001 and 2004 there appeared at least five new editions; Amazon made it one of their first digital titles which their customers, for less than the price of a bus-ticket, could download. At the end of the 1970s it was still in use as a school-text, and for a generation born long after Buchan had died in 1940 memories of it remain active.[188]

In 1906 Buchan had published anonymously a novel (loosely) about Africa and empire. It was didactic, and is barely readable today.[189] What distinguishes *Prester John* is its narrative pace. It is the story which holds the mind. But when Buchan derided his efforts as a popular story-teller, or harked back to the genres of nineteenth-century realism as providing the only worthwhile model for the novel, he was underestimating his own achievements.[190] For he was more inventive than he ever admitted.

Buchan worked from many literary models. There were classical influences. There were Bunyan and the Bible. And then there were the intertwined traditions of the historical novel and nineteenth-century Scottish prose, both of which came to be organized specifically as boys' literature. Sir Walter Scott, James Fenimore Cooper, and Robert Louis Stevenson: it was these writers who were most active in his mind.

One of the dominating themes of the historical novel was the frontier, both in its virtuous sense, and in its more fearsome aspects. In significant numbers of novels in an emergent nineteenth-century genre of 'adventure', the racial slaughter of civilized beings by assorted savages composed a critical component in the narrative structuring. Barely into the first chapter of Fenimore Cooper's foundational *The Last of the Mohicans*, for example, the reader confronts this:

> A wide frontier had been laid naked by this unexpected disaster, and more substantial evils were preceded by a thousand fanciful and imaginary dangers. The alarmed colonists believed that the yells of the savages mingled with every fitful gust of wind that issued from the interminable forests of the west... Numberless recent massacres were still vivid in their recollections; nor was there any ear in the provinces so deaf as not to have drunk in with avidity the narrative of some fearful tale of midnight murder, in which the natives of the forests were the principal and barbarous actors. As the credulous and excited traveler related the hazardous chances of the wilderness, the blood of the timid curdled with terror, and mothers cast anxious glances even at those children which slumbered with security of the largest towns. In short, the magnifying influence of fear began to set at naught the calculations of reason, and to render those who should have remembered their manhood, the slaves of the basest passions.[191]

Maybe this seems too distant from Buchan. But if we turn to his biography of Walter Scott—dedicated to two of his closest friends, Stanley Baldwin and G. M. Trevelyan—we can catch again the prominence of the theme. As might be expected, he emphasizes the imperial dimensions, in which Scott's family was active in the service of the empire, both in the military and in administration. Canada, India, and the West Indies loom large. Buchan reminded his readers that Scott toyed with the idea of joining the Indian service. And he tells this tale:

> The case of his youngest brother was a far deeper vexation. Daniel Scott, having taken to evil courses, was shipped off the West Indies. But Jamaica proved no cure, he went downhill in mind and body, and during a negro rebellion on the plantation where he was employed he did not show the family courage. He returned home with this stigma on his name, was taken into his mother's house and soon died. Scott would not see him; he called him his 'relative', not his brother; he declined to go to his funeral or wear mourning for him. In those high-flying days he could forgive most faults, but not cowardice, and he felt that by the unhappy Dan the family scutcheon had been indelibly stained.[192]

Long ago Georg Lukács argued that the nineteenth-century historical novel became one of the vehicles by which 'men came to comprehend their own existence as something historically conditioned', and by which modern populations came to know themselves *as nationals*.[193] The structures of feeling which developed in conjunction with this cultural transformation were both complex and varied, the expansion of the self assuming many different forms. Nevertheless, to become self-conscious in this way was to think of oneself as a new sort of historical being. For the most part, to think historically was to think ethnically. Certainly, by the end of the century in Britain these ethnic determinations, irretrievably tied to a subtext or shadow-text subsumed by the structures of racial fear, moved to the centre of concern in the increasingly popular genre of historical realism.

Around the turn of the century—or 'at the time of the Boer War', as one authority proposes in making a parallel argument—a number of key developments occurred in the fiction of mass culture which can be charted, amongst other places, in Buchan's novels.[194]

First, the form of the historical novel itself split, between the frontier novel proper, on the one hand, representing virtue and the open landscape; and, on the other, its darker counterpoint, the urban detective story dominated by vice and mean streets.[195] Arguably these were functions of a single imaginative projection, the psychic split producing geographies which were the mirror-image of each other. This imagined political ecology had been anticipated by J. A. Froude in *Oceana*, as I showed in the first chapter. In Buchan, novel by novel, the split was at its most marked.

Second, in the crime novel—or in its correlate, the spy-story—the frontier came home. The skills of *veld*-craft were called upon to be reconstituted in a form appropriate for the urban environment in order to track, neither beasts nor savages, but enemies within, who masqueraded as civilized and who endeavoured to interpolate themselves as nationals. The frontiers of the white race, at this point, can be seen not merely to be working in order to save civilization from barbarism 'over there', but to traverse the national community 'at home'. None the less, the lessons learnt on the colonial frontier still maintain their authority. Thus Buchan's estimable hero, Richard Hannay, could operate successfully in London, while Scotland Yard exhibited an effete incompetence, precisely because he was at home with the metaphysics of the frontier in a way that the domestic detective, suburban-bound, could never be.

Third, irrational eruptions, a required element in stories of criminal, Gothic malfeasance, became increasingly racialized, manifest in an entire gallery of alien figures. From this period the demented characters in popular fiction were haunted less by ghosts and spirits, and increasingly by the grotesque aliens and hybrids which the frontier had proved incapable of containing—or which, indeed, the pathological demarcation of the white man itself had generated. Thus the proconsular obsession with erecting a white man's country registered in a displaced history, in this lower, vulgar, repressed form. These super-aliens were anticipated in Professor Moriarty, cohered in Fu Manchu and in Buchan's varied hybrid nihilists, and became dramatically visible in later descendants, such as in Ian Fleming's Blofeld.[196]

Fourth, although the racialization of the irrational became prominent at this time within the fictions of mass culture, the internal instability of the figure of the white man signalled the characteristic impress of modernity—in Joseph Conrad pre-eminently, but in John Buchan or Edgar Wallace as well. For all the mastery of the *veld*, and for the self-possession inscribed in the configurations of white masculinity, the hero's demons were never quite absorbed by the magical powers of the frontier. The frontier may have promised him renewal. But as often as not it instigated collapse, exacerbating a strange precariousness of the self.

Buchan may have believed he was rescuing the traditions of historical realism as a counter to the abstractions of high modernism. But in so doing, the form itself changed. His shockers, for all their conservatism, occupied a place in the mass culture of popular modernity which he himself never quite relished.

In one other respect his novels reorganized the terrain of popular fiction. In the very first moments of his writing career as a young and precocious student, Buchan—against all expectations—coquetted with aestheticism and with the ideas of Walter Pater. This first brush with a feminized aesthetic was a brief affair. He moved quickly on to other things and, more deliberately, to a self-consciously muscular form of writing. This was inspired by a very particular sexual politics. It was driven by the desire to repudiate the feminine which, as I have suggested, represented a powerful component of high imperial thinking in the late Victorian and Edwardian world. Elaine Showalter sees in this a conscious reassertion of the masculine properties of the imagination. She writes: 'The revival of "romance" in the 1880s was a men's literary revolution intended to reclaim the kingdom of the English novel for male writers, male readers, and men's stories.' She reads this shift in terms of a reaction against the 'mannered' realism of George Eliot, led by Rider Haggard and Robert Louis Stevenson.[197] Indeed, Arthur Conan Doyle identified Stevenson as 'the father of the modern masculine novel'. Out of this literary reaction developed a genre of male romance written explicitly for boys, meaning not only stories from which girls were excluded, but also indicating that these were stories in which the capacity to imagine a homoerotic world was at a premium.[198] Buchan moved into this mode of writing, made it is his own, and modernized it—inventing a kind of episodic, cinematic prose in the process.[199] The legacy of these masculine romances, and of the concomitant ways of imagining the self, has had a long subsequent history.[200]

Prester John is one of the great frontier novels of the period.[201] There is continuing controversy whether its narrative draws upon the events of the Transvaal of 1904, or those of Natal of 1906. This is the type of controversy which is familiar in discussions of historical realism, but which can never satisfactorily be resolved.[202] There is doubt too about when exactly it was drafted, and about its different versions. Under the title, 'The Black General', it appeared in instalments between April and September 1910 in *The Captain*. The timing is significant. In July 1910 the *Daily Mirror* employed for the first recorded time in Britain the term 'race riot'. This report, and others in other papers, referred to the victory in the USA of the black boxer Arthur John 'Jack' Johnson, who trounced his white rival. In the aftermath of his victory riots broke out in the US and in Jamaica, and the London County Council warned cinemas not to show the film of the fight, for fear of similar rioting in London. In this peculiarly modern crisis (when, once more, the new media made the running) the racial divide between metropole and colony diminished significantly, anticipating popular panics of a later age.[203] It is perfectly conceivable that this was in Buchan's mind as he was drafting *Prester John*.

The opening chapter of *Prester John* is set in the remembered Scotland of Buchan's past, fusing together the terrors of childhood—drawing from the conventions of the *Bildungsroman*, Robert Louis Stevenson in particular—with the terrors of racial fear, echoing Fenimore Cooper.

> I mind as if it were yesterday my first sight of the man. Little I knew at the time how big the moment was with destiny, or how often that face seen in the fitful moonlight would haunt my sleep and disturb my waking hours. But I mind yet the cold grue of terror I got from it, a terror which was surely more than the due of a few truant lads breaking the Sabbath with their play.

'The man' sighted was the visiting black preacher, John Laputa, who in an earlier sermon that morning had 'forecast a day when the Negroes would have something to teach the British in the way of civilization'. Skipping the evening service in the kirk David Crawfurd, the young hero and narrator, witnessed the preacher, now divested not only of his clerical apparel but of all his clothes, dancing a pagan ritual on the beach, and carrying an assegai-like 'great knife'. Crawfurd's terror, from the outset, was made the more awful as it was compounded by the feeling that he himself was 'somehow shut in with this unknown being in a strange union'.[204]

As indeed he was. John Laputa, it transpires, is the leader of a 'Kaffir rising' in South Africa, where David Crawfurd journeys to seek his fortune. He meets again with Laputa under various circumstances and comes to be instrumental in putting down the rebellion. That is the story.

This instant terror precipitated by the sight black of masculinity might seem predictable, the very stuff of a late Victorian childhood. But the memories of John Buchan's childhood, by the time he came to write the novel, had been organized by the intervening experience of South Africa. There is evidence to suggest that the older mores of the Free Church, in which he had grown up, were very different from those which were becoming increasingly speakable in the age of Chamberlain and Milner. On being appointed to Milner's staff in the autumn of 1901, Buchan received a letter from an elder of the church who had known him since his childhood.

> I feared for the future of South Africa where there has been so much corruption, where Christian principles have been stifled by the craze for gold, and where there is the ever-present opportunity of the white oppressing the black. But if I knew that a man like you was helping to hold the helm, I should have confidence in its future. Rhodes and the others are great men, possessed with large ideas, but they are hardly to be trusted in the treatment of the blacks and other questions…If these empire-builders require to use the black races as stepping-stones to further their plans, many people will say that they are justified, but I cannot, and if I can do anything to hinder them I will do it willingly.

In deference to Buchan's appointment, one assumes, he added: 'I believe however that Lord Milner will do what is right to the dark race, but he will need some one to help him, some one with the fear of God before his eyes.'[205] There is no knowing if these views, or views like these, dominated Buchan's childhood. It is likely that they did. What is evident, however, is that by the time *Prester John* was drafted, the philanthropic radicalism which informed this testament could find no voice, bent by the force of the men who possessed the 'large ideas'.

The fictional Crawfurd's departure to South Africa occurs as a result of the death of his father, 'suddenly of a paralytic shock'. His journey to the frontier demanded he leave his mother, while she offers all she is able: a 'tearful farewell' on the quayside. (For the record, so far as this pertains, Buchan's mother in fact followed him to South Africa, a matter of some discomfiture, it seems, to her son.) Henceforth, until the narrative closure, his mother has only a single fleeting appearance, in a wonderful moment of displacement. 'At luncheon-time, when I was about half-way, I sat down with my Zeiss glass—my mother's farewell gift—to look for the valley.' In the story which follows, home in its many varieties—family, domesticity, the home authorities, the newspaper-reading public—is encoded as irredeemably feminine, in contrast to the masculinity of the frontier, where things get done and insurrections are quelled. In Buchan's imagination there are no women on the frontier. Or more accurately, there is a black house-servant ('who did two men's work'); and there is the recurring memory of white women and children massacred in earlier black uprisings.[206]

For all the simplicity of the novel, there is much to be said. I shall restrict myself here to the issue of race and sexuality, looking particularly at the relations between black and white and at the frontier which divides them.

The hero of the novel is David Crawfurd, who through the course of the narrative learns to become a white man. The process of this acquisition of wisdom and whiteness is explicit. 'Yet it was an experience for which I shall ever be grateful, for it turned me from a rash boy into a serious man. I knew then the meaning of the white man's duty.' The catalogue which follows— 'the gift of responsibility' and so on—is less interesting than the process which allows this manful evolution to happen.[207]

The dominating presence of white masculinity in the novel is a veteran of the Matabele campaign, Captain James Arcoll, a reticent figure who remains in the background, but who is active—decisive—when required. Within the conventions of the genre the reader recognizes his ethnic mastery by his capacity to disguise himself as a native. The 'miserable-looking Kaffir' turns out to be 'an active soldierly-looking man of maybe fifty years' who—we don't need to be told—is white. The young David witnesses this transformation in wonderment, seeing for himself Arcoll reassuming his proper whiteness.[208] When Crawfurd is on the point of losing his capacity to reason through fever and exhaustion, and thus in danger of losing his claims on a manly whiteness, Arcoll is there to steady him. 'Arcoll, still holding my hands, brought his face close to mine, so that his clear eyes mastered and constrained me.' This benevolent mastery dispels the various fevers dispossessing Crawfurd, and allows him back his manhood.[209]

Other whites have a less decisive role to play. Historically, one of the striking features of the novel is that the Afrikaners are all but absent. If Arthur Conan Doyle's *The Great Boer War* was about the Afrikaners with only fleeting references to blacks forcing their way into the text, eight years later, in *Prester John* the situation is very nearly reversed. There is a reference to 'Dutch farmers in the mountains'; to a momentary shared communion with these 'honest, companionable fellows'; or, where they clearly assume a subordinate role, Crawfurd says in an aside, 'I set the Dutchmen to unload and clear the ground for foundations, while I went off to Sikitola to ask for labourers.' The narrative constructions of whiteness are British, an imaginative projection which has already, magically, resolved old antagonisms into honest companionship, under the unspoken supremacy of the new conquerors.[210]

Amongst the white characters there is the local schoolteacher from Scotland, Mr Wardlaw, who is no man of action, and operates on the frontier in commensurately feminine mode. There is too the character of Japp, the store-keeper to whom the young Crawfurd is apprenticed. Japp is all bad, effectively relinquishing his entitlement to be recognized as a white man. He is a drunkard; he abuses the black female house-servant; he buys and sells diamonds illegally; and he is deferential to those blacks whom he believes may be able to advance his fortunes. This existential collapse remains unexplained. But there are hints. One is that Japp, colonial-born and fond of resorting to the *sjambok* on his housemaid, represents the traditional Boer, losing sight of the responsibilities incumbent upon the civilized supremacist. This is a possibility which might allow the reader to understand that the frontier has a more disturbing, enervating character; there are traces of this in Buchan, but it is an idea which Conrad was prepared to explore more seriously. Another possibility is uttered by Japp himself: 'You may hear drums any night, but a drumming like that I only once heard before. It was in '79 in the 'Zeti valley. Do you know what happened the next day? Cetewayo's impis came over the hills, and in an hour there wasn't a living white soul in the glen. Two men escaped, and one of them was called Peter Japp.'[211] Such an experience might unman even the most resolute of frontier adventurers.

Finally within the spectrum of white civilization, showing all the virtues of the white man, is Crawfurd's dog, Colin. He is loyal and resourceful, and knows his duty. He 'heartily dislikes' Japp and frightens 'Kaffirs'. He is Crawfurd's only friend. But despite these virtues he is dumb and simple, his simplicity suggesting a kind of primitive attribution of whiteness. He is, after all, 'a Boer hunting-dog'.[212]

The reader knows that black will be pitted against white, barbarism against civilization. But whatever the degree of evil the black characters embrace, they have one redeeming quality. They are racially pure. They may be black, and thus have to carry the burden of their backwardness. But (so we read) they have the opportunity to know their place in the racial hierarchy, and to know that if they follow their truest instincts under wise white leadership goodness will ultimately prevail. This is not a possibility, however, shared by those of mixed race, who are 'neither one thing nor the other', and who are destined to a life of permanent dislocation. The 'most atrocious villain', consequently, is the mercenary Henriques. 'He had a face the colour of French mustard—a sort of dirty green—and blood-shot, beady eyes with the whites all yellowed with fever.' He is, just about, white: but at the same time, he's a 'double-eyed traitor to his race'.[213] It is Henriques, his yellowness accentuated, who kills Colin the dog. He is the authentic hybrid, who can follow no instinct but self-interest. As Edgar Wallace, in similar vein, saw things, 'black is black and white is white, and all that is in between is foul and horrible'.[214] Henriques personifies the white man compromised in his very blood, a quasi white man who can never become white.

The frontier between black and white runs through the colony. Those whose job it is to know the native are experts in knowing the frontier. When Crawfurd arrives in Blauuwildebeestefontein he reflects: 'Whatever serpent might lurk in it, it was a veritable Eden.' Moving from the settlement, across the *veld*, to the hills is a journey undergone by Crawfurd on a number of occasions, and each time it is explicitly recounted as a journey across 'the frontier', from 'civilization' to 'barbarism'. In order to be properly manful, the young hero has to cross the border and, as much as in any more ritualized initiation, must walk through many terrors. With this accomplished, the grown man will be able to accommodate himself to the feminine world of domesticity with no fear that he himself will become feminized. 'Here was a fresh, clean land, a land for homesteads and orchards and children. All of a sudden I realized that at last I had come out of savagery.'[215]

The accompanying dangers, though, are great, for the quest requires him to enter the world of blackness and to re-emerge uncontaminated, remaining white. In this drama blacks have a necessarily anonymous existence. Virtually the only black person to speak is Laputa. There are plenty of occurrences of the stock image of 'the Kaffir'—who cannot understand the meaning of what 'we' do; who is 'mortally afraid of a white man's dog'; and who 'cannot wink, but... has a way of slanting his eyes which does as well'. There are also the unseen masses, keeping alive the memories of black rebellions in previous generations. Buchan makes explicit reference to the slave rebellion in Haiti and to the Indian uprising of 1857. These memories get translated into a white common sense, as predictable and as intoxicating as the *veld* itself. 'My houseboy', declares Wardlaw, 'might be in the rising, and I would never suspect it till one fine morning he cut my throat.' Or as Crawfurd expresses the same fears: 'I felt odd quiverings between my shoulder blades where a spear might be expected to lodge.'[216]

Laputa is distinct. By both Arcoll and Crawfurd he is regarded as noble and kingly, an honourable product of the frontier. Time and again the text confirms his prowess. 'The man's face was as commanding as his figure, and his voice was the most wonderful thing that ever came out of human mouth. It was full and rich, and gentle, with the tones of a great organ.' But his is a characterization which splits in a number of ways. For all the explicit eroticization of his masculinity, he is feminine too. He is both educated and savage, both of the frontier and not. 'For he now became a friendly and rational companion. He kept his horse at an easy walk, and talked to me as if we were two friends out for a trip together.' He quotes Virgil, and weighs up the intellectual reputation of a professor at Edinburgh. It is in fact this confusion which is his undoing, for he is that most dangerous of things, an educated black man, whose learning requires him to forget the eternal racial truths of the frontier and leads him to embrace the heady delusions of Ethopianism and Pan-Africanism.[217]

But these confusions notwithstanding, he is a powerfully attractive figure. This, potentially, is Crawfurd's downfall. In order to be sure of both his whiteness and his manhood he has to overcome his transgressive attraction towards Laputa, evident from the moment he witnesses his strange antics on the beach by his childhood home. 'My mind was mesmerized by this amazing man...I had a mad desire to be of Laputa's party. Or rather, I longed for a leader who should master me and make my soul his own...I had to struggle with a spell which gripped me equally with the wildest savage.' 'I was hypnotized by the man.' These were the fevers which possessed the young hero, and which carried him from reason to unreason (to 'a dream-world'), from the will to master to the will to be mastered.[218] This is the ordeal he has to undergo: to resist his illicit desire for Laputa and for going native.

In this there is a simple dichotomy between his good father (Arcoll) and his bad father (Laputa). He feels mastered by both, but only one can make him his own. The first description of Laputa is that 'he is as big as your father'. Later, Crawfurd admits: 'I was helpless as a baby in his hands'. Or again: 'I listened spell-bound as he prayed. I heard the phrases familiar to me in my schooldays at Kirkcaple. He had some of the tones of my father's voice, and when I shut my eyes I could have believed myself a child again.' The presences of Arcoll and Laputa rotate, the presence of one ensuring the absence of the other. David's first sight of each is in a state of undress—though Arcoll preserves a proper state of modesty, while Laputa, as we see through David's eyes, exults in his own nakedness. The narrative crux is the moment when Crawfurd's soul is torn between the two: when in his feverish exhaustion he might lose his will to be masterful, and succumb to passivity and his transgressive desires. If this had occurred, David would have failed in his ordeal. The steady intervention of Arcoll restores the hero's pluck and equilibrium. Laputa dies (as does, inevitably Henriques) and the colony is saved.[219]

With the villains dead there remained 'months of guerrilla fighting, and then months of reprisals, when chief after chief was hunted down and brought to trial'. With the counter-insurgency complete, Crawfurd was able to settle his domestic affairs, and a benevolent Milnerism could be introduced to settle the affairs of the colony. David Crawfurd now proved sufficiently manly that he could return to his mother and to his mother country, bearing a large tranche of Laputa's treasure-trove, such that his mother 'need never again want for comfort'. He had been careful, of course, to sell all his diamonds to de Beers, thus refraining from flooding the market and destabilizing the international trade. New discoveries of diamonds also underwrote the colony's reconstruction. At Blauuwildebeestefontein a modern training college was established—safe from the hands of missionaries—to train the natives in the production of cash-crops for export to the metropole: tobacco, fruit, and cotton. In a magical transformation the *veld* becomes a simulacrum of Scotland. There are sheep and orchards, and 'The loch on the Rooirand is stocked with Loch-leven trout'. The 'Kaffir farms on the Berg' came under the imposition of curfew, but an incipient democracy moved into place: 'We have cleaned up all the kraals, and the chiefs are members of our county council, and are as fond of hearing their own voices as an Aberdeen bailie.'[220] After all the dangers the *veld* at last was restored to its true racial authority. *Prester John* was published the year the Union of South Africa was founded. It works as a foundational fiction of the new dominion. In it, David Crawford became a white man, and South Africa a white man's country.

5

Frontier philosopher

Jan Christian Smuts

In early August 1942 Winston Churchill was in Cairo. He had been worried that the command of the Middle Eastern armies was not working effectively and he had concluded that senior military figures needed to be relieved of their posts. He had decided to travel to North Africa in order to be on the spot to manage these changes himself, and he arranged for Field-Marshall Jan Smuts, the prime minister of South Africa, to join him, believing him uniquely capable of providing sound advice about the matter in hand. Churchill's physician, Sir Charles Wilson (better known by his subsequent title of Lord Moran), travelled to Cairo too: he was convinced that Smuts was more ruthless than Churchill, and that—in this situation—it was ruthlessness Churchill needed. On the evening of 7 August, after a day reviewing the troops, Churchill, Smuts, Wilson, and others met for dinner at the British embassy. Churchill and Smuts did most of the talking and, as usual, Wilson did most of the observing. They talked of history, and debated whether patterns and structures could be discerned in the historical past. Then they came to discuss Gandhi.[1] The Raj was facing a serious internal crisis of authority. The 'Quit India' resolution of the Indian Congress had been sanctioned as official policy at Bombay that day, committing the Congress to non-violent mass struggle 'on the widest possible scale' if the British rejected the Congress's ultimatum. Whereas Nehru was cautious, Gandhi was militant. As the meeting in Bombay came to an end, Gandhi gave his blessing: 'Here is a mantra, a short one, that I give you. You may imprint it in your hearts and let every breath of yours give expression to it. The mantra is: "Do or Die".'[2] Both Churchill and Smuts had had confrontations with Gandhi before: Churchill in the early 1930s, during the political controversies of the Government of India Bill, and Smuts before the First

World War, when Gandhi had been organizing Indians in Natal. Churchill despised Gandhi, while Smuts's feelings were more ambivalent. 'He is a man of God', claimed Smuts during dinner: 'You and I are mundane people. Gandhi has appealed to religious motives. You never have. That is why you have failed.' Churchill chose not to take offence. With a reported 'great grin' he responded to Smuts: 'I have made more bishops than anyone since St Augustine'. According to Wilson, 'Smuts did not smile. His face was very grave.'[3] Wilson then recorded in his diary his own internal monologue:

> While they talked I kept asking myself what kind of man is Smuts. Is he the Henry James of South Africa? Does he think of his fellow Boers as James came to think of the American scene as perhaps a little primitive? A South African here speaks of him as 'remote'; even to his own people he is a stranger. No one really knows him. It appears that this solitary, austere Boer with his biblical background lives in a world of his own. It is as if he has been cut off from his kind... Anyone who steps in his path is ruthlessly pushed aside.[4]

This little bit of table-talk is significant. Smuts had been an old antagonist of the British, and of Churchill's, in the South African War. Thereafter, he was held in the highest esteem. The previous autumn, at King George's personal command, he had been promoted to the rank of field-marshall. The fact that Churchill wanted him in Cairo is revealing, for Smuts was one of the few war-leaders whom he trusted without equivocation—though shared memories of the South African War also counted for much, certainly for Churchill. There were few people, at this time certainly, who could tell Churchill to his face that he was a failure. Wilson was probably right to think that it was his ruthlessness which counted for most, though the views of both, Churchill and Smuts, on the empire, and on the various threats to its continuation, coincided. They were of a caste and of a generation which felt disconcerted, and sometimes bewildered, by world events which placed in jeopardy all that they had lived for: the authority of white rule, organized around the liberal precepts of the British empire.

They both knew this to be a matter of civilization. Churchill was positioned at the very centre of things, at the apex of the imperial civilization. Smuts saw these questions not only as a dedicated upholder of empire, but also from his perspective as a colonial nationalist—a South African—and as a figure, ethnically, who was not British. What Churchill imbibed, Smuts had to learn. His commitments were more cerebral, often more profound, and never open to levity. He realized intellectually that maintenance of

British imperial rule into the future was going to be accomplished not only by armies, counter-insurgency, and by intensive police intervention, but by the evolution of a new civilization. It is not that Smuts, any more than Churchill, had qualms about armies, counter-insurgency, and intensive police intervention. Ruthlessness was indeed true to his character. But at the same time he was no doubt serious in his comments on Gandhi. However eccentric Gandhi might have seemed from Whitehall or Pretoria, he could call upon a depth of appeal to the Indian masses which made him exceedingly dangerous. When it came to civilization, Gandhi was no cheap, primitive huckster, as Churchill sometimes liked to dream: he was, Smuts came to apprehend, in a distant, fearful way, matchless.

This sense of civilization makes Wilson's thoughts on Smuts, and the parallel he made with Henry James, intriguing. Henry James, in the words of F. R. Leavis, was the 'intellectual poet-novelist of "high civilization"'.[5] James, the New Englander, was irresistibly drawn to Europe—to England in particular—due precisely to his search for the virtues of an old country. While England possessed history and the shaded textures of the past America, James reflected, was all light and no shadow. 'It takes a great deal of history', he wrote, 'to produce a little literature.' High civilization, in other words, was the necessary preserve of the old, and together they constituted the conditions necessary 'to set a novelist in motion'. But this movement from new to old, which is what James's literary imagination was about, was never merely a vindication of the old at the expense of the new. He knew well enough the American predilection for a 'superstitious' valuation of Europe.[6] What made literature, or civilization, work was the confrontation between new and old. The old on its own would die without a transfusion from the new. It was the terms of this encounter which would prove critical.

Smuts was no novelist. Nor were his imaginative capacities comparable to those of Henry James. But the problem was his, and in this Wilson was perceptive. Smuts had all the attributes of a colonial nationalist arising from a new nation, a nation which—for all its fantastic possibilities—was (in Smuts's own mind) a place of hyper-lightness, without shadings or history. To prosper it needed civilization, which England represented in abundance. But similarly England without the radical temper of the new, from the colonial margins, would atrophy and die. Smuts's thought was organized in these terms. Imagining South Africa through the beauties of its landscapes and through the clarity of the light on the *veld* was, as we have seen, a characteristic means for articulating the romance of the white man's nation. Yet as Smuts also knew, it was not all whiteness and light: the new carried with it the dark incubus of race. Not only did he have to contend with his own self-imposed mission of bringing together colony and metropole, old and new. He also had to devise a politics—a conception of civilization—in which the truths of white supremacy could conform to the requirements of a liberal, neighbourly, and inclusive imperial ideal.

Who was Smuts? And why his esteem in metropolitan England?

Jan Smuts

For a British generation born around the turn of the century, or a little after, Smuts would have been an entirely familiar figure, more so than any other colonial statesman, and more than most domestic politicians. It is revealing that a man so familiar could so quickly disappear from view. Today, if one asks well-informed, educated Britons, professional historians amongst them, about Smuts his name triggers vague memories, but the details have vanished.

Smuts was born into a Cape Afrikaner family in 1870. Cape Afrikaner sensibilities in this period were complex, and cannot be read back, in a reverse teleology, from the Afrikanerdom of the apartheid years. A sense of ethnic particularity did nothing to disturb loyalty to the British crown and to the empire more generally. When Cecil Rhodes became prime minister of the Cape in 1890, the Afrikaner Bond could offer its allegiance to Rhodes, and present its own role as one which was broad and inclusive. One recent historian has noted 'the low voltage of their [the Cape Afrikaners's] sense of ethnic solidarity with their Afrikaner kinsfolk in the republics'—in the Transvaal and in the Orange Free State.[7] As a youth and young man Smuts revered Rhodes. His respect for England and its civilization deepened when he studied at Cambridge University. But for a young Cape Afrikaner, even for one whose ethnic identifications with the larger Afrikaner cause ran at low voltage, Rhodes was a dangerous hero to choose. Ultimately Cape Afrikaner loyalties to Rhodes, to Britain, and to the empire could not withstand the intensifying antagonism of the British towards the Afrikaners of the Transvaal. It is a matter of dispute within the historiography whether the turning point arose with the abortive Jameson Raid of 1895 (when Rhodes attempted a pre-emptive strike against the Transvaal Republic); or with the appointment of the belligerent Sir Alfred Milner as governor of the Cape and as Britain's high commissioner in South Africa in 1897; or with the final onset of the war itself in 1899. But the effect is not contentious: what previously had run at low voltage was turned up high, generating as the norm what previously had been an exception—hostility to Britain. This was an enmity which turned Smuts as much as it did any other Afrikaner inhabiting the Cape.

Smuts's own retrospective memory was that it was the Jameson Raid which broke his loyalties to Rhodes and to the empire. 'It was *the* disaster', he wrote to the novelist Sarah Gertrude Millin in 1932.[8] He had, by the late 1890s, become incensed by the free-booting capitalist adventurism of the leading British imperialists—Rhodes, Milner, and Joseph Chamberlain were his villains—and, in consequence, when war was imminent he unhesitatingly supported the Afrikaners, his own patrimony, against the British. The full pitch of his anger was expressed in a pamphlet—*A Century of Wrong*—which he wrote on the eve of the South African War. His denunciation of British imperialism was fierce. He drew liberally from J. A. Froude, though turning him on his head, in order to demonstrate that what appeared to be beneficent was in truth nefarious. In the British edition he addressed the issue of native policy:

> That the Dutch in South Africa have treated the blacks as the English in other colonies have treated the aborigines is probably true…But, whereas in Tasmania and the Australian colonies the black fellows are exterminated by the advancing Britons, the immediate result of the advent of the Dutch in the Transvaal has been to increase the number of natives from 70,000 to 700,000, without including those who were attracted by the goldmines. In dealing with native races all white men have the pride of their colour and the arrogance of power.

Interwoven with condemnation of the British was a passionate call to the Afrikaner people to resist the threat of extinction which had now befallen them. At stake was 'the blood of our race':

> The hour has struck which will decide whether South Africa, in jealously guarding its liberty, will enter upon a new phase of its history, or whether our existence as a people will come to an end, whether we shall be exterminated in the deadly struggle for liberty which we have prized above all earthly treasures, and whether South Africa will be dominated by capitalists without conscience, acting in the name and under the protection of an unjust and hated Government 7,000 miles away from here.[9]

In his determination to destroy the British empire he was driven to advocate the instigation of guerrilla warfare in India, forcing the metropole to fight on every front—a strategy revived, in different circumstances in the 1960s, by *guevaristas* of many different stripes. With Kant in his backpack, he fought long and hard against the British, surviving extended periods behind enemy lines. Against enormous odds, the Afrikaners held out for three years. Yet in the summer of 1902 Smuts was one of the Boer commanders who understood the extent of their military defeat, and who advocated—in spite of everything—making peace.

In the face of defeat he believed that a single option presented itself: accommodation to the British, in the hope that the authentic traditions of English liberalism would, before too long, prevail over the mercenary opportunism (as he saw it) of Milner and his allies. There were many times of turbulence and humiliation, as Smuts himself described the experiences which followed. But reconciliation, he believed, finally arrived. The moment, sanctified in memory, came to assume mythic resonance in his subsequent recountings of his own biography, winning him to the cause of English civilization for the duration of his life. When the Liberals resumed power in 1906 Smuts was quick to visit the new prime minister, Sir Henry Campbell-Bannerman. 'I used no set arguments, but simply spoke to him as man to man and appealed only to the human aspect, which I felt would weigh deeply with him.'[10] So true ran the spirit of liberality in Campbell-Bannerman (as Smuts was fond of explaining thereafter) that he was immediately impressed by the virtue of Smuts's pleading, and declared at once his administration's intention to offer self-government to the vanquished South African colonies. The ills brought about by Rhodes, Milner, and Chamberlain had been absolved.

From that moment on he became the principal advocate in South Africa of maintaining his nation's links with the British crown and, whenever the opportunity arose, promoting the cause of English civilization. The British empire, he believed, had come to an end the evening he talked with Campbell-Bannerman. The rapacious polity, which could heroize Rhodes or Milner, had of its own accord transmuted into a freedom-loving confederation of autonomous nations, held together only by shared respect for the common historic values of England. To argue in these terms was at the same time to distance himself from the intransigent elements within Afrikaner nationalism, favouring in its place a fusion of Dutch and British into a newly vibrant colonial nationalism, founded on the shared affiliations of whiteness. His first political speech dilated on the need to ensure 'the consolidation of the white race'.[11] Fully conscious of his role as a nation-maker (with the founding fathers of the United States, and Abraham Lincoln too, at the back of his mind), Smuts played a critical role in the creation of the Union of South Africa in 1910, and was later to be prime minister, between 1919 and 1924, and again between 1939 and 1948, while he served as deputy prime minister in the coalition years, between 1933 and 1939. This was a career which could create its own myths. Just after his death, with due filial hyperbole, his son claimed: 'There is, in fact, very little in South Africa that did not spring from his fertile brain.'[12]

There were though many in South Africa who abhorred him. He created legions of political enemies, and many were hostile to his vision of Anglo-Afrikaner dominion. A multitude of others loathed him personally. According to the (old) *Dictionary of National Biography*, when Smuts returned to South Africa in 1895 to practise law, 'His lack of social graces was a serious handicap, and few briefs came his way.'[13] Nor did he make any attempt to disguise his attraction for the larger imperial—and later, the global—stage, which his detractors perceived (with justice) to carry with it a commensurate disregard for what he saw as the provincialism of his own nation. 'Here in England my work has been much approved by high and low,' he wrote in a typically gloomy mood in 1929 to his wife back home, 'only in my own country this belittling occurs and what the cause or motive is I fail to see. It is a funny world—enough to disgust one.'[14] The attraction of the metropole proved compelling for Smuts. He loved the inheritors of Quaker radicalism. He loved the imperial men who walked the corridors of power. He loved being lauded by all and sundry, the men who stood in awe of his intellect and—this austere, unerotic man—the women who fell for him. The public representatives of metropolitan England, Tory and Labour, imperialist and radical, created Smuts in their own image. 'The most considerable person in Greater Britain', was the verdict of A. G. Gardiner in 1916, a view emanating from the heart of the New Liberalism, while a year later C. P. Scott of the *Manchester Guardian* believed him to be 'perhaps the most popular man in the country'.[15] He became the civilized incarnation of the imperial frontier, statesman, and philosopher, the fount of wisdom on every conceivable matter.

In March 1917 he arrived in London to attend the first Imperial Conference. Smuts's success as the military leader of the South African forces in east Africa came before him. As his son later described it: 'England hailed him as the hero of the hour, the conqueror in the first big success of the war. The propaganda value of this former Boer general, now fighting for Britain, was exploited to the full. England needed cheering news. Into this world of weariness, dejection and disaster my father burst with a new message of hope and encouragement.'The propaganda worked well. He was compared to Caesar, Cromwell, and Napoleon. Winston Churchill, never slack in exploiting the moment, had this to say:

> At this moment there arrives in England from the outer marches of the Empire a new and altogether extraordinary man...The stormy and hazardous roads he has travelled by would fill all the acts and scenes of a drama. He has warred against us—well we knew it. He has quelled rebellion against our own flag with unswerving loyalty and unfailing shrewdness. He has led raids at desperate odds and conquered provinces by scientific strategy...His astonishing career and his versatile achievements are only the index of a profound sagacity and a cool, far-reaching comprehension...[16]

The following month the British prime minister, David Lloyd George, persuaded him to join the war cabinet, notwithstanding his lack of representation at Westminster, a post he held for some eighteen months. For all this time in Britain he was honoured as an exceptional public man. Both houses of parliament held a banquet for him, at which he scoffed at the idea that he was present as a guest of the British, 'but simply as one of yourselves'.[17] South Africans organized a dinner at the Savoy to celebrate his success in the mother country. In 1917 he received the freedom of the City of London, of Edinburgh, and of six other cities in Britain. The same year, the universities of Cambridge, Edinburgh, Glasgow, Wales, Dublin, and Manchester awarded him honorary degrees.[18] Offers of high honours came his way incessantly. In January 1918 he delivered a lecture to the Royal Geographical Society in the midst of a German air-raid, contending with 'the noise of anti-aircraft guns, and once or twice the rattle of pieces of shrapnel dropping on the dome'.[19] An intimate of his even has Smuts claiming that the King had requested him to remain in Britain so that he could become prime minister.[20]

He was a representative at the Versailles peace negotiations, though he hated the outcome. (During the various meetings he came close to Keynes, telling him in July 1919 'You have a great future before you'.[21]) He was a zealous advocate of the League of Nations, campaigning tirelessly to promote its cause. 'In my heart of hearts', he confided to a friend at the end of 1920, 'I feel that the League is my own child'.[22] Even when holding high office in South Africa he was always ready to travel to Britain, becoming one of the earliest patrons, from 1933, of the scheduled air-service from the Cape to London.[23] In the summer of 1921, when in London for the Imperial Conference, Smuts (with the approval of Lloyd George) intervened in the Irish crisis, hoping that as an erstwhile enemy of the British empire he could prevail upon Eamon De Valera to recognize the goodwill of the government; when the Stormont parliament was opened in the North, it was Smuts who drafted the King's speech, which emphasized the larger imperial dimensions of the Irish situation. This was the time when, as one biographer put it, 'Smuts had become the demigod of the British imperialists.'[24] In 1929, in his role as scholar and Africanist rather than as statesman, he presented the Rhodes lectures at Oxford University, and used the opportunity of the visit to deliver the Sidgwick Memorial Lecture at Cambridge, as well as to fit in other talks, on less scholarly matters, to other prestigious public institutions. Two years later, as president of the British Association for the Advancement of Science, he delivered the Association's centenary address, while at the same time working behind the scenes to influence the outcome of the Round Table on India. In 1934 he was elected Rector of St Andrews University.

In September 1939 Smuts led the campaign inside South Africa to persuade first the cabinet, and then parliament, to swing away from a position of neutrality—and indeed from alliance with the Axis powers—and to support the Allies. When, as a result of the success of his struggle, he once more became prime minister, he moved again close to the power-centres of the imperial state, an influence redoubled when his old friend Churchill assumed office in May 1940. (It was on the basis of personal friendship, for example, rather than official obligation that Churchill kept Smuts informed of the Tube Alloys project, concerning US manufacture of the atom bomb.) From South Africa he broadcast on the BBC to Britain, rivalling Churchill and J. B. Priestley in popularity, and he himself tuned in every night at six o'clock to hear the BBC reports from Daventry. In his own way he became something of an unlikely star, becoming 'a particular hero of the cinema news-reels'.[25] Penguin devoted one of its early paperbacks to his biography.[26] While in London in October 1942, he addressed both houses of parliament—the introduction given by Lloyd George, the thanks by Churchill, and the assembled worthies, in characteristically schoolboy fashion, offering a spirited rendition of 'For he's a jolly good fellow'. Fifteen million people in Britain listened to the speech on the BBC; Pathé,

Movietone, and Gaumont newsreels all covered it at length, Movietone extending the time of its newsreel especially to accommodate the occasion.[27] In Washington, President Roosevelt's Pacific War Council postponed its business so its members could listen to Smuts on a short-wave wireless in the president's office.[28] Leo Amery, witnessing the speech from the Royal Gallery, exulted in the wisdom of this 'prophet of Empire', and drew a flattering contrast to Churchill (who 'looked curiously gross and commonplace, a blend of eighteenth-century English and twentieth-century American'), while Chips Channon—diarist, socialite, and lofty cynic—initially finding the speech 'so bromidic' that he was convinced it must have been drafted by Sir Anthony Eden, shortly after was completely charmed by the South African and came to hold him in high esteem.[29] Even George Orwell, far distant from the political allegiances of the likes of Amery and Channon, could at this time quite unselfconsciously maintain of Smuts that 'Few modern statesmen are more respected in Britain.'[30] During the war he was both a powerful figure within the ruling circles of the British elite, and treated in the media as a popular national hero.

In the immediate postwar years he was a commanding personality at the inauguration of the United Nations, drafting the Preamble to the UN's founding document.[31] He was one of the speakers to launch the BBC's Third Programme, taking the opportunity to reflect on the inherent liberality of the Commonwealth which arose, he suggested, as a direct consequence of the bankruptcy of British imperialism during and after the Boer War.[32] When Stanley Baldwin died Smuts was chosen to replace him as Chancellor of Cambridge University. His portrait still hangs beside that of Milton at Christ's College. During the royal tour of South Africa in February 1947 he had the time of his life, ubiquitous in the newsreel and television reports, performing his many official duties with all the pomp he could muster, but also—when the occasion allowed—happy to fool around both for the cameras and for the delight of his guests. (His government, however, insisted that George VI should not shake hands with any Africans at official occasions and as a consequence the African National Congress boycotted the visit. This did nothing to disturb the royal family's continuing affection for Smuts: till late in the century, it seems, the older members still recalled him as 'dear Smuts'.[33]) In 1947 the Left Book Club published Arthur Keppel-Jones's *When Smuts Goes*, a fearful anticipation of what South Africa would be like in Smuts's absence and under the leadership of the National Party.[34] In the celebrated 'Teach Yourself History' series of the 1940s, Basil Williams discussed Smuts and Louis Botha in the single volume; Smuts was the only living figure included in the series. Williams concluded: 'one might call him one of the most all-embracing geniuses of our age'.[35] With his defeat by the National Party in 1948 his following in Britain became yet more intense.[36]

For some, the heroic memories of Smuts remained with them long after his death. Appropriately, Robert Menzies of Australia, another great colonial of the age whose adoration of England equalled that of Smuts, delivered the first Smuts memorial lecture at Cambridge University. As this followed in the wake of the Sharpeville massacre in South Africa, Menzies's eulogy to Smuts's imperialism had to be tempered in order to take account of the consequent turmoil in racial politics. His praise remained undimmed.[37] In 1970 Earl Mountbatten declared Smuts to be 'Undoubtedly one of the greatest men of the century', while later in the decade Reginald Maudling, once high in the firmament of British Conservatism, bemoaned the loss of the political 'titans'—whom he identified most memorably as Churchill, Smuts, and Menzies.[38] At the end of the 1980s the irrepressible Lord Blake could be found reflecting publicly on the fate of the world 'since Smuts'.[39] His most eminent biographer, the Australian Keith Hancock, decided on this epitaph: 'a countryman, a son of the soil, an Afrikaner, and something more than that—an African, perhaps the greatest African that had yet appeared'.[40] And even, in a rather different sector of the national culture, the impossibly long-living family cat of William Brown—the fictional 'Just William'—carried the name of Smuts.[41]

Philosopher of race

In British political life Smuts was a trouble-shooter, called upon to deal directly with intractable crises which could not easily be resolved by conventional party-political means—with the Irish, with striking Welsh miners, with Bela Kun's Bolshevik regime in Hungary, with India. In these instances he worked as a public rather than a party figure, and in this respect he was particularly regarded by both the two war leaders, Lloyd George and Churchill. As he was to comment later, 'On the merits of Right and Left I am myself somewhat Laodicean.'[42] In these terms, he was a component of the 'Caesarist' temper which ran through British politics in the first half of the century, in which national solutions overrode the putative constitutional norm of two-party alternation.[43] Yet in conducting these public duties Smuts represented himself and was seen as an authentically imperial statesman, who carried within him a vision of the whole empire unimpeded by mere national interest.

This was a more complex and ambivalent politics than might first appear. Smuts was proud of his own colonial nationalism, and never for a moment forgot that he himself was a founding father of the new nation of South Africa. For all his love of the metropole, he was neither English nor British, but South African—indeed, one of the first South Africans. Those at the centre were right to see him (from their metropolitan perspective) as a man of the colonial frontier. Owing to the particular exigencies of the national composition of the new South Africa—in which, from 1910, white British and white Afrikaner learnt to organize an alliance in order to maintain supremacy over the non-white population—Smuts had long appreciated the importance of subsuming national allegiance to the larger requirements of race. Effectively, this compact between British and Afrikaner had been sealed at the treaty of Vereeninging, when Chamberlain and Milner agreed to defer discussion of the black franchise until after the Boers had been granted responsible government. Yet Smuts was also drawn to the particular encodings of white authority which were manifest in the British empire. At the core of these idealized projections of white civilization lay the fictions of England. As an article of faith Smuts believed that these were not the exclusive preserve of the metropole. In this lay his wager with history, for he came to be convinced, as enthusiasts at the centre hoped, that other nations would claim for themselves the values, cultures, and customs which the British called their own. As he looked back on the war in South Africa he arrived at the puzzling paradox that it had 'taught the British people that the Boers were fighting, in some measure, for Britain's own traditional ideals'.[44]

To think in this way involved not a denial of colonial nationalism in favour of the nationalism of the metropole: Britishness without the centring of Britain can be understood as an ethnic structuring, in which individual nations represented local variants of the larger entity, or in the vocabulary of the day, local patriotisms. Kith and kin; the mother country; the Commonwealth; the crown—these and cognate terms all alluded to these wider affiliations, manifest in the peculiarly providential history of the British. Sometimes these attributes were described as British, sometimes as English, but whichever term was invoked, the purpose of their incantation was to insist on their universal applicability. The values nurtured in a single national history could be dispersed universally, the particular transformed into the general. Just as Sir Walter Scott made Scotland (in Smuts's eyes) 'a possession for the whole human race', so the empire—'the greatest actual political achievement of time'—universalized the ethnic codes of its core nations.[45] Smuts, colonial and former enemy of the empire, came to inhabit this inheritance with the supreme confidence of one who had undergone a conversion, learning to speak its mysteries with greater fluency than accredited nationals whose mother-tongue it was. Like generations of Scots and Welsh before him, he was pulled into a force-field of English ethnicity, reviving it as no domestic could. With him the moral truth of the frontier, in all its force, came home.[46]

If within this imperial mentality there could exist many national variables, a factor which was a deal more awkward to resolve was the question of non-white peoples. There were limits to the self-proclaimed universalism of the British. Irish Catholics, French Canadians, Afrikaners could orbit around these ethnic structures, sometimes included, sometimes excluded, sometimes white, sometimes not.[47] Historians are fully apprised of the manifold registers of Britishness, and of its capacious reach.[48] It has been shown that non-white peoples in British domains could adopt for themselves allegiance to Britain: among the black populations of South Africa and of the British colonies south of the Sahara, amongst indigenous or First-Nation peoples in Australia, Canada, and New Zealand, and in India and the Caribbean. Britishness could speak to men and women, metropolitan and colonial, black and white, anglophone and non-anglophone, Christian and non-Christian. Britishness could, moreover, provide the non-white native the opportunity to become a fully functioning modern inhabitant of the empire, overcoming his or her status as a native. As I have noted in previous chapters, there emanated from political leaders in London many formal commitments to the aspiration that allegiance to Britain would come from white and non-white subjects of the empire alike. Yet while all this is true, it was British rule which had turned newly colonized populations into natives in the first instance. In this lay the doubleness, or paradox, of Britishness—a point I will return to in the following volume.

As I have suggested, the common experience of the colonized was their transformation into the figure of the native. As Vivian Bickford-Smith has demonstrated most Creole elites of the late nineteenth century could not think of themselves as natives, but black Englishmen and Englishwomen. But by the 1910s, when for example the British had abandoned the Creoles of the Cape in favour of white Afrikaners, and those of West Africa for 'traditional' leaders, these erstwhile Englishmen and Englishwomen had no option but to learn their new roles as natives. Out of the new persona of the native came a new form of anti-colonial nationalism: but the ground from which it evolved was the doubling of the colonized subject, as simultaneously quasi-Briton and native. From the 1870s in the Cape, Bickford-Smith argues, race came to override class in the dynamics of social hierarchy, with separate laws—in 1887, 1892, and 1893—turning back the black vote.[49] In settler societies this process of nativization was general, and arguments about imperial Britishness need to be located within it. The racial limits to Britishness occurred at the point where the native came into being. Mahmood Mamdani's insight is pertinent, suggesting the need 'to go beyond the conventional thought that the real crime of colonialism was to expropriate the indigenous, and consider that colonialism perpetrated an even greater crime. That crime was to politicize indigeneity, first as a settler libel against the native, and then as a native self-assertion.'[50] This turning back of Britishness, and imposition—or reimposition—of the boundaries of nativehood was a historical process which, in the Cape, gathered pace from the 1880s. The Cape was Smuts's home territory. He came of age at a time when legislation was intent upon transforming black Britons into natives. For all his commitments to a benign Britain which would bring within its embrace ever greater numbers of peoples, Smuts was never one to proclaim the Britishness of the native. These—Briton and native—were, in his own mind, necessarily separate figures. For all his political career he was preoccupied with what came to be known as 'the native question'. His was a politics dedicated to the management of the native. His conception of empire, which came to be praised so fulsomely in the metropole, was fiercely racialized, in which the division between black and white was absolute. It was on these terms that the Union of South Africa was founded.[51]

Yet within the culture of metropolitan Britain whiteness, which in the colonies determined the structures of inclusion and exclusion, was largely unspoken. It was signified powerfully enough—in the symbol of the crown, in the providence of the English, in the daily habits of a freedom-loving people—but for the mosrt part worked silently, through many displacements. Smuts however was born into a culture in which the divide between black and white was spoken incessantly: he lived his life as a white man in a way that Churchill, for example, was not required to do. As he knew the black man, he knew the better what it was to be white. At the end of the 1940s an English admirer, writing from Ceylon and with knowledge of Africa, wrote to Smuts explaining: 'English people, with their copy-book maxims and their smug humanitarian theories, cannot understand the instinct inherited from forebears who have had to fight black races for their very existence'.[52] As a consequence, Smuts became one of those who assumed a strategic position in creating for the domestic political elite a way of articulating race which conformed to the codes of English ethnicity, and in the process reorganized those codes themselves. Or to give this greater specification: in an age in which political rights increasingly were universalized, Smuts struggled to reconcile his faith in the supremacy of white civilization with a regard for liberty and democracy. He persevered in his attempt to provide democratic justification for his own belief in the immutability of racial difference. On his death he bequeathed to the British a conception of race which could be recuperated by domestic politicians when called upon to have something intelligent or acceptable to say on the issues of empire and immigration. The legacies of an instinctive supremacism or racial superiority transmuted into matters of culture, civilization, and disposition. Whether it was in tempering the enthusiasm of black nationalist leaders, or justifying white landladies' refusal to let rooms to black applicants on account of the *other* tenants, a way of articulating racial difference emerged which appeared to confirm the essential liberality and neighbourliness of the English. In this sense Smuts functioned, for the British, as a philosopher of race.

Many in Britain, especially those who held the authority to shape public opinion, read his writings or heard him lecture. Many more gained an image of him from the wireless and the newsreel. By the end of his life, even those who had never read a word he had written would have known *him*. They would have known that he stood against South Africa's National Party and thus against the injustices of apartheid. And they would have known too (for they were told it often enough) that he represented 'the best' of England's destiny overseas, equally firm in his determination to hold back the vague menace which the idea of Africa itself continued to signify. Audiences watching him in the cinemas may have been impressed or bored to tears; they may have cheered or booed. But in his persona these complex histories were condensed. He was known, in other words, as myth. In such ways philosophies become common sense.

White supremacy in South Africa

Smuts began and ended his life a white supremacist. No apologist can turn this around. He was a prime mover in the organization of segregation in South Africa; from the moment the Union was founded he set out to dispel all doubts that the new nation would be anything but a 'white man's country'.[53] Like the vast majority of his generation of imperial men, he took it as axiomatic that sexual relations between black and white would bring all manner of evil, contaminating from within the structures of white civilization. In 1896, in introducing an article of Olive Schreiner's in the *South African Telegraph*, he declared that he looked upon 'the intermixture of black and white in South Africa as in every way the darkest spot of our civilisation, the cancer which, unless arrested and kept within the narrowest limits, will ultimately corrode and corrupt the very life-centres of our society'.[54]

If racial 'intermixture' represented one danger, non-white immigration represented another. Smuts's vision of the new South Africa was of a nation embracing the widest spectrum of white cultures. This he made clear on the eve of the founding of the Union. 'The whole meaning of Union in South Africa is this: we are going to create a nation—a nation which will be of a composite character, including Dutch, German, English and Jew, and whatever white nationality seeks refuge in this land—all can combine. All will be welcome.'[55] This was the logic which derived from the intoxicating idea of creating a white man's country, the corollary of which encouraged embargoes to be placed on non-whites—Indian and Chinese—who might have thought of making this new country their own. In this, Smuts was expressing sentiments little different from whites in New South Wales or in British Columbia, or indeed in Westminster, when such issues had to be addressed. But what gave dramatic intensity to their articulation by Smuts, and by others in South Africa, was the perception that they, as whites, composed a vulnerable outpost of civilization which existed perilously on the tip of darkest Africa, always on the point of being overwhelmed or submerged by the inchoate forces of blackness which pressed in on them. From his earliest moments as nation-maker, even when imagining the contours of a future national literature, such anxieties touched Smuts at the deepest core of his thought.

> It must never be forgotten that the race struggle is destined to assume a magnitude on the African continent such as the world has never seen and the

imagination shrinks from contemplating; and in that appalling struggle for existence the unity of the white camp, to which the past has so signally contributed, will not be the least necessary condition—we will not say of obtaining victory, but of warding off (the ultra pessimists say of postponing) annihilation.[56]

His was a culture which lived in a permanent emergency, peculiarly attuned to apprehensions of its own destruction.

The overriding issue, however, lay precisely in the native question. From his first public pronouncements he expressed his belief that democratic theory, deriving from the historical traditions of Western Europe and the United States, was 'inapplicable to the coloured races of South Africa'.[57] These views he repeated, in almost identical terms, in the period up to and including his delivery of the Rhodes lectures in 1929.[58] Thereafter, he tended to be less explicit, though even on the occasions he appeared most sceptical of the effectiveness of segregation, the underlying sentiment remained unmodified. For Smuts, race was not an issue which could be resolved by political society. It was too profoundly a historical matter for the state, with its short-term purview and its mechanistic administration, to intervene in effectively. Racial difference was a consequence of centuries of human development, distributing a high level of civilization to some and a low level to others. As he put it in 1935, South Africa contained 'human races ranging from the very lowest to the highest'.[59] Essentially, race was a question of civilization, an inherited human problem whose resolution stretched far into the future. In the interim, the management of racial difference was best effected, not by politics, but by the good moral judgement of the race to whom history had bequeathed the superior qualities of civilization.

The correspondence between Smuts and J. X. Merriman at the beginning of 1906 is revealing. Merriman was a close political ally and friend of Smuts; a man of Whiggish temperament, he was to be Louis Botha's rival for the office of prime minister in the first government of the Union. Merriman wrote to Smuts in order to comment on a memorandum the latter had drafted arising from the discussions with Campbell-Bannerman. 'What struck me at once in reading your admirable remarks on liberal principles', Merriman commented,

was that they were open to the same objection in kind as the American Declaration of Independence, viz., that you ignore three-quarters of the population because they are coloured. I know what a very delicate subject this is and believe me I touch on it with great reluctance...I can see an infinity of trouble in this Native question however carefully we handle it. I gather that the policy of Milner and of those on whom his mantle has fallen is to unite the two white races in opposition to the black. From their point of view this is Machiavellian in its astuteness.

Now taking myself as an example of those who are not negrophilists but at the same time believers in our Native policy, I do not like the Natives at all and I wish we had no black man in South Africa. But there they are, our lot is cast with them by an overruling Providence and the only question is how to shape our course so as to maintain the supremacy of our race and at the same time do our duty.

Merriman outlined the two options which he believed presented themselves. First, one could recognize the right to vote of all those who qualified, regardless of colour, on the model of the old Cape; or, on the model of the Transvaal, the Orange Free State, and Natal, opt for 'the total disenfranchisement of the Native'.

To this Smuts replied:

I sympathize profoundly with the Native races of South Africa whose land it was long before we came here to force a policy of dispossession on them. And it ought to be the policy of all parties to do justice to the Natives and to take all wise and prudent measures for their civilization and improvement. But I don't believe in politics for them. Perhaps at bottom I do not believe in politics at all as a means for the attainment of the highest ends; but certainly as far as the Natives are concerned politics will to my mind only have an unsettling influence. I would therefore not give them the franchise, which in any case would not affect more than a negligible number of them at present. When I consider the political future of South Africa I must say that I look into shadows and darkness; and then I feel inclined to shift the intolerable burden of solving that sphinx problem to the ampler shoulders and stronger brains of the future.[60]

Smuts, for another four decades or more, *was* the future: more than most, 'the intolerable burden' was his, and he never found the political means to resolve it. The more intractable the issue became, the more he wrestled with his conscience, and the more incapable he became of ever finding a solution. In every move he made the ethical imperatives were trumped by the ethnic imperatives of whiteness transcendent. He placed himself in an impossible situation.

The same logic, and the same dilemmas, can be seen in Smuts's response to the agitation led by Gandhi. Gandhi learnt his politics in South Africa. He arrived in the early 1890s as a young barrister, having trained in London. His sympathies were powerfully inflected towards the ideals of British civilization. Keith Hancock, Smuts's biographer, put it like this: 'Gandhi, if anything, was more deeply in love than Smuts was with the British constitution and the British habit of compromise, which he believed to be harmonious with the basic values of his own civilisation.'[61] On his arrival in South Africa Gandhi discovered that the realities of life for Indians—subjects of the crown—in Natal were far distant from these ideals. In attempting to correct the situation he found himself pulled into politics, launching in 1894 the Natal Indian Congress. His loyalty to Britain did not diminish; indeed, in part it marked the source of his political inspiration. He served in an ambulance unit in the South African War, an experience he underwent again during the uprising in Natal in 1906. On this latter occasion, witnessing the brutality of the reaction of the white authorities, his faith in the righteousness of British justice cracked.[62] The following year, as a result of Campbell-Bannerman's decision to concede self-government—the very act which had done so much to impress Smuts of the virtue of the British—the Transvaal passed the so-called Black Act, which restricted new Indian immigration and placed systematic restrictions on those Indians already there, and included new requirements for them to register with the authorities. Gandhi led the resistance against the Act, persuading large numbers of Indians not to register and organizing, in effect, his first campaign of civil disobedience. The campaign spread beyond the Transvaal, and came to embrace the entire array of issues which underpinned Indian discrimination. The struggle continued as an intense public issue until the outbreak of the First World War, a period which coincided with the founding of the Union.

Smuts took it upon himself to confront this challenge, both by police intervention and by negotiating directly with Gandhi. The two principal antagonists, with their shared passion for the codes of British public conduct, held each other in mutual regard, a respect which developed, in later years, into what might even have been an uneasy distant friendship. An ingredient in the persona of the mythic Smuts has him accepting a pair of sandals made by Gandhi while the latter was in prison, a possession in which Smuts subsequently invested great emotional attachment. In the early 1920s Smuts wrote to Gandhi, reflecting on their prewar confrontations, and attempting to explain why he was obliged to act as he did:

> When I was about the same time as you studying in England, I had no race prejudice or colour prejudice against your people. In fact, if we had known each other we should have been friends. Why is it then that now we have

become rivals we have conflicting interests? It is not colour prejudice or race prejudice, though some of our people do ignorantly talk in those terms, but then there is one thing which I want you to recognise. It is this. I may have no racial legislation, but how will you solve the difficulty about the funda-mental difference of our cultures? Let alone the question of superiority, there is no doubt that your civilisation is different from ours. Ours must not be overwhelmed by yours. That is why we have to go in for legislation which must in effect put disabilities upon you.[63]

And that, for Smuts, was that.

There were two public episodes later in his political life when Smuts formally explained his views on race. On each occasion the same dilemmas asserted themselves. In the first of these, in the Rhodes lectures at Oxford, he presented an unambivalent defence of white supremacy, and of the con-sequent politics of segregation. The native, he argued, was neither inferior, 'nor a man and a brother'. In saying this, he rejected the biological deter-minism characteristic of mainstream racial thought of the time. At the same moment he rejected a universal humanism, a humanism—in terms of race—which had been forged in the abolition struggles a century earlier. The conviction that the black slave was 'a man and a brother' went to the very heart of the abolition movement. In repudiating this so starkly, Smuts was explicitly turning himself against an entire tradition of Nonconformist and radical belief.

In place of these 'two extremes', he drew from a cultural anthropology which—formally—paid heed to the distinctive virtues of the way of life of both black and white. To apply external criteria—the criteria, for example, of universalism deriving from the Enlightenment—to the cultures of Africa would be, Smuts argued, entirely inappropriate. Civilization for the native needed to develop on 'specifically African foundations'. Thus 'segregation' and 'separate parallel institutions' provided the most benevolent solution for all, preserving not only the distinctive cultures of the respective races, but also 'public health, racial purity, and public good order'. For this to work, white settlement, white capital, and 'white employment' were necessary conditions; and more specifically, within the sovereignty of the empire, strong white dominions in Africa were the most desirable means for secur-ing future development. In South Africa itself, parallel development of black and white needed, he insisted, the most careful regulation of black employ-ment in white locations. Native women and children must on no account move into white areas. 'This the law should vigorously preserve, and

systems—whether it is administered through passes or in any other way—
should only allow the residence of males for limited periods, and for the
purposes of employment among the whites.'[64]

At this moment, by calling upon a cultural justification for segregation,
Smuts was at his most assured philosophically, finding a neat intellectual
resolution to his problems in coming to terms with the native question. And
by describing a humanist universalism as an 'extremism', equivalent in its
perils to an unreconstructed racism, he was able to position himself in the
moderate, rational centre, adopting an idiom which was peculiarly reassuring to his British audience. From such a perspective those in the metropole
who *did* believe in the justice of equal rights could be condemned, in a fearful discursive economy, as *kafferboeties*—or as this appears in its genteel translation, 'negrophilists'—a formulation which effectively closed the issue.[65]

The private correspondence, however, suggests a rather different picture
from the public man in the Sheldonian Theatre, sharing his knowledge of
the native deriving from a lifetime's experience on the racial frontier. It
shows, on the contrary, a man who continued to exhibit extraordinary confusion about how such policies were to be implemented, and who continued to be assailed by ethical misgivings—misgivings, however, which never
found sufficiently powerful a voice to compete with the unrelenting truths
of race.[66]

The second occasion was marked by Smuts's speech to the South African
Institute of Race Relations in January 1942. Here again, he opened by distinguishing his own views from the prevailing philosophies of equality
between black and white, on the one hand, and on the other, of racial superiority. Going back to Rhodes he reinvented the idea of 'trusteeship'. This
idea he saw as being codified in the ethical aspirations of the League of
Nations, particularly in the League's declaration that 'the lot, the advancement, the upliftment of the backward peoples is the sacred trust of civilization'. He emphasized the ethical obligations embodied in the idea of trust,
suggesting that its connotations were 'almost religious'. Trusteeship, he
argued, was necessary because of the low level of 'cultural advance' of the
blacks of South Africa. From this ethical point of view, Smuts concluded
that segregation in South Africa had been 'a very great disappointment', and
that it has fallen upon 'evil days'. Above all, segregation simply was not
working in the urban areas: 'You might as well try to sweep the ocean back
with a broom.' Self-interest needed to give way to the ethics of trusteeship;
though, he added, if the situation were not speedily resolved the danger of

the white population sinking to the level of the black would become a reality. Yet he conceded that there were many problems, especially in translating 'the beautiful word "trusteeship" into practice'.[67]

It wasn't clear at the time, and it isn't clear now, where such thoughts left him. From the late 1930s, the migration of white Afrikaners *and* of blacks from the countryside to the cities placed extraordinary pressure on the established systems of segregation, turning the urban areas into new arenas of confrontation. This situation was exploited by the Nationalists, who from this point imagined the white man to be fighting anew old battles, but henceforth in the theatre of economic competition.[68] When Smuts condemned segregation, it was more its particular manifestations than the thing itself which perturbed him. Two days after his talk to the Institute of Race Relations he was writing, in private, that 'Of course, everybody in this country is agreed that European and African should live apart and preserve their respective cultures', only to add: 'But much more than that is called for today in the new Africa.'[69]

Smuts's confusions on segregation left him vulnerable to political attack from his domestic enemies, especially when it came to debating and implementing policy. He complained often enough in his letters that he was criticized from every quarter—both for being too hard on the blacks of South Africa, and too soft.[70] When segregation became an issue of policy, he vacillated and prevaricated. Over matters of implementation he was notably inconsistent, more often than not reacting to proposals arising from others. Yet so profound in his mind was the absolute justice of white supremacy that, in confronting those more militant than him on the manner of instituting segregation, invariably he was outflanked.

At no time was this more apparent than in the 1930s when J. B. Hertzog was prime minister. Through the 1920s Hertzog and Smuts were not simply political opponents. Hertzog in particular was in the habit of heaping sulphurous abuse on Smuts, both as a politician and as an individual. Even in what one supposes is the modified form in which this enters the genteel biographies, we find reference to 'caked dung' and 'bastard sheep'. Yet by 1933 the crisis in the South African state was deemed to be so serious that the two agreed to work together in a coalition government, with Hertzog as prime minister and Smuts as his deputy. In a bid to effect the unity of the white race and to further the development of a specifically South African nationalism, the following year the fusion of their respective parties— Smuts's South African Party and Hertzog's National Party—was pushed through by the two leaders.[71] As prime minister, Hertzog set about tightening the systems of segregation and continuing the process of winding back the political rights of the native population in the Cape. As the momentum of this new legislative offensive gathered pace Smuts's protégé, J. H. Hofmeyr, resigned, representing himself as a liberal on the issue of native rights who could stomach no more. Smuts remained, understanding well enough the consequences for his own reputation. He quibbled about technicalities and about legalisms. But, at bottom, his own incapacity to reconcile his faith in white supremacy with his own ethical mission towards the native left him no room to manœuvre. On the native question, he wrote to a friend during this period, 'one easily slips into measures which appear harsh and retrogressive'.[72]

Conceptual distinctions between Smuts's preferred versions of segregation and apartheid proper are not easily drawn. Segregation constituted the very foundations of his ideal of South Africa as a white man's nation. Smuts himself was prepared to go on record declaring that the difference between his own views and those of the Nationalists dedicated to apartheid was a matter of degree.[73]

The historiography on this is sophisticated and voluminous; it is complicated, on the one hand, by differing interpretations of the effectiveness of segregation, as policy, in the period between 1910 and 1948; and on the other, by differing assessments of the cohesion and homogeneity of the apartheid state from 1948. There is an argument that, the unevenness of implementation notwithstanding, there existed an unbroken lineage from Milner in the first decade of the century, to the Smuts and Hertzog variants of segregation, culminating in apartheid in the Nationalist period.[74] An alternative reading suggests that a more fractured development occurred. Saul Dubow, for example, believes that segregation did not become a coherent policy until the 1920s, and that this system in turn needs to be distinguished from apartheid, if only due to the 'dogmatic intensity' of the latter.[75] Each approach—stressing either continuity or discontinuity—has many variants. Much of the contention arises from the question of whether explanatory primacy should be given to the economic functions of separate development, or to its ideological or cultural autonomy. The issue cannot be resolved here. One might only note in this context that by the 1940s—by the time of Smuts's speech to the Institute of Race Relations—the acceleration of urbanization had indeed demonstrated the obsolescence of the inherited practices of segregation. This much Smuts appreciated. If segregation were to be continued, this conjunctural emergency indicated that more vigilant systems would have to be introduced, requiring tighter administration of those blacks active in the urban economies and, indeed, greater state intervention in moving the black populations from the urban to the rural zones. In effect, Smuts never had to confront the politics which was necessary to ensure that segregation continued into the 1950s, and we shall never know how he would have responded politically to such a situation.

It is clear that in his own mind he regarded segregation conducted without the beneficence of British liberality to be a danger. Segregation could only work, he believed, as part and parcel of a fully civilizing project. When at the Versailles Peace Conference Hertzog had first suggested that the Transvaal and the Orange Free State secede from the British empire, Smuts wrote that this would entail 'the complete isolation of Dutch-speaking Africa and in that isolation its stranglement and decay...It means that a civilised South Africa becomes a dream, and that the white people of this country have decided to commit political suicide.'[76] The building of a country properly belonging to 'the white man' *depended on* continuing connection to the sources of European civilization. Conversely, segregation deriving only from the instincts of a narrow Afrikanerdom, as Smuts perceived apartheid to be, could only bring about (in Smuts's view of things) the destruction of South Africa. In this perspective, segregation was not the issue. The overriding duty, for Smuts and his allies, was to invent a mode of segregation which conformed to the enlightened codes of European civilization.

The necessity of Europe, in Smuts's imagination, for white Africa was demonstrated with force in his final years as prime minister. In 1943 he returned to the issue to which he had devoted so much time in the first years of the Union: the Indian population in South Africa. This happened, we need to note, during the war when many urgent matters pressed in; and at least potentially it concerned the citizens of a powerful imperial ally. Smuts's government sought to overturn the rights of Indians resident in Natal, rights which had been in place since the 1860s. Pressure had been put on the government, from below, by the English-speaking whites—not by Afrikaners—of Natal. The Trading and Occupation of Land Bill (the Pegging Bill) was drafted, whose purpose was to extend severe restrictions on the freedoms of Indians living in the Transvaal and Natal. Indians in South Africa were predictably outraged, and the government in India made a number of formal and informal overtures to ensure that the bill was not made law. After much prevarication, and after many compromises were made and failed, the South African government finally passed, in 1946, the Asiatic Land Tenure and Indian Representation Act. As the name implied, this imposed new restrictions on the purchase and tenure of land and, in an attempt to placate critics, created a separate electoral register for Indians, allowing them the right to elect three white representatives. Given the agitation which had gripped India since August 1942, this was hardly a measure which political leaders in India could countenance. Smuts himself insisted on seeing the problem as an entirely domestic matter. In introducing the bill he claimed: 'That is what we intend in this Bill—fair play and justice for our Indian fellow-citizens, but we do not want to change the structure of our society...we want to preserve the European orientation of our society.'[77]

India withdrew its high commissioner, and took the issue to the first meeting of the General Assembly of the United Nations.[78] Smuts himself travelled to the United States to speak in the debate. Mrs Ranjit Pandit unleashed a ferocious attack on him and on South Africa, and India's position was vindicated. At the UN Smuts faced a new world, in which the voice of non-white peoples was assuming a new-found power, and which left him not so much angered as bewildered.[79] The author of the Preamble to the UN Charter found himself the first to be arraigned for violating its principles.

Smuts, we can see, was a practical philosopher of white supremacy. At the same time he was a nation-builder in the classic nineteenth-century mould. As much as Bismarck or Cavour or Lincoln, he believed his people to be the historic agent in a larger universal, providential history. In 1899, with the war with Britain clearly in view, he wrote to Jan Hofmeyr:

> Our people throughout South Africa must be baptized with the baptism of blood and fire before they can be admitted among the other great peoples of the world. Of the outcome I have no doubt. Either we shall be exterminated or we shall fight our way out; and when I think of the great fighting qualities that our people possess, I cannot see why we should be exterminated. So, even if the worst happens, I am quite calm and await the future with confidence.[80]

Having undergone this baptism of fire, and having made accommodation with the British and their empire, Smuts always looked to this larger, messianic stage, and henceforth was to be suspicious of the local and often (as he perceived it) 'unhistoric' aspirations of the Afrikaners. On returning from leading South African troops against the Germans in East Africa in 1916, he adopted the epic tone: 'We have followed in the steps of the Voortrekkers...

South Africa, instead of being a small, cramped, puny country, gnawing at its own entrails...will become the great country which is its destiny.'[81] And the destiny of the newly fashioned white race of South Africa was one which, for Smuts, was *Pan-African*. In 1888, when Cecil Rhodes visited Victoria College at Stellenbosch, the young Jan Smuts delivered a speech of welcome on behalf of the student body. Its theme, guaranteed to find a welcome audience in Rhodes, was—white—Pan-Africanism.[82]

As a founder of South Africa Smuts was not alone in believing the Union of 1910 marked merely a provisional moment in the expansion of the nation. It appeared to the founding fathers, Botha as much as Smuts, that the three high commission territories—Basutoland, Bechuanaland, and Swaziland—would all become incorporated into the Union, the only question being one of timing.

Rhodesia, for Smuts and anglophiles like him, represented simply the next logical step. When, in 1922, incorporation into the Union was put to Rhodesian voters, Smuts was active—both as politician and, by happenstance, as a private tourist—in advocating its virtues. The view from London, in the person of the colonial secretary, Winston Churchill, was positive too. With Ireland, India, and Egypt in turmoil, a greater South Africa under Smuts's leadership seemed a good bet. Losing the referendum was a blow to Smuts, convincing him that the Rhodesians possessed no vision of empire, existing merely as unhistoric 'little Jingoes'.[83] It also halted, at least temporarily, his ambitions for Northern Rhodesia and Kenya, though it did not entirely quell his hopes of creating a 'second Rand' on the Katanga copperbelt.

After the First World War German South Africa was mandated to the Union. Smuts hoped desperately it would duly be taken over formally. In part it was to secure this that, after the Second War, he travelled to the United Nations—though on this, as on the legislative discrimination against the Indians of Natal and the Transvaal, he and the Union were humiliated.

Many public figures in South Africa and in Britain held the Portuguese in scant regard, failing to see how they could be accepted as true imperialists, and thus looking to the time when South Africa would acquire, minimally, Mozambique. During the First World War the South African cabinet unanimously agreed to the idea of purchasing Mozambique, though it was not thought fit to consult Portugal on the matter.[84] Smuts himself was particularly inventive in his various schemes to divest Portugal of its African colonies.

And there were arch-expansionists—as ever, with Smuts in the van—who dreamt of the entire eastern continent, from the Cape to Cairo, coming under the rule of Britain and the white man. In a speech to the Afrikaner Circle in Pretoria in 1933 Smuts's views on expansion differed little from the schoolboy romantic of the 1880s, nor indeed from the elder statesman of the 1940s:

> We must cultivate an Africa outlook; we must expand, otherwise trouble will in the future arise within our boundaries...I have a passion for Africa. I love Africa...There is something that lies deep in the Afrikaner. This is the northern prospect. The drive was always to the north...In the future we shall be involved with Pan-African questions. Our system and our culture cannot in the long term be maintained within our borders. We shall have to go farther.[85]

Smuts and Leo Amery

On these issues Smuts's most intimate ally was in London, not Pretoria: it was, predictably enough, Leo Amery. For the greater part of half a century they can be found hatching schemes and plotting and dreaming, the cartographies of empire resonating in their imaginations. The moment Amery was appointed secretary of state for the colonies, in November 1924, Smuts was on to him:

> All the highlands of Eastern Africa from the Union to Abyssinia are healthy for Europeans and can be made a great European State or system of States during the next three or four generations. It is one of the richest parts of the world, and only wants white brains and capital to become enormously productive. But the present tendencies seem all in favour of the Native and the Indian, and the danger is that one of the greatest chances in our history will be missed. The cry should be 'the highlands for the whites' and a resolute white policy should be pursued. The fruits of such a policy will be a *White* State in time more important than Australia. There is land enough for all the vast Native population on the flanks of the highlands. But the Natives by themselves will continue to stagnate as they have stagnated for the last ten thousand years. A great White Africa along the Eastern backbone, with railway and road communications connecting North and South, will be a first-class addition to the Empire and will repay all the capital put into it. It is an expansion of the Rhodes policy. Why should it not become *your* policy?[86]

In this Amery needed no bidding. His vision of the British empire was boundless. A few years earlier he had been writing to Lloyd George outlining his belief 'in that Southern British World which runs from Cape Town through Cairo, Bagdad and Calcutta to Sydney and Wellington'.[87] A decade on he was happy to contemplate the idea that a northern arc be added to the empire, comprising Iceland and Greenland as stepping-stones to Canada, at the same moment that Smuts was reminding him again of a settler dominion in Africa south of the equator which would be the equal of Canada and Australia.[88]

The two of them were irrepressible. The historical and geographical precedents they bandied back and forth, with all the erudition of Oxford and Cambridge confirming every utterance, signalled the wonderful ease of an imperial caste incapable of noticing that the world had moved. Even in the midst of the Second World War Amery's memories of classical civilization were powerfully present. At the end of 1943, in apprising Smuts of his vision of postwar Europe, he insisted that 'The area in question is really very much Scandinavia plus the old Roman Empire West and South of the limes.' (The *limes* marked the boundaries of the classical empire of Rome.) Norway and Iceland, he suggested to Smuts, would be particularly welcome elements in the new settlement, as 'Their standards of life are ours'.[89] Not much later he was back corresponding with Smuts, anticipating the possibility of Norway joining, and Ireland rejoining, the Commonwealth and, in a heroic bid to transcend the petty misfortunes of the past, the USA as well, 'though I should not welcome that unless and until the Commonwealth has grown to be in resources and world position once more at least a match to America'.[90]

Norway, Iceland, the United States—these were the dreams of an older imperial generation, unbalanced by the decline of British power. Churchill, at the same time, was reflecting on the possibilities of bringing royalist Greece into the Commonwealth in order to aid the white terror unleashed against the partisans. By the end of the 1940s Amery's public standing was not high, his imperial flourishes too easily regarded as the fancies of an old man.

And yet: strategic diplomacy and the *realpolitik* of international relations are not immune to the dreams of previous times—to the dreams of old men—as the histories of empires have demonstrated often enough.[91] To suppose that presidents Roosevelt, Truman, or one of their successors would have hitched the fortunes of the USA to colonial Britain—if it were a serious consideration—was pretty deranged. To worry away at Iceland was the pastime only of the true initiate. But the idea of creating a white dominion across the breadth of eastern Africa was a scheme which had been close to the heart of Smuts since the Union of South Africa was founded. This was of a different order. For both Smuts and Amery, for obvious reasons, the Union was to be the core of any such venture. After Britain's loss of India in 1947, the strategic focus of empire was relocated to the eastern Mediterranean and to central Africa, as a conscious reinvention of colonialism for the postwar epoch.[92] Indian independence marked not the end of empire, but its renewal—a forgotten dimension in the history of Britain in the 1950s. The dream of the white man's country animated not only the generation of Amery, Churchill, and Smuts, but younger political tyros, and younger emigrants from the metropole too, who only knew the heyday of empire from stories.

The defeat of Smuts in 1948, and the hostility of the new Nationalist government in South Africa towards Britain, however, ensured that the Union would be excluded from the new colonial experiment. The eventual founding of the Central African Federation, comprising Southern and Northern Rhodesia and Nyasaland, occurred after Smuts had died. For British strategists the Federation was designed to serve as a bulwark *against* South Africa. That such a thing could have happened was incontrovertible evidence that Smuts's hopes for a white Pan-Africanism, spreading outward from the Union, had been dashed. But even so, the imperial and racial vision of a new white dominion in Africa, equal in potential to Australia and Canada, was one which he had cherished.

Protagonist of the white race

When Smuts died in September 1950 Amery had no qualms in comparing him to Chamberlain, Rhodes, and Milner, precisely the figures whom Smuts had vilified most passionately at the time of the South African War:

> For me it is the loss not only of an old friend but of the man with whom, since Milner's death, I have been most closely in sympathy on public affairs and to whom I could write and speak most freely. He was a very remarkable man, on the whole one of the few great men I have known, though not perhaps of the sheer creative force of Chamberlain or Rhodes, or of the deeper balance as well as of the administrative power of Milner. His life was certainly one of the most remarkable chapters in Commonwealth and world history in the last fifty years.[93]

This was a tribute, clearly, which came deep from the heartland of Britain's imperial culture, recognizing Smuts as a man who represented the very apogee of his civilization: of his nation, his empire, and his race.

A strikingly similar assessment came from an entirely contrary perspective: from the great philosopher of black Pan-Africanism, W. E. B. DuBois in the USA. DuBois, it seems, had always kept his eye on Smuts, referring to him, on different occasions, as 'a great liberal statesman' and alternatively as 'that great hypocrite'. DuBois was present at the founding conference of the United Nations in San Francisco when Smuts made his plea for an article on human rights, an act he judged, unsurprisingly, to be 'an astonishing paradox'.[94] DuBois and Paul Robeson were both active lobbyists before and during the founding conference.[95] With this still in his mind, DuBois addressed the Manchester Pan-African Congress, in October 1945, and reminded his audience of that *other* Pan-Africanism represented so forcefully by Smuts.[96] This he conceptualized, specifically, as a 'white Pan-Africanism'.[97]

More dramatically, twenty years earlier DuBois had identified Smuts as 'the greatest protagonist of the white race'. 'Liberal England', he wrote, 'wanting world peace and fearing French militarism, backed by the English thrift that is interested in the restored economic equilibrium, found as one of its most prominent spokesmen Jan Smuts of South Africa, and Jan Smuts stands for the suppression of the blacks.' He went on:

> Jan Smuts is to-day, in his world aspects, the greatest protagonist of the white race. He is fighting to take control of Laurenço Marques from a nation that recognizes, even though it does not realize, the equality of black folk; he is fighting to keep India from political and social equality in the empire; he is fighting to insure the continued and eternal subordination of black to white in Africa; and he is fighting for peace and good will in a white Europe which can by union present a united front to the yellow, brown and black worlds. In all this he expresses bluntly, and not yet without finesse, what a powerful host of white folk believe but do not plainly say in Melbourne, New Orleans, San Francisco, Hongkong, Berlin and London.[98]

Those to whom Smuts was a hero would have found little to argue with in this account. But the implications are significant.

The emphasis of DuBois's depiction falls on the white Pan-Africanism of Smuts—'in his world aspects'—and on his capacity to speak the truths of race. But it is interesting why he should have singled out Smuts. In DuBois's native United States there were any number of white supremacists a deal more intransigent than Smuts; in Europe and its colonies, many more imperial tribunes a deal more belligerent in the cause of whiteness. Nor, as I have suggested, in his personal enmities was Smuts conspicuously or unusually racist. The contrast to Churchill, for example, is marked in the relations of the two men to Gandhi. Smuts, resolute in his determination to hold the line of civilization, was in his personal relations with Gandhi respectful in a distant kind of way, and maybe even friendly. Churchill, on the other hand, could barely constrain himself when he came to consider Gandhi, either deriding him in public, or jesting in private in a manner which suggests the degree to which Gandhi truly did trouble him.[99] It seems, perhaps, as if DuBois was implying that Smuts was particular in his resolve to speak what others dared not speak. This may be so. But DuBois also made it clear that it was, essentially, *liberal* England which took Smuts to heart, and that his espousal of race was 'not...without finesse'.

Smuts was learning to articulate a politics of race. He was learning to educate what Milner had earlier identified as the primitive instincts of whiteness—which, in the age of empire, increasingly came to turn on visceral antagonism—into a publicly constituted politics, with an appointed language and philosophy. DuBois more than many knew about the fictions or masquerades of whiteness and he knew too, as a consequence, that racial whiteness as a component of a democratic politics in the twentieth century was an issue which needed to be addressed. A specifically 'white' politics needed a particular voice. Smuts found this voice (though Churchill did not). A critical moment in its construction occurred in Smuts's alighting upon the fact that those who, in the twentieth century, believed the black man to be 'a man and brother' were, in fact, *extremists*. This he believed to be a peculiarly metropolitan distemper, for those in the metropole could not properly know the native. It thus lay with him, as a moral duty, to overcome this ignorance. Condemnation of humanist universalism as a political extremism, beyond the bounds of the given constitutional codes, came quietly to be enveloped in the discursive norms of public life in Britain. In the 1950s and 1960s it could be heard time and again. For greatest political effect it was spoken in the voice of liberal tolerance. In this logic, the truth of race imperceptibly evolved into an essentially democratic mission. Smuts, as the statesman and philosopher from the frontier, was an important agent in making this happen. At the same time, he was self-consciously a protagonist of civilization, in which civic life of any worth was accorded universal reach; in which self-interest always needed to be subsumed to ethical imperatives; and in which the domain of thought and beauty was of deeper value than the exigencies of day-to-day political competition. In themselves these were attractive attributes. Harnessed to a militant ethnic absolutism, they were far from that. Yet what was persuasive about Smuts—and, equally, what was unnerving—was the depth of his commitment to an authentically democratic current in English radicalism.

English radicalism, English feminism

Amery of course was right to place Smuts alongside Rhodes, Chamberlain, and Milner. He, and others close to Smuts, could not have failed to have seen how he moved into their ideological orbit. At the end of 1908, in a letter to Smuts, Olive Schreiner declared herself to be 'the last of the Republicans, sick of Empire and Union Jack'. She thought Smuts was getting more like Milner, and told him so. 'Don't be cross, what must be said, must be said.'[100] During his time in the British war cabinet, he worked alongside Milner, and Lord Curzon too. Amery, not surprisingly, was delighted to see their growing rapprochement. 'Great fun to see Lord M. and Smuts hobnobbing like the best of old friends'; or a bit later: 'It was nice to see Smuts taking Lord M.'s arm and walking along with him, with the sort of affectionate deference that one would pay to a favourite uncle. Oom Alfred!'[101]

But there is reason to think that Smuts himself never quite saw it in this light. For him another England was always active in his imagination: not the England of empire and Union Jack, but the England of Nonconformist radical liberalism, free-thinking and communitarian, which thrived on its hostility to the imperialism and militarism of Milner. When the radical liberal, J. A. Hobson, died in April 1940 Smuts wrote to his old friend Margaret Gillett: 'Our circle is rapidly contracting, and soon the rest will be gone too.'[102] In his own mind Smuts remained faithful all his life to the intimacy of 'our circle', even while his own politics gave every indication of carrying him faraway.

In 1891, when he had arrived at Cambridge, so far as he made a social life for himself it was within the world of New Liberalism. He arrived as a member of a small nation, whose pioneer rural values were in the process of being turned inside out by the new capitalists and plutocrats of the Rand. Smuts's instincts were anti-imperialist and anti-capitalist. He was studious and devout, attending his local Presbyterian church. He became friends with E. W. Hobson, who was the brother of J. A. Hobson, who in turn himself came close to Smuts and stayed with him on becoming the correspondent for the *Manchester Guardian* in South Africa on the eve of the South

African War. Smuts was taught, too, by F. W. Maitland who instilled in him a philosophical regard for the values inscribed in the traditions of English constitutionalism.

Maitland hoped that Smuts would dedicate himself to becoming the great theorist of English law. He duly went on to pursue his career at the Middle Temple, but whilst there he threw himself, not into jurisprudence, but into a study of Walt Whitman.

Whitman was not the obvious choice for a young man as devout and rectilinear in ethical matters as Smuts. Whitman, he wrote much later,

> did a great service to me in making me appreciate the Natural Man and free-ing me from much theological or conventional preoccupations due to my very early pious upbringing. It was a sort of liberation, as St Paul was liberated from the Law and its damnations by his Damascus vision. Sin ceased to domi-nate my view of life, and this was a great release as I was inclined to be severely puritanical in all things.[103]

Smuts wrote a book-length manuscript on Whitman in a few months, though he was unable to find a publisher. His purpose in writing it was twofold. He took Whitman as an exponent of the spirit of American civili-zation and American democracy. As a nation-builder in the making, he was drawn not to the examples of the old nations, but to a young country, con-tent to concede that the United States possessed a civilization worth emu-lating—though here we might also recall D. H. Lawrence's conviction that Whitman was 'the first white aboriginal'.[104]

Second, he was concerned with the question of the human personality and its evolution. For Smuts, Whitman, like Goethe, represented 'a whole and sound piece of manhood' (or so the young Smuts thought), 'such as appears but seldom, even in the course of centuries'. 'And it is to such men', he continued, 'that we turn our attention more eagerly and closely, men who do not excel in this or that special quality or department, but who excel *as men*.' Indeed, in such figures there evolves a congruence between the human and the natural worlds. In reading Whitman, 'the student feels that he is in the biological world'. Thus for Smuts, Whitman represented above all *the harmony* of evolution—a process in which the cooperative val-ues of civilization were incubated—as opposed to 'the grim scientific con-ception of Darwin'. In bringing together the social and the individual, or more concretely America and Whitman, and the natural and the human, Smuts was arguing, at least by implication, that a civilized democracy itself was the product of a long evolutionary process, existing on a higher human scale than other political forms.[105] It was as a result of this reasoning that he contrasted Whitman to Thomas Carlyle, taking them to be the great prophets of the contemporary age. While Carlyle looked back, Smuts contended, Whitman was the future.[106]

Whitman, perhaps, was something of a specialist taste within the circles of New Liberalism in the 1890s. But the boundaries of these late nineteenth-century intellectual groupings were, as ever, porous. In approaching Whitman in these terms Smuts was discovering for himself the key conceptual postulates of a benign reading of evolution, which lay close to the philosophical precepts of the New Liberalism. Yet at the same time, intellectually at least, his interest in Whitman opened up to him preoccupations common to the inventive libertarianism of the 'new life' socialists and feminists of the period, preoccupations about a certain independence of thought in matters to do with domestic and sexual conventions, and which carried also a visionary sense of the co-operative ideal.[107] Smuts's Old Testament upbringing held him back from experimenting too far, for in the end he was always the seminarian. Even so Whitman gave him a glimpse of some other way of being, free from the strictures of the law of the prophets, and instilling in him a sympathy for an ethically grounded libertarianism.

His close friendship with Emily Hobhouse, and with her brother L. T. Hobhouse, marked the true beginnings of 'our circle' and of its consequent intimacy. For Leonard Hobhouse, the South African War stood as 'the test issue of this generation'.[108] Arguably, New Liberalism cohered as an authentic politics around opposition to the war. In this, the example of Emily Hobhouse was supreme. In her, anti-militarism and anti-imperialism fused with a humanitarian, practical feminism.[109]

In discovering that conventional set-piece engagements produced little success, the British military commanders came to devise a strategy which depended on prosecuting a war of position against the entire Afrikaner population, civilian as well as military. By the time combat ended, many more than 20,000 Afrikaner women and children had perished, and this out of a total Afrikaner population of some 200,000. Emily Hobhouse was ashamed. She became the principal figure in exposing the scandal and creating from it a new public, composed not only of radicals, feminists, and anti-imperialists, but by those initially sympathetic to the war who had become converted by her arguments. She became, as a consequence, a great heroine to the Afrikaners.[110]

She and Smuts first met in July 1903. Emily Hobhouse had arrived in South Africa with charitable funds for Boer farmers, and various schemes designed to revive the rural economy. She stayed with the Smuts family, and grew attached to Smuts himself and to his wife and children. For Smuts in particular the experience was imbued with a deep symbolism. In the words of Keith Hancock: 'Her presence in the home at Sunnyside was living proof of the faith which Smuts had never wholly surrendered, even in the darkest years, that there was another England besides Chamberlain's and Milner's, the England of John Bright. He and Miss Hobhouse became fellow workers for its resurrection.'[111] From that moment on, for nearly another quarter of a century until her death, Smuts showed Emily Hobhouse many kindnesses in a perpetual chain of small domestic and financial matters, increasingly so as she became more frail, as well as in supporting her in the larger matter of 'resurrecting' an authentically moral and honourable English nation. When she died in 1926 her ashes were buried at the foot of the Vrouemonument in Bloemfontein which commemorated the women and children who had died in the camps. On 26 October Smuts spoke at the monument in her memory. By this time, for him, her status as an 'Englishwoman' was paramount and unequivocal: in herself she personified the feminized ethics of the universal English nation. Single-handedly, Smuts proclaimed, she had turned around the meaning of the Boer War. 'For the future of South Africa the whole meaning and significance of the Anglo-Boer War was permanently affected by this Englishwoman.' Her angelic providentialism; her inner spirit; and her femininity: these made her what she was. For her, as for Edith Cavell, Smuts was sure that espousal of a simple patriotism was not enough.[112]

Perhaps his lifetime's deepest friendship derived directly from his attachment to Emily Hobhouse. In December 1905 Smuts sailed to England in order to talk with Campbell-Bannerman. On board he met again Margaret Clark who had been Emily Hobhouse's assistant in South Africa for the previous year, and who had visited his family on earlier occasions. Clark came from an established Liberal, Quaker family in Somerset; she was a feminist who had been educated at Cambridge. She was also John Bright's granddaughter. On disembarking in Dover Smuts was introduced to her mother, Bright's daughter (Helen Bright Clark), who was waiting to welcome her, and they all took the train together (second class) to London. Smuts truly must have seen the hand of providence in this. He was in England, witnessing the creation of a new Liberal government after an interminable stretch of Conservative administrations. In London he passed his time with Hobson and Hobhouse, who were now increasingly influential public figures. He spent his weekends in Street in Somerset with the Clarks, in a milieu which combined twice-daily Bible readings with fierce free-thought when it came to politics, among the living descendants of John Bright's radicalism. Street itself, with its historic ties to Quakerism still intact, had long been an important point in the itineraries of black emancipationists from the USA. In 1886–7 Frederick Douglass had visited the anti-lynching propagandist, Catherine Impey. (He had first met John Bright and his family in Rochdale in the late 1840s.) In 1899 Booker T. Washington had travelled to Street to meet with Helen Bright Clark. Smuts followed in this lineage: Frederick Douglass, Booker T. Washington, Jan Smuts.[113] And, as he would have it, his crowning achievement was to have persuaded Campbell-Bannerman, man to man, to concede self-government to the defeated South African states. This was a sublime moment for Smuts, in which politics and the subdued eroticism of burgeoning, intimate female friendships created a new future for him. His 'resurrection' of Bright's England was not merely a matter of state. It was lived.

For the rest of his days he remained in close contact with Margaret Clark, pouring out his thoughts in a vast correspondence, year in and year out. Shortly after they met, she married Arthur Gillett, a partner in a small local bank. (The bank was taken over by Barclays in 1919, just at the point it was starting to expand its colonial operations and Gillett, two years later, was appointed a director.) The marriage gave no indication of interrupting the friendship between Smuts and Margaret; on the contrary, Arthur Gillett himself was drawn into the relationship.

Yet Smuts was also attracted to Margaret's elder sister, Alice. She too was an independent woman, having been the director of the family firm in Street. She had travelled in the Middle East. She was active in the campaign for the women's vote; and in the war she was on the Friends' Committee for War Relief.

The intensity of these relationships quickened whilst Smuts was in London serving in the war cabinet in 1917–18, and then subsequently when he attended the peace negotiations at Versailles. During the week he would be in Whitehall, administering the massed armies of the western front and the mobilization of civilians at home, an imperial man amongst imperial men. In the evenings he would retire to his suite at the Savoy where, we are told, he was happy to eat *biltong* sent to him by his wife.[114] Here, he would either work or talk with Alice Clark. Clark, at this time, was registered at the London School of Economics and researching her book, *Working Life of Women in the Seventeenth Century*, the founding text of British feminist historiography.[115] They discussed the book at length. On publication Clark acknowledged Olive Schreiner and, enigmatically, unnamed others; Smuts believed that it was he who was mainly responsible for keeping her at it and ensuring she finished it.[116] Their views on the war were contrary—three of Clark's cousins were conscientious objectors—and one can assume that these nocturnal conversations did not preclude periodic sharp exchange and mutual exasperation.[117] At the weekends he would leave London for the Gilletts' residence in Banbury Road in Oxford. The summer of 1918, despite the distant carnage, seems to have been a particularly joyful moment. Smuts and his friends would decamp to Streatley or Moulsford, swim in the Thames and camp outside, go for long hikes and talk incessantly; once they all went to hear Cecil Sharp lecture on English folk music. Indeed, it had its own touch of 'new life' about it. On Monday morning he was back on the train for the war cabinet. 'My thoughts have continually run back to Millfield', he wrote to Alice Clark from the Savoy in January 1918, 'and my soul has been saturated with the Blessedness of which Spinoza speaks. I have drafted a War Aims statement in answer to the Brest[-Litovsk] negotiations.'[118] Possibly it was not only the business of managing mass slaughter which broke the harmony of these excursions. The correspondence between him and Alice Clark, in late 1918 and early 1919, becomes more urgent and more troubled, hinting at passions which could not be contained by the tranquil idylls of these pastoral interludes.

To these tough, principled, subversive intellectual women—Emily Hobhouse, Margaret Gillett, Alice Clark—should be added Olive Schreiner. She created her own singular radicalism, inspired by her revulsion against the politics of Rhodes, in particular, and the militarism of empires, in general; by a feminism formed in the teeth of the putatively progressive Men and Women's Club, and in the rather more congenial atmosphere of Edward Carpenter's libertarian community at Millthorpe; and by an aesthetic imagination which left most of her generation of writers standing. From an early moment in the century she was an admirer of W. E. B. DuBois's *The Souls of Black Folk*.[119] These women were strange company for Smuts to keep. They were not the sort of people, additionally, to keep their opinions to themselves. Gillett's outbursts against Smuts, in a lifetime's correspondence, were few and restrained.[120] Those of Emily Hobhouse and Olive Schreiner, especially during the nightmare years of the First World War, were frequent and unrestrained.[121] The passions which drew these women to Smuts are well nigh impossible to unravel. One is reminded of Beatrice Potter's infatuation with Joseph Chamberlain, and of Schreiner's with Karl Pearson and Cecil Rhodes.[122] In each instance Beatrice Potter and Olive Schreiner found the politics of their loved one monstrous and their manner impossibly overbearing. Room for manœuvre for independent women, with public ambitions, were circumscribed not only socially, but emotionally. There may have been some of these dynamics at work in the case of Smuts, his very rectitude and public invulnerability sparking an erotic charge. But these were not relationships, so far as we can tell, of unrequited love. He listened. He genuinely shared at least a measure of their enthusiasms. They, and their politics, entered his life.

So as one sees his imperial career progressing from one public triumph to the next, one is periodically taken aback by manifestations of this other life, which interrupted the fluency of his repeated declarations of faith in the British empire, in white Pan-Africanism, and in separate racial development. This radical inheritance was, in part, an expression of what John Buchan identified as the 'sagacious lawlessness' of colonial life, which thrived because of its remove from the conventions of the metropole; and it also connected, in the British context, with an intransigent historic Nonconformity. If, amongst the imperial elite of Westminster, Whitehall, and Oxford, the idea of democracy was defined by the practices of English constitutionalism, then Smuts did indeed carry in himself a larger vision.

Shortly after his arrival in Britain during the First World War, in June 1917, he was interviewed by the US journalist, Edward Marshall. Marshall introduced Smuts by referring to him as 'a democrat of democrats'. The position Smuts adumbrated in the interview is one which has been revived in recent historical scholarship. He suggested that in Europe the war signalled the final collapse of the old imperial, feudal order, 'the Armageddon of humanity's long struggle against feudalism'. The British case was more particular. Britain, he thought, had been slipping back into militarism under the leadership of Disraeli, a development which had culminated in the war with South Africa in 1899. The eventual outcome—Campbell-Bannerman's generosity combined with the founding of the Union—had reversed this trend, and created a new democratic nation in South Africa. For this reason, Smuts explained, the South African War needed to be understood as the historical equivalent of the great democratic revolutions of America and

France. The future rested in the young nations of the world. And, with the promptings of his feminist interlocutors still in his head, he added that the war must mean 'the great end of the oppression of all womanhood'.[123]

His reputation as a democrat, in Britain, was made in this moment. There was, one imagines, a deal of early twentieth-century spin in the public idealization of this 'democrat of democrats'. But there was enough substance for it to work, and from that moment on the image of Smuts the democrat simply came to pass as the common currency of the metropolitan ruling bloc and of the makers of public opinion.[124]

Smuts's speeches and writings of the First World War are consistent in their structure, oscillating back and forth between his condemnations of imperialism and his own declared faith in white supremacy and separate development. Imperialism, militarism, Prussianism: these were his enemies. These were ills, he believed, which existed not only in the German and central European empires, but potentially in Britain too, as his judgement on Disraeli made clear. As the war ended he became less sanguine about the possibilities of a future democratic Europe. Like so many others of the age, he became increasingly anxious about the failure of Europe and the disintegration of its civilization.[125] But in Britain his faith deepened. The British polity represented, he argued, not an empire but a community of free nations: or as he termed it at the time, a 'British Commonwealth of Nations'.[126] Smuts was persuaded by the very simplicity of this idea. It represented nothing less than the democratic reinvention of the idea of empire, appropriate for an age characterized by mass democracy and the creation of new, young nations.

As this implies, his faith in democracy was simultaneously a faith in Britain. Smuts's meditations on the nature of democracy worked to elaborate the idea of the citizen as 'an ethnic', such that the citizen came to public life with a pregiven set of dispositions which derived from his or her unspoken allegiance to the way of life bequeathed by a history ordained by providence. This coupling together of citizenship and ethnicity was perhaps the most powerful single feature of democratic theory in Britain at the time, in the 1920s and 1930s, when mass democracy stabilized. It informed both left and right. And, for the bulk of those at the centre of British politics, it did much to define democracy in an age dominated by Communism and fascism. Thus Smuts was not only an influence in the milieu of New Liberalism in the early part of the century. His sense of democracy was entirely compatible with the progressive radicalism of the 1930s. Yet, as I suggested earlier when noting the impact of his speech of October 1942, he was too—without ever hitching his fortunes to the causes advocated by the public dissidents of the time—a disquieting presence in the larger arena of democratic Britain in that momentous year of radical populism.

It is revealing that in the 1930s Ernest Simon tried to tempt Smuts to ally himself formally with the Association for Education in Citizenship. Simon was a civic radical whose roots led back to the Frankfurt revolutionaries of 1848, and who came to personify one version of the continuation of Manchester liberalism into the twentieth century. Even more than Hobhouse in an earlier period, he was a decisive agent in holding the *Manchester Guardian* to its traditionally progressive commitments.[127] By the early 1930s he was increasingly convinced by the theoretical justifications for socialism. But he abhorred Communism; he was irritated by what he regarded as the ineptness of Labour's high command; and he was saddened by the incapacity of the left, broadly conceived, to generate for itself a suitably ethical defence of citizenship and democracy. For this reason in May 1934 he, along with Eva Hubback, launched the Association for Education in Citizenship, designed as a kind of non-Communist democratic popular front, pulling in all those of the centre dedicated to the expansion of citizenship. In the following October he drafted a letter which was to go to W. P. Crozier, the editor of the *Guardian*, in which he urged the paper (of which Simon was a director) to adopt more of the 'Baldwin-Smuts stuff' in its advocacy of citizenship.[128] Three years later he invited Smuts to become a vice-president of the Association. This represents a key moment in the reworking of the conception of citizenship, in which a radical liberal tradition sought to make common cause with both Baldwin and Smuts.[129] It suggests, I think, the vitality of an imagined ethnic memory in the fashioning of citizenship in Britain in this period, for the alliance of disparate public intellectuals embraced by the Association turned, above all else, on a shared perception of the unique values of the traditions of native constitutionalism. And it suggests once again Smuts's continuing role for the British as an exemplary democrat.

The contradictory positioning of Smuts, as democrat and supremacist, may also make us reflect on his public standing in the radical moment of 1942. Although his interest in domestic British matters was slight, it is clear that his commitments never lay with the discredited Toryism of those stigmatized as the Guilty Men, despite his own espousal of appeasement until late in the day. After all it was his closest allies, Amery and Churchill, who did much in the last moments to dispatch these very figures from their formal positions of power. Smuts's politics took him to Churchill and to the Labour leaders, in that order. While others seized the moment to debate the configuration of the postwar domestic world, Smuts was given the opportunity—by being invited to address both houses of parliament—to present his view of the postwar international order. Two days after his speech the Eighth Army in North Africa launched its offensive against Field-Marshall Rommel's forces. The upbeat tenor of Smuts's address suggests that he may well have known this was imminent. Yet insofar as Smuts was part of the domestic public culture, his presence reminds us of the complex, contradictory forces which went to make up the rag-tag populism of the radicalism of the mid-1940s, in which official and popular politics veered between accommodation and antagonism, and in which the inheritances of an older colonial order could still register deep in popular life.

When Smuts had arrived in London on 13 October 1942 he was initially met by the veteran imperialist, J. L. Garvin. He then went, as an honoured elder statesman with experience of government during the First World War, hot-foot to the cabinet, which was sitting in Westminster.[130] There, at a critical moment in the strategic balance of the entire war, the cabinet had discussed the issue of racially segregated latrines for the US troops stationed in the United Kingdom.[131] No doubt Smuts's imminent arrival would have proved reassuring to those British leaders whose knowledge of 'native races' was wanting. But it is not as if these were truths which Smuts chose to keep to himself. Earlier in the year, in March, a volume of his writings was published in Britain under the title—echoing the spirit of the times—*Plans for a Better World*. A version of the same book had appeared in South Africa in 1940 as *Greater South Africa: Plans for a Better World*. The change of title was reasonable enough, and no doubt determined by the publishers. The British edition sold well, generating a second print-run within the month. Photographs were circulated, no doubt with the approval, or more, of the Ministry of Information, of eager squaddies reading it under the shade of their half-tracks in the North African desert.[132] The opening chapter frames simply enough the argument which follows. It is called 'The White Man's Task' which rehearsed, in Smuts's usual manner and without equivocation, the supremacist case. In itself, perhaps not too much should be made of this. His was only one voice, although one carrying both authority and at least a degree of popular backing. Even so, it is a troubling reminder of the ease with which older colonial sensibilities could be carried forward into the imaginings of the new postwar social settlement.[133]

This is evident, too, from a volume which appeared the following year under the radical imprint of Victor Gollancz. Written by Alexander Campbell it carried the title *Smuts and the Swastika*. In form, it is one of those characteristic pedagogic texts of the time which sought to instil in what was imagined to be 'the ordinary voter' the necessary knowledge to become a functioning citizen. The author, either himself South African or with a knowledge of the country, is on a long train-ride across the *veld* when he meets two British soldiers, 'Alan' and 'George'. He takes the opportunity to put them right on the history of South Africa. He informs them of the Nazi sympathies which run through public life, indicting Herzog. Smuts—predictably by this stage—assumes the role of hero. He was the one who was responsible for ousting Herzog. Currently, according to the narrator, he was endeavouring to overcome the impoverishment of the native, which was all the doing of Herzog's long period of political dominance. And 'he intends to do everything he can to give the natives a square deal', even though this had allowed his enemies to brand him a Communist.[134] At this point 'George', emphatically declaring that he is 'no ruddy Socialist', none the less wonders out loud whether 'Imperialism' itself may be to blame.[135] To this, the narrator duly explains that what happened in South Africa under Herzog represented the corruption of the imperial ideal, and that the personification of the true imperialism, battling against Nazism at home and abroad, is Smuts. Just as Nazism must be defeated, so after the war it would be necessary for the British to maintain its empire, rebuilding it on the basis of 'trusteeship' and 'goodwill'. 'The greatest Imperialist to-day isn't an Englishman at all; he's a Boer. His name is Smuts.'[136]

Smuts himself was exercised by his role as democrat and supremacist; from the 1940s his anxieties on this became deeper; and after the UN condemnation, there was a period when the dilemma dominated his private correspondence. In this, though, he saw himself as no more and no less than the personification of his own white South Africa. 'Faust's two souls', he wrote, 'inhabit this good fine beloved people.'[137] In his last years as prime minister he could not help but realize that world opinion was turning against him. Bemused, he determined to convince friends who did not know South Africa that the colour bar was supported, as he believed, by good people who held no malice. It was simply 'part of the divine order of things', a feeling that was as much a part of South Africa as the beauty of its landscape. 'I can watch the feeling in my own family, which is as good as the purest gold.'[138] On another occasion he put it like this: 'On the one side I am a human and a humanist, and the author of the preamble to the [UN] Charter. On the other I am a South African European, proud of our heritage and proud of the clean European society we have built up in South Africa, and which I am determined not to see lost in the black pool of Africa.' There is resolution here: but no way that the irreconcilables could be reconciled. The closing observation, fateful in tone, is revealing: 'The world is reeling between the two poles of white and colour.'[139]

Yet having recognized that Smuts, at one level and late in life, perceived well enough the impossibility of reconciling his predominating philosophies of life, we also have to remember how difficult it is to deal with such issues without the condescension of posterity, whatever its enormity. Positions which look to us bizarrely self-contradictory can be experienced in their own historical time as banal in their obviousness. So it was, in part, with Smuts. Indeed, the argument can be stated more forcefully. The philosophies which animated his regard for democracy could also serve as justification for his faith in white supremacy.

New Liberalism: theories of evolution

We can return here to L. T. Hobhouse. There has been an interesting, if surprising, attempt to revive Hobhouse and New Liberalism in the writings of Cornel West, a singular North American black thinker of our own times, a thinker who is agile and always alert to the emancipatory potential of received theories. On Hobhouse he has this to say:

> I think a tradition that we ought to be rereading is a tradition of British new liberals. A tradition of John Morley, the old radical and independent, L. T. Hobhouse, J. A. Hobson... and others at the turn of the century who were concerned about severing democratic forms of liberalism from British forms of imperialism.
>
> It fundamentally shapes around the Boer War in the 1890s. There is a wonderful book by Hobhouse called *Democracy and Reaction* which ought to be read by every American citizen, not because it is right, but because it has some insight. Most libraries don't even have the book but it was published in 1903 and it is fascinating, in fact.
>
> In this book—in the same year Du Bois was talking about the problem of the twentieth century, the problem of the color line—Hobhouse says that the problem of the twentieth century will be the relation of democracy to white racial domination and the women's struggle...

He is trying to rethink the notion of democracy and he is a liberal, but he can't go with Chamberlain and the other pro-imperialists. He has to rethink democracy in relation to race and empire and gender...[140]

Cornel West is right. It is an impressive book. And, so far as my argument is concerned here, it is important to establish the degree to which the situation in South Africa defined British social democracy in its making.

Hobhouse's premise was that aggressive imperialism abroad encouraged illiberal politics at home. Like Smuts, he identified a long period of reaction in Britain, which he dated from the 1880s to the end of the South African War. And he suggested that the increasing tendency to legitimate racial subjugation was a characteristic of the period, and that this invocation of racial superiority was fixed, philosophically, at the very centre of an emergent anti-democratic politics. The new imperialism represented 'a hard assertion of racial supremacy' which touched every aspect of national life. 'Thirty years ago the whole Empire was anti-slavery. Now, far from putting it down, we have on more than one occasion suffered the introduction of one form or another of servile labour under the British flag. It is difficult to conceive any great white nation waging war in these days on the slavery question.'[141] Hobhouse's parodies of various justifications for the racial dominance of the white man, steeped in putatively liberal sentiment, anticipate many of the arguments which Smuts was to make later in his life, to the boundless, colossal acclaim of British public leaders.

Hobhouse maintained that before the 1880s there had been in existence a very different sort of empire, one which had been founded on Cobdenite principles and which had been driven by humanitarian, not exploitative, imperatives. In a powerful passage he explained how the shift from the one to the other occurred, identifying a particular 'medium' which had 'facilitated the change':

> For if the Empire was so liberally formed, so free, tolerant, and unaggressive, could we have too much of it? Should we not extend its blessing to those that sit in darkness? And so, by a seductive blending of the old Adam of national vanity with the new spirit of humanitarian zeal men are led on to the destruction of their own principles.[142]

To this rhetorical question—'could we have too much of it?'—Hobhouse produced no answer.

Hobhouse was as genuine in his condemnation of white rule as Smuts was heart-felt in its defence. On this, their two outlooks cannot be conflated.

They shared, however, a common conceptual starting-point. They both accepted the logic of evolutionary theory; and they both strove to wrest the concept of evolution away from what they saw as the hard, scientistic rendering which Darwin had initiated, in which competition and survival determined human life. Smuts, in common with all New Liberal thinking, emphasized the alternative idea of harmony, arguing that the evolution of humanity brought with it the potential for more harmonious social and individual development, the transcendence of social antagonism, and the fulfilment of civilization. The evolution of the human mind—of reason and discrimination—created the possibility for ever greater human agency in the organization of social affairs. This conception of evolution, idealist but nominally anti-Hegelian, shaped the fundamental principles of one of the strongest currents of early British social democracy.

Smuts's own commitment to a philosophy of evolutionism was constant. In rudimentary form it inspired his examination of Whitman in the 1890s. It was also the explicit thesis of his philosophical-cum-scientific treatise, *Holism and Evolution*, which he published in 1926. This latter text was scrutinized and revised by Alice Clark; recommended for publication by the progressive Balliol intellectual, A. D. Lindsay; and enthusiastically endorsed by the prominent Communist sympathizer and natural scientist, J. B. S. Haldane. It is difficult to think of a more convincing radical pantheon than this.[143]

In different circumstances, however, evolutionary theory of this type could also underpin belief in the different historical stages of distinct civilizations. It could function, in turn, as justification for more developed civilizations to defend themselves against incursions from cultures perceived to be less advanced. In the culture of white South Africa, poised, as its tribunes always declared, on the edge of civilization, apprehensions of the reversal of history, in which the lower would engulf the higher, proved compulsively appealing.

In the predominant discourses of social Darwinism of the late nineteenth century, evolution and race were inextricably linked. Breaking from the ethnic ordering of the master-categories of evolution required a more complex intellectual politics than New Liberal theorists were able to produce.[144] Despite its stress on harmony, in key instances New Liberal thought represented an uneven break with eugenics and social Darwinism. The idea of an inescapable polarity between those deemed fit and those deemed unfit seeped into their writings, the line demarcating the two deriving ultimately from an unspoken capitulation to the dynamics of racial difference. As Michael Freeden has conceded, the division between the efficient and the deficient represented the anxious 'twilight zone' of New Liberalism.[145]

This may suggest no more than the fact that at various moments the democratic impulse of New Liberalism was compromised, and that the category of race, tied so closely to that of evolution, continued to have disturbing consequences, even for such self-conscious democrats. But there is more to it than that, for separate racial development could become the favoured policy of progressive intellectuals, as a determinedly democratic strategy.

Seven years after *Democracy and Reaction*, Hobhouse published his definitive *Liberalism*. On relations between black and white he wrote:

> A specious extension of the white man's rights to the black may be the best way of ruining the black. To destroy tribal custom by introducing conceptions of individual property, the free disposal of land, and the free purchase of gin, may be the handiest method for the expropriator...perhaps our safest course, so far as principles and deductions prevail at all, is to fix our eyes on the elements of the matter, and in any part of the world to support whatever methods succeed in securing the 'coloured' man from personal violence, from the lash, from expropriation, and from gin; above all, so far as it may yet be, from the white man himself. Until the white man has fully learnt to rule his own life, the best of all things that he can do with the dark man is to do nothing with him. In this relation, the day of more constructive Liberalism is yet to come.[146]

Such views hover close to the fantasies of a modernist primitivism, which projected elaborate images of the native as a sublime product of nature, untouched by the contaminations of the modern world. These imaginative projections were generated by a certain iconoclasm. Not only were black men and women understood to be more truly human than white, but they were also perceived to demonstrate to upholders of white civilization the fact that they, as whites, had become overcivilized—too rational, too mechanical, too rapacious, too effete. Hobhouse's argument in *Liberalism* represented a philanthropic version of this same position, in all its ambivalent radicalism, in which black needed to be segregated from the evils of white.

On occasion Smuts argued in these terms, particularly when he was discussing 'the Bushmen', rather than 'the native', of South Africa.[147] More often, he spoke in a similar manner but turned it the other way around, explaining that white civilization had to be protected from the surreptitious infiltration of black barbarism. This was a position clearly antithetical to Hobhouse. Yet, whichever way the argument was deployed, the effect was to arrive at a point in which the allure of separate races appeared tantalizing, conclusive, and just. To begin from the evolutionary premise too easily allowed the chimera of racial, or cultural, hierarchies to emerge. Pro-native or anti-native, Hobhouse or Smuts, each argument came to mirror the other: for the sake of harmony, civilization, and practical democracy in South Africa a line had to be drawn between black and white.

A man of repute

We may now be able to understand why Smuts's reputation as a democrat in Britain was secured, and why it was not only those on the imperialist right who subscribed to it. There are three issues.

First, there is the matter of pro–Boer solidarity. In 1899 to have supported the Afrikaners was recognized to have been the imprimatur of radical faith. The Boers were regarded by their sympathizers as an oppressed nation, fighting the combined forces of a predatory imperialism (Britain) and an exploitative capitalist rump (the Randlords of the Transvaal). To be pro-Boer required courage. It also required the conscious transformation of a received patriotism, which, in its Chamberlainite forms, also laid claim to its own radical heritage. Such affiliations were neither easily jettisoned nor easily redrawn. One wonders, for example, whether Margaret Gillett's silences in her correspondence with Smuts—never quite confronting him on the native question—had their origin in this primal allegiance to an oppressed people, even at the moment that she could see the edifice of supremacism being put in place, stone by stone. For this generation of radicals, who had endured bad years in the belly of the beast, to have turned on Smuts in later times would have been to have lost something of themselves. Thus where one might have expected to witness outrage at the slow systematization of segregation in South Africa—in the *Manchester Guardian*, for example, or in the *New Statesman*—one finds instead modest, or sometimes fulsome, encomia to Smuts and to the nation he represented.[148]

Second, as General Hertzog, Dr Malan, and the Nationalists emerged to the right of Smuts, there was yet more reason for progressive opinion in Britain to be circumspect in its denunciations. There was always someone more supremacist just around the corner. The *Manchester Guardian*, in its response to the electoral victory of the Nationalists in May 1948, believed the results had 'gone as badly as they could'. It declared that 'the evolution of relations between black and white is the greatest problem of this century'. But there was not a word to indicate that Smuts's own position was profoundly formed by his faith in white supremacy. 'The policy of Smuts and Hofmeyr', the *Guardian* opined, 'is the realistic and practical course.'[149]

Third, as we have seen in the case of Hobhouse, when segregation was cohering as a system, there was a liberal or radical justification for its implementation. In South Africa this was the case.[150] So too in Britain. We can take, for example, the writings of Walter Cotton. Cotton was a British missionary of impeccably liberal pedigree. He refused to condemn inter-racial marriage, and he conceived race to be a contingent category, rather than hard-and-fast destiny. In 1931 he published *Racial Segregation in South Africa: An Appeal*. This bitterly condemned Smuts's plans for extending European settlement in Africa (and in so doing, drew on DuBois), and was written in a spirit of Christian fellowship. And yet his 'appeal' was driven by the belief that segregation, its difficulties notwithstanding, was fundamentally virtuous and needed to be implemented with greater urgency.[151] What is perceived as evidently barbarous a century on, with the historic consequences of apartheid deeply burnt in popular memory, appeared—or could appear—in quite different light a century ago. This ambivalence, and the contingencies it engendered, provided Smuts, in the British context, the conditions in which his mythic, heroic persona could flourish.

He was, indeed, a political figure peculiarly immune to public criticism. It is not as if his policies, even by the standards of the day, were beyond reproach. Nor were critical voices absent. They were there, but made little permanent impact. In part this was a result of the reputation he had fashioned as a public man who knew the native in a manner the metropolitan inhabitant could not. When he came to deliver his Rhodes lectures in 1929, the *Cape Times*, an organ friendly enough to Smuts and to his South African Party, commented on the ignorance of those who lauded him: 'The picture, for instance, of the native question in South Africa which General Smuts presented to the guileless and unworldly eyes of Oxford, seemed to South Africans to have almost scandalously little resemblance to local realities.'[152]

The most sustained public criticism of Smuts inside Britain arose, in fact, in response to the Rhodes lectures. J. H. Oldham, secretary of the International Missionary Council and skilled in the organization of public opinion, speedily drafted a book-length reply. At the time, Oldham was in the midst of a campaign to persuade the British government to recognize the ultimate paramountcy of black African rights in central and eastern Africa.[153] That Smuts should try to bend opinion in a contrary direction marked a clear danger. Oldham's *White and Black in Africa* was modulated in its response. Its attack remained focused on the proposals emerging from the lectures themselves, most especially the idea that 'white' development provided the key for the success of the eastern seaboard of central Africa. It did little to show that the policies to which Smuts committed himself followed directly from his intransigent faith in the justice of white supremacy. Yet despite the limited scope of the Oldham's reply, it was informed and telling.[154] It may have influenced the new Labour colonial secretary, Lord Passfield (the former Sidney Webb), who certainly moved in the direction outlined by Oldham. Yet even this relatively measured exposé of Smuts seems merely to have been a passing moment. It did little to undermine his larger public authority. What was true of Oldham appears to be true of those other voices raised against Smuts. They may have been heard, but they didn't break the esteem in which he was held.[155] And certainly, after September 1939, his allies in Britain—if ever they did worry about his various practices as a mortal, profane politician following his own domestic agenda in a faraway dominion— could forgive him much.[156]

Nor was Smuts's immunity to criticism restricted to the native question. In his first term as prime minister his government was responsible for two massacres of civilians, and for putting down the miners' insurrection on the Rand in February 1922.[157] None of these episodes seems seriously to have turned, for any length of time, mainstream labourist or liberal opinion against him, nor to have done anything to prevent his resurrection as a hero of Britain in the dramatic days of the autumn of 1942. Nor did the bitter syndicalist memories of the anti-labour repression of 1913–14 appear to find any significant public outlet after the First World War.

It was not until the mid to late 1940s that opposition to South Africa began to cohere as a prominent strand in domestic British radicalism.[158] The key moment was the Nationalist victory in 1948 though, so far as critics in Britain were concerned, this required no pressing review of Smuts's role up until that point. He was enemy to the Nationalists, with his own quirky if compromised radical pedigree, and that sufficed. Two years later he was dead, and posterity could work upon the mythic Smuts unimpeded.[159]

Smuts came to fame early in life. There was, for his enthusiasts in Britain, always something a bit posthumous about him thereafter, as if he had progressed from being a young elder statesman to a different realm entirely, transcending the obligations of the known world. Slim as ever (as white South Africans of his generation liked to put it), he was not averse to playing up to this, as he made clear in October 1942 when he was resurrected for the British public. 'And now that I reappear on this scene after many years, you are interested in this somewhat mythical figure and curiosity from the past.'[160] Myths, Roland Barthes suggested in an equally playful manner, are 'well-fed, sleek, expansive, garrulous', inventing themselves ceaselessly and obeying their own internal logics.[161] Smuts, in mythic mode, could simultaneously be posthumous and immortal, as only a deity could be. Reports came from the elections in South Africa in 1994 that an unusually reclusive citizen had arrived at a polling station to vote for Smuts. On discovering that, on this occasion, the revered old man wasn't standing, he turned heel and tramped back into the bush.

Remembered and forgotten

When Smuts died on 11 September 1950, Lord Samuel broadcast a tribute on the Home Service, while BBC television announced the passing of 'one of the greatest and best-loved statesman' of South Africa.[162] Further formal tributes came from Attlee, Churchill, and the King, which were all duly reported in *The Times* the next day, alongside Dr Malan's timely if wilfully undiplomatic assertion that 'South Africa is no longer a British colony'.[163] The *Daily Express*, demonstrating high-quality journalism, announced in its front-page headline: 'Smuts hears he is better—dies'.[164] In the House of Commons on 13 September Attlee, as prime minister, was called upon to speak again his faith in Smuts, recounting how he first heard of him as a schoolboy when Smuts himself was a lawyer in President Kruger's government in the Transvaal. (He refrained, though, from saying any more about his schoolboy enthusiasms of the time.) He went on: 'I have often heard him say that British Imperialism died with the South African War and no one did more than he to give form to the concept of the evolution of an Empire into a Commonwealth.' Most remarkable was his 'intense belief...in all that we call the British view of life'.[165]

In South Africa the Nationalist government offered a state funeral, which the family refused.[166] In its place a full-scale military funeral was held in Pretoria on the fifteenth, which received a deal of coverage in the British press and newsreels, as did the activities of the civic day set aside to honour his memory the following June.

Even the dead and buried were not precluded from adding their voice to the commemoration and immortalization of Smuts. Immediately his death was known the *Cape Times* published a posthumous letter from Sir Herbert Baker, who himself had died four years earlier. Baker was an Englishman who had created, as many saw it, an 'indigenous' South African architecture. (In London he had also designed the Bank of England, India House, and South Africa House.) He had been close to Rhodes and to those grouped in Milner's Kindergarten. Smuts had been a patron.[167] The commission to design the Union Buildings in Pretoria had been awarded to Baker in the year before the Union itself was founded; he later went on to collaborate with Sir Edwin Lutyens in the construction of New Delhi. From his grave Baker announced to the South African public that when he had designed the Union Buildings he had created two pedestals for equestrian statues, which remained vacant—an instructive reminder of the empty or homogencous time of an aspiring national form. One of these plinths, declared Baker, should be for Louis Botha, the other for Smuts, the 'two riders' who had fought heroically 'for the honour of South Africa and the Commonwealth'.[168]

Collections for a memorial fund in South Africa had been initiated even before the funeral occurred, though Smuts's widow made it clear that she wished for a 'live' memorial rather than a statue, obelisk, or plaque.[169]

But the private aspirations of colonial widows, however esteemed their husbands, do not seem to have carried much influence on the decisions of the public men in the metropole. From October, the matter of a suitable statue of Smuts in the capital became a periodic issue.[170] In June 1951 Attlee finally proposed in parliament that there should be such a statue, and in this was supported by Churchill and by the leader of the Liberals, Clement Davies. 'It is right', Davies suggested, 'that future generations, here in London, should see in the form of a statue the man whom we were privileged to know, and to see again the strong features, the perfectly shaped head and the virile bearing of this man, who was an inspiration to his fellow men throughout the whole of his long and varied career.'[171] After a number of unexplained delays, Churchill can be found a year later, having replaced Attlee as prime minister, making the same proposal again. In the speech Churchill referred to the convention which prevented statues being erected to native British figures until ten years after their deaths: yet for men from overseas, Churchill believed, this rule could be relaxed, for 'they stand above the ebb and flow of daily life'. The motion was passed unanimously.[172]

In July 1952, there appeared the first indication that a statue to Smuts might prove contentious. The first expressions of anxiety turned on a matter of propriety, when MPs were worried about the susceptibilities of *others* in the Commonwealth. The Labour MP Eirene White—friend of Paul Robeson and daughter of Thomas Jones (an ardent fan of Smuts)—had this to say:

> I would draw the attention of the Committee to the fact that we have citizens in other countries of the Commonwealth who may, perhaps, have rather less reason for gratitude to the late Field Marshall ... he did not always show in his domestic career the magnanimity which he displayed towards his former military opponents in this country. In dealing with Africans and with the coloured peoples and with those people in the Union of South Africa whose origins were in the Asian countries of the Commonwealth, his actions sometimes left something to be desired. I think it would be unfortunate if, in choosing a site, we chose one which might be considered not quite appropriate by some of our fellow citizens of the Commonwealth. I say this because there have been some suggestions in the Press that this monument might be placed in Parliament Square.
>
> I would draw the attention of those who may be responsible to the fact that there is at least one position in Parliament Square which might be considered not quite appropriate for the purpose. There may be some members of the Commonwealth who would find it extremely incongruous to have a statue of Field Marshall Smuts placed in immediate proximity to that of Abraham Lincoln.
>
> I hope, therefore, that whilst we express in a proper way our own appreciation of the work which the Field Marshall did in his relationship with this country, we shall bear in mind the possible feelings of other members of the Commonwealth in making our decision upon this matter.[173]

This provoked a predictable reaction from the Tory member for Surrey East, Charles Doughty. 'Field Marshall Smuts was one of the greatest members of the British Empire that has ever lived ...Whatever he did was for the best of that country—let us make no mistake about that—even if some of his actions may be criticised by those who are ill-informed ...I rise to protect his name against any slight that may inadvertently have been directed against it.'[174] But the questions exercising other members were barely to do with Smuts at all. They were largely aesthetic. Tom Driberg, for example, a seasoned critic of British colonialism, agreed with Eirene White, but felt more impelled to press his own case for commissioning a young sculptor who would produce a work of some artistic interest.[175] This was a view echoed by Marcus Lipton, the MP for Brixton, who declared himself 'not concerned with the merits or demerits' of Smuts, but wanted something striking to emerge. 'If the Minister were to say that two or three monuments are to be removed to make room for a better one in memory of Field Marshall Smuts, then I should be more inclined to support the Motion now before the House.'[176] The tyros of modernity warmed to their theme. Malcolm Bullock was convinced that 'London possessed some of the worst statues in the world' and decried 'the old hack sculptors who go round not only London but the provinces as well'.[177]

If it had not been for the muscle-brained antics of Charles Doughty, business may well have concluded with a majority solemnly voting for the new iconoclasm. However, when another member, Charles Pannell, eventually endorsed the views of Eirene White, a colossal rumpus broke out between Doughty and the chairman, on the one hand, and the Labour representatives on the other, for Doughty had recently made himself notorious for his wild attacks on Fenner Brockway and on Brockway's attempts to persuade parliament to legislate against the colour bar. With tempers rising, the connection between Smuts and segregation at last broke into the open. Before Doughty 'suggests that Field Marshall Smuts was the final judge upon all matters that affect the colour bar', Hansard records Pannell as saying, 'he ought to consider his own intolerance as an Hon. Member of the House of Commons'.[178] These ructions notwithstanding, none of the members saw fit to oppose the statue of Smuts; they agreed at this stage it should proceed, *nem. con.*

The memorial committee, chaired by Smuts's old friend and erstwhile high commissioner in Pretoria, Lord Harlech, went about its business slowly. It was not until December 1955, in reply to a written question from the Liberal Clement Davies, that the minister of works, Nigel Birch, first publicly announced both the location and the sculptor.[179] The location was indeed to be Parliament Square—due in part, perhaps, to the interest which Churchill himself had been taking in its redesign.[180] Smuts was to be placed in the heart of the square, alongside Palmerston, Derby, Disraeli, and Peel, statues that looked to Virginia Woolf to be 'black and sleek and shiny as sea lions that have just risen from the water'.[181] The traffic would separate him from Abraham Lincoln (and from Lord Canning), who were positioned in an outer orbit, thus maintaining—at least in the case of Lincoln—the proper decorum.

If Eirene White would have seen this as a vindication of her own views, the choice of sculptor, in Jacob Epstein, was more complex. He was hardly youthful, as Driberg would have been quick to aver. Indeed, he was barely younger than Churchill or Smuts. And there is reason enough to think that, by the 1950s, he was tolerably close to the spectre of the 'old hack', ready to take any commission which came his way, that had disconcerted the MPs. But he did once boast a reputation as an aesthetic heretic.[182] And this was a heresy which had had its roots in an appropriation of black Africa—or, as the art critic Anthony Blunt described it in the *Spectator* in 1935, Epstein revived European art 'by an infusion of dark blood'.[183]

The *thought* that Smuts's immortality was to be realized through the medium of 'dark blood'... nothing could have been more horrifying to him. Yet the ambiguities resonate. As Epstein recounted his own life, he had been brought up at the end of the century in a Jewish immigrant culture, in the shadow of Brooklyn Bridge; he was drawn to anarchism; he loved Whitman; and on the lower east side, black culture—he claimed—was part of his life. He came to London, via Paris, in 1902, settling as an artist in St Pancras.[184] He did indeed produce some stunning sculptures, which stand as icons of the twentieth century, and which indubitably fuse a perceived African primitivism with a modernist aesthetic. Just before the First World War Sir Herbert Samuel—who in 1950 was to pay tribute to Smuts on the Home Service— was the guest of honour at the Royal Society of British Sculptors. Referring specifically to Epstein, he made his own bid for a traditional aesthetics, identifying clearly enough the enemy: 'For my own part, whilst the sculpture of the early inhabitants of Easter Island and Benin may be quite interesting from the point of view of anthropology, I am not sure they ought to be models for present-day art.'[185] Since a stay in Paris in 1912, black Africa had entered Epstein's aesthetic repertoire. In the 1920s he was in Harlem, his encounter organized by the white impresario, Carl Van Vechten. There he sculpted Paul Robeson. Through his life Haile Selassie (in the dramatic moment of 1936), Rabindranath Tagore, and Nehru were all to sit for him.[186]

Yet on the other hand, one could counterpoise to them Joseph Conrad or T. S. Eliot, Ernest Bevin or Princess Margaret. Tabulations like this do not necessarily mean much, especially in the commodified art world on which Epstein depended. In 1952 it was a Tory of the deepest hue, Rab Butler, who unveiled his *Madonna and Child* in Cavendish Square. By the time the commission for Smuts came his way he had been knighted. In residing at 18 Hyde Park Gate, he lived directly opposite Churchill. Such vignettes may provide a clue about the social accommodation of an impressively successful immigrant into Britain, but little more. It may be possible, as some conventional interpretations have it, to divide Epstein's career into two parts: callow rebel and aged conservative. Or it may be more appropriate to see Epstein from a rather different angle, as a white artist transformed by the aesthetics of the black Atlantic, but who—working through the faultlines of English civilization—became a kind of archetype of a conservative modernity: the émigré who reconstructs the forms of the national culture but who simultaneously subscribes to its deepest reflexes.[187]

However one chooses to see this, of one thing there can be no doubt: from early on, Epstein regretted the Smuts assignment. He was required to consult with the Ministry of Works and with the Royal Fine Art Commission, and he needed approval, in the early stages, from Attlee too. The minutiae of the details of Smuts's military uniform generated a number of controversies with the various authorities concerned (an abiding passion of the civic English), and Epstein himself was determined that the figure would be created *in motion*, to represent the energy of its human original.[188] By March 1956, when the project should have been completed and unveiled, the plinth was still nowhere to be seen. A firm in Pretoria had been contracted to produce a twenty-five ton piece of granite to provide the base. Four huge pieces were quarried before one was found without a flaw. When it was finally ready and about to be transported to Durban, it fell to the ground and was smashed. Epstein's frustrations possessed him, and he reverted to his role of *prima donna*. He blamed the company in Pretoria ('It's very easy to make a sculpture; it's very difficult to make a base'), while the managing director blamed him ('Not only I but everyone else thinks he is being very unreasonable to say the least').[189] After many postponements, on 17 July Patrick Buchan-Hepburn, the minister of works, finally announced in parliament that the statue would be unveiled on 7 November by Churchill, as a memorial to 'a great enemy of racial discrimination', no less.[190] The mishaps, however, were not yet over. A week before the statue was due to be unveiled, a controversy arose over the correct spelling of Smuts's middle name.[191] By the day itself, Churchill had pulled out on grounds of poor health, though his wife, Clementine, was of the opinion that he was ready for any excuse to absent himself.[192] And, in a different order of things, the constant delays resulted in the unveiling coinciding with the domestic climax of the Suez crisis.

At dawn on 6 November the Anglo-French seaborne forces landed at Port Said, prepared to take control of the entire canal zone. The British cabinet met at 9.45 a.m. The chancellor of the exchequer, Harold Macmillan, had been on the telephone to Washington before the meeting convened, anxious about the run on the pound; he became convinced that the only means of ensuring US support for an International Monetary Fund loan for Britain was the announcement of an immediate ceasefire. The pressure on the prime minister, Sir Anthony Eden, intensified. The country was split. Sunday the 4th had witnessed a huge demonstration in Trafalgar Square, whose angry cries quietly echoed through the emergency cabinet meeting.[193] President Eisenhower—facing re-election at this very moment—was furious, as were all the leading US politicians who mattered. On the morning of the 6th, it became clear that the cabinet too was backsliding. The ceasefire was agreed. First the French, and then the Americans, were informed. At 6.00 p.m. Eden told the Commons that a ceasefire would be effective from midnight, London time. If there is a single day which marks the symbolic collapse of Britain's imperial ambitions, 6 November 1956 must be regarded as a convincing contender.

But Eden's humiliations were only just beginning. In the morning of 7 November, just as Smuts was officially being resurrected in Parliament Square, Eden was engaged in a round of telephone conversations with Eisenhower. The first of these was friendly enough: Eden congratulated the president on his re-election, and persuaded him that Britain was still sufficiently a prestigious world-power to be invited to Washington in order to contribute to the diplomatic resolution of the Middle Eastern crisis. In the two conversations which followed, however, Eisenhower first expressed his doubts about the idea, and then—with little more than an icy courtesy—overrode Eden entirely, thereafter having almost nothing more to do with him. Eden was finished, and the imperial polity he represented widely perceived to be in tatters.[194] Within the fortnight he was at Ian Fleming's Jamaican home (Goldeneye), followed, after he had relinquished his position as prime minister in the new year, by a restorative sojourn in New Zealand.

The urgency of this crisis made the unveiling of Smuts a forlorn occasion. Eden, clearly, was absent, as was the entire cabinet and anyone else of influence. A tiny cluster of official guests witnessed the event, made up of diplomats and MPs, Enoch Powell included.[195] Churchill had indeed excused himself, though his brief words were read out, which turned on the idea that Smuts's qualities 'transcended nationality'.[196] The official unveiling was conducted by W. S. Morrison, the speaker of the House of Commons, who (perhaps also with Smuts's views on Goethe and Whitman in mind) informed those assembled that the last thing Smuts had said to him was this:'Morrison, it is a great thing to be a man—a great thing'.[197] The band of the Irish Guards played, while pedestrians got on with their business, with little more than a cursory look to the ritual being enacted—and while the double-decker buses endlessly circulated around Parliament Square, ensuring that Smuts was never required to look Abraham Lincoln in the eye.

In the six years of procrastination in getting the monument constructed, from his death in 1950 to the unveiling of 1956, Smuts had slipped out of the dominating rhythms of popular memory. For those who knew him, and for a particular generation of imperial men, memories of him remained invincible, as we have seen. For the majority who didn't know him, and for new generations, his image became progressively weaker. There is an inevitability about this, which is nothing more than the inevitability of mortal time, and of the creation of new generational cultures, which in the 1950s was particularly marked. But there was another dynamic at work. By this point in 1956 it was becoming increasingly awkward to project, unadorned, heroic epics of contemporary imperial life. On 7 November all the theatrical apparatuses were in place for the enactment of the commemoration of Smuts as the personification of the monumental history of empire. All, that is, bar the living principal actors: Churchill and the new generation of imperial men. The statue, the military band, the enormous Union Jack draping the bronze figure: the stage was set. In place of the politicians, however, were their wives and daughters: Lady Churchill, Eden's wife, Clarissa, the daughter of Smuts—though how they responded to Morrison's injunctions on transcendent masculinity is not recorded. There is an echo here of classical tragedy, the women stoically arranged around the memorial of the dead hero who discovered—late in life—his own mortality, ruing the hubris of their fallen loved one. The monumentalization of Smuts, and of the empire he represented, turned out to be an empty affair. It was an elegy not only for Smuts but for the British empire itself. By 1956, in the larger national culture, Smuts had become a hollow man, his effigy in bronze signifying— Epstein's aspirations notwithstanding—'gesture without motion'. Nor was this simply a consequence of the immediate political emergency. It suggests the presence of a larger historical fracture and the coming of a generation which could be forgetful about empire.

The Times, still sure of its role in the national culture, accorded the unveiling due prominence, publishing a photographic spread—alongside the photos of Eisenhower and Richard Nixon, the victors in the US presidential elections—which was effortlessly attuned to formality and tradition. BBC television showed the unveiling live, predictably calling on Richard Dimbleby to provide the commentary, and repeated an edited version in the evening.

More telling, perhaps, was the Movietone newsreel. Newsreels were still, at the end of the 1950s, a singularly powerful means by which the domestic population came to know about foreign and imperial events. In 1956 only some 15 per cent of the adult population watched television, while in the region of a thousand million cinema tickets were sold. During the war the newsreel had been a significant dimension of the experience of the home front. Early television news had directly copied the newsreel format, in the first instance simply borrowing the neighbouring form untransformed for the new medium. It had principally been through the newsreels that the story of the end of empire had assumed a popular form, both continuing into the postwar period scenes which confirmed 'the pluck of our boys out there', and in the process developing a particular vernacular which was peculiarly its own. C. Day Lewis had identified the characteristics of this form much earlier, at the end of the 1930s:

> There is the mayor opening the oyster season:
> A society wedding: the autumn hats look swell:
> The old crocks' race, and a politician
> In fishing-waders to prove that all is well.[198]

Increasingly, during the 1950s and into the 1960s, the newsreel vernacular became more jokey, playful, and topical, or in contemporary terms, more tabloid. As television began to compete as the premier means by which hard news was imparted, the magazine format of the newsreel claimed its role as sovereign medium of the topical, a genre which was neither quite news, nor quite entertainment. The populist, documentary, democratic element, which had been one impetus which had given birth to the newsreel, had all but vanished. Even so, the development of the newsreel genre proved an uneven process, for there were occasions when light-hearted topicality was not appropriate. After all, this was still the time when cinema programmes closed with the national anthem.

Some of these dilemmas are apparent in the Movietone newsreel, and indicate the contrasts to the heroic tone of November 1942. The Smuts unveiling was allocated just twenty seconds. The shots were conventional, formal, and quite without interest. The musical background was composed of a serious score, a touch funereal in deference to a public man departed. And the voice-over, tempered and respectful, could have come straight out of the pages of *The Times*. This was news and the nation, tightly demarcated and determinedly straight-faced. Next came—the order itself is revealing— a longer feature on the cycle and motor-cycle show at Earl's Court, which was altogether more fluent: in thirty-four seconds it conveyed wonderment at the spectacle of the modern and pride in the inventiveness of the British, while its narrative worked by topical allusion (the wealth of the *arriviste* Sir Bernard and Lady Docker; threats of petrol shortages), humour, irony, and pun. The divide between the new consumerism and the old imperialism could not have been more conspicuous. This in turn was followed by news of the Hungarian uprising (cynicism of the Kremlin bosses) and—at last, one might have thought—by Suez (our boys bringing restraint and civiliza-tion; cynicism of the Kremlin bosses).

This is micro-history with a vengeance, marking the onset of a media epoch in which cognitive structures become attuned to programme flows composed of twenty or thirty second segments. In itself, it can tell us rela-tively little. But to think in these terms may suggest that, in an age of new media forms and increasingly intense consumption, the monumental narra-tives which in earlier decades had seemed the natural mode for representing the official rhetorics of imperial Britain no longer carried the same author-ity. It is not that they entirely disappeared: one need only think of Churchill's funeral (though there is every reason to think that this did indeed mark the end of a particular domestic colonial culture). Nor is it the case that such media-driven forms had not been active in the organization of national-popular cultures in previous periods. Rather, it has more to do with a cul-tural diversification and the shifting imperatives of cultural authority, the axis turning sharply—in an age of Americanized mass culture—to the pop-ular. Given the proliferation of new electronic media, the ability institution-ally to hold in place official or monumental public narratives diminished, as they became more difficult to orchestrate. To put this in metaphorical idiom, the cultural authority of the (imaginary) Home Service citizen—located in a very particular imperial, national, and domestic history—was confronted by an unprecedented array of competing public possibilities, a perspective which offers one way of understanding what 1956 was about. In such a culture, the monumental memory of Smuts—taken on its own terms, and unmediated (say) by the romance of epic Hollywood—had limited popular reach. He had finally become the past.

The dissolution of the domestic colonial order in the late 1950s was complex, working across many different sites in the culture. The centring of new popular forms—commodified and Americanized—was unsettling, and not only to stereotypical retired colonial officials in Purley or Camberley. But significantly, within the inner reflexes of this new culture a peculiarly potent if displaced narrative of race and empire was dramatized within the borders of actually existing England, working as a kind of 'phantom' to the more publicly visible, official histories.[199]

If earlier in the century intimations of 'dark blood' had been received through the aesthetics of high modernism, by 1956 the medium of rhythm and blues, or in its more commodified form, rock'n'roll, was moving to the centre of popular experience.[200] While the resurrection of Smuts in Parliament Square testified to a culture determined to uphold the essentials of white civilization, through more subterranean channels versions of the black experience did indeed break into the lived cultures of white England— heavily mediated, perhaps, and with unknown consequences, but present none the less. In May 1956 *Melody Maker* reported the views of Asa Carter, of Alabama's Citizens' Council, that rock music was no more than the means of 'pulling down the white man to the level of the negro... It is part of a plot to undermine the morals of the youth of our nation. It is sexualistic, unmoralistic, and the best way to bring people of both races together.'[201] Carter was then closely identified with the Klan, and on his way to becoming a confidant of George Wallace.[202] His, patently, was an abrasively extreme view. But in Britain it could be heard in more modulated registers, from a variety of different locations: from politicians (Marcus Lipton, agnostic about Smuts, held no such equivocation about the dangers of rock'n'roll), in the popular press, from the BBC, from religious groups, in *Melody Maker* itself.[203] With a degree of irony, Margery Perham, in her Reith lectures of 1961, put it like this: 'Africa knew how to use the syncopated magic of the drum to summon ecstasy. Even unconsciousness. And perhaps in the abandonment of our youth to this spell, she inflicts a subtle revenge!'[204] While the final preparations for Smuts's statue were in train, exuberant crowds 'ranted and raved' outside the Gaumont cinemas in Dagenham, Leyton, and Stratford, fired up by seeing *Rock Around the Clock*.[205] These early manifestations of rock culture in Britain were inchoate, and too fluid to be positioned either socially or politically. But they were not without meaning, structure, or memory. They were a premonition, introducing a new historical time, and signalling a dimension of popular life and a new arena in which inherited ethnic memories—both black and white—would be played out and reinvented.

The tempo of these new cultures could make the old seem very old, dissolving those memories of Smuts and of his world which even in the 1940s had registered powerfully in public life. The valorization of black in white cultures was clearly one issue. In more conventional historiographical terms, it can also be noted that the long consensus on South Africa did not survive the coming of the Nationalist government in 1948. By 1956, eloquent if isolated individual public voices could be heard in England condemning apartheid and segregation. Even on the occasions when Smuts was not implicated in these condemnations (as generally he wasn't), their effect—for those who chose to listen—was at least to throw into doubt the inherited image of South Africa as a colonial idyll. From the mid-1950s, exiles from Nationalist South Africa slowly began to find their way to London, anticipating an exodus which gathered momentum as the repression inside the country intensified, and which ultimately reshaped the contours of Britain's internal political culture. They, too, were to be important in creating in white Britain new public perspectives on race.[206] Gradually, the religious and political descendants of the early twentieth-century pro-Boers began to generate a new dissident constituency, though necessarily shifting the object of their allegiances. As much as in 1899, British political life in the 1960s was again to be divided by South Africa.[207]

The surest voice of condemnation, which on occasion could be heard in the press and on television, was that of Trevor Huddleston. Through him, pre-eminently, another view of South Africa came into focus. From 1943 until he was recalled twelve years later, Huddleston had been priest-in-charge of the Anglican missions in Sophiatown and Orlando, on the edge of Johannesburg. There he was located not only in the crucible of African National Congress activism, but also at the heart of a visceral, urban black modernity which, against all odds, forged a culture of peerless imagination. The stories slowly fed back to England: of Yehudi Menuhin playing in Huddleston's church in 1950; of Hugh Masekela's trumpet, which was to assume the mythical equivalence of Gandhi's sandals. In 1956, unhappily back in England, Huddleston published his denunciation of the South

African regime—*Naught for your Comfort*—whose opening sentence implicated Smuts in his overall indictment. The book sold over 100,000 copies in
hardback generating, in effect, a new public.[208] This was a public which
could no longer plead innocence about South Africa, and which was likely
to remain resolutely unmoved by the imperial rituals occurring in Parliament
Square.[209] But by this time it wasn't even necessary to read the histories.
Shortly after Smuts was unveiled, on 5 December 1956 the four-year treason
trial opened in South Africa, the 156 defendants fighting for their lives.

These different developments raise a number of questions. There is perhaps an inevitability about the limited duration of the affective power of
those commemorated monumentally. One thinks of the waxwork figure of
Lord Roberts, British hero of the Sepoy Rebellion in India and of South
Africa, quietly spirited away from Madame Tussaud's early in the 1940s, a
matter of no public controversy as no one much remembered who he was
or what he had done. This same generational imperative must hold in the
case of Smuts too. But the speed with which he entered forgetfulness is
impressive. The declining authority of histories which sought to affirm the
values of the colonies as the special preserve of the white man was evident.
By the end of the 1950s the empire was coming so completely to signify the
past that it was almost impossible to remember that once it had symbolized
the future. Joseph Chamberlain's passionate invocation of 'Birmingham
man' at the dawn of the century carried—in the 1950s and 1960s—quite
different connotations, more parochial and domestic than he could have
ever imagined.

But if formal memories of empire fractured, or dispersed, this is not to say
that they had no effect. Dispersal suggests displacement. In different conditions,
these same memories could come alive in different form. South Africa became
one means by which white Britons in the late 1950s and 1960s could live out
their own ethnic dramas, as I indicated at the beginning of the last chapter. If
the fallout from Sophiatown eventually fed into the radical counter-cultures of
the 1960s, belief in the virtues of the white man's country, though largely
redundant in its own formal colonial terms, assumed a new popular accent as
a consequence of black immigration. So profoundly had race been encoded in
colonial language that, with the onset of black immigration as a social fact,
there was a logic in thinking that England itself had turned into one of its own
colonies. If the symbolic authority of the idea of the white man's country had
weakened in terms of the colonies, it had a new life ahead in terms of the
metropole. The day after the unveiling of the Smuts statue, on 8 November

1956, BBC television transmitted the first of what turned out to be a long line of domestic dramas about race—about black and white—in Britain: John Elliot's *A Man from the Sun*, in which one could catch an early glimpse of the white man in England, in his own domestic space, perceiving himself as victim of unnamable, unnerving forces greater than himself, triggered by the arrival of black neighbours. Viewers had no need to remember Smuts in order to recognize the ethnic codes which were played out before them. In certain circumstances, in particular neighbourhoods, whiteness itself, as the drama showed, had become a new axiom of everyday life.[210]

★★★★★

Lofty praise of the moral virtue of Jan Smuts, as the personification of enlightenment in racial politics and as the embodiment of the British way, was indicative of a political culture whose own memory had been formed deep in the history of colonialism. In this Attlee was as implicated as Churchill. This was a public memory which, when required, incubated its own forgetfulness. It was a memory in which amnesia could be organized. In 1956 a statue was erected to the memory of the man identified by DuBois as 'the greatest protagonist of the white race'. But in so doing other memories were vanquished. If one visits this site today one can just about make out a faint inscription—a literal trace—on the stonework where the figure of Smuts now stands:

> From 1865 to 1950 there stood on this site the memorial fountain in memory of Sir Thomas Fowell Buxton Bart MP and others in commemoration of the emancipation of the slaves under the British flag in 1834. The memorial now stands in the Victoria Tower Gardens.

The memory of this proud exemplar of the white race continues to suppress prior memories of the emancipation of black slaves and of the destruction of indigenous peoples. For Buxton was not only a great advocate of emancipation: he was also the prime mover in launching the Aborigines' Protection Society, motivated in the first instance as a response to white settler violence against the Xhosa in the Cape. That Buxton's memory should be effaced by the commemoration of a descendant of those Cape settlers, whose allegiance to white supremacy ran deep, is symptomatic of a culture in which the often unconscious imperatives of white civilization still prevailed.

In early September 1958 a group of young men in Notting Hill determined to go 'nigger hunting', as they subsequently explained their actions
in court. They set off for their local rugby club for a few drinks in order to
set themselves up. Finding it closed, before they embarked on their nocturnal violence, they drove to a local pub in Bloemfontein Road in Acton. It
was called The General Smuts.[211]

Four years after that, on a Sunday in June in 1962, Nelson Mandela was
on a clandestine visit to London. Like previous generations of illegal political visitors he took time out for tourism, strolling around Westminster with
his friend Oliver Tambo. They came upon the statue of Smuts. 'Oliver and I
joked that perhaps some day there would be a statue of us in its stead'.[212]
Nearly, but not quite.

6

Defeated by friends

The Central African Federation

The working out of the great problems of federal government...seems to
have been left in charge of the English people.

(Joseph Chamberlain, Toronto, 1887.[1])

[The Central African Federation will be] written on my heart when I die.

(Lord Home, Westminster, 1988.[2])

In the empire of the late nineteenth and twentieth centuries the domestic
politics of the metropole remained largely insulated from the intervention
of colonial politicians. The movement of personnel tended to radiate out
from metropole to colony. Political representatives of the dominions and
white colonies travelled to Britain to petition the imperial government, to
attend imperial conferences, and to add a putative lustre to the set-piece cer-
emonies empire required. Smuts, as we have seen, arrived seeking recognition,
to be adorned and honoured. He never appeared overly concerned about the
political allegiances of those who received him, imagining himself to be above
the petty divisions of British party politics. Despite his celebrated independence of character he exhibited a deep deference to all things metropolitan.
The ease with which he moved amongst those with power and influence was
what he valued most, his credentials as Greater Britain's favoured colonial
serving him well. Much the same could be said of the Australian Sir Robert
Menzies, who in his later days adopted a role as Britain's colonial uncle, visiting his distant relatives every so often to dispense a tipsy mixture of sentiment
and admonishment, dreaming all the while of times long past.

In 1960–1, when the transfer of power in Africa was at its most precarious, not only in Britain's central African possessions but also in Algeria and

in the Congo, this pattern of relations between centre and colony broke down. To Sir Roy Welensky, the prime minister of the Central African Federation, the policies of Harold Macmillan's Conservative government posed a threat of such extremity to white rule in the territory that he believed himself compelled to intervene in the politics of the metropole. From afar, he opened a campaign to turn the Conservative party against the Macmillan leadership. Welensky's overriding objective was to win independence for the Federation in order that the white settlers could go about their business as of old, unimpeded by hostile blacks and by their putative allies in London. Though his animus towards Macmillan was pronounced, his preoccupation with central Africa ensured that political issues in Britain were only ever of secondary importance. Welensky had no express intention of breaking the government; any intervention he planned was designed tactically, as a means to the greater end, as he perceived it, of independence for the Federation. But his was a dangerous game to play, with high stakes. There was a moment, early in 1961, when a sizeable body of Conservatives rallied to his cause, sympathetic to the ethos of the settler, which Welensky personified. Many of them, however, did not share Welensky's agnosticism about Macmillan's political future. 'The goals of preserving the Federation', writes one historian, 'and overthrowing Harold Macmillan had run in parallel for [Lord] Salisbury and his radical followers.'[3] Others, for a range of disparate reasons, personal as well as political, wished Macmillan and all he represented to be dispatched from office. For a brief but significant moment Welensky, the militant colonial tribune, symbolized an alternative source of political authority *in Westminster*, around whom disaffected Conservatives could regroup.

It is not customary, in discussions of the end of the British empire, to claim that the process of decolonization itself generated a crisis from which, within domestic public life, a new politics emerged. But this is my argument: that out of the crises attendant upon decolonization came a new politics of the right, and settler populism became a vehicle for the ideological recasting of the political right in the metropole. The benevolent reading of Britain's withdrawal from empire—in which, after a good innings, the far-sighted leaders of the nation realized that the game was up and proceeded to confer independence on grounds of the strictest philanthropy—never had much purchase in the historiography, though versions of it can still be heard in public life. What does remain prevalent, however, is the assumption, if only by default, that the end of empire was achieved without momentous breaks and discontinuities in the political life of the home-nation, without—to call upon a term notorious for its imprecision—the triggering of a crisis within the domestic state.

I think this assumption wrong. But to make such a claim it is necessary to recognize that this is a conceptual as much as an empirical problem. We need to know what kind of crisis occurred, how it should be calibrated, and where it is to be located. We need to be able to distinguish between a crisis which was merely conjunctural, and one with deeper structural properties; this in turn requires us to grasp the specific temporalities that operated. Readers will appreciate that these are questions not easily resolved. However they underwrite, I believe, the larger issue concerning the connections between end of empire and the home society of the metropole.

To insist that there was a crisis is not to inflate what occurred. There was no emergency in British politics—as there was in France in this same period—in which the repercussions of the struggle between colony and metropole threatened to destroy the constitutional system. In France there existed a direct, visible connection between the colonial catastrophes in Vietnam and in Algeria and the run of profound political crises which threatened the state in the metropole. In 1958 the *pied noir* insurrection in Algeria had already broken the Fourth Republic. Continued uprisings and mutinies in the colony throughout 1961 and 1962 impacted directly on the politics of the centre. In Britain there was no comparable experience of attempted coups and assassinations. Londoners were never obliged to scan the skies, on the lookout for mutinous troops parachuting into the city, as the French were in their capital on Sunday 23 April 1961. Whatever happened amongst the Conservative dissidents during these same months, and among their colonial allies, it never represented a crisis of that order.[4]

But nor should the gravity of the British situation be underestimated. In this penultimate chapter I focus on the collapse of the Central African Federation and on the consequent repercussions on a new, emergent Conservative right in the metropole.

The Central African Federation

In 1953, three years after Smuts died, and in part as a response by the British government to the victory of the National Party in the 1948 election in South Africa, the Central African Federation was created. The Federation comprised the three British territories of Southern and Northern Rhodesia, and Nyasaland, now respectively Zimbabwe, Zambia, and Malawi. Enthusiasts for the Federation believed its inauguration to be proof of the future longevity of the British empire. It was an experiment in which high hopes were invested. Its supporters—initially emanating from the Labour party—imagined that a dominion based on racial partnership would soon emerge, building in central Africa a new imperial bloc which would come to equal the historic dominions of Australia, New Zealand, and Canada.[5] The ambition of the architects of Federation was impressive, its presence confirming that well into the postwar period imperialists in London supposed that Greater Britain still remained a strategic reality, on which the future of Britain itself depended.

In the event all such grandiose hopes proved short-lived. The speed of the development of black nationalism and the effectiveness of its mobilization destabilized the intricate constitutional calculus in which white sovereignty had been institutionalized.[6] As the tempo of black agitation intensified the white settler leaders became more intransigent, imposing impossible strains on the relationship with the British state. By the end of the 1950s all the great aspirations had evaporated. For the government in London it became just another crisis to be resolved. In December 1963 the Federation was wound up, ending the last great empire-building initiative of the British.

Today the Central African Federation is remembered mainly by imperial historians, though only by a small minority of them. The institutional structure of federation was notorious for its administrative complexity. A succession of senior ministers, civil servants, and political appointments was charged with its management. Vast amounts of official time were eaten up in attempting to make it workable, drawing in many different offices of state. Five governments needed to be coordinated (the three territorial governments, the Federal government, and the government in London), calling upon the Commonwealth Relations Office (with responsibility for the Federal government and Southern Rhodesia), the Colonial Office (Northern Rhodesia and Nyasaland), a governor-general (for the Federation) and a governor (for Southern Rhodesia), not to mention from March 1962, as the entire experiment imploded, a designated secretary of state in the person of Rab Butler. The number of competing sources of authority, each with its own vested interests, not only induced administrative confusion but also meant that interdepartmental rivalries escalated. In addition the myriad of proposals for political reform, endlessly disputed, endlessly Byzantine, preoccupied many a constitutional lawyer. When Butler was in the midst of his attempts to bring the Federation to an end he found the task as burdensome as his involvement in the India Bill of 1935, legislation which had for years absorbed the energies of senior ministers.[7] Statecraft of this sort caused trouble in the past. It also taxes the skills and diligence of historians in the present, requiring immersion in the labyrinthine minutiae of long-forgotten administrative and constitutional procedures which, even as they were designed, were largely superannuated. One might think, then, that of all the infinity of topics for historical research, study of the Federation would hardly represent an inviting, irresistible prospect. It certainly does not appear to supply the stuff of popular history, amenable to the demands of television or to the zippy narrative of the page-turner. The likelihood of Simon Schama turning his hand to the Central African Federation is, I suspect, slim.[8]

Nor, moreover, is there is anything elevating about the distinctly British aspects of the story, which might appeal to those on the lookout for exemplary homilies deriving from the nation's past. None of the principal actors involved could look back on it as a mission well accomplished. Indeed in every respect it was a disaster. Over the years the evolving crisis broke political careers and turned historic friendships inside out. For the key protagonists it was indeed a moment best forgotten, a secret engraved on one's inner being to be revealed—as Lord Home implied in the quotation which stands as an epigraph to this chapter—only after death. Forgotten by the politicians, brought back to some sort of half-life by a small coterie of specialist historians and, for those of us in the old metropole, possessing no visible connection to the imperatives of contemporary times, this is indeed a vanished story.

There are of course other dimensions apart from the British. To specify one's object of study as the Central African Federation necessarily privileges the various departments of the British state, in its metropolitan and expanded forms. It puts at the centre of things the relations, as Joshua Nkomo declared at the time, between 'white man and white man'.[9] To approach this history from an alternative angle—prompted, say, by concern with the independence of Zambia or Malawi—would present a different picture, in which the role of the Federation would be more oblique, if no more uplifting.

But my own concern in this volume, as I have emphasized throughout, is with the shifting structures of racial whiteness. White men talking to white men can be revealing. Whiteness, I maintain, is not an incidental, or genteel, aspect of the history of the Federation. It lies at its very core, for this was a history which was largely a struggle about racial whiteness: about its prospects and futures, its responsibilities and dangers, its possibilities and impossibilities. To think in these terms, in an attempt to work through the administrative bias of the existing accounts, might encourage—this is my hope—other stories to surface. I find something compelling about histories, once actively present and charged which, without notice, disappear from public life, or whose protagonists claim, with an uneasy laugh, that they have them written on their hearts. What hides behind the forgetfulness? What may be disinterred from these troubling episodes in the national past?

The history of the Central African Federation is not only one of bureaucrats and constitutions but one, too, of turbulent passions. As white authority ebbed away in central Africa the white political leaders turned in on themselves generating a macabre drama in which friends became enemies, and enemies traitors. There was (so far as we know) no exchange of poisoned Bibles, in the manner of Renaissance tragedy, but there was plenty of double-dealing, treachery, and revenge that belie the normally calm prose of the administrative memorandum. The events in the region coincided with much blood-letting in Algeria and in the Congo which haunted the imaginations of the white settlers across the three territories, and not only of them. In the event little or no 'white blood' was spilt—black Africans, as usual, suffered grievously in comparison—though there was much evidence of the symbolics of what I have referred to earlier as unhappy blood. The impossibilities of whiteness were there for all to see. The settlers in the colonies came to believe that they had been sold out to the forces of black nationalism by Quislings in London who were unable to comprehend what whiteness demanded of them. And many of the white colonials, alongside a number of their allies in the metropole, with a deeper appreciation of the tragic mode, arrived at the conviction that they had been witness to the inexorable defeat of the white man.

The predominating conflict between the British government in London and the white political leaders in the Federation turned on the fate of the black populations of the three territories. The black Africans of Northern Rhodesia and of Nyasaland had their rights, as 'natives', overseen directly by London, through the instrument of the Colonial Office. The black Africans of Southern Rhodesia, a self-governing colony since 1923, had no such legal protection. Their lives depended on the decisions made by the territory's white settlers. In Southern Rhodesia, with the largest and the most assertive settler population, the institutions of white supremacy were entrenched. Black political leaders in Africa and critics of empire in Britain fought hard to convince public opinion that there was little which separated the position of blacks in Southern Rhodesia from those in apartheid South Africa.[10] From this perspective federation looked less like a benign experiment in racial partnership than a constitutional *coup* orchestrated by the settlers in Southern Rhodesia in order to extend their rule in the region. The black political parties in Northern Rhodesia and Nyasaland resisted the imposition of federation, and struggled to bring about its destruction, as did the blacks in Southern Rhodesia. The settler representatives believed that the economic concentration brought about by federation justified the bestowal of dominion status, reasoning that as the Gold Coast was heading towards independence—achieved in March 1957—then the white kith and kin in central Africa were equally, or more, deserving to take charge of their own affairs. In essence, the British government found it inadvisable or impracticable to jettison its responsibilities to the black Africans and to place them under the rule of the minority of white settlers, urging instead the installation of new guarantees to bring about racial partnership. From the latter 1950s the policies of London and Salisbury increasingly diverged, and relations between the two got rough.

As this divergence developed, the perception that there were two different types of Briton—metropolitan and urbane, on the one hand, and on the other colonial and purposively down to earth—deepened. The notion served a useful rhetorical purpose. The political managers from the metropole assumed that their sophistication and urbanity allowed them to grasp the larger picture, and that the settler position was based only on parochial self-interest; the settlers, in turn, were certain that they were the bearers of an essential—racial—truth which the very sophistication of their adversaries in London served to muddy and compromise. In part, this is how the emergent conflict between the two sides was lived out, the settlers in the Federation convinced of the mendacity and double-dealing of those at the centre, and not without reason. As the chairman of the Settlers' and Residents' Association of Nyasaland recalled: 'Dealing with HM's Ministers was a distasteful and sordid experience. These men were utterly unscrupulous; assurances and promises were flagrantly violated on the pretext of expedience. Their conduct repelled confidence and forfeited respect. In the intervening years intense bitterness has matured into unalloyed contempt.'[11]

In all the recrimination two deeper issues stand out. First, two contrary conceptions of politics operated. A number of the representatives of the British state (Lord Home, for example) held philosophical views about the virtues of white civilization which, on paper, were indistinguishable from those held by the settler leaders, and most remained convinced by the benevolence of British rule in Africa. But at the same time, from the perspective of Downing Street, the Federation was one amongst a multitude of issues which needed to be overseen; it was rarely the most pressing; its direct electoral impact, despite the periodic fears of the Tories, proved slight; and it was a long way away.[12] Economic realities intervened, and opposing forces in black Africa needed to be reckoned with. The worldwide diplomatic situation was changing fast: anti-colonial opinion in the United Nations and in the Commonwealth strengthened, as Smuts had discovered, and the attention of the British government turned to the European Economic Community. To say this is to recognize that the balance was tipping against the continuation of formal colonial rule. Even where sympathy for the old colonial ways was present, reasons of state—not of the idealized state of Greater Britain, but of the profane metropolitan state—took precedence. By the time of the Federation the divergence between inherited ethnic-imperial sympathies and the everyday requirements of the state could not readily be reconciled. As the crisis unfolded it came to be apparent that for the British matters of state, narrowly understood, predominated. For Macmillan it was barely an ideological—a national—issue at all. It just needed to be resolved.

On the other hand for Sir Roy Welensky and for the settlers more generally, the conflict was entirely an ideological—a national and a racial—issue, for their investment in the idea of white civilization became the means by which they could defend an entire system of social privilege. For them, the state (the British state) was turning against the nation (the white nation of overseas Britons). In this lay the perfidy of the various ministers. The state, as they saw it, was operating as an engine of ethnic treachery, intent on destroying the nation-people. If Macmillan and the senior British officials followed a politics of expediency, doing what they could to manage a situation in which they had little effective power, Welensky was drawn into the vortex of a very different kind of endeavour: the politics of ethnic populism. How far he was prepared to travel down this road remained, for the greater part of his premiership, an open question.

Second, both sides in the conflict were struggling over competing visions of white authority. One of the paradoxes of the situation is that—until perhaps the arrival of Rhodesian Front and Ian Smith in Southern Rhodesia at the beginning of the 1960s—the majority of the leading white contenders drew from the same diminishing linguistic repertoire of colonial liberalism. All formally distanced themselves from white supremacy; all formally embraced racial cooperation; all formally looked forward to the slow evolution of black majority rule, when the time was propitious. All claimed to be following the British way and all spoke in the same tongue. But declarations of principle which sounded the same, or looked to be the same on paper, carried consequences which could be entirely contrary.[13] Often the meaning resided in the undertone, or in what was left unsaid, or in a shrug of a shoulder largely lost to the historical record.[14] Or as Sir Roy Welensky explained to Lord Salisbury, 'one word can have a hundred different meanings'.[15] This was the cause of much ill-feeling amongst the participants, fuelling many grievances. The fact, though, that all the major players believed that they were required to speak in the same terms, and to speak as if they shared the same ultimate objectives, suggests that the strategic possibilities open to the British and to the settlers were contracting: in the face of a confident, advancing black nationalism, the terrain of an old white paternalism was becoming increasingly narrow, with room for manœuvre diminishing at every point. This marked a crisis not only of colonial policy but of colonial liberalism itself.

Federation: the final crisis

When at the end of 1957 the government in London announced that the promised constitutional review of the Federation would be held in 1960, the cabinet still believed that a future for the Federation was possible. Welensky, the strongest advocate for settler interests, had been Federal prime minister since November 1956, and he looked forward to the Federation gaining dominion status. While making concessions to the settlers on some matters, the Colonial Office pressed for constitutional reform for black Africans, particularly in Northern Rhodesia and in Nyasaland. But every constitutional advance, even the most modest, brought into the fray political forces dedicated to the destruction of the Federation. In turn constitutional reform in Nyasaland spurred black political leaders in Northern Rhodesia, and exacerbated the grievances of those in Southern Rhodesia. Federation amplified political dissidence, each territory aiming to leapfrog over its

neighbour. The announcement of the date of the Federal review itself galvanized the black opposition, uniting otherwise disparate political currents.
For if independence were to be granted to the Central African Federation,
the blacks in Nyasaland and Northern Rhodesia would find themselves
under direct settler control emanating from Salisbury. This transformed the
entire dynamic of black politics. For the British government, on the other
hand, the great practical justification for constitutional reform was that it
would encourage moderate political leaders to emerge from the black
masses. Events in central Africa in 1959, however, were to confirm that
those deemed moderates were becoming a declining constituency.

From the latter part of 1958 the mobilization of the black Africans in the
territories intensified. This was most evident in Nyasaland, the weakest
link in the Federation. When in July 1958 Hastings Banda returned from
his long exile he confronted a situation in which radical activity was high.
For his last years in London, Banda had worked as a general practitioner in
Willesden, involved in the anti-colonial networks which the city spawned,
before shifting his base to the Gold Coast. Within a month of his return
he became leader of the Nyasaland African Congress; in 1963, a year before
Nyasaland won independence, he was elected prime minister; in 1965 he
was made president, and five years later president for life. On arriving in his
native land, attired in his characteristic black homburg and dark three-
piece suit, he was barely able to speak in his indigenous tongue and out of
touch with local realities. A tumultuous crowd was in place to meet him
at the airport. At this historical moment Banda, a man of a deeply conservative disposition, became the unlikely figurehead for the popular movement for independence.[16] His decision in December to accompany
Kenneth Kaunda, the leader of the Zambian African National Congress
and future president of Zambia, to Accra to attend the first Pan-African
Congress to be held in Africa—where the delegates signed a declaration
calling for the dismemberment of the Federation—did nothing to allay the
fears of his white antagonists. The Federal government as a whole determined to exert its authority. Sir Edgar Whitehead, who had orchestrated
the *coup* against the liberal Garfield Todd and replaced him as prime minister of Southern Rhodesia, was the first to impose a state of emergency, on
25 February 1959, despite the relative quiescence in the territory.[17] Some
500 black militants, men and women, were arrested and jailed without
trial.[18] Emergencies were declared in Nyasaland on 2–3 March and in
Northern Rhodesia on 11 March.

In Nyasaland, the pretext for the emergency was a report from the Special Branch purporting to reveal a planned massacre of whites. Welensky, ready for a showdown with Banda, was apprised of this information some two weeks before the emergency, and the government in London shortly thereafter. Sir Robert Armitage, the governor of Nyasaland, accustomed to the rhetorical flourishes of the Nyasaland African National Congress, had no desire to be pressured into action by Welensky.[19] But given the deterioration of the situation Armitage informed London that he would declare a state of emergency on 2 March, though he made no mention of the murder plot. Julian Amery, the under-secretary at the Colonial Office, had (in the absence of Alan Lennox-Boyd, the secretary of state) already primed the cabinet about the forthcoming massacre, making 'his colleagues' flesh creep'.[20] Lennox-Boyd later informed the House of Commons that he possessed evidence that the Nyasaland Congress planned 'to carry out widespread violence and murder of Europeans, Asians and moderate African leaders: that in fact a massacre was being planned', while Amery, ever attentive to the sentiments of settler life, summoned the spectre of Mau Mau and spoke of the threat of a 'blood-bath'.[21] In the event approximately 1,000 suspects were detained, including thirty-four of the thirty-five graduates of the nation: Armstrong had cabled Lennox-Boyd to inform him that he was about to arrest all the known 'bad and brave men'.[22] On the first day of the emergency twenty Africans were shot dead by the security forces at Nkata Bay, and a further thirty-one in the days which followed. The repression in the three territories had been carefully coordinated and it is clear that the Federal government was seeking a confrontation with the nationalists all of whom, by virtue of their very nationalism, were deemed to be extremists.[23] The decision to impose emergencies in Nyasaland and in Northern Rhodesia was, of necessity, endorsed in London, suggesting that the British, as well as the Federal, government was not averse to a show of force.[24] But in neither territory was militant African nationalism destroyed. Indeed more than any other single act the imposition of the emergencies hastened the destruction of the Federation.[25]

On 14 March, as Lennox-Boyd at the Colonial Office was considering how an official inquiry into the violence perpetrated by the security forces in Nyasaland should be conducted, news came through of the massacre of Mau Mau detainees in the Hola camp in Kenya. This seriously compromised the government's credibility as an exponent of racial partnership. At the same time, in determining the inquest into the Nyasaland emergency, the cabinet made a series of miscalculations both in the nature of the inquiry and in the eventual choice of the chairman. Lord Devlin was appointed chair, and duly reported in July 1959. Devlin concluded that there had been no plot to massacre the white population, or anyone else; that the measures taken by the authorities had been illegal, and that ('no doubt only temporarily') the colony was 'a police state'; that the great majority of black Africans opposed the Federation; and that Banda himself was no extremist.[26] For the government this represented a disaster, prompting Macmillan, with Devlin in his sights, to ruminate in his diary about the vices of lapsed Catholics, Fenians, and hunchbacks.[27] Macmillan and Lennox-Boyd had no option but to reject the report's findings, calling upon all the resources of government to counter Devlin's conclusions.[28]

Ministers, keen to keep the remit of Devlin's commission as tightly circumscribed as possible, had earlier agreed that a broader inquiry into the future of the Federation, in preparation for the 1960 constitutional conference, could be beneficial. Fierce exchanges occurred between Conservative and Labour, and between the governments in London and Salisbury, about the terms and composition of the commission, while Macmillan proved himself as adept as ever in the art of subterfuge, playing off his antagonists and securing, in this instance, a desired outcome. Lord Monckton—a reliable conservative brought out of retirement, whose diplomatic skills had been credited with resolving the abdication crisis in 1936—was chosen to chair the inquiry. Reporting in October 1960 the commission emphasized, as Devlin had, the continuing hostility of black Africans to the Federation, and advised that settler intransigence, particularly in Southern Rhodesia, needed to be confronted in order for the Federation to survive.[29] When the constitutional review opened in December 1960 the viewpoints of the various participants were already so radically divergent that the formal proceedings were effectively abandoned as soon as they began.

A crisis of brinkmanship occurred in February 1961, when the fate of a new constitutional settlement in Northern Rhodesia hung in the balance, and when both the Federal and the British governments planned the mobilization of their troops in readiness for military intervention.[30] However Welensky, for all his bluster, was never prepared to embrace treason. Outmanoeuvred on every front his authority amongst the settlers began to ebb away. In August 1961 the (renamed) Malawi Congress Party won a majority in the Nyasaland election, its leaders refusing to contemplate a future inside the Federation. After a year of negotiation the new constitution in Northern Rhodesia eventually came to favour the black electorate and the election of October 1962 provided Kaunda a political majority. While black leaders advanced in the two northern territories the whites in Southern Rhodesia continued their swing to the right, the politics of the region increasingly polarized. When at the beginning of 1962 Whitehead set out to repeal the Land Apportionment Act—the cornerstone of white hegemony—he triggered a wave of populist reaction in the colony, which culminated at the end of the year in his dismissal and replacement by the Rhodesian Front leader, Winston Field, declaring that he would guarantee the future of settler supremacy. By the end of 1962 the Federation was opposed by the political majorities in all its three constituent territories. By this stage nothing could be done to save it. As Welensky half feared, those who were most prominent in managing the final destruction of the Federation—Home and Butler—were the two British politicians in whom he had first invested the greatest measure of trust.[31] On 31 December 1963 the Central African Federation ceased to exist.

The stories of the Central African Federation and of its sequel, Rhodesia, offer an embittered, mock-heroic rendition of the larger theme of racial whiteness, the universal aspirations invested in the ancient figure of Joseph Chamberlain's 'Birmingham man' long gone. An older, expansive conception of white civilization, confronted by defeats all around, collapsed into a sense of the world more defensive and inward, in which the perception of past glories existed only as a rebuke to the present.

Repercussions

The conception of white authority personified by Welensky marked not only a reassertion of the old colonial ways: it was, more specifically, a white backlash, formed in what we might call the 'highest stage' of decolonization. The politics generated in the Central African Federation, arising from local imperatives, reverberated inside the metropolitan state. For a brief moment, in February 1961, the Conservative party split along lines which were dictated by the situation in central Africa. In itself this was perhaps a matter of no great significance, a local crisis, certainly, but not necessarily anything more, creating the usual wrangles which the party whips were tutored, in their specialist ways, to resolve.

But for a number of reasons the divisions inside the Conservative party, initially instigated by far-off concerns overseas, became deeper and more long-lasting, and more attuned to domestic rather than to colonial realities, prefiguring an ideological shift in the party which incubated slowly over many years. In part this was due, for a time at least, to a measure of opportunism: backbenchers frustrated with Macmillan's leadership, and with what they imagined to be his accommodation with political adversaries, had no reason to be scrupulous about the issues they chose to exploit. However in other respects the opposition to Macmillan was more systematic. The dangers to the colonial order endlessly rehearsed by Welensky—the extinction of the civilization of the white man; the threat to social 'standards' posed by the black presence; the outbreaks of disorder increasingly apparent in every department of civil society; the menace of Communism—spoke to conservatives in Britain anxious about the social situation in their own country. The language of colonial disorder provided a means by which the disorders of the metropole could be understood and articulated. The constitution of Northern Rhodesia, opaque and legalistic, was one issue; the disintegration of colonial verities at home, possessing a much deeper potential for popular appeal, was quite another.[32]

At this point in the early 1960s one can see the first signs of an evolving *ideological* crisis in the state.[33] This was not a crisis which was generalized. Neither the majority of the Labour party nor the majority of the Conservative leadership was won by the racial jeremiads of Sir Roy Welensky. What did occur, however, was that an identifiable section of the Tory party, on the right, garnering support from a number of influential journalists, effectively began to disengage from the commitments to the postwar settlement espoused by the leadership.[34] Following the formation of the Monday Club in January 1961 this factionalism was underwritten by a degree of party organization. Where the Monday Club, and the larger, more inchoate phenomenon of the emergent New Right, proved most effective during this period was in challenging ideologically the consensus of the postwar years and in promoting a stricter, more radical Conservatism.

Put briefly the advocates of the new Conservatism believed, or said that they believed, that the entire spectrum of British politics had swung far to the left. Their intention was to turn it back to the right. Insofar as this was successful the politics of the radical right, its radicalism notwithstanding, could appear—*hélas!*—to be occupying the sanctified, consensual middle ground revered within the traditions of British constitutionalism. In this endeavour race and colonial issues played a prominent part. Assertion of black self-activity, in colony or metropole, was always in danger of being

indicted as extremism. As I pointed out in the Prologue, by the time of
Enoch Powell's Birmingham speech the *Daily Telegraph* was propagating the
idea that Powell represented the authentic middle ground of Conservatism,
hostile in equal measure to the racists and the anti-racists. This struggle to
present those on the right of the Conservative party as men and women of
moderation, speaking only for the values of ordinary folk, had a measure of
political purchase. But over the longer term the organized presence of such
mentalities in public life, in which the prescriptions of a civilization signified by racial whiteness became spoken with greater militancy—in political
society, in elements of the media, in various populist initiatives on the
ground—had a deep cumulative, transformative effect. When political tribunes on the right drew from the values of the colonial past as a means of
countering what they took to be the rising tides of metropolitan disorders,
and when such views acquired the authority of common sense, over time
the terrain of politics as a whole was indeed pulled to the right.

In what follows I offer selected snapshots of contending positions in the
Conservative party, and in its immediate orbit, in order to draw out the connections between the political crisis in the colonial state and the consequent
ideological crisis in the metropolitan state.

Cub Alport: consensus eclipsed

Cuthbert (Cub) Alport, Britain's high commissioner in the dying days of
the Federation, was a man genuinely dedicated to the ideals of racial partnership, as he understood them from his locations within the milieu of
English Conservatism. But taking on the job of high commissioner was to
cause him untold distress. His hopes for British rule in Africa were to be
broken; his own political reputation damaged; and, as a direct result of these
events, a lifetime friendship came to an end. His task in Africa was not aided
by his inability to grasp that his own liberal ethos, imbibed through the
codes of his social caste, functioned as the trigger for, and not the antidote
to, the deepening havoc in the region.

When in January 1961 Alport was invited by the prime minister, Harold
Macmillan, to take on the post of high commissioner—an idea which Alport
himself had put to Macmillan—there was no longer a grand future for the
Federation. The prospect of a military solution occurred early on in his
appointment. When in February reports were received in London indicating

that Welensky was mobilizing Federal troops to intervene in Northern Rhodesia, as a possible prelude to his organizing a *coup*, the Ministry of Defence prepared airborne forces in Kenya (Operation Kingfisher) in readiness for restraining the Federal government.[35] Alport's was to be a holding operation, preventing catastrophes rather than building empires, and perhaps if federation collapsed exploring whether alternative forms of cooperation between the territories could be sustained. Before his departure the final advice he received from the Commonwealth minister, Duncan Sandys, was characteristic of a prevailing malaise: 'All I can say, old boy, is to go out and do your best.'.[36]

Alport had always felt an affinity for Africa and he had established himself as an expert on African and imperial affairs. [37] He had been born into a British imperial family in Johannesburg, educated at Haileybury and Cambridge University, becoming president of the Cambridge Union in 1935.[38] He served in East Africa during the war. Within a few months of his election as an MP in 1950 he was appointed secretary to the Conservative backbench Committee for Imperial Affairs, and later served on a parliamentary commission to Kenya during the Mau Mau crisis. Over the years he had travelled widely in Africa and before Macmillan offered him the post in Salisbury he had been a minister at the Commonwealth Office, where he dealt with a number of prominent black African leaders. He regarded himself, and was regarded by his Tory colleagues, as an enlightened Conservative—though this was a view not always shared by his Labour opponents, many of whom discovered him to be an intemperate parliamentarian.[39] He had been a founding inspiration for the One Nation Conservatism of the 1950 intake of MPs, adumbrating from early on a political philosophy built on the concept of consensus that remained with him for his entire public life. (He did however withdraw from the One Nation group in 1953 until it 'remembered the Empire'.[40]) In later years Mrs Thatcher, when she was prime minister, certainly believed him to be a devotee of consensus politics. She found his attacks on the divisiveness of her policies sufficiently unguarded that, in 1984, the Conservative whip was withdrawn from him, the only occasion when this has occurred in the House of Lords, and thereafter he was content to sit as an independent conservative. An advocate of conciliation at home he carried these same commitments into imperial and foreign affairs. He had no time for those in his own party who blindly championed the settler cause in Africa. In the 1960s and 1970s he was hostile to the white minority governments in both Rhodesia and South Africa, on one occasion attacking the government of Edward Heath for its sales of arms to the Union. When he died in 1998 the *Guardian*'s obituarist Andrew Roth, a commentator of independent outlook, recorded Alport's 'sympathy for Africans'.[41] Yet these sympathies had their limits. He was no friend of black nationalism and believed deeply in the civilizing role of the British in Africa. The formation of the Federation, he was sure, provided a model for the whole continent curbing, as he had hoped, 'the excesses of both black and white nationalism'. 'It was', in his view, 'the last and certainly not the least important phase in the creative work of Britain in Africa'.[42]

When Macmillan offered Alport the post of high commissioner he judged his man well. The flattery was carefully underplayed, he did not conceal the difficulties involved, and he invoked the twin incentives of history and duty. As Alport later recounted the incident he put it like this:

> He [Macmillan] then went on to say that it would mean leaving the House of Commons and that I could either go to the House of Lords or no doubt would be recommended to the Queen for some lesser distinction. He would advise the latter since 'a peerage makes people think you are so old'. It would also enable me to re-enter the House of Commons when I returned. The post at Salisbury was at this critical time of great importance. My presence there with my knowledge of the problems and personalities of Central Africa might be instrumental in saving the Federation. He did not underestimate the difficulties. Indeed they had caused him more anxiety than almost anything else. Besides, he went on, such a post would follow a great imperial tradition of public service overseas. There had been Milner... Cromer... and when I came back there was the prospect of re-entering public life with the enhanced value which my experience abroad would give me. [*Ellipses in the original.*] After all he had been able to offer another High Commissioner the post of First Lord of the Admiralty while he was still at sea on his return journey from Australia.[43]

One can imagine the scene: Harold Macmillan playing Harold Macmillan, a figure tired of the vulgarities which political life imposed upon him, but pressing on, 'as one must'. And in the end getting his way.

It does not seem from this account that Macmillan actually had much to say about Alport's great proconsular predecessors, 'Milner... Cromer...' They were spirits to be summoned, talismans, invoked for effect on Macmillan's part. Alport thought that mention of them was not to be taken seriously. Enoch Powell's response, on hearing that his friend was to accept the assignment, was more emphatic: '"This," he said to me, "is the most romantic thing that has happened to any of us."'.[44] That Powell should speak in these terms long after he had concluded that the empire was finished, and as no enthusiast for the Central African Federation, is curious.[45] Whatever else, it seems, he could still imagine the empire offered romance to Englishmen of his generation. Alport did not share Powell's views on the termination of empire; but as much as Powell its spell still touched him.

Yet as with earlier generations of imperial adventurers the romance of Africa could also prove unsettling. A photograph of Alport on the boat leaving England, with his wife and children, shows a conventionally modern Home Counties family, a 1960s family far removed in appearance from their imperial-Victorian predecessors. What the photograph does not depict, however, is that historic fears had already descended. On the eve of their departure Alport's wife, Rachel, 'dreamed that a horde of blood-thirsty blacks came storming up the village street at Layer de la Haye [in Essex] and started to break their way into our house. She apparently had a strenuous time saving her daughters and herself from a fate worse than death. She certainly woke up next morning in a very exhausted and embittered frame of mind.'[46] These were anxieties which her husband shared, if rather more abstractly. Throughout his memoir Alport, in his unassuming manner, alludes to the 'mysteriousness' of Africa, to its 'brutality'. Laying a wreath at the graveside of Cecil Rhodes he described the location as a site in which none of 'the familiar values and customs of my own religious experience seemed to be present... Nowhere except beside the sepulchre of this Englishman in the heart of Africa have I had this sense of being in a haunted, sinister, pagan place...'.[47] The heart of darkness was always close by. With a conviction shot through with myopia he could claim that 'below the surface in Africa lay tendencies towards instability and violence which European control had suppressed but not extinguished... I saw no signs of the existence among Africans of those powerful moral forces which are able to redeem the peoples of contemporary Europe from some reversion to barbarism or a sudden recourse to cruelty.' 'My mind', he concluded, 'went back to Milner. He had forecast exactly the consequences of the premature withdrawal of British influence from South Africa—for both black and white.'[48]

The One Nation group of Tories, arriving at Westminster five years after the Conservative rout of 1945, prided themselves on their determination to create a new political generation, abjuring the class politics of the interwar years and committed to a cross-party consensus on welfare and full employment.[49] Since the early 1930s Alport had discovered his political mentor in the figure of Rab Butler, in many ways the leading Tory ideologue of the postwar settlement—though it was the friendship with Butler which was to be undermined due to the events in central Africa. Yet this never prevented older imperial instincts from intruding. J. R. Seeley had been an early influence; when he was growing up the spirit of Cromer was one to be admired; he took Rhodes and Milner to be his idols (enough to lay a wreath at the grave of the former); and although he was sceptical of Macmillan's invocation of the proconsular tradition of Milner and Cromer, in his account of his days as high commissioner he returns to them himself often enough.[50] However, as he continually complained, he had none of the power of his proconsular predecessors.

In Salisbury Alport had an impossible time. The dominating enthusiast for the Federation was Welensky whose distrust of the British turned him into an enemy. Alport felt abandoned by his allies in London who, he concluded, were making policy according to the needs of local political contingencies rather than with an understanding of the larger situation. Despite the many blandishments he knew that all he could expect from London was to be treated as 'little more than a titled messenger boy'.[51] The African leaders were more hostile each day, and on one occasion the high commission was the scene of a protest by black mothers, with their babies, against the new Southern Rhodesian constitution.[52] His predecessor commiserated with him for the 'fiendish time' he was experiencing.[53] But in all the recrimination what disturbed him most was the extent of the hostility directed to him, as the official representative of the imperial government, making him at one point equate his own fate with that of Pontius Pilate. The black nationalists, for the most part, boycotted all attempt at discussion. Welensky would unleash his fury. From other whites he encountered 'revulsion' and 'hatred'.[54] He was compelled to disconnect his telephone at night and was advised not to fly the Union Jack at the high commission for fear that passers-by might feel tempted to shoot at it. As he prepared to leave his post in June 1963, failure apparent at every turn, he realized that 'the end of Federation would end, to all intents and purposes, the long adventure of the British in Africa'.[55] A short while later, having made the journey back to England, he found himself—not at the Admiralty—but in the labour exchange in Holborn, searching for a job. His own failure signalled the larger failure of racial partnership.

In July 1945, on hearing the news of the Conservative disaster in the general election, Alport had sent Rab Butler a telegram welcoming the defeat, 'jubilant at its scale'.[56] He had earlier explained to Butler that he thought there existed in the party a 'very small' right wing, and a much larger number of those whom he described as 'the real "conservatives" or Tories—people like you and I'.[57] He believed that the ousting of the old guard in 1945 provided the opportunity for 'the real "conservatives"' to 'purge our organisation', and to regroup in order to win dominance both in the party and, eventually, in government.[58] As he saw it this was exactly what began to happen in the postwar years, symbolized first by the formation of the One Nation Tories in 1950, and then confirmed by the Conservative return to government the following year. Throughout, Alport was fighting on two fronts, the domestic and the imperial, certain that the two were inextricably linked and that the ethic of consensus (one nation at home, partnership overseas) was necessary in both arenas. But this advance, in Alport's view, was short-lived. By the end of the 1950s the influence of the One Nation group had declined, its members (Powell amongst them) taking different political paths, and preferment for some, and not for others, the cause of friction. Alport's experiences in central Africa convinced him not only of the limitations of Conservative colonial policy but of the Conservative government more generally. After returning home from Africa he came to conclude that the hopes of One Nation Conservatism were undergoing a protracted defeat, in both imperial and domestic affairs, the collapse occurring in the early years of the 1960s, and more or less coinciding with his posting in the Federation. By 1967, in the privacy of his diary, he was condemning Macmillan as 'that wicked old man' and decrying the coming of 'decadence and rootlessness', while in public he confessed that: 'Between 1956 and the Election of 1964 the Conservative Party was forced to take actions which ran directly counter to the basic tenets of its faith in the Commonwealth, in overseas policy, and, to some extent, in Britain.'[59] As the promise for a centrist, consensual Conservatism stalled so, Alport believed, the conditions emerged for a new Tory right to establish itself inside the party. As a consequence, no longer able to see the Conservative party itself as the exclusive home for 'the real "conservatives"', he began to think in terms of a national government as the most effective means for organizing the moderate centre, checking the extremes of both right and left.[60] This call for a national government from a returning imperial functionary, despite its impeccably centrist aspirations, marked a classic proconsular reflex. The spirits of Cromer and Milner were not so distant.[61] In January 1968 he was writing in these terms to *The Times*.[62] Later, when Edward Heath was in office, he still hoped to resuscitate the politics of 1950, telling Heath that it was the duty of those surviving One Nation Conservatives to do battle with 'the Powellite—Monday Club—right-wing of the Conservative Party'.[63] But by this time the great hopes of the progressive Tories of the postwar years were in disarray.

The enemies he confronted in the late 1960s and 1970s—'the Powellite-Monday Club' right inside his own party—were, though, familiar to him, partly in terms of personnel, and certainly so ideologically, for he had first witnessed these forces cohering around Roy Welensky during the last days of the Federation.

Sir Roy Welensky: settler populism

On 1 May 1952 the administrative secretary in Northern Rhodesia, A. T. Williams, wrote to the Colonial Office concerning an incident when two white government workers, S. J. H. Upton, a livestock officer, and G. D. Pretorius, a Public Works Department storeman, felt obliged to leave a government hostel because five blacks were staying there. The case had been raised in the House of Commons. Williams pointed out that the white men came from good families and that their behaviour was in no way to be censured. 'I should say', he explained, 'that many senior officers of this Government would be very reluctant to accept Africans into their homes as guests. This has nothing to do with racial feelings. Very, very few Africans in this Territory have yet got to the stage where they can comfortably meet Europeans on equal terms socially and culturally.' He went on to emphasize that it was always desirable 'to treat Africans as ordinary human beings' rather than according to prescribed racial principles, adding that 'one has friends whom one delights to honour and to entertain in one's home but whose company on a shooting trip, for example, would be abhorrent. But it should be unnecessary to explain any further.' He closed by reminding the civil servants in London that the real danger to race relations arose not from the actions of the two disgruntled whites but from 'the inexperienced, sentimental European or the ill-mannered European'.[64]

This racialized view of human intercourse, common sense to the settler but needing to be spelt out for the officials in the Colonial Office, underpinned Welensky's politics. When in 1938 he was first elected to the legislative council in Northern Rhodesia, and questioned about his policies, he replied by stating his conviction that 'I've no need for a policy. I'm simply pro settler'.[65] For all its variant political manifestations 'pro settler' meant a conception of the world much like that exemplified by the circumlocutions of Mr Williams, in which the racial boundaries of everyday life were vigilantly policed, and which—it appeared—had 'nothing to do with racial feelings'.

Welensky has disappeared from public memory in Britain even more completely than Smuts. There were never any monuments or memorials to him, no pubs named after him nor likenesses adorning the walls of Cambridge colleges, no breathless endearments from fading royals. Welensky took on the post of prime minister of the Central African Federation on 1 November 1956, his first days coinciding with the Suez crisis, which did much to reveal Britain's declining power in Africa. Almost from the very beginning of his time in office he, sure that a nation's authority derived from the determination of its leaders, found himself to be at loggerheads with the British government. Two years into his premiership he had already concluded that 'the battle for Africa was already on'.[66] He perceived the decline of empire to be evidence of the lack of political will on the part of Britain's rulers, of their abnegation of all that had once made the empire great. Older generations brought up with the empire may still possess the occasional recollection, the more deeply conservative amongst them happy to admit—after many years—their continuing admiration. These, though, are individual memories, with no influence on the public life of the present.

One can understand why Smuts was feted and Welensky consigned to oblivion. Smuts's enthusiasm for the protocols of Greater Britain broadly conformed to what imperial managers and ideologues in London believed to be desirable and feasible, while Welensky's continuing professions of faith in the idea of Britain overseas, only a few years later, increasingly came to be a political embarrassment. Loyalty to the idea of an expansive Britain brought the one garlands, the other to the lip of treachery. In formal terms they were both 'pro settler' but the situations in which they operated called for distinct political investments.

Welensky had been brought up a classic poor white, born in Salisbury in 1907, the thirteenth child of a feckless Lithuanian Jew with a propensity for losing money, and of an Afrikaner mother who had converted to Judaism. The future tribune of Greater Britain did not have, according to the criteria of the times, 'a drop of British blood'.[67] His father had arrived in Bulawayo in 1895 and had been on active service with the Bulawayo Field Force. He then moved to Gwelo (Gweru), lured by the attraction of the 'second Rand',

and thence to Salisbury. The family lived in poverty. This was exacerbated when Welensky's mother died, when he was 11; shortly after he left school to start work. Welensky was big in every meaning of the word, a large man with a forceful sense of his place in the world. He took up boxing as a source of income, eventually becoming, by default as it turned out, the Rhodesian heavyweight champion. He contemplated travelling to the United States to try for the world title but romance intervened, and he chose instead to stay in Rhodesia and marry his sweetheart, Elizabeth Henderson, a Scots-Afrikaner waitress from Bulawayo who—so the story goes—customarily served him his favourite beverage of ginger-beer with an ice-cream snowball. At 17 he found a job on the Rhodesian railways, first as a fireman, then graduating to engine-driver. The railway was owned by the British South Africa Company (BSAC), the chartered company which had been Rhodes's instrument for the appropriation of the Ndebele and Shona lands that, in 1890, became the white man's country of Rhodesia. The Company ruled the new nation until 1923, when Rhodesia became a self-governing colony. The direct political influence of the BSAC declined in the following years, though it remained the decisive economic power in the nation. Welensky hated the Company on orthodox class grounds, certain it was a parasitic force robbing industrious colonials of their wealth and enriching faraway plutocrats in Britain. Despite his promotion to driver he and his new wife suffered acute privation: their first baby, Ruth, contracted enteritis at nine months and died. Welensky was active in the Railway Workers Union—though, as he recalled in later years, as a dedicated constitutionalist with no sympathy for militant syndicalism—and took a leading role in the strike of 1929. He was reinstated after the strike was called off, but at a lower grade than hitherto and subsequently transferred from Wankie (Hwange), in Southern Rhodesia, to Broken Hill, south of the Northern Rhodesian copper-belt. In 1933 he became chairman of his local union branch, a post he was re-elected to every year until he became deputy prime minister of the Federation in 1953, and in 1941 founded the Northern Rhodesia Labour party, a working-class party whose goal was closer union with Southern Rhodesia.

Welensky was a genuinely proletarian political figure, gaining his education—Mill, Marx, and Morris, Wells, and Galsworthy—on the footplate, pride in his labouring skill indistinguishable from his sense of himself as a white man. His work, his union commitments, and his opposition to the Company provided a powerful populist underpinning to his politics.

This populism, in turn, confirmed his credentials as a settler who knew the native, allowing him to boast of his intimacy with blacks of his own generation. His most memorable evocation to this effect occurred in his interview with John Freeman on British television in May 1960: 'But I have, if you don't mind me being perfectly blunt, swum bare-arsed in the Makabusi in Salisbury with many picannins in my poorer days... I got to know them fairly well'.[68] Such affirmations of his proximity to the native conjures up not contempt but camaraderie, deriving from a shared experience, or an imaginary shared experience, of colonial life in the sticks. His biographer, an unstinting admirer of his subject, informs us that as a young man Welensky had worked in a 'Kaffir store' and that he had enjoyed joining local blacks 'in a score of skylarking adventures'. This, to say the least, is unlikely. But even so such jaunts, if they ever occurred, were circumscribed. To quote again from his biographer, 'Roy knew the African intimately; admired them for what good qualities they demonstrated but recognised their obvious limitations. He did not have to go a few steps from the garden gate of No. 24 to see them and, in talking to them, perceive the extent to which ancient slave-neurones darkened their minds.'[69]

During his union activities in Broken Hill Welensky fell foul of members of the British Union of Fascists and was subjected to anti-Semitic taunts.[70] He was never a practising Jew; at some point he became a freemason; and later in life, when he had become a public figure, he drifted into a conventional social Anglicanism. His is a story of progressive and eventually, it seems, complete assimilation.[71] Yet he was always willing to claim that his experience of anti-Semitism convinced him of the iniquities of fascism and redoubled his faith in the values of Britishness. He was also able to exploit his Jewishness in order to condemn racism. On one occasion, much later in his political career, he explained to the black author, Peter Abrahams, that 'I am a member of an oppressed race myself. I am a Jew and I have never forgotten being persecuted by fascist elements in Rhodesia before the war.'[72]

An 'oppressed race'; an oppressed social class; and, in his later struggles with representatives of the metropole's ruling elite, oppressed as a colonial: but through it all Welensky still imagined himself to have the dispositions of a white man—indeed, it was his capacities as a white man which he believed enabled him to transcend the bigotries he faced—and he was diligent in his refusal to acknowledge the larger racial oppressions on which the Rhodesias were founded.

In 1951 he was interviewed by the South African newspaper, *Die Burger*, and some ten years later summarized the views he expressed in the interview at the start of his memoir of his political life in the days of Federation. He identified three different schools of thought in the colonial management of race. First was that represented by the Colonial Office in London, driven by a spirit of democracy. The problem with this viewpoint, according to Welensky, was that it required thinking that democracy was just 'a simple business of counting heads', which 'to anybody with any experience of backward peoples' could be no more than 'arrant nonsense'. The second was apartheid. About this he had nothing particular to say—certainly, in *Die Burger*, the mouthpiece for apartheid, he was not prepared to commit himself to any moral censure of the National Party—beyond pointing out that 'this at least had a definite objective, which was lacking in the Colonial Office's vague and generalised policy'. Finally, there was the position to which he subscribed. This aimed to institutionalize racial partnership based on Cecil Rhodes's dictum, 'equal rights for all civilised men'. 'I stressed again', he went on,

> my belief that the European was bound to be the senior partner; but I pointed out that we in this school held that in so far as the African was fitted to play a part in government, judged by the contribution he made to his country's development, he should play that part...we didn't believe that suppression paid, but we were gravely concerned at the breakneck speed with which the British Government wanted to hand over control to the African. We believed in progress step by step, at the rate at which the African showed himself capable of, as well as willing to take, responsibility.

Looking back at this, at the time he was writing his memoir in the early 1960s, he emphasized that he was 'not anti-African'. 'I was simply against those who believed that, far better than we who lived there, they knew about Africa.'[73]

There is little evidence that Welensky exhibited much desire, personally, to be courteous to the individual black Africans he came across, at least in his public life, notwithstanding his boasts about his youthful racial camaraderie. We do know that Elizabeth, his wife, once made a formal complaint to the police that one of her 'houseboys' had stolen a slice of Christmas cake.[74] At the Federal Review Conference in London in 1960 Macmillan was astonished to discover that Welensky had never before met Banda or Kaunda. Alport, although not necessarily a reliable witness in this context, was horrified by Welensky's dealings with black leaders. Alport's views receive some corroboration from Welensky himself: during a tea-party in London for official guests at the Festival of Britain he was convinced that while Africans were lauded he had been snubbed, which resulted in his sending a furious complaint to the Colonial Office.[75] This suggests, minimally, the intractability of settler habits, even when these things could count politically: little wonder that 'very, very few' Africans could meet 'comfortably' with Europeans.

For much of his life Smuts spoke about race and white supremacy with relatively little embarrassment or qualification, as if he were merely addressing a fact of life, a matter beyond human intervention. Welensky, for his part, was required to formulate the settler case in more guarded terms.[76] He had an empirical, pragmatic turn of mind—this was part of his populist appeal—with little of Smuts's commitment to intellectual reflection. Even so the arguments he assembled should not be underestimated. He never held back from praising the achievements of 'the white man'. Towards the end of his premiership of the Federation he gave a spirited speech at the Royal Horticultural Show in Nairobi which took for its theme the idea that 'The white man has not much to be ashamed of'. This was recorded and played at many subsequent meetings in Kenya outselling, according to the record producers, local sales of Elvis.[77] Or at the end of 1962, echoing much older sentiments, he declared that there are 'definite limits beyond which the white man will not be pushed'.[78] But while praising white civilization he could, on occasion, be more circumspect about the position of the native. While Smuts was content to proclaim the truths of race, Welensky—even as he revered the doings of the white man—endeavoured to demonstrate that he had entirely freed himself from racial thought. 'Equality', Welensky claimed, 'cannot be conferred; it must be earned—and accepted as being earned. Equality has nothing to do with race or colour.'[79] Without any hint of equivocation this was to turn inside out the principles of racial justice, denying racial logic in the very moment of its utterance. In a single knight's move, race was shifted from the body ('colour') to conduct or, to stay with Rhodes's own formulation, to 'civilization'.

It is difficult to judge the effect reasoning of this sort had during the Welensky years, though neither allies nor adversaries would have had difficulty in deciphering the essential codes.[80] To argue in this way was not peculiar to Welensky, as we can see from the similar assertions made by A. T. Williams, denying the presence of 'racial feelings' arising from a racial incident, or later, as I shall indicate in the next chapter, from the racial language employed by Ian Smith.[81] But outside the region, in the metropole, where popular knowledge of African nationalism was often driven by simple stereotypes, apparent racial even-handedness of this kind, exemplifying the British way, did generate a measure of political purchase. In Britain, for all the ambiguities in play, the public expression of racial arguments—*as racial*—carried certain taboos, which explains why the 1961 bill to curb black immigration, for example, proved so awkward for the political managers, requiring a peculiarly public form of dissimulation. In this situation, for those sympathetic to the imperatives of white civilization, to hear coming from the colonies a defence of racial whiteness which purported to be entirely non-racial was an innovation to be welcomed.

Alongside a racial politics which denied the efficacy of race Welensky also presented himself as a man of the moderate political centre. The presence of the Nationalist government in South Africa paid dividends for him in this respect as it had done for others, and so too did the diehards in his own camp with whom he was in contention.[82] By positioning himself in the middle of two contending extremes—on the one hand, the upholders of apartheid and, on the other, the revolutionary black nationalists — he worked hard to fashion himself as a non-ideological figure, motivated only by his regard for British values, and as an enemy of extremism wherever it was to be found.[83] He made much of the fact that in the Federation he spoke on behalf of 'the moderate African', even though his own policies were responsible for divesting many Africans of the last vestiges of their 'moderation'.[84]

To have witnessed Welensky operating in his own society, and to have experienced the omnipresence of the colour line, would have been to recognize—for friend and foe alike—that his was a politics founded on white power. To be confronted directly by the segregation between black and white in daily life, sanctioned by the law and winning all but universal consent from the racially privileged, leaves nothing to the imagination. But in Britain that immediacy was absent and, as we have seen in the case of Smuts, the representations of colonial issues in the metropole were always heavily mediated. Even at an unconscious level inherited myths of black Africa—assegais and their counterparts—had a role to play. Conversely, the familiarity of racial whiteness, and of the values of Britishness in which they were encoded, carried a certain credence at home, as the affirmations of the affiliations between 'kith and kin' were to show later during the Rhodesian crisis.[85] This ideological *disconnection* between metropole and colony was important, and touched directly the workings of the domestic polity.[86] Welensky was a white supremacist who believed that the democratic 'business of counting heads' was 'arrant nonsense'. When apologists defended him as a man of moderation, as many did on the Conservative right, they did great damage to democracy. And when, in later years, these same views appear in the historiography it suggests that they have, even now, a degree of credibility.[87]

It was as a paragon of moderation that Welensky was invited to speak at the annual conference of the Institute of Directors at the Albert Hall in London at the end of 1961, addressing an audience of more than five thousand. He spoke as one who had been witnessing, on the front line, the defeat of the West, a defeat whose enormity had not been grasped by those cosseted in the home society. One listener was so enthusiastic that he paid £5,000 to have the speech reprinted as a full-page advertisement in the *Daily Express*. It stands as an important document from the period of decolonization, indicating the terms on which Welensky mounted his defence of continuing white rule. In the manner of Froude, it works as an address to the people rather than to the state, opening with the acknowledgement that 'the undoubted courage and integrity of the British people have not in recent years been reflected in some of the actions taken on their behalf'. Welensky was emphatic that the Federation was 'the direct descendant of British Imperialism', evident in the 'British administration, British traditions and British standards which were implanted in Central Africa seventy years ago, with the first coming of civilisation'. Against this British inheritance were arrayed the forces of Pan-Africanism: demagogic, brutal, cynical, 'racialist', and working at the behest of Moscow. The nationalists, he argued, had played upon white guilt about colonialism in the metropole and had successfully undermined 'authority': 'the naked truth is that it was pressure, pressure from the nationalist movements, and fear of the colonial stigma, which did most to turn the minds of the metropolitan powers from their colonial tasks'. Although largely unnoticed or comprehended in the metropole, 'the West has suffered, I regret to say, a major defeat'.

The purpose of the speech was to announce that accommodation to the Pan-African movement had continued for long enough and that now was the moment to reassert white authority. 'It is not too late to stand firm.' But white authority, and the 'British traditions' on which it was founded, could only counter the 'racialism' of the nationalists if it itself refused all truck with race. When the Federation was founded 'It was clear that a choice had to be made, a choice between the domination by one race over another on the one hand, and partnership on the other, with the goal of a way of life in which a man's ability, not the colour of his skin, would count.' From the beginning of Federation 'we acknowledged that the days of the privilege of a white skin were over. Neither in moral nor in practical terms did we believe the old order to be tenable; but we refused to exchange one form of racialism for another . . . And as you in Britain are now discovering, the hardest prejudices of all to eradicate are those of race and caste.' He outlined the advances which had been made: 'an African Minister in my Government; there are African Ministers in the Northern Territories and they are virtually in control of the Executive Council of Nyasaland'. Only by renouncing 'racialism' could whites bring progress and freedom— 'freedom from want, freedom from ignorance, freedom from the brutal savagery of tribalism; freedom from superstition and witchcraft, freedom from intimidation; and the freedom of equality before the law'.[88]

Welensky was skilled in making the rhetorical principles of his adversaries his own—acknowledging 'the colonial stigma' in a way that Smuts, for one, was never required to do—and in defending the colonial order as the exemplification of a social system that had superseded race. It is unlikely that the historical record, which told a contrary story, would have had much influence on the assorted businessmen who filled the Albert Hall, or on the readers of the *Express*. It is probable that their knowledge of the constitutional and social realities of the Federation was, in the way of these things, slight. But there is a greater likelihood that the symbolics of the speech would have registered more deeply. When he finished, according to *The Times*, he 'sat down to an ovation which vibrated the Albert Hall'.[89] Welensky depicted valiant British traditions compromised by governments too ready to appease their foes, manifest at this moment in the form of a savage black movement dedicated to Pan-Africanism. This touched old fears. As one who *knew* he told, too, of defeats of Britain in faraway places. 'Authority' itself was in danger, but too few were capable of seeing the speed with which it was unravelling. It was not too late, however, 'to stand firm'.

'There is nothing wrong', Welensky told his audience at the Albert Hall, 'with the courage of the British people and its leaders.'[90] He may have believed this about 'the British people'. He certainly didn't about their 'leaders'. From the moment he became prime minister of the Federation he increasingly came, day by day, to be persuaded of the mendacity and irresolution of the imperial government. Earlier in the year, in Salisbury, Welensky had been lunching with the Commonwealth minister, Duncan Sandys. He recalled that he'd been arguing that, with 'a firm exercise of authority', it would have still been possible to have kept Nyasaland in the Federation. "'No, Roy," said the Commonwealth Secretary. "You see, we British have lost the will to govern."' This—coming from Winston Churchill's erstwhile son-in-law, no less—was regarded by Welensky and by the other Rhodesians present as a scandalous admission. It was not only Sandys's insouciance which proved objectionable. It was the fact that he could have put an idea like this into words—that such a thing could be *said* by a minister of Her Majesty's Government—which confirmed its truth. Welensky was so out-raged that he suffered an immediate migraine and, in his version of the story, Alport returned home and vomited.[91]

Moderation was not evident in the internal workings of the Federation. And it was, too, conspicuously absent in Welensky's involvement in the neighbouring Congo, where he did all he could to abet the ultras of racial supremacy who planned to mount their last stand for the white man in the breakaway province of Katanga. Belgian special forces intent on reversing colonial independence; wild veterans from Indochina and Algeria nursing dreams of vengeance; settler militants from Southern Rhodesia; assorted US spooks plotting to disarm the forces of Pan-Africanism: these were Welensky's chosen allies.[92]

During 1959, after a long period of apparent colonial stability, Belgium's authority in the Congo began a precipitate collapse: 'no colonial power in history was destroyed more quickly'.[93] The government in Brussels sought a swift exit before the situation further deteriorated. Elections were held in May 1960 and, to the dismay of seasoned colonial hands, Patrice Lumumba, an inspirational advocate for decolonization, triumphed.[94] The formal handover of power took place, in public, on 30 June. In the presence of King Badouin of Belgium, and of the prime minister Gaston Eyskens, Lumumba issued an unscripted, uncompromising denunciation of colonial rule, broadcast across the nation, indicting a system which had condoned slavery and announcing that the people of the Congo were no longer to be 'niggers', making it clear that the struggle for independence, far from being over, was just getting started.[95] Taking their cue from Lumumba the army mutinied against their white officer corps. The military split, chaos threat-ened, whites fled, and—in the name of order—Belgian paratroopers occu-pied the nation's major cities in a bid to reimpose colonial rule. On 11 July Katanga—the mineral-rich heartland of the old colony, the fiefdom of the gigantic Union Minière consortium—announced its secession under the leadership of Moïse Tshombe, looking to Belgium and to mercenary forces to protect its future. In September Lumumba was deposed in a *coup* led by his one-time political ally Jospeh-Désire Mobutu, who delivered Lumumba to his mortal enemy, Tshombe. Neither Mobutu nor Tshombe, nor the Belgians nor the Americans, nor indeed the British, wished Lumumba to remain alive.[96] During his incarceration by Mobutu, Lumumba had been systematically beaten. On his arrival in Katanga, the violations—perpetrated by Katangan and Belgian officials, Tshombe himself participating—intensified. He was finally shot on 17 January, his dismembered corpse immersed in a barrel of sulphuric acid.[97] Late in the day the United Nations—initially called into the Congo by Lumumba to counteract Belgian aggression, then in the name of order siding with the Belgians and Tshombe—turned their fire on Katanga and secured Tshombe's downfall.[98] Mobutu staged a second *coup* in 1965, installed himself as head of state, and continued in office until 1997 when, in retribution for his support of the Rwandan Hutu during the genocide three years earlier, he was overthrown by intervention from neighbouring Rwanda, Burundi, and Uganda. The afterlife of the catastrophe of 1960 was long and bloody.

For Welensky the crisis in the Congo was immediate and urgent. Northern Rhodesia shared a border with the Congo—indeed, with Katanga—of many hundreds of miles, great stretches of which were unmarked. Economic traffic between the two regions was constant, the Rhodesian railways used to transport the Union Minière minerals. The advocates of a 'white' Pan-Africanism—Rhodes, Smuts, and later Ian Smith—all imagined a time when Katanga would be sequestered by the British. Even before the crisis of 1960 Welensky had informed a *Daily Express* journalist that he was contemplating the incorporation of Katanga into the Federation.[99] When unrest took hold of the Congo the fears of settlers, irrespective of nationality, were fuelled, precipitating the conviction that black barbarity was again rampant, as it had been in Kenya and was in Algeria. Many Europeans fled, crossing the border to Northern Rhodesia and bringing with them lurid tales. From July 1960 Welensky's support for Tshombe was total, believing him to be a bastion against Pan-Africanism and Communism.[100] Northern Rhodesia functioned as a conduit for mercenaries and materiel. Welensky attempted to prevail upon the British government to recognize Tshombe's Katanga as a sovereign nation and to provide him the support he needed. When, in the autumn of 1961, Tshombe repudiated a UN agreement to reintegrate Katanga in the republic Welensky ordered the Federation's military to the border. The British government, taking the lead from Washington, decided that a united Congo was necessary. Tshombe, in this scheme of things, was expendable. For Welensky this confirmed both the cynicism and the weakness of the imperial government. Nor was he blind to the fact that, if Tshombe were expendable, so too was he.

During 1960–1 in Salisbury and London, Katanga functioned as a decisive cockpit where the politics of decolonization and the politics of the cold war intersected, placing it high on the agenda of colonial and foreign affairs. By the end of 1961 it had become a defining issue in giving form to the emergent Conservative right which Welensky attempted to mobilize in his bid to counter Harold Macmillan and Iain Macleod.[101] For the right Katanga signalled a surrender by the West of unmitigated enormity.

Welensky's memoirs, published in 1964, immediately after the termination of the Central African Federation, are driven by his sense of betrayal by enemies whom he once believed to be friends. 'The battle to build the Federation', he explained, 'was won in the open', realizing an idea which had arisen from 'the mainstream of British politics'.

> A few years later, however, the Federation was destroyed, not by our avowed enemies but by those who called themselves our friends and said they believed in what we had built. They killed it slowly, in the dark and by stealth; and they wept hypocritical tears as they finished the deed. That is the measure of what happened to Britain between 1952 and 1959; what happened to us is almost of small account beside that tragedy.[102]

By the end of 1963, when the Central African Federation was dismantled, as these words suggest, Welensky's destruction was almost complete. A few months later he attempted to revive his political life by standing in the Arundel by-election in Southern Rhodesia. He stood as an opponent of Ian Smith's Rhodesian Front, certain that any unilateral declaration of independence for Southern Rhodesia would fatally undermine the power of the settlers. In a vicious campaign he was mocked as a Jew, a Communist, and a traitor, and as a politician who had been humiliated by the British and who now lived in the shadow of Ian Smith.[103] He was roundly beaten. In the aftermath of this final political defeat he retired from public life. After the death of Elizabeth he married Valerie Scott, a Tory party worker thirty years his junior, started a new family, and quietly lived out his last days in Blandford Forum in Dorset, a tranquil, pastoral ending to a life dedicated to the directives of white supremacy.

'Mau Mau Macleod': Tory dissension at home.[104]

Harold Macmillan spent much of his premiership preoccupied with the pace of black advancement in the African colonies, at one moment appearing to accelerate the process, at others pulling back. He was almost entirely untouched personally by the romance of the settler—in private he was disparaging—though nor did he ever evince sympathy for black nationalism. The government's room for manœuvre was slight, and its capacity to influence events in distant lands diminishing. In central Africa historic social forces were colliding and, as Macmillan himself reluctantly came to realize in his later years in office, the best he could hope for was to prevent a cataclysm.

He was also constantly aware of the potential for rebellion at home from within the Conservative party, and with good reason for—as he acknowledged often enough—there were plenty of malcontents within his own ranks. However in the event, on colonial issues, as Philip Murphy has pointed out, only a relatively small group of Tory backbenchers actively opposed the government; between 1959 and 1964 there was no significant party rebellion against two- or three-line whips; and among the dissidents there were virtually no influential party figures and none was destined for high office.[105] The pro-empire forces, it seems, were of little consequence. But was this so?

As I have noted the greatest challenge to the government occurred at the beginning of 1961 when Welensky orchestrated a Tory vendetta against the colonial secretary, Iain Macleod. Macleod had been appointed to the post in October 1959. His immediate predecessors, Oliver Lyttleton (Lord Chandos) and Alan Lennox-Boyd (Lord Boyd), were old-school imperialists, men of wealth with significant business interests in Africa, and whose natural sympathies were unequivocally for the settler. Macleod was of a different stamp.[106] He came from an empire family—his father had worked as a medical officer in Assam, and after the war one of his brothers emigrated to Kenya, another to Canada—but he was brought up in Skipton where, after India, his father had become a general practitioner. His social mores were, in the way of these things, upper-middle- rather than upper-class, and within the Conservative party he was recognized as an intellectually able progressive. Until he became colonial secretary he had never visited a single British colony, the cause of some dismay when his appointment was announced.[107] Earlier he had been shocked by the Hola catastrophe and by the fallout from the emergency in Nyasaland, convinced by the depth of the domestic political crisis they had induced.[108] However in his first year at the Colonial Office he could not apprehend the degree to which events in central Africa were accelerating. Only hesitantly did he conclude, in relation to Kenya and to the Federation, that constitutional change needed to be speeded up. This demanded, in turn, that he confront the settlers.

In its initial ideological incarnation the Central African Federation had, in Westminster and in Whitehall, been the inspiration of Labour-Fabian, anti-apartheid progressivism, championed by Andrew Cohen, assistant under-secretary at the Colonial Office, who headed the African Department; by his counterpart, G. H. Baxter at the Commonwealth Relations Office; by Patrick Gordon Walker at the Commonwealth Office; and with more circumspection by James Griffiths at the Colonial Office. At the beginning of 1951 Gordon Walker had travelled through central and southern Africa, a journey which did much to convince him that the danger from Nationalist South Africa was serious. Reporting on his investigations he made it clear that alongside Britain's objective of advancing the interests of black Africans in the region there existed an objective of equal importance: the need to *contain* South Africa. The latter, he insisted, should never be subordinated to the former.[109] Yet 'containing' South Africa could only become a reality by collaborating with the white settlers in the adjacent territories, most of all in Southern Rhodesia. This reasoning rested on the assumption that the whites in the Union were racial extremists, while those in the Rhodesias were attuned to the ways of British liberality and paragons of goodwill, a proposition of dubious veracity. Indeed, in large part the idea of the Federation represented a concession to what we can understand as the white nationalism of the settlers: just as London was learning to accommodate black nationalism, so too it had to accommodate the demands from a resurgent white nationalism.[110] How these objectives—cultivating the settlers of southern and central Africa while simultaneously demanding the advancement of black Africans—were to be reconciled was never made clear: not in the minds of the Labour progenitors of the Federation, and certainly not by their Tory successors, who had few scruples in passing responsibility to settler activists.[111]

Like many Conservatives of his generation Macleod worked from the premise that political life was inhabited by distinct species: moderates and extremists. As much as Welensky, or Alport, he placed a premium on the virtues of what he called moderation. Yet predictably contention arose in demarcating where the division between moderation and extremism should fall. Macleod had never been persuaded by the common settler reflex that every African nationalist was a hothead, bent only on destruction, and after the Nyasaland emergency he was even less inclined to accommodate such fallacies. Within four weeks of his appointment he had announced the end of the long-term emergency in Kenya. The following month he released the majority of those who had been detained in Nyasaland, resolving to leave in prison only those whom he identified as 'the true hard core'.[112] In the early months of 1960—while Macmillan was in South Africa sharing his thoughts on the 'wind of change' and, in Algeria, the *pieds noirs* militants were embarking upon a full-scale *jacquerie*—he argued for the release of Hastings Banda, meeting resistance not only from the Federation but from Macmillan and from the Commonwealth secretary, Lord Home. During this same period at Lancaster House he presided over the discussions concerning the future constitution for Kenya, looking to formalize a common electoral roll for black and white. In both Kenya and Nyasaland Macleod was prepared, on specifics, to take on the settlers and their allies in London and on which, at the end of February 1961, he staked his own political future.

In following this line of action his purpose was to create a new political centre, splitting both the African nationalist moderates, and the moderates in the settler camp, from their respective radicals—although in the minds of the colonial managers the intention of creating 'moderates' was never divorced from the option of resorting to the intensification of state violence, as the imposition of the emergencies made clear.[113] Those who refused to compromise, nationalist or settler, were to be cast out.[114] This required a significant reappraisal of the criteria by which moderation was defined: on the one hand, substantial cohorts of blacks agitating for independence were to be brought into the spectrum of recognized, legitimate constitutional politics; on the other, the settlers could no longer qualify as moderates as an automatic consequence of their whiteness. In the spring of 1960, for example, Macleod arrived at the conclusion that Banda was as moderate as the British government was likely to get.[115] Translating this approach into practical policies presented many difficulties and every twist and turn produced new dangers and perpetual dissension. But to proceed by this logic held the promise of overcoming what—since the foundation of the Federation—had been irresolvable, the simultaneous privileging of both black and white. The immediate costs of the Macleod strategy were carried by the diehard settlers, confirming their belief in the ignorance of those residing at the empire's centre and creating the mental conditions for the summoning of such crazed, fantasized apparitions as 'Mau Mau Macleod'. Macleod sought to shift the centre of political gravity in the colonies away from settler absolutism: in doing so he generated a backlash in Westminster in which cohered a deepening politics of the right.

This came to a head over the question of the Northern Rhodesian constitution at the start of 1961. The previous October the Monckton Commission had recommended that an African majority should be established in the Northern Rhodesian legislature. Welensky believed that were this to occur Southern Rhodesia would be forced to secede from the Federation; Macleod, on the other hand, was equally insistent on the need to press ahead, seeking 'to get an agreement between the Africans and as many Europeans as I could'.[116] During the course of the confrontation battle lines were drawn, the threats of a settler *coup* inside the Federation accumulated, and British and Federation military units were placed on alert.

For many years Welensky had built up close connections with Conservative politicians in London, a tireless campaigner for settler interests. When he had been in London for the Festival of Britain in July 1951 he took the opportunity to caucus, boasting that he had seen everyone in the Conservative party from Winston Churchill downwards.[117] He was particularly close to Lord Salisbury, while politically he gravitated to the rump of the old Suez rebels. The Suez Group had its origins in the opposition to the withdrawal of the British garrison from the canal zone in 1954, generally meeting in the Amery household in Eaton Square. In May 1957 a small nucleus of the original dissidents—Paul Williams, John Biggs-Davison, Viscount Hinchingbrooke, Patrick Maitland, Anthony Fell, Angus Maude, Sir Victor Raikes, and Lawrence Turner—continued to hold out against what they perceived to be the government's appeasement of Egypt, and temporarily resigned the party whip.[118] From this point on they represented the diehard empire faction, distinct from the majority of the party due to their willingness actively to challenge the government. At the very moment when decolonization was gathering pace, they remained isolated, bereft of political influence; yet organizationally the group proved significant, providing the vehicle by which a militant ethos of empire was maintained during the travails of decolonization. Above all, they were receptive to the message Welensky brought from central Africa.

In January 1961 Welensky launched his offensive against Macleod, urging the Tory dissidents to take the fight to the heart of Westminster. By the end of the month the incitements from central Africa were coming thick and fast: to Lord Salisbury, Robin Turton, John Biggs-Davison, and Patrick Wall, amongst others. In the words of the historian J. R. T. Wood—Wood was Welensky's man in the field of history—'Welensky said he wanted Macleod attacked from every quarter'.[119] On 9 February some fifty backbenchers attended the Commonwealth Affairs Committee where the opposition to Macleod was vocal. That same day Turton, an ex-minister and one-time subsidized visitor to the Federation, submitted an early-day motion—drawn up by Biggs-Davison in consultation with John Roberts, the leader of the Northern Rhodesian United Federal party—proposing that the government stay true to the principles of Lennox-Boyd's 1958 constitution: that, in other words, the pace of reform immediately be slowed down. Within a few days over ninety MPs had added their signatures (including Mrs Thatcher), representing more than one-third of the Conservative backbenchers.[120] For the first time the centre of the party had been drawn into the camp of the settler ultras. In the following month the rebellion ebbed and flowed. In the opening days Macmillan could not be at all certain how events would turn out, but he was sure in his own mind that Macleod had 'undoubtedly leaned over too far toward the African view'.[121] Welensky himself kept the pressure up, and on 16 March addressed a second meeting of the Commonwealth Affairs Committee, which in itself represented an affront to Macmillan and Macleod.[122] Some 200 backbenchers attended and gave Welensky an enthusiastic response: subsequently Patrick Wall—not an impartial observer, but on this occasion perhaps accurate enough—informed Welensky that he had carried between two-thirds and three-quarters of the meeting with him.[123]

In Westminster the principal conspirator against Macleod was Lord Salisbury—'Bobbety', whom we have come across before as Sir Ralph Furse's fag at Eton and as a wartime enthusiast (as Lord Cranborne) for the idea of imperial blood. He himself was of the bluest of blue blood: as the fifth Marquess of Salisbury he was the grandson of the great Tory prime minister, born at the Cecil family seat, Hatfield House, in 1893, which is where he died in 1972. The family owned vast tracts of property in Hertfordshire, in Cranborne in Dorset, and in London's West End. The Southern Rhodesia capital had been named after his grandfather, and in the 1940s Salisbury himself had purchased many thousands of acres of farmland in the colony. In January 1956, on being awarded the freedom of Salisbury, he declared that Rhodesia's founders were the 'greatest men' of the 'modern world'.[124] In the late 1930s he had opposed appeasement, which cleared his way for office in Churchill's wartime coalition: he was at various times dominions secretary, colonial secretary (he declined the offer of viceroy of India), leader of the House of Lords, and (like his father and grandfather before him) leader of the Conservative party in the House of Lords. He was appointed Commonwealth secretary when the Central African Federation was coming into being, drafting with Lord Swinton the preamble to the federal constitution. In the view of Robert Menzies he had rightful claim to be 'one of the wisest men of our time', who 'has modesty, good sense, good judgment, high character, imagination and sense of responsibility completely blended in him'.[125] Others were equally extravagant though less generous. The editor of the *Daily Telegraph*, Sir Colin Coote, took him to embody 'the definition of a gentleman as one who never gives offence unintentionally'.[126] Salisbury, as this suggests, was an impeccable master in the art of giving offence. To Roy Jenkins he appeared merely 'sour and malevolent'.[127]

As Simon Ball shows in his revealing portrait, the lives of Salisbury and Macmillan had been closely enmeshed for a generation.[128] They arrived at Eton in the same year, were contemporaries at Oxford, and served as officers in the Grenadier Guards during the First World War. Salisbury's sister married Macmillan's brother-in-law. They allied with Anthony Eden in opposition to the appeasement of Neville Chamberlain, and in time both came to be supported by Churchill, serving together in his wartime government, when Salisbury was the more senior figure of the two. In the early 1950s they again worked closely in their determination to oust Churchill from the premiership, convinced that his incapacities posed a danger to the party, as they did once more in 1956 in keeping Eden resolute in organizing the invasion of Egypt and acting as cheerleaders for his conspiracy with Israel. Over the years they had plotted together, and they had advanced together. The rupture between them opened when Macmillan became prime minister in January 1957. Ancient Tory battles were alive in their imaginations. In the year that he had become prime minister Macmillan noted that 'I expect his feelings towards me were those of his grandfather towards Disraeli . . . he, the great Salisbury, thought Disraeli was not a good Tory.'[129] Worried, perhaps, by those with intimate memories of his past deeds being too close to him, Macmillan felt uneasy in having contemporaries in his cabinet; when he felt able to ride out the political consequences, he dispensed with them. In his very first days in office he instructed those around him to brief the press against Salisbury, letting it be known that in future he would no longer be a figure of influence.[130] Within a few months he had exploited his position as premier to outmanœuvre Salisbury, pressuring him to resign on what Macmillan took to be a secondary matter (the release of Archbishop Makarios, the EOKA figure head, fighting for Greek–Cypriot self-determination) rather than on an issue which he thought might have produced a deeper public outcry (Egypt, particularly, on which Salisbury's views were close to those of the Suez Group). According to John Barnes, however, although not revealed at the time, a 'major factor' in his resignation turned on his desire for an immediate ban on West Indian immigration, an issue which the cabinet was fearful of opening to public scrutiny.[131] In the coming years he maintained his pro-empire, anti-immigration loyalties, and spoke out against developing closer ties with Europe. Playing on the historic credentials which had accrued from his resignation from Neville Chamberlain's government in 1938, he henceforth took it upon himself to condemn the 'appeasement' of those whom he believed were insistently capitulating to the empire's enemies.[132] In 1962 he was invited to act as the founding president of the Monday Club, an office he accepted and held until his death eleven years later.[133]

Salisbury was not accustomed to operating outside the charmed inner circle of the ruling elite. There was enough of his grandfather in him to feel that the councils of the state were in the nature of an heirloom, and that sharing them with others was tantamount to an act of impropriety. Just as the third Marquess had been alarmed by the demagoguery of Joseph Chamberlain, so Bobbety was not one to stomach anything more populist than a glass of decent port with the good folk of the Carlton Club. Yet those with an appetite for power knew from historic experience that propriety could never function as an absolute, and that in moments of danger authority had to make concessions to what otherwise would have been treated as irredeemably demagogic or vulgar.[134] After all, whatever his class susceptibilities, Lord Salisbury (the third Marquess) chose to make his own political alliance with Joseph Chamberlain; and so in a desperate—albeit, one assumes, an entirely unconscious—re-enactment his grandson, Bobbety, engineered his pact with the ethnic populism espoused by Chamberlain's ideological descendant: the colonial Sir Roy Welensky.

Early in 1957 Lord Salisbury and Sir Roy Welensky had begun to correspond in earnest at a time when Welensky was in the first moments of his premiership of the Federation, and when Salisbury was about to cut himself adrift from Macmillan and the Conservative government. From that point until 1963, when the Federation was dissolved, some 150 of their letters have survived and been archived.[135] By the spring of 1957 formalities had been dispensed with and 'Bobbety' and 'Roy' were starting to share confidences. A number of the letters are perfunctory, thanking the other for kindnesses shown, or explaining the impossibility of sending a proper letter due to public demands or illness. Lady Salisbury joins the correspondence to thank Sir Roy for gifts of flowers following his visits to Hatfield, although Lady Welensky appears to have played no part in these written communications which, aside from the occasional endearment, came to turn on matters of state. A significant cache, by contrast, constituted lengthy disquisitions of many pages, sometimes typed, sometimes hand written, on the politics of the moment. From the spring of 1960 they increasingly carry the frenzied, although no doubt necessary, instructions 'Private', 'Confidential', 'Personal', and 'Secret', in varying conjunctions. In its entirety the correspondence supplies an important record of two leading upholders of white supremacy arriving at the realization that the British government was retreating, if unpredictably and haphazardly, from its historic commitment to empire, and in so doing abandoning the empire militants on whom, in an earlier epoch, it had depended.

If Salisbury can be construed as the senior of the two owing to his length of service in high office and to his close proximity to the centres of metropolitan power, it was Welensky, as serving premier reporting from the frontline, who made the running. His wholehearted loyalty to settler civilization in central Africa represented, in Salisbury's imagination, empire at its most resolute, signalling a strong ethical charge, and Salisbury proved ready to applaud.

'Bobbety', wrote Welensky in August 1960, 'I would almost sell my soul for a little bit of guts in the British government'.[136] Such was the dominating refrain of the correspondence. There were those with 'guts', who determined to fight for their convictions, and there were their enemies, the 'defeatists' and the 'appeasers', quick to surrender to the forces of barbarism and to 'double cross' those who insisted on maintaining the principles of empire. Macmillan and Macleod soon were accorded the role of primary agents of unprincipled appeasement. Welensky was happy to condemn Alport as worthless. Maudling, when he replaced Macleod as colonial secretary, speedily joined the ranks of the treacherous. When, in 1962, Rab

Butler was given cabinet responsibility for the Federation, both Welensky and Salisbury were initially unsure what to make of the appointment, puzzled by Butler himself and unable to determine where his loyalties lay. By the end of the year, when Butler had come to support the secession of Nyasaland, their puzzlement lessened, and they concluded that he merely confirmed their apprehension that even potentially good men, in serving the immediate interests of the British government would inevitably go bad.

Through 1961–3 Welensky's letters were punctuated by his reverie that he might cut loose from Britain and go his own way. In this respect the collaspe of Katanga was critical, the United Nations evidently abetting the barbarians, or so it seemed to the correspondents. In May 1963 he repeated his conviction that the London government was 'gutless', concluding that 'I have crossed the Rubicon'. (This was designated 'Top Secret and Personal'.) He informed Salisbury that he was about to pay a visit to Verwoerd, sure that South Africa and Portugal were the only authentic allies which remained.[137] This was a move which Salisbury found worrying, apprehensive that Welensky's popularity in the metropole would be compromised if he allied himself too closely with Verwoerd.[138] Yet by the end of the month Welensky was explaining to Salisbury that Verwoerd was convinced that Southern Rhodesia had gone too far down the road to multiracialism, putting paid to any prospect of there ever occurring amalgamation with South Africa. He confessed that he was 'glad of this', as it decisively clarified the situation.[139] Like many previous crossings of the Rubicon, Welensky once more pulled back, resolving to struggle on even while fearing that defeat loomed.

Indeed Welensky came to believe that his travails occurred *because of* his whiteness. The promises made to 'a white man' in Africa, he complained, had become 'almost meaningless'.[140] He informed Salisbury that he was worried about 'the long-haired gentlemen' in London and their influence on 'our African brethren', allowing him to rehearse his belief that as a result of British intervention, 'the law-abiding African' had become 'compelled to play ball with the thugs'.[141] Day by day the line distinguishing London from Moscow seemed to be disappearing. The aim of the Communists, he told Salisbury in August 1963, was to get rid of 'the white man' in Africa as a prelude to their total takeover.[142] By an inexplicable twist of fate, what previously had signalled privilege now represented all that was most base: 'our curse is obviously that our skins are white and that's no good on this continent'.[143]

This was not exactly the language which Salisbury habitually employed, but nor was there any point when he demurred, for he shared with Welensky the conviction that corruption had taken hold of the centre. Yet if Salisbury proved more circumspect in his use of language, with a readier recourse to the virtues of the British, his sentiments none the less accorded with those of Welensky. 'Tolerance is the national quality that represents the highest degree of civilisation', he opined. 'I really believe the British have it in their bones'.[144] Even so, his denunciations of those Conservatives who allied themselves with Macmillan were as fierce as Welensky's, and more than once he wished that Welensky would prove more decisive. He was grateful to Welensky for passing on detailed information of the extent of the duplicities of British (and UN) officials operating in central Africa, for it confirmed all he most abhorred. Yet, just as Welensky had a sharper sense of the daily realities of the collapse of colonial order in central Africa, so Salisbury had of the manifold disorders which he perceived to be stalking the metropole. Interspersed with commentaries on the Congo, or on Nyasaland, Salisbury was keen that the ills at home should receive due heed. Just as Welensky despaired of a government which had no 'guts', so Salisbury, in his more patrician vocabulary, bemoaned the lack of *leadership* in the nation. Striking workers at Fords were intent on 'holding the whole community to ransom'; postmen took it into their heads to work to rule; the entire working class was 'emasculated by the welfare state'; too many young men were turning out to be 'very pinkish'.[145] The growth of disorder derived directly from the laxness of the nation's leaders, personified by Macmillan, and perceived to be conspicuously wanting when compared to upright, morally sound white colonials such as Welensky. Both Salisbury and Welensky were appalled by the revelations generated by the Profumo affair, each certain in his own mind that the moral structure of the nation was disintegrating, and that the cause of the collapse lay with Conservatives who were not properly Conservative. While Salisbury condemned the 'do-gooders' and the 'spivs', Welensky admitted that 'I find it difficult to believe that an imperial mission, one that had such meaning and such future for so many people, could be destroyed in such a miserable way and cause such little comment in England', remarking only how curious he found it that Macmillan should find himself traduced for the Profumo affair and not 'for the betrayal of the white man'.[146]

As Simon Ball contends, the question of Africa transformed the relationship between Salisbury and Macmillan from one of distrust to one of 'open hatred'.[147] In the autumn of 1960, in the aftermath of the Monckton report, Welensky took the 'extraordinary step', as he put it himself, of sending the secret diplomatic correspondence he had received from Macmillan to Salisbury, certain that this would demonstrate Macmillan's mendacity: for after Monckton had published its findings it had become clear that the many assurances made by Macmillan about the future of the Federation to Welensky had come to nothing.[148] Salisbury was appalled by what he read, burning his own copies and advising Welensky to publish the correspondence and reveal the prime minister to be a liar. This Welensky felt unable to do. Later Macmillan acknowledged that 'From our sources of information we know that Welensky and his High Commission give every private document and all private discussions to Lord Salisbury', and it was on these grounds that he instructed MI5 to monitor Salisbury as a potential threat to national security.[149] Relations between Macmillan and Salisbury had turned toxic. In December 1960 the latter formed his Watching Committee, a device to organize dissent within the party and to send a warning to Macmillan that he meant business. In doing so he also played on old collective memories, for in April 1940 his father had created just such a committee in order to launch the *coup* against Neville Chamberlain. In the event included amongst those whom Salisbury attracted was a ramshackle clutch of Tory screwballs (Hinchingbroke, Lord Lambton), their eccentricity the cause of much satisfaction to Macmillan ('rather a ragamuffin lot').[150] Salisbury's purpose, however, was to avoid a direct attack on Macmillan by going for Macleod, exploiting the animosity deriving from what his critics believed to be his determination to break up the Federation.

The occasion when he came into the open—a celebrated exercise in offence, even as he insisted he was embarked on no such thing—occurred in the House of Lords on 7 March 1961, when he indicted the colonial secretary for ethnic treachery, impugned his character by dwelling on his well-known expertise as a gambler (deceiving the 'white people' of Africa), and added the memorable jibe that he 'has been too clever by half'.[151] Salisbury's speech did much damage to Macleod, yet its intemperance marked the symbolic highpoint of the revolt against the government. Four days later it was revealed that Salisbury had refused to have his name put forward for the presidency of his local Hertfordshire Conservative Association, a gesture (complete with indignant letters to *The Times*) imitated by Lords Selborne and Forester in the days that followed, hardly acts of consequence.[152] The following autumn rumbles of discontent over Northern Rhodesia recurred amongst the Tory backbenches. The crisis in Katanga continued to be divisive, strengthening the hand of the Watching Committee (and attracting new recruits, such as Lord Boyd, the erstwhile colonial secretary, Lennox-Boyd), leading Home to calculate that on this issue the bulk of the party at Westminster was closer to Salisbury than to Macmillan.[153] By December Macmillan was fearful that the dissidents were influencing 'the whole *centre* of the party', but he held on until the Christmas recess, and reckoned—correctly—that few would instigate an assault on his leadership over the Congo.[154] The prolonged 1961 domestic crises of empire appeared, in the end, merely to peter out. The rebellion had been vanquished.

The metropolitan right

By Christmas 1961 Salisbury effectively capitulated, his political capital spent. During the summer Macmillan had decided that Macleod should be removed from his post as colonial secretary. In part this was because of the continuing strategic differences between him and Duncan Sandys, who had replaced Home at the Commonwealth Office. And in part it was because, having broken the log-jam in central Africa and drawn the fire from Macmillan through the succession of crises in the previous months, he had become expendable.[155] The right were exultant that it should be him to go, rather than Sandys, for there was little else to cheer them. On 10 October 1961, the day after Macleod's resignation, Patrick Wall informed Welensky that his departure would bring a close to 'the ruthless pro-African Nationalist line'.[156] In the event his successor, Reginald Maudling, proved as troublesome to Macmillan as had Macleod, pulled along by events to much the same degree, and soon coming to realize the impracticalities of making overtures to the white minorities. When in the new year Maudling also started to issue threats of resignation Macmillan despaired, noting in his diary that he was *'plus noir que les nègres'*.[157] Macleod's ejection from the Colonial Office did little to slow the impetus of decolonization.

But this is not the end of the story. The empire right in the party was, it is clear, defeated politically. The transfer of sovereignty in central Africa was, so far as the white protagonists were concerned, conducted as a passive affair, managed from London administratively and pragmatically rather than as a momentous ideological struggle. The events of 1961, when the political fissures inside the Conservative Party were most visible and dangerous, came close to marking the failure of this pragmatic approach, drawing into the constitutional arena the threat of unruly political forces. Yet while Home and Butler, the architects of administrative decolonization, eventually succeeded in their chosen strategy, they did not win a decisive ideological victory.[158] The ideological fall-out from central Africa was complex and long-lasting, for from the defeat of the Tory imperialists emerged a revivified Conservative right, drawing as much from the experience of the party's grassroots as from the imperatives of the parliamentary party at Westminster. It is at this juncture that we can locate the beginnings of the movement from the traditional right, principally fighting a sectional, rearguard defence against the loss of empire, to the New Right, which was eventually to take root in the moment of Powellism and Thatcherism in the later 1960s and 1970s. In its early phases this was a political formation which owed much to the mentalities that were manifest in the settler resistance in central Africa, and later in Rhodesia. It was, in addition, a politics created in reaction to the administrative logic that had dominated the end of British rule in central Africa, and which came to draw upon a growing populist groundswell.

There are three interconnected issues: decolonization as a passive revolution; the ideological resurgence of the right in the aftermath of the political defeats of 1961; and the crystallization of a distinctly 'new' right. I shall say more about these matters at the end of the next chapter on Rhodesia (where I discuss the Monday Club) and also in the closing volume of *Memories of Empire*. Here I present only brief concluding remarks.

The defeat of the imperial old guard was largely an effect of the institutional structures which underwrote decolonization. The Colonial Office's preoccupation with the existence of identifiable moderates is important in this respect. The purpose of this strategic thinking, as I have indicated, was to create a new political class to which authority could be transferred when black majority rule came into being; where such a grouping was absent, as Macleod believed it was in Uganda, many problems presented themselves.[159] The intention was to take the initiative away from the black militants in the townships and to organize the appropriate governing institutions in which the semblance of postcolonial order could be maintained. Strategically, the endless drafting of new constitutions represented one of the major means by which this was to be achieved. Above all, it was necessary to install local representatives with whom business could be done. This represented, in Gramsci's terms, the workings of a passive revolution, in which the optimum political solution depended on the minimal popular mobilization of the key contenders. Constitutions, commissions, inquiries: these were the characteristic stratagems of passive decolonization, slowing things down when necessary, and shunting off awkward issues to an appropriate siding until the situation quietened. The most enduring symbol of this strategic logic was Lancaster House, the opulent townhouse in St James's in the shadow of Buckingham Palace; itself steeped in the ornate, neo-classical paraphernalia of history and tradition, it provided the *mise-en-scène* for the encounters between the old settler representatives and the new cadres of black leaders, convening in order to work through the details of the transfer of sovereignty, under the chairmanship of the British.[160] This dedication to a passive transition, however, was not restricted to the colonies: although perhaps less pressing, for the government in London it was equally desirable for the metropole.

The absence of Conservative backbench rebellions over Britain's withdrawal from central Africa can be explained, at one level, by the fact that, in the words of Philip Murphy, 'most of the important decisions made by government ministers relating to Africa were never debated in Parliament'.[161] Far from being the result of open discussion, the crucial decisions took shape, step by step, in the institutions of the administrative state: in the cabinet, in Whitehall, and in the offices of the British functionaries in the colonies, and by means of the creation of *ad hoc* bodies, such as commissions and inquiries. Within the party itself, as Murphy notes, 'there was a rapid expansion in the institutions through which party members could express their views on colonial affairs'—he cites the parliamentary committee system, the Conservative Commonwealth Council, and the various policy committees.[162] These did give voice to backbench opinion, as we have seen, and they served as useful barometers for assessing the ideological balance of forces: but ultimately they were not where power resided. Although the Conservative leadership was alert to the build-up of dissidence within the party, the occasions for set-piece confrontations were obviated. The rebels themselves were obliged to fall back on their own procedures—early-day motions, the Watching Committee—in order to attempt to exert leverage over a process which always seemed to exist just out of their reach. Such manœuvring did little to overcome the primacy of an administrative system which, amongst other things, offered the prime minister every opportunity to display his skills in the dark arts of tactical intrigue.

Welensky, too, was caught in this system of political calculation. By instinct he was the committed exponent of settler populism and, as he himself emphasized, from this derived his entire conception of politics. He personified the sensibilities of white backlash, bent on breaking the springs of black militancy: his views on race, even by the unexacting standards of the time, were purposively immoderate. Yet—with the occasional significant exception—he remained dutiful to the requirements of British constitutionalism even when they were the cause of much grief. At every stage he was outpaced by London, frequently finding himself rendered a passive spectator, able only to rail against the bad faith of erstwhile friends. There were times when he could have espoused greater militancy, raising the level of confrontation between Salisbury and London. After Monckton had reported he could, for example, have published his correspondence from Macmillan; in February 1961 he could have played his trump and orchestrated a political *coup*, as Ian Smith was to do later in Rhodesia; in the following June he could have flown to Britain to put his case direct to the metropolitan public, as he considered for a while, mobilizing not merely backbench dissidents, but a wider spectrum of domestic popular opinion; and toward the end of 1961 he could have ignored the diplomatic pressures from Britain and the US and made common cause with Tshombe. Any one of these options would have activated new forces, and undermined the managed constitutional calculus emanating from London. But so too any one of them would, in all likelihood, have destroyed him. After his failure to instigate his parliamentary rebellion early in 1961 few viable alternatives remained. Keeping to the protocols dictated by London caused his undoing; embarking on a more radical alternative he may well have faced the same outcome. The power he was able to summon was slipping away. As much as his allies in London, Welensky—for all his rhetorical intransigence—was politically neutralized.

Such, too, was the fate of Lord Salisbury. He had made his pact with Welensky, hopeful that Macmillan could be dispatched, though he possessed considerably less inclination for the exigencies of popular intervention than his ally. Salisbury was given to tradition, to hierarchy, and to the social obligations governed by his patrician sentiments, and his defence of empire was essentially nothing more than backward-looking. In this he was not alone. When, for example, in December 1962 Rab Butler was on the point of confirming Nyasaland's right to secede from the Federation, Salisbury was joined in his denunciations of the government by Lords Boyd, Chandos, Swinton, and Malvern (the title adopted in 1955 by the ennobled Sir Godfrey Huggins, Welensky's predecessor as Federal prime minister), all fiercely committed to the Federation as a beacon of white civilization. All were resolutely of an old, traditional right, fighting a rearguard action against the dissolution of the last vestiges of Greater Britain. All were born in the late Victorian period (save Boyd, who was born in 1904), and despite important differences in social standing—Chandos and Swinton came from the heartlands of aristocratic privilege—all were exemplars of an older formation of Conservative high imperialism.

But against expectations, this old right discovered it had a future, or one of sorts at least. When, at the start of 1961, he had been assembling the members of his Watching Committee Salisbury received a letter from Paul Bristol seeking support for a new Conservative pressure group, which took the name of the Monday Club.[163] Bristol himself worked in a ship-broking firm, having just left the army. Of his two leading colleagues, one was works director of a light engineering firm, the other a freelance photographer, having recently lost his job as Conservative agent for Stoke Newington. They represented a lower-middle-class world which was totally foreign to Salisbury. Even so their ambition was to counter the liberalism of the Conservative Bow Group; they believed the government's policy on the African colonies fundamentally misguided; and they shared a political animosity towards Macmillan.[164] At the time Salisbury's energies were absorbed in organizing on his more familiar terrain of Westminster, with Hatfield serving as his retreat when internecine struggles took their toll. None the less he offered his help, as did Welensky.[165] He raised capital for the Monday Club from the British South Africa Company and eventually agreed, alongside Lord Boyd, to offer his official imprimatur. Although this commitment was never primary for Salisbury—Simon Ball is no doubt right to perceive it as a 'side-show' in his public life—it was nevertheless symptomatic of a significant transition in the politics of the Conservative right.[166]

The Monday Club was to go through many evolutions. During the years of its greatest influence, from the 1960s through to the middle 1970s, its presence in the Conservative party was important in giving organizational form to the opinions of the radical right, and in functioning as an ideological bridgehead between the parliamentary party, on the one hand, and local Tory associations and various improvised neigbourhood *groupuscules* of concerned 'citizens' or 'ratepayers', on the other. Although politically it always represented a subordinate element in the Conservative party, it served—in the moment of decolonization—to transform the old empire Toryism of the Salisbury generation into something resembling a political programme, working most effectively when it combined the inherited language and instincts of empire with the lived, everyday concerns of the metropole. Most of all the Monday Club became the means by which the sensibilities of colonial defeat, overseas, were translated into a domestic idiom, dramatizing the apprehension that the home-nation was on the point of destruction.

It is at this moment that the political impact of the end of empire in the metropole can most readily be located. To look only at the manifest content of politics—at the details of evolving political programmes and policies—misses too much, not least because the scope for imperial intervention was contracting fast. Throughout these pages I have suggested that for the metropolitan population the overseas empire was often most profoundly experienced as a complex, symbolic phenomenon, projected out from the self. Disputes over the arcane details of colonial constitutions were never likely to draw in the home population, as matters of urgency. When Welensky inspired his audience of business people in the Albert Hall, relating his story of a civilization in danger, overrun by enemies, his listeners were not required to think exclusively of faraway Lusaka or Blantyre. They could equally turn their minds to locales closer to home. Welensky's fears of the erosion of 'authority' and his injunction to 'stand firm' could be read in varied registers. Indeed, as he confirmed in his memoir, in his own mind the tragedy of his political life lay not in the destruction of the Federation but in the corruption that he believed it revealed at the heart of the empire. This reproduced a familiar pattern of proconsular thought, counterpoising the luminosity of the frontier to the dark decay of metropolitan life.

'Authority' may appear to be an innocent abstract noun. But for Welensky, as perhaps for many in his audience, it signified the dispositions of a specifically white civilization, just as in the metropole the forces of disorder were increasingly coming to be associated with the idea of 'the immigrant'.[167] Ideas of white communities in danger at home came to be superimposed in the imagination on memories of endangered whiteness overseas. Older mentalities took on new forms. During the time of Kipling and of the Edwardian proconsuls the conviction that the governing class had become ethnic traitors, squandering the nation's birthright, signalled the force of the ideological crisis of the state. These accusations were heard again at the height of decolonization, from Welensky and Salisbury at the beginning of the 1960s, and then again from Enoch Powell in June 1970, intent on uncovering the enemy within the very highest echelons of the home government. These were, perhaps, expressions of militancy restricted to the musings of a zealous minority. But even so, such thinking also touched popular sentiment, turning on the notion that ordinary white English people had ceased to be represented in their own nation, and that something akin to an ethnic divide had opened up between the governing class and the people, and between state and nation. How else are we to understand the designation of Powell as 'the only white man in there', the 'there' referring to the political domain of Westminster?

These were mentalities which were to rise to the surface in the Powellite conjuncture of 1968–70 and they are recorded in, amongst other places, the archive of correspondence which Powell himself received. They constitute the ideological grounding of the politics of the New Right. This is a difficult, imprecise term, and I will need to return to it. There is little consensus about when, as a phenomenon, the New Right first appeared and confusion, too, in distinguishing between it and its predecessors, the so-called traditional Tory right. The Monday Club represented a significant nucleus of New Right politics, though there existed many alternative currents. Yet the crucial distinction between the 'old' and the 'new' right had less to do with contrasting axioms or principles, and more with a shift in the institutional structures which underwrote their respective politics. For the old right (Salisbury, Boyd, Chandos, and their like) the political centre of gravity was located at Westminster, and this dictated the form of politics to be pursued: Welensky's rhetoric notwithstanding, the Salisbury–Welensky rebellion, organized strategically around historic parliamentary procedures, held back from mobilizing political forces located outside the formal constitutional arena. The broadening class positions of the New Right—evident, for example, in the social origins of the founding members of the Monday Club—created the conditions which favoured the emergence of a decidedly more populist right-wing politics, in which, for some, Westminster itself was as much a problem as it was a solution. Indeed, in many respects this was ethnic populism reinvented for the metropole after empire, bent on reracializing both political and civil society.

These developments transformed the ideological organization of Conservatism. Long ago, in his classic study of the Conservative party, Andrew Gamble noted that from the early 1960s—or more specifically, as he indicates, from 1961—what he called the 'politics of government' began to draw apart from the 'politics of support' or as I have suggested, using a different vocabulary, 'state' and 'nation' began to diverge.[168] Thus passive

decolonization can be understood as a factor in the 'politics of government' and the emergent New Right as a constituent of the new 'politics
of support'. This helps us grasp, analytically, the nature of the parliamentary rebellion led by Salisbury. His attacks on Macmillan and Macleod
may have been both malicious and Quixotic, and some of his most prominent lieutenants—Macmillan's 'ragamuffins'—objects of ridicule. Yet in
his very actions he brought to the fore the dichotomy between the politics of government and support, which others, such as the young cadres of
the Monday Club, learnt to exploit. Moreover, in his uncompromising
appeal to the historic traditions of Greater Britain, embodied pre-eminently in the white settlers of central Africa, the descendants of the 'greatest men' of the 'modern world', he made it clear that the means by which
the offensive against the state was to be mounted turned on a powerful
invocation of race and nation. Race, I suggest, in its many manifestations,
worked as an active element in the shaping of the new politics of
support.

Through the 1960s, in both its colonial and its metropolitan aspects, race
was often a divisive issue for the Conservatives, as we can tell from the various splits produced by Rhodesia, by immigration policy, and by the management of domestic race relations. When it came to the making of policies it
was rare for consensus to occur. Even the Monday Club—largely made, and
later broken, by its popularization of race politics—found in its early years
that arriving at an agreed position on immigration a perilous business. Part
of the reason for the depth of the internal schisms within the Conservative
party was, indeed, due to the fact that the right (self-styled race-tribunes,
the Monday Club, local constituency associations) increasingly mobilized,
from 1961 and after, on race and nation, articulating their dissatisfaction
with the politics of government in the language of race, and taking their
battle to the heart of the party. In April 1963, for example, long after the
formal defeat of the Salisbury faction, Macmillan was writing to Menzies,
expressing his anxiety that once more the government's colonial policy was
generating significant disaffection on the backbenches: he thought it possible, on this occasion, that as many as 200 of his own MPs were inclined to
support a Rhodesian Front declaration of independence for Rhodesia.[169]
This demonstrates the degree to which, relatively soon after the defeat over
Northern Rhodesia, the right in the party was able to regroup.

However it might also indicate that, whatever dissension arose over *policy*,
the defence of white civilization, evoking old memories, continued to

possess the potential to draw in a much wider section of the party than the strict, acknowledged right.[170] In his history of the Conservative party John Ramsden observed that:

> Alongside the conventionally right-wing elements that formed the Monday Club, and overlapping with them to a great extent, were the many Tories of all types, highly placed throughout the Party (especially in Southern England) for whom the future of South Africa and Southern Rhodesia presented... problems, since so many of them had relatives who had chosen to settle there or had economic interests that they wished to preserve.[171]

Or we could recall that when the backbench revolt over the Federation was taking place in February 1961, the senior Tories who constituted the Cabinet Commonwealth Migration Committee, representing the broad range of Conservative opinion, finally resolved to press ahead with the Commonwealth Immigrants Act, devised to restrict specifically non-white migration to the UK. The racial thinking embodied in the Act represented the very core of respectable Conservatism.[172] A militant commitment to the historic vision of Greater Britain was, by the early 1960s, becoming the hallmark of the old right generation of Tories, increasingly disconnected from contemporary realities. But many of the precepts on which that historic vision had been founded assumed a new-found gravity as Greater Britain rapidly contracted and Britain itself appeared to be destined for an impending break-up.

Through the 1960s the New Right comprised not merely the radical sections of the Conservative party but also an amorphous, decentred constellation of ideas across the wider society, an emergent formation in the process of assuming an identifiable political cohesion, composed of many contrary currents which functioned to broaden the party's politics of support. It took root in Westminster, but was perhaps more readily apparent in popular agitation in civil society arising from a succession of interconnected moral panics, reminiscent of Enoch Powell's troubled conception of 'The Thing'. It was evident in local anti-immigration and rate-payers organizations; in the business of writing letters to those in authority drawing attention to the depredations of race, or to the outrages of sexual permissiveness; in the reactions to crime or to the perils of youth; in deepening anxieties about the iniquities of welfare, or about trade-union power.[173] The letters sent to Conservative MPs in 1960–1, and those addressed to Powell in 1968, which I introduced in the Prologue, are symptomatic of this emergent popular mentality, conjoining strange, disjointed apprehensions of the end of empire ('It is a wind of change for England + unless something is done England will not remain England for long') with more tangible, located commentaries on the proximity of the black presence and national decline. It was a mentality mesmerized by the spectacle of domestic confusion, in which the entire social landscape appeared to be slipping out of place. This was a way of seeing unhinged by the slow corrosion of the systems of social difference which had been cast in the epoch of empire's high noon. Just as the fantasy of the white man had given form to the understandings of systems of difference in the late Victorian period, so too in the period at the end of empire new, resurgent identifications with whiteness had much life left in them.

★★★★★

A few days after Harold Macmillan had made his 'Wind of change' speech in Cape Town, he and Macleod were cabling each other about the discussions concerning the future of Kenya. Macleod, at this stage, was ready to force the issue and make his stand against settler absolutism. Macmillan responded, in what appeared to be a tone of cool rationality, asking him 'What would the effect be on Southern Rhodesia?'.[174] The question of Rhodesia was to haunt not only Macmillan but his successors for a generation and more, with terrible consequences. This is the theme of my final chapter.

7

Ian Smith

The last white man?

I yearned for adventure, for love, for romance, and I seemed condemned to an existence of drab utility. The village possessed a lending library, full of tattered works of fiction, and I enjoyed perils and love-making at second hand, and went to sleep dreaming of stern silent Rhodesians, and of strong men who always 'felled their opponents with a single blow'.

(Agatha Christie, *The Man in the Brown Suit*, 1924[1])

What sixth sense about rebellion *à l'anglaise* made me pack my dinner jacket?

(Peregrine Worsthorne, *Sunday Telegraph*, 28 Nov. 1965[2])

PS . . . I too feel strongly about events in Rhodesia—we all do.

(Mrs Thatcher to Winston Spencer-Churchill, 9 Nov. 1978[3])

She gave me history lessons as well. History that could not be found in the textbooks; a stint in the field and a rest, the beginning of the story, a pause.

(Tsitsi Dangarembga, *Nervous Conditions*, 1988[4])

On 12 September 1976 Ian Smith, the first Rhodesian-born prime minister of Rhodesia, noted in his diary that he had attended the Pioneer Day celebrations in Cecil Square, in the capital Salisbury (Harare), to honour the raising of the flag which commemorated the founding of the nation.

As usual it was a dignified, happy occasion involving prayers and a short talk from the attending parson, with many people gathered around in silence, paying their respects on this solemn occasion. Nothing flamboyant, just a simple acknowledgement of the arrival of the pioneer column a mere 86 years previously, and the raising of the Union Jack to signal the establishment of another outpost of the British Empire. Visitors to our country invariably comment on the high standards of civilisation which have been built up in such a short space of time.[5]

Rhodesia, as Smith indicates, had been in existence for eighty-six years.[6] At the time he was writing the white nation was involved in a ferocious war, battling against guerrilla armies whose purpose was to destroy the settler state. The fighting had been prolonged and brutal. The previous month, a small special operations contingent of the Rhodesian armed forces had carried out a raid deep in Mozambique killing some 500 guerrillas and an unknown number of non-combatants.[7] At this point, in 1976, the end of Rhodesia was not far off. The war was taking a terrible toll. The collapse of the Portuguese empire in Mozambique and Angola, a year earlier, had radically shifted the regional balance of power. The decision by the Republic of South Africa, under US pressure, to cut its losses and pull back its support for Ian Smith was becoming apparent throughout 1975 and 1976—in August 1976 the Republic withdrew its military helicopter crews—and this spelt the end of the white regime in Rhodesia. The previous March Smith had declared at a press conference: 'I don't believe in black majority rule ever in Rhodesia, not in a thousand years.'[8] Yet eleven days after the Pioneer Day ceremony, following a bruising meeting with the South African prime minister John Vorster, he was forced to retreat, announcing on Rhodesian television that preparations would begin for instituting majority rule.[9] After much obstruction, in June 1979 his government finally ceded formal power and the office of prime minister passed to Bishop Abel Muzorewa.

These historical realities did not appear to be uppermost in Smith's mind when he wrote his diary on Pioneer Day for his words sought only to register the values for which he had been struggling, and by which he justified the continuing slaughter. As he rightly pointed out, the history of his nation was short-lived. A child who had witnessed the first raising of the flag in Fort Salisbury, in 1890, could well have also observed the scene on the same spot which Smith recorded in 1976, and been present too at Rhodesia's final liquidation. Indeed, this is a duration encompassed within the notion of living memory. For Smith, white Rhodesia—that living collective memory—was dignified, pious, and respectful, abjuring any hint of flamboyance. It represented the civic virtues of a small, faraway community (an 'outpost') and an ordinary people (the 'many people gathered around in silence') which, against the odds, had been able to establish not just civilization, but a civilization of 'high standards'—or as Smith more commonly put it, a civilization of the highest standards, a conception which was far from innocent racially.[10]

Smith was a figure whose influence broke into the political life of the metropole. He represents too the last phase of the tradition of colonial tribune of which, in their different ways, both Jan Smuts and Sir Roy Welensky were part. This was certainly the view of Sarah Gertrude Millin, who has appeared before in these pages. Millin—a staunch upholder of the white settlers in southern and central Africa and, from the time of the Sharpeville massacre in March 1960, a late convert to apartheid—was always ready to laud those colonial leaders who, in her view, overcame the characteristic racial appeasement of the metropolitan politicians and prosecuted, unabashed, the interests of the white man.[11] She dedicated her 1923 novel on the Rand uprising, *The Jordans*, to Smuts and went on to write his biography. From the early 1960s she became a regular correspondent with Welensky.[12] Toward the end of her career as a novelist, in 1962, she dedicated *The Wizard Bird* to him, claiming him, with a certain infelicity, to be 'The Dyke of Africa'.[13] And in 1966, as her commitment to the idea of race became more desperate, she edited a volume which took for its title *White Africans are Also People*, much of her own contribution a chaotic mix of ferocious bigotry, biblical myth, and random history.[14] The situation in Rhodesia provided its focal point. Her support for the regime of Ian Smith was total: 'there is no cause these days I believe in as much as Rhodesia's'.[15] Smith was, for her, the man of the moment, and the essays in *White Africans* sought to prove the point. The book carried contributions from Welensky and, predictably, from Lord Salisbury, amongst others. Even as Smith dealt the empire a mortal blow he remained a militant advocate of Greater Britain. Politically Millin portrayed him to be the last white man, which is pretty much how Smith came to understand himself.

In metropolitan Britain through the 1960s and 1970s Rhodesia signalled a political faultline, with right and left defined by their respective stance on the Rhodesian situation. For the right Rhodesia condensed many of the anxieties which underwrote decolonization, particularly those which concerned race. However the coincidence of this colonial crisis, on the one hand, with an emergent domestic crisis triggered by non-white immigration on the other, created the circumstances in which, symbolically and politically, the two became superimposed. Just as the colour bar in Rhodesia was first tentatively relaxed so the colour bar in Britain was becoming more widely institutionalized. The language of the beleaguered whites in the colony came to serve as a means for comprehending the racial situation at home. There were ideologues on the right who worked to make this happen, associated with the Monday Club, seeing in the betrayal of the white folk in Rhodesia, as they perceived it, an analogue of the betrayal of their kith and kin in England. But this was also a transposition which took place as a result of less conscious intervention, the contemporary domestic imaginings of black and white invisibly shaped by the continuing force of an inherited colonial common sense. Rhodesia, much like South Africa, came to signify for the metropole race itself. Those sympathetic to the whites summoned a potent repertoire of historical memories of the settler nation: memories that were highly charged in their mythic content and which, in their very evocations of times past, did much to induce new patterns of forgetfulness. As the empire came to its end Rhodesia became a powerful symbolic site in which competing memories of empire were fought out, and where the future as much as the past was at stake.

Ethnic populism at the end of empire

In the opening chapter I suggested that one of the consequences of a Greater Britain, in Dilke's terms, or of an expansive England, in Seeley's, was the emergence of what I termed a specifically ethnic populism, in which the white peoples of the empire were attributed a common imperial identity, a theme I discussed in the last chapter when I introduced the figure of Sir Roy Welensky.

Invoking the people—the white people—of the empire in this way did not in itself stipulate a given politics. The imagined community of the white empire represented a phenomenon resembling more an ideological force-field, traversed by many contrary political currents, than a single political reality. I have already referred to the tension between the centripetal forces in the empire, exerting a measure of unity, and the centrifugal forces, producing the conditions for those more distant parts to disconnect from the centre, and to create new forms. This dynamic was common in many manifestations of Greater Britain at the turn of the twentieth century, with each contrary force simultaneously at work, as we have seen in the cases of Australia and South Africa.

It was apparent too, emphatically so, in the politics of Rhodesia, whose history was punctuated by either the threat of, or the reality of, rebellions

mounted in the name of an implacable loyalism. Ian Smith himself personified these contradictions, which had been active in the very founding precepts of Greater Britain. Even in the 1960s and 1970s he felt able to exhort
the white British people, wherever they were to be found, as purposively as
any of the great imperial tribunes from an earlier age. In asserting their own
colonial nationhood Rhodesians not only adopted the language of British
patriotism; they transformed it and made it their own. Yet for all the shared
Britishness, when relations with London deteriorated the divide between
colony and metropole was in part articulated as an ethnic one, with those
inhabiting the periphery believing themselves to be the true custodians of
the deep core of British values. Ian Smith was convinced that he was
engaged in an ethnic struggle: not just against the African nationalists within
the nation, but on a second front against representatives of the British government ignorant of the realities of colonial life. Rhetorically at least, Smith
was always careful to position himself as the representative of the Rhodesian
people who, in contending with the British state, did so as the underdog,
with only the steadfast will of his people to sustain him in his fight with a
greater, malevolent force. The properties of Rhodesian populism were
complex, as I shall explain, and replete with ambiguities. But they brought
back to life a long historical memory of the virtues of the white empire and
of those who had peopled it. This closing chapter on Rhodesia allows us to
track the evolution of this phenomenon late into the twentieth century.

At first sight it might seem as if an ethnic populism construed in these
terms could have no purchase in the metropole, or not in England where
there existed no profound ethnic divisions between rulers and ruled. But
this assumes too great a degree of ethnic stability, as I suggested in the first
chapter when I commented on Kipling's views on Unionism: and so too,
I argue, in the 1960s when black migration worked to unsettle English ethnicity. The indigenous English who believed that they were suffering *as
whites* came to imagine that the politicians were, somehow, in cahoots with
the new black migrants. The governors of the land lived faraway—so the
stories went—from the areas of migration; they were out of touch with the
real feelings of the English people; they didn't know blacks as their white
neighbours did and, wittingly or unwittingly, they were working to destroy
the nation. The rulers, in other words, had become the enemies of all true
English men and women. It was to such anxieties that the Monday Club,
and then later Powellism, responded. It was notions such as these that
allowed Powell himself, in the crisis which followed his Birmingham speech

in April 1968, to be identified—in contrast to all other political leaders—as 'the only white man'. This was a populism which sought to claim back the nation from the politicians. As the people, in their guise of 'ordinary' English men and women, were mobilized *against* the British state, the lineaments of an ethnic populism—in the metropole—can be discerned. The old centrifugal forces of empire—the drive to pull away from the centre—began to operate *in England*, as a vociferous section of the nation voiced their disconnection from the state. And in this situation the stories emanating from white Rhodesia proved peculiarly fertile.

For Smith it had fallen to the Rhodesians to take on the mantle of historic Britain. Despite the strong words Welensky—just about—held back from treason. Smith, who became Rhodesia's prime minister in April 1964, did not, and in so doing presented himself as the most loyal of Britons, forced to resort to absolute action on account of the ethnic collapse of those charged to govern the British state. His Unilateral Declaration of Independence (UDI) for Rhodesia, announced in November 1965, opened up divisions in Britain itself. For the emergent radical right 'Smithy' was indeed a good egg, as those sympathetic to him liked to put it. In their reveries they imagined Rhodesia to represent not just 'the last loyal white colony' (as Kipling himself had once declared) but, more starkly, the last racial utopia, where order and good sense prevailed.[16] The idea of Rhodesia evoked all that was most captivating in the imperial past, living proof of the past in the present, and providing a necessary corrective for an England beset by disorder and subversion.

The settler nation

In 1882 Ernest Renan delivered his famous lecture at the Sorbonne in which he declared that nations, in order to work as collectivities, require a necessary measure of forgetfulness about their origins.[17] Eight years later, in September 1890, many thousands of miles away the Union Jack was raised on a new white settlement: the encampment was named in honour of Britain's prime minister, Salisbury, while the nascent territory, at first unofficially and then officially, took the name of its accredited founder, Cecil Rhodes. What in this story was, in Renan's terms, to be forgotten?

Rhodes's Pioneer Column accomplished its occupation of Mashonaland through a simple, brazen act of expropriation. The Column, having set out from Mafeking, comprised 180 men, and was accompanied by a British South Africa Company (BSAC) paramilitary police force of some 500, and by a retinue of African soldiers and servants. Two weeks after raising the flag in Fort Salisbury the Column disbanded and each of the pioneers was granted land on which to farm, and in addition bound if required for future military service. The mythic commemorations of the Pioneer Column, such as the one rehearsed by Ian Smith, recalled a rag-tag grouping of hardy souls, inspired only by the honest dream of a homestead and a few of acres of land. But the Column was above all else the creature of the BSAC, backed by the Company's capital and force of arms and functioning as the vehicle by which the Company's power could extend its authority north of the Limpopo. In this lay the nucleus of the new nation-state. Taxes were levied on the Shona peoples, and various strategies devised to compel size-able numbers to leave the land and work in the mines. Even so, sustained violence between the Shona and the Ndebele, on the one hand, and the settlers, on the other, was contained until the end of 1893, when the first Matabele War broke out, the Company forces determining to invade Matabeleland. The combined power of the BSAC paramilitaries, volun-teers, and British troops—aided by the maxim gun—speedily destroyed King Lobengula's armies, and razed Bulawayo to the ground.[18] After the defeat of Lobengula, Matabeleland was subject to rapid colonization with-out precedent in east or central Africa: captured lands were sold to new streams of pioneers, cattle commandeered, the gold deposits opened up and Ndebele labour coerced to work in the mines, and the railway and telegraph (both effectively in the hands of Rhodes) integrated the conquered lands into the larger strategic region of southern Africa where capital accumula-tion was fast advancing.[19] The Company's rule of Matabeleland was offi-cially recognized by the imperial government, which effectively was presented with a fait accompli. In response to this systematic dispossession, in March 1896 the Matabeleland rebellion (the first *Chimurenga*) was launched in a bid to win back Ndebele independence, with the Shona join-ing in the insurrection.

The fact of this black insurgency burnt itself into the collective memory of white settler society in Rhodesia.[20] Almost 10 per cent of the settler popu-lation was killed, either in military engagement or in attacks on their home-steads, while hundreds of homes, mines, and ranches were destroyed, triggering a vast repertoire of stories recounting the brutality of the native that entered the memory of future generations of the settler nation. It was true that, in some instances, the murders of whites were undertaken by Africans who had been known and trusted by those they killed, fuelling the settler conviction that 'the native' was always ready to turn on his or her master.[21] Fears for the sanctity of white women ran deep, triggering tales of the 'Black Peril' which later were to serve as the defining moral justification for the colour bar.[22] The retribution meted out by the settlers, driven by the desire to wreak racial vengeance, was indiscriminate and unrestrained. I have referred earlier to the counter-guerrilla action set in train by Robert Baden-Powell; there was, however, nothing exceptional in the scale of violence to which he resorted.[23] One visitor believed that the reimposition of order which followed the insurgency was as savage, and as racially inspired, as that perpetrated by the British in the aftermath of the Sepoy Rebellion of 1857.[24] Indeed white immigrants from India brought with them their own memories of 1857, which fed into the fears generated in 1896–7, and worked to confirm the truth of the essential barbarity of the native, whether Indian or African.[25] As much as in the early encounters between incoming settlers and Aborigines in the Australian colonies, the potential for systematic white violence was ever present. The same undertow of genocidal desire, and the same penchant for euphemism, can be detected.[26] These marked a significant dimension of the settler experience, and functioned as the corollary of the belief that the settlers themselves had been drawn into a race war.

The foundational event of the white nation—the fact of expropriation—was never an act around which silence accrued, or which appeared, in private or in public, to be inconsequential. On the contrary the founding stories of the nation were told and retold incessantly, with fierce compulsion, each telling confirming the prowess of the whites. In subsequent years the first raising of the flag in Salisbury was commemorated as Occupation Day; it was only in 1961, some two generations after the event itself, that a degree of diplomacy prevailed and the more innocuously designated Pioneer Day was inaugurated to take its place.

We do not know the extent to which, in private, at sundowner time with the darkness falling fast, talk would turn to past misdeeds when settler expropriated native, or the scale of approbation such stories would elicit. The informal, conversational tone of Welensky's childhood reminiscences, related to a journalist whilst prime minister of the Federation, perhaps offers a clue: 'They used to talk about going out from here, capturing Natives and hanging them on the spot . . . If a black walked on the pavement in Salisbury when I was a boy the first white man who came along would kick his behind for him. Now they sit in the House of Assembly...'[27] We know, though, that in terms of official public representations memories of violence were prominent. But these public memories, which organized the official nation, took the perpetrators of injustice to be the Africans, and those who suffered the settlers. This was a collective memory which was institutionalized. In Gwelo (Gweru) in the 1950s, for example, there existed a public memorial to the settlers 'Murdered by Natives', and one also to the gallant horses, donkeys, and oxen which had help to carry civilization to the bush. It is here that Renan's forgetfulness impinges, a forgetfulness that transposes the figure of the expropriator to that of victim. Forgetfulness in this instance signals not a lack of stories—a silence, an unspeakability—but the presence of a multitude of other stories which functioned to screen all but the virtue of the settler.

Thus the great founding legend of the Rhodesian nation told of the exploits of Major Allan Wilson in the Matabele War of 1893. Wilson and a small troop, in pursuit of Lobengula, found themselves cut off from the main forces and surrounded by the enemy at a spot by the Shangani river, where they were attacked and killed by Ndebele forces. A myriad of putatively factual accounts quickly circulated in both Rhodesia and Britain, long before any of the first-hand testimonies had been received. In all the reports, the gallantry and manful heroism of those fighting for empire, confronted by a much larger native force armed with assegais, became the unassailable truth. All were valiant, apparently either dying writing last letters to their loved ones, or singing the national anthem, or hymns, or even in one unlikely version a collective rendition of 'Hip! Hip! Hooray!'[28] The story entered the popular domain, in boys' books and magazines, as a feature of the 'Savage South Africa' show in Earl's Court in 1899, and in the early rituals of Baden-Powell's scouting movement. Throughout the history of Rhodesia memorials to the patrol were omnipresent; in 1904, in a calculated act of nation-building, the bones of those who had died were collected and reinterred in the Matopos, alongside Rhodes himself, beneath a vast granite monument designed to tell new generations the story.[29] The legend of Wilson at Shangani indicated nothing about the larger dynamics of the Matabele War, nor about the dispossession which followed. What registered was the image of the *impi* and his assegai, articulating an entire repertoire of racial thought and, as their natural contrary, the heroics of the white man, brave but outnumbered. A few key signs did all the ideological work. All else was forgotten.[30]

In much the same way the commemoration of the Pioneer Column worked to highlight the values of the independent settler, whilst eliminating from the narrative the role of the BSAC. This, though, reflected the growing political power of the settler. From the moment the royal charter was granted to the Company in 1889 relations between it and the London government were perpetually strained. While in principle the government was content to extend British rule at no public cost, Rhodes's disregard for diplomatic niceties created many new dangers for Westminster. Even while the government endorsed Company expansionism it was reluctant to encourage the emergence of an alternative system of authority in the region over which it had little control. In the aftermath of the 1896–7 rebellion the settlers began to draw away from the Company, particularly in the urban centres of Bulawayo and Salisbury, in the belief that the Company was more concerned to indulge its shareholders than protect the settlers; and there emerged too the popular notion that the Company was less than vigilant in pursuing racial segregation and was prone to 'coddle' the native.[31] Even before the rebellion the settlers had been pressing for 'responsible government', that is, for a measure of self-government. The Colonial Office— Joseph Chamberlain in particular—saw in the idea the possibility of curbing the power of the Company. In 1898 a partially elected legislative council was created, to which two settler representatives were recruited, and in which the BSAC retained a majority of official members. This might be viewed as a relatively modest innovation, in which the authority of the BSAC remained undisturbed. But critically it broke the Company's monopoly of power and marked, as Terence Ranger argues, the first step in settler supremacy.[32] Within ten years minority representation on the legislative council had been turned into a majority, and power shifted decisively to the settlers.

During the First World War the campaign for responsible government gathered pace, institutionalized in the Responsible Government Association, founded in 1917.[33] Eventually the Colonial Office agreed to a referendum based on a straightforward alternative between assimilation with the Union of South Africa or self-government. Held in October 1922, those voting for responsible government won a clear majority, securing some 60 per cent of the popular vote. As a result, the following October Rhodesia duly became a self-governing colony of the crown. This was a fateful outcome. Although the British government held certain reserve powers, particularly in relation to native affairs, these were never used. In practice the government had ceded political power to the small minority of white settlers—comprising a population of some 35,000 in all—while leaving approximately 900,000 Africans subject to the unchallenged rule of settler supremacy.[34]

This location of settler power, lodged deep inside the state, did much to shape the populist spirit of white Rhodesia, drawing symbolically on the founding myths of the nation. The dominating political rhetorics told a story of the ordinary people of the nation—homesteaders, workers, mothers—who, dependent only on their own resources, had defeated forces much greater than themselves: hostile native armies, the British South African Company, the Union government in South Africa, and the might of the imperial state in London. Articulating such populist sentiment was the defining motif of the Rhodesians' birthright, valorizing a people militantly protective of their historic popular rights.[35]

The Rhodesian state was a conquest state. From the beginning and throughout its history it depended on the mobilization of the white popu-lace to maintain order.[36] The 1926 Defence Act introduced compulsory military service; there was, in addition, a police reserve of armed volunteers, allied to the British South Africa Police, a body of importance for the defence of the settler nation.[37] Schools encouraged cadet corps; scouting and guide troops taught drill, discipline, and *veld*craft; and there existed an extensive civic network of rifle and pistol clubs.[38] When Ian Smith was growing up in Selukwe (Shurugwi) the Volunteers organized the town's sports events, and local dances took place in the drill hall.[39] These educative initiatives—training the white population in the practicalities of military discipline and popularizing the mentalities of armed defence—seamlessly moved back and forth between state and civil society. In the early decades of the nation, in the maintenance of white hegemony the distinction between public official and private citizen was always fluid. In the particular case of the mining compounds, for example, the authority of the police was regularly overridden by the authority of the private owners, who could call upon their own enforcers.[40] In the bush formalities of the law carried little influence, the police and magistrates invariably endorsing the actions of the settlers. In daily life there was no clear distinction between violence sanc-tioned by the state and violence unleashed by the white citizen. Even as late as 1960, during the riots in Salisbury's black townships in July, thirteen Africans were shot dead: six by the police and seven by Europeans putatively defending life and property.[41] In the incessant social emergency ordained by the racial imperative the entire white population was, in effect, conscripted to defend the status quo, and—officially or unofficially—integrated into the operations of the state.

But for the most part it is the ambiguities of Rhodesian populism which stand out.[42] Conventionally populism denotes a movement, from 'below', which challenges the authority of the domestic state, binding the people against the power bloc. In Rhodesia the symbiosis between state and settler dictated a different pattern, for the primary antagonist of 'the people' was not the state but the mass of black Africans subordinated to them. The ordinary folk venerated in the myths of the nation were the principal agents of exploitation, dedicated to upholding the system of racial supremacy, and able when necessary to call upon the full force of the state. This racial situation generated much circumlocution, in which social realities were turned inside out and many feats of forgetfulness accomplished, as we shall see when we come to Ian Smith.

Moreover for the greater part of the history of Rhodesia, in its incarnation as a self-governing colony, the government was in most respects cautiously deferential to the expectations which emanated from Britain, although conscious all the time of an opposition primed to exploit the perpetual racial grievances of the settlers. The political crisis of the late 1950s and early 1960s, which brought to power Ian Smith and the Rhodesian Front, marked the moment when a new political arrangement emerged.

The Unilateral Declaration of Independence

Writing in 1977, in the final days of white Rhodesia, the Tory historian Lord Blake commented on the continuing longevity of the myth of Allan Wilson:

> It is by far the most prominent feature in the iconography of Rhodesian history. Paintings galore, sculptures, friezes, tapestries depict it. There is scarcely a public building where one does not see in some medium or other the depiction of a scene which has now become semi-stylized—the troops firing from behind a rampart of dead horses; Allan Wilson himself, taller than all the rest, shooting a Ndebele warrior with his revolver; the enemy in the background with assegai and gun. There is the flavour of romantic imperialism, the *Boy's Own Paper*, Kipling, Henty and much else which was common coin in England of the 1890s. From there it has long disappeared but in Rhodesia, along with many other pickled pieces of the English past, it still lingers on.[43]

This temporal divide between an old Rhodesia, still locked into the romantic imperial past, and a modern England or Britain which had apparently
broken free from the detritus of empire, was a common perception of the
time, repeated by Rhodesians themselves, by visiting journalists, and (as we
can see in the case of Blake) by academic commentators. Harold Wilson, the
Labour prime minister who found himself having to deal with Rhodesia's
UDI, was also tempted to think in these terms. Just before UDI took place
he stated on British television that Britons and Rhodesians were 'living in
almost different centuries'. Reflecting on this some years later, Ian Smith
concurred, though supplying his characteristic twist in order to show that
Rhodesia, unlike Britain, had remained committed to the values of the
imperial past. 'Perhaps that was true. We were living in the old Britain, the
old empire.'[44] Yet as I have argued throughout this volume the various historical pasts which enter the present do so as a function of the requirements
of the present: they are worked for, articulated to the partisan concerns of
the present, and spoken in new idioms. Rhodesia never simply represented
the past. Those who extolled the nation's heroic imperial history did so in
the struggle to maintain a racial order in the political present, drawing on
old memories to orchestrate modern lives. It was Wilson's hubris to imagine
that Smith belonged only to the historical past.

The sentiment that Rhodesia, or the white settler societies more generally, represented England or Britain *as it was* was not Smith's alone. This
structure of thought was of a long duration. Reveries such as these, though,
impose their own silences and forgetfulness. Indeed they *could* only be forgetful. To imagine the nation in this way—Rhodesia as England was—
necessarily entailed disavowing, in the imagination, the presence of the
black Africans. These fantasies, though, had a palpable historical reality. Lord
Blake, writing in the midst of a full-scale, militarized black uprising which
was to destroy the settler nation, provides an indication. 'Even today', he
wrote, 'it is extraordinary how easily in this highly-segregated social system
one can forget that Africans exist, save as cooks, servants, gardeners and
waiters, although they outnumber the whites by twenty-five to one and
everybody is now aware of their political aspirations.'[45] For sure, 'everybody'
was aware of the force of black nationalism. Photographs of the time show
white mothers, armed with automatic weapons, taking their children to the
supermarket or mall, ready to repel attacks by black insurgents. And yet at
the same time it was, says Blake, possible to 'forget that Africans exist'. This
is evidence of a particular mentality which negates that which is most

urgent. It attests to the impossible fantasy of racial segregation, driven by the wish that once and for all whiteness could be divested of the incubus of its ever-proximate other. And it generated, as well, its own distinctive counter-violence. On 18 April 1964, at the OK Bazaar Supermarket in Salisbury, at the blast of a whistle twenty African men started punching white women shoppers, a bid to be existentially recognized replete with political ambiguity.[46]

The idea that Rhodesia 'was' the past was a strange one, especially after the Second World War. The 1950s saw breakneck modernization. As with the other settler societies in the empire, white migration was considered by the Rhodesian government to be essential for the social development of the nation. Between 1946 and 1951 135,600 white migrants arrived in Rhodesia, marking an astonishing 65.1 per cent increase in the European population.[47] In 1951 only about one-third of the white population had been born in Rhodesia, with little under a third (30.5 per cent) having migrated from the Union of South Africa, and most of the remainder (28.8 per cent) coming from the British Isles. Through the 1950s the percentage of population who were indigenous white Rhodesians continued to fall. As late as 1970, 75 per cent of whites over 16 had been born elsewhere.[48] Whatever the customary myths of the nation's public representatives Rhodesia was not a society marked by generational continuity. Historically and sociologically Rhodesia was in every sense a new country, not an old one. Attachments to the past had to be learnt anew.

There is certainly evidence that on the eve of UDI, in British eyes at least, popular commitment to the old memories of the national past was still strong, from the support demonstrated for the set-piece invocations of nationhood (Rhodes, Allan Wilson, Pioneer Day) to the informal, and generously received, affirmations of Rhodesian patriotism in everyday situations.[49] Yet the social realities of daily life were far removed from the pioneer myths, or from the romantic imperialism identified by Blake. In the 1950s and 1960s more than 90 per cent of the European population was urban. The great boom in tobacco exports brought the country much wealth, as indeed had membership of the Federation. But by 1956 only 5 per cent of the white population was engaged in agriculture, compared to the 32 per cent in manufacturing.[50] The trappings of modern life advanced rapidly. Reputedly Salisbury, according to its mayor Frank Clements, had been, until 1959, the world's fastest developing city. 'Really it's just like Surbiton, Surbiton set in Africa. The average Salisbury man is not a wild westerner.'[51]

Nearly every white family owned a car, long before car ownership in Britain was widespread. From the beginning of the 1960s swimming pools, particularly, became symbols of the new wealth, with a greater concentration of pools amongst white families in Salisbury than amongst the inhabitants of Beverley Hills. One entrepreneur, Kenneth Humphries, commenting on this trend (amongst 'Europeans of course') announced: 'We follow American trends, and you'l find that our pools follow exactly the American pattern.' 'It's patio living', he explained. 'It goes with barbecues, outdoor furniture in plastic and metal, easy tables and perhaps a gay umbrella. We show people how to live.'[52]

In his public utterances Smith did not dwell on the pleasures of 'patio living' though, against expectations, he was an enthusiastic supporter of the coming of casinos to Rhodesia and he declared himself a fan of Disneyland.[53] It might seem as if there were two Rhodesias that whites inhabited: the public world which paid obeisance to the old rituals of empire and the private world, where those of sufficient means enjoyed an easy life of sunshine and modern, ostentatious affluence. But these, the old and the new, were not contraries. For all their apparent discrepancies they were connected through the medium of race. In seeking new migrants the Rhodesian government emphasized the standard of living whites enjoyed, offering British migrants wages approximately 50 per cent higher than they would have received at home, as well as cheap black domestic labour. Both were a direct function of the racial situation. In the early postwar years many migrants from Britain remembered how they welcomed the absence of material privation and the ethos of a new country which encouraged individual advancement. What is striking, however, is the speed with which new European migrants came to be integrated into the culture of indigenous white Rhodesians. Primarily this was a consequence of the requirements of white solidarity.[54] In a system in which racial whiteness was the overarching sign of social hierarchy internal ethnic divisions, within the incoming white populations, could only ever be of secondary importance. The labour market was protected for all whites, while the institutions of state education did much to 'Rhodesianize' the children of the new migrants.[55] The authority of racial whiteness determined: the means by which, in lived culture, whiteness was encoded and made local was largely through the propagation of the historic myths of the nation, giving rise to the journalistic cliché that it only ever took half an hour for a white migrant to become Rhodesian. The symbolic power of the old stories of the pioneers could speak not only to old settlers but also to the new generations preoccupied with the mechanics of suburban modernity, as the various jaunty pop and rock songs acclaiming national icons (Cecil Rhodes, the military), or the hugely popular 'Rhodesians Never Die', confirm.[56]

This was not, though, only a cultural matter, narrowly understood; it was political too. Notwithstanding the pace of social transformation, from the first moment of self-government in 1924 until the repercussions following the developing crisis in the Central African Federation from the late 1950s, the stability of the state was pronounced. Writing long ago Colin Leys, like many other commentators, was struck by the longevity of old imperial customs in Rhodesia.[57] Yet he understood this less as evidence that Rhodesia was living in its past than as the social expression of the sclerosis of the political system. His argument runs as follows. Since 1924, under various guises, there had existed what essentially was a 'government' party, which in its contingent forms had derived from the Responsible Government Association of 1917: the Rhodesia Party, the United Party, the United Rhodesia Party, the United Federal Party, the shifting evolution from one to the other more to do with personalities and small-scale factionalism than a fundamental change in vision. The legislative pillars of this political regime were the Land Apportionment Act of 1930, which segregated landownership between black and white on the South African model, and its counterpart, the Industrial Conciliation Act, which segregated employment. The common rhetorical motifs of the government party over these years emphasized anti-socialism, private enterprise, hostility to high taxation, restricted social services, opposition to outside interference, and the great value of the British heritage. This ideological commitment to a *laissez-faire* state expressed the structure of a regime, according to Leys, which could resolve issues which arose inside it, but not those which arose externally, that is, from within the African population or from outside the nation. 'Power tends to gravitate', he added, 'toward those who are least ready for change, having more to lose.'[58]

Alongside the government party, he argued, there existed, again in variable manifestations, an opposition party 'whose one permanent characteristic is its appeal to the racial fears of the European population'.[59]

Leys was writing in 1959 and he was aware that the long period of political stability was at that very moment beginning to pull apart.[60] From 1933 to 1953 Rhodesia had been led by the prime minister Godfrey Huggins, who was ennobled as Lord Malvern in 1955. In 1953 Huggins left his post in Southern Rhodesia to become the first prime minister of the Central African Federation, a position he passed on to Welensky three years later. Huggins and the new Federal party he brought into being, the United Federal Party (UFP), represented the old colonial elite. He had been born into a prosperous Conservative family in Bexley, in Kent, in 1883 and had migrated to Rhodesia in 1911. Throughout his life he held to an old-school imperial patriotism (Kipling and Edgar Wallace were his literary favourites), sure that the public schools produced the best kind of settler. What Rhodesia needed, he had once stated, 'was young men who had fagged at school and had been flogged at school, people who knew how to command and obey and knew how to handle their black labourers'.[61] He was suspicious of an isolationist 'little Rhodesianism', fearing that a Southern Rhodesia which remained inward-looking would be of no more significance, as he put it, than Newfoundland. His ideal was for maximal racial segregation, arguing for the removal of all blacks from the common electoral roll in 1932 and perceiving the Land Apportionment Act, comprehensive though it was, only as the first step towards a more systematic institutionalization of racial separation. Huggins was not one to harbour resentment against the established order for in imperial affairs, even from his outpost in Salisbury, he *was* the established order. 'He could talk the language of Downing Street', as his biographers note, with all due understatement.[62] He represented, in the terms Leys propounded, one-party government in his own person.

The years 1958–60 marked a genuine political crisis, events in Rhodesia and events in the Federation interacting such that disorder in the one reverberated to cause disorder in the other. The prolonged sclerosis of the political system in Rhodesia, described by Leys, generated a deepening polarization which undermined the inherited political settlement. On the one hand, the Southern Rhodesian African National Congress, relaunched by Joshua Nkomo in September 1957, gave expression to an active, organized mass movement which had no stake in the pre-existing political institutions and that could only operate from the outside. The announcement by the British government at the end of the year that the constitutional review of the Federation would take place in 1960 provided a common focus for the respective nationalist oppositions. On the other hand, the growing rift between London and Salisbury, from this time on, meant that local political support for the settlers became less easy to maintain than hitherto, doing much to undermine the *raison d'être* of the United Federal Party. In the face of this the removal of the liberal figure of Garfield Todd in early 1958 marked a bid by the UFP leadership to reassert its authority over the white electorate. Todd's successor was Sir Edgar Whitehead. Whitehead's father had been a distinguished member of the diplomatic corps and he himself had been born in the British embassy in Berlin, emigrating to Rhodesia as a young man in 1928 to take up the life of a country landowner. Socially, he was of the UFP-Huggins tradition. In the election of June 1958 the UFP won, with seventeen seats, but the new, right-wing Dominion Party gained—as if from nowhere—thirteen: if the parties had fought without the preferential vote the Dominion Party would have secured outright victory. This suggests the degree to which the social base of the old Rhodesian families was being eroded by a new generation of incoming migrants: demobbed soldiers, artisans, tax exiles, Britons leaving India after independence, South Africans.[63] This, combined with the more militant organization of the black Africans, signalled the onset of a continuing split in the ruling bloc, rupturing the one-party system and bringing a more militant white populism into the heart of the state.

The February 1959 state of emergency, brought about as a result of the state-inspired racial *grande peur*, served as a significant portent. As black agitation increased, the disarray of Whitehead's UFP was evident. In late July 1960 the townships of Salisbury were the scene of strikes and protests which, when they collided with the forces of law and order, turned into serious riots and resulted in African deaths.[64] On 20 July half the city's African population failed to arrive at work, and a demonstration of some 20,000 collected; a few days later the strikes and demonstrations spread to Bulawayo. Whitehead, as dedicated a pragmatist as Huggins, oscillated between fierce repression and a mild loosening of the codes of public segregation. These events provoked him into introducing a savage array of repressive legislation: a Vagrancy Bill, drawing from Tudor tradition to police the modern black urban dispossessed, the Emergency Powers Bill, and the Law and Order (Maintenance) Bill, the latter proving useful to Mugabe in a later epoch. At the beginning of the new year Whitehead declared his intention of dismantling the starkest institutions of segregation including the Land Apportionment Act, the historic symbol of white supremacy. Like Huggins before him he too had reached the conclusion that maintaining the strict and elaborate provisions of the Act no longer conformed to Rhodesia's economic realities.[65] In this polarized, febrile conjuncture Whitehead's announcement did much further to alienate whites who already believed, day by day, that power was slipping from their grasp.

At this point the political initiative passed to the Rhodesian Front, the new coalition of right-wing forces which had succeeded the Dominion Party, led by Winston Field. Field himself, public-school-educated and wealthy, would, in earlier circumstances, have seemed a natural supporter of the UFP, for most of the Rhodesian Front was well to his right. But as the UFP's political authority crumbled its right wing regrouped around the Rhodesian Front. A letter to the *Rhodesian Herald*, published on 6 February 1962, gives a glimpse of this larger political shift:

> I have faithfully followed the Huggins-Welensky line for over 25 years. But at the next election I shall be asked to vote away the Europeans' long-standing protection against their swamping by hordes of primitive people, and agree to having them live next door to me and attending school with my children. This I cannot do... call it prejudice if you will but however liberal-minded we are, we can never cease to shrink from close and intimate contact with the Africans.[66]

In December, with popular sentiment of this kind cohering on the ground, the Rhodesian Front defeated the UFP in the polls and formed its first government—despite the fact that, according to James Barber, it made no election promises, and simply gave voice to white anxiety.[67] Alongside Field the new cabinet contained a number of figures from the old British-Rhodesian oligarchy: Clifford Dupont, the Duke of Montrose (preferring to be known, in deference to the populist spirit of colonial life, as plain Lord Graham), and Jack Howman. But its electoral popularity, outside the traditional political class, derived from its determination to resist black advance. In repudiating the objective of racial partnership, even while it continued to pay obeisance to racial harmony, the incoming government created for itself a new political opportunity. From this point on the UFP could only be squeezed out. The party was caught between the white militants, led by Rhodesian Front, on the one hand, and on the other, the African political representatives who, although forced to operate outside the formal system, were the only practicable competitors for power. In dispensing with any pretension of partnership the government in Rhodesia freed itself from many entanglements, including that of having to accommodate the British.

The degree to which successive British prime ministers—Macmillan, Sir Alec Douglas-Home (previously Lord Home), Wilson—appreciated this is unclear. Both the Conservative and the Labour governments, while convinced that they had a historic responsibility to resolve the situation, lacked the political will either to intervene decisively themselves or, alternatively, to recognize Britain's lack of power and to pass greater authority to the United Nations. Both Field, and then Ian Smith, who ousted Field from the Rhodesian Front leadership in April 1964, continued to press London for independence. From the start of his term of office Smith prepared for unilateral action, signalling a deeper shift to the right.

The Rhodesian army was reorganized, and senior officers whose loyalties to the Rhodesian Front were deemed questionable were retired.[68] Through 1964 the entire black nationalist leadership was imprisoned, most remaining in gaol, or under various forms of restriction, for many years. The offensive against the declining UFP (which reverted to the original name of the Rhodesia Party) continued apace, until it finally vanished from the political map. A dubious referendum appeared to give the Rhodesian Front a popular mandate to declare independence. Further repression fell on the nationalists. On 3 November 1965 the governor, Sir Humphrey Gibbs, the Queen's representative in the territory, endorsed the government's plans to impose a state of emergency knowing that—in all likelihood—it was to be used in preparation for UDI, notwithstanding Smith's remonstrations to the contrary. In doing so he signed the means by which he himself was effectively to be deposed.[69]

The immediate period before UDI were days of high drama, with Harold Wilson travelling to Rhodesia in an attempt to strike a deal and, at the last moment back in London, orchestrating a prolonged telephone call imploring Smith to step back. Smith, on the other hand, played it to the hilt, demonstrating at every turn his credentials as a son of the empire. The broadcast declaration itself was made on 11 November, Armistice Day. The text of UDI followed closely that of the American declaration of independence, though deleting the reference to the equality of all men. It spoke in the name of 'the people of Rhodesia', 'kith and kin' to the people of Britain, who had 'shed their blood' for all 'freedom loving people'.[70] The signing was conducted under the portrait of the Queen. Throughout the nation black and white huddled around radio sets to hear Smith's broadcast, the sense of occasion palpable.[71] 'In the lives of most nations there comes a moment when a stand has to be made for principle, whatever the consequences. This moment has come to Rhodesia... We may be a small country, but we are a determined people who have been called upon to play a role of world-wide significance.'[72] Throughout Smith conducted himself as if he had been singled out by the hand of history.

It was common for settlers to imagine that the societies they were building restored a purer past, unavailable to those in the metropole, where independent men and women could live their lives as they wished, without interference from higher authority. Echoes of these reveries could be heard, too, in Smith's broadcasts on 11 November. He claimed to be righting wrongs and returning Rhodesia to a time when ordinary people—ordinary white people—could go about their business unencumbered by intervention from afar. In his own mind, he had commandeered the power of the state in order to effect a racial *restoration* across the nation as a whole. As a Salisbury estate agent—an aficionado of patio living, perhaps—remarked, having heard the UDI broadcast: 'I'm glad that independence has been declared because this country belongs to the white man.'[73]

Ian Smith

In the *Rhodesia Herald* of 29 October 1966 these well-known words of Ian Smith can be found:'If Churchill were alive today I believe he would probably emigrate to Rhodesia—because I believe that all those admirable characteristics of the British we believed in, loved and preached to our children, no longer exist in Britain.' But these values still did exist, Smith continued, in Rhodesia 'to a greater degree than they ever existed in the mother country'.[74] Whether Churchill would ever have contemplated moving from the metropolitan comforts of Hyde Park Gate to Salisbury or Bulawayo, or to a farm in the bush, we can only speculate. After his escapades in South Africa, as a very young man, he never demonstrated much enthusiasm for Africa south of the Sahara. In any case, sanctions would have interfered with his daily infusions of Pol Roger and there are priorities, after all. The comment, however, is classic Ian Smith: it is calculation masquerading as innocent virtue. Plausibility is not the issue.

Smith's most complete presentation of the values he espoused occurs in his autobiography, *The Great Betrayal*, published late in his life in 1997.[75] Even more than most political memoirs, little in it is reliable. It is not just that it is self-serving and tendentious. It is that the gap between the autobiographical figure of Smith and his historical counterpart is so incredible that the reader must wonder what enabled him to write it. Originally contracted to HarperCollins, the manuscript was rejected the instant the editors came to read it. John Blake, once a tabloid columnist close to Rupert

Murdoch and Robert Maxwell, took it on, publishing it alongside Ronnie Kray's autobiography, *Murder, Madness and Marriage*—Kray was a sadistic East End villain—and *The Duchess of York Uncensored* by Madame Vasso Kortesis, a Greek fortune-teller who acted as the Duchess's spiritual adviser. Smith's is not a volume that has attracted scholarly attention.

Yet this is writing which comes directly out of colonial defeat and for that alone it is of interest. It carries the psychology of defeat on every page, dramatizing too the impossibilities of whiteness. Peter Godwin describes how, with the advent of majority rule, whites in Rhodesia slowly underwent 'a metamorphosis from settler to expatriate'. Their culture, he argues, became more private and inward. 'The traditional "Rhodie" shrank back into a *laager* of home and video, *braaivleis* and sports club, muttering privately about how the blacks were ruining God's own country.'[76] Smith's autobiography was published well into the Mugabe era when the remnants of the old settler society were under intermittent attack, leading to what the government deemed to be the third *Chimurenga*. In those circumstances, for an older Rhodesian generation, the book took on talismanic properties. It served as testament to a remembered past even while it had lost all grip on the historical present. What others 'muttered in private' Smith spoke out loud in public. In the years since publication this is a culture which has now migrated to the virtual world of the net. Search 'Rhodesia' on the internet and an entire diasporic world opens up. There are sites which reunite lost friends, and which advertise local events for old Rhodesians: ladies' coffee mornings in Perth, the April *braai* in Newbury. All manner of 'Rhodesiana' is for sale, especially CDs and DVDs designed to bring back the old country through the media of music and moving image. Military memorabilia is at a premium. Blogs from far-flung Rhodesians extol 'Smithy' as a saintly, misunderstood figure—and Britain (a nation strangled by 'political correctness') is commonly derided. *The Great Betrayal*, still appearing in new editions ten years after it was first published, works as something like an icon in this dispersed, subterranean world of whiteness unhinged.[77] It is too easy to read it as a unique text, the projection only of one man's idiosyncrasies. Its conditions of production make it more than that, representative not only of an individual in crisis but of a distinct historical formation.

This all seems very faraway. Yet it is still a culture which is articulated in the syntax of Britishness: not the putatively corrupted Britishness evident in the follies of successive metropolitan governments, but the fantasized Britishness of the mind which resided, unsullied, in the privileged location of the imperial past. Echoes of this thinking can be heard in other quarters, closer to home. When Smith died at the end of 2007 the *Daily Mail* carried two laudatory articles. They were not uncritical. Yet, as a consequence of the terrors perpetrated by Mugabe's ZANU-PF, the *Mail* journalists—while conceding 'that Mr Smith ran a pretty ruthless police force'—were given licence to exhume the Smith years essentially as a good thing, a beacon to the benevolence of white rule.[78] In the UK political defence of Smith, though a minority pursuit, is not extinct.

Smith habitually spoke in the fundamentalist voice of the virtuous Christian homesteader, portraying himself as the son of pioneers, a man of the people, with his roots in the soil of his native land. To British readers, his memories of his childhood in Selukwe sound in tone uncannily like Lady Thatcher's memories of Grantham—except that while Smith's portrayal is suffused with a boyish love for the land and for the sporting outdoors, Thatcher's is domestic and conveys a greater sense of privation, her femininity an unwanted burden. Yet the manner in which in adult life each mobilized these private memories into a usable public rhetoric is close, creating a political language which denied its political provenance. Clean-living, homespun morality, and, above all, straightness of character are what matter. In Smith's version:

> Law and order in your society, discipline at your school, play the game by your fellow man, you cannot let them down, and in the final analysis it may even be necessary to die for your cause. These were the conditions under which you lived, under which as a member of the British Empire, you were privileged to live.[79]

The prose may lack grace, and the politics of the present ('law and order') rearranges memories of the colonial past. Yet in this view of things politics represents the means to restore the virtues of the past to a society in danger of losing all it once had.

'Playing the game' meant much to Smith, allowing him to conceptualize his politics as if it were not politics at all. He had been born in the mining district of Selukwe in 1919, his father migrating from Scotland as a 17 year old in 1898 and his mother, from Cumberland, just after the South African War. His father was a small businessman, and both his parents stalwarts of the local community, his mother founding the local Women's Institute. The family home was disciplined and Christian, inculcating in the younger son the duties of proper manhood.[80] Throughout his schooling, first at Selukwe and then at boarding school in Gwelo, Smith's dominating passion was for sport.[81] Rugby and cricket entered his soul and memories of sporting achievements punctuate his autobiography. Yet it is clear that sport, for Smith, was perceived to be a sign of civilization and denoted too a certain utopian impulse. Sport he took to be 'clean', a key word in his lexicon, employed for describing the combination of individual human endeavour and colonial order.[82] In the midst of his prolonged negotiations with the London government memories of British sporting traditions reminded him of the honest, decent past he believed had been forsaken in the metropole. In a mantra which would be obscure to all but the initiated he recollected 'the philosophy of abiding by the rules of the game' exemplified at 'Lord's and the Oval, Twickenham and Murrayfield, Wimbledon, St Andrews, Epsom and Bisley', bringing into his imagination, through the medium of these sacred sites, the achievements of an entire civilization.[83]

Throughout his life he repeated his conviction that, while he wanted nothing more than to be on his farm, or watching the rugby or cricket with his family, public duty impelled him to immerse himself in the compromised sphere of politics, for 'any suggestion of shirking responsibility must be resisted'.[84] Politics he found 'sordid', negating the 'cleanliness' which the passions of a sporting life offered. 'Our political world was riddled with compromise, appeasement, indecision, all part and parcel of the deviousness which permeated our society—I felt strongly about this permissiveness, but at the same time tried to avoid over-reaction.'[85] In this domain of darkness and subterfuge, far removed from the simple ethics of the playing-field, there reside many temptations. Smith, like Bunyan's Pilgrim before him, retained the true faith even as those about him stumbled. Throughout many ugly encounters, narrated in his memoirs in all their minutiae, he held to his principles. He overrides obfuscation and intrigue by looking his antagonists straight in the eye and speaking the truth, unblemished, while others balk. His look alone quells enemies, shaming them and revealing the grubbiness of the latest underhand transaction that he and his people had to suffer. 'I always find it reassuring', he states, 'to be associated with people who have the courage of their convictions.'[86] His force of character disarms those around him, while his own straight-speaking sets 'the cat among the pigeons', 'calls their bluff', or makes them 'spitting mad'.[87] With quiet, immovable resolution 'Smithy' goes about his duties, all the while untouched by the corruption in which he has to dwell and which eats away at that which he holds most dear.

The greatest test of masculine character, however, Smith believed occurred in battle. His memories of the war worked as a powerful touchstone for his later life. In 1941 he interrupted his studies in order to join the 237 (Rhodesia) Squadron of the Royal Air Force. After initial training as a fighter pilot he was posted throughout the Middle East and north Africa. In the autumn of 1943 he was involved in a flying accident and suffered serious injury, bringing him close to death. After a short convalescence he returned to active service, only to be shot down over Italy in June 1944. Having fought alongside the partisans for a number of months, with winter coming, he made for the Allied lines and was eventually able to rejoin his unit. These years—hazarding with death, battling (as he hoped) to maintain the empire, drawing from a resolute masculine camaraderie—were to prove elemental for Smith, a formative experience to which the later realities of civilian life could never compare. In the Rhodesian popular imagination the nation's airmen were the stuff of romance, taller, tougher, and leaner than their metropolitan cousins, 'burnt and brown...glorious and rebellious': 'it was as if the gallant youth from 1914 had donned a uniform the colour of the sky and taken wing...The air was their medium...'[88]

He repeatedly returned to the anti-fascist credentials of white Rhodesians, weaving the collective memory of the fight against Nazism with the struggle to preserve white supremacy in Rhodesia into an indivisible story, which served to vindicate a peculiarly British valour. Smith admired 'Winston Churchill above all others' and was sure in his own mind that he 'had not fought in Churchill's war, and that Churchill had not led that war, to promote black majority rule or any kind of black mischief'.[89] In the conflicts of the 1970s, abandoned by those whom he believed to be allies, he remembered his flying days as a time uncomplicated by moral or political encumbrance. During his dark days of 1976, when the writing for Rhodesia was on the wall, he later recollected that 'I longed for those carefree days when I was flying around the skies in my Spitfire, saying to myself: "Let anyone cross my path and he will have to take what comes his way".'[90] At such points in the memoirs the superimposition of a fictive self—in this instance, indeed, a comic-book self—on the lived self is total, generating in the memoir an unreal persona devoid of human complexity and programmed only to undertake the increasingly frenzied, desperate obligations of a white man who sees all around him collapsing.[91] These are identifications, moreover, which work to separate the human life from the racial violence which Smith himself had set in train. In his diary of 7 February 1976, for example, he wrote:

Spent a few hours this morning watching our Currie Cup cricket game against Western Province, and Rhodesia put up a very good performance. Eric Rowan, one of South Africa's great batsmen, was there, and he came and had a good talk with me—cricket and politics! That evening a message came in reporting a successful encounter, where we had bagged 18 terrorists with no causalities on our side. An enjoyable and successful day.[92]

The old euphemisms of the settler had a long history.

It was partly his experience of having fought in the war that persuaded him to enter politics. All those who had fought with him were unanimous, it seems, that it was necessary to bring about 'a decent, clean world'. From the very beginning, he informs the reader, he was alert to the menace of international Communism, wishing that the Western leaders would 'clean up Russia, with its communism', for otherwise the defeat of fascism would only leave 'the job half finished'. Winston Churchill, was soon to be dismissed by an ungrateful, ignorant electorate; an ailing Roosevelt, on the other hand, without Churchill's backbone, had been 'conned by Stalin'.[93] As Smith makes clear, from this point on his hatred of Communism was matched only by his hatred of Pan-Africanism. In his later political life he refused to make any distinction between the two.

In an orthodox colonial cameo he describes how, on first returning home after his overseas postings, the dogs made 'a great fuss' of him and 'dear Mesa, our faithful old servant...put his arms around me and cried'.[94] He went back to university in the eastern Cape to complete his degree, and then took up farming near Selukwe, purchasing a 2,000 hectare property which many years later was to be the cause of contention with the Mugabe regime. It was then too that he met his wife, Janet, South African-born and a young widow with two children, her husband having died in a rugby match.[95] In Smith's rendition she exhibits all the attributes of Rhodesian character. He describes her as an outdoor sporty girl, full of pluck and dedicated to doing the right thing, whatever the personal cost—or in John Buchan's terms, 'a thorough sportsman'. 'Probably the qualities I admired most in her, though, were her courage and honesty of purpose. She was opposed on principle to side-stepping or evading an issue, no matter how difficult the problem, and her tendency was to opt for a decision requiring courage, as opposed to taking the easy way out.' A perfect companion, in other words, for the doughty Smith: 'At my stage of life I had the wisdom necessary to make a realistic assessment, devoid of emotion and immature fantasies, of our ability to live and work together.'[96]

This postwar moment, too, frames Smith's retrospective account of political developments in southern Africa. He regarded the National Party's defeat of Smuts in the South African general election of 1948 as signalling 'one of the most profound events affecting the history of Africa'. Smuts the 'great war hero' was, like Churchill, spurned by the 'ingratitude' of the popular electorate. As a result under the Nationalists South Africa fell into 'the apartheid trap', which Smuts—he claims—had wisely avoided. Many good things, he insisted, would have followed a Smuts victory in 1948: the Central African Federation would have never have been formed; Rhodesia would have gained legal independence; Portuguese hegemony in Angola and Mozambique would have been maintained; and the 'Marxist–Leninist gangsters' would not have bedevilled the region.[97]

When Smith was elected to the Southern Rhodesian legislature in 1948 for the opposition Liberal party he was anything but an advocate of 'little Rhodesianism', and certainly no outspoken critic of apartheid.[98] At this early stage of his political career he was a militant Rhodesian expansionist. He believed the discussions for closer cooperation between the two Rhodesias presented the opportunity 'to take the first step in the formation of a country in this part of Africa which in time would be one of the greatest countries in the world'. He imagined that federation, at first encompassing the Rhodesias and Nyasaland, would soon after include Kenya, Uganda, and Tanganyika, in the north, and Bechuanaland, in the south.

> I then feel that we should have to pause and consolidate ourselves before taking another step, and probably the final step. It will be best taken when it can be taken on a basis of equality in strength and numbers and therefore it would give equality in representation. This final step...is a Federation with the Union of South Africa.

Southern Rhodesia, in this vision, was to form the nucleus of a vast new white state in eastern, central, and southern Africa, built in the image of the British (preserving 'our British way of life') but whose command was to lie not with the Colonial Office but with the setters of Southern Rhodesia. Although the ultimate purpose was amalgamation with South Africa— apartheid notwithstanding—Rhodesia, having incorporated both its close and distant neighbours, would stand as co-broker with the Union, on at least an equal footing. Smith, however, made no secret of his desire that ultimately 'Rhodesia would take the lead.'[99]

In the event more prosaic issues predominated. He came to give cautious backing to the Federation, joined Huggins's Federal party—despite his fears, as he described them retrospectively, that the party represented the interests of 'the establishment, big business and finance, and the monopoly press'— and became a member of the Federation's assembly.[100] His scepticism about the conditions on which the Federation had been founded remained in place, increasing every moment that Westminster was drawn more closely into the management of the Federation's affairs. In 1962 he relinquished the United Federal party whip and by the end of the year had moved close to the leadership of the Rhodesian Front.

On race, notwithstanding his commitment to white supremacy, Smith—in the manner of Welensky—was obliged to temper his public statements in order to demonstrate that he was an enemy of racism and untouched by racial prejudice. He liked to display his opprobrium toward apartheid, explaining to foreign visitors, with breathtaking cynicism, that it was as a result of apartheid that the South African government had 'lost touch with' its blacks, in much the same way that he denounced the black nationalists as 'racialists'.[101] Reiterated throughout his life was his insistence that black Africans had only recently encountered civilization ('Muzorewa and his ancestors had not even invented the wheel by the time the white man had arrived'); that they were, as a result, still close to a primitive state of nature; and that in consequence they would not be 'ready' to take control of their own affairs until long into the future, and in the meantime for 'standards' to be safeguarded white dominion was necessary.[102] This racial argument was supplemented by homilies in which he commended the loyalty and integrity of individual blacks known to him and to his family, old retainers and the like, insisting all the while (in words which decidedly *were* from a prior epoch) that 'our blacks' were the happiest souls on earth and that 'our average black' was a 'conservative...satisfied with the manner in which things were progressing'.[103]

This, though, is only part of the story. Smith liked to boast that white Rhodesia had sprung from 'the strong individual character' of the pioneers.[104] *Character* comes from a classically colonial, proconsular pedagogy, the staple of children's literature and school speech-days.[105] It is a concept which largely, but not exclusively, works as a synonym for the authority of the white man. The ultimate embodiment of character, in Smith's imagination, was Ian Smith himself who, in remaining true both to his own self and to his people, demonstrated the historic virtues of the white man. But the idea of character is not precisely symmetrical with the figure of the white man. The occasional, token, black man could possess character.[106] White women could possess character, while in Smith's world black women do not enter the field of vision, or do so only as history's victims, prey to the machinations of agitators.[107] But it was the populist inflections of character which carried most weight for him. It is the people—the white people who founded Rhodesia and who built it up—who possess character, and the politicians (especially those outside Rhodesia) who lack it. In this scenario the totemic Smith, who has character in abundance, works as the emissary from the people to the politicians, his every action driven by his instinctive identification with the deepest desires of his own people. His politics, which he professes is not a politics at all, represents the distillation of the white nation, summed up in the only words that matter:'I am a Rhodesian'.[108] His logic—much as it was for an earlier generation of proconsuls, or later for the Powellites—is impenetrable, for character/people/race/nation operate as equivalents. Character, in this reading, is a peculiarly colonial virtue, for outside the redoubt of Rhodesia all Smith can see is the collapse of the integrity which character bestows and the steady erosion of its closest correlate, the white man.

This is the drama which *The Great Betrayal* enacts. Solid in their support for Smith in his travails are the unnamed, unrepresented ordinary folk of modern times: the whites of Rhodesia,'strong characters' made up of 'moderate, middle-of-the-road conservatives'; their kith and kin in Britain, struggling against their own unprincipled governments; and assorted men and women scattered across the English-speaking world.[109] The majority of Rhodesian blacks—'our blacks', sworn enemies of 'the extremist'—are, we are told, four-square behind him, although they themselves are accorded no agency, dependent on others to represent them. His wife Janet's resolution never falters and although not active in the public world herself she is positioned very close—intimately, in fact—to the apogee of white masculinity, Smith himself. Various heroes of the past are conscripted to his cause, amongst whom the mythic Churchill is, naturally, pre-eminent. Smuts appears as 'our old friend'.[110] Included in this pantheon (as it had been for Welensky) is the figure of António Salazar, the long-serving dictator of Portugal who, in Smith's view, had charge of a 'clean' country, demonstrated 'character' and 'determination', and who 'had the courage to put the interests of his country first'.[111] Both the Queen and Mrs Thatcher—each exemplars of character—he regarded as true friends of Rhodesia, their hostile actions explained only as a consequence of advice proffered by mincing, mendacious courtiers, appeasers all.

If these comprise Smith's natural allies, his natural enemies are dispatched by a single word: 'socialist', though the term is generously applied. All Labour politicians, as a matter of course, are thus condemned, 'hell-bent on appeasing Marxism–Leninism, at the expense of the old traditional values of the British Empire'.[112] The physique of the Labour foreign secretary, David Owen—'meagre and slouching'—signifies an entire epic of metropolitan decline.[113] Field-Marshall Lord Carver, called out of retirement in 1977 by the UK and US governments in an attempt to break the UDI deadlock, Smith took to be another socialist, notwithstanding his erstwhile command of the British armed forces and his significant role in the Kenyan counter-insurgency against the Mau Mau. He even entertained doubts about the political integrity of Henry Kissinger, hinting that perhaps he too had been contaminated by the virus of communism. Socialist and communist appear as indiscriminate, elastic terms: they serve only to place his political enemies beyond the pale of reasonable human endeavour.

Essentially his story turns on those who were once friends but who, when times got rough, capitulated, betraying not only themselves but all that white civilization represents. A long succession of Tories (the most nefarious identified as Rab Butler, Duncan Sandys, and Lord Carrington) are exposed as dupes of the terrorists. The South African leader, John Vorster, who finally wields the knife, once 'firm and straight', in the end turns out to be 'weak and vacillating'.[114] In Rhodesia, Huggins, Welensky, Whitehead, and Field all demonstrate deficiency of character, and fail the cause. So too, when nerve is required, does the nation's senior military commander, General Peter Walls, a grandson of pioneers who as a very young man had commanded an SAS unit during the Malayan insurgency. Defeatism even enters his own councils and undoes a number of his Rhodesian Front zealots (Hector MacDonald, David Smith). He confesses that he had been 'stabbed in the back'.[115] 'Treason and corruption... quietly and insidiously' penetrated 'underground'. 'By the time one becomes aware of the destruction which has taken place, it is too late.'[116]

As defeat mounts the possibility of 'positive and constructive thinking in the typical Rhodesian fashion' becomes a more gruelling, lonely task.[117] In the memoir he becomes an increasingly isolated figure, intransigent, but abandoned by old friends and allies whose commitments to the protocols of whiteness collapse. In the end he finds solace only with Janet, faithful to the last, and with the diminishing band of wartime RAF intimates who remain resolute, dreaming old dreams while they pass around their pewter tankards of ale.[118] On the last day of white rule in Rhodesia—31 May 1979—in a final gesture of defiance Smith determined to wear his RAF tie, symbolizing an entire lost world.

The autobiographical story Smith tells follows the generic conventions of masculine colonial romance. He fashioned his life as if he were a hero in a John Buchan novel, possessing all the fantastic, requisite powers of the white man, the embodiment of simple but absolute truths.

In 1910 *Prester John* told of the making of a white man's country, the youthfulness of the novel's protagonist, David Crawford, an allegory for the optimism and youthfulness of a new British white South Africa, with an epic future ahead. The persona of Ian Smith orchestrated in *The Great Betrayal* is of the same fictional genealogy as David Crawford. Indeed the autobiographical hero of Smith's memoirs—Smith himself—can be located as being, in symbolic terms, the son of David Crawford. The place and timing of Smith's birth, his Scottish ancestry, his deep internalization of the colonial order of things, his achieved masculinity, his sense of self: all these position the fictionalized Ian Smith as the plausible offspring of an adult David Crawford. But Smith has none of David's youth: he is an old man, close to death. *The Great Betrayal* is obliged to rewrite the story of *Prester John* in reverse telling, not of the founding, but of the destruction of a white man's country where black insurrection, far from being quelled, had triumphed. In Smith's volume white men are a declining constituency. As Rhodesia becomes only a memory Smith holds out to the end, and as he does so he speaks to those remaining souls he can persuade to listen—desperate, haunted, acting out times past—compelled to explain his fate as the last white man.

Metropole: the New Right

Smith, like Welensky, tells the story of the destruction of the colonial nation when 'treason and corruption' worked their way through the society, unseen and 'underground'—or 'from within and without' in the older words of Kipling. Enemies of the nation appear in a fantastical array of manifestations located at every point in the state, stirring up dark forces below. This is the mentality, in a specifically colonial idiom, of Enoch Powell's 'The Thing' adumbrated in his 'Enemies within' speech, and more broadly too of certain strands of conservative New Right thinking in the UK in the 1960s and 1970s. In identifying ethnic enemies existing *inside* the ruling bloc this was a sensibility, both in colony and metropole, driven by an intrinsic populism, in which the nation and its people, facing destruction, were invoked by the race tribunes as the counter to appeasement in high places. That Ian Smith himself was positioned at the apex of the Rhodesian state did nothing to militate against his fashioning his own populist rhetoric—just as later in Britain Thatcher and the Thatcherites could, rhetorically, side with the people against the state, notwithstanding their own hold on the institutions of state power.[119]

Striking is the degree to which elements of Rhodesian politics, through the postwar period, anticipated the preoccupations of the New Right in Britain in later years. Colin Leys's portrayal of the political values of what he identified as the institutional governing party of Rhodesia, referred to earlier, is instructive: anti-socialism, private enterprise, hostility to high taxation, restricted social services, opposition to outside interference, and the significance of British values, not to mention racial 'standards'.[120] In this respect Rhodesia operated as an anticipation of a New Right politics which, after many convolutions, was to take root in the metropole. From the late 1940s British migrants were travelling to Rhodesia in order to escape the constraints of what they feared would be the unwanted disciplines imposed by the new welfare state: a regime of 'spam, blackouts and Nissen huts' and ruinous taxes.[121] Cyril Dunn, the *Observer* journalist, discovered that many of the migrants from Britain regarded themselves as 'sturdy individualists', who were anxious to make their own way in the world and to whom the welfare state was 'anathema'. 'Private endeavour is consistently extolled and the tenets of Socialism derided.'[122] Basil Davidson, at the beginning of the 1950s, encountered the same phenomenon, reporting that Salisbury 'was full of eager people with their minds bent on big money, on big careers, on cutting loose from poor old England where "opportunities" were now, alas, so few and far between'.[123] Migrants such as these, 'refugees from the British Welfare State', were sure to receive an official welcome in Rhodesia.[124] When in 1957 the Federation launched a scheme to attract former army officers to migrate to central Africa it was made clear that 'escapers and complainers' should not apply.[125] Yet at the same time such notions of the colony as a land of material opportunity also worked alongside the idea that Rhodesia embodied a fantasized England of the past. When Richard

Cartwright, a future Rhodesian Front MP, arrived in the country in 1951 he remembered that 'I felt, My God, I'm home. Everything was so English, you know', while a number of new migrants—later in the decade—were happy to tell the press that they had left Britain because of the growing numbers of West Indians, imagining their new homeland to be a place (though how was this possible?) untouched by a black presence.[126]

By the time of the Rhodesian Front, attacks on the social disarray of Britain were a common element in Rhodesian public life, driven by the conviction that the mother country had forfeited its historic individualism for the false collective values of the welfare state. In 1964 Lieutenant-Colonel A. J. W. Macleod, speaking in the Rhodesian parliament, identified the welfare state as 'the root cause of all the moral degeneracy in the world today'. A year later he informed members that it was due to the welfare state that 'the national character suffers', declaring that welfare, in conjunction with pornography and drugs, created the conditions for 'complete demoralisation', warning in the same breath of the dangers of 'Red China's' destabilization of the West. Brigadier Andrew Dunlop concurred: 'Spoon feeding has been the ruination of the greatest race that ever existed, the British race. Through the Welfare State they have degenerated fast and furiously.' R. P. Ellis in the *Rhodesian Herald* thought that the 1944 Education Act was to blame, creating an entire generation of left-wing teachers. 'Make no mistake about it, anyone in the United Kingdom below the age of 35 has been well steeped in the idealistic, optimistic, and above all fantastic doctrine of socialism.' In August 1964 P. K. van der Byl, who after UDI took on the role of enthusiastic state censor, indicted the BBC and freedom of broadcasting, explaining that the BBC was responsible for 'criminality in London... Mods and Rockers, and all those other things, when you consider the total moral underminings which have been taking place in England' in the past fifteen or twenty years.[127]

These were sentiments rehearsed too in the metropole, blimpish and eccentric in the early 1960s, but gaining public credibility as the New Right cohered as a political force. Smith's jamming together the twin maladies of the 'philosophy of appeasement' and 'the cult of the permissive society', his emphasis on law and order, and his projection of the figures of the 'extremist' and the 'bully boy' all indicate a conception of politics in which the respectable citizen was called upon to confront the forces of disorder, wherever they were manifest.[128] In such a view the line between 'legitimate political opponents' and 'the enemy of the state'—or even, as he put it, 'the external enemy in disguise'—was becoming more confused, in need of constant intervention from the forces of order.[129] Enemies were 'within'.

Rhodesia deeply divided public opinion in Britain, the usual redoubts of liberalism openly hostile to Smith's white supremacism, while much of the right wavered.[130] The *Daily Mirror*, for example, recalling its radical heyday of the 1940s, took UDI as an opportunity to move onto the offensive against the right, explicitly declaring the need for Britons to destroy the 'myth' of kith and kin.[131] Yet on the other side of the political divide many of Smith's natural sympathizers found themselves in an awkward situation, hamstrung by the illegality of UDI and by what they felt to be Rhodesia's affront to the monarch. The Conservative press, in particular, had difficulty in formulating persuasive editorial positions. Even John Biggs-Davison, as zealous an admirer of 'Smithy' as one could hope to find, believed it necessary to confess to the Commons that 'I deplore UDI'—the cause, as Hansard records, of a degree of mirth.[132] However it is also clear that, notwithstanding the frequent public reservations which prevailed, there also emerged a strong strain of militant opinion. Despite the difficulties in openly supporting Smith's declaration of UDI the Tory right endeavoured to oppose every measure that sought to bring the regime to an end. There had been vocal support for Smith at the Conservative party conference in October 1965, immediately before UDI.[133] The vote on oil sanctions in parliament the following December generated a three-way split inside the Conservative ranks, comprising a small minority which supported the Labour policy of imposing oil sanctions, the main body of the party which followed the official line of abstention, and the right which was made up of the old Welenskyites and the Katanga lobby—the biggest division inside the Conservative party since the debates over the US loan in 1945.[134] From this point on the right remained a permanent fraction within the party, with periodic rebellions on Rhodesia punctuating official business in the coming years: in October 1969, in November 1970, and culminating in the major, last-ditch revolt in November 1978 when 116 Tories defied the frontbench, and John Biggs-Davison and Winston Churchill (the grandson of the wartime prime minister) resigned from the shadow government.[135] Many of the Rhodesia dissenters were also those opposing the party on immigration, on race relations, and on Europe, delineating the contours of the parliamentary New Right. From the mid-1960s the right in parliament, in a conscious bid to look outward from Westminster, paid greater attention to organizing public rallies in central London—in Caxton Hall, in Central Hall, and in an

explicit bid to wrest the initiative from 'the left', in Trafalgar Square—on
Rhodesia (notably Duncan Sandys's 'Peace with Rhodesia' demonstration
held in Trafalgar Square in January 1967), and on allied race matters.[136] In the
wider public sphere, as Alice Ritscherle has shown, in the opinion columns
of the national newspapers, and in sections of the provincial press, there
appeared steady support for Smith and for the white Rhodesians he represented. The journalists Peregrine Worsthorne, of the *Sunday Telegraph*, and
Kenneth Young (a Monday Club member), in the *Daily Express*, were the
most steadfast, but they were not alone.[137] The bulk of the sentiments
unearthed by Ritscherle turned less on the legality of the government's
action than on the national qualities of Rhodesians, replaying the familiar
stories of the white settlers, insisting on the essential Britishness of Rhodesia
('Most Rhodesians are of the toughest British stock'), and proclaiming the
equivalence of the fate of Britain in 1940 and that of Rhodesia in 1965.[138]
And insofar as we have access to less mediated popular voices it is possible
periodically to catch evocations, not of the equivalence between the two
nations, but of a deeper contrast deriving from their respective strategies for
managing race. In the immediate aftermath of UDI one vox-pop inter-
viewee informed a *Panorama* journalist that England needed 'a Britisher, Ian
Smith in here as Prime Minister to do the same in this country, with aliens,
Greeks, Italians and coloured people'.[139] The formulation 'to do the same in
this country' remained diplomatically opaque.

   The medium by which the values of white Rhodesia actively entered the
political life of the metropole, in the moment of decolonization, was the
Monday Club. UDI, in particular, galvanized the Club, providing it with a
political issue which spoke to a wide array of disaffected conservatives.
Cedric Gunnery, one of the founders of the Club and its long-time treasurer, was convinced that UDI marked the turning point in its fortunes,
reckoning that the membership doubled in the aftermath of UDI, to some
600.[140] From this point on the Monday Club became the principal institu-
tion that worked to articulate the varied sensibilities of the emergent New
Right, connecting Westminster to a burgeoning grassroots which otherwise
had only a contingent relation to the world of formal party politics. The
driving force for this, as I suggested in the last chapter, was a powerfully
accentuated, colonial reading of race. The Monday Club created a politics
which addressed the perceived distempers in the metropole brought about
by 'aliens, Greeks, Italians and coloured people', and did so by drawing from
an archive of memories of mythic white pasts overseas.

Organizationally, however, the transformations which Gunnery attributed to UDI had begun to occur rather earlier than he recalled. Initially the Monday Club served as a ginger group, committed to what it defined as 'traditional Conservative principles', and hoping to encourage local party associations to debate party policy with greater engagement.[141] Its political premise was based on the axiom that Macmillan's administration, by pushing too far to the left, had abandoned the tenets of true Conservatism.[142] The Monday Club was founded in September 1961 at the Onslow Court Hotel in Kensington, its inaugural meeting devoted to 'The situation in Africa'.[143] It was officially recognized by Conservative Central Office in the following August.[144] Before 1964, as Philip Murphy contends, it was ideologically 'heavily influenced by Welensky's allies', and from the start strove to connect decolonization in Africa to domestic issues.[145] In November 1963 the Club hosted a reception for Ian Smith in London, followed the next year by similar occasions for Clifford Dupont and for the leader of the breakaway Katangan region, Moïse Tshombe. Welensky and Salisbury, as we have seen, secured the funds. The hardened Suez rebels—John Biggs-Davison, Patrick Wall, Paul Williams—joined the council and in 1962 Salisbury and Lord Boyd accepted honorary appointments, supplying a patina of old Tory prestige. That same year Paul Bristol, perhaps the most resolute of the early cadres, visited central Africa, with introductions to Welensky and to Tshombe. End of empire and the travails of white peoples under siege—whether overseas or at home—possessed an unusual, heightened *immediacy* in the imaginations of the Club's founding militants.

In this early phase the Monday Club was primarily London-based, aiming to attract a young metropolitan constituency. At first, full membership was restricted to those who were under 35, and even by 1970 40 per cent of its membership was still under 40, relatively youthful by Conservative party standards. After the electoral defeat of the Conservative party in 1964, however, the 'club'-like ethos diminished as its leading figures endeavoured to transform it from a forum for discussion into a mass organization; in doing so it came to transmute into a party within a party, building up a mass individual membership (members were not required also to join the Conservative party), with its own rules and regulations, and a permanent bureaucracy. Membership, and most of the official membership figures, referred to the national club, though in addition there were many affiliates, in localities and in universities in particular, as well as in the women's and youth sections. Its focus was directed more to the Conservative constituency associations than to the party at Westminster and it came to use the annual Conservative conferences as an institutional vehicle for exerting pressure on the party leadership. Alec Douglas-Home was a great favourite of the Club— notwithstanding Welensky's diatribes—and he was happy to speak at its official events, twice being invited as guest of honour at the Club's annual dinner (in 1964 and 1969), and providing a significant channel between the grassroots and the senior inner councils of the larger party. At the same time, from the middle 1960s, the Club moved perceptibly to the right: attacking the 'liberal establishment' at home; condemning tentative moves toward *détente* with the Communist bloc; lending support to Portugal and to South Africa; and, from 1965, identifying with Ian Smith's Rhodesian Front and calling for the end of Britain's sanctions against Rhodesia.[146] In defending white Rhodesia the Monday Club elaborated a corpus of tradi- tional social values, extant and admired in the colony but, it appeared, pro- foundly compromised in the metropole.[147] There was much enthusiasm amongst members when, in January 1971, fifteen stalwarts travelled to Salisbury to meet with Ian Smith, presenting him with a picture of a Hunter aircraft flying over the Zambezi valley, painted by Richard Gardiner of the Club's Aviation Group.[148]

The 1965 breviary by Harold Soref and Ian Grieg, *The Puppeteers*, is indicative of the shift to the right. Grieg had been one of the four original founders of the Monday Club. Soref was an old empire hand, who had declared at the 1953 Tory party conference that 'we will never overcome the premature scuttle from India', a position from which he appeared never to relent.[149] His faith in Rhodesia was total, imagining it to stand as the racial utopia which Britain itself had once symbolized. 'Rhodesia represents', he once stated, 'Britain in its halcyon days: patriotic, self-reliant, self-supporting, with law and order and a healthy society. Rhodesia is as Britain was at its best.'[150] The purpose of the book, which distilled the thinking of the Africa Group of the Club, was to 'reveal'—though why such revelations were nec- essary is difficult to fathom—the names of (white) individuals (Terence Ranger, the historian; Colin Legum, of the *Observer*; Harold Wolpe, the ANC activist and sociologist to be) and organizations (the Anti-Apartheid Movement; the Movement for Colonial Freedom) which were adherents to black nationalism. It carried the subtitle: *An Examination of Those Organizations and Bodies Concerned with the Elimination of the White Man in Africa*.[151] Faith in the virtues of white civilization touched every aspect of the Monday Club mentality. John Biggs-Davison's *The Centre Cannot Hold*, published in

1969, was equally evident of the rightward turn, anticipating Powell's 'Enemies within' speech made the following year, and alert to the peculiarly colonial perception that a civilization was on the brink of destruction. The object of his attack was what he termed 'the politically pink and the morally permissive'. Yet he was confident that the cultural counter-attack against the prevailing liberal and radical ethos had begun to pay dividends, not least because of the work of the Monday Club. 'The "winds of change" are indeed veering. The tide is on the change.'[152] And so it was.

An early domestic impetus for the radicalization of the Club arose from the October 1964 results of the election in Smethwick, in the West Midlands, a neighbouring constituency to that of Enoch Powell. The Conservative candidate Peter Griffiths (a grammar-school-educated local man) beat the incumbent Labour representative Patrick Gordon Walker (the son of a judge in the Indian civil service, and the former Commonwealth secretary, whose support for the creation of the Central African Federation derived from his opposition to Nationalist South Africa). Griffiths secured his victory on an explicitly racist platform, marking a dramatic instance in the divide between the politics of government and the politics of support which I discussed in the last chapter.[153] Immediately after the election the Monday Club's Executive Council invited its Commonwealth Affairs Group to prepare a study of immigration. In December there appeared an initial document, and early in the new year a new 'Memorandum on immigration' was drafted, which announced that henceforth immigration was to be viewed, not only as an appropriate, but as an urgent, matter of political and public concern. 'We believe that the present influx of immigrants raises difficulties which are suitable for political action'—which signalled precisely the approach that the Conservative government, and no doubt its Labour successor as well, hoped to avoid. In an opening passage the 'Memorandum' explained that the Monday Club was 'thoughtful' but that at the same time it 'believes in outspokenness'. There was nothing 'thoughtful' about the references to 'venereal disease', to general standards of 'hygiene', and to 'noisy bottle parties' pursued by West Indians.[154] But the import was clear and uncompromising. The Commonwealth Immigration Act of 1962 needed to be tightened. 'Outspokenness' seems to have been just another euphemism. Henceforth anti-immigration became the leitmotif of the Club's policies.

As Powell developed his own racial politics in the mid-1960s there occurred a growing convergence between him and the Monday Club, an alliance which in the early 1970s deepened over the question of Europe.[155]

Powell spoke on a number of Monday Club platforms and was invited as guest of honour to the annual dinner in 1968, in the aftermath of his Birmingham speech.[156] It was due to the Monday Club, he argued, that many were brought into the Conservative party who might otherwise have been estranged from it.[157] From the Club's point of view, in the words of Biggs-Davison, 'Part of the importance of Enoch Powell, most intelligent, but very popular statesman, is that he declared it open season for the sacred cows of the pink Establishment.'[158] Indeed, from March 1968 to March 1969, according to the official historian, membership of the Club increased by 90 per cent, a significant rate of growth which coincided exactly with the height of the Powellite movement.[159] From the time of Powell's intervention in Birmingham, the Club ratcheted up its populist racism, opposing the Race Relations Act—a key issue, both for the Monday Club and for Powell—calling for the repeal of the Commonwealth Immigration Act of 1968 (which, partly as a result of pressure from the right, was superseded by the Immigration Act 1971), proposing that all coloured immigration be halted, and demanding that repatriation be set in train. George Young's 1969 publication, *Who Goes Home?*, was emphatic in this regard, and the cause of controversy amongst Club members.[160] This dedication to a racial politics culminated in the September 1972 'Halt immigration now!' meeting at Westminster Central Hall, addressed by Ronald Bell, John Stokes, John Biggs-Davison, and Harold Soref. In many respects the conception of the world marked by this rightward turn came increasingly to mimic that of the right in Rhodesia: the Rhodesian Front and its allies had, in the Monday Club, found its counterpart in the metropole.

By 1971 the Monday Club was claiming a combined individual and branch membership of approximately 10,000—including thirty MPs, six of whom were in the government, and thirty-five peers—organized in thirty branches.[161] It issued a small library of pamphlets and policy documents on every conceivable subject.[162] Crime, the profligacy of the welfare state, Northern Ireland, the irresponsibility of the BBC, and defence were common themes, each articulated in terms of the nation in peril. The spectre of internal enemies remained powerful, a recurring motif.[163] The historic imperial-Tory enthusiasm for tariffs and state protection gave way to an ever more profound regard for the ideals of the free market and self-reliance, though not without dissension. And although it was divided on the issue of the European Economic Community, the anti-Europe diehards, the nucleus composed of veterans of the Suez Group and of Salisbury's Watching

Committee (Robin Turton, Viscount Hinchingbrooke, Paul Williams, Anthony Fell), first became an identifiable tendency under the wing of the Monday Club in the period 1961–2, coinciding with the crisis of central Africa; by the close of 1962 more than forty Conservatives had put their names to an anti-EEC motion. Here, too, the investments in a post-imperial nationalist politics were pronounced.

The influence of the Club peaked in 1971–2. Allowing members to enrol on an individual basis, with no affiliation to the Conservative party, had from the late 1960s opened the organization to infiltration by the far-right fascist sects, particularly by the National Front.[164] A succession of plots and attempted putsches took hold during the period from 1972 to 1973, in which a number of the old guard, committed to their vision of traditional Conservatism, found it prudent to drift away.[165] During the Thatcher years the leadership were content to slow the tempo of their activities in the belief that on the basics, bar one or two important exceptions, Mrs Thatcher herself was following as closely as she could the Monday Club brief, though the flurry of agitational literature continued unabated.[166] By the late 1980s and early 1990s the Club had become little more than a rump, led for a while by Denis Walker, a former minister of education in the Rhodesian government and the leading, and probably the only, activist of the International Monarchist League, run out of his office in Bishop's Stortford. John Stokes, the prominent Monday Club MP who had been one of the main speakers in the 'Halt immigration now!' conference, took time out from his political responsibilities to follow his extra-mural predilections as vice-president of the Royal Stuart Society, a contemporary niche for those who entertained ancient Jacobite reveries. In these later years the Club was given to courting the unabashed far right, lauding assorted figures such as the freelance ultras Count Nikolai Tolstoy, Franjo Tudman, and Vladimir Cyrillovich, grand duke of Russia and pretender to the imperial throne. The Club allied itself with the Western Goals Institute, an offshoot of the World Anti-Communist League, whose purpose was to whitewash various tyrannies, particularly those in central America during the years of the Contra counter-insurgency. Patrick Wall, meanwhile, spent the last decade of his life as president of the British UFO Association. By the time of the Conservative election victory of 1979, bringing Mrs Thatcher to power, the Monday Club had fulfilled its historic task.

While it was still an effective force in public life, the Monday Club operated as a coalition, binding together discordant historical currents by connecting, politically, the colonial past to the postcolonial future. On the one hand it worked from the legacy of the old imperialist ideologues within the Conservative party, for whom elements of the proconsular traditions still carried meaning, attenuated but none the less present (as, paradoxically, they had also been for Cub Alport, despite his active repudiation of the Monday Club-Powellites). Even though the rhetoric of the old imperial right could still be militant, its instincts were naturally attuned to the prerogatives of a declining politics of government, embodying a long history in which a statist practice of governance, at home and overseas, had come to be deeply internalized. Salisbury's blue-blooded Cecil pedigree, as most of his enemies came to realize—but as he never could—was the cause of his undoing. And yet the cathartic charge of Salisbury's empire generation, invoking the phantasmagoric, utopian properties of a past governed by racial whiteness, was greater than he or his contemporaries were ever able to comprehend. This articulation of a heightened, if displaced, historical sense of the world and a crippling myopia may, I suppose, be a characteristic of a declining class. 'Without knowing it himself' a historical figure located in such a predicament 'may speak one thing to the conscious mind while whispering another to the unconscious'.[167] The past, after all, is never entirely the past. This old high imperialism, its class determinants conspicuous, marked one side of things. On the other, the modern, populist forces, indebted to the earlier generations of Conservatives for the overriding colonial and racial verities incubated in the making of Greater Britain, none the less proved less concerned with the class rituals of Westminster, looking out to a politics in which support as much as government determined, and in which the imperatives of domestic metropolitan life—after empire—took precedence. The militants of the New Right confronted the future by drawing on the deep resources of the empire's past, and recasting it for the present.

I shall conclude this volume by pointing to the instabilities of this conjunction of the old empire politics and the new racial politics, picking out a single thread from the larger story. In doing so, we might glimpse something of the power of the imperial past still active in the time of decolonization, and also something of its impossibilities. These closing remarks, compressed as they are, turn on the figure of Alan Lennox–Boyd, later Lord Boyd, patron of the Monday Club.

Lennox–Boyd was properly an imperialist of the traditional right. In his biography Philip Murphy opens with a wonderfully irreverent portrait penned by Michael Foot in 1952:

he is a real Tory without prefix, suffix, qualification or mitigation. His Tory instincts work in response to any proposition, however strange or unaccustomed, as if operated by an electrical appliance. There is nothing complicated in his nature. He is simplicity itself. Indeed, he would be the despair of the most amateur psychologist. Nothing bizarre or appalling happened to him in his infancy apart from membership of the Junior Imperial League. The real question is whether he has ever escaped the atmosphere of these childish capers. He is a Junior Imp who never grew up, a Primrose League Peter Pan.[168]

Murphy sets out to turn this verdict around in order to demonstrate that, whatever his deeper sensibilities, Lennox-Boyd's term at the Colonial Office was not one of reaction but, on the contrary, was marked by pragmatism, a willingness to compromise, and a readiness greater than that many of his colleagues to make concessions to colonial nationalism.

There can be no doubt of Lennox-Boyd's Tory-imperial credentials. At Oxford, as Murphy shows, his devotion to the imperial creed was neither 'especially original nor sophisticated'. Through the 1920s and the 1930s he displayed an orthodox right-wing sympathy for the Italian and Spanish variants of fascism. Most of his ideas came from 'his mentor', John Buchan; he enthusiastically, explicitly, followed Milner and Cromer in their belief that Englishmen possessed an innate talent for colonial administration; and as president of the Oxford Union he organized the unveiling of a bust of Curzon.[169] These early proconsular sympathies remained with him. He came to be a diehard opponent to the India Bill of 1935, receiving on his marriage (into the Guinness family) a silver tray from the India Defence League which carried the inscription: 'In recognition of a gallant endeavour'.[170] Much later, as colonial secretary, he had direct responsibility for the counter-insurgency against the Mau Mau in Kenya, and subsequently proved, in private, to be candid—as Murphy concedes—about his cover-up of the state terror visited upon the colony.[171] He was a staunch supporter of Eden's attack on Egypt, writing to him in the midst of the crisis to explain that 'I remain convinced that if Nasser wins, or even appears to win, we might as well as a government (and indeed as a country) go out of business.'[172] In central Africa there is no evidence that he ever understood the need to confront the settlers and at the beginning of 1959—in good faith or not—he gave official credence to the Nyasaland *grande peur* turning on the putative, impending racial massacres.[173] From the very first discussions of closer association in central Africa his sympathies lay with Welensky; and as the Federation's denouement was first publicly endorsed, when Rab Butler announced the right of individual territories to secede, he wrote to Welensky, informing him that 'I can hardly find words to express my feelings of shame and distress at the events of the last few weeks which are the culmination of a long period of disastrous surrenders.'[174] In 1962, alongside Lord Salisbury, he was invited to become patron of the Monday Club, an offer he accepted.

Murphy is right to argue that the power of the office of colonial secretary, in this period above all, was increasingly circumscribed. Lennox-Boyd appreciated this and acted accordingly, committing himself to day-to-day pragmatism rather than to the pursuance of grand imperial designs. But the pragmatic decisions of a diehard were not necessarily those of one of more progressive inclination. In insisting on the fundamental convergence of Lennox-Boyd and Iain Macleod as colonial secretaries, Murphy states that their 'essential aim was to allow Britain to retain control over her colonies until the moment when all formal authority had been relinquished, and to exert influence over them thereafter'.[175] Perhaps so. Yet 'retaining control' in Lennox-Boyd's case required the imposition of emergencies in Cyprus, Northern Rhodesia, and Nyasaland, overseeing the counter-terror in Kenya, while 'exerting influence' in the case of Egypt demanded full-scale military invasion. This indicates less an accommodation to colonial nationalism than a determination to contain or destroy it. That this brought only limited and temporary success Lennox-Boyd knew well enough. Failure to stand up to Nasser, he feared, would put Britain 'out of business'; the 'disastrous surrenders' which brought about the collapse of the Central African Federation induced in him 'shame' and 'distress'. It was emotions such as these which propelled him into the Monday Club.

Lennox-Boyd's journey from proconsular epigone to grandee of the Monday Club is instructive, placing two distinct histories in the one frame, and alerting us to important, subterranean political continuities. It signals not merely the coming of the end of empire, but a more complex narrative of one who felt deeply a sense of political defeat and 'shame', and who continued his 'gallant endeavour' to propagate the values of colonial order. That this endeavour took place after the empire had largely vanished, on the territory of the metropole, required him to confront those in his own party whom he held responsible for the defeats inflicted on his nation. Like many of those who, before too long, felt a compelling desire to write to Enoch Powell expressing *their* 'distress' about what they believed to be the termination of England, so Lennox-Boyd came to conclude that all he most valued was about to 'go out of business'.

There is, though, a twist. In 1968 Boyd resigned from the Monday Club because of his opposition to Powell and his unease with the deepening convergence between the Club and the Powellites. At the same time Paul Bristol also resigned, on similar grounds, due to his hostility to George Young's pamphlet, *Who Goes Home?* As the Monday Club moved sharply to the right it is no surprise, perhaps, that some of its early adherents pulled back, resisting the new militancy. Their decisions have been explained by their reluctance to shed their commitments to a tradition of paternalistic multiracialism.[176] No doubt this is right: the resolutely hard Conservatism espoused by Boyd throughout his political life was not necessarily incompatible with more idealistic aspirations for a white paternalism—as we have seen, for example, in the case of Boyd's *sensei*, John Buchan.

But it was not only a matter of differing ideological perspectives. As I have been suggesting, the coming of the Monday Club, of the New Right more generally, and then of the Powellite moment from 1968, signalled a break in the structures of politics, in which a greater weight fell to the politics of support outside the institutions of Westminster, and which can be tracked in—amongst other places—the new political significance of the popular press and of television. The authority of the traditional political class, formed in the interstices of empire, was diminishing, and during this period the inherited class allegiances, to Conservative or Labour, began to slacken.[177] These social transformations, expressions of the democratization of everyday life of the postwar years and of the dissolution of a certain culture of deference, can be seen at work inside the Monday Club itself. In the Monday Club distinct historical formations coexisted in the single organization. As I have indicated, on the one hand there were those who had been formed by the empire, Westminster, Oxford, the army, and the law; their world, for example, was represented by the annual Monday Club ball, held at the Café Royal under the presidency of Lady Cranborne, Salisbury's daughter-in-law. It is this world, too, for which Sir Ralph Furse, in his 1962 memoir, provides such an extraordinary elegy.[178] On the other hand, there were those who came from an emergent, lower-middle-class or working-class suburban milieu far removed from the culture of the traditional political class, for whom the proximate, domestic exigencies of race predominated. These distinct formations neither prescribed ideological positions (Boyd and Bristol were at one in their opposition to a fierce anti-immigration

stance), nor were wholly insulated, one from the other. Indeed it was precisely their coexistence and interaction which proved so potent. Thus the
Monday Club not only generated differing political positions, narrowly
understood; it also comprised distinct forms of political practice, in which
the politics of government—the habituated traditions of the old governing
class—actively vied with the politics of support, evident in the emergent
populist inclinations of the New Right. Lord Boyd had been nurtured by
the former. The new world which was unfolding, both in the Monday
Club and outside its ranks, was one which he, as much as Salisbury, could
never quite comprehend or accommodate himself to. Even as the new politics embraced the historic, colonial protocols of racial whiteness, it did so
within the overriding syntax of popular life.

When Welensky in the Central African Federation, and then later Smith
in Rhodesia, were fighting their final battles against black majority rule,
they imagined that the destruction of these historic white man's territories
would spell the death of the white man. Without a white man's country
where were white folk to go, and what were they to do?[179] Both Welensky
and Smith indulged in the idea that they were the final survivors of a lost
civilization, battling against the extinction—not only of all that was noble—
but of something deep in their own being. Yet behind their backs an unexpected transubstantiation occurred. Racial whiteness took on a new life
elsewhere, in men and women faraway. The figure of the white man, and all
it represented, already heavy with accreted meaning, had more work to do.
If the imperative of racial whiteness died in central Africa, in the dark
metropole at empire's end it experienced a strange, disturbing resurrection.

Notes

INTRODUCTION

. *The Complete Letters of Sigmund Freud to Wilhelm Fleiss, 1887–1904* (Cambridge, Mass.: Harvard UP, 1985), 271. I'm using the modified translation which appears in Michael S. Roth, 'Freud's Use and Abuse of the Past', in Roth (ed.), *Rediscovering History: Culture, Politics, and the Psyche* (Stanford, Calif.: Stanford UP, 1994), 336. I draw some formulations here from my own 'End of Empire and the English Novel', in Rachael Gilmour and Bill Schwarz (eds.), *End of Empire and the English Novel since 1945* (Manchester: Manchester UP, 2011).
2. Virginia Woolf, *The Years* (London: Penguin, 2002), 275.
3. Interview with Enoch Powell, 26 Apr. 1988.
4. Enoch Powell, 'Fears that have Not Changed', *The Times*, 19 Apr. 1988; and see the leader, 'Mr Powell's Prophecy', 22 Apr. 1988.
5. This file is held in Powell's constituency papers in the Stafford Record Office, D4490/48. I'll return to it in the closing volume. Interview with Powell.
6. See Wendy Webster, *Englishness and Empire, 1939–1965* (Oxford: Oxford UP, 2005), and her *Imagining Home. Gender, 'Race' and National Identity, 1945–1964* (London: UCL Press, 1998); Stuart Ward (ed.), *British Culture and the End of Empire* (Manchester: Manchester UP, 2001); Stephen Howe, *Anticolonialism in British Politics: The Left and the End of Empire, 1918–1964* (Oxford: Clarendon Press, 1993), and his 'When (if ever) did Empire End? "Internal Decolonization" in British Culture since the 1950s', in Martin Lynn (ed.), *The British Empire in the 1950s: Retreat or Revival?* (Houndmills: Palgrave Macmillan, 2006); and Philip Murphy, *Party Politics and Decolonization: The Conservative Party and British Colonial Policy in Tropical Africa, 1951–1964* (Oxford: Clarendon Press, 1995).
7. He was angered by Britain's involvement in the Biafran-Nigerian catastrophe, and too by the government's support for the United States in Vietnam.
8. Richard Crossman, *The Crossman Diaries: Selections from the Diaries of a Cabinet Minister* (London: Hamish Hamilton and Jonathan Cape, 1979), 66; entry for 30 Jan. 1965.
9. The image of Gandhi was removed so as not to cause discontent in the subcontinent.
10. Jacqueline Rose, *States of Fantasy: The Clarendon Lectures in English Literature* (Oxford: Clarendon Press, 1994), 5.

11. A persuasive history written in these terms is Henry Rousso, *The Vichy Syndrome: History and Memory in France since 1944* (Cambridge, Mass.: Harvard UP, 1991); see too Nancy Wood, *Vectors of Memory: Legacies of Trauma in Postwar Europe* (Oxford: Berg, 1999); and with a wider conspectus, Tony Judt, 'Epilogue: From the House of the Dead. An Essay on Modern European Memory', in his *Postwar: A History of Europe since 1945* (London: Heinemann, 2005). On the connections between memory and postcolonial France, Alec G. Hargreaves (ed.), *Memory, Empire and Postcolonialism: Legacies of French Colonialism* (Lanham, Md.: Lexington Books, 2005); and the chilling account in Jim House and Neil MacMaster's excellent *Paris 1961: Algerians, State Terror, and Memory* (Oxford: Oxford UP, 2006). Conceptually, I have been guided by the contributions to Susannah Radstone and Bill Schwarz (eds.), *Memory: Histories, Theories, Debates* (New York: Fordham UP, 2010), and by Michael Rothberg, *Multidirectional Memory: Remembering the Holocaust in the Age of Decolonization* (Stanford, Calif.: Stanford UP, 2009).

12. Important here is Stuart Hall, Chas Critcher, Tony Jefferson, John Clarke, and Brian Roberts, *Policing the Crisis: Mugging, the State and Law and Order* (London: Macmillan, 1978).

13. See Geoffrey Pearson, *Hooligan: A History of Respectable Fears* (London: Macmillan, 1983); and Raymond Williams, *The Country and the City* (London: Chatto & Windus, 1973).

14. W. E. H. Stanner, *After the Dreaming: Black and White Australians. An Anthropologist's View. The Boyer Lectures 1968* (Sydney: ABC, n.d. [1968]), 26, 27; and Henry Reynolds's lecture, effectively a sequel to Stanner, *The Breaking of the Great Australian Silence in Australian Historiography, 1955–1983* (London: Trevor Reese Memorial Lecture, Australian Studies Centre, University of London, 1984).

15. See the Prologue, below.

16. And see my, ' "Shivering in the Noonday Sun": The British World and the Dynamics of "Nativization" ', in Kate Darian-Smith, Patricia Grimshaw, and Stuart Macintyre (eds.), *Britishness Abroad: Transnational Movements and Imperial Cultures* (Melbourne: Melbourne UP, 2007).

17. See Ann Laura Stoler, *Carnal Knowledge and Imperial Power: Race and the Intimate in Colonial Rule* (Berkeley, Calif.: University of California Press, 2002), and her 'Tense and Tender Ties: The Politics of Comparison in North American History and (Post) Colonial Studies', *Journal of American History*, 88/3 (2001), for the colonial anticipations, focusing on the domestic microphysics of power, which also appears in her edited collection, *Haunted by Empire: Geographies of Intimacy in North American History* (Durham, NC: Duke UP, 2006).

18. In *Capital Affairs: The Making of the Permissive Society* (New Haven: Yale UP, 2010), Frank Mort draws from his earlier study—*Dangerous Sexualities: Medico-Moral Panics in England since 1830* (London: Routledge & Kegan Paul, 1987)—to propose that the management of sexual life in the 1950s and 1960s was, for all the talk of liberation, still haunted by older, late Victorian histories. My argument on colonialism and race works in parallel.

19. Although I am wary of much of the literature on trauma, I've found Jenny Edkins, *Trauma and the Memory of Politics* (Cambridge: Cambridge UP, 2003), helpful. Paul Gilroy, *After Empire: Melancholia or Convivial Culture?* (London: Routledge, 2004), suggests the degree to which memories of the Second World War functioned as screens, displacing the historical realities of colonial life.

20. The best account can be found in Catherine Hall and Sonya Rose, 'Introduction: Being at Home with the Empire', in Hall and Rose (eds.), *At Home with the Empire: Metropolitan Society and the Imperial World* (Cambridge: Cambridge UP, 2006).

21. The last twenty years have witnessed a renaissance in imperial historiography in the anglophone world. Many historians have pursued these arguments, the bulk of them prompted by feminist politics. Those which have touched me most include Antoinette Burton, *At the Heart of Empire: Indians and the Colonial Encounter in Late-Victorian Britain* (Berkeley, Calif.: University of California Press, 1998); Graham Dawson, *Soldier Heroes. British Adventure, Empire and the Imagining of Masculinities* (London: Routledge, 1994); Catherine Hall, *Civilising Subjects: Metropole and Colony in the English Imagination, 1830–1867* (Cambridge: Polity, 2002); Diana Jeater, *Marriage, Perversion, and Power: The Construction of Moral Discourse in Southern Rhodesia, 1894–1930* (Oxford: Clarendon Press, 1993), and her *Law, Language, and Science: The Invention of the 'Native Mind' in Southern Rhodesia, 1890–1930* (Portsmouth, NH: Heinemann, 2007); Yasmin Khan, *The Great Partition: The Making of India and Pakistan* (London: Yale UP, 2007); Paula M. Krebs, *Gender, Race and the Writing of Empire: Public Discourse in the Boer War* (Cambridge: Cambridge UP, 1999); Marilyn Lake and Henry Reynolds, *Drawing the Global Colour Line: White Men's Countries and the International Challenge of Racial Equality* (Cambridge: Cambridge UP, 2008); Philippa Levine, *Prostitution, Race, and Politics: Policing Venereal Disease in the British Empire* (New York: Routledge, 2003); Elleke Boehmer, *Empire, the National, and the Postcolonial: Resistance in Interaction* (Oxford: Oxford UP, 2002); Ann McClintock, *Imperial Leather: Race, Gender and Sexuality in the Colonial Context* (New York: Routledge, 1994); Diana Patton, *No Bond But the Law: Punishment, Race, and Gender in Jamaican State Formation, 1780–1870* (Durham, NC: Duke UP, 2004); Adele Perry, *On the Edge of Empire: Gender, Race, and the Making of British Columbia, 1849–1871* (Toronto: University of Toronto Press, 2001); Mary Procida, *Married to the Empire: Gender, Politics and Imperialism in India, 1883–1947* (Manchester: Manchester UP, 2002); Kristin Ross, *Fast Cars, Clean Bodies: Decolonization and the Reordering of French Culture* (Cambridge, Mass.: MIT Press, 1995); Mrinalini Sinha, *Colonial Masculinity: The 'Manly' Englishman and the 'Effeminate' Bengali in the Late Nineteenth Century* (Manchester: Manchester UP, 1995), and her *Specters of Mother India: The Global Restructuring of an Empire* (Durham, NC: Duke UP, 2006); Stoler, *Carnal Knowledge and Imperial Power*; Carol Watts, *The Cultural Work of Empire: The Seven Years' War and the Imagining of a Shandean State* (Edinburgh: Edinburgh UP, 2007); Marcus Wood, *Blind Memory: Visual*

Representations of Slavery in England and America, 1780–1865 (Manchester: Manchester UP, 2000); and Anna Davin's path-breaking 'Imperialism and Motherhood', *History Workshop Journal*, 5 (1978). On the domestic disposition of race I have been much influenced by Sonya O. Rose, *Which People's War? National Identity and Citizenship in Wartime Britain, 1939–1945* (Oxford: Oxford UP, 2003).

22. I've been struck by Hannah Arendt's endeavour to understand, both historically and theoretically, race-thinking and empire as components of modern totalitarianism. Her discussion of the British empire in *The Origins of Totalitarianism*, first published in 1951, covers much of the ground I introduce in the first volume: Froude, Dilke, and Seeley; Cromer and Curzon; South Africa and Australia. When nations imagine themselves racially—or, as she says more specifically in regard to England, when 'Englishmen have turned into "white men"'—that is the moment which signifies the end of what she called 'Western man'. 'For...race is, politically speaking, not the beginning of humanity but its end, not the origin of peoples but their decay, not the natural birth of man but his unnatural death', Hannah Arendt, *The Origins of Totalitarianism* (London: Allen & Unwin, 1958), 157. In terms of the historiography, I am indebted to V. G. Kiernan, *The Lords of Human Kind: European Attitudes to the Outside World in the Imperial Age* (Harmondsworth: Penguin, 1972), which did much to bring the white man—in his late Victorian, imperial disposition——explicitly into the line of vision of the metropolitan intellectual culture.

23. Very helpful is Judith Butler, *The Psychic Life of Power: Theories in Subjection* (Stanford, Calif.: Stanford UP, 1997),

24. In response to Ward's, *British Culture and the End of Empire*, Philip Murphy makes the same point: *Contemporary British History*, 17/2 (2003), 153–5.

25. Bernard Porter, *The Absent-Minded Imperialists. Empire, Society, and Culture in Britain* (Oxford: Oxford UP, 2004); and for his defence against his many critics, 'Further Thoughts on Imperial Absent-Mindedness', *Journal of Imperial and Commonwealth History*, 36/1 (2008).

26. e.g. Gwyn A. Williams, 'The Concept of "Egomonia" in the Thought of Antonio Gramsci: Some Notes in Interpretation', *Journal of the History of Ideas*, 21 (1960).

27. At one point Porter might seem to concur. He suggests the possibility that if the middle class of the early 19th cent. 'were imperialists' they were so 'without knowing it'. But this is a line of thought he chooses not to pursue: Porter, *Absent-Minded Imperialists*, 112.

28. He informs the reader that 'It is always dangerous to infer too much from literature'. But when he comes to Virginia Woolf, not a writer renowned for her blokeishness, he assures us that she 'came from one of those very imperially connected families, so presumably she knows what she is talking about'. Which—presumably—makes it all right: Porter, *The Absent-Minded Imperialists*, 43. Woolf certainly knew enough about empire to humiliate the imperial navy:

Hermione Lee, *Virginia Woolf* (London: Vintage, 1997), 282–6. And enough about stories to know that narrating only what is observable works hypnotically to obscure what is most real—most human—about a life. See esp.Virginia Woolf, 'Mr Bennett and Mrs Brown', in her *Woman's Essays: Selected Essays*, i, ed. Rachel Bowlby (London: Penguin, 1992).

29. Porter, *Absent-Minded Imperialists*, 317.

30. I have in mind David Cannadine's *Ornamentalism: How the British Saw their Empire* (London: Allen Lane, 2001), which in placing the centrality of its argument on ornament, ceremony, and flummery exults in resurrecting the pre-Powellite fancies of the 1960s. For a sharp critique in this vein, see Geoff Eley, 'Beneath the Skin. Or: How to Forget the Empire without Really Trying', *Colonialism and Colonial History*, 3/1 (2002).

31. Roland Barthes, *The Pleasures of the Text* (London: Jonathan Cape, 1976), 10.

32. Linda Colley, *Captives: Britain, Empire and the World, 1600–1859* (London: Pimlico, 2003), 376–7, where she draws the readers' attention to 'the urgent matter of race'. Elsewhere she has taken to task those whom she considers to be 'wallowing in post-imperial guilt', Linda Colley, 'Blueprint for Britain', *Observer*, 12 Dec. 1999. Her article originally began life as a Downing St lecture to Mr Blair. Given his subsequent penchant for things imperial, maybe he was listening all too intently.

33. See Himani Bannerji, 'Politics and the Writing of History', in Ruth Roach Pierson, Nupur Chadhuri, and Beth McAuley (eds.), *Nation, Empire, Colony: Historicizing Gender and Race* (Bloomington, Ind.: Indiana UP, 1998). For representative overviews: Clare Midgley (ed.), *Gender and Imperialism* (Manchester: Manchester UP, 1998); Philippa Levine (ed.), *Gender and Empire* (Oxford: Oxford UP, 2004); and Angela Woollacott, *Gender and Empire* (Basingstoke: Palgrave, 2006). More explicitly in terms of historical practice: Antoinette Burton, *Dwelling in the Archive: Women Writing House, Home, History in Late Colonial India* (New York: Oxford UP, 2003) and Sonya O. Rose, *What is Gender History?* (Cambridge: Polity, 2010).

34. See Catherine Hall and Keith McClelland (eds.), *Race, Nation and Empire: Making Histories, 1750 to the Present* (Manchester: Manchester UP, 2010).

35. The lecture was originally delivered in May 1973; it's most widely available as J. G. A. Pocock, 'British History: A Plea for a New Subject', *Journal of Modern History*, 47 (1975), 612, 616, and 614; and see his *The Discovery of Islands: Essays on British History* (Cambridge: Cambridge UP, 2005).

36. In this regard Angela Woollacott identifies the phenomenon of the 'masculinist romanticization' of the settler: 'Gender and Sexuality', in Deryck M. Schreuder and Stuart Ward (eds.), *Australia's Empire: Oxford History of the British Empire, Companion Volume* (Oxford: Oxford UP, 2008).

37. E. M. Collingham offers an insight into the transformation from the 'effeminate, flamboyant and wealthy' body of the early nabob of the East India Company to the 'sober, bureaucratic representative of the Crown' in the person of the sahib, discerning in this a larger 'shift from an open to a closed and

regimented body', *Imperial Bodies: The Physical Experience of the Raj, c1800–1947* (Cambridge: Polity, 2001).

38. Lake and Reynolds, *Drawing the Global Colour Line.*

39. James Belich, *Replenishing the Earth: The Settler Revolution and the Rise of the Anglo-World, 1783–1939* (Oxford: Oxford UP, 2009).

40. Amongst the growing literature on the continuation of Victorian sensibilities in Caribbean anti-colonial thought, most of which emphasize conceptions of gender, see Michelle A. Stephens, *Black Empire: The Masculine Global Imaginary of Caribbean Intellectuals in the United States, 1914–1962* (Durham, NC: Duke UP, 2005); Belinda Edmondson, *Making Men: Gender, Literary Authority and Women's Writing in Caribbean Narrative* (Durham, NC: Duke UP, 1999); Leah Reade Rosenberg, *Nationalism and the Formation of Caribbean Literature* (New York: Palgrave, 2007); Alison Donnell, *Twentieth-Century Caribbean Literature* (London: Routledge, 2005); Anne Spry Rush, *Bonds of Empire: West Indians and Britishness from Victoria to Decolonization* (Oxford: Oxford UP, 2011); Simon Gikandi, *Maps of Englishness* (New York: Columbia UP, 1996); and——directly relevant—— Simon Gikandi, 'Pan-Africanism and Cosmopolitanism: The Case of Jomo Kenyatta', *English Studies in Africa,* 43/1 (2000).

41. The phrase comes, famously, from Frederick Cooper and Ann Laura Stoler, 'Between Metropole and Colony: Rethinking a Research Agenda', in Cooper and Stoler (eds.), *Tensions of Empire: Colonial Cultures in a Bourgeois World* (Berkeley, Calif.: University of California Press, 1997), 4.

42. John Comaroff and Jean Comaroff, *Of Revelation and Revolution,* ii. *The Dialectics of Modernity on a South African Frontier* (Chicago: University of Chicago Press, 1997), 19.

43. Peter Brooke, in a thoughtful intervention, makes the comparison between Powell and Lord Ripon insisting on the imperial, rather than on the post-imperial, properties of Powell's thinking. In making this argument, however, he imagines imperial and post-imperial as antinomies, which I find unhelpful: 'India, Post-Imperialism and the Origins of Enoch Powell's "Rivers of Blood" Speech', *Historical Journal,* 50/3 (2007). My own approach, on the contrary, is to emphasize the degree to which the postcolonial necessarily carries within it continuities from the colonial past. In this I follow Camilla Schofield, 'Enoch Powell and the Making of Postcolonial Britain', unpublished Ph.D., Yale, 2009.

44. Anna Marie Smith, *New Right Discourse on Race and Sexuality: Britain, 1968–1990* (Cambridge: Cambridge UP, 1994), 14.

45. David Armitage offers a methodological discussion of the idea of Greater Britain, though for a different period and with a greater emphasis on the Atlantic dimensions, in 'Greater Britain: A Useful Category of Historical Analysis?', *American Historical Review,* 104/2 (1999); for England in the context of the British state, Laurence Brockliss and David Eastwood (eds.), *A Union of Multiple Identities: The British Isles, c1750–c1850* (Manchester: Manchester UP, 1997); and for postcolonial England, Graham MacPhee and Prem

Podder (eds.), *Empire and After: Englishness in a Postcolonial Context* (Oxford: Berghahn, 2007).

PROLOGUE

1. This effacement of memory conforms to the investigations of Marc Auge, *Non-Places: Introduction to an Anthropology of Supermodernity* (London:Verso, 1995).
2. Charles W. Boyd (ed.), *Mr Chamberlain's Speeches,* ii (London: Constable, 1914), 125ff.
3. Interview with the author, 26 Apr. 1988. 'Remember, I was born and brought up in Birmingham'—and in this Powell laid claim to a political, not merely a geographical, inheritance.
4. Simon Heffer, *Like the Roman: The Life of Enoch Powell* (London: Weidenfeld & Nicolson, 1998), 558.
5. The friend was Clem Jones, the editor of the Wolverhampton *Express and Star* during this period. His statement about the episode can be found in Mike Phillips and Trevor Phillips, *Windrush: The Irresistible Rise of Multi-Racial Britain* (London: Harper Collins, 1998), 245–53. It is one of the few inside views we have, although (as I describe below) the friendship between the two broke on the day of the speech, because of it. Powell had dropped his daughters off to be looked after by the Jones family, and when he came to collect them was told that he would no longer be welcome in their household: *1968: Rivers of Blood. The Real Source*, BBC Radio 4, 4 March 2008. Nearly a quarter of a century later Powell invited Clem Jones to join the celebrations for his eightieth birthday.
6. Bill Smithies and Peter Fiddick (eds.), *Enoch Powell on Immigration* (London: Sphere, 1969), 43 and 35. The historical antecedents of such a figure can be gleaned from the local study of Wolverhampton which comprises part of Jon Lawrence's *Speaking for the People: Party, Language and Popular Politics in England, 1867–1914* (Cambridge: Cambridge UP, 1998).
7. Robert Shepherd, *Enoch Powell: A Biography* (London: Pimlico, 1997), 360. I have used the Michael Oakley translation (London: Dent, 1957); the relevant passages occur in the opening section of book 6.
8. Stuart Hall, 'A Torpedo Aimed at the Boiler-Room of Consensus', *New Statesman*, 17 Apr. 1998.
9. Hanif Kureishi, 'London and Karachi', in Raphael Samuel (ed.), *Patriotism: The Making and Unmaking of British National Identity,* ii. *Minorities and Outsiders* (London: Routledge, 1989), 272.
10. See too the memories of Bill Morris in the *New Statesman*, 17 Apr. 1998, and in *1968: Rivers of Blood*; and of Paul Boateng in Shepherd, *Enoch Powell*, 355. Or as Mike Phillips said of Powell: 'His memory will probably have me looking over my shoulder in the streets of my own city, London, for the rest of my life', *Guardian*, 9 Feb. 1998.

11. Andrew Roth, *Enoch Powell: Tory Tribune* (London: Macdonald, 1970), 357. The source for this is the *Birmingham Post*, 22 Apr. 1968. The paper also reports Sidney Miller as uttering his own variant of knowing the native: 'The folk who live here know what it is like.'

12. Shepherd, *Enoch Powell,* 351.

13. Or at least: this is how Mrs Thatcher—Lady Thatcher—recounted the events later: Margaret Thatcher, *The Path to Power* (London: HarperCollins, 1995), 146. By the time she came to write her memoirs, she regarded Powell's sacking as 'a tragedy' (p. 147). Interviewed on the television programme, *Playing the Race Card* (BBC2, 31 Oct. 1999), she agreed that, while there did exist popular prejudices against coloured immigrants at the time, 'those prejudices were not there with Enoch Powell'. She concluded with the observation: 'I always think Enoch was an asset, an asset'.

14. Douglas Schoen, *Enoch Powell and the Powellites* (London: Macmillan, 1977), 38.

15. *The Times*, 22 Apr. 1968.

16. *Daily Telegraph*, 22 Apr. 1968

17. Powell's readiness to destroy in order to conserve marks him as an archetypal figure of the radical right. Or as Tom Nairn indicated, 'in Powellism the English conservative Establishment has begun to destroy itself', *The Break-Up of Britain: Crisis and Neo-Nationalism* (London: Verso, 1981), 288.

18. Benedict Anderson, *Imagined Communities: Reflections on the Origins and Spread of Nationalism* (London: Verso, 1984). On the affective communities created by letter-writing I've been much influenced by David Fitzpatrick, *Oceans of Consolation: Personal Accounts of Irish Migration to Australia* (Melbourne: Melbourne UP, 1995). Fitzpatrick maps what he calls 'a geography of affection', which is also in part of a map of memory. All the inhabitants of the old neighbourhood—Derry, near Ennistymon in Ireland—mentioned in letters home from a new emigrant to Australia are, literally, mapped onto the formal cartography of the village. In consequence one can *see* the lines of affection by which the home village is remembered. For the idea of 'homely' racisms: Phil Cohen, *Home Rules: Reflections on Racism and Nationalism in Everyday Life* (London: Centre for New Ethnicities Research, University of East London, 1993).

19. Smithies and Fiddick, *Powell on Immigration*, 40.

20. Ibid. 36.

21. Shepherd, *Enoch Powell*, 353.

22. Phillips and Phillips, *Windrush*, 251.

23. *The Writing on the Wall*, Channel 4, transmitted in four episodes from 3 Nov. to 15 Dec. 1985; the television series was accompanied by Philip Whitehead, *The Writing on the Wall* (London: Channel 4 Books, 1985). See too Shepherd, *Enoch Powell*, 354.

24. Shepherd, *Enoch Powell*, 353; Diana Spearman, 'Letters of Blood', *New Society*, 9 May 1968.

25. Heffer, *Like the Roman*, 466.

26. Katharine Thomson, curator of the Powell archive at Churchill College, Cambridge; email comm. with the author, 27 Oct. 2004 and 26 June 2005, quoting correspondence from Powell dated 29 Nov. 1976. The Stafford archivists are not able to indicate the extent of the correspondence to Powell in the aftermath of his Birmingham speech.

27. A selection of approximately 700 of these letters are housed in the archive at Churchill College. These were selected by Powell in support of his legal case against the *Sunday Times*, as a result of the newspaper, on 2 Feb. 1969, accusing him of 'spout[ing] the fantasies of racial purity'. The case was settled in Powell's favour in Apr. 1970. Given the purpose for which they were selected, it is unlikely that Powell would have chosen those which were most explicitly racist. Heffer, *Like the Roman*, 508. Assuming that there are 100,000 of the letters at Stafford, which could be a low estimate, at the rate at which I have read this selection, it would take a single researcher at least three years to read and document them all. I'll return to my reading of these letters in the final volume.

28. Spearman, 'Letters of Blood'.

29. *Daily Telegraph*, 25 Apr. 1968; Patrick Cosgrave, *The Lives of Enoch Powell* (London: Pan, 1990), 252.

30. *The Writing on the Wall*; and *Playing the Race Card*.

31. Spearman, 'Letters of Blood'.

32. Shepherd, *Enoch Powell*, 353.

33. Spearman, 'Letters of Blood'.

34. Heffer, *Like the Roman*, 464.

35. E. P. Thompson, 'The Crime of Anonymity', in Douglas Hay, Peter Linebaugh, John G. Rule, E. P. Thompson, and Cal Winslow, *Albion's Fatal Tree: Crime and Society in Eighteenth-Century England* (Harmondsworth: Penguin, 1977), 307–8. See too E. P. Thompson's 'Sir, Writing by Candlelight', in his *Writing by Candlelight* (London: Merlin, 1980). The best discussion of the connection between letters and race in the contemporary period is Stuart Hall, Chas Critcher, Tony Jefferson, John Clarke, and Brian Roberts, *Policing the Crisis: Mugging, the State and Law and Order* (London: Macmillan, 1978), ch. 5 See too, for evidence from Australia, Ghassan Hage, *White Nation: Fantasies of White Supremacy in a Multicultural Society* (Annandale, NSW: Pluto, 1998), 20.

36. For evidence from the West Midlands, see Paul Foot, *Race and Immigration in British Politics* (Harmondsworth: Penguin, 1965); his *The Rise of Enoch Powell: An Examination of Enoch Powell's Attitude to Immigration and Race* (Harmondsworth: Penguin, 1969); and Ian Grosvenor, *Assimilating Identities: Racism and Educational Policy in Post-1945 Britain* (London: Lawrence & Wishart, 1997), 111 and 114.

37. Stephen Brooke, 'The Conservative Party, Immigration and National Identity, 1948–1968', in Martin Francis and Ina Zweiniger-Bargielowska (eds.), *The Conservatives and British Society, 1880–1990* (Cardiff: University of Wales Press, 1996), 160.

38. Diana Spearman, 'Enoch Powell's Election Letters', in John Wood (ed.), *Powell and the 1970 Election* (Kingswoon, Surrey: Elliot Right Way Books, 1970), 32 and 34.

39. Spearman, 'Letters of Blood'.

40. See the illustrations in Shepherd, *Powell*

41. Virgil, *Aeneid* 7. Freud quotes this line at the end of *The Interpretation of Dreams*, which is the version I use here; Oakley has it—'If I cannot prevail upon heaven, I will stir up hell'.

42. Hall, *Policing the Crisis*, 132–4.

43. I rely here on the collaborative research of many of my final year students at Goldsmiths College at the end of the 1990s, from which I have learnt much.

44. Carolyn Steedman, 'State-Sponsored Autobiography', in Becky Conekin, Frank Mort, and Chris Waters (eds.), *Moments of Modernity: Reconstructing Britain, 1945–1964* (London: Rivers Oram Press, 1999), 42. In this chapter Steedman discusses the pedagogies of writing which developed in the school system in the early postwar period, and examines the expectation that everyone had a story to tell. One can safely assume that many of Powell's correspondents were of an age to have been schooled in this tradition. In Apr. 1968, in a great collective outpouring, they told their stories, as they had been taught to do.

45. Cosgrave, *Lives of Powell*, 253.

46. Schoen, *Powell and the Powellites*, p. xvii.

47. Richard Crossman, *Diaries*, iii (London: Hamish Hamilton and Jonathan Cape, 1977), 29; Gilmour in *Playing the Race Card*.

48. Heffer, *Like the Roman*, 555.

49. See Enoch Powell, 'Vote Tory' (16 June 1970), in Wood, *Powell and the 1970 Election*.

50. Schoen, *Powell and the Powellites*.

51. Shepherd, *Enoch Powell*, 354, gives the figure of 800; the *Daily Express*, 24 Apr. 1968, the figure of 2,300.

52. The previous week Constantine, having been elected rector of St Andrews University, had delivered an address on 'Race in the World', although it had been regarded as controversial to speak of race on such an occasion: Gerald Howarth, *Learie Constantine* (London: Allen & Unwin, 1977), 202ff. Howarth also supplies details of anonymous racist letters received by Constantine, ibid. 75.

53. See Fred Lindop, 'Racism and the Working-Class Strikes in Support of Enoch Powell in 1968', *Labour History Review*, 66/1 (2001).

54. *Daily Mail*, 24 Apr. 1968. *The Times*, 2 Sept. 1958, reported: 'In one street where some of the ugliest fighting has taken place your Correspondent found a group of men in a public house singing "Old Man River" and "Bye Bye Blackbird" and punctuating the songs with vicious anti-Negro slogans. The men said that their motto was "Keep Britain White", and they made all sorts of wild charges against their coloured neighbours. Incidentally, they were very bitter against the

Labour Party for "letting them in"'. I will return to the events of 1958 in the succeeding volumes.

55. *Daily Express*, 24 Apr. 1968.
56. Roth, *Tory Tribune*, 361.
57. *Daily Telegraph*, 24 Apr. 1968.
58. Shepherd, *Enoch Powell*, 355.
59. *Daily Telegraph*, 24 Apr. 1968.
60. Quoted in Martin Walker, *The National Front* (London: Fontana, 1977), 110.
61. *Daily Telegraph*, 25 Apr. 1968.
62. *The Writing on the Wall*; the clip comes for the second instalment.
63. The best synoptic account is Anthony Smith, *The Ethnic Revival* (Cambridge: Cambridge UP, 1981); and see Wener Sollors (ed.), *The Invention of Ethnicity* (New York: Oxford UP, 1989).

CHAPTER I

1. Bill Smithies and Peter Fiddick (eds.), *Enoch Powell on Immigration* (London: Sphere, 1969), 35–6.
2. Or when in 1945, in *Brief Encounter*'s Milford—in the heart of mythical middle England—Trevor Howard informs Celia Johnson that he must go 'a long way away', it transpires that his destination is Johannesburg.
3. Evelyn Shuckbrugh, *Descent to Suez: Foreign Office Diaries, 1951–1956* (New York: Norton, 1987), 18.
4. For incisive reflections on the 'kinetic' intimacies of movements across empires, Tony Ballantyne and Antoinette Burtons (eds.), *Bodies in Contact: Rethinking Colonial Encounters in World History* (Durham, NC: Duke UP, 2005); and their edited sequel, *Moving Subjects: Gender, Mobility, and Intimacy in an Age of Global Empire* (Champaign, Ill.: University of Illinois Press, 2009).
5. Salman Rushdie, *The Satanic Verses* (London: Viking, 1988), 343 and 129.
6. It would be instructive to discover when the term first appeared. Theodore Allen uses it to describe the aspirations of displaced settlers, moving south to North Carolina and closer to the perceived frontier, in the second half of the 18th cent.—though it's not clear where the term (in quotation marks) arises: *The Invention of the White Race*, ii. *The Origins of Racial Oppression in Anglo-America* (London: Verso, 1997), 257.
7. Paul Carter, *Living in a New Country: History, Travelling and Language* (London: Faber & Faber, 1992), 8; and Annie Coombes (ed.), *Rethinking Settler Colonialism: History and Memory in Australia, Canada, New Zealand and South Africa* (Manchester: Manchester UP, 2006).
8. *Hancock's Half Hour: The Emigrant*, BBC television, 18 Mar. 1960. The theme of emigration recurs in John Osborne's *The Entertainer*, first produced at the Royal Court on 10 Apr. 1957. Set at the time of Suez and resonating with images of national decline, Canada appears as an evocative counterpoint—21-inch TVs

and new Buicks. But Archie Rice, the principal character, can't contemplate a future without Bass on draught. John Osborne, *Plays,* ii (London: Faber & Faber, 1998). British complaints about Canadian beer had a long history: James Belich, *Replenishing the Earth: The Settler Revolution and the Rise of the Anglo-World, 1783–1939* (Oxford: Oxford UP, 2009), 283.

9. Stephen Constantine, 'Empire Migration and Imperial Harmony', in Stephen Constantine (ed.), *Emigrants and Empire: British Settlement in the Dominions between the Wars* (Manchester: Manchester UP, 1990), 1–2.

10. Between 1947 and 1948, a period which comprised the beginnings of the apartheid state, 40,000 Britons emigrated to South Africa. Edna Bradlow, 'Empire Settlement and South African Immigration Policy, 1910–1948', in Constantine, *Emigrants and Empire*, 193. The scheme had been initiated by the South African prime minister, Jan Smuts, in 1946, before he was ousted by the National Party in 1948.

11. Kathleen Paul, *Whitewashing Britain: Race and Citizenship in the Postwar Era* (Ithaca, NY: Cornell UP, 1997), 25.

12. Paul, *Whitewashing Britain*, 61.

13. A. James Hammerton and Alistair Thomson, *Ten Pound Poms: Australia's Invisible Migrants* (Manchester: Manchester UP, 2005), 31; between 1945 and 1982 some one and a half million emigrants left Britain and Ireland for Australia (ibid. 34).

14. *Observer*, 18 Mar. 2001. Five of the six most desirable countries were the USA, Australia, Canada, New Zealand, and Ireland. Second equal to Australia was Spain—a sign of the times.

15. The study by Hammerton and Thomson, *Ten Pound Poms*, offers the most detailed reconstruction.

16. Paul, *Whitewashing Britain*, ch. 2.

17. Cited ibid. 29.

18. Cited ibid. 40.

19. Cited ibid. 41.

20. As Kathleen Paul shows, unease began to register in the minds of British policy-makers when it became apparent that, as thousands of white Britons were leaving the metropole, thousands of black Britons were arriving from the Caribbean. In Mar. 1955 the UK High Commissioner in Canberra wondered whether Australia, in seeking British subjects, 'would like a number of the West Indians who at the moment seemed to wish to come to the UK'. Cited ibid. 57–8.

21. Cited in Gwenda Tavan, *The Long, Slow Death of White Australia* (Melbourne: Scribe Publications, 2005), 42.

22. Cyril Dunn, *Central African Witness* (London: Victor Gollancz, 1959), 207. Dunn goes on to say that, though these comments were rare, it was to be expected that the majority would soon become 'fervent believers in racial superiority'. And see E. R. Braithwaite, *'Honorary White': A Visit to South Africa* (London: New English Library, 1977), 1, for the racial motivations of English emigrants to South Africa in the early 1970s.

23. R. T. Appleyard, *British Emigration to Australia* (Canberra: Australian National University, 1964), 171. Thirty-five of his respondents mentioned race as a factor in their deciding to emigrate: significant, but not overwhelming. See too Peter Griffiths, *A Question of Colour?* (London: Leslie Frewin, 1966), 208.

24. When D. H. Lawrence journeyed to Australia in early 1922 he wrote back home: 'The east, the bit I've seen, seems silly. I don't like it one bit. I don't like the silly dark people or their swarming billions or their hideous little Buddha temples, like decked up pigsties – nor anything. I just don't like it. It's better to see it on the cinema: you get there the whole effect, without the effort and the sense of nausea … Europe is, I fancy, the most satisfactory place in the end … I break my heart over England when I am out here. Those natives are *back* of us – in the living sense *lower* than we are. But they are going to swarm over us and suffocate us. We are, have been for five centuries, the growing tip. Now we're going to fall. But you don't catch me going back on my whiteness and Englishness and myself. English in the teeth of all the world, even in the teeth of England—How England deliberately undermines England', quoted in Howard Booth, 'Lawrence in Doubt: A Theory of the "Other" and its Collapse', in Howard Booth and Nigel Rigby (eds.), *Modernism and Empire* (Manchester: Manchester UP, 2000), 210. Whilst in Sydney in 1938–9, Enoch Powell read all Lawrence's fiction.

25. Alistair Thomson, '"The Empire was a Bar of Soap": Life Stories and Race Identity among British Emigrants Travelling to Australia, 1945–71', in Hsu-Ming Teo and Richard White (eds.), *Cultural History in Australia* (Sydney: University of New South Wales Press, 2003), 205, 210, 207, 212, and 209; and for the larger story, Hammerton and Thomson, *Ten Pound Poms*. This offers an excellent account of the varying subjective reasons which prompted Britons to migrate to Australia. The authors conclude that race was 'not infrequently' a factor in persuading people to leave Britain, though not decisive, ibid. 72.

26. An important precursor can be found in the pages of the *Imperial Airways Gazette* during the spring and summer of 1936, which published the letters of 'Harry', flying from London to Johannesburg on Imperial Airways, to his mother back home. Travelling through east Africa the flight stopped at Moshi to refuel. Inside the station all 'was cool, clean and civilised and delightfully arranged, the refreshments on a snow white table cloth showed that some Englishwoman (or at least British) was doing her bit to make the tropics better and brighter'. The following day at Entebbe he 'found besides Englishmen, smart and shaven in shorts and helmets and Englishwomen, smart and cool in white frocks, a really good English breakfast'. Cited in Chandra B. Bhimull, 'Empire in the Air: Speed, Perception, and Airline Travel in the Atlantic World', unpublished University of Michigan Ph.D, 2007, 113.

27. Stephen Constantine, 'Empire Migration and Imperial Harmony', in his *Emigrants and Empire*, 2; and Stephen Constantine, 'Migrants and Settlers', in Judith M. Brown and Wm. Roger Louis (eds.), *The Oxford History of the British Empire,* iv. *The Twentieth Century* (Oxford: Oxford UP, 1999), 165.

28. James Belich, *Making Peoples: A History of the New Zealanders. From the Polynesian Settlement to the End of the Nineteenth Century* (London: Allen Lane, 1996), 278.

29. Anthony McFarlane, *The British in the Americas, 1480–1815* (London: Longman, 1992), 308.

30. Iain R. Smith, 'Milner, the "Kindergarten" and South Africa', in Andrea Bosco and Alex May (eds.), *The Round Table: The Empire/Commonwealth and British Foreign Policy* (London: Lothian Foundation, 1997), 47.

31. Eric Richards, *Britannia's Children: Emigration from England, Scotland, Wales and Ireland since 1660* (London: Hambledon, 2004), 175. And see Robert Bickers (ed.), *Settlers and Expatriates: Britons Over the Seas: Oxford History of the British Empire, Companion Volume* (Oxford: Oxford UP, 2010).

32. Belich, *Replenishing the Earth*, 153 and 165.

33. W. E. B. DuBois, 'The Souls of White Folk' in his *Darkwater: Voices from within the Veil* (New York: Harcourt, Brace & Howe, 1920; 1st publ. 1903), 29–30.

34. Belich, *Making Peoples*, 280–1.

35. Marjory Harper, 'Enticing the Emigrant: Professional Agents and the Promotion of Emigration from the British Isles, with Particular Reference to Scotland and Canada, c1880–1930', Second British World Conference, Cape Town, Jan. 2002.

36. Avril Maddrell, 'Empire, Emigration and School Geography: Changing Discourses of Imperial Citizenship, 1880–1925', *Journal of Historical Geography*, 22/4 (1996). As Andrew Thompson has emphasized, the volume of post back and forth between metropole and settler colony had always been high. In 1909 more than 8 million pounds of mail was sent from the UK to Canada, Australia, and New Zealand, with more than 2.5 million pounds received into the UK; added to this (for the period 1909–10) there were also nearly 500,000 parcels being sent out from the UK, and nearly 200,000 received: *The Empire Strikes Back? The Impact of Imperialism on Britain from the Mid-Nineteenth Century* (Harlow: Pearson, 2005), 59–60.

37. John Buchan, 'The New Doctrine of Empire', in his *Comments and Characters* (London: Nelson, 1940), 87; 1st publ. in the *Scottish Review*, 2 May 1907.

38. Cited in Andrew S. Thompson, *Imperial Britain: The Empire in British Politics, c1880–1932* (Harlow: Pearson Education, 2000), 33.

39. Though for an early critical interrogation of great importance, from a Colonial Office insider, see Lord Olivier, *White Capital and Coloured Labour* (London: Hogarth Press, 1929), which carries an explicit critique of the idea and practice of a 'white man's country', ibid. 21. Much of his argument draws from his own experience of having lived in the West Indies, mostly in Jamaica. A first version of the book appeared in a series edited by Ramsay MacDonald in 1906.

40. This phrase comes from 'Adamastor', a Christian critic of apartheid, in *White Man Boss* (London: Victor Gollancz, 1950), 38; significantly, it was employed to describe the Afrikaners, not the English.

41. Catherine Hall, *Civilising Subjects: Metropole and Colony in the English Imagination, 1830–1867* (Cambridge: Polity, 2002), 43. Kirsty Reid, *Gender, Crime and Empire:*

Convicts, Settlers and the State in Early Colonial Australia (Manchester: Manchester UP, 2007), provides a fine account. She emphasizes the process by which the perceived canker of the convict population—even after transportation was abolished—threatened to create an alien nation, and was replaced by initiatives to induce a more feminine, domestic social order from which a properly white nation could emerge. Edward Gibbon Wakefield had been shocked that 'the English' in Australia had made 'from their own loins a nation of Cyprians and Turks', cited ibid. 161.

42. Winston Churchill, *Churchill Speaks, 1897–1963: Collected Speeches in Peace and War,* ed. Robert Rhodes James (Leicester: Windward, 1981), 703ff. Churchill codified these sentiments in his own contribution to the historiography, *A History of the English-Speaking Peoples,* 4 vols. (London: Cassell, 1974; 1956–8). As late as 1953 he was writing to Eisenhower: 'Of course my Number One is Britain with her eighty million white English-Speaking people working with your one-hundred-and-forty million', *The Churchill-Eisenhower Correspondence, 1953–1955,* ed. Peter Boyle (Chapel Hill, NC: University of North Carolina Press, 1990), 34.

43. Mark McKenna, *This Country: A Reconciled Republic?* (Sydney: University of New South Wales Press, 2004), 77. And see Jane Connors, 'The 1954 Royal Tour of Australia', *Australian Historical Studies,* 100 (1993).

44. For the historiography, see Vincent Harlow, *The Founding of the Second British Empire, 1763–1793,* i. *Discovery and Revolution* (London: Longmans, Green, 1952), and ii. *New Continents and Changing Values* (London: Longman, 1964); and Peter Marshall, 'The First and Second Empires: A Question of Demarcation', *History,* 44 (1964). A comprehensive account can be gained from the first two vols. of *The Oxford History of the British Empire*: Nicholas Canny (ed.), *The Origins of Empire: British Overseas Enterprise to the Close of the Seventeenth Century*; and P. J. Marshall (ed.), *The Eighteenth Century* (Oxford: Oxford UP, 1998). In the latter volume see esp. P. J. Marshall, 'Britain without America: A Second Empire?' P. J. Marshall, *The Making and Unmaking of Empires: Britain, India, and America, c1750–1783* (Oxford: Oxford UP, 2005), the summation of a lifetime's scholarship, argues the distinction between the first and second empires conceals more than it reveals. He suggests that British policy in both India and in America sought greater integration in this period, though with radically different consequences in each case.

45. C. A. Bayly, *Imperial Meridian: The British Empire and the World, 1780–1830* (London: Longman, 1989), 6.

46. Ibid. 8 and 195.

47. Linda Colley, *Britons: Forging the Nation, 1707–1837* (New Haven: Yale UP, 1992). These two analyses—Colley's and Bayly's—are complementary. And significant too, for a much sharper idea of the domestic impact of empire, is Kathleen Wilson, *The Sense of the People: Politics, Culture and Imperialism in England, 1715–1785* (Cambridge: Cambridge UP, 1995).

48. Frederick Cooper, 'African Workers and Imperial Design', in Philip Morgan and Sean Hawkins (eds.), *Black Experience and the Empire: Oxford History of the*

British Empire. Companion Volume (Oxford: Oxford UP, 2004); and Bill Schwarz, '"Shivering in the Noonday Sun": The British World and the Dynamics of "Nativization"', in Kate Darian-Smith, Patricia Grimshaw, and Stuart Macintyre (eds.), *Britishness Abroad: Transnational Movements and Imperial Cultures* (Melbourne: Melbourne UP, 2007).

49. Thomas Holt, *The Problem of Freedom: Race, Labor, and Politics in Jamaica and Britain, 1832–1938* (Baltimore: Johns Hopkins UP, 1992), 236. The emphasis of Holt's argument falls on the connections between modern racism and *post*-slave societies. 'The development of racist thought was not a natural outgrowth or legacy of slavery; it arose in part from the seemingly nonracist (or racially neutral) premises of liberal ideology', p. xix.

50. In 1867 the creation of self-governing Canada prompted little excitement in ruling circles in Britain and didn't touch popular life at all. For Disraeli, it was a small matter, as it was for the Conservative prime minister, Lord Derby, and for the bulk of the House of Commons. The governor-general's instructions to the military exhibited a typically refined insouciance: 'the troops in Canada shall parade at a given hour (say eleven o'clock) on the 1st July, fire royal salute, hoist royal standard, and perform such other evolutions as may best express their joy at the accomplishment of Confederation'. Cited in Kenneth McNaught, *The Pelican History of Canada* (Harmondsworth: Penguin, 1976), 130–1. This suggests that self-governing Canada was created before enthusiasm for the white empire in the metropole reached its height. Disraeli's regard for imperial prowess was, in any case, unapologetically despotic and Orientalist. And Phillip Buckner, 'The Creation of the Dominion of Canada, 1867–1901', in Buckner (ed.), *Canada and the British Empire: Oxford History of the British Empire, Companion Volume* (Oxford: Oxford UP, 2008).

51. For divergent views on the concept of Greater Britain: Duncan Bell, *The Idea of Greater Britain: Empire and the Future of the World Order* (Princeton: Princeton UP, 2007); and Daniel Gorman, *Imperial Citizenship: Empire and the Question of Belonging* (Manchester: Manchester UP, 2006).

52. See Catherine Hall, 'Rethinking Imperial Histories: The Reform Act of 1867', *New Left Review*, 208 (1994); and Catherine Hall, Keith McClelland, and Jane Rendall, *Defining the Victorian Nation: Class, Race, Gender and the Reform Act of 1867* (Cambridge: Cambridge UP, 2000).

53. Bell, *Idea of Greater Britain*, 17; and Marilyn Lake and Henry Reynolds, *Drawing the Global Colour Line: White Men's Countries and the International Challenge of Racial Equality* (Cambridge: Cambridge UP, 2008), 7.

54. Belich, *Replenishing the Earth*, 157–8.

55. Thompson, *Imperial Britain*, offers the most complete picture; and his 'Imperial Propaganda during the South African War', in Greg Cuthbertson, Albert Grundlingh, and Mary-Lynn Suttie (eds.), *Writing a Wider War: Rethinking Gender, Race and Identity in the South African War, 1899–1902* (Athens, Ohio: Ohio UP, 2002). See as well Jan Rüger, 'Nation, Empire and Navy: Identity Politics in the United Kingdom, 1887–1914', *Past and Present*, 185 (2004).

56. Moisei Ostrogorski, *Democracy and the Organization of British Politics* (London: Macmillan, 1902), 551 and 440, and on the Primrose League: Janet Robb, *Primrose League, 1883–1906* (New York: AMS Press, 1942), and Beatrix Campbell, *Iron Ladies: Why do Women Vote Tory?* (London: Virago, 1987).

57. Belich, *Making Peoples*, 286–7.

58. See the letter sent by Ellen Moger to her parents from Adelaide on 28 Jan. 1849, in Lucy Frost (ed.), *No Place for a Nervous Lady: Voices from the Australian Bush* (Ringwood, Victoria: Penguin, 1985), 34–7.

59. This dependence on an individual's labour-power included domestic service. A good overview is Julia Bush, ' "The Right Sort of Woman": Female Emigrants and Emigration to the British Empire, 1890–1910', *Women's History Review*, 3/2 (1994).

60. Bernard Bailyn, with Barbara DeWolfe, *Voyagers to the West: Emigration from Britain to America on the Eve of the Revolution* (London: I. B. Tauris, 1987), 5. This impressive book carries many insights which help us understand the later period, as does Bernard Bailyn and Philip Morgan (eds.), *Strangers within the Realm: The Cultural Margins of the First British Empire* (Chapel Hill, NC: University of North Carolina Press, 1991).

61. For a revealing analysis of the interplay between colonial order and disorder, Joy Damousi, *Depraved and Disorderly: Female Convicts, Sexuality and Gender in Colonial Australia* (Cambridge: Cambridge UP, 1997).

62. Adele Perry, *On the Edge of Empire: Gender, Race and the Making of British Columbia, 1849–1871* (Toronto: University of Toronto Press, 2001); and Patricia E. Roy, *White Man's Province: British Columbia. Politicians and Chinese and Japanese Immigrants, 1858–1914* (Vancouver: University of British Columbia Press, 1989).

63. Cited in Perry, *On the Edge of Empire*, 155.

64. Cited ibid. 175; a view—'savages in our midst'—repeated a month later: Adele Perry, 'Whose World was British? Rethinking the "British World" from an Edge of Empire', in Darian-Smith *et al.*, *Britishness Abroad*, 145. This chapter puts further emphasis on the transnational composition of the settlers in British Columbia and on the degree to which those who governed the territory came from other parts of the empire than Britain, calling into question the parameters of a 'British world'.

65. A powerful plea for the feminizing of empire in these terms can be found in Ethel Colquhoun, *The Vocation of Woman* (London: Macmillan, 1913), particularly ch. 12, 'Women and the Empire'.

66. 'The settler makes history and is conscious of making it': Frantz Fanon, *The Wretched of the Earth* (Harmondsworth: Penguin, 1971; 1961), 40.

67. Sir Charles Dilke, *Greater Britain: A Record of Travel in English-Speaking Countries during 1866 and 1867* (London: Macmillan, 1868); Sir John Seeley, *The Expansion of England: Two Courses of Lectures* (London: Macmillan, 1883); and J. A. Froude, *Oceana, or England and her Colonies* (London: Longmans Green, 1886). See too, Sir Charles Dilke, *Problems of Greater Britain* (London: Macmillan, 1890).

68. One of the most original accounts is V. G. Kiernan, *The Lords of Human Kind: European Attitudes to the Outside World in the Imperial Age* (Harmondsworth; Penguin, 1972). It is instructive, for my purposes here, that the 1st edn. of this was published in 1969. The period between the publication of the 1st hardback edn. and its paperback issue coincided with the height of the Powellite moment. To point out, more than thirty years on, some of the peculiarities of the book does nothing to diminish its power. The absence of Lord Milner e.g. is very strange. For a sharply focused reading of the emergence of the figure of the Aryan, looking to India, New Zealand, and Britain, which usefully concentrates on the web of connections between these three imperial sites, see Tony Ballantyne, *Orientalism and Race: Aryianism in the British Empire* (Houndmills: Palgrave, 2002); and for the wider ideological background, Robert J. C. Young, *The Idea of English Ethnicity* (Oxford: Blackwell, 2008).

69. Clarendon e.g. in the 17th cent., declared his hope that Massachusetts would be ruled as if it were a corporation 'of Kent or Yorkshire', cited in Robert Bliss, *Revolution and Empire: English Politics and American Colonies in the Seventeenth Century* (Manchester: Manchester UP, 1990), 132. And as I indicate below, Froude consciously saw himself continuing themes first adumbrated by James Harrington in the 17th cent.

70. Herbert Paul, *The Life of Froude* (London: Pitman, 1905), 364.

71. Dilke, *Greater Britain*, Preface.

72. The classic investigation remains Christopher Hill, 'The Norman Yoke', in John Saville (ed.), *Democracy and the Labour Movement: Essays for Donna Torr* (London: Lawrence & Wishart, 1954).

73. Cited in David Nicolls, *The Lost Prime Minister: A Life of Sir Charles Dilke* (London: Hambledon Press, 1995), 15.

74. Dilke, *Greater Britain*, 399.

75. Ibid. 573.

76. Ibid. 284.

77. Ibid. 544.

78. Ibid. 281.

79. Ibid. 88 and 572.

80. Ibid. 223.

81. Ibid. 88.

82. Ibid. 357.

83. Ibid. 85.

84. He believed that whites on the frontier were 'provoked' by native attacks; what he couldn't countenance was indiscriminate punishment, in which innocent natives became the object of settler retribution, ibid. 357. Twice on his travels he found himself in danger—travelling by mail-coach from Fort Leavenworth to Salt Lake City (for which he paid the supremely aristocratic sum of $500), and again in New Zealand from Maori attack. For a good contextualization of the latter, James Belich, *The New Zealand Wars and the Victorian Interpretation of Racial Conflict* (Auckland: Auckland UP, 1986).

85. Dilke, *Greater Britain*, 281.
86. See Patrick Brantlinger, *Dark Vanishings: Discourse on the Extinction of Primitive Races, 1800–1930* (Ithaca, NY: Cornell UP, 2002). And Renato Rosaldo's interpretation of a mourning organized by the 'longing for what they themselves have destroyed': 'Imperialist Nostalgia', in his *Culture and Truth: The Remaking of Social Analysis* (London: Routledge, 1993), 87.
87. Dilke, *Greater Britain*, 224.
88. Ibid. 225.
89. Ibid. 223.
90. Roy Jenkins, *Sir Charles Dilke: A Victorian Tragedy* (London: Fontana, 1968), 45. His other Tory rival was C. F. Freake, who had built the Cromwell Road.
91. Jenkins, *Dilke*, 42–3.
92. Deborah Wormell, *Sir John Seeley and the Uses of History* (Cambridge: Cambridge UP, 1980); G. A. Reiss, *Sir John Seeley: A Study of a Historian* (Wolfboro, NH: Longwood, 1987; 1st publ. 1912); and Peter Burroughs, 'J. R. Seeley and British Imperial History', *Journal of Imperial and Commonwealth History*, 1/2 (1973). Between 1882 and 1922 the British repeated sixty-six times their promise to withdraw from Egypt: A. J. P. Taylor, *The Struggle for Mastery in Europe* (Oxford: Oxford UP, 1987), 289.
93. Froude, *Oceana*, 337.
94. Ibid. 2.
95. Ibid. 2–3.
96. Ibid. 4–5.
97. Ibid. 11.
98. Ibid. 13–14 and 5.
99. Ibid.; emphasis mine.
100. Ibid. 3.
101. 'The first thing that struck me—and the impression remained during all my stay in Australia—was the pure English that was spoken there. They do not raise their voice at the end of a sentence, as the Americans do, as if with a challenge to differ from them. They drop it courteously like ourselves. No provincialism has yet developed itself.' Ibid. 73. Now the exact reverse is the case, and Australian speech-patterns appear unnoticed in the conversations of native Britons whose first-hand knowledge of Australia may be non-existent, but who came to know Australia as children through the soaps.
102. Ibid. 15.
103. There is a revealing moment in Froude's *The English in the West Indies* when his reverie is interrupted by the quotidian. Describing his unsatisfactory experiences of Trinidad he notes in an aside: 'The commonplace intrudes upon the imaginative'. *The English in the West Indies: Or the Bow of Ulysses* (London: Longmans, Green, 1888), 67.
104. Froude, *Oceana*, 7–8.
105. Important is an unpublished paper by Phil Cohen, 'Antisemitism and the Internal Orient: The Strange Case of the Jewish East End'. See too Steven

Marcus's memorable 'Reading the Illegible', in H. J. Dyos and Michael Wolff (eds.), *The Victorian City: Images and Realities,* ii. *Shapes on the Ground/A Change of Accent* (London: Routledge & Kegan Paul, 1978); and more explicitly on the colonial determinations, John Marriott, 'The Meaning of Dirt', in his *The Other Empire: Metropolis, India and Progress in the Colonial Imagination* (Manchester: Manchester UP, 2003), 161–6.

106. Frederick Jackson Turner, *The Frontier in American History* (New York: Henry Holt, 1953); Dee Brown, *Bury My Heart at Wounded Knee: An Indian History of the American West* (St Albans: Paladin, 1978); and Alistair Hennessy, *The Frontier in Latin American History* (London: Edward Arnold, 1978). For the 'honorary' British colonies, E. J. Hobsbawm, *Industry and Empire* (Harmondsworth: Penguin, 1974), 148; a discussion of settler societies in the southern hemisphere, which includes Uruguay, Argentina, and Chile, can be found in Donald Denoon, *Settler Capitalism: The Dynamics of Dependent Development in the Southern Hemisphere* (Oxford: Clarendon Press, 1983). Of course, the frontier never entirely disappears from the metropolitan imagination. Not only is it perpetually relocated, but it is also periodically rediscovered: even as we left the 20th cent., new peoples were 'discovered'.

107. Seeley, *Expansion of England,* 10–11 and 184.

108. Ibid. 121, 105, 103, and 109.

109. Ibid. 295 and 235.

110. Ibid. 46.

111. Ibid. 43.

112. For Seeley's difficulties with India, ibid. 184, 203, and 304; and for the later rediscovery of this idea, Enoch Powell, 'Myth and Reality', in his *Freedom and Reality* (London: Batsford, 1969).

113. Seeley, *Expansion of England,* 80–1.

114. Ibid. 175: for Seeley's discussion of historiography, Bill Schwarz, 'The Expansion and Contraction of England', in Schwarz (ed.), *The Expansion of England: Race, Ethnicity and Cultural History* (London: Routledge, 1996). Conrad described Europe's early conquistadors as 'conquering a bit of truth here and a bit of truth there', a wonderful insight which anticipates much contemporary post-colonial enquiry: 'Geography and Some Explorers', in his *Last Essays* (London: Dent, 1926), 19. Wilson Harris, in similar mode, has identified a form he calls 'conquistadorial realism', *The Radical Imagination: Lectures and Talks* (Liege: University of Liege Press, 1992), 14.

115. Seeley, *Expansion of England,* 174.

116. Ibid. 69.

117. Belich, *Making Peoples,* 332. David Malouf holds to this aspect of the colonial past as a resource for the Australian future. Talking of early convicts transported, he says: 'And there must have been some among them, like Simeon Lord and Mary Reibey or Esther Abrahams, for whom Botany Bay was not just the underside of the world but the realisation of that dream of radical

English thinkers in the seventeenth century, the world turned upside down', *A Spirit of Play: The Making of Australian Consciousness* (Sydney: ABC Books, 1998), 17.

118. Thomas Carlyle, 'Occasional Discourse on the Negro Question', *Fraser's Magazine*, 40 (Dec. 1849). I follow here Catherine Hall's 'Competing Masculinities: Thomas Carlyle, John Stuart Mill and the Case of Governor Eyre', in her *White, Male and Middle Class: Explorations in Feminism and History* (Cambridge: Polity, 1992). And see too her *Civilising Subjects*. When I interviewed Enoch Powell in 1988 he told me that he had never heard of this essay: interview with the author, 26 Apr. 1988.

119. Carlyle, 'Occasional Discourse', 675; and J. A. Froude, *Thomas Carlyle: A History of his Life in London, 1834–1881*, ii (London: Longmans, Green, 1884), 23. In the weeks before he had drafted the article, Carlyle had spent the summer visiting Ireland. He was not pleased by what he'd witnessed, and by the lack of what he described as an 'Anglo-Saxon' influence. As he wrote in his journal: 'Ugly spectacle, sad health, sad humour, a thing unjoyful to look back on'. The vision of the West Indies succumbing to the fate of a 'Black Ireland' was one which ran through his 'Occasional Discourse': Froude, *Carlyle*, 21; Carlyle, 'Occasional Discourse', 672.

120. Froude, *Carlyle*, 26. Froude's reading of this early radical spirit derived from Carlyle's general iconoclasm, and on his determination that all men—black labourer or white aristocrat—must, as a matter of their manful self-fulfilment, work. The Cromwellian theme and the immovable respect for the 'Saxon-British' are both present in the 'Occasional Discourse', 674. They lead (in Carlyle's mind) directly to the theme of 'British blood' (p. 676).

121. John Stuart Mill, 'The Negro Question', *Fraser's Magazine*, 41 (Jan. 1850).

122. Hall, *White, Male and Middle Class*, 265.

123. A perceptive analysis of the press reporting can be found in H. L. Malchow, *Gothic Images of Race in Nineteenth-Century Britain* (Stanford, Calif.: Stanford UP, 1996), 211. When British supporters organized a dinner in honour of Eyre on his arrival from Kingston in Aug. 1866, demonstrators outside carried placards declaring it to be 'The Feast of Blood', *The Times*, 23 Aug. 1866.

124. These included Charles Kingsley, Charles Dickens, John Ruskin, and Alfred Lord Tennyson. Hall, *White, Male and Middle Class*, reconstructs the episode with the most insight, while for Kingsley see her 'Men and their Histories: Civilising Subjects', *History Workshop Journal*, 52 (2001). And very importantly, on the complexities of Eyre's prior views on race, Hall's 'Imperial Man: Edward Eyre in Australasia and the West Indies, 1833–66', in Schwarz, *Expansion of England*. Ruskin's interventions on these matters show how deeply racial categories were entering aesthetic theory. His inaugural lecture at Oxford as Slade Professor in 1870 e.g. takes time to reflect on the quality of English blood, and to put before his audience the choice for England either to 'perish' or to 'found colonies as fast and as far as she is able', *Lectures on Art* (London:

George Allen, 1910), 35 and 37; and see too Paul Gilroy, 'Art of Darkness: Black Art and the Problems of Belonging to England', *Third Text,* 10 (1990). Ruskin's influence on Cecil Rhodes was to be overwhelming. Dickens's final novel, *The Mysteries of Edwin Drood,* 1st publ. in instalments in 1870, reflects the impact of the 1857 Sepoy Rebellion and—especially—the Eyre events on the domestic imagination: here too one can find the figure of 'white men' in its new emergent meanings (Harmondsworth: Penguin, 1993, 102). See too K. J. Fielding, 'Edwin Drood and Governor Eyre' *The Listener,* 25 Dec. 1952.

125. Hall, *White, Male and Middle Class,* 275.

126. John Stuart Mill, *Autobiography* (Oxford: Oxford UP, 1971), 158 and 159–60.

127. Ibid. 176–7. His step-daughter, Helen Taylor, added: 'At one time I reckoned that threats of Assassination where [sic] received at least once a week: and I remarked that threatening letters were always especially numerous by Tuesday morning's post. I inferred that they were meditated during the Sunday's leisure and posted on the Mondays…It may be observed…that in England Sunday is generally used for all kinds of letter-writing, innocent as well as guilty', 177. Just as—we might recall—in this same period, in the weeks preceding his inauguration as president, Lincoln received threatening letters and threats of assassination, all encoded in terms of race.

128. Dilke, *Greater Britain,* 16.

129. Catherine Hall, responding to a roundtable discussion of *Civilising Subjects* with Simon Gikandi, Thomas Holt, and Philippa Levine, *Journal of British Studies,* 42/4 (2003), 508.

130. Peter Marsh, *Joseph Chamberlain: Entrepreneur in Politics* (New Haven: Yale UP, 1994), 176.

131. Cited ibid.

132. Cited ibid. 110.

133. Cited ibid. 191.

134. ibid. 286.

135. Cited ibid. 294.

136. ibid.

137. ibid. 306. For an insightful interpretation of the obverse of 'Saxondom' in the realm of high politics at this same time, see Antoinette Burton, 'Tongues Untied: Lord Salisbury's "Black Man" and the Boundaries of Imperial Democracy', *Comparative Studies in Society and History,* 42/3 (2000).

138. At the same time, he was explicit in his views on the unfitness of blacks to rule in the West Indies: Marsh, *Chamberlain,* 411.

139. This is how Powell himself understood Chamberlain's intervention of the time: interview with the author.

140. Hall, *Civilising Subjects,* 273.

141. Charles W. Boyd (ed.), *Mr Chamberlain's Speeches,* ii. (London: Constable, 1914), 125–6, 135, 128, 130, and 131.

142. Ibid. 128.

143. Ibid.

144. See Saul Dubow, 'Colonial Nationalism, the Milner Kindergarten and the Rise of "South Africanism", 1902–1910', *History Workshop Journal*, 43 (1997). And for a comprehensive view of the Round Table, Bosco and May, *The Round Table*, and John Kendle, *The Round Table Movement and Imperial Union* (Toronto: University of Toronto Press, 1975). For those who participated in the South African Kindergarten, memories of the experience remained unassailable. Robert Brand had been one of these young men. His grandson, the author James Fox, recalls how as a boy in the 1950s the names were part of his own domestic habitat, 'familiar from repetition, like unknown relations or dead prime ministers . . . Some of the names were more memorable because my grandfather would often have to shout them—still addressing some of his closest surviving colleagues by their surnames after fifty years—into the telephone, trying to make contact, the lines from the Byfield exchange often bad, and the party at the other end sometimes deaf', *The Langhorne Sisters* (London: Granta, 1999), 175.

145. Cited in John Marlowe, *Milner: Apostle of Empire* (London: Hamish Hamilton, 1976), 23.

146. Milner, *Nation and Empire*, 153; he used these terms in a speech in East Wolverhampton on 17 Dec. 1906, invited to the constituency by the prospective Unionist candidate, Leo Amery. Milner's volume is dedicated to his 'old friend' Charles W. Boyd who first prevailed upon Milner to publish his speeches, and who appears to have done the bulk of the labour in preparing them for publication; he also edited Joseph Chamberlain's speeches.

147. J. O. Stubbs, 'Lord Milner and Patriotic Labour, 1914–1918', *English Historical Review*, 87 (1972).

148. Milner, *Nation and Empire*, 4–5, and cited in Marlowe, *Milner*, 39.

149. Cited in Marlowe, *Milner*, 152.

150. Milner, *Nation and Empire*, 85 and 90–1.

151. There is the possibility that this was drafted by John Buchan: Peter Henshaw, 'John Buchan from the "Borders" to the "Berg": Nature, Empire and White South African Identity, 1901–1910', *African Studies*, 62/1 (2003), 19 and 29.

152. Cecil Headlam (ed.), *The Milner Papers*, ii. *South Africa, 1899–1905* (London: Cassell, 1933), 545.

153. Milner, *Nation and Empire*, 19, for his speech of 20 Apr. 1900; and see too his Johannesburg speech of 8 Jan. 1902 in Headlam, *Milner Papers*, ii. 319–22; and the report of this speech in the *Cape Argus*, 25 Apr. 1902, reproduced in M. J. Farrelly, *The Settlement After the War in South Africa* (London: Macmillan, 1900), 290–3.

154. Milner, *Nation and Empire*, pp. xxxv and xxxiii.

155. Ibid. 290.

156. Ibid. 489 and 491.

157. Milner speech of 18 May 1903 (the 'Watchtower speech'), in Headlam, *Milner Papers*, ii. 466–70.

158. See *The Works of Rudyard Kipling* (Ware, Herts: Wordsworth Poetry Library, 1994): this is the famous opening section of the 1899 poem 'The White Man's Burden'; see too in the same year, 'A Song of the White Men'.

159. For a contemporaneous critique of the racial assumptions of such thinking, referring specifically to Joseph Chamberlain and to the renowned Africanist, Sir Harry Johnston, see the chapter 'The British Empire and Coloured Labour', in Theophilus E. Samuel Scholes, *Glimpses of the Ages, or the 'Superior' and 'Inferior' Races, So-Called, Discussed in the Light of Science and History* (Haymarket (London): John Long, 1905). Scholes was a Jamaican who had studied medicine in London and Edinburgh and who settled in London.

160. Milner, *Nation and Empire*, pp. xxxv–xxxvi.

161. 'Milner's Credo', *The Times*, 27 July 1925. Milner's sense of his generation 'holding the fort' for empire in unpropitious times was constant: it appeared in his 'Introduction' to *Nation and Empire* in 1913, p. xxviii.

162. Milner, *Nation and Empire*, p. xxxiii.

163. Ibid. 141–2. Two years later, in one of his first speeches in Canada, he used almost exactly the same words: 'The man of white race who is born a British subject can find a home in every portion of the world where he can live under his own flag...', ibid. 314. For more in this vein, from a later period, Viscount Milner, *The British Commonwealth* (London: Constable, 1919).

164. Stanley Baldwin, 'England', in *On England* (Harmondsworth: Penguin, 1938; 1926), 17; see Bill Schwarz, 'The Language of Constitutionalism: Baldwinite Conservatism', in *Formations of Nation and People* (London: Routledge & Kegan Paul, 1984).

165. On populism I follow Ernesto Laclau, *Politics and Ideology in Marxist Theory: Capitalism, Fascism, Populism* (London: New Left Books, 1977).

166. 'The Government of Subject Races', *Edinburgh Review* (Jan. 1908). This was published the same year as Cromer's vindication of his period of rule of Egypt, *Modern Egypt*, 2 vols. (London: Macmillan, 1908). See Robert Tigner, 'Lord Cromer: Practitioner and Philosopher of Imperialism', *Journal of British Studies*, 2/2 (1963). Egypt proved critical in the evolution of proconsular thought: from Alfred Milner, *England in Egypt* (London: Edward Arnold, 1892), through Cromer, to Lord Lloyd, *Egypt since Cromer*, 2 vols. (London: Macmillan, 1933 and 1934). Informative commentaries can be found in John Marlowe, *Cromer in Egypt* (London: Elek Books, 1979); John Charmley, *Lord Lloyd and the Decline of the British Empire* (London: Weidenfeld & Nicolson, 1987); and a provocative reconceptualization in Timothy Mitchell, *Colonising Egypt* (Cambridge: Cambridge UP, 1988). M. E. Chamberlain argues that it was Joseph Chamberlain's visit to Egypt in 1889 which converted him to imperialism: 'Lord Cromer's *Ancient and Modern Imperialism*: A Proconsular View of Empire', *Journal of British Studies*, 12/1 (1972), 65, while according to John Buchan 'In twenty years one Englishman has done what twenty centuries have failed to do', in his 'Lord Cromer and Egypt' (11 Apr. 1907), repr. in Buchan, *Comments and Characters* (London: Nelson, 1940), 113.

167. In 1910 Cromer was invited, as incoming president, to deliver an address to the Classical Association. He took the task seriously and, continuing the themes of his contribution to the *Edinburgh Review*, he questioned friends and scholars (including John Buchan) about the origins of race prejudice and the effects of racial intermarriage. Those consulted, as reported by Chamberlain in 'Lord Cromer's *Ancient and Modern Imperialism*', concurred that race prejudice was a product of specifically modern times, and was strongest amongst the peoples of northern Europe. What is most striking, however, is that the discussion was entirely dispassionate, as if the curious phenomenon of racial antipathy were completely unconnected to the 'government of subject races': Lord Cromer, *Ancient and Modern Imperialism* (London: John Murray, 1910).

168. The phrase comes from Leo Amery in a letter of 26 Feb. 1904 to Milner, outlining the goals of the Compatriots' Club. Quoted in A. M. Gollin, *Proconsul in British Politics: A Study of Lord Milner in Opposition and Power* (London: Anthony Blond, 1960), 105.

169. See David Dilks, *Curzon in India*, i. *Achievement*, ii. *Frustration* (London: Hart-Davis, 1969 and 1970). Outside Curzon's old home in Carlton House Terrace, hidden deep in the foliage of the gardens, stands a commemorative bust of appropriately proconsular severity.

170. Roger Owen, *Lord Cromer: Victorian Imperialist, Edwardian Proconsul* (Oxford: Oxford UP, 2004), 399.

171. Curzon and Milner both took office in the Lloyd George coalition at the end of 1916; Cromer died in Jan. 1917.

172. Cited in Golin, *Proconsul in British Politics*, 119.

173. Cited ibid. 157.

174. Bill Schwarz, 'Conservatism and "Caesarism", 1903–1922', in Mary Langan and Bill Schwarz (eds.), *Crises in the British State, 1880–1930* (London: Hutchinson, 1985); Frans Coetzee, *For Party or Country? Nationalism and the Dilemma of Popular Conservatism in Edwardian England* (New York: Oxford UP, 1990); and Alan Sykes, 'The Radical Right and the Crisis of Conservatism Before the First World War', *Historical Journal*, 26/3 (1983).

175. James Loughlin, *Ulster Unionism and British National Identity since 1885* (London: Pinter, 1995). Later in the century this same centrifugal dynamic operated not only in the colony but in the metropole too. This I take to be one of the defining arguments of Tom Nairn's *The Break-Up of Britain* (London: Verso, 1981), in which Nairn examined how—from the time of the end of empire—the various nationalities of the United Kingdom, including the English qua English, voiced their disconnection from the central state. His chapter on Enoch Powell suggests that Powellism can be understood as a movement in which those at the very centre of the United Kingdom—the English—expressed their antagonism to the state *as ethnic English men and women*, in a classic manifestation of ethnic populism 'at home'. And many did so having witnessed, as they perceived it, white loyalists overseas, in Rhodesia and elsewhere, having been sold out by the politicians at home.

176. As Donal Lowry points out, many senior figures involved in the prosecution of the war in South Africa went on to support opposition to Home Rule (Roberts, Jameson, French, Milner, as well as Kipling), while others took their lessons in counter-insurgency to Ireland and to Palestine: ' "The World's No Bigger than a Kraal": The South African War and International Opinion in the First Age of "Globalization"', in David Omissi and Andrew Thompson (eds.), *The Impact of the South African War* (Basingstoke: Palgrave, 2002), 279–80.

177. David Gilmour, *The Long Recessional: The Imperial Life of Rudyard Kipling* (New York; Farrar, Strauss & Giroux, 2002), 246. This is as frightful as his study of Curzon, which I come to later. Gilmour closes by endorsing Sir Lewis Namier's contention that it was Kipling's inspiration which saved the nation in 1940, specifying his influence on Winston Churchill, Leo Amery, and—of all people—Lord Lloyd. These 'Kipling imperialists', according to Gilmour, 'were unable to preserve the Empire for long' but 'they kept their country alive' (p. 311). But what was this England that Churchill, Amery, and Lloyd had saved? And who would wish to live there?

178. Cited ibid. 245.

179. Cited ibid. 246–7.

CHAPTER 2

1. Henry Reynolds, *Why Weren't We Told? A Personal Search for the Truth about our History* (Ringwood, Victoria: Viking, 1999), 39–40.

2. For Seeley's influence on Baldwin (and Froude's too), Philip Williamson, *Stanley Baldwin. Conservative Leadership and National Values* (Cambridge: Cambridge UP, 1999), 117–20, and more generally: Roba Soffer, *Discipline and Power: The University, History and the Making of an English Elite* (Stanford, Calif.: Stanford UP, 1994).

3. Cited in Williamson, *Baldwin*, 259.

4. Cited in Keith Middlemas and John Barnes, *Baldwin: A Biography* (London: Weidenfeld & Nicolson, 1969), 377.

5. Roy Campbell, *Light on a Dark Horse* (Harmondsworth: Penguin, 1971; 1951), 161.

6. *The Times*, 23 Aug. 1866.

7. Frantz Fanon, *Black Skin, White Masks* (London: Paladin, 1972; 1952), 130; and see his *The Wretched of the Earth* (Harmondsworth: Penguin, 1971; 1961), 31.

8. Just as Benedict Anderson suggests that it was Creole communities overseas which developed conceptions of nation-ness before many kindred communities within Europe, so one might suggest by analogy that the practice of imagining the nation as white occurred first in the colonies, and only later seeped back to the metropole: *Imagined Communities: Reflections on the Origin and Spread of Nationalism* (London: Verso, 1983), ch. 4.

9. Cited in Robert Huttenback, *Racism and Empire: White Settlers and Coloured Immigrants in the British Self-Governing Colonies, 1830–1910* (Ithaca, NY: Cornell UP, 1976), 22. Gandhi, for one, was appalled by Chamberlain's speech, seeing it only as an expression of bad faith: Marilyn Lake and Henry Reynolds, *Drawing the Global Colour Line: White Men's Countries and the International Challenge of Racial Equality* (Cambridge: Cambridge UP, 2008), 132.

10. Lord Milner, *The Nation and the Empire* (London: Constable, 1913), 296–7.

11. For an important discussion of Reynolds as historian, Bain Attwood and Tom Griffiths (eds.), *Frontier, Race, Nation: Henry Reynolds and Australian History* (Melbourne: Australian Scholarly Publishing, 2009).

12. See Lynette Russell (ed.), *Colonial Frontiers: Indigenous–European Encounters in Settler Societies* (Manchester: Manchester UP, 2001), esp. Luke Godwin, 'The Fluid Frontier: Central Queensland, 1845–63'.

13. Sir Alfred Lyall, 'Frontiers Ancient and Modern', *Edinburgh Review* (July 1909); republ. in his *Studies in Literature and History* (London: John Murray, 1915), 291.

14. Lord Curzon, *Frontiers: The Romanes Lecture* (Oxford: Clarendon Press, 1907), 5 and 56–8.

15. Marilyn Lake, 'Australian Frontier Feminism and the Marauding White Man', in Clare Midgley (ed.), *Gender and Imperialism* (Manchester: Manchester UP, 1998).

16. Elspeth Huxley, *White Man's Country: Lord Delamere and the Making of Kenya*, i. *1870–1914* (London: Chatto & Windus, 1980; 1935), 95 and 149–50.

17. Adele Perry, *On the Edge of Empire: Gender, Race and the Making of British Columbia, 1849–1871* (Toronto: University of Toronto Press, 2001), ch. 1.

18. Catherine Hall, 'Imperial Man: Edward Eyre in Australasia and the West Indies, 1833–1866', in Bill Schwarz (ed.), *The Expansion of England: Race, Ethnicity and Cultural History* (London: Routledge, 1996), 138.

19. Mary Procida, *Married to the Empire: Gender, Politics and Imperialism in India, 1883–1947* (Manchester: Manchester UP, 2002), 6; and see too Durba Ghosh, *Sex and the Family in Colonial India: The Making of Empire* (Cambridge: Cambridge UP, 2006).

20. See the various accounts collected in Lucy Frost (ed.), *No Place for a Nervous Lady: Voices from the Australian Bush* (Ringwood, Victoria: Penguin, 1985).

21. Sir Robert Baden-Powell, *Girl Guiding* (London: C. Arthur Pearson, 1918), 26 and 59.

22. Adele Perry, 'Whose World was British? Rethinking the "British World" from an Edge of Empire', in Kate Darian-Smith, Patricia Grimshaw, and Stuart Macintyre (eds.), *Britishness Abroad: Transnational Movements and Imperial Cultures* (Melbourne: Melbourne UP, 2007), 146–8.

23. Cited in Henry Reynolds, *Frontier: Aborigines, Settlers and Land* (St Leonards, NSW: Allen & Unwin, 1996), 11.

24. Cited ibid. 10.

25. Cited ibid. 7.

26. Mark McKenna, *Looking for Blackfellas' Point: An Australian History of Place* (Sydney: University of New South Wales Press, 2002), ch. 7; and Ann Curthoys, 'Expulsion, Exodus and Exile: White Australian Historical Mythology', *Journal of Australian Studies*, 61 (1999), 3.

27. Memorandum, 9 Apr. 1841; cited in Henry Reynolds, *An Indelible Stain? The Question of Genocide in Australia's History* (Ringwood, Victoria: Viking, 2001), 90.

28. An instructive fictional account can be found in Kate Grenville, *The Secret River* (Edinburgh: Canongate, 2006), which discusses the 'forgetting' of the violence which made white Australia. It has provoked much discussion in Australian public life.

29. J. A. Froude, *Oceana, or England and her Colonies* (London: Longmans, Green, 1886), 4–5.

30. Cited in Reynolds, *Frontier*, 4 and 52.

31. Henry Reynolds, *The Other Side of the Frontier* (Ringwood, Victoria: Penguin, 1982), 109.

32. Reynolds, *Frontier*, 30.

33. Cited ibid, 7.

34. Cited ibid. 49.

35. Reynolds, *Indelible Stain?*, 92.

36. Cited in Reynolds, *Frontier*, 51–2.

37. Ibid. 4.

38. Governor Arthur of Tasmania e.g. in the late 1820s: Reynolds, *Indelible Stain?*, 64.

39. Through his reading of the press across the Cape, New South Wales, and New Zealand, Alan Lester argues that from the mid-1830s to the 1840s settler pressure produced an effective counter-offensive against the humanitarian cause, creating a new ideological dominance, winning over *The Times* in London, and defining a version of Britishness which closely reflected settler interests. The strength of this reading derives from his emphasis on the channels of communication between the respective colonies: 'British Settler Discourse and the Circuits of Empire', *History Workshop Journal*, 54 (2002). Arguably, in turn, Dilke and Froude took these views of Britishness and presented them back to the metropolitan reading public. See too Lester's *Imperial Networks: Creating Identities in Nineteenth-Century South Africa and Britain* (London: Routledge, 2001); and David Lambert and Alan Lester (eds.), *Colonial Lives across the British Empire: Imperial Careering in the Long Nineteenth Century* (Cambridge: Cambridge UP, 2006).

40. Reynolds, *Indelible Stain?*, 56.

41. Ibid. 99–101.

42. Cited ibid. 47.

43. Catherine Hall, *Civilising Subjects: Metropole and Colony in the English Imagination, 1830–1867* (Cambridge: Polity, 2002); and her 'Imperial man'.

44. Reynolds, *Other Side of the Frontier*, 114–16.

45. Cited in Reynolds, *Frontier*, 63–5. A vivid contemporary account of the Port Denison region in these years can be found in David Adams (ed.), *The Letters of Rachel Henning* (Sydney: Sirius Books, 1963). It is clear that by this period Henning distinguished between those 'faithful' or 'civilized' Aborigines who had made their accommodation with the settlers, and those she identified as 'the wild blacks', who couldn't be trusted not to turn on whites (pp. 123, 147, 161, and 184–5).

46. See Perry, *On the Edge of Empire*, 175. In Mar. 1842 Charles La Trobe had noted that, in the western parts of New South Wales, 'the savage tribes are not only upon our borders, but intermingled with us in every part of this district', cited in Jan Critchell, 'Encounters in the Western District', in Bain Attwood and S. G. Foster (eds), *Frontier Conflict. The Australian Experience* (Canberra: National Museum of Australia, 2003), 53.

47. See Reynolds, *Frontier*, 63 and 64.

48. Homi Bhabha, 'DissemiNation', in Bhabha (ed.), *Nation and Narration* (London: Routledge, 1990), 297.

49. Andrew Roberts, in his biography, gives the briefest account of the tour: *Salisbury: Victorian Titan* (London: Weidenfeld & Nicolson, 1999), 17–19. The only other references to Australia in this large book concern a couple of Salisbury's early book reviews and his satisfaction that, in 1887, the colony agreed to contribute to the upkeep of an imperial naval squadron. The volume is dedicated to Margaret Thatcher.

50. *The Times*, 1, 2, and 3 Jan. 1901.

51. Robert Menzies, *To the People of Great Britain at War from the Prime Minister of Australia* (London: Longmans, 1941). In a radio broadcast of 23 Feb. 1941 Menzies declared that 'You and we are of one blood, and we are not to be put down by ambitious adventurers or predatory rogues' (p. 14).

52. See esp. David Fitzpatrick, *Oceans of Consolation: Personal Accounts of Irish Migration to Australia* (Melbourne: Melbourne UP, 1995), esp. 20, 609, 612–13, and 624. No such accounts exist for English emigrants, where the intense localism we witness in these letters may have been rather less—as in the particular case of Henry Parkes, discussed below.

53. For important reflections on this longer history, Ken Gelder and Jane M. Jacobs, *Uncanny Australia: Sacredness and Identity in a Postcolonial Nation* (Carlton South, Victoria: Melbourne UP, 1998).

54. In 1860 there were some 340 miles of track in Australia; by 1900, over 10,000 miles. Beverley Kingston, *The Oxford History of Australia*, iii. *1860–1900: Glad, Confident Morning* (Melbourne: Oxford UP, 1988), 32–4. For a sense of how Australia was integrated into a global telegraph system, see the map in Wm. Roger Louis, 'Introduction', to Judith M. Brown and Wm. Roger Louis (eds), *The Oxford History of the British Empire*, iv. *The Twentieth Century* (Oxford: Oxford UP, 1999), 6; and for the link between the telegraph and the imperial

press see Simon J. Potter, *News and the British World: The Emergence of an Imperial Press System, 1876–1922* (Oxford: Clarendon Press, 2003). For telephone exchanges: Manning Clark, *A Short History of Australia* (New York: Mentor Books, 1963), 154; and for the telegraph, Alan Atkinson, ' "He Filled us Full of Laughter": Contact and Community in Australian Experience', in Hsu-Ming Teo and Richard White (eds.), *Cultural History in Australia* (Sydney: University of New South Wales Press, 2003), 41. The classic case of railroad-building as purposeful colonial nation-building is Canada: see Douglas Hill, *The Opening of the Canadian West* (London: Heinemann, 1967); and Milner's belief in the indispensability of rail construction for the national development of both Canada and South Africa, in his 31 Oct. 1908 Ottawa speech, 'South African Development', in his *Nation and Empire*, 330–1. The most breathtaking vision of empire can be seen in Kitchener's decision to build the railway in Sudan with the same gauge as that of South Africa: James *Morris, Farewell the Trumpets: An Imperial Retreat* (Harmondsworth: Penguin, 1979), 37.

55. See Zygmunt Bauman, 'Soil, Blood and Identity', *Sociological Review*, 40/4 (1992).

56. Cited in Stuart Macintyre, *The Oxford History of Australia*, iv. *1901–1942: The Succeeding Age* (Melbourne: Oxford UP, 1986), 10.

57. Cited ibid. iv, p. xx. These words were spoken on Inauguration Day in Kalgoorlie in Western Australia by the editor of a local newspaper, representing common sentiments.

58. Curthoys, 'Expulsion, Exodus and Exile', 15; and her 'Constructing National Histories', in Attwood and Foster, *Frontier Conflict*, 195.

59. For official attempts to instigate managed miscegenation in Western Australia and the Northern Territories in the 1920s and 1930s—explicitly conducted in terms of 'stamping out' bad blood with 'white blood'—see Russell McGregor, 'Breed out the Colour, or the Importance of Being White', *Australian Historical Studies*, 33/121 (2002), 294.

60. In an analysis of nation-building in early 20th-cent. Europe, the reader confronts this alarming sentence, concerning anti-Semitism in Hungary in the 1920s: 'had the country been more democratic, it would probably have been more anti-Semitic still'. Mark Mazower, *Dark Continent: Europe's Twentieth Century* (Harmondsworth: Penguin, 1999), 59.

61. Sir Henry Parkes, *The Federal Government of Australasia: Speeches on Various Occasions, November 1889–May 1890* (Sydney: Turner & Henderson, 1890), 15–17; 6 Nov. 1889.

62. I draw here from A. W. Martin, *Henry Parkes: A Biography* (Melbourne: Melbourne UP, 1980); and his *Parkes and the 1890 Conference* (Canberra: Parliament House, 1990).

63. Elspeth Huxley, *Their Shining Eldorado: A Journey through Australia* (New York: William Morrow, 1967), 47. The library now boasts two additional volumes.

64. In the *Empire*, 5 Sept. 1853, cited in Paul Pickering, '"The Oak of English Liberty": Popular Constitutionalism in New South Wales, 1848–1856', *Journal of Australian Colonial History*, 3/1 (2001), 13. This gives a fine account of the milieu of political thought in which Parkes was active, and to which he contributed.

65. Sir Henry Parkes, *Fifty Years in the Making of Australian History*, i (London: Longmans, Green, 1892), 10.

66. Cited in Martin, *Parkes*, 22.

67. Sir Henry Parkes, *An Emigrant's Home Letters* (Sydney: Angus & Robertson, 1897), 10. When Charles Fay, a Hampshire tanner, was transported to New South Wales for his part in the 'Swing' riots of 1830, his young son was under the impression that his father had 'gone to fight the Blacks': E. J. Hobsbawm and George Rudé, *Captain Swing* (London: Lawrence & Wishart, 1969), 272.

68. Parkes, *Emigrant's Home Letters*, 86 and 94.

69. Cited in Martin, *Parkes*, 34. His 'Song of the Australian Settler' is significant: 'Our home is where the wandering black/And all wildest things come nearest', in Henry Parkes, *Fragmentary Thoughts* (Sydney: Samuel Lee, 1889), 168. This volume of verse represents, in Parkes's own words, 'the broken record of the inner life', p. v.

70. Cited in Martin, *Parkes*, 40.

71. Sir Charles Dilke, *Greater Britain: A Record of Travel in English-Speaking Countries during 1866 and 1867* (London: Macmillan, 1868), 390.

72. Martin, *Parkes*, 76.

73. Ibid. 153.

74. Clark, *History of Australia*, 143.

75. J. Russell Endean, *Sir Henry Parkes and Mr Chamberlain, MP* (Torquay: Shinner & Dodd, 1900). The full subtitle reads: *For Intense Heat, for Rash Judgement and for Unsound Policy, I am Commended to Her Majesty's Colonial Secretary.*

76. Cited in Martin, *Parkes*, 194; and Henry Parkes, *Australian Views of England: Eleven Letters Written in the Years 1861 and 1862* (London: Macmillan, 1869), 2.

77. Henry Parkes, 'A Lay for the Times', *Murmurs of the Stream* (Sydney: James Waugh, 1857), 17.

78. Henry Parkes ('Wanderer'), *The Beauteous Terrorist* (Melbourne: George Robertson, 1885), 32.

79. Henry Parkes, 'One People, One Destiny', *Sonnets and Other Verse* (London: Kegan Paul, Trench, Trubner, 1895), 22. This marked a poetic tribute to the toast he proposed to the inter-colonial conference in Sydney town hall in Mar. 1891.

80. Parkes, *Fifty Years*, i. 239–40.

81. Froude, *Oceana*, 142.

82. Parkes, *Fragmentary Thoughts*.

83. Though one of the last issues of *Empire* under his control pressed for an inquiry into 'the state of outrage between the white and black races in New South Wales', Martin, *Parkes*, 154. For the Aboriginal presence 'in our midst' in Sydney in the 1870s and 1880s, and for the measures taken to counteract this presence, Maria Nugent, *Botany Bay: Where Histories Meet* (Crows Nest, NSW: Allen & Unwin, 2005), 45–57.

84. For an exploration of Parkes as a memory in contemporary commercial cultures, Meaghan Morris, 'At Henry Parkes Motel', in her *Too Soon, Too Late: History in Popular Culture* (Bloomington, Ind.: Indiana UP, 1998).

85. Cited in Martin, *Parkes*, 391. Nine years later Richard Seddon, the premier of New Zealand, in dispatching troops to South Africa, stated in the House of Representatives the obligation deriving from the 'crimson tie'. Cited in Donal Lowry, ' "The World's No Bigger than a Kraal": The South African War and International Opinion in the First Age of "Globalization" ', in David Omissi and Andrew Thompson (eds.), *The Impact of the South African War* (Basingstoke: Palgrave, 2002), 275. I am not suggesting that there were no antecedents for these kinds of sentiment. We might recall Burke's words in the House of Commons, reflecting upon relations between Britain and the American colonies, spoken in late Mar. 1775, less than a month before hostilities broke out at Concord and Lexington: 'My hold of the colonies is in the close affection which grows from common names, from kindred blood, from similar privileges, and equal protection. These are the ties which, though light as air, are as strong as links of iron', Edmund Burke, *Speech of Edmund Burke, Esq., on Moving his Resolutions for Conciliation with the Colonies, 22 March 1775* (New York: Charles Scribner's Sons, 1903), 68. In this speech there are many anticipations of the themes I discuss in relation to Parkes.

86. Parkes, *Federal Government*, 21; 6 Nov. 1889.

87. Ibid. 52; 9 Dec. 1889.

88. See Parkes, *Federal Government*, 21 and 135.

89. Ibid. 131. This comes from Parkes's speech at the Melbourne meeting of the inter-colonial conference.

90. *Official Record of the Proceedings and Debates of the Australasian Federal Conference, 1890, held in Parliament House, Melbourne* (Melbourne: Robert Brain, Government Printer, 1890); *Pall Mall Gazette*, 8 Feb. 1890, 296; and *The Times*, 11 Feb. 1890, 321; *John Bull*, 21 Feb. 1890, saw federation as a culmination of Dilke's dream of empire (p. 422).

91. Parkes, *Federal Government*, 73.

92. Parkes, *Fifty Years*, i. 121.

93. Cited in Charles Lyne, *Life of Sir Henry Parkes: Australian Statesman* (London: Fisher Unwin, 1897), 262–3.

94. Cited in Martin, *Parkes*, 314–15.

95. Parkes, *Fifty Years*, i. 124.

96. More generally on this, see Lake and Reynolds, *Drawing the Global Colour Line*, ch. 8.

97. *Empire*, 2 Feb. 1852, cited in Paul Pickering, '"The Finger of God": Gold's Impact on New South Wales', in Iain McCalman, Alexander Cook, and Andrew Reeves (eds.), *Gold: Forgotten Histories and Lost Objects of Australia* (Cambridge: Cambridge UP, 2001), 41. Parkes had first-hand experience of the induced labour shortage: in May 1851 he had no compositors to set up the next issue of *Empire*, as they had left the city in search of gold.

98. Martin, *Parkes*, 231.

99. Or as he put it in an early poem, this time with black Africa in mind: 'We might have been of Afric's race supine/In degradation born, in bonds to die', *Fragmentary Thoughts*, 207.

100. Cited in Huttenback, *Racism and Empire*, 84.

101. California constitutes an integral part of this larger, common story. A year later, in 1882, the state legislature passed an Exclusion Act which empowered the state specifically to exclude Chinese. This was contemporaneous with the restrictions imposed in New South Wales.

102. Cited in Huttenback, *Racism and Empire*, 89–90.

103. Sir Henry Parkes, *Fifty Years in the Making of Australian History*, ii (London: Longmans, Green, 1892), 58.

104. Ibid. 206–9.

105. Lake and Reynolds, *Drawing the Global Colour Line*, 157–9.

106. Parkes, *Fifty Years*, ii. 211–13.

107. Ibid. 219–22.

108. Pickering, 'Oak of English Liberty', 19. It is clear too that the precedent of the Thirteen Colonies was active in his mind in this period, ibid. 21.

109. Gwenda Tavan, *The Long, Slow Death of White Australia* (Melbourne: Scribe Publications, 2005), 9.

110. W. K. Hancock, *The Cambridge History of the British Empire*, vii/1. *Australia* (Cambridge: Cambridge UP, 1933), 500–1.

111. Cited in Clark, *History of Australia*, 172–3.

112. Stuart Hall, *Three Blind Mice: Rethinking New Ethnicities* [video], Inaugural Lecture, Centre for New Ethnicities Research, University of East London, n.d. [1996].

113. Huttenback, *Racism and Empire*, 315.

114. For the impact of Seeley in Australia in the late 1880s, see Luke Trainor, *British Imperialism and Australian Nationalism: Manipulation, Conflict and Compromise in the Late Nineteenth Century* (Cambridge: Cambridge UP, 1994), 172–3. A Melbourne reviewer of Froude's *Oceana* believed it represented no more than 'a mere superficial skimmer of whipped syllabub', quoted by Donald Wood, 'John Jacob Thomas', in J. J. Thomas, *Froudacity: West Indian Fables by James Anthony Froude* (London: New Beacon, 1969; 1889), 19. During the debate on Australian policy towards the South African war, 'The

names of Dilke, Froude, Lecky and Seeley were frequently invoked': Barbara Penny, 'The Australian Debate on the Boer War', *(Australian) Historical Studies*, 14/56 (1971), 531. When, in 1964, Donald Horne came to write *The Lucky Country* (Ringwood,Victoria: Penguin, 1980), he opened his account with the Asian presence, and with Froude. Horne had been editor of the *Bulletin* from 1961–2. This had been founded in 1880 as an advanced democratic publication, on the model of *Reynolds News* in London. Its initial masthead had declared: 'Temper democratic, bias offensively Australian'; this soon switched to 'Australia for the Australians', which in turn in 1908 became 'Australia for the White Man'. Horne dropped this when he became editor.

115. Angela Woollacott suggests that the figure of the specifically Australian girl, imagined as a foil to her more staid English sister, emerges at the beginning of the 20th cent.: *To Try Her Fortune in London: Australian Women, Colonialism and Modernity* (New York: Oxford UP, 2001), 157–9. Ann Curthoys argues that it was only from the 1930s that women became incorporated into the pioneer legend, 'Expulsion, Exodus and Exile', 7, for which more generally, J. B. Hirst, 'The Pioneer Legend', *(Australian) Historical Studies*, 18 (1979).

116. Douglas Cole, ' "The Crimson Thread of Kinship": Ethnic Ideas in Australia, 1870–1914', *(Australian) Historical Studies*, 14/56 (1971), 515, 516–17, and 521. See too the same author's 'The Problem of "Nationalism" and "Imperialism" in British Settlement Colonies', *Journal of British Studies*, 10/2 (1971).

117. Cited in Richard White, *Inventing Australia: Images and Identity, 1688–1980* (St Leonards, NSW: Allen & Unwin, 1980), 75. It was only at this time, in the 1890s, that the contemporary idea of 'the pioneer' first became part of the currency of national myth-making: Hirst, 'The Pioneer Legend'.

118. Perhaps as many as two-thirds of Sydney's inhabitants braved the rain to bid farewell to the first contingent of volunteers to sail to South Africa: Craig Wilcox, *Australia's Boer War: The War in South Africa, 1899–1902* (Melbourne: Melbourne UP, 2002), 25.

119. Penny, 'Australian Debate on the Boer War'; and for a contrasting view, C. N. Connolly, 'Manufacturing "Spontaneity": The Australian Offer of Troops for the Boer War', *(Australian) Historical Studies*, 18/70 (1978); and the same author's 'Class, Birthplace and Loyalty: Australian Attitudes to the Boer War', *(Australian) Historical Studies*, 18/71 (1978). See too Bill Nasson, *The South African War, 1899–1902* (London: Arnold, 1999), 279–80. For Kipling's praise for the Australians, David Gilmour, *The Long Recessional: The Imperial Life of Rudyard Kipling* (New York: Farrar & Strauss, 2002), 150; and see too Donal Lowry, ' "The Boers were the Beginning of the End?": The Wider Impact of the South African War', in Lowry (ed.), *The South African War Reappraised* (Manchester: Manchester UP, 2000), 226. Throughout the war, the Canadian press similarly extolled the superiority of the Canadian troops over the British: Philip Buckner, 'Canada', in Thompson and Omissi, *Impact of the South*

African War, 242; as did John Buchan in 1901: 'The tall men in the Canadian contingents, with their curious brightness of eye, which comes from looking over vast prospects of country, were more than mere Volunteers or Manitoba stock-riders. They were to the observant man the visible sign of a masculine and unwearied nation', cited in Henshaw, 'John Buchan from the "Borders" to the "Berg": Nature, Empire and White South African Identity, 1901–1910', *African Studies*, 62/1 (2003), 16. The longer history of these foundational national stories is well told in Alistair Thomson, *ANZAC Memories: Living with the Legend* (Melbourne: Oxford UP, 1994).

120. For an extraordinary instance of the process by which these themes were worked back into the imagination of the metropole, see D. H. Lawrence, *Kangaroo* (Harmondsworth: Penguin, 1997; 1923); and D. H. Lawrence and M. L. Skinner, *The Boy in the Bush* (Cambridge: Cambridge UP, 1990; 1st publ. 1924).

121. Cited in Marilyn Lake, 'White Man's Country: The Trans-National History of a National Project', *Australian Historical Studies*, 122 (2003), 346.

122. Lake, 'White Man's Country'; and her 'The White Man Under Siege: New Histories of Race in the Nineteenth Century and the Advent of White Australia', *History Workshop Journal*, 58 (2004); 'On Being a White Man, Australia, circa 1900', in Teo and White, *Cultural History in Australia;* 'Women and Whiteness', *Australian Historical Studies*, 117 (2001); and Lake and Reynolds, *Drawing the Global Colour Line*. Jock Phillips, *A Man's Country? The Image of the Pakeha Male: A History* (Auckland: Penguin, 1987), identifies 'the bloke under siege' in New Zealand as specifically a postwar phenomenon (ch. 6), though clearly this is employed in a more descriptive sense.

123. Lake and Reynolds, *Drawing the Global Colour Line*, 2.

124. Charles H. Pearson, *National Life and Character: A Forecast* (London: Macmillan, 1893), 16 and 85; Lake and Reynolds, *Drawing the Global Colour Line*, ch. 3.

125. Lake, 'White Man Under Siege', 4; and 'Being a White Man', 102.

126. Lake and Reynolds make much of the contrast between Dilke and Seeley, on the one hand, and Pearson on the other, arguing that while Dilke and Seeley emphasized the future triumph of the white man, Pearson was already apprehensive that that future had been jeopardized by the incursions of non-white peoples in what were essentially white men's countries. This is an important distinction to make. In part it derives from the timing of their respective writings, and also from the fact that Pearson's *National Life* was much more deeply shaped by the colonial situation. But I think that the contrast between metropolitan optimism and colonial pessimism can be overdrawn. The dream of white nationhood was always compromised by the realities of racial others, and the fantasy of omnipotence never far from fears of vulnerability. Lake and Reynolds, *Drawing the Global Colour Line*, 76.

127. As the White Australia policy was nearing the end of its life Robert Menzies, who finally retired as Australian prime minister in 1966, was quizzed on British television about its appropriateness; he replied without, one imagines, a blush: 'Oh, we don't call it that now', Horne, *Lucky Country*, 114. And see Tavan, *Long, Slow Death of White Australia*.

128. These histories are comprehensively reconstructed in Huttenback, *Racism and Empire*.

129. The languages of whiteness which emerged from these circumstances, encompassing a potent combination of evident self-interest with claims to be universal in moral authority, were not without precedent. The first anglophone colonial nationalism, in the United States in the 1770s and 1780s, carried too many of these same characteristics. For good discussions of the coexistence of ideas of the free-born Englishman and palpable social, especially racial, inequalities, see Eric Foner, *Slavery and Freedom in Nineteenth-Century America* (Oxford: Oxford UP, 1994; inaugural lecture of the Harmsworth Professor of American History, 17 May 1974), 3–4; and Edward Countryman, *The American Revolution* (Harmondsworth: Penguin, 1987), 16–18.

130. 'The Government of India Act, 1935, evoked more discussion than any measure since the Irish Home Rule Bills. In Parliament it occasioned 1,951 speeches, containing 15½ million words, filling over four thousand pages of Hansard', Robert Rhodes James, *Churchill: A Study in Failure, 1900–1939* (Harmondsworth: Penguin, 1981), 267. At this time, according to the record of one confidante, Eustace Percy, Stanley Baldwin 'in certain moods . . . would talk in private of nothing else', cited in Middlemas and Barnes, *Baldwin*, 697. The longer story, orchestrated around the competing themes of 'difference' and 'similarity', is told with insight by Thomas Metcalf, *Ideologies of the Raj: The New Cambridge History of India*, iii/4 (Cambridge: Cambridge UP, 1994).

131. E. S. Turner, 'The Crystal Palace Experience', *London Review of Books*, 25 Nov. 1999, in which Turner recalls his own visit as a schoolboy to the Wembley Exhibition. There is now a fair amount of historical research, if scattered, on Wembley, and it is worth pointing out that one of the most popular contemporary postcolonial novels, Andrea Levy's *Small Island* (London: Review, 2004), opens in 1924 with the white protagonist's childhood encounter with a black man at the Wembley Exhibition. In this context it is worth highlighting the symbolic role of the Canadian Mountie. With its origins rooted in the early 20th-cent. imperial romance for young boys, the myth of the Mountie has demonstrated a remarkable capacity to reinvent itself and to cross over different media. An inventory reveals that there have been more than 250 Hollywood movies devoted to the theme, it thereby ceasing to be a narrowly national memory. I am grateful to Vanessa Hughes for this information.

132. James Walvin, *Passage to Britain: Immigration in British History and Politics* (Harmondsworth: Penguin, 1984), 69; for reflections on the prehistory of these

themes, see Andrew Blake, 'Foreign Devils and Moral Panics: Britain, Asia and the Opium Trade', in Schwarz, *Expansion of England*.

133. See Bernard Gainer, *The Alien Invasion: The Origins of the Aliens Act of 1905* (London: Heinemann, 1972); David Feldman, *Englishmen and Jews: Social Relations and Political Culture, 1840–1914* (New Haven: Yale UP, 1994); and David Glover, 'Liberalism, Anglo-Jewry, and the Diasporic Imagination, 1890–1914', Comparative Studies in Social Transformation colloquium, University of Michigan, 27 Jan. 2000.

134. Prem Podder, 'Passports, Empire, Subjecthood', in Graham MacPhee and Prem Podder (eds.), *Empire and After: Englishness in a Postcolonial Context* (Oxford: Berghahn, 2007).

135. Catherine Hall, Keith McClelland, and Jane Rendall, *Defining the Victorian Nation: Class, Race, Gender and the Reform Act of 1867* (Cambridge: Cambridge UP, 2000); and for a view of how electoral faultlines played across metropole and the overseas imperial possessions, Ian Christopher Fletcher, Laura E. Nym Mayhall, and Philippa Levine (eds.), *Women's Suffrage in the British Empire: Citizenship, Nation, Race* (London: Routledge, 2000).

136. Charles W. Boyd (ed.), *Mr Chamberlain's Speeches*, ii (London: Constable, 1914), 130, 127, and 140.

137. Laura Tabili, *'We Ask for British Justice': Workers and Racial Difference in Late Imperial Britain* (Ithaca, NY: Cornell UP, 1994).

138. For vibrant accounts, which pursue a compelling political argument, see Marcus Rediker, *Between the Devil and the Deep Blue Sea: Merchant Seamen, Pirates, and the Anglo-American Maritime World, 1700–1750* (Cambridge: Cambridge UP, 1993), and Peter Linebaugh and Marcus Rediker, *The Many-Headed Hydra: The Hidden History of the Revolutionary Atlantic* (London: Verso, 2000).

139. See e.g. a characteristic jeremiad: O. Etzbacher, 'The Yellow Peril', *The Nineteenth Century and After*, 55 (1904).

140. Cited in Tabili, *'We Ask for British Justice'*, 91, 81, 92, and 1; all the information in this paragraph comes from Tabili's thoughtful account.

141. This commodification of whiteness could also be sympathetically viewed by those who otherwise were hostile to an insurgent labourism. Thus Lionel Curtis, one of Milner's great protégés, could claim: 'The tendency of Trade Unions to exclude coloured labour should be fostered by all patriotic men in Australia and America', *With Milner in South Africa* (Oxford: Blackwell, 1951), 226.

142. 21 Jan. 1903, cited in John Marlowe, *Milner: Apostle of Empire* (London: Hamish Hamilton, 1976), 161.

143. Jonathan Hyslop, 'The Imperial Working Class Makes itself "White": White Labourism in Britain, Australia, and South Africa Before the First World War', *Journal of Historical Sociology*, 12/4 (1999), 413; Burns cited in Jonathan Schneer, *London 1900* (New Haven: Yale UP, 1999), 257.

144. 6 Oct. 1905. Speech to the 95 Club Dinner at the Grand Hotel, Manchester, in Winston *Churchill, Churchill Speaks, 1897–1963: Collected Speeches in Peace and War*, ed. Robert Rhodes James (Leicester: Windward, 1981), 76.

145. Churchill, *Collected Speeches*, 76. Chamberlain's specific crime, according to Churchill in a speech he made on 14 Dec. 1905, was that 'he never hesitated to drag the colonial empire into the vortex of British politics', making it a sectional—not a national—issue: *Collected Speeches*, 79.

146. 9 Jan. 1906. Speech at Lever Street Schools, Manchester in Churchill, *Collected Speeches*, 84. His first ministerial speech, on 22 Feb. 1906, was devoted to the issue of Chinese labour.

147. Cited in Lowry, 'The Wider Impact of the South African War', 206.

148. I rely here on Logie Barrow, 'White Solidarity in 1914', in Raphael Samuel (ed.), *Patriotism: The Making and Unmaking of British National Identity*, i. *History and Politics* (London: Routledge, 1989); Hyslop, 'The Imperial Working Class Makes itself "White" ', from which the quote from the *Amalgamated Society of Engineers Monthly Journal and Report* (Feb. 1914), 398, derives; and Hyslop, 'The British and Australian Leaders of the South African Labour Movement, 1902–1914: A Group Biography', in Darian-Smith et al., *Britishness Abroad*.

149. See Andrew Thomson, *The Empire Strikes Back? The Impact of Imperialism on Britain from the Mid Nineteenth-Century* (Harlow: Pearson, 2005), 66–72.

150. For some hints, Bob Holton, *British Syndicalism, 1906–1914: Myths and Realities* (London: Pluto Press, 1976).

151. See e.g. the career of Tom Mann: Dona Torr, *Tom Mann and his Times* (London: Lawrence & Wishart, 1956); and for Mann's cooperation with Havelock Wilson during the strikes of 1910–11, and again in 1912, see Holton, *British Syndicalism*, 122–7.

152. Trainor, *British Imperialism and Australian Nationalism*, ch. 11.

153. Cited in Hyslop, 'The Imperial Working Class Makes itself "White" ', 411. My information on these connections between Australian, South African, and British labourism comes from this illuminating exploration; and see too the same author's 'A Ragged Trousered Philanthropist: Robert Tressell in Cape Town and Johannesburg', *History Workshop Journal*, 51 (2001). Jeremy Krikler's comments on the later period are also relevant: 'The Commandos: The Army of White Labour in South Africa', *Past and Present*, 163 (1999).

154. Hyslop, 'The Imperial Working Class Makes itself "White" ', 415 and 416; see too J. B. Jeffreys, *The Story of the Engineers, 1800–1945* (London: Lawrence & Wishart, 1946). A more subjective sense of what this movement meant can be gleaned from Baron Hirson and Gwyn A. Williams, *The Delegate for Africa: David Ivon Jones, 1883–1924* (London: Core Books, 1995). Jones left Aberystwyth—as a follower of Lloyd George in politics and of Unitarianism in religion—for New Zealand in 1907, in order to recuperate from tuberculosis. Whilst there he was drawn to socialism. He travelled to Australia. In Oct.

1909 he wrote home: 'New Zealand is a trifle parochial. Like Joe Chamberlain, I want my spirit enlarged, if not by the illimitable veld, then by the illimitable elbow-room of Canada', where a brother of his had earlier emigrated (ibid. 84). In the event, he sailed to South Africa. There he became active politically, his views on race shifting from scepticism about the virtues of 'the black man' to a more accommodating stance, ending his days as a Bolshevik of unbounded enthusiasm. For a parallel career, comprising Australia, New Zealand, and South Africa, and culminating in Bolshevism, Torr, *Tom Mann*.

155. The chair of the committee which coordinated these activities, the South Africa Constitutional Rights Committee, was one Victor Fisher; he subsequently became active in a 'national' Labour party, an organization founded by Milner to bring about representation for patriotic labour. See J. O. Stubbs, 'Lord Milner and Patriotic Labour', *English Historical Review*, 87 (1972).

156. Cited in Hyslop, 'The Imperial Working Class Makes itself "White"', 417, from *Forward*, 11 Apr. 1914.

157. Cited in Barrow, 'White Solidarity in 1914', 281, emphasis added.

158. There was a problem too when the colonies were thought to come under the sway of excessive civilization. 'Curzon maintained that better steam and postal communications had . . . reduced the Englishman's attachment to India, bringing the attractions of home life and home associations closer and encouraging him to regard himself as an unfortunate exile', David Gilmour, *Curzon* (London: John Murray, 1994), 223–4. For similar views, expressed much later in the century, Sir Ralph Furse, *Aucuparius: Recollections of a Recruiting Officer* (London: Oxford UP, 1962), 263. More generally, from a literary—and contrary—perspective, Joseph Bristow, *Effeminate England: Homoerotic Writing after 1885* (Milton Keynes: Open UP, 1995).

159. Some of these discrepancies in perspective are rehearsed in Julia Bush, *Edwardian Ladies and Imperial Power* (Leicester: Leicester UP, 2000), and the ambiguities can be followed in Michael Roper, *The Secret Battle: Emotional Survival in the Great War* (Manchester: Manchester UP, 2009).

160. I follow here the short, stimulating account by Ben Shephard, 'Showbiz Imperialism: The Case of Peter Lobengula', in John MacKenzie (ed.), *Imperialism and Popular Culture* (Manchester: Manchester UP, 1986); and see too H. L. Malchow, *Gothic Images of Race in Nineteenth-Century Britain* (Stanford, Calif.: Stanford UP, 1996).

161. Shephard, 'Showbiz Imperialism', 98–9.

162. For further argument on this, see my 'Politics and Rhetoric in the Age of Mass Culture', *History Workshop Journal*, 46 (1998).

163. Cited in Shephard, 'Showbiz Imperialism', 99–101.

164. See Michael Dutfield, *A Marriage of Inconvenience: The Persecution of Seretse and Ruth Khama* (London: Unwin, 1990).

165. Cited in Shephard, 'Showbiz Imperialism', 101–3.

166. Cited ibid. 100.

CHAPTER 3

1. Cited in David Gilmour, *The Long Recessional: The Imperial Life of Rudyard Kipling* (New York: Farrar, Strauss & Giroux, 2002), 125.
2. Cited in Angela Woollacott, *To Try Her Fortune in London: Australian Women, Colonialism, and Modernity* (New York: Oxford UP, 2001), 3.
3. See particularly the work of Kathleen Wilson: *The Sense of the People: Politics, Culture, and Imperialism in England, 1715–1785* (Cambridge: Cambridge UP, 1995); *The Island Race: Englishness, Empire and Gender in the Eighteenth Century* (New York: Routledge, 2003); and her edited collection, *A New Imperial History: Culture, Identity, and Modernity in Britain and the Empire, 1660–1840* (Cambridge: Cambridge UP, 2004).
4. John MacKenzie, 'Introduction' to his edited collection, *Imperialism and Popular Culture* (Manchester: Manchester UP, 1986), 7–8. Andrew Thompson gives a different reading of these surveys, suggesting that they reflect a degree of popular knowledge of empire: *The Empire Strikes Back? The Impact of Imperialism on Britain from the Mid-Nineteenth Century* (Harlow: Pearson, 2005), 208–9.
5. *The Times*, 1 Jan. 1901.
6. Ibid.
7. See Ann Laura Stoler, *Race and the Education of Desire: Foucault's* History of Sexuality *and the Colonial Order of Things* (Durham, NC: Duke UP, 1995), ch. 3. Stoler highlights Foucault's 1976 lectures at the College de France, in which he noted a shift in the 18th and 19th cents. in Europe from a 'symbolics of blood' to an 'analytics of sexuality'—though Foucault notes that this was a transformation in which 'overlappings, interactions, and echoes' of the former were carried into the workings of the latter. Thus in the modern period a preoccupation with blood 'haunted the administration of sexuality'. But Stoler adds this gloss (pp. 49, 51): 'What is problematic in Foucault's argument is not his description of the reappearance of a "symbolics of blood" in the nineteenth century and its continued salience today, but rather the selective (northern) European-bound genealogy he draws for it. The myth of blood that pervades nineteenth-century racism may be traced, as Foucault does, from an aristocratic preoccupation with legitimacy, pure blood, and descent, but not through it alone. It was equally dependent on an imperial politics of exclusion that was worked out earlier and reworked later on colonial ground.' For a European—though predominantly German—view, Uli Linke, *Blood and Nation: The European Aesthetics of Race* (Philadelphia: University of Pennsylvania Press, 1999).
8. J. M. Coetzee, 'Blood, Flaw, Taint, Degeneration: The Case of Sarah Gertrude Millin', *English Studies in Africa*, 23/1 (1980), 42 and 51; repr. in his *White Writing: On the Culture of Letters in South Africa* (New Haven: Yale UP, 1988); Gaston Bachelard, *The Psychoanalysis of Fire* (Boston: Beacon Press, 1968), 105–6.
9. See Martin Barker, *The New Racism: Conservatives and the Ideology of the Tribe* (London: Junction Books, 1981).
10. Phil Cohen, 'Laboring Under Whiteness', in Ruth Frankenberg (ed.), *Displacing Whiteness: Essays in Social and Cultural Criticism* (Durham, NC: Duke UP, 1997),

260; and Les Back, 'Inside Out: Racism, Class and Masculinity in the "Inner City" and the English Suburbs', *New Formations*, 33 (1998).

11. Illuminating are Judith Walkowitz, *Prostitution and Victorian Society: Women, Class and the State* (Cambridge: Cambridge UP, 1980); Jeffrey Weeks, *Sex, Politics and Society: The Regulation of Sexuality since 1800* (London: Longman, 1981); Frank Mort, *Dangerous Sexualities: Medico-Moral Panics in England since 1830* (London: Routledge & Kegan Paul, 1987); and Geoffrey Pearson, *Hooligan: A History of Respectable Fears* (London: Macmillan, 1983). For a synoptic approach, Mary Langan and Bill Schwarz (eds.), *Crises in the British State, 1880–1930* (London: Hutchinson, 1985).

12. John Marriott, *The Other Empire: Metropolis, India and Progress in the Colonial Imagination* (Manchester: Manchester UP, 2003).

13. See esp. Mrinalini Sinha, *Colonial Masculinity: The 'Manly' Englishman and the 'Effeminate' Bengali in the Late Nineteenth Century* (Manchester: Manchester UP, 1995). For the broader context, V. G. Kiernan, *The Lords of Human Kind: European Attitudes to the Outside World in the Imperial Age* (Harmondsworth: Penguin, 1972); and Michael Roper and John Tosh (eds.), *Manful Assertions: Masculinities in Britain since 1800* (London: Routledge, 1991).

14. Ann Laura Stoler, 'Tense and Tender Ties: The Politics of Comparison in North American History and (Post) Colonial Studies', *Journal of American History*, 88/3 (2001), 865.

15. Partha Chatterjee, *The Nation and its Fragments: Colonial and Post-Colonial Histories* (Princeton: Princeton UP, 1993), 10.

16. Sinha, *Colonial Masculinity*, 182.

17. Cited in Adele Perry, *On the Edge of Empire: Gender, Race and the Making of British Columbia, 1849–1871* (Toronto: University of Toronto Press, 2001), 155. An illuminating discussion of the dynamics of femininity and whiteness in the plantation societies of an earlier period can be found in Cecily Jones, *Engendering Whiteness: White Women and Colonialism in Barbados and North Carolina, 1627–1865* (Manchester: Manchester UP, 2007), and see too David Lambert, *White Creole Culture, Politics and Identity during the Age of Abolition* (Cambridge: Cambridge UP, 2005).

18. See Catherine Hall, 'Of Gender and Empire: The Nineteenth Century', and Barbara Bush, 'Gender and Empire: The Twentieth Century', both in Philippa Levine (ed.), *Gender and Empire: Oxfrod History of the British Empire, Companion Volume* (Oxford: Oxford UP, 2004). Important too is A. James Hammerton's 'Gender and Migration' in the same volume.

19. Richard Phillips, *Sex, Politics and Empire: A Postcolonial Geography* (Manchester: Manchester UP, 2006).

20. This issue is discussed in the essays collected in Antoinette Burton (ed.), *Gender, Sexuality, and Colonial Modernities* (London: Routledge, 1999).

21. Cited in Laura Tabili, 'Women "of a Very Low Type": Crossing Racial Boundaries in Imperial Britain', in Laura A. Frader and Sonya O. Rose (eds.), *Gender and Class in Modern Europe* (Ithaca, NY: Cornell UP, 1996), 166; Laura Tabili, 'Empire is the

Enemy of Love: Edith Noor's Progress and Other Stories', *Gender and History*, 17/1 (2005); and Lucy Bland, 'White Women and Men of Colour: Miscegenation Fears in Britain after the Great War', *Gender and History*, 17/1 (2005).

22. Philippa Levine, *Prostitution, Race, and Politics: Policing Venereal Disease in the British Empire* (New York: Routledge, 2003), 232.

23. Ibid. 183.

24. Ibid. 235.

25. Alan Sinfield provides an admirably non-functionalist gloss, which has more general application: 'The interpretative challenge is to recover the moment of indeterminacy. For it is not that our idea of "the homosexual" was hiding beneath other phrases, or lurking unspecified in the silence, like a statue under a sheet, fully formed but waiting to be unveiled: it was in the process of becoming constituted... To presume the eventual outcome in the blind or hesitant approximations out of which it was partly fashioned is to miss, precisely, the points of most interest.' *The Wilde Century: Effeminacy, Oscar Wilde and the Queer Moment* (London: Cassell, 1994), 8. Weeks, *Sex, Politics and Society*; Matt Cook, *London and the Culture of Homosexuality, 1885–1914* (Cambridge: Cambridge UP, 2003); Matt Houlbrook, *Queer London: Perils and Pleasures in the Sexual Metropolis, 1918–1957* (Chicago: University of Chicago Press, 2005), esp. ch. 9, which examines the language of disease, plague, canker, and foreign invasion associated with the male homosexual; and Joseph Bristow, *Effeminate England: Homoerotic writing after 1888* (New York: Columbia UP, 1995).

26. For the slightly earlier period Nadia Valman provides an important perspective by thinking together Judaism and masculinity: 'Manly Jews: Disraeli, Jewishness and Gender', in Tony Kushner and Todd Endelman (eds.), *Disraeli's Jewishness* (London: Vallentine Mitchell, 2002).

27. I have offered a parallel argument in 'Night Battles: Hooligans and Citizens, 1898', in Mica Nava and Alan O'Shea (eds.), *Modern Times: Reflections on a Century of English Modernity* (London: Routledge, 1996).

28. This is the argument of Mary Procida, both for the Raj and for the empire more generally: *Married to the Empire: Gender, Politics and Imperialism in India, 1883–1947* (Manchester: Manchester UP, 2002); while Barbara Bush, in 'Gender and Empire in the Twentieth Century', reconstructs the early 20th-cent. moves to the feminization of empire.

29. Cited in Gilmour, *Long Recessional*, 151.

30. Cited in Brian Harrison, *Separate Spheres: The Opposition to Women's Suffrage in Britain* (London: Croom Helm, 1978), 34.

31. Cited in Gilmour, *Long Recessional*, 228.

32. Cited in Antoinette Burton, *Burdens of History: British Feminists, Indian Women, and Imperial Culture, 1865–1915* (Chapel Hill, NC: University of North Carolina Press, 1994), 13.

33. Curzon often remarked on his shock—having seen British Tommies bathing— at the whiteness of male working-class bodies.

34. See esp. Noel Ignatiev, *How the Irish Became White* (London: Routledge, 1995). For long I was intrigued by John Ford's 1956 movie, *The Searchers*, which is an explicit investigation of the entry into whiteness; its loss; and its restoration. I wondered where this came from. But things come clearer if one sees Ford as an Irish director. The 'Texicans' have all the attributes, in their idealized homestead existence, of the primal Irish, who themselves move back and forth between inhabiting competing ethnic force-fields, first white, then 'native'. The film is a thoughtful exploration of the mobility of whiteness, whose plot turns on the vicissitudes of frontier populism. The conventional biographies have Ford born in the USA under the name Sean Aloysius O'Feeney; some however dispute this, insisting on an Irish birth, subsequently hidden from public view: see Jean Mitry's interview with Ford, 1st publ. in *Cahiers du Cinema* in 1955, and reproduced in Andrew Sarris (ed.), *Interviews with Film Directors* (New York: Avon Books, 1969), 199. See as well the chapters in Fintan O'Toole, *The Lie of the Land: Irish Identities* (London: Verso, 1999), 'Going Native' and 'Meanwhile Back at the Ranch'; and Robert Pippin, *Hollywood Westerns and American Myth* (New Haven: Yale UP, 2010).

35. Cited in Thomas Holt, *The Problem of Freedom: Race, Labor, and Politics in Jamaica and Britain, 1832–1938* (Baltimore: Johns Hopkins UP, 1992), 282. There is much written on this. See Ignatiev, *How the Irish Became White*, and Luke Gibbon, 'Race Against Time: Racial Discourse and Irish History', in Catherine Hall (ed.), *Cultures of Empire: A Reader. Colonizers in Britain and the Empire in the Nineteenth and Twentieth Centuries* (Manchester: Manchester UP, 2000). A good starting point can also be found in G. K. Peating, 'The Whiteness of Ireland Under and After the Union', and the roundtable discussion which follows with contributions from L. Perry Curtis Jnr, John Belchem, and David A. Wilson, *Journal of British Studies*, 4/1 (2005).

36. Reflecting on the death of General Gordon, Froude noted that it was an event more intensely felt in the colonies 'as if at the circumference the patriotic spirit was more alive than at the centre', J. A. Froude, *Oceana, or England and her Colonies* (London: Longmans, Green, 1886), 131. We might remember that Robert Gordon Menzies, born in a weatherboard house in Jeparit, Victoria, in 1894, was named after the famed general.

37. Homi Bhabha, 'Day by Day . . . with Frantz Fanon', in Alan Read (ed.), *The Fact of Blackness: Frantz Fanon and Visual Representation* (London: Institute for Contemporary Arts, 1996), 199; and there is much in Sara Ahmed, 'A Phenomenology of Whiteness', *Feminist Theory*, 8/2 (2007).

38. Sarah Gertrude Millin, *The Dark River* (New York: Thomas Selzer, 1920), 26.

39. An acute reading of the impossibilities invested in white Englishness in the Victorian period is Jennifer DeVere Brody, *Impossible Purities: Blackness, Femininity, and Victorian Culture* (Durham. NC: Duke UP, 1998).

40. Sinfield, *The Wilde Century*, 64–5; and Christopher Lane, *The Ruling Passion: British Colonial Allegory and the Paradox of Homosexual Desire* (Durham, NC: Duke UP, 1995).

41. Cora Kaplan makes a parallel argument: 'absolute whiteness in *Jane Eyre* is less the attribute of a viable raced human subject than an apparition, a specter called forth by contemporary prohibitions against those affective ties, whether of desire or identification which must inevitably cross or blur the lines of difference', ' "A Heterogeneous Thing": Female Childhood and the Rise of Racial Thinking in Victorian Britain', in Diana Fuss (ed.), *Human, All Too Human* (London: Routledge, 1996), 187.

42. W. E. B. DuBois, 'The Souls of White Folk', in his *Darkwater: Voices from within the Veil* (New York: Harcourt, Brace & Howe 1920; 1903), 29–30.

43. Thus Jose Harris: 'imperial visions injected a powerful strain of hierarchy, militarism, "frontier mentality", administrative rationality, and masculine civic virtue into British political culture, at a time when domestic political forces were running in quite the opposite direction, towards egalitarianism, "progressivism", consumerism, popular democracy, feminism and women's rights', *Private Lives, Public Spirit: Britain 1870–1914* (London: Penguin, 1994), 6.

44. bell hooks, 'Representing Whiteness in the Black Imagination', in Lawrence Grossberg, Cary Nelson, and Paula Treichler (eds.), *Cultural Studies* (London: Routledge, 1992), 338; and see the collection, David Roediger (ed.), *Black on White: Black Writers on What it Means to Be White* (New York: Schocken, 1999), which includes this essay.

45. The most cited titles are, from within the field of labour history: David Roediger, *The Wages of Whiteness: Race and the Making of the American Working Class* (London: Verso, 1990); and his *Towards the Abolition of Whiteness: Essays on Race, Politics, and Working Class History* (London: Verso, 1994). See in addition, Theodore Allen, *The Invention of the White Race*, i. *Racial Oppression and Social Control* (London: Verso, 1994), and ii. *The Origins of Racial Oppression in Anglo-America* (London: Verso, 1997); Alexander Saxton, *The Rise and Fall of the White Republic: Class Politics and Mass Culture in Nineteenth Century America* (London: Verso, 1990); Ignatiev, *How the Irish Became White*; and more recent, and more wide-ranging, Matthew Frye Jacobson, *Whiteness of a Different Color: European Immigrants and the Alchemy of Race* (Cambridge, Mass.: Harvard UP, 1998). From within feminist history, Catherine Hall, *White, Male and Middle Class: Explorations in Feminism and History* (Cambridge: Polity, 1992); Radhika Mohanram, *Imperial White: Race, Diapsora, and the British Empire* (Minneapolis: University of Minnesota Press, 2007); Vron Ware, *Beyond the Pale: White Women, Racism, and History* (London: Verso, 1992), and her 'Defining Forces: "Race", Gender and Memories of Empire', in Iain Chambers and Lidia Curti (eds.), *The Post-Colonial Question: Common Skies, Divided Horizons* (London: Routledge, 1996); and Marilyn Lake and Henry Reynolds, *Drawing the Global Colour Line: White Men's Countries and the International Challenge of Racial Equality* (Cambridge: Cambridge UP, 2008). An intriguing analysis, which connects centrally with these issues, is Eric Lott, *Love and Theft: Blackface Minstrelsy and the American Working Class* (New York: Oxford UP, 1993). Empirical studies include Grace

Elizabeth Hale, *Making Whiteness: The Culture of Segregation in the South, 1890–1940* (New York: Vintage, 1999); and for my own period, T. G. Ashplant, 'Dis/connecting Whiteness: Biographical Perspectives on Race, Class, Masculinity and Sexuality in Britain c1850–1930', *L'Homme: ZFG* 16/2 (2005). Anthropological readings of contemporary times include: Ruth Frankenberg, *White Women, Race Matters: The Social Construction of Whiteness* (London: Routledge, 1993); and John Hartigan, *Racial Situations: Class Predicaments of Whiteness in Detroit* (Princeton: Princeton UP, 1999). From cinema studies, Richard Dyer, 'White', *Screen*, 29/4 (1988); and his *White: Essays on Race and Culture* (London: Routledge, 1997). Representative collections include: Frankenberg, *Displacing Whiteness*; Mike Hill (ed.), *Whiteness: A Critical Reader* (New York: New York UP, 1997); Noel Ignatiev and John Garvey (eds.), *Race Traitor* (London: Routledge, 1996); and Birgit Brander Rasmussen, Eric Klinberg, Irene J. Nexica, and Matt Wray (eds.), *The Making and Unmaking of Whiteness* (Durham, NC: Duke UP, 2001). David Stowe provides a survey: 'Uncolored People: The Rise of Whiteness Studies', *Lingua Franca* (Sept./Oct. 1996). I am grateful to Les Back for showing me his manuscript, co-authored with Vron Ware, *Out of Whiteness: Color, Politics, and Culture* (Chicago: University of Chicago Press, 2002). Their ruminations on the 'grey zones' in the ethics of whites studying whiteness are entirely convincing.

46. Cited in Richard Wright, *The Colour Curtain: A Report on the Bandung Conference* (London: Dennis Dobson, 1961), 151, from Sukarno's opening address. The 1927 Brussels Congress of Oppressed Nationalities sought to convene the peoples of Africa and Asia; but Bandung marked the first occasion when there was official or governmental representation. For the anxieties of the British government about Bandung, see the cabinet minutes of 13 Jan. 1955, and the discussions with Washington on 23–4 Aug. 1955, reproduced in David Goldsworthy (ed.), *British Documents on the End of Empire, A/3. The Conservative Government and the End of Empire, 1951–1957*, part I. *International Relations* (London: Institute of Commonwealth Studies/HMSO, 1994), 59–60 and 285–7. And see Dipesh Chakrabarty, 'The Legacies of Bandung: Decolonization and the Politics of Culture', in Christopher J. Lee (ed.), *Making a World After Empire: The Bandung Moment and its Political Afterlives* (Athens, Ohio: Ohio University Center for International Studies, 2010).

47. Conventionally, the Japanese defeat of the Russian navy in 1905 is seen a historic turning-point. One of the most surprising documents I have come across is a letter received on this matter by Jan Christian Smuts from his old Cambridge friend, H. J. Wolstenholme, written a year before the Union of South Africa was founded, on 14 May 1909. If only Smuts could have heeded his friend's warnings: W. K. Hancock, *Smuts: The Sanguine Years, 1870–1919* (Cambridge: Cambridge UP, 1962), 322. The Russian defeat, and the reassertion of a self-consciously white military supremacy in the Pacific, forms an important component in Lake and Reynolds,

Drawing the Global Colour Line, ch. 8. In particular they concentrate on the arrival of the US fleet in Sydney and Melbourne in the winter of 1908 (and thence to Auckland). The invitation for the Australian leg came direct from the prime minister, Alfred Deakin, much to the irritation of the Colonial Office. Theodore Roosevelt told the *New York Times* that the purpose of the fleet's visit was to 'show England... that those colonies are white man's countries'. Deakin responded by acknowledging the 'blood relations' which tied the whites of Australia to the whites of the United States: cited in *Drawing the Global Colour Line*, 197 and 205.

48. Harold Macmillan, *Riding the Storm, 1956–1959: Memoirs*, iv (London: Macmillan, 1971), 252. The notes for this speech, made in the aftermath of the rift between the USA and the UK over Suez, are fascinating, providing a good indication of Macmillan's view of things. A little later he could be found exhorting white settlers in Kenya to compromise on majority rule in order to preserve the fundamentals of 'white civilization': cited in Robert Shepherd, *Iain Macleod: A Biography* (London: Pimlico, 1995), 182. I am not suggesting that these anxieties occurred only at the time of decolonization, for they shadowed colonial through the 20th cent., as we can see in the apprehensions underlying the founding of the Commonwealth of Australia in 1901. There emerged a considerable literature in the early part of the 20th cent., of which Maurice Muret, *The Twilight of the White Races* (London: Fisher Unwin, 1926), is representative.

49. For a consideration of memories of empire in these terms, from one who subscribed to such notions, Peregrine Worsthorne, 'Thought Control is Not the Answer', *New Statesman*, 5 Mar. 1999.

50. Frantz Fanon, *Black Skin, White Masks* (London: Paladin, 1972; 1952) and his *The Wretched of the Earth* (Harmondsworth: Penguin, 1971; 1961); Richard Wright, *Black Power* (1954), *The Color Curtain* (1956) and *White Man, Listen!* (1964), and all repr. in a single volume, *Black Power* (New York: Harperperennial, 2008); and, in particular, James Baldwin, *Notes of a Native Son* (Harmondsworth: Penguin, 1995; 1954) and *Nobody Knows My Name: More Notes of a Native Son* (New York: Dell, 1961). The common Parisian connection may well be relevant. Richard Wright attended Bandung as a reporter, and published his account in *The Colour Curtain*; and Baldwin attended the Congress of Negro Writers and Artists in Paris in 1956 which Alioune Diop, in his opening address, referred to as a 'second Bandung': Baldwin, 'Princes and Powers' in his *Nobody Knows My Name*, 25. Wright dedicated *White Man, Listen!* to 'my friend' Eric Williams, the distinguished historian and first prime minister of an independent Trinidad and Tobago. How these themes have been carried into a later epoch can be tracked in the special issue—'The White Issue'—of *Transition*, 73 (1998), esp. the editorial, 'White Skins, White Masks'.

51. The evidence is there for Fanon, though in what many perceive to be in distinct registers, in *Black Skin, White Masks*, and in his *The Wretched of the Earth*.

Wright's engagement with European colonialism can be gauged from his *Black Power* collection. And Baldwin's, although perhaps more fragmentary, runs through his essays from the 1950s onwards: for this, see Cora Kaplan and Bill Schwarz, 'America and Beyond', in Kaplan and Schwarz (eds.), *James Baldwin: America and Beyond* (Ann Arbor: University of Michigan Press, 2011).

52. Baldwin, 'Stranger in the Village', in his *Notes of a Native Son*, 152.

53. And so too Fanon. In a striking passage he declared: 'The settler and the native are old acquaintances. In fact the settler is right when he speaks of knowing "them" well. For it is the settler who has brought the native into existence and who perpetuates his existence.' *The Wretched of the Earth*, 40.

54. According to Phil Cohen: 'Racism proceeds by erasure... Ironically, in view of its project, what this erasure produces is memory. Not a false memory, or a full memory, but a memory that bears the traces of a repression. A screen memory. In other words, a graphic image bound up with a strong impression of some formative moment, which nevertheless covers over an even more traumatic event. Covers over, but does not wipe out...' Indeed, Cohen implies that race can *only* be remembered by means of screen memories: 'Laboring Under Whiteness', 274.

55. This fact of disavowal presents particular difficulties for comprehending how race is remembered: much that determines, it would seem, passes out of memory, and appears only in strange, abstracted displacements. In 'Stranger in the Village' Baldwin describes how in an exclusively white Swiss village horse-hair wigs come to stand in for the memory of an otherwise forgotten blackness.

56. For an illuminating historical reflection, Gail Bederman, *Manliness and Civilization: A Cultural History of Gender and Race in the United States, 1880–1917* (Chicago: Chicago UP, 1995).

57. Baldwin, *Notes of a Native Son*, 154.

58. I am drawing here from George Shulman, 'Baldwin, Prophecy, and Politics', in Kaplan and Schwarz, *James Baldwin*.

59. Toni Morrison, *Playing in the Dark: Whiteness and the Literary Imagination* (London: Picador, 1992), 72; see too her 'The Site of Memory', in Martha Geven, Trinh Minh-ha, and Cornel West (eds.), *Out There: Marginalization and Contemporary Cultures* (New York: New Museum of Contemporary Art, 1960). Morrison is Baldwin's literary executor: for the connections between the two, Lovalerie King and Lynn Orilla Scott (eds.), *James Baldwin and Toni Morrison: Comparative Critical and Theoretical Essays* (New York: Palgrave Macmillan, 2006).

60. Kobena Mercer, *Welcome to the Jungle: New Positions in Black Cultural Studies* (New York; Routledge, 1994), 215.

61. Dyer, *White*, 10.

62. Roediger, *Towards the Abolition of Whiteness*, 13; James Baldwin, 'On Being "White" and Other Lies', *Essence* (Apr. 1984); this is included in Roediger, *Black*

on White, which is the version I have used. Contrast this to Dan T. Carter, 'Reflections of a Reconstructed White Southerner', in Paul A. Cimbala and Robert F. Himmelberg (eds.), *Historians and Race: Autobiography and the Writing of History* (Bloomington, Ind.: Indiana UP, 1996).

63. Fanon, *Black Skin*, 77. My emphasis here is on the reciprocity, not the symmetry, between black and white.

64. Morrison, *Playing in the Dark*, 59.

65. See references above; Roediger has contributed to the journal, *Race Traitor*.

66. Ignatiev and Garvey, *Race Traitor*, 289. This raises a familiar political dilemma: what in white civilization *is not* contaminated by the effects of the system of race privilege? Reading *Race Traitor*, I'm reminded of W. E. B. DuBois recalling his time as a young man in Europe: 'Europe modified profoundly my outlook on life...something of the possible beauty and elegance of life permeated my soul...I came to know Beethoven's symphonies and Wagner's *Ring*. I looked long at the colors of Rembrandt and Titian. I saw in arch and stone and steeple the history and striving of men and also their taste and expression. Form, color and words took new combinations and meanings...I was not less fanatically Negro...' *The Autobiography of W. E. B. DuBois: A Soliloquy on Viewing my Life from the Last Decade of its First Century* (New York: International Publishers, 1986; 1968), 156–7.

67. Ignatiev and Garvey, *Race Traitor*, 291.

68. Baldwin, 'On Being White', 180.

69. Nadine Gordimer, 'Rejoice, Beloved Country!' *Independent on Sunday*, 13 June 1999. A celebrated account coming out of the South African situation of this recasting of the white self is Rian Malan's *My Traitor's Heart* (London: Vintage, 1991), which takes for its subtitle: *Blood and Bad Dreams: A South African Explores the Madness in his Country, his Tribe and Himself*. Malan quotes Colonel Swanepoel, chief interrogator of the South African security police: 'The West is a spent force...it has lost its blood', to which Malan adds the gloss: 'In fact, all white nations save the Afrikaners and the Israelis had lost their blood and would shortly wind up on the trash heap of history' (p. 81). The autobiographical narrative of *My Traitor's Heart* explores the resistances involved in the renunciation of a whiteness bequeathed by history.

70. Fanon, *Black Skin*, 82.

71. Melanie Klein, 'A Contribution to the Psychogenesis of Manic-Depressive States', in Juliet Mitchell (ed.), *The Selected Melanie Klein* (Harmondsworth: Penguin, 1986). Klein introduces this notion of manic reparation after a discussion of the psychic significance of fantasies of 'good blood' and 'bad blood'. Derek Walcott writes of the 'manic absurdity' of giving up 'thought because it is white', *What the Twilight Says* (London: Faber & Faber, 1998), 27, while Nancy Wood uses similar terms, introducing the idea of 'memorial militancy', in 'Remembering the Jews of Algeria', *Parallax*, 4/2 (1998), 178, republ. in her *Vectors of Memory: Legacies of Trauma in Postwar Europe* (Oxford: Berg, 1999).

I have been guided here by Karl Figlio's suggestive essay, 'Historical Imagination/ Psychoanalytical Imagination', *History Workshop Journal*, 45 (1998).

72. James Baldwin, *The Fire Next Time* (Harmondsworth: Penguin, 1964), 16–17.

73. Baldwin's step-father was of the first generation of free men and women who came north in 1919. Baldwin presented this picture: 'In my mind's eye I could see him, sitting at the window, locked up in his terrors; hating and fearing every living soul including his children who had betrayed him, too, by reaching towards the world which had despised him': *Notes of a Native Son*, 88. This was the past Baldwin had in mind.

74. Wright, *White Man, Listen!*, 42.

75. My thinking on this has been shaped substantially by Stuart Hall, esp. his 'New Ethnicities', in David Morley and Kuan-Hsing Chen (eds.), *Stuart Hall: Critical Dialogues* (London: Routledge, 1996); and *Three Blind Mice: Rethinking New Ethnicities* (video), inaugural lecture of the Centre for New Ethnicities Research, University of East London, n.d. (1996).

76. For an exemplary approach, Jacqueline Rose, *States of Fantasy* (Oxford: Clarendon Press, 1998).

77. Bill Schwarz, ' "Already the Past": Memory and Historical Time', in Susannah Radstone and Katharine Hodgkin (eds.), *Regimes of Memory* (London: Routledge, 2003).

78. It is important to remember that Halbwachs insisted also that what he termed 'interior life' (he made an exception for dreaming) was also social: Maurice Halbwachs, *On Collective Memory* (Chicago: University of Chicago Press, 1992), 50.

79. Fredric Jameson, 'Postmodernism, or the Cultural Logic of Late Capitalism', *New Left Review*, 146 (1984); and his 'Postmodernism and Consumer Society', in Hal Foster (ed.), *Postmodern Culture* (London: Pluto Press, 1985). The connection to Adorno is emphatically presented in Jameson's *Late Marxism: Adorno, or, the Persistence of the Dialectic* (London: Verso, 1990; 1944), which in turn follows from Theodor Adorno and Max Horkheimer, *Dialectic of Enlightenment* (London: Verso, 1979). Paul Connerton offers a persuasive overview: *How Modernity Forgets* (Cambridge: Cambridge UP, 2009). And see Susannah Radstone and Bill Schwarz, 'Mapping Memory', in Radstone and Schwarz (eds.), *Memory: Histories, Theories, Debates* (New York: Fordham UP, 2010).

80. Fredric Jameson, 'Future City' *New Left Review*, 2/21 (2003), 76.

81. Renato Rosaldo, 'Imperialist Nostalgia', in his *Culture and Truth: The Remaking of Social Analysis* (London: Routledge, 1993).

82. Luisa Passerini, 'Memories between Silence and Oblivion', in Katharine Hodgkin and Susannah Radstone (eds.), *Contested Pasts: The Politics of Memory* (London: Routledge, 2003), 241.

83. In translation we have Pierre Nora, *Realms of Memory*, 3 vols. (New York: Columbia UP, 1996–8); and *Rethinking France: Les Lieux de mémoire*, 4 vols. (Chicago: Chicago UP, 2001–10). I have discussed Nora in greater detail in my

'Memory, Modernity and Temporality', in Radstone and Schwarz, *Memory*. The absence of any colonial dimension to Nora's reconstruction of France's national memory is all but complete.

84. Pierre Nora, 'The Era of Commemoration', in Nora (ed.), *Realms of Memory: The Construction of the French Past*, iii. *Symbols* (New York: Columbia UP, 1998), 609.

85. Ibid. 610.

86. Neal Ascherson, 'The Crocodiles Gathered', *London Review of Books*, 4 Oct. 2001.

87. This guides Raphael Samuel, *Theatres of Memory*, i. *Past and Present in Contemporary Culture*, and ii. *Island Stories: Unravelling Britain* (London: Verso, 1994 and 1998); the argument was first posed analytically by Walter Benjamin, *Charles Baudelaire: A Lyric Poet in the Era of High Capitalism* (London: Verso, 1983), 145–6.

88. I draw here from Richard Terdiman *Present Past: Modernity and the Memory Crisis* (Ithaca, NY: Cornell UP, 1993).

89. I have discussed this in 'Media Times, Historical Times', *Screen*, 45/2 (2004).

90. John Durham Peters, *Speaking into the Air: A History of the Idea of Communication* (Chicago: University of Chicago Press, 1999), 138; and Bill Schwarz, 'The "Poetics" of Communication', in James Curran and David Morley (eds.), *Media and Cultural Theory* (London: Routledge, 2006). See too Alison Landsberg, *Prosethetic Memory: The Transformation of American Remembrance in the Age of Mass Culture* (New York: Columbia UP, 2004).

91. See Matt Matsuda, *The Memory of the Modern* (New York: Oxford UP, 1996); and for a more theoretical-literary interpretation, Terdiman *Present Past*. There is much relevant in Stephen Kern, *The Culture of Time and Space* (London: Weidenfeld & Nicolson, 1983).

92. Indications can be found in D. A. Headrick, *The Tools of Empire: Technology and European Imperialism in the Nineteenth Century* (New York: Oxford UP, 1981); in Thomas Richards, *The Imperial Archive: Knowledge and Fantasy of Empire* (London: Verso, 1994), and in his earlier *The Commodity Culture of Victorian England: Advertising and Spectacle, 1851–1914* (London: Verso, 1991); and in Anne McClintock, *Imperial Leather: Race, Gender and Sexuality in the Colonial Contest* (London: Routlege, 1995).

93. James Ryan, *Picturing Empire: Photography and the Visualisation of the British Empire* (London: Reaktion, 1997); and Chandrika Paul, *Media and the British Empire* (Basingstoke: Palgrave, 2006).

94. David Cannadine, 'Lord Curzon as Ceremonial Impresario', in his *Aspects of Aristocracy: Grandeur and Decline in Modern Britain* (New Haven; Yale UP, 1994), ch. 4.

95. Valerie Chancellor, *History for their Masters: Opinion in the English History Textbook 1800–1914* (Bath: Adams & Dart, 1970), and Peter Readman, 'The Place of the Past in English Culture, c1890–1914', *Past and Present*, 186 (2005).

96. Helpful on this is Andreas Huyssen, *Twilight Memories: Marking Time in a Culture of Amnesia*, (London: Routledge, 1995), though his title indicates the direction of his argument.

97. George Lamming, *In the Castle of my Skin* (London: Longman, 1987; 1953), 48–50.

98. Jean Rhys, *Wide Sargasso Sea* (Harmondsworth: Penguin, 1976; 1966), 55.

99. Peter Hulme, *Remnants of Conquest: The Island Caribs and their Visitors, 1877–1998* (Oxford: Oxford UP, 2000), 205.

100. Ann Curthoys, 'Expulsion, Exodus and Exile in White Australian Historical Mythology', *Journal of Australian Studies*, 61 (1999), 15; and her 'Constructing National Histories', in Bain Attwood and S. G. Foster (eds.), *Frontier Conflict: The Australian Experience* (Canberra: National Museum of Australia, 2003).

101. W. E. H. Stanner, *After the Dreaming: Black and White Australians. An Anthropological View. The Boyer Lectures 1968* (Sydney: ABC, n.d. [1968]), 26, 7, 24–5, and 53. Attwood and Foster, in their 'Introduction' to *Frontier Conflict*, work from this text, and have important comments to make about it. Stanner was an anthropologist who had worked in Kenya, who had been close to Jomo Kenyatta, and been influenced by W. H. Macmillan (who had written about the West Indies) and by Norman Leys (a prominent critic of British rule in east Africa). Thanks to Ann Curthoys for showing me her paper, 'W. E. H. Stanner and the Historians'. In the 1980 Boyer lectures, Bernard Smith returned to these themes, emphasizing again the costs of forgetfulness: *The Spectre of Truganini: The Boyer Lectures 1980* (Sydney: ABC, n.d. [1980]). And see Robert Foster, Rick Hosking, and Amanda Nettlebeck, *Fatal Collisions: The South Australian Frontier and the Violence of Memory* (Kent Town: Wakefield Press, 2001); and Tom Griffiths, *Hunters and Collectors: The Antiquarian Imagination in Australia* (Cambridge: Cambridge UP, 1996).

102. Attwood and Foster, 'Introduction', 2. Bain Attwood, *Possession: Batman's Treaty and the Matter of History* (Melbourne: Miegunyah Press, 2009), offers a subtle reading of the dialectic of memory and forgetting.

103. Stanner, *After the Dreaming*, 27.

104. At the British World conference in Melbourne in 2004, Kate Darian-Smith convened a fascinating panel, whose contributors were drawn from across the old white settler colonies, investigating the prevalence of white 'captive' narratives in precisely these terms. Given the relative rarity of whites being captured by indigenous peoples, why—the panellists asked—were these stories so numerous, and why so highly charged?

105. Ernest Renan, 'What is a Nation?' (lecture delivered at the Sorbonne on 11 Mar. 1882) in Homi Bhabha (ed.), *Nation and Narration* (London: Routledge, 1990), 11. With Renan in mind, Bhabha makes this comment: 'It is through this syntax of forgetting—or being obliged to forget—that the problematic identification of a national people becomes visible', 'DissemiNation', *Nation and Narration*, 310.

106. Michael Billig, *Banal Nationalism* (London: Sage, 1995), ch. 3, 'Remembering Banal Nationalism'. Lamming in *In the Castle of my Skin* is good on the banalities of imperial iconography in the colony. Helpful too is Melvin Pollner, *Mundane Reason: Reality in Everyday and Sociological Discourse* (Cambridge: Cambridge UP, 1987).

107. Pierre Bourdieu, *The Logic of Practice* (Cambridge: Polity, 1990), 56; my emphasis.

108. For a fuller elaboration, Paul Antze, 'The Other Inside: Memory as Metaphor in Psychoanalysis', in Susannah Radstone and Kate Hodgkin (eds.), *Regimes of Memory* (London: Routledge, 2003).

109. Sigmund Freud, 'Screen Memories', in *The Complete Psychological Works of Sigmund Freud*, iii. *Early Psycho-Analytical Publications* (London: Hogarth Press, 1962), 306.

110. Sigmund Freud, 'Remembering, Repeating and Working-Through', in *The Complete Psychological Works of Sigmund Freud*, xii. *Papers on Technique and Other Essays* (London: Hogarth Press, 1958), 150.

111. Adam Phillips, 'Close-ups', *History Workshop Journal*, 57 (2004), 143.

112. For a parallel argument drawn from literary evidence, though one which places greater emphasis on melancholia, see Lane, 'Epilogue: Britain's Disavowal and the Mourning of Empire', in his *The Ruling Passion*.

113. Two good collections are directly relevant: Kate Darian-Smith and Paula Hamilton (eds.), *Memory and History in Twentieth-Century Australia* (Melbourne: Oxford UP, 1994); and Sarah Nuttall and Carli Coetzee (eds.), *Negotiating the Past: The Making of Memory in South Africa* (Oxford: Oxford UP, 1998).

114. Halbwachs, *On Collective Memory*, 188.

115. Stuart Hall, 'The Hinterland of Science: Ideology and the Sociology of Knowledge', in Centre for Contemporary Cultural Studies, *On Ideology* (London: Hutchinson, 1978).

116. Marcel Proust, *Remembrance of Things Past*, i. *Swann's Way* (Harmondsworth: Penguin, 1989; 1913), 46–51. These themes had first been discussed by Henri Bergson in 1896 in his *Matter and Memory* (New York: Zone Books, 1991), ch. 2. Walter Benjamin develops the argument in 'On Some Motifs in Baudelaire', in his *Illuminations* (London: Fontana, 1973). In his 'Short Speech on Proust', delivered on his fortieth birthday, Benjamin adopted the most radical interpretation by claiming that involuntary memories 'are images which we have never seen before we remember them': cited in Miriam Hansen, 'Benjamin, Cinema and Experience', *New German Critique*, 40 (1987), 179.

117. Pierre Nora, 'Between Memory and History: *Les Lieux de memoire*', *Representations*, 26 (1989), 50.

118. Enoch Powell, 'Commentary', in Brian Brivati and Harriet Jones (eds.), *What Difference did the War Make?* (Leicester: Leicester UP, 1995), 14–15.

119. *Daily Telegraph*, 9 Feb. 1998.

120. Henry James, *Hawthorne* (London: Macmillan, 1967; 1879), 142.

CHAPTER 4

1. John Buchan, 'Evening on the Veld', *Blackwood's Edinburgh Magazine*, 171 (1902), 595.

2. Cited in Preben Kaarsholm, 'Kipling and Masculinity', in Raphael Samuel (ed.), *Patriotism: The Making and Unmaking of English National Identity*, iii. *National Fictions* (London: Routledge, 1989), 217; and in Tim Jeal, *Baden-Powell* (London: Hutchinson, 1989), 419. At this moment, however, Kipling was on the point of discovering an authentic Englishness in the Sussex past.

3. This has continued through the century. For an examination of one of the final moments of this long historical experience see Molly Dineen's moving *Home from the Hill*, first shown on British television on 22 Jan. 1987, and the memoir which accompanied the programme: Hilary Hook, *Home from the Hill* (London: Sportsman's, 1987).

4. Daniel Gorman, *Imperial Citizenship: Empire and the Question of Belonging* (Manchester: Manchester UP, 2006), ch. 6: 'John Buchan, Romantic Imperialism and the Question of Who Belongs', provides a careful, if perhaps too temperate, reading of Buchan's views on empire.

5. John Buchan, *Memory Hold-the-Door* (London: Dent, 1984; 1940), 120. Of South Africa he stated: 'But it is the land itself which holds my memory', 115.

6. Ibid. 124–5.

7. Ibid. 128.

8. John Buchan, *The Thirty-Nine Steps* (London: Pan, 1975; 1915), 7.

9. Buchan, *Memory Hold-the Door*, 127.

10. Ibid. 108.

11. According to Buchan, Milner's great gift was that he 'espoused the state', ibid. 98. A useful account of this episode is Walter Nimocks, *Milner's Young Men: The 'Kindergarten' in Edwardian Imperial Affairs* (Durham, NC: Duke UP, 1968). See too Frederick Madden and D. K. Fieldhouse (eds.), *Oxford and the Idea of Commonwealth* (London: Croom Helm, 1982), which should be supplemented with Terence Ranger's inaugural lecture as Rhodes Professor of Race Relations at Oxford University, *Rhodes, Oxford and the Study of Race Relations* (Oxford: Clarendon Press, 1987).

12. An insightful commentary can be found in Helen Callaway, 'Dressing for Dinner in the Bush: Rituals of Self-Definition and British Imperial Authority', in Ruth Barnes and Joanne Eicher (eds.), *Dress and Gender: Making and Meaning in Cultural Contexts* (Oxford: Berg, 1992).

13. In Feb. 1910, Susan Buchan wrote to her husband ('My own darling Gogg') to tell him of her meeting with Asquith ('Old Sickie'): his 'face was flushed and eyes fixed—whether by having dined too well or by the fact that hordes of Liberals kept passing him by, I don't know…Directly he saw us he said how much he had enjoyed his dinner here—then said "What a brilliant fellow John is—he ought to be in the House…he is far too jolly a fellow not to be in it and we shall have such fun if he were there".' Buchan had been close to Asquith's

son, Raymond, at Oxford: cited in Andrew Lownie, *John Buchan: The Presbyterian Cavalier* (London: Constable, 1995), 105. Ironically, given Buchan's ambitions for politics, I think Amery was close to the mark when he suggested that 'he was not really interested in the subject matter of politics', L. S. Amery, *My Political Life*, i. *England Before the Storm, 1896–1914* (London: Hutchinson, 1953), 266.

14. L. S. Amery (ed.), *The Times History of the War in South Africa, 1899–1902*, 7 vols. (London: *The Times*, 1900–09). According to one authority, Amery's account of the origins of the war—a vindication of the politics of Milner and Chamberlain and the poetics of Kipling—set the dominant historiographical tradition for more than a generation: Iain Smith, 'The Origins of the South African War (1899–1902): A Reappraisal', *South African Historical Journal*, 22 (1990), 27; and more generally his *The Origins of the South African War, 1899–1902* (London: Longman, 1996). For an intriguing discussion of Amery's relationship to his Jewishness, W. D. Rubenstein, 'The Secret of Leopold Amery', *Historical Research*, 181 (2000).

15. A. J. P. Taylor, *From the Boer War to the Cold War: Essays on Twentieth-Century Europe* (Harmondsworth: Penguin, 1996), 298.

16. Milner's relationship to the press was also of great importance, as A. N. Porter demonstrates in 'Sir Alfred Milner and the Press, 1897–99', *Historical Journal*, 16/2 (1973). Much intrigue revolved around the appointment of an editor for the *Johannesburg Star*. In July 1898 one of the paper's directors wrote to W. T. Stead in London outlining a modest job description for the future editor: 'He must have faith in the English speaking race and be able and willing to render substantial aid to Sir Alfred Milner in forwarding Imperial Policy in South Africa... His mission would be to educate, guide and unite the men who read English on the Rand and who are for the most part today an incoherent and factious crowd.' In the event it was agreed with G. E. Buckle, the editor of *The Times*, that W. F. Monypenny ('emphatically a gentleman', according to Buckle) could act as *The Times* correspondent in Johannesburg and at the same time edit the *Star* (ibid. 330–1 and 333). Buckle and Monypenny were later to collaborate in writing the classic 6-vol. *Life of Benjamin Disraeli, Earl of Beaconsfield* (London: Murray, 1910–20). For more on the role of *The Times*: Dorothy Helly and Helen Callaway, 'Journalism as Active Politics: Flora Shaw, *The Times* and South Africa', and Jacqueline Beaumont, '*The Times* at War, 1899–1902', in Donal Lowry (ed.), *The South African War Reappraised* (Manchester: Manchester UP, 2000).

17. There is a substantial, controversial historiography here: see Richard Price, *An Imperial War and the British Working Class: Working-Class Attitudes and Reactions to the Boer War, 1899–1902* (London: Routledge & Kegan Paul, 1972), which aims to refute J. A. Hobson's fears of a rampant popular jingoism emerging in response to Mafeking, adumbrated in his *The Psychology of Jingoism* (London: Grant Richards, 1901); for an overview which is intelligent but whose empirical cast of mind seems cyclopean when it comes to matters of history and the imagination, Michael Howard, 'Empire, Race and War in Pre-1914 Britain', in Hugh

Lloyd-Jones, Valerie Pearl, and Blair Worden (eds.), *History and Imagination: Essays in Honour of Hugh Trevor-Roper* (London: Duckworth, 1981); Victor Kiernan, *The Lords of Human Kind: European Attitudes to the Outside World in the Imperial Age* (Harmondsworth: Penguin, 1972); Henry Pelling, *Popular Politics and Society in Late Victorian Britain* (London: Macmillan, 1968); and for what remains perhaps the best general discussion yet, Gareth Stedman Jones, 'Working-Class Culture and Working-Class Politics in London, 1870–1900: Notes on the Remaking of a Class', in his *Languages of Class: Studies in English Working Class History, 1832–1982* (Cambridge: Cambridge UP, 1983). More recently, John MacKenzie, 'Empire and Metropolitan Cultures', in Andrew Porter (ed.), *The Oxford History of the British Empire*, iii. *The Nineteenth Century* (Oxford: Oxford UP, 1999); and for an illuminating gloss on MacKenzie's more general interpretations, Robert H. MacDonald, *The Language of Empire: Myths and Metaphors of Popular Imperialism, 1880–1918* (Manchester: Manchester UP, 1994).

18. See Kenneth O. Morgan, 'The Boer War and the Media, 1899–1902', *Twentieth Century British History*, 13/4 (2002); and Donal Lowry, ' "The World's No Bigger than a Kraal": The South African War and International Opinion in the First Age of "Globalization" ', in David Omissi and Andrew Thompson (eds.), *The Impact of the South African War* (Basingstoke: Palgrave, 2002).

19. An incisive account was written long ago: Asa Briggs, *Mass Entertainment: The Origins of a Modern Industry* (Adelaide: Griffin Press, 1960). Hobson's *Psychology of Jingoism* is about the relation between jingoism and the new mass media, and the book is an attempt to understand 'the modern manufacture of public opinion' (p. 109). And see too: *The Boer War: The First Media War*, BBC2, 18 Mar. 1997.

20. Bill Nasson, *The South African War, 1899–1902* (London: Arnold, 1999), 8, and ch. 9; relevant in this regard is the same author's 'Commemorating the Anglo-Boer War in Post-Apartheid South Africa', *Radical History Review*, 78 (2000).

21. Reginald Pound and Geoffrey Harmsworth, *Northcliffe* (London: Cassel, 1959) tell this story.

22. Benedict Anderson, *Imagined Communities: Reflections on the Origin and Spread of Nationalism* (London: Verso, 1986), 39–40; and Geoffrey Nowell-Smith, 'On History and the Cinema', *Screen*, 31/2 (1990). In making the connection between the cinema, modern subjectivities, and memory, Nowell-Smith uses one of Kilping's South African stories, 'Mrs Bathurst' (1904), reproduced in his *Short Stories*, i. *A Sahib's War and Other Stories* (Harmondsworth: Penguin, 1971).

23. David Fitzpatrick, *Oceans of Consolation: Personal Accounts of Irish Migration to Australia* (Melbourne: Melbourne UP, 1995).

24. Ernest Gellner, *Nations and Nationalisms* (Oxford: Blackwell, 1983), 123.

25. Roland Barthes, *Mythologies* (London: Paladin, 1986).

26. See *Selections from the Smuts Papers*, vi. *December 1934——August 1945*, ed. Jean van der Poel (Cambridge: Cambridge UP, 1973), 278; letter to Margery Gillett, 6

Jan. 1941. For the place of the war correspondent in South Africa, Raymond Sibbald, *The War Correspondent: The Boer War* (Stroud: Allan Sutton, 1993).

27. A good commentary which places Wallace in the centre of the new mass culture is David Glover, 'Looking for Edgar Wallace: The Author as Consumer', *History Workshop Journal*, 37 (1994). On publication Wallace sent a copy of his *The Four Just Men* to Joseph Chamberlain with a note asking if he could 'find some way of dragging [it]...into a political speech I should be everlastingly obliged'. Chamberlain never replied: Margaret Lane, *Edgar Wallace: The Biography of a Phenomenon* (London: Hamish Hamilton, 1964), 153. Edgar Wallace, *Sanders of the River* (London: Brown, Watson, 1933; 1911); Merian C. Cooper and Edgar Wallace, *King Kong* (London: Transworld, 1966; 1932)——although it appears that the novel was in fact authored by one Delos W. Lovelace; and *The Four Just Men* (Oxford: Oxford UP, 1995; 1906). The myth of Sanders was prominent in British cinema from the time the story was filmed by Alexander Korda (with Paul Robeson) in 1935: Richard Dyer provides an indication in 'White', *Screen*, 29/4 (1988).

28. Rudyard Kipling, *Something of Myself: For my Friends Known and Unknown* (Harmondsworth: Penguin, 1981; 1937), 113; George Shepperson, 'Kipling and the Boer War', in John Gross (ed.), *Kipling: The Man, his Work and his World* (London: Weidenfeld & Nicolson, 1972).

29. George Orwell, 'Rudyard Kipling', in *The Collected Essays, Journalism and Letters*, ii. *My Country Right or Left, 1940–43* (Harmondsworth: Penguin, 1980), 227; and Colin MacInnes, 'Kipling and the Music Halls', in Gross, *Kipling*. Orwell noted: 'Few people who have criticized England from the inside have said bitterer things about her than this gutter patriot', *Collected Essays*, ii. 220.

30. Benita Parry is good on the recent revival of Kipling: 'The Contents and Discontents of Kipling's Imperialism', in Erica Carter, James Donald, and Judith Squires (eds.), *Space and Place: Theories of Identity and Location* (London: Lawrence & Wishart, 1993).

31. The film was produced in 1972. In selling the rights in 1960 to producer and scriptwriter Carl Foreman (the story is that Churchill had heard good things about Foreman's *The Guns of Navarone*), Churchill was unaware that Foreman had earlier been blacklisted in the USA. At the end of the 1950s, Cecil B. de Mille had hoped to make a film about Baden-Powell, starring David Niven: Jeal, *Baden-Powell*, 567.

32. Reproduced in Winston S. Churchill, *Frontiers and Wars* (Harmondsworth: Penguin, 1972); *Savrola* was 1st publ. as a book in the USA in 1899: republ. London: Leo Cooper, 1990; Winston S. Churchill, *My Early Life, 1874–1908* (London: Fontana, 1983; 1930), 85 and 67; and D. J. Wenden, 'Churchill, Radio and Cinema', in Robert Blake and Wm. Roger Louis (eds.), *Churchill* (Oxford: Oxford UP, 1933), 226. For Churchill's contracts with the *News of the World*, see Matthew Engel, *Tickle the Public: One Hundred Years of the Popular Press* (London: Victor Gollancz, 1996), 227. On the empire, Ronald Hyam, 'Churchill and the

British Empire', in Blake and Louis, *Churchill*, 167; and Robert Rhodes James (ed.), *Churchill Speaks, 1897–1963: Collected Speeches in Peace and War* (Leicester: Windward, 1981), 810.

33. Julian Symons, *Portrait of an Artist: Conan Doyle* (London: André Deutsch, 1974), 61; Arthur Conan Doyle, *The Great Boer War* (London: Smith, Elder, 1902): this was printed eighteen times between Oct. 1900 and Oct. 1902, though Leo Amery, for one, was doubtful about its 'picturesque imaginativeness of style', *Times History*, ii, p. vii. Within a year of his journey to South Africa, Conan Doyle was active in supporting the new 'anti-alien' British Brothers' League. The same year he also wrote a defence of the military campaign, fulminating against liberal critics: *The War in South Africa: Its Causes and Conduct* (London: Smith, Elder, 1902). Conan Doyle opened a public fund to ensure that every newspaper editor in Europe and North America could receive a free copy.

34. G.A. Henty, *With Buller in Natal; or a Born Leader* (London: Blackie, 1901; 1900); and his final novel, *With Roberts to Pretoria: A Tale of the South African War* (London: Blackie, 1902). For Henty's influence on a generation see Taylor, *From Boer War to Cold War*, 47.

35. For a discussion of Erskine Childers, Edgar Wallace, and John Buchan in these terms, Michael Denning, *Cover Stories: Narrative and Ideology in the British Spy Thriller* (London: Routledge & Kegan Paul, 1987), ch. 2. The opening sentence of Erskine Childers, *The Riddle of the Sands* (Harmondsworth: Penguin, 1995; 1903) alludes to blackness, barbarism, and civilization (p. 15).

36. W. J. Reader, *'At Duty's Call': A Study in Obsolete Patriotism* (Manchester: Manchester UP, 1988), 19; Patrick Dunae, 'Boys' Literature and the Idea of Empire, 1870–1914', *Victorian Studies*, 24/1 (1980). On the general issue of empire and masculinity, Graham Dawson, *Soldier Heroes: British Adventure, Empire and the Imagining of Masculinities* (London: Routledge, 1994).

37. Robert Baden-Powell, *Scouting for Boys* (London: C. Arthur Pearson, 1909; 1908); and *Girl Guiding* (London: C. Arthur Pearson, 1918); Jeal, *Baden-Powell*; and Michael Rosenthal, *The Character Factory: Baden-Powell and the Origins of the Boy Scout Movement* (London: Collins, 1986). As *The Times* commented in its unusually populist celebration of the ending of the siege of Mafeking, 'The story of Mafeking has all the elements of romance', 21 May 1900.

38. Cited in Nasson, *South African War*, 248.

39. *The Boer War: The First Media War*; and John Barnes, *Filming the Boer War: The Beginnings of the Cinema in England, 1894–1901*, iv (London: Bishopsgate Press, 1992). The theme of empire and spectacle is explored in Paul Greenhalgh, *Ephemeral Vistas: The Expositions Universelles, Great Exhibitions and World's Fairs, 1851–1939* (Manchester: Manchester UP, 1990); on MadameTussaud's, MacDonald, *The Language of Empire*, 94; on advertising, Anne McClintock, *Imperial Leather: Race, Gender and Sexuality in the Colonial Conquest* (London: Routledge, 1995), and M. D. Blanch, 'British Society and the War', in Peter Warwick (ed.), *The South African War: The Anglo-Boer War, 1899–1902* (London: Longman, 1980),

230–2; for board-games, Annie Coombes, 'The Franco-British Exhibition: Packaging Empire in Edwardian Britain', in Jane Beckett and Deborah Cherry (eds.), *The Edwardian Era* (Oxford: Phaidon, 1987), 160; Ian McDonald, *The Boer War in Postcards* (Wolfeboro: Allan Sutton, 1990); and Andrew Thompson, 'Publicity, Philanthropy and Commemoration: British Society and the War', in Omissi and Thompson, *Impact of the South African War*, 113.

40. Rayne Kruger, *Goodbye Dolly Gray: The Story of the Boer War* (London: Pimlico, 1996), 505. The declared 'godfather' of the book, the author's literary agent, is identified as the author Paul Scott. This, and Thomas Pakenham, *The Boer War* (London: Futura, 1982), provide the best narrative accounts of the war.

41. This is confirmed by the documentation in Stephen Koss (ed.), *The Pro-Boers: The Anatomy of an Anti-War Movement* (Chicago: University of Chicago Press, 1973). The *Manchester Guardian* was an important organizer of liberal opinion, especially in its reports from South Africa filed by J. A. Hobson, subsequently collected together in 1900 as *The War in South Africa: Its Causes and Effects* (London: Nisbet, 1901). Interestingly, the only author of fiction who appears in Koss's volume is Jerome K. Jerome. It is necessary to observe, too, that positions within Nonconformity were complex, reflecting the larger transitions from radicalism to Unionism: see Greg Cuthbertson, 'Pricking the "Nonconformist Conscience": Religion Against the South African War', in Lowry, *The South African War Reappraised*.

42. Enoch Powell, interview with the author, 26 Apr. 1988.

43. Dunae, 'Boys' Literature', 115.

44. Symons, *Portrait of an Artist*, 63.

45. Blanch, 'British Society and the War', 215. He notes too that 'for some time at least during the South African War 14.2 per cent of the entire male population aged 18 to 40 years was in uniform', and suggests: 'A major reason for joining the Regular army . . . was that working men were stimulated by the experiences retold by their father and uncles and brothers. Thus was militarism re-cycled, as it assumed a place in popular culture', 229 and 214. In all, 448,435 British and colonial troops served in the war: Thompson, 'Publicity, Philanthropy and Commemoration', 100.

46. Curzon and Kitchener both agreed on the possibility of calling upon the Indian army, probably the only thing they ever did agree upon. But in a war between 'white races' the prevailing opinion was hostile: David Omissi, 'India: Some Perceptions of Race and Empire', in Omissi and Thompson, *Impact of the South African War*.

47. For the connections with Australia: a press correspondent from Sydney, Frank Wilkinson, published his *Australia at the Front: A Colonial View of the Boer War* (London: John Lang, 1901); but see too Amery, *Times History of the War in South Africa*, iii, ch. 2, and Reader, *'At Duty's Call'*, 12. The historiography can be followed in Laurie Field, *The Forgotten War: Australia and the Boer War* (Melbourne: Melbourne UP, 1995); Barbara Penny, 'The Australian Debate on the Boer War',

(Australian) Historical Studies, 14/56 (1971); C. N. Connolly, 'Manufacturing "Spontaneity" for the Australian Offer of Troops for the Boer War', *(Australian) Historical Review*, 18/70 (1978); and the same author's 'Class, Birthplace and Loyalty: Australian Attitudes to the Boer War', *(Australian) Historical Review*, 18/71 (1978). Luke Trainor, 'Australia and New Zealand', in Omissi and Thompson, *Impact of the South African War*, is helpful for the latter. The Canadian situation is summarized in Philip Buckner, 'Canada', in Omissi and Thompson, *Impact of the South African War*, and in Robert Page, *The Boer War and Canadian Imperialism* (Ottawa: Canadian Historical Association, 1987); and a more complex rendition is given in Carmen Miller, 'Loyalty, Patriotism and Resistance: Canada's Response to the Anglo-Boer War, 1899–1902', *South African Historical Journal*, 41 (1999). The French in Quebec, however, tended to regard the South African War in terms of their own defeat of 1759, drawing on all the consequent antipathies towards the British. For some of these issues: Deryk Schreuder, 'British Imperialism and the Politics of Ethnicity: The "Warring Nations" of the African Highveld', *Journal of Canadian Studies*, 25/1 (1990).

48. James Loughlin, *Ulster Nationalism and British National Identity since 1885* (London: Pinter, 1995), 32; and the report from the *Cape Times*, 16 Mar. 1900, reproduced in M. J. Farrelly, *The Settlement After the War in South Africa* (London: Macmillan, 1900), 309–13. Catholic Ireland was a different matter. The case of Michael Davitt is instructive. He resigned as an MP in Oct. 1899, condemning the war as 'the greatest crime of the nineteenth century'. He proceeded to join the Irish Brigade in Boer service, finding amongst the Afrikaners a moral purity which contrasted with the conduct of the Anglo-Saxon countries——'that of a Godless culture, of refined vice, of divorce courts and immorality, of drunkenness and prostitution': cited in Francis Sheehy-Skeffington, *Michael Davitt: Revolutionary, Agitator and Labour Leader* (London: MacGibbon & Kee, 1967), 166; and Michael Davitt, *The Boer Fight for Freedom* (New York: Funk & Wagnalls, 1902), 37. According to R. F. Foster, the Boer War was 'nearly as crucial an event for Irish nationalism as the death of Parnell', *Modern Ireland: 1600–1972* (Harmondsworth: Penguin, 1989), 448. Insurgents of the Easter Rising consciously looked back to the Boer example: Tim Pat Coogan, *Michael Collins: A Biography* (London: Arrow, 1991), 13 and 54. More generally on Ireland and empire, or anti-empire, Keith Jeffrey (ed.), *An Irish Empire? Aspects of Ireland and the British Empire* (Manchester: Manchester UP, 1996).

49. Much has been made of the connections between the Scots and the Afrikaners, as a result of a shared religious culture. Thus Smuts was typical in suggesting (albeit to a Scottish audience) in 1929 that 'It is often difficult to know where the Scots end and the Dutch begin', *Africa and Some World Problems* (Oxford: Oxford UP, 1930), 3–4. On a more celebrated occasion, some sixty years after the war, Harold Macmillan made the same sort of claims in his so-called 'Wind of Change' speech, made on 3 Feb. 1960 in Cape Town, reproduced in Harold Macmillan *Pointing the Way, 1959–61: Memoirs*, v (London: Macmillan, 1972).

Here he made much of the shared debt to the Synod of Dort of 1618——though he failed to remind his audience that the Synod was most notable for formally sanctioning the principle that Christianity and chattel slavery were incompatible. For the wider context: Andrew Dewar Gibb, *Scottish Empire* (London: Alexander Maclehouse, 1937); R. A. Gage (ed.), *The Scots Abroad: Labour, Capital and Enterprise, 1750–1914* (London: Croom Helm, 1985); Michael Fry, *The Scottish Empire* (Phantassie: Tuckwell, 2001), esp. 344; and John M. MacKenzie with Nigel Dalziel, *The Scots in South Africa: Ethnicity, Identity, Gender and Race, 1772–1914* (Manchester: Manchester UP, 2007).

50. Dai Smith, *Aneurin Bevan and the World of South Wales* (Cardiff: University of South Wales Press, 1993), 18.

51. Kruger, *Goodbye Dolly Gray*. As Keith Jeffery makes the same point: 'The paradox of this imperial service was that the more individual parts of the Empire generously contributed on their own behalf to collective imperial needs, the more independent-minded they might become.' 'Kruger's Farmers, Strathcona's Horse, Sir George Clarke's Camels and the Kaiser's Battleships: The Impact of the South African War on Imperial Defence', in Lowry, *The South African War Reappraised*, 193.

52. The key conceptual elaboration, based principally on his visits to Canada and Australia, was Richard Jebb, *Studies in Colonial Nationalism* (London: Edward Arnold, 1905). A year later Jebb travelled to South Africa on behalf of the *Morning Post*. See esp. Deryk Schreuder, 'Colonial Nationalism and "Tribal" Nationalism in the Making of the South African State, 1899–1910', in John Eddy and Deryk Schreuder (eds.), *The Rise of Colonial Nationalism: Australia, New Zealand, Canada and South Africa First Assert their Nationalism* (London: Allen & Unwin, 1988).

53. The complexities of the issue are illustrated by the currency of the term 'local patriotism', which could be used as a synonym for colonial nationalism *and* by those dedicated to the idea of a more integrated empire. Thus through the early part of 1902 Milner himself became an advocate of 'local patriotism': see his Johannesburg speech of 8 Jan. in Cecil Headlam (ed.), *The Milner Papers*, ed. Cecil Headlam, ii. *South Africa, 1899–1905* (London: Cassell, 1933), 319–22; and the report of his speech in the *Cape Argus* of 25 Apr., reproduced in Farrelly, *The Settlement After the War*, 290–3. Joseph Chamberlain employed the same notion in his dramatic intervention of 15 May 1903, though in this instance symbolically to unify 'Birmingham men' throughout the empire: *Mr Chamberlain's Speeches*, ed. Charles W. Boyd, ii (London: Constable, 1914), 125–30. For a significant aspect of the larger story: John Kendle, *The Round Table Movement and Imperial Union* (Toronto: University of Toronto Press, 1975). The view of the Kindergarten and the Round Table movement—preferring 'to see the world divided between white and black areas, one in the temperate and the other in the tropical zone', ibid. 304—was one which was to have a new lease of life in the 1960s, when the Amery patrimony played its part.

54. Cited in Porter, 'Milner and the Press', 335.

55. Olive Schreiner believed the Boers to have been cut adrift from Enlightenment thought as a consequence of their language: Ruth First and Ann Scott, *Olive Schreiner* (New Brunswick, NJ: Rutgers UP, 1990), 195.

56. Cited in Nasson, *South African War*, 256. Though perhaps Theodore Roosevelt's views are most telling in terms of prevailing conceptions of racial destiny. In two letters at the end of 1899 he expressed his liking for these 'belated Cromwellians', but none the less was convinced that they were 'battling on the wrong side in the fight of civilization and will have to go under', cited in Max Beloff, *The Great Powers: Essays in Twentieth-Century Politics* (London: Allen & Unwin, 1959), 226.

57. Amery, *Times History of the War in South Africa*, i. 1–2.

58. Lionel Curtis, *With Milner in South Africa* (Oxford: Blackwell, 1951), 201.

59. John Barrell, *The Infection of Thomas De Quincey: A Psychopathology of Imperialism* (New Haven: Yale UP, 1991), 11.

60. This is convincingly argued by Paula M. Krebs, '"The Last of the Gentlemen's Wars": Women in the Boer War Concentration Camps Controversies', *History Workshop Journal*, 33 (1992). And in continental Europe, pro-Boer sentiment could be justified in terms of the supposed weakness of the British in dealing with the black natives of South Africa: Preben Kaarsholm, 'Pro-Boers', in Raphael Samuel (ed.), *Patriotism*, i. *History and Politics* (London: Routledge, 1989), 121.

61. Conan Doyle, *The Great Boer War*, 1–2.

62. A fine discussion of Conan Doyle's understanding of the sexual politics of the war is in Paula M. Krebs, *Gender, Race, and the Writing of Empire: Public Discourse in the Boer War* (Cambridge: Cambridge UP, 1999), ch. 4.

63. Conan Doyle, *The Great Boer War*, 383, 419, 531, and 121; 535, 647, and 717; and 646.

64. Cited in Peter Warwick, *Black People in the South African War* (Cambridge: Cambridge UP, 1983), 15.

65. Ibid. 15–18.

66. Bill Nasson, *Abraham Esau's War: A Black South African War in the Cape, 1899–1902* (Cambridge: Cambridge UP, 1991), 126; and more generally, Christopher Saunders, 'African Attitudes to Britain and the Empire Before and After the South African War', in Lowry, *The South African War Reappraised*.

67. This may suggest that the metropolitan experience inverted that of South Africa. Fransjohn Pretorius argues that in South Africa after the peace of Vereeniging memories of black mobilization were expunged from public life: 'Boer Attitudes to Blacks in Wartime', in Lowry, *The South African War Reappraised*.

68. Cited in Kruger, *Goodbye Dolly Gray*, 503.

69. *Selections from the Smuts Papers*, ed. W. K. Hancock and Jean van der Poel, ii. *June 1902–May 1910* (Cambridge: Cambridge UP, 1966), 71. And for an important perspective on the emergent white man's country, Morag Bell, 'A Woman's

Place in "a White Man's Country": Rights, Duties and Citizenship for the "New" South Africa', *Ecumene*, 2/2 (1995).

70. Nasson, *Abraham Esau's War*, 189. Who was learning from whom: Smuts from Chamberlain, or Chamberlain from Smuts? Smuts was not the only one disappointed by Chamberlain. Chamberlain was petitioned at the same time by Sol Plaatje, the great black South African intellectual. It was tempting to follow this story further, for it connects at many points with my own concerns: his shadowing of Smuts; his long campaigns in England; his relations with W. E. B. DuBois; his time in Harlem in the 1920s. Much can be gleaned from his *Mafeking Diary: A Black Man's View of a White Man's War* (London: James Currey, 1990); and from Brian Willin, *Sol Plaatje: South African Nationalist, 1876–1932* (London: Heinemann, 1984).

71. See Gautam Chakravarty, *The Indian Mutiny and the British Imagination* (Cambridge: Cambridge UP, 2004).

72. *The Works of Rudyard Kipling* (Ware: Wordsworth Poetry Library, 1994), 305.

73. Robert Baden-Powell, *Indian Memories: Recollections of Soldiering, Sport, etc.* (London: Herbert Jenkins, 1915), 14–15.

74. 'The Indian Mutiny in Fiction', *Blackwood's Edinburgh Magazine*, 161 (Feb. 1887).

75. Jeffrey Richards, 'Boy's Own Empire: Feature Films and Imperialism in the 1930s', in MacKenzie, *Imperialism and Popular Culture*, 149.

76. Robert Baden-Powell, *The Matabele Campaign, 1896: Being a Narrative of the Native Rising in Matabeleland and Mashonaland* (London: Methuen, 1897). For his account of black atrocities, and for his own insistence that, these cruelties notwithstanding, he was no 'nigger-hater', ibid. 33 and 63–4; and *Indian Memories*, 17.

77. Terence Ranger, *Revolt in Southern Rhodesia, 1896–7: A Story of African Resistance* (London: Heinemann, 1967), 322–3. Olive Schreiner's extraordinary novel, *Trooper Peter Halket of Mashonaland* (Johannesburg: A. D. Donker, 1974) should be read in this context, as a riposte to the likes of Baden-Powell. Notoriously, the first 1897 edn., published in London, carried a photograph of a lynching; this was subsequently dropped until the 1974 reissue.

78. Churchill, *Early Life*, 82; Randolph Churchill, *Winston S. Churchill*, i. *Youth, 1874–1900* (London: Heinemann, 1966), 209. Churchill and Baden-Powell had first met in India, at a polo match in Meerut: Winston Churchill, *Great Contemporaries* (London: The Reprint Society, 1941; 1937), 325; and Baden-Powell, *Indian Memories*, 35.

79. Churchill, *Early Life*, 9–10 and 14. For an unusually reflective view of these things, more about white than black, see the letter from John Dove of the Round Table to his colleague Robert Brand, written from India in Sept. 1919: 'Do you remember your nursery ideas of a savage? Can a man who is nearly stark naked and brown and painted and whose long black hair calls up "Man Friday" running across the sands from the cannibal bonfires, ever be really fit for a vote? I have changed since I came here, but I still, I confess, feel old prejudices welling

up at me. This is especially so from time to time one of those strange outbursts of inconceivable brutality occurs.' This latter reference is to the events in Amritsar the previous spring: cited in Kendle, *The Round Table*, 304.

80. There were appropriately dynastic memories here. In 1891 his father had travelled to South Africa, in the company of Alfred Beit and visiting Cecil Rhodes, in order to organize his investments in the Rand, which made him a fortune. He furnished his reports to the *Daily Graphic* (for a fee of 2,000 guineas), which he later published as *Men, Mines and Animals in South Africa* (London: Sampson Low, 1892): R. F. Forster, *Lord Randolph Churchill: A Political Life* (Oxford: Oxford UP, 1988), 372–4. Randolph's sister, Lady Sarah Wilson, acquitted herself during the war as adventurer, captured celebrity, and *Daily Mail* correspondent: Brian Roberts, *Churchills in Africa* (London: Hamish Hamilton, 1970). At the end of 1899 Winston Churchill's mother travelled to South Africa on a hospital-ship (complete with X-ray facilities) for which she had campaigned in London high society, while his younger brother served as a lieutenant. Jennie Churchill and her two sons were to have a reunion in South Africa: Ralph G. Martin, *Lady Randolph Churchill: A Biography,*. ii. *1895–1921* (London: Cardinal, 1974), chs. 14–15. In turn Winston's son, Randolph, was momentarily a *News of the World* correspondent in Johannesburg in 1959: Anita Leslie, *Randolph* (New York: Beaufort Books, 1985), 147–8. And *his* son—upon embarking for a journey by light plane throughout Africa in 1963—could boast: 'At each of the three stages in the history of modern Africa—the European conquest, the continent's economic development and the African liberation—there was a member of my family at hand to write about it': Winston S. Churchill, *First Journey* (London: Pan, 1966), 3.

81. See esp. *The Malakand Field Force* (1898); *The Story of the River War: An Account of the Re-conquest of the Soudan* (1899); *London to Ladysmith* (1900); and *The Story of Ian Hamilton's March* (1900), all reproduced in *Frontiers and Wars*. See too his *Early Life*, ch. 15, on Omdurman; and *Parliamentary Debates, House of Commons*, 28 Feb. 1906, cols. 1233–44. The following July he made a similar point in the Commons, referring to 'the white community of men, women and children, who are, after all, a little more than a drop in the great ocean of coloured people by whom they are surrounded, and whose lives and whose fortunes may at any moment be swept into the abyss by some sudden uprising of millions of natives' (7 July 1906), *Churchill Speaks*, 101.

82. John Barnes and David Nicholson (eds.), *The Empire at Bay: The Leo Amery Diaries*, ii. *1929–1945* (London: Hutchinson, 1988), 988, and for the larger context, Michael Faber, *Speak for England: Leo, Julian and John Amery. The Tragedy of a Political Family* (London: Free Press, 2005), ch. 18. A year earlier Amery had claimed that 'Winston has a curious hatred of India . . . and is convinced that the Indian Army is only waiting to shoot us in the back', cited in Wm. Roger Louis, *In the Name of God Go! Leo Amery and the British Empire in the Age of Churchill* (New York: Norton, 1970), 170, which also details the struggle between Amery and Churchill over India in the 1940s. This is an engaging though uncritical

perspective from deep inside All Souls; for a contrary view, Bill Schwarz, 'Empire: For and Against', *Twentieth Century British History*, 6/3 (1995). Marcus Garvey came to believe that Churchill was the greatest Negro hater in the British empire: Colin Grant, *Negro with a Hat: The Rise and Fall of Marcus Garvey and his Dream of Mother Africa* (London: Jonathan Cape, 2008), 284.

83. *The Churchill–Eisenhower Correspondence, 1953–1955*, ed. Peter Boyle (Chapel Hill, NC: University of North Carolina Press, 1990), 167 (8 Aug. 1954).

84. Jeremy Krikler, 'Social Neurosis and Hysterical Pre-cognition in South Africa: A Case-Study and Reflections', *Journal of Social History*, 28/3 (1995), 493, 509, and 510; see too his complementary 'Agrarian Class Struggle in the South African War', *Social History*, 14/2 (1989).

85. Shula Marks, *Reluctant Rebellion: The 1906–8 Disturbances in Natal* (Oxford: Oxford UP, 1970); and for the comparison to Morant Bay, Ronald Hyam, *Elgin and Churchill at the Colonial Office, 1905–8: The Watershed of the Empire-Commonwealth* (London: Macmillan, 1968), 9.

86. Hyam, *Elgin and Churchill*, 251 and 538.

87. 'Gebuza' (F. E. Colenso), *The Peril in Natal* (London: Fisher Unwin, 1906), 6 and 9.

88. Roderick Jones, 'The Black Peril in South Africa', *The Nineteenth Century and After* (May 1904), 715–21. See Jones's memorial to Buchan included in Susan Tweedsmuir, *John Buchan by his Wife and Friends* (London: Hodder & Stoughton, 1947); and N. Levi, *Jan Smuts* (London: Longman, 1917), 307.

89. Winston Churchill, *My African Journey* (London: Hodder & Stoughton, 1908), 48. On this occasion, Churchill took his camera. His dispatches were originally sent to the *Strand Magazine*, while those of his travelling companion, Eddie Marsh, were directed to the *Manchester Guardian*.

90. Cited in Hyam, *Elgin and Churchill*, 408.

91. Ibid.

92. For Milner's Watch Tower speech: *Milner Papers*, ii. 466–9; for important anticipations of these arguments, see Anthony Trollope, *South Africa*, 2 vols. (London: Chapman Hall, 1878).

93. This comprised the period Jan.–June 1904: Demetrius Bougler, 'The "Yellow Peril" Bogey'; Oswald P. Low and W. T. Gill, 'A White Australia: What it Means'; O. Etzbacher, 'The Yellow Peril'; and Sir Harry Johnston, 'The White Man's Place in Africa'; Johnston cited in Bernard Porter, 'The Edwardians and their Empire', in Donald Read (ed.), *Edwardian England* (London: Croom Helm, 1982), 34. In similar vein, see the anonymous 'The Revolt Against the Paleface', *Review of Reviews* (Aug. 1900). In fact, anti-Russian sentiment could also allow some sympathy for the Japanese, who by a bizarre twist could appear less 'oriental' than the Russians. Baden-Powell, for one, always rather liked the martial asceticism of the Japanese. In any case, as Richard Storry has pointed out, 'the victorious navy had largely been built and equipped at Barrow, Elswick and Sheffield; and most, if not all, of the Japanese officers had been trained or professionally advised by Englishmen', *A History of Modern Japan* (Harmondsworth: Penguin, 1979), 141.

94. Cited in Kate Darian-Smith, Liz Gunner, and Sarah Nuttall, 'Introduction' to their edited collection, *Text, Theory, Space: Literature and History in South Africa and Australia* (London: Routledge, 1996), 4. The connections between South Africa and Australasia, on the one hand, and Argentina, on the other, are of deep interest. For these colonial connections in the southern hemisphere, by-passing the metropole, see the thematic issue of *Australian Cultural History*, 10 (1991).

95. Robert Huttenback, *Racism and Empire: White Settlers and Coloured Immigration in the British Self-Governing Colonies, 1830–1910* (Ithaca, NY: Cornell UP, 1976); Eddy and Schreuder, *Colonial Nationalism*, esp. Avner Offner's discussion of '"The Pacific Rim" societies'. Critical here, in thinking through the consequences of 'the end of the Columbian epoch' and the end of territorial conquest is the influential paper by H. J. Mackinder, 'The Geographical Pivot of History', *Geographical Journal*, 23/4 (1904). When Mackinder read this to the Royal Geographical Society in Jan. 1904, Leo Amery was present; nearly four decades later Amery was still rehearsing Mackinder's arguments. See his letter to Smuts, 15 Dec. 1943, in *Smuts Papers*, vi. 471.

96. Cited in Kenneth Harris, *Attlee* (London: Weidenfeld & Nicolson, 1984), 9 and 11. There is much more in this tenor in Earl Attlee, *Empire into Commonwealth*, The Chichele Lectures (Oxford: Oxford UP, May 1960), which presents a perfect summation of Labour Whiggism.

97. Cited in Harris, *Attlee*, 244.

98. George Ives, aged 111, who had served in the Imperial Yeomanry in the South African War, died in Vancouver on 12 Apr. 1993: *Independent*, 17 Apr. 1993. Dorah Ramothibe, of Soweto, who had been interned, was 118 in 1999: *The Times*, 17 Sept. 1999. The Channel 4 series entitled *The Boer War* ran in four parts through late Sept. and early Oct. 1999.

99. Recording these thoughts of Churchill was Jock Colville, quoted in Donal Lowry, '"The Boers were the Beginning of the End"? The Wider Impact of the South African War', in Lowry, *The South African War Reappraised*, 229.

100. See Buckner, 'Canada', 233.

101. Churchill, *My Early Life*, 67; and see Buchan, *Memory Hold-The-Door*, 52.

102. Paul Fussell's *The Great War and Modern Memory* (Oxford: Oxford UP, 1977) provides the most compelling and moving evidence.

103. D. H. Lawrence, *The Rainbow* (Harmondsworth; Penguin, 1971), 445–6. When this was published it was reviewed alongside *The Thirty-Nine Steps*: Lownie, *Buchan*, 119, which may remind us of the contingency of literary forms.

104. Cited in Laura Cameron and John Forrester, '"A Nice Type of English Scientist": Tansley and Freud', *History Workshop Journal*, 48 (1999), 65.

105. For song, Richard Hoggart, *The Uses of Literacy* (Harmondsworth: Penguin, 1973), 162, which first appeared in 1957.

106. Thompson, 'Publicity, Philanthropy and Commemoration', 114, and Andrew Thomson, *The Empire Strikes Back? The Impact of Imperialism on Britain from the Mid-Nineteenth Century* (Harlow: Pearson, 2005), 181.

107. Kruger, *Goodbye Dolly Gray*, 512. At the centenary commemoration, when Afrikaners were looking to Britain for an apology, the Duke of Kent represented Britain, a sure sign that the matter was seen by those who governed to be of no importance at all: *Telegraph*, 5 Oct. 1999. For a similar forgetfulness asserting itself in Canada (as recorded by the novelist Margaret Atwood) see Donal Lowry, 'Not Just a "Teatime War"', in Lowry, *The South African War Reappraised*, 14.

108. For the extinction of Roberts, MacDonald, *Language of Empire*, 94.

109. Cited in Ben Shepard, *Kitty and the Prince* (London: Profile Books, 2003), 175.

110. *Oxford English Dictionary*; and F. E. Colenso, *History of the Zulu War* (London: Chapman Hall, 1880), 413.

111. Gail Ching-Liang Low, 'His Stories? Narratives and Images of Empire', in Carter, *Space and Place*, 198ff.

112. Cited in C. A. Dunn, *Central African Witness* (London: Victor Gollancz, 1959), 49; and ibid. 54.

113. Bertram Mitford, *The King's Assegai: A Matabili Story* (London: Chatto & Windus, 1894); *The White Hand and the Black* (London: Eveleigh Nash, 1906); and *Forging the Blades: A Tale of the Zulu Rebellion* (London: Eveleigh Nash, 1908). *The King's Assegai* has recently been republished, in 2007 and in 2010. See too Anna Howarth, *Sword and Assegai* (London: Smith, Elder, 1899).

114. Bill Nasson, 'Delville Wood and the South African Great War Commemoration', *English Historical Review*, 480 (2004), 59.

115. Peter Godwin, *Makiwa: A White Boy in Africa* (London: Picador, 1996), 214. *Assegai* was the name taken by the magazine of the Rhodesia and Nyasaland army during the time of the Central African Federation.

116. The obsession, amongst a generation of boy scouts, with sheath-knives is relevant, the scout movement legitimizing in suitably domestic idiom the weapons of the frontier for home use. In '(Uni)forming Youth: Girl Guides and Boy Scouts in Britain, 1908–39', in *History Workshop Journal*, 45 (1998), 126, Tammy Proctor quotes from Roy Hattersley's autobiography on the way which for him scouting was 'irrevocably associated with knives', and from a passage in Harold Wilson's memoirs in which, over half a century later, he records his regret at his father's inability to afford a sheath-knife on his joining the scouts.

117. J. C. Smuts, *Jan Christian Smuts* (London: Cassell, 1952), 282.

118. See too Elizabeth Wilson's reflections on the detritus of empire which ended up in domestic England, perceived merely as disconnected domestic curios for a younger generation: 'A crocodile's skull...on the wall like a symmetrical, dried-up sponge. A leopardskin rug complete with fangs in a pink wax mouth, with claws and tail, sprawled over the chintzes', *Mirror Writing* (London: Virago, 1982), 3.

119. Harry Hopkins, *The New Look: A Social History of the Forties and Fifties in Britain* (London: Secker & Warburg, 1963), 272.

120. *Hancock's Half Hour: The Emigrant*, BBC television, 18 Mar. 1960.

121. Although this colonial memory still has the capacity to recur in popular fiction, doing much the same racial work: Nickie MacMenemy, *Assegai* (London: Macmillan, 1973); William Moore, *The Soldiers Against the Assegais* (London: Sphere, 1975); and Wilbur Smith, *Assegai* (London: Macmillan, 2009).

122. Cited in Lownie, *Buchan*, 241. He always hoped to write a children's history of South Africa, but he never made any progress. At Smuts's instigation, though, he did write *The History of the South African Forces in France* (London: Nelson, 1920).

123. Cited in Lownie, 183 and 150; John Buchan, *Nelson's History of the War*, 24 vols. (London: Nelson, 1915–19). Much of this was pillaged for the shorter volume, for younger readers, which Buchan co-wrote with Henry Newbolt: *Days to Remember: The British Empire in the Great War* (London: Nelson, 1923). The initial request to write the Nelson History went to Conan Doyle, but he refused, and the job went to Buchan. It is not jingoistic, in any hard sense, and pays tribute to the footsoldiers of the war. *Days to Remember* ends by defending the League of Nations. But to try to maintain it is not propaganda is a touch myopic: Keith Grieves, 'Nelson's *History of the War*. John Buchan as a Contemporary Military Historian, 1915–22', *Journal of Contemporary History*, 28/3 (1993).

124. Martin Green, *A Biography of John Buchan and his Sister Anna: The Personal Background of their Literary Work* (Lewiston, NY: Edwin Mellen Press, 1990), 105.

125. Buchan, *Memory Hold-the-Door*, 220; and cited in Lownie, *Buchan*, 209.

126. Cited in Lownie, *Buchan*, 82.

127. Buchan, *Memory Hold-the-Door*, 80 and 51.

128. Ibid. 277.

129. Ibid. 77

130. Ibid. 168.

131. Ibid. 182; this is fictionalized as Fosse Manor—'the deepest and greenest corner of England'—in John Buchan, *The Three Hostages* (Harmondsworth: Penguin, 1988; 1924), 10.

132. See esp. the photograph of Buchan as Lord High Commissioner of the Church of Scotland in 1933, reproduced in Lownie, *Buchan*. Virginia Woolf's remarks on the exhibitionism of such attire—'How many, how splendid, how extremely ornate they are—the clothes worn by the educated man in his public capacity'—are especially pertinent in this instance. In the same text she takes Buchan to task for his unassuming, unconscious militarism: *Three Guineas* (Oxford: Oxford UP, 1992; 1938), 177–80; 159–60; and 369. Woolf was an old schoolfriend of Buchan's wife, Susan.

133. Christopher Harvie, 'Second Thoughts of a Scotsman on the Make: Politics, Nationalism and Myth in John Buchan', *Scottish Historical Review*, 70/1 (1991).

134. For Negro spirituals, Lownie, *Buchan*, 260.

135. Buchan, *Memory Hold-the-Door*, 254.

136. Ibid. 184.

137. Buchan joined the team of people who were variously recruited to draft Baldwin's speeches; and indeed he took a hand in writing some of those of Ramsay MacDonald as well, suggesting he was a political coalition in his own person: Lownie, *Buchan*, 222. For information on Baldwin's regard for Buchan: Janet Adam Smith, *John Buchan and his World* (London: Thames & Hudson, 1979), 84; and Baldwin's own contribution to Tweedsmuir, *Buchan by his Wife and Friends*.

138. Buchan, *Three Hostages*, 13–15 and 23.

139. John Buchan, *Sick Heart River* (London: Hodder & Stoughton, 1941), 256, and 284–5.

140. Richard Usborne, *Clubland Heroes* (London: Constable, 1953).

141. Gertrude Himmelfarb, 'John Buchan: An Untimely Appreciation', *Encounter* (Sept. 1960).

142. David Daniell, 'John Buchan', *Words International* (Mar. 1980); and his study of the novels, *The Interpreter's House: A Critical Assessment of John Buchan* (London: Nelson, 1975).

143. Lownie, *Buchan*. James Buchan, John's grandson, in reviewing the Lownie biography, called it 'straightforward and loyal in the extreme', complaining only of its punctuation: 'The First Hundred Years', *London Review of Books*, 24 Aug. 1995.

144. David Cannadine, *G. M. Trevelyan: A Life in History* (London: HarperCollins, 1992), 159; and his 'John Buchan', in his *History in our Time* (Harmondsworth: Penguin, 2000). My own account of Trevelyan can be found in ' "Englishry": The Histories of G. M. Trevelyan', in Catherine Hall and Keith McClelland (eds.), *Race and Nation in British History* (Manchester: Manchester UP, 2010).

145. Harvie, 'Second Thoughts of a Scotsman on the Make', and J. H. Parry, 'From the Thirty-Nine Articles to *The Thirty-Nine Steps*: Reflections on the Thought of John Buchan', in Michael Bentley (ed.), *Public and Private Doctrine: Essays in British History Presented to Maurice Cowling* (Cambridge: Cambridge UP, 1993), are sympathetic. See too Juanita Kruse, *John Buchan and the Idea of Empire: Popular Literature and Political Ideology* (Lewiston, NY: Edwin Mellen Press, 1989). There are biographies in addition to Lownie, though Buchan has to share one with his sister: Janet Adam Smith, *John Buchan* (London: Hart-Davis, 1965); and Green's thoughtful, *John Buchan and his Sister*. The family reminiscences are if anything less restrained, comprising memoirs by his wife, his sister, and two of his four children: Tweedsmuir, *Buchan*; Anna Buchan, *Unforgettable, Unforgotten* (London: Hodder & Stoughton, 1945); William Buchan, *John Buchan: A Memoir* (London: Buchan & Enright, 1982); and Alice Fairfax-Lucy, *A Scrap Screen* (London: Hamish Hamilton, 1979).

146. Robert Heussler, *Yesterday's Rulers: The Making of the British Colonial Service* (Syracuse: Syracuse UP, 1963), 22–3.

147. Sir Ralph Furse, *Aucuparius: Recollections of a Recruiting Officer* (Oxford: Oxford UP, 1962), 230–1. Furse was the son-in-law of Buchan's friend and co-author, Sir Henry Newbolt. Buchan also served on the Fisher Committee in 1929 to assess the Colonial Office's recruitment procedures, which recommended that Furse's system be continued. It is certain they would have known one another. In Feb. 1943 Furse drafted his own memorandum in which he recognized that the old ways could not continue, due to new dangers arising from 'the unin-structed white—and not least his womenfolk', cited in Anthony Kirk-Greene, *On Crown Service: A History of H.M. Colonial and Overseas Civil Services, 1837–1997* (London: I. B. Tauris, 1999), 43. For an account of the end of Furse's career, Peter Hennessy, *Never Again: Britain 1945–51* (London: Jonathan Cape, 1992), 224–5; and for a glorious instance of his judgement going awry, Thomas Hodgkin, *Letters from Palestine, 1932–36* (London: Quartet, 1986).

148. When this goes wrong, the consequences were catastrophic, as Joseph Conrad demonstrated in *Lord Jim: A Tale* (Oxford: Oxford UP, 1996; 1900), 43 and 45.

149. Furse, *Aucuparius*, 230–1.

150. Cited in Heussler, *Yesterday's Rulers*, 22–3. In much the same way, Bram Stoker predicted from the physiognomy of the 13-year-old Winston Churchill that the boy would go far: Paul Murray, *From the Shadow of Dracula: A Life of Bram Stoker* (London: Cape, 2004), 253.

151. Kirk-Greene, *On Crown Service*, 96.

152. Lownie, *Buchan*, 233. This was in contrast to his brother William, who was sent down from Oxford and went to work with Alfred Hitchcock, who was a great admirer of Buchan's: his obituary appeared in the *Guardian*, 8 July 2008.

153. John Buchan, *Greenmantle* (Harmondsworth: Penguin, 1981; 1916), 25.

154. Buchan, *Three Hostages*, 68. For an insightful account of panics about drugs and femininity at this same time, Marek Kohn, *Dope Girls: The Birth of the British Drug Underground* (London: Lawrence & Wishart, 1992).

155. Buchan, *Three Hostages*, 53, 56, and 104.

156. Buchan, *Greenmantle*, 167–71 and 221.

157. Nimocks, in discussing Milner's Kindergarten in South Africa, quotes a letter from Peter Parry to Geoffrey Robinson, referring to Patrick Duncan as 'very estimable and white all over', *Milner's Young Men*, 25.

158. Buchan's account of the collapse of the democracies in the 1930s is both rel-evant and extraordinary: 'The European traditions have been confronted with an Asiatic revolt, with its historic accompaniment of janissaries and assassins. There is in it all, too, an ugly pathological savour, as if a mature society were being assailed by diseased and vicious children.' *Memory Hold-the-Door*, 286.

159. Sandy Arbuthnot and Peter Pienaar (a Boer from the northern Transvaal who had proved an uncommonly good tracker against the Matabele in 1896 and who sided with the British in the war) are both described in feminine terms; Hannay, on hearing of the attractions of Medina, insists he won't fall for him as he is no 'flapper', *Three Hostages*, 43; and Hannay's wife as a 'sportsman',

Three Hostages, 201. If men lose their whiteness through losing their capacity to reason, women do so through the contagions of inter-racial sex.

160. Buchan, *Three Hostages*, 77.

161. Buchan, *Memory Hold-the-Door*, 168.

162. Buchan's *The Power House* (London: Dent, 1984) was the first of his novels to deal with highly placed quislings at home, and is premised on the thinness of the barrier dividing civilization from anarchy, foreseeing a future in which Britain 'would sink to the level of Ecuador' (p. 38). Buchan wrote it on a cruise to the Azores in June 1913, and it was first published in 1916. According to Christopher Harvie, he drafted it in order to entertain A. J. Balfour: *The Centre of Things: Political Fiction in Britain from Disraeli to the Present* (London: Unwin Hyman, 1991), 150.

163. Cited in Nimocks, *Milner's Young Men*, 17. He repeated the point more than ten years later: *The Nation and the Empire* (London: Constable, 1913), p. xxxvii.

164. Amery, *Times History of the War in South Africa*, vi. 57; Peter Henshaw, 'John Buchan from the "Borders" to the "Berg": Nature, Empire and White South African Identity, 1901–1910', *African Studies*, 62/1 (2003), suggests much greater ideological influence.

165. Though for a powerful reflection on what one *can* extrapolate from the history of the British camps, Reviel Netz, 'Barbed Wire', *London Review of Books*, 20 July 2000; and more emphatically, from neighbouring Namibia in the same years, David Olusoga and Casper W. Erichsen, *The Kaiser's Holocaust: Germany's Forgotten Genocide and the Colonial Roots of Nazism* (London: Faber & Faber, 2010), particularly the epilogue, 'The Triumph of Amnesia'.

166. Cited in Lownie, *Buchan*, 78.

167. John Buchan, *The African Colony: Studies in the Reconstruction* (Edinburgh: Blackwood, 1903); for Cromer's estimation, Lownie, *Buchan*, 85; and Henshaw, 'John Buchan from the "Borders" to the "Berg" ', 12.

168. Buchan, *African Colony*, p. xvii.

169. Ibid. 6–7, 17, 49, 60, 65, 75, and 76; and for Buchan's recognition of a shared Scots and Boer heritage, Lownie, *Buchan*, 81.

170. Henshaw, 'John Buchan from the "Borders" to the "Berg" ', 21–2.

171. Insightful are Jeremy Foster, 'The Poetics of Liminal Places: Landscape and the Construction of White Identity in Early Twentieth Century South Africa', unpublished Ph.D, Royal Holloway, University of London, 1998; and his *Washed with Sun: Landscape and the Making of White South Africa* (Pittsburgh: University of Pittsburgh Press, 2008), which has chapters on Baden-Powell and on John Buchan.

172. Buchan, *African Colony*, 80 and 83.

173. South African writers were soon to object to this 'cult of the *veld*', and to the inability of South Africans to represent their nation except through the imaginative structures of the metropole. One of the earliest and most powerful expressions of this frustration came from none other than Sarah Gertrude

Millin, writing under the name of S. G. Liebson. 'And sometimes we even pretend to discern the golden light when all we really see is the distant reflection from someone else's glowing imaginations. That is, we simply forge another's vision': 'The South Africa of Fiction', *The State*, 7/2 (1912), 135. I am grateful to Saul Dubow for this reference. An important parallel text comes from Smuts, musing on the need for a national literature, and first drafted in July 1892: 'The Conditions of Future South African Literature', in *Selections from the Smuts Papers*, ed. W. K. Hancock and Jean van der Poel, i. *June 1886— May 1902* (Cambridge: Cambridge UP, 1966), 41–8.

174. Buchan, *African Colony*, 191, 199, 201ff, 205 and 208–9. When deep-shaft mining first began, one ounce of gold was extracted from every ton of ore extracted: Smith, *Origins of the South-African War*, 45. When Buchan was writing this the mines were showing an annual mortality rate of 57.7 per 1,000; two years later approximately one-eighth of the black workforce was dying each year: John Farley, 'Bilharzia: A Problem of "Native Health," 1900–1950', in David Arnold (ed.), *Imperial Medicine and Indigenous Societies* (Manchester: Manchester UP, 1988), 194.

175. Buchan, *African Colony*, 285, 291, 293, and 295; and see Curtis, *With Milner in South Africa*, 225–6, for identical views.

176. John Buchan, *Prester John* (Harmondsworth: Penguin, 1985). For popular memory, *Memory Hold-the-Door*, 207; Buchan used the term to describe the influence of Henry Newbolt.

177. Lownie, *Buchan*, 194.

178. C. L. R. James writes of his reading *The Captain* at school, at the moment when Buchan's work was serialized: *Beyond a Boundary* (London: Stanley Paul, 1986; 1963), 47; forty years later at the same school, Buchan was still present— V. S. Naipaul, *A Way in the World* (London: Minerva, 1995), 103. Chinua Achebe, 'The Song of Ourselves', *New Statesman*, 9 Feb. 1990. On reading *Prester John* he says: 'I did not see myself as an African to begin with. I took sides with the white men against the savages. In other words, I went through my first level of schooling thinking I was of the party of the white man in his hair-raising adventures and narrow escapes. The white man was good and reasonable and intelligent and courageous. The savages arrayed against him were sinister and stupid or, at the most, cunning. I hated their guts', ibid. 31 and 32. Ngũgĩ wa Thiong'o, *Decolonising the Mind: The Politics of Language and Literature in Africa* (London: James Currey, 1986), 12. See too for Rhodesia: Daphne Anderson, *The Toe-Rags: A Memoir* (London: Cardinal, 1990), 236.

179. Margaret Thatcher, *The Path to Power* (London: HarperCollins, 1995), 113. Harold Macmillan had been reading him five years earlier: Peter Catterall (ed.), *The Macmillan Diaries: The Cabinet Years. 1950–1957* (London: Pan, 2004), 353.

180. Bloke Modisane, *Blame me on History* (Harmondsworth: Penguin, 1980; 1963), 8.

181. For the details, Lownie, *Buchan*, 292–3. *The Three Hostages* had been the first 'Book at Bedtime' broadcast on the Light Programme in 1949; later it was

again presented on radio, written on this occasion by John Prebble, who had scripted *Zulu*. I am grateful to Tim Crook for this information.

182. The first movie was in 1925; the three versions of *The Thirty-Nine Steps* came in 1935, 1959, and 1978.

183. James Kellas, 'The Party in Scotland', in Anthony Seldon and Stuart Ball (eds.), *Conservative Century: The Conservative Party since 1900* (Oxford: Oxford UP, 1994), 686.

184. Lownie, *Buchan*, 294.

185. *Yesterday in Parliament*, BBC Radio 4, 20 July 2005.

186. Himmelfarb, 'Buchan', 49.

187. Lownie, *Buchan*, 195.

188. There have been, of course, counter-memories. Jomo Kenyatta, apparently, was much influenced by the book, and it set him thinking about forms of insurrection: *Lownie*, Buchan, 112. One rumour has it that the African National Congress sponsored a translation. The British Library has a copy of *UPrester John: Ihunyushwe ngu*, published by ADB in Johannesburg in 1960, tr. J. F. Cele.

189. John Buchan, *A Lodge in the Wilderness* (London: Nelson, 1917). Buchan had experimented with two early published writings on the frontier: *The Half-Hearted* (London: Hodder & Stoughton, 1900); and 'Fountainblue' in his *The Watcher of the Threshold* (London: Blackwood, 1902).

190. John Buchan, *The Novel and the Fairy-Tale* (London: English Association, 1931).

191. James Fenimore Cooper, *The Last of the Mohicans* (Harmondsworth: Penguin, 1994; 1826), 14. Buchan mentions Fenimore Cooper in *The Power-House*, 112. He appeared too in F. E. Colenso's pamphlet about Natal, quoted earlier, to signal the racialized fear of barbarism. If the British have the capacity to disguise themselves as natives, Hawk-eye could deceive his antagonists by pretending to be a bear. When Furse visited Canada it brought to life for him *The Last of the Mohicans*, as Barbados activated in his mind memories of *Treasure Island* and *Robinson Crusoe*: *Aucuparius*, 187.

192. John Buchan, *Sir Walter Scott* (London: Cassell, 1932), 95–6.

193. Georg Lukács, *The Historical Novel* (London: Merlin, 1962), 23–4.

194. James Donald, *Sentimental Education: Schooling, Popular Culture and the Regulation of Liberty* (London: Verso, 1992), 60.

195. There are vast critical literatures on each of these genres. Briefly, on the frontier a thoughtful interpretation along the lines I suggest here is Robert Dixon, *Writing the Colonial Adventure: Race, Gender and Nation in Anglo-Australian Popular Fiction, 1875–1914* (Cambridge: Cambridge UP, 1995); and see Richard Phillips, *Mapping Men and Empire: A Geography of Adventure* (London: Routledge, 1997). One can understand the urban hooligan functioning as the counterpoint to the young colonial hero overseas: Bill Schwarz, 'Night Battles: Hooligans and Citizen, 1898', in Mica Nava and

Alan O'Shea (eds.), *Modern Times: Reflections on a Century of English Modernity* (London: Routledge, 1996).

196. This theme is followed through in Colin Watson, *Snobbery with Violence: English Crime Stories and their Audience* (London: Eyre Methuen, 1979); and for a good historical contextualization, David Glover, 'Aliens, Anarchists and Detectives: Legislating the Immigrant Body', *New Formations*, 32 (1999); and more particularly, *Vampires, Mummies and Liberals: Bram Stoker and the Politics of Popular Fiction* (Durham, NC: Duke UP, 1996). David Cannadine argues that Ian Fleming's greatest debt was to Buchan: *In Churchill's Shadow: Confronting the Past in Modern Britain* (London: Penguin, 2003), 286.

197. Rider Haggard's *King Solomon's Mines* London: Pan, 1951) is a key popular text in this regard. In 1885 Haggard, having just read *Treasure Island*, bet his brother five shillings he could equal it. He wrote it while commuting, and sent it to Cassell's *Magazine of Art*, which backed up publication with an unprecedented advertising campaign. Rider Haggard, a future Unionist candidate in the 1895 election, had travelled to South Africa as secretary to the Governor of Natal; in 1877 he raised the Union Jack over Pretoria when Britain annexed the Transvaal Republic. On returning from South Africa for the last time in June 1914 he wrote in his diary: 'My name will perhaps always be connected with Africa if it remains a white man's "house" and even if it does not—perhaps', cited in Peter Beresford Ellis, *H. Rider Haggard: A Voice from the Infinite* (London: Routledge & Kegan Paul, 1978), 214.

198. Elaine Showalter, *Sexual Anarchy: Gender and Culture at the Fin de Siècle* (London: Bloomsbury, 1991), 79–80, where she quotes from Arthur Conan Doyle; and see H. Rider Haggard, 'About Fiction', *Contemporary Review* (Feb. 1887) and Sir Alfred Lyall, 'Novels of Adventure and Manners', *Quarterly Review* (Oct. 1894), republ. in his *Studies in Literature and History* (London: John Murray, 1915). In relation to children's fiction the story is told in Joseph Bristow, *Empire Boys: Adventures in a Man's World* (London: HarperCollins, 1991); in Kimberley Reynolds, *Girls Only?: Gender and Popular Children's Fiction in Britain, 1880–1910* (Hemel Hempstead: Harvester Wheatsheaf, 1990); and Kathryn Castle, *Britannia's Children: Reading Colonialism through Children's Books and Magazines* (Manchester: Manchester UP, 1996). An exactly parallel argument occurs in historiography at the time, marked most of all in Seeley's diatribes against a feminized, literary version of historical imagination, as opposed to his own masculine, rational, and truthful interpretation.

199. Film rights were sold in 1913, and then again in 1919. Alexander Korda expressed a wish to film it in the 1930s, presumably hoping for Paul Robeson to star in it: Lownie, *Buchan*, 239 and 241.

200. A survey of 800 readers of *The Captain* (Apr. 1908) asking for the twelve best boys' books ever written elicited a list which included: *Treasure Island, Westward Ho!, The Adventures of Sherlock Holmes, Ivanhoe, King's Soloman's Mines, Coral Island*, and *The Last of the Mohicans*. These tastes were still apparent in a similar

survey in 1940: Jeffrey Richards, 'Introduction' to his *Imperialism and Juvenile Literature* (Manchester: Manchester UP, 1989), 8. Tony Blair's nomination of *Ivanhoe* as his favourite book has a long history.

201. See Craig Smith, 'Every Man Must Kill the Thing he Loves: Empire, Homoerotics and Nationalism in John Buchan's *Prester John*', *Novel: A Forum on Fiction*, 28/2 (1995); and T. J. Couzens, '"The Old Africa of a Boy's Dream": Towards Interpreting Buchan's *Prester John*', *English Studies in Africa*, 24/1 (1981).

202. Krikler, 'Social Neurosis'; and Marks, *Reluctant Rebellion*. According to Paul Rich the novel represents the 'successful elaboration, in colloquial terminology... of the essential tenets of Milnerism': ' "Milnerism and a Ripping Yarn": Transvaal Land Settlement and John Buchan's Novel *Prester John*', in Belinda Bozzoli (ed.), *Town and Country in the Transvaal: Capitalist Penetration and Popular Response* (Johannesburg: Ravan Press, 1983), 412–13. This may be formally right, but it misses the transformative effects of the 'colloquial terminology' which allow us to see what Milnerism required the imagination to repress. See too Nicholas Thomas's reading of the novel in his *Colonialism's Culture: Anthropology, Travel and Government* (Cambridge: Polity, 1994).

203. J. P. Green, 'Boxing and the "Colour Question" in Edwardian Britain: The "White" Problem of 1911', *International Journal of the History of Sport*, 5/1 (1988).

204. Buchan, *Prester John*, 9–15.

205. Cited in Smith, *Buchan*, 112.

206. Buchan, *Prester John*, 21, 22, 46, and 36.

207. Ibid. 198.

208. See Gail Ching-Liang Low, 'White Skins/Black Masks: The Pleasures and Politics of Imperialism', in Carter, *Space and Place*.

209. Buchan, *Prester John*, 68, 70, and 164.

210. Ibid. 35, 43–4, and 55.

211. Ibid. 64–5.

212. Ibid. 38 and 141. See on this Klaus Theweleit's discussion of men and their horses: *Male Fantasies* (Cambridge: Polity, 1987).

213. Buchan, *Prester John*, 23, 91, and 56.

214. Cited in McDonald, *Language of Empire*, 35.

215. Buchan, *Prester John*, 33, 60, and 189.

216. Ibid. 83, 141, 119, 56, and 84; for Haiti and the Mutiny, 56.

217. Ibid. 25 and 151. For historical discussion of Ethiopianism and the North American influences, Krikler, 'Social Neurosis'; and Edward Roux, *Time Longer than Rope* (Madison, Wis.: University of Wisconsin Press, 1978), ch. 8.

218. Buchan, *Prester John*, 108–9 and 178. Critical here is the notion of 'the gaze that locks the hero and the villain into a moment of mutual recognition': Tony Davis, 'The Divided Gaze: Reflections on the Political Thriller', in Derek Longhurst (ed.), *Gender, Genre and Narrative Pleasure* (London: Unwin Hyman, 1989), 121. Davis quotes from Freud on paranoia and its relation to 'fiendish

intentions and demonic power', and links this in turn to the suppression of a homoerotic urge and the immobilization of the hero.

219. Buchan, *Prester John*, 11, 157, and 106.

220. Ibid. 191–203. The dedication to Lionel Phillips, a South African mining magnate, is appropriate.

CHAPTER 5

1. Lord Moran, *Winston Churchill: The Struggle for Survival, 1940–1965* (London: Sphere, 1968), 69–70; diary entry for 7 Aug. 1942.

2. Cited in Michael Edwardes, *Nehru* (Harmondsworth: Penguin, 1973), 147–8.

3. Moran, *Churchill: The Struggle for Survival*, 69–70.

4. Ibid.

5. F. R. Leavis, *The Great Tradition* (Harmondsworth: Penguin, 1980), 21.

6. Henry James, *Nathaniel Hawthorne* (London: Macmillan, 1967; 1879), 23, 6, and 1.

7. Iain Smith, 'Jan Smuts and the South African War', unpubl. paper, 3; I am very grateful to Iain Smith for showing me this, which subsequently appeared in *South African Historical Journal*, 41 (1999). See too Mordechai Tamarkin, 'The Cape Afrikaners and the British Empire from the Jameson Raid to the South African War', in Donal Lowry (ed.), *The South African War Reappraised* (Manchester: Manchester UP 2000).

8. *Selections from the Smuts Papers*, ed. Jean van der Poel, v. *September 1919—November 1934* (Cambridge: Cambridge UP, 1973), 521; from a letter of 13 Sept. 1932.

9. *A Century of Wrong*, Issued by the State Secretary [F. W.] Reitz, 1899, pp. xiii–xiv and 1–2. This had been drafted by Smuts in Sept. It was publ. in Britain with an introduction by the radical journalist W. T. Stead, who depicted himself in his preface as a 'friend and supporter' of Rhodes and 'the former colleague and upholder' of Milner. Stead himself is of great interest, cropping up on many different occasions. He corresponded with Smuts. The reference to Milner concerns the time when he was apprenticed to Stead on the *Pall Mall Gazette*. See Frederick Whyte, *The Life of W. T. Stead* (London: Cape, 1925); and Raymond Schultz, *Crusaders in Babylon: W. T. Stead and the* Pall Mall Gazette (Lincoln, Neb.: University of Nebraska Press, 1972).

10. W. K. Hancock, *Smuts: The Sanguine Years* (Cambridge: Cambridge UP, 1962), 215. Bernard Friedman, *Smuts: A Reappraisal* (London: Allen & Unwin, 1975), is good on this episode. A suitably unmythic reading is provided by Ronald Hyam, 'The Myth of the "Magnanimous Gesture": The Liberal Government, Smuts and Conciliation, 1906', in Ronald Hyam and Ged Martin (eds.), *Reappraisals in British Imperial History* (London: Macmillan, 1975). I should add that Hancock himself was a considerable figure in the mid-century drive to reassess the British empire: see his *Argument for Empire* (Harmondsworth: Penguin, 1944), and Saul Dubow, 'Keith Hancock, Race and Empire', in Catherine Hall and Keith McClelland (eds.), *Race and Nation in British History* (Manchester: Manchester UP, 2010).

11. *Selections from the Smuts Papers*, ed. W. K. Hancock and Jean van der Poel, i. *June 1886–May 1902* (Cambridge: Cambridge UP, 1966), 82; the speech, an attack on his future friend, Olive Schreiner, was delivered in Oct. 1895.

12. J. C. Smuts, *Jan Christian Smuts* (London: Cassell, 1952), 124.

13. *Dictionary of National Biography, 1941–1950* (Oxford: Oxford UP, 1959).

14. *Smuts Papers*, v. 436; 29 Dec. 1929. This was just after the experience of a particularly nasty election defeat in South Africa; it was also a moment when, sick of Sir Austen Chamberlain's foreign policy, he was happy to contemplate a Labour government.

15. Cited respectively in N. Levi, *Jan Smuts* (London: Longman, 1917), 293, and in Ronald Hyam, *The Failure of South African Expansion, 1908–48* (London: Macmillan, 1972), 66.

16. Cited in Smuts, *Jan Christian Smuts*, 180–1. When Churchill referred to 'quelling rebellion' he had in mind the following. At the outbreak of the First World War, General Maritz, inspired by Boer, anti-British feeling, led a rebellion against the government, marching 600 men into South-West Africa and joining the German troops stationed there. The prime minister of South Africa, Louis Botha, and Smuts ordered the rebels—including many former comrades-in-arms, Maritz included—be destroyed.

17. Speech on 15 May 1917; J. C. Smuts, *War-Time Speeches* (London: Hodder & Stoughton, 1917), 25.

18. For a typical encomium of the time, in this instance from the master of Magdelene College, Cambridge, A. C. Benson, *The Happy Warrior: A Sight of General Smuts at Cambridge, May 1917* (Cambridge: Cambridge UP, 1917).

19. Hugh Robert Mill, *The Record of the Royal Geographical Society, 1830–1930* (London: Royal Geographical Society, 1930), 196–7. I owe this reference to Felix Driver.

20. The friend was Lady Daphne Moore, wife of the governor-general and commander-in-chief of Kenya, 1943–9: see Piet Beukes, *The Holistic Smuts: A Study in Personality* (Cape Town: Human & Rousseau, 1990), 186.

21. *Selections from the Smuts Papers*, ed. W.K. Hancock and Jean van der Poel, iv. *November 1918–August 1919* (Cambridge: Cambridge UP, 1966), 266; letter to Keynes, 17 July 1919.

22. *Smuts Papers*, v. 59; letter to Margaret Gillett, 26 Dec. 1920. And see I. C. Smith, 'J. C. Smuts' Role in the Establishment of the League of Nations and the Mandate for South-West Africa', *South African Historical Journal*, 5 (1973).

23. Imperial Airways extended its service to Cape Town in Jan. 1932: Peter Wingent, *Movements of Aircraft on Imperial Airways' African Route, 1931–39* (Winchester: Peter Wingent, 1991).

24. F. S. Crafford, *Jan Smuts: A Biography* (London: Allen & Unwin, 1946), 198.

25. Harold Smith, 'Apartheid, Sharpeville and "Impartiality": The Reporting of South Africa on BBC Television, 1948–61', *Historical Journal of Film, Radio and Television*, 13/3 (1993), 293. The online archive of Pathé newsreels contains a significant amount of material on Smuts, going back to 1917.

26. H. C. Armstrong, *Grey Steel (Jan Christian Smuts): A Study in Arrogance* (Harmondsworth: Penguin, 1939). Despite both the title and the stress on Smuts's wilfulness, the portrait is not politically unsympathetic, recognizing him as a great man. Commenting on his 1929–30 visit to Britain, Armstrong notes that 'He left for South Africa established as an elder statesman of England', 275. Smuts himself found the biography presented 'a most unlovely picture': *Selections from the Smuts Papers*, ed. Jean van der Poel, vi. *December 1934–August 1945* (Cambridge: Cambridge UP, 1973), 76; letter to Margaret Gillett, 2 May 1937. Armstrong's biography was originally publ. by Faber in 1937. See too William F. Burbidge, *Field-Marshall Smuts: Soldier and World Statesman* (Bognor Regis: John Crowther, n.d. [1943]).

27. Smuts, *Jan Christian Smuts*, 423. The speech is reproduced in full in Crafford, *Smuts*, 343–55. Smith, 'Apartheid, Sharpeville and "Impartiality"', suggests that the entire Pathé and Movietone newsreels were given over to the full forty-four-minute speech but this does not seem to have been the case, each newsreel giving the occasion some ten minutes.

28. *Daily Express*, 22 Oct. 1942. The *Express* itself provided prominent coverage on its front page; reproduced the speech in full; and added a laudatory editorial. Reporting in the *Daily Mirror* on the same day was also significant. Two years later, on 22 May 1944, Smuts found himself on the cover of *Time*.

29. *The Empire at Bay: The Leo Amery Diaries, 1929–1945*, ed. John Barnes and David Nicholson (London: Hutchinson, 1988), 839–40; entry for 21 Oct. 1942. At the time Amery and Churchill were continually falling out: see Bill Schwarz, 'Empire: For and Against', *Twentieth Century British History*, 6/3 (1995). How much Amery and Smuts had been discussing Churchill behind his back is unknown. But a few weeks later Smuts referred to Churchill in much the same terms: 'Winston lives in the 18th century and doesn't grasp what is happening', Thomas Jones, *A Diary with Letters, 1931–1950* (Oxford: Oxford UP, 1969), 505; entry for 17 Nov. 1942. And *Chips: The Diaries of Sir Henry Channon*, ed. Robert Rhodes James (Harmondsworth: Penguin, 1984), 415–16 and 418–19; entries for 21 Oct. and 17 Nov. 1942.

30. George Orwell, *The War Commentaries*, ed. W. J. West (New York: Schocken, 1986), 172; broadcast of 24 Oct. 1942. Orwell scripted these talks anonymously for the Indian Section of the Eastern Section of the BBC: they purported to give an 'Indian' view of world events. Would the Smuts who had at one time wished to foment revolution in India be remembered by his listeners, at this turbulent moment in the nation's history? Or would they only have recalled the enemy of Gandhi?

31. See Mark Mazower, *No Enchanted Place: The End of Empire and the Ideological Origins of the United Nations* (Princeton: Princeton UP, 2009), ch. 1, 'Jan Smuts and Imperial Internationalism'.

32. 'In the Boer War it [British imperialism] probably played its last hand: in that war and the peace which followed the crust of imperialism was broken and the

deeper forces of the real British spirit once more emerged to the surface', Jan Christian Smuts, 'Reflections on World Affairs', *The Listener*, 3 Oct. 1946, 428.

33. Donal Lowry, '"Not Just a Teatime War"', in Lowry (ed.), *South African War Reappraised*, 16; the information on the royal family is told by an impeccable source, and sounds all too convincing.

34. Arthur Keppel-Jones, *When Smuts Goes* (London: Victor Gollancz, 1947). Though two years earlier the Left Book Club had publ. Alexander Campbell's *It's Your Empire* (London: Victor Gollancz, 1945) which opened with Smuts (suggesting that many people in England believed him to be 'the only white man' in South Africa), but which adopted a relatively harsh view of his racial inclinations, 7 and 10.

35. Basil Williams, *Botha, Smuts and South Africa* (London: Hodder & Stoughton, 1946).

36. It was in 1948 also that Field-Marshall Viscount Montgomery, war-hero and chief of the Imperial Defence Staff, presented to prime minister Clement Attlee his 'grand design' for maintaining white supremacy, under British influence, in Africa. In his report he described Africans as 'savage', and white settlers as in need of 'a good jolt to make them face up to their Empire responsibilities'. The Labour government had to inform the field-marshall of the difference between support for South Africa's determined policy of white supremacy, and the British goal of ultimate self-government for the African colonies. Many of Montgomery's ideas, it seems, had originated with Smuts: *Guardian*, 7 Jan. 1999.

37. Robert Menzies, 'First Smuts Memorial Lecture', in F. K. Crowley (ed.), *Modern Australia in Documents,* ii. *1939–1970* (Melbourne: Wren, 1973), 393–6.

38. Earl Mountbatten, 'Introduction', to Zelda Friedlander (ed.), *Jan Smuts Remembered* (London: Allan Wingate, 1970), 8; Reginald Maudling, *Memoirs* (London: Sidgwick & Jackson, 1978), 19. Bob Brand, a veteran of the Milnerite Kindergarten and who accompanied John Buchan on his 1903 trek in Swaziland, in Aug. 1963 spent the last night of his life in the family home of his grandson, James Fox. His memories of South Africa were animated, fixing on 'his treks in the high veld, the politics of his youth'. And among his last words were his memories of Smuts: James Fox, *The Langhorne Sisters* (London: Granta, 1998), 545.

39. Robert Blake, *The World since Smuts* (Johannesburg: South African Institute of International Affairs, 1989). This latter comprised the third Jan Smuts memorial lecture in South Africa itself: the first had been given in 1984 by Laurens Van Der Post. Two years earlier Blake had commemorated Churchill in the same way and in the same spirit in Fulton, Missouri.

40. Cited in W. K. Hancock, *Smuts: The Field of Force, 1919–1950* (Cambridge: Cambridge UP, 1968), 385–6.

41. As does a dog encountered on Hampstead Heath in 1944 in Sarah Waters, *The Night Watch* (London: Virago, 2007).

42. *Smuts Papers*, vi. 444–5; letter to Margaret Gillett, 21 July 1943.

43. See Bill Schwarz, 'Conservatism and "Caesarism," 1903–1922', in Mary Langan and Bill Schwarz (eds.), *Crises in the British State, 1880–1930* (London: Hutchinson, 1985). Smuts's vertical movement through the imperial institutions made him an exception: his closest rival, frustrated at every turn the moment he set his eyes on the metropole, was Menzies. On these themes: Benedict Anderson, *Imagined Communities: Reflections on the Origin and Spread of Nationalism* (London: Verso, 1985), 88.

44. Interview with Edward Marshall, June 1917; in Smuts, *War-Time Speeches*, 115. Or viewed from the other way around, Churchill, in congratulating Smuts on first becoming premier, assured him that many difficulties would be surmounted. 'That wise and tolerant liberalism which is the peculiar product of our island is one of the keys': *Smuts Papers*, v. 17; 30 Oct. 1919.

45. P. B. Blanckenberg, *The Thoughts of General Smuts* (Cape Town: Juta, 1951), 30; and *Smuts Papers*, v. 443—from a speech to the Empire Parliamentary Association, 28 Jan. 1930. Smuts clearly thought of South Africa in these terms as well, at least as a universal nation in the making. The most powerful statement of this aspiration can be found in one of his earliest writings, from July 1892, 'The Conditions of Future South African Literature', in which he takes England as a cultural model: see *Smuts Papers*, i. 41–8; and Isabel Hofmeyr, 'Building a Nation from Words: Afrikaans Language, Literature and Ethnic Identity, 1902–24', in Shula Marks and Stanley Trapido (eds.), *The Politics of Race, Class and Nationalism in Twentieth-Century South Africa* (London: Longman, 1987). In aphoristic rendition: 'The miracle of history is the miracle of South Africa', Blanckenberg, *Thoughts of Smuts*, 183; or, alternatively, his view that South Africa constituted 'one of the true and great romances in modern history': *War-Time Speeches*, 80—speech at the Savoy, 20 May 1917.

46. Smuts's comment on Lloyd George is apposite: 'History will show him the biggest Englishman of them all', cited in Crafford, *Smuts*, 141.

47. Indeed, in a deeper sense, these were necessary to the formation of English nationalism; without these antagonists, it could not have existed. As Partha Chatterjee notes, if ever such a nationalism did become universal 'it would in fact destroy itself', *Nationalist Thought and Colonialism: A Derivative Discourse* (London: Zed, 1986), 17.

48. I am thinking of the many papers delivered (to date) to the five British World conferences, held in London (1998), Cape Town (2002), Calgary (2003), Melbourne (2004), and Auckland (2005). I have commented on the theme of Britishness, as it has been deployed in these discussions, in '"Shivering in the Noonday Sun": The British World and the Dynamics of "Nativization"', in Kate Darian-Smith, Patricia Grimshaw, and Stuart Macintyre (eds.), *Britishness Abroad: Transnational Movements and Imperial Cultures* (Melbourne: Melbourne UP, 2007), from which I draw here. For an important paper which emphasizes the allegiance of non-British ethnics to the codes of Britishness, see Donal

Lowry, 'Empire Loyalism and the Assimilation of Non-British White Subjects in the White Colonies Of Settlement: An Argument Against "Ethnic Determinism"', first presented at the Second British World Conference in 2002, and republ. in a selection of the proceedings: Carl Bridge and Kent Fedorowich (eds.), *The British World: Diaspora, Culture and Identity* (London: Frank Cass, 2003). It should be stressed that Lowry's concern is only with 'non-white British subjects'.

49. Vivian Bickford-Smith, 'The Betrayal of Creole Elites, 1880–1920', in Philip Morgan and Sean Hawkins (eds.), *Black Experience and the Empire: Oxford History of the British Empire. Companion Volume* (Oxford: Oxford UP, 2004). I also learnt much from Bickford-Smith's paper to the Second British World Conference, 'Revisiting Anglicisation in the Nineteenth-Century Cape Colony', reproduced in Bridge and Fedorowich, *The British World*.

50. Mahmood Mamdani, 'Beyond Settler and Native as Political Identities: Overcoming the Political Legacy of Colonialism', *Comparative Studies in Society and History*, 43/4 (2001), 664.

51. In July and Aug. 1909, a delegation, naming itself as a 'Delegation of the Representatives of the Coloured and Native British Subjects Resident in the British Dominions of South Africa', travelled to London to lobby against the upcoming bill establishing the Union of South Africa. They petitioned, specifically, as black Britons, knowing full well that the transfer of power from London to Pretoria could only advance the processes of nativization. To no avail. Labour MPs opposed the bill. After its victory Keir Hardie declared: 'for the first time we are asked to write over the portals of the British Empire "Abandon Hope all ye who enter here"', cited in Guy Willoughby, 'Envisioning Empire: The Case for the "Coloured and Native British Subjects in South Africa" and the Act of Union of 1909', Second British World Conference, Cape Town, 2002.

52. The correspondent was Lady Moore: Hancock, *Field of Force*, 487.

53. Smuts, *War-Time Speeches*, 85; speech held at the Savoy dinner to honour him, 22 May 1917. In later years he became an enthusiastic promoter of research carried out in Queensland which demonstrated the capacity of white men to thrive in the tropics. As he argued in his first Rhodes lecture, 'Australia has the unique distinction of having bred up during the last seventy years a large, resident pure-blooded white population under tropical conditions', 2 Nov. 1929; in J. C. Smuts, *Africa and Some World Problems* (Oxford: Oxford UP, 1930), 62.

54. *Smuts Papers*, i. 121; 2 July 1896.

55. Cited in Hancock, *The Sanguine Years*, 361; Feb. 1910. From early on Smuts in public was both pro-Jew and pro-Zionist. On 3 Nov. 1919 he addressed the South African Zionist Federation and suggested that Jews had solved the problem of nationhood by being both national and international simultaneously. He went on to argue that the Old Testament was not only a sacred text of Judaism, but also 'has been the very marrow of Dutch culture here in South Africa', *Smuts Papers*, v. 25. Through the remainder of his public life he continued to be

a staunch supporter of Zionism and (later) of Israel. There are arguments, though, that he capitulated to anti-Semitic policies while serving as J. B. Hertzog's deputy in the 1930s, and that Smuts himself refused to promote an individual because of his Judaism: see Friedman, *Smuts*, 125 and 130. The latter episode concerns the husband of Sarah Gertrude Millin; there is no reason to suppose the case against Smuts proven on this.

56. *Smuts Papers*, i. 46; July 1892.
57. Ibid. 93; Oct. 1895.
58. Smuts, *War-Time Speeches*, 88; speech at the Savoy, 22 May 1917. And Smuts, 'Native Policy in Africa', *Africa and Some World Problems*, 77–8; second Rhodes lecture, 9 Nov. 1929.
59. J. C. Smuts, 'The South African Spirit', in his *Plans for a Better World* (London: Hodder & Stoughton, 1942), 138; Imperial Press Conference, 22 Mar. 1935.
60. *Selections from the Smuts Papers*, ed. W. K. Hancock and Jean van der Poel, ii. *June 1902–May 1910* (Cambridge: Cambridge UP, 1966), 239 and 242; Merriman to Smuts, 4 Mar. 1906; and Smuts to Merriman, 13 Mar. 1906. The theme was continued in Merriman's letter of 18 Mar. (pp. 244–6: 'God forbid I should advocate a general political enfranchisement of the Native barbarian. All I think is required for *our* safety is that we shall not deny him the franchise on account of colour.'). The exchange took place against the backdrop of the black rising in Natal that same Feb.
61. Hancock, *The Sanguine Years*, 323. Or as Gandhi himself talked about his love for the British constitution: 'I can see now that my love of truth was at the root of this loyalty', M. K. Gandhi, *An Autobiography, or the Story of my Experiments with Truth* (Harmondsworth: Penguin, 1976; in 2 vols. 1927, 1929), 166.
62. Gandhi, *Autobiography*, 286–91.
63. Cited in Hancock, *The Sanguine Years*, 346. For Gandhi, see Robert Huttenback, *Gandhi in South Africa: British Imperialism and the Indian Question, 1860–1914* (Ithaca, NY: Cornell UP, 1971), 177ff., and ch.8; and Marilyn Lake and Henry Reynolds, *Drawing the Global Colour Line: White Men's Countries and the International Challenge of Racial Inequality* (Cambridge: Cambridge UP, 2008), ch.5.
64. Smuts, *Africa and Some World Problems*, 77, 92, 93, 48, and 100.
65. *Selections from the Smuts Papers*, ed. Jean van der Poel, vii. *27 August–17 October 1950* (Cambridge: Cambridge UP, 1973), 99; letter to J. H. Hofmeyr, 15 Oct. 1946.
66. Insightful on this is Saul Dubow, *Scientific Racism in Modern South Africa* (Cambridge: Cambridge UP, 1995).
67. *Smuts Papers*, vi. 333, 334, 336, and 334.
68. Hancock, *Field of Force*, 289.
69. *Smuts Papers*, vi. 345; letter to Margaret Gillett, 23 Jan. 1942.
70. In the June 1929 election Smuts was denounced by his political enemies—General Hertzog and Dr Malan—as 'the man who puts himself forward as the apostle of a black Kaffir state...extending from the Cape to Egypt...and already foretells the

day when even the name of South Africa will vanish in smoke upon the altar of the Kaffir state he so ardently desires', cited in Hancock, *Field of Force*, 218.

71. Nor, for all his love of the empire, did Smuts ever relinquish his own Afrikaner patrimony. As deputy prime minister in 1938 it was appropriate for him to attend the ceremony to lay the foundation stone for the Voortrekker monument—a decisive symbolic moment in the memoralization of the Afrikaner nation. And on 16 Dec. 1949—Dingaan's Day—in a spectacle of high drama witnessed in person by some 250,000 (or 10%) of the white population of South Africa, he spoke at the unveiling of the monument, noting that the Voortrekkers 'did not pursue a policy of extermination which in other countries solved the aborigine problem for the new settlers'. See Adamastor, *White Man Boss* (London: Victor Gollancz, 1950), 17. Smuts, *Jan Christian Smuts*, 522, puts the total numbers of those present much higher, at 400,000. When Movietone showed this to British cinema audiences (estimating a mere 30,000 spectators) the historical significance of the event received rather less attention than the varieties of facial hair sported by the men.

72. *Smuts Papers*, vi. 78; letter to Margaret Gillett, 15 May 1937.

73. On 14 Sept. 1949, K. Howard-Browne, the vice-chairman of the Putfontein branch of the United Party wrote to Smuts to express how sad he was that he, Smuts, was critical of apartheid. Smuts's reply was as follows: 'I quite appreciate your point of view, and myself and other party leaders have repeatedly declared that up to a point apartheid is common ground and the traditional policy of South Africa. Socially and residentially it has always been accepted South African policy. The National Party are however proceeding far beyond that policy.' He noted particularly the attacks on constitutional rights—the experiences of Hertzog's Native Bills of the 1930s notwithstanding. *Smuts Papers*, vii. 309–11; 26 Sept. 1949.

74. This approach places greatest emphasis on the report of the Native Affairs Commission, which sat from 1903 to 1905; and on the subsequent Natives Land Act of 1913, establishing segregation in the countryside (although it was not operative in the Cape). See esp. Martin Legassick, 'British Hegemony and the Origins of Segregation in South Africa, 1901–14', in William Beinart and Saul Dubow (eds.), *Segregation and Apartheid in Twentieth-Century South Africa* (London: Macmillan, 1995); this needs to be read alongside Maynard Swanson's gripping account, 'The Sanitation Syndrome: Bubonic Plague and Urban Native Policy in the Cape Colony, 1900–09', in the same volume. Hancock, in his inimitable style, is prepared at one point to concede the essentially British origins of segregation: 'The doctrine of separateness, as now defined under Lord Milner's auspices, could get along quite comfortably with *baasskap*', *The Sanguine Years*, 316. The most convincing accounts of Milnerism remain Shula Marks and Stanley Trapido, 'Lord Milner and the South African State', *History Workshop Journal,* 8 (1979); and their 'Lord Milner and the South African State Reconsidered' in Michael Twaddle (ed.), *Imperialism, the State and the Third World* (London:

British Academic Press, 1992), which should be read with Saul Dubow, 'Colonial Nationalism, the Milner Kindergarten and the Rise of "South Africanism," 1902–1910', *History Workshop Journal,* 43 (1997). An alternative view which prefers to emphasize the relative failure of Milner—and the correlative success of a virtuous Campbell-Bannerman—is G. H. L. Le May, *British Supremacy in South Africa, 1899–1907* (Oxford: Clarendon Press, 1965). For important confirmation that ideologies of segregation were features of the modernization of South Africa, the comparative discussions of John Cell and G. M. Fredrickson are useful: respectively, *The Highest Stage of White Supremacy: The Origins of White Supremacy in South Africa and the American South* (Cambridge: Cambridge UP, 1982); and *White Supremacy: A Comparative Study on American and South African History* (Oxford: Oxford UP, 1981). More recently, with a welcome Latin dimension, there is Anthony W. Marx, *Making Race and Nation: A Comparison of the United States, South Africa and Brazil* (Cambridge: Cambridge UP, 1998). The modernity of Afrikaner theories of segregation is also argued in André du Toit, 'No Chosen People: The Myth of the Calvinist Origins of Afrikaner Nationalism and Racial Ideology', *American Historical Review,* 88/4 (1983).

75. Saul Dubow, *Racial Segregation and the Origins of Apartheid in South Africa, 1919–36* (London: Macmillan, 1989), 178; this account gives more attention to Smuts's Native Affairs Act of 1920, regarding this as the decisive 'watershed' in the institutionalization of segregation (p. 4). This should be read alongside Dubow's *Scientific Racism in Modern South Africa* (Cambridge: Cambridge UP, 1995).

76. Cited in Hancock, *Field of Force,* 18–19; 3 Dec. 1920.

77. Cited in Friedman, *Smuts,* 172; 25 Mar. 1946. Hofmeyr's criticisms of the discriminatory aspects of the bill constituted a key theme in the Nationalist denunciation of the government in the election in 1948. On 28 Apr. 1943 the British high commissioner in Pretoria, Lord Harlech, wrote to Attlee offering his views on the Pegging Bill: 'Even when rich they live in appalling squalor and their social and domestic habits make them the most unpleasant neighbours. Once a street or neighbourhood becomes Indianised the lot of the remaining Europeans is indeed unenviable, as is that of the white folk in or on the edges of negro Haarlem [sic] in New York . . . the number of "educated" or higher class Indians in South Africa is few and far between and many of the Natal Indians appear to have far lower standards of living and cleanliness than the Native Zulus in spite of their superior wealth and money getting capacity. They are apparently content with this and make "slum" conditions even when they have not the excuse of poverty.' Cited in Paul B. Rich, 'The Impact of South African Segregationist and Apartheid Ideology on British Racial Thought, 1939–60', *New Community,* 13/1 (1986), 2. Rich suggests that Harlech held 'an intense admiration for Smuts' (ibid.)—which indeed he did.

78. Just as India, in 1944, had campaigned against the continuation of Australia's racial immigration policies: Gwenda Tavan, *The Long, Slow Death of White Australia* (Melbourne: Scribe Publications, 2005), 38; and see too 46–7.

79. From New York Smuts wrote to Margaret Gillett: 'All along the East coast of Africa from Mombassa to Durban and ultimately to Cape Town they are invading, infiltrating, penetrating in all sorts of devious ways to reverse the role which we have thought our destiny…East and West meet at this moment of history and frankly I am a Westerner, although I love and respect the whole human family, irrespective of colour or race.' *Smuts Papers*, vii. 101; 27 Oct. 1946. His public response to Mrs Pandit adopted a rather different tone: 'It is to prevent such conditions of clash arising in South Africa, where so many races, cultures and colours come together, that the Union is doing its best on fair, decent and wise lines to keep the different elements, as much as convenient and possible, apart and away from unnecessary intermixture, and so prevent bloody affrays like those in India or pogroms such as we read of in other countries.' Cited in Smuts, *Jan Christian Smuts*, 497.

80. *Smuts Papers*, i. 236-7; 10 May 1899.

81. Cited in Crafford, *Smuts*, 133.

82. P. R. Warhurst, 'Smuts and Africa: A Study in Sub-Imperialism', *South African Historical Journal,* 16 (1984), 82.

83. Cited in Hyam, *Failure of South African Expansion*, 67; I draw closely from Hyam here.

84. Winston Churchill, for one, believed the Portuguese to be 'wily' and 'oily', their colonies 'sinks of iniquity'. This was a sentiment expressed at the end of 1906, when he was a minister at the Colonial Office; it was a common enough view of the imperial caste in London, then and later. Conversely, the Portuguese were wary of Smuts and of his expansionist ambitions. See Hyam, *Failure of South African Expansion*, 27; and for the bid to buy Mozambique, and for Portuguese views on Smuts, Warhurst, 'Smuts and Africa', 85 and 87. Smuts's hopes for a greater South Africa disturbed, at various times, the French and the Belgians as well. A less benevolent view of British policy in southern Africa than that provided by Hyam can be found in Martin Channock, *Unconsummated Union: Britain, Rhodesia and South Africa, 1900–45* (Manchester: Manchester UP, 1977).

85. Cited in Warhurst, 'Smuts and Africa', 95.

86. Cited in Hancock, *Field of Force*, 223.

87. Cited in Wm. Roger Louis, *In the Name of God, Go! Leo Amery and the British Empire in the Age of Churchill* (New York: Norton, 1992), 70.

88. Amery was rather taken with the thought that the Icelanders might be 'tempted to come in as a Small Dominion', cited in Louis, *In the Name of God*, 70. And *Smuts Papers*, v. 380; 22 May 1928—for one example amongst many.

89. *Smuts Papers*, vi. 470; 15 Dec. 1943.

90. Amery, *Empire at Bay*, 1065; 2 May 1949. A few weeks earlier, on 3 Mar., Amery had addressed cadets for the colonial service at Rhodes House in Oxford. As he noted in his diary, his dilemmas were those of Smuts, though expressed without undue worry about the capacity of universalism to function universally (p. 1066).

91. That these imaginings were present is recognized even in the mainstream historiography of empire. Commenting on the famed Robinson and Gallagher thesis, Wm. Roger Louis notes: 'These strategic calculations [of colonial administrators and politicians] were to an extent phantasmagorical. Strategic ideas reflected subjective interpretations of the history of European expansion', 'Robinson and Gallagher, and their Critics', in Wm. Roger Louis (ed.), *Imperialism: The Robinson and Gallagher Controversy* (London: New Viewpoints, 1976), 3.

92. Roger Louis's estimation of Amery's long-term influence is important in this context. Referring to the official papers drafted by him at the end of the First World War, he suggests that there is 'a fair claim for him as the architect of the British geo-political system that endured until the crack-up at Suez in 1956. The basic idea was to establish an arc of British influence stretching from the Cape through East Africa and the Sudan to Egypt, from Egypt through the Middle East to India, and from India through South-East Asia to the Dominions in the antipodes', *In the Name of God*, 68.

93. Amery, *Empire at Bay*, 1067; entry for 11 Sept. 1950.

94. W. E. B. DuBois, *W. E. B. DuBois Speaks: Speeches and Addresses, 1920–1963* (New York: Pathfinder Press, 1970), 130 and 197. These were all statements made in the mid-1940s.

95. Marika Sherwood, 'The United Nations. Caribbean and African-American Attempts to Influence the Founding Conference in San Francisco in 1945', *Journal of Caribbean History*, 29/1 (1995).

96. DuBois, *DuBois Speaks*, 178.

97. W. E. B. DuBois, *The World and Africa: An Inquiry into the Part Which Africa has Played in World History* (New York: Kraus-Thornton, Millwood, 1991; 1947), 244–5. He also noted (p. 43): 'In 1945 Jan Smuts, prime minister of South Africa, who had once declared that every white man in South Africa believes in the suppression of the Negro except those who are "mad, quite mad," stood there before the assembled peoples of the world and pleaded for an article on 'human rights' in the UN charter. Nothing so vividly illustrates the twisted contradictions of thought in the minds of white men.'.

98. W. E. B. DuBois, 'The Negro Mind Reaches Out', in Alain Locke (ed.), *The New Negro: An Interpretation* (New York: Johnson, 1968), 401–2: the collection was 1st publ. in 1925, DuBois's essay a little while earlier.

99. In public, his speeches of 30 Jan. 1931 (Manchester Free Trade Hall) and 23 Feb. 1931 (Epping) are the most notorious: *Churchill Speaks, 1897–1963: Collected Speeches in Peace and War*, ed. Robert Rhodes James (Leicester: Windward, 1981); and in private—Churchill rejoicing at 'the coming of a "world-wide movement of reaction"' and saying 'that Gandhi should be bound hand and foot at the gates of Delhi and trampled on by an enormous elephant ridden by the viceroy'—cited in Philip Ziegler, *Diana Cooper* (Harmondsworth: Penguin, 1983), 143.

100. Cited in Ruth First and Ann Scott, *Olive Schreiner* (New Brunswick, NJ: Rutgers UP, 1990), 252.
101. Cited in Louis, *In the Name of God*, 66; these comments were made in 1917.
102. *Smuts Papers*, vi. 214; 4 Apr. 1940. The letter went on to extol the qualities of the *Manchester Guardian*.
103. *Smuts Papers*, vi. 400; letter to Margaret Gillett, 26 Dec. 1942. Or as he put it a little while earlier (p. 111): 'I like that funny English expression "enjoy myself." It sounds so good, and I have no experience of it.' In writing about Whitman to Margaret Gillett in 1942, Smuts confessed that there was much about him that he had missed, owing to 'my simplicity and ignorance of such abnormalities', and also commented that he was now rather more sceptical about Whitman's significance (p. 400). A year later he was referring to 'an unsound strain in his [Whitman's] make-up' (p. 443); letter to Margaret Gillett, 21 July 1943.
104. D. H. Lawrence, *Studies in Classic American Literature* (Harmondsworth: Penguin, 1971), 182. This is where Lawrence commends a morality which is not 'didactic' but which 'Changes the blood first'. Whitman, he thought, 'a great moralist'. 'He was a great changer of the blood in the veins of men' (p. 180).
105. Jan Smuts, *Walt Whitman: A Study in the Evolution of Personality* (Detroit: Wayne State UP, 1973), 26 and 30. Smuts also believed that in the most evolved human personality there existed no division between the conscious and the unconscious, or between reason and emotion. So far as the unconscious existed, it represented 'the vast region of mental twilight in which the primordial forces of our cosmic nature disport themselves' (p. 33).
106. Ibid.
107. The dominant reception of Whitman was through Edward Carpenter and, to a lesser extent, Havelock Ellis. Indeed in one respect, Carpenter's reading of Whitman was the same as Smuts's: they both saw in Whitman's poetry the vision of an evolutionary 'higher type of humanity' creating 'a new form of life'. See Sheila Rowbotham and Jeffrey Weeks, *Socialism and the New Life: The Personal and Sexual Politics of Edward Carpenter and Havelock Ellis* (London: Pluto, 1977), 111; Chushichi Tsuzuki, *Edward Carpenter, 1844–1929: Prophet of Human Fellowship* (Cambridge: Cambridge UP, 1980); and Sheila Rowbotham, *Edward Carpenter: A Life of Liberty and Love* (London: Verso, 2009).
108. Cited in Michael Freeden, *The New Liberalism: An Ideology of Social Reform* (Oxford: Clarendon Press, 1978), 82. See too Stefan Collini, *Liberalism and Sociology: L. T. Hobhouse and Political Argument in England, 1880–1914* (Cambridge: Cambridge UP, 1979); and P. F. Clarke, *Liberals and Social Democrats* (Cambridge: Cambridge UP, 1977). Hobhouse had been active in the Manchester district of the Protection of Native Races Society since at least 1898: J. A. Hobson and Morris Ginsberg, *L. T. Hobhouse. His Life and Work* (London: Allen & Unwin, 1931), 38.
109. Although this is not to imply that British feminism was unilaterally anti-imperial: see esp. Antoinette Burton, *Burdens of History. British Feminists, Indian Women, and Imperial Culture, 1865–1915* (Chapel Hill, NC: University of North

Carolina Press, 1994); and, less explicitly concerned with early feminism, but of great relevance, Julia Bush, *Edwardian Ladies and Imperial Power* (Leicester: Leicester UP, 1999).

110. An uncomplicated version of her story appears in John Fisher, *That Miss Hobhouse* (London: Secker & Warburg, 1971); and see as well Paula Krebs, ' "The Last of the Gentlemen's Wars": Women in the Boer War Concentration Camp Controversy', *History Workshop Journal,* 33 (1992).

111. Hancock, *The Sanguine Years,* 182.

112. *Smuts Papers,* v. 330.

113. See Vron Ware, *Beyond the Pale: White Women, Racism and History* (London: Verso, 1992).

114. Crafford, *Smuts,* 143.

115. Alice Clark, *Working Life of Women in the Seventeenth Century* (London: Cass, 1968; 1919); in her acknowledgements she refers to Olive Schreiner's *Woman and Labour,* 1st publ. eight years earlier (London: Virago, 1978).

116. *Smuts Papers,* v. 33; Smuts to Alice Clark, 10 Oct. 1920.

117. *Selections from the Smuts Papers,* ed. W. K. Hancock and Jean van der Poel, iii. *June 1910–November 1918* (Cambridge: Cambridge UP, 1966), 467; Alice Clark to Smuts, 19 Mar. 1917.

118. *Smuts Papers,* iii. 583; letter to Alice Clark, 2 Jan. 1918.

119. Shortly after the Boer War came to an end Emmeline Pethick Lawrence visited Schreiner and gave her a copy of *Souls of Black Folk*; as it was 1st publ. in 1903, it must have been one of the very first edns.: see First and Scott, *Schreiner,* 254. Schreiner's involvement in the Men and Women's Club is discussed in Judith Walkowitz, *City of Dreadful Delight: Narratives of Sexual Danger in Late-Victorian London* (London: Virago, 1992), and in Lucy Bland, *Banishing the Beast: English Feminism and Sexual Morality, 1885–1914* (Harmondsworth: Penguin, 1995); and her trips to Millthorpe are recounted in Rowbotham and Weeks, *Socialism and the New Life.*

120. When she wrote to him during the debates on the constitution of the new Union of South Africa e.g. she complained about the exclusion of women from the franchise and about 'the foolish words about European descent', *Smuts Papers,* ii. 586; 27 Aug. 1909.

121. Unrestrained enough to raise the eyebrows of Keith Hancock, at any rate: *The Sanguine Years,* 460–1. Important in this respect are Schreiner's reflections on 'the Englishman' in her posthumously published *Thoughts on South Africa* (London: Fisher & Unwin, 1923), where she develops a critique of the notion of the 'pure-blooded Englishman' (pp. 356–7). For good discussions, Paula Krebs, *Gender, Race, and the Writing of Empire: Public Discourse in the Boer War* (Cambridge: Cambridge UP, 1999), ch. 5, and her 'Olive Schreiner's Racialization of South Africa', *Victorian Studies,* 40/3 (1997); and Carolyn Burdett, *Olive Schreiner and the Progress of Feminism: Evolution, Gender, Empire* (Basingstoke: Palgrave, 2001).

122. Or, in a slightly different register, Smuts's later relationships with Lady Daphne Moore and Crown Princess Frederica of Greece, though the social standing of those he fell for seems to have shifted.

123. Smuts, *War-Time Speeches*, 109–24. The fact that Smuts was being interviewed by a US journalist no doubt coloured his words. In terms of historiography, I am thinking particularly of Arno Mayer, *The Persistence of the Old Regimes: Europe to the Great War* (New York: Pantheon, 1981).

124. As ever, Thomas Jones's diary provides an insight into the manner in which the politicians viewed themselves: 'I rose to go and S. B. [Stanley Baldwin] picked up from his desk, laden with new books, a copy of Smuts' [St Andrews] Rectorial Address on *Freedom* and gave it to me after inscribing it, "From one lover of Freedom to another," which recalled to my mind a parting gift from L. G. [Lloyd George] of a portrait of Mazzini: "From one admirer of Mazzini to another"', *Diary with Letters*, 139; 17 Nov. 1934.

125. See the correspondence from the second half of 1919 to early 1920: 'Europe is a sad broken world' (to Margaret Gillett, 6 Sept. 1919); 'I sometimes fear that this war is simply the vanguard of calamity and that the Great Horror is still to come' (to Alice Clark, 21 Oct. 1919); 'God has retired into the background, and the prospect before the world is dark indeed' (to Margaret Gillett, 30 Dec. 1919); 'It sometimes looks to me as if there is going to be a permanent set-back to European civilisation, as if the conditions of human life are slowly but steadily, and perhaps permanently, deteriorating' (to Alice Clark, 10 Jan. 1920). *Smuts Papers*, v. 5, 16, 31, and 33.

126. *War-Time Speeches*, p. vii. He argued against an overly centralized, or federated, system in order to allow maximum equality between each nation in the Commonwealth, preferring to see the crown functioning as a symbolic means for cohesion. But this was to be on the model of a 'democratic kingship': 'I shall not be surprised to see the time come when our Royal princes, instead of getting their consorts from among the princelings of Central Europe, will go for them to the Dominions and other portions of the British Empire', *War-Time Speeches*, 34–5; 15 May 1917.

127. See Brian Simon, *In Search of a Grandfather: Henry Simon of Manchester, 1835–99* ([Leicester?]: Pendene Press, 1997); and Mary Stocks, *Ernest Simon of Manchester* (Manchester: Manchester UP, 1963). Simon's wife Sheena joined Labour in 1935; Simon himself in 1946; later still at the end of his life he gravitated towards the Campaign for Nuclear Disarmament.

128. I draw from Sarah Benton's unpubl. researches here in the archives of the Association for Education in Citizenship, for which I am very grateful. The 'Baldwin–Smuts stuff' comes from a letter Simon wrote to his wife on 26 Oct. 1934, and follows Smuts's Rectorial Address at St Andrews which he had delivered on 17 Oct.: see J. C. Smuts, *Freedom* (London: Alexander Maclehose, 1934). Simon's letter to his wife appears to have been airing ideas for a later letter to Crozier; the letter to Smuts was written on 3 June 1937.

129. For this see Bill Schwarz, 'The Language of Constitutionalism: Baldwinite Conservatism', in *Formations of Nation and People* (London: Routledge & Kegan Paul, 1984); and for a representative text, Sir Ernest Simon *et al.*, *Constructive Democracy* (London: Allen & Unwin, 1938)—an analysis brim full of Baldwin, and with contributions from, amongst others, Lord Halifax, Arthur Bryant, Clement Attlee, and William Beveridge. In the event Smuts declined Simon's overtures, arguing that despite his sympathy for the Association he always refused to join overseas organizations.

130. Crafford, *Smuts*, 316.

131. For extensive discussion of this cabinet meeting, and its aftermath, Graham Smith, *When Jim Crow Met John Bull: Black American Soldiers in World War II Britain* (London: I. B. Tauris, 1987), 72–9. Churchill's only contribution to the discussion was to make a joke about blacks and banjos.

132. See e.g. Field-Marshall Lord Bramall and Adrian Gilbert (eds.), *The Desert War, 1940–42* (London: Sidgwick & Jackson, 1992).

133. For a lone contrary view, Nancy Cunard and George Padmore, *The White Man's Duty: An Analysis of the Colonial Question in the Light of the Atlantic Charter* (London: W. H. Allen, 1942); I shall follow up this theme in the next volume. These issues are not prominent (and Smuts is absent) in both Paul Addison, *The Road to 1945* (London: Quartet, 1977), and in Angus Calder, *The People's War: Britain 1939–1945* (London: Panther, 1971), though the latter is at pains to show from the outset that 'when Britain "stood alone" in 1940, she stood on the shoulders of several hundred million Asians' (p. 22). A. J. P. Taylor, *English History, 1914–1945* (Harmondsworth: Penguin, 1977; 1965), has rather a lot about Smuts—where not factual, suitably irreverent—whereas Peter Clarke's more recent *Hope and Glory: Britain 1900–1990* (Harmondsworth: Penguin, 1996), all but misses Smuts completely, and its neglect of empire is striking.

134. Alexander Campbell, *Smuts and the Swastika* (London: Victor Gollancz, 1943), 14. Two years later the Left Book Club publ. Alexander Campbell's *It's Your Empire* (London: Victor Gollancz, 1945) which opened with Smuts, but which adopted a relatively harsh view of his racial inclinations (pp. 7 and 10). I assume that this is the same author, but if so it is not clear what accounted for the change of emphasis.

135. Campbell, *Smuts and the Swastika*, 14.

136. Ibid. 15.

137. *Smuts Papers*, vii. 281; letter to Margaret Gillett, 20 July 1948. Smuts anticipated this notion in a letter to Lord Brand on 13 Nov. 1939: 'South Africa has a divided soul', *Smuts Papers*, vi. 199.

138. *Smuts Papers*, vii. 10; letter to Margaret Gillett, 17 Nov. 1946.

139. Ibid. 126; letter to Daphne More, 2 Mar. 1947.

140. Cornel West, *Beyond Eurocentrism and Multiculturalism,* i. *Prophetic Thought in Postmodern Times* (Monroe, Me.: Common Courage Press, 1993), 57–8.

141. L. T. Hobhouse, *Democracy and Reaction* (London: Fisher Unwin, 1904), 45 and 61. I have used the reprint of this (ed. P. F. Clarke, Brighton, Harvester Press, 1972), which includes the 1909 introduction to the 2nd edn., which is where Hobhouse specifically dates the period of reaction from 1886 to 1903.

142. Ibid. 48.

143. J. C. Smuts, *Holism and Evolution* (London: Macmillan, 1926). Yet even when Smuts was most deeply immersed in examining evolution as an organic and harmonious process other, less liberal motifs press in. Thus he defines an organism as 'a little living world in which law and order reign', cited in Hancock, *Field of Force*, 185. In 1929 a symposium on the book was organized in South Africa, attended by Haldane and by Lancelot Hogben (who was hostile to Smuts's thesis). For the best account of this radical moment in the history of the natural sciences, Gary Werskey, *The Visible College* (London: Allen Lane, 1978).

144. Hobhouse himself was unambiguous in his formal statements: 'belief in race itself is necessarily a reactionary tendency', cited in Collini, *Liberalism and Sociology*, 178.

145. Freeden, *New Liberalism*, 177–85.

146. L. T. Hobhouse, *Liberalism* (Oxford: Oxford UP, 1964), 540. In the same work he noted too (p. 240): 'the colonies include the most democratic communities in the world. Their natural sympathies are not with the Conservatives, but with the most Progressive parties in the United Kingdom.' We need to recall in this context the active role of evolutionary theory and variants of eugenics in the making of the feminisms of the period, which pulled some feminists into uncompromising defences of racial purity—especially during and after the campaign to persuade parliament to enact a White Slave Traffic Bill in 1912: see esp. Bland, *Banishing the Beast*.

147. See Dubow, *Scientific Racism*, 51; and in Smuts's first political speech, the belief that the native, in coming into contact with European civilization, 'has both physically and morally deteriorated; the closer that contact has been, the greater has been that deterioration', *Smuts Papers*, i. 97. In so far as we need to consider the question of intellectual influences, there is no reason to assume that it was all one way, from Hobhouse to Smuts.

148. Thus the *New Statesman* welcomed the 1920 Native Affairs Bill as 'wise and generous', cited in T. J. Haarhoff, *Smuts the Humanist: A Personal Reminiscence* (Oxford: Blackwell, 1970), 62. Or again, the report in the *Manchester Guardian* of Smuts's speech at the Royal Institute of International Affairs in 1934 was entirely laudatory: 'General Smuts, erect, neat, pink and white, speaking in a high voice with a touch of accent more Latin than Dutch, gave it a speech worthy of his powers. No politician in England for many a day has combined his sweep, his detachment, and his subtlety. What impressed one most was the way in which his mind cuts down to essentials and declares them without circumlocution ... this clarity of mind enables him to grasp and state what he

regards as the essentials of a situation in a way which one wishes that any member of our own Government could emulate.' Cited in Smuts, *Jan Christian Smuts*, 363.

149. *Manchester Guardian*, 29 May 1948.

150. See esp. Paul B. Rich, *White Power and the Liberal Conscience: Racial Segregation and South African Liberalism, 1921–1960* (Manchester: Manchester UP, 1984) and his *Hope and Despair: English-Speaking Intellectuals and South African Politics, 1896–1976* (London: British Academic Press, 1993); and Saul Dubow, 'Race, Civilization and Culture', in Marks and Trapido, *Politics of Race, Class and Nationalism*.

151. Walter Cotton, *Racial Segregation in South Africa: An Appeal* (London: Sheldon Press, 1931).

152. Cited in Kenneth Ingham, *Jan Christian Smuts: The Conscience of a South African* (London: Weidenfeld & Nicolson, 1986), 164.

153. Hancock, *Field of Force*, 224 and 229; and the editorial notes by John Barnes and David Nicholson in Amery, *Empire at Bay*, 139–43.

154. J. H. Oldham, *White and Black in Africa: A Critical Examination of the Rhodes Lectures of General Smuts* (London: Longman, 1930). And see too, from the same year, Leonard Baines, *Caliban in Africa: An Impression of Colour Madness* (London: Victor Gollancz, 1930), which, while denouncing 'the shame of all white blood', carried a brief indictment of Smuts (pp. 245, 109–10).

155. See Barbara Bush, *Imperialism, Race and Resistance: Africa and Britain, 1919–45* (London: Routledge, 1999), 183 and 196. For a later exception, Adamastor, *White Man Boss*, categorically states that Smuts's United Party was dedicated to 'white supremacy', and that Smuts himself was a practitioner of racial segregation (pp. 8 and 26); this was in *1950*. Although not explicitly a document critical of Smuts, see too, Frank Weston, Bishop of Zanzibar, *The Black Slaves of Prussia: An Open Letter Addressed to General Smuts* (London: Universities' Mission to Central Africa, n.d. [1918?]). This brought to his attention the fate of those blacks in German East Africa who had fought for the British: if Germany were allowed to regain control of the territory, they would be in danger. Weston, however, was sensitive to the problem of raising the question of black rights: 'When missionary bishops speak of African rights, men lend an unwilling ear, and "wink the other eye"' (p. 3). To this came the reply (as from 'General Smuts' Headquarters, Savoy Hotel, London, W. C.'): 'I have read the open letter of the Bishop of Zanzibar to me with the deepest interest. It contains a very solemn plea to the conscience of the British people, backed by an array of solid facts.' An unwilling ear, perhaps?

156. This is not to suggest that on matters of policy Smuts got his way. Clearly this was not the case: it was not so in the aftermath of the Rhodes lectures, nor in the 1940s, when he was pressing the British government for yet more regional privileges in exchange for the South African contribution to the war effort. He could function as a totem of imperial civilization while, at the same time,

on policy matters other determinations had to be taken into account. British respect for Menzies, or Roosevelt for that matter, never ensured their interests prevailed over those of the domestic government: and so with Smuts. This would suggest that a paradox exists. Responses to Smuts could be more ambivalent for those officials who had to deal with him directly than in the national culture more generally. For a hint, Stephen Howe, *Anticolonialism in British Politics: The Left and the End of Empire, 1918–64* (Oxford: Clarendon Press, 1993), 139–40.

157. For this, Jeremy Krikler, *White Rising: The 1922 Insurrection and Racial Killing in South Africa* (Manchester: Manchester UP, 2005).

158. An illuminating assessment of the fluctuating views of South Africa projected in the British press can be found in Peter Henshaw, 'The Springbok Reviled: British Attitudes towards Apartheid South Africa, 1948–1994', paper presented to the Second British World Conference, Cape Town, 2002.

159. According to Paul Rich, 'the important feature of the British Empire-Commonwealth in the interwar years is that no significant challenge was made to South African domestic policies', 'The Impact of South African Segregationist and Apartheid Ideology', 1. Clearly the UN condemnation was a significant anticipation. Rich also draws attention to the replacement of Lord Harlech as high commissioner by Sir Evelyn Baring. But he goes on to argue that in the early 1950s opposition came principally from private organizations, outside the state, and only very slowly touched the policy-makers. He cites the presence of Attlee's sister, Mary, a missionary in South Africa and active in making segregation a public issue in Britain. This is in contrast to her brother, whose regard for Smuts and for a British South Africa was high. For a nice cameo, see the Movietone newsreel of Oct. 1946, picturing Smuts delivering to Attlee and to the British government a cheque from the people of South Africa.

160. Cited in Crafford, *Smuts*, 344. Keith Hancock opens the second volume of his biography by announcing that he had drafted a chapter on 'the mythology of Smuts', but had decided to exclude it: *Field of Force*, p. xi. For an illuminating discussion of the biographical construction, see Saul Dubow and Shula Marks, 'Keith Hancock Looks at South Africa', unpubl. paper delivered to the Institute of Commonwealth Studies, Dec. 1988. I am very grateful to Saul Dubow for lending me a copy.

161. Roland Barthes, *Mythologies* (London: Vintage, 1993), 148.

162. Cited in Smith, 'Apartheid, Sharpeville and "Impartiality"', 254.

163. *The Times*, 12 Sept. 1950.

164. *Daily Express*, 12 Sept. 1950. The *Express* paid a fulsome editorial tribute, while Frank Owen (one-third of 'Cato', the collective author of Victor Gollancz's 1940 polemic *Guilty Men*) in a long article represented him as a Liberal 'worried about the colour war in South Africa'. Owen had met him in Cape Town shortly before his death. 'He said many wise things. The wisest: "A man's wife

is always above him. She is the steam in the kettle." ' The *Daily Mirror* of the same day claimed that he had died 'with broken heart', destroyed by the political victories of the Nationalists.

165. Hansard, House of Commons, 13 Sept. 1950. For Nicholas Winterton, 'Here was a guide and philosopher for the whole world'.

166. Smuts, *Jan Christian Smuts*, 527.

167. In Mar. 1911 Baker wrote to Smuts, quoting Wren: 'Arch has its political uses: public buildings being the ornament of a country; it establishes a nation, draws people and commerce, makes the people love their native country, which passion is the original of all great actions in a Commonwealth.' One can imagine how pleasing this would have been to Smuts: cited in Thomas Metcalf, *An Imperial Vision: India's Architecture and Britain's Raj* (London: Faber & Faber, 1989), 193.

168. *The Times*, 13 Sept. 1950.

169. *The Times*, 14 and 18 Sept. 1950. Zionists had named a plot of land near Haifa after him in 1933; and from 1946 his name adorned a street in Athens.

170. Hansard, House of Commons, 24 Oct. 1950. The question was first put to Attlee by John Rodgers, who subsequently became secretary to the General Smuts memorial committee in 1953.

171. Hansard, House of Commons, 7 June 1951.

172. Hansard, House of Commons, 26 June and 2 July 1952. Felix Driver has drawn my attention to the unveiling of the statue to David Livingstone by the headquarters of the Royal Geographical Society on 23 Oct. 1953. The occasion was presided over by Oliver Lyttleton, the colonial secretary, who took the opportunity to invoke Curzon's tributes to Livingstone. A few weeks later Lyttleton was the subject of an unprecedented censure motion by Labour for his handling of African affairs.

173. Hansard, House of Commons, 2 July 1952. When in 1919 Thomas Jones applied to be principal of University College at Aberystwyth he had both Lloyd George and Smuts as his references—though he still failed to get the job: Gwyn Williams, *When Was Wales?* (Harmondsworth: Penguin, 1985), 221. Irene White's obituary was publ. in the *Guardian*, 27 Dec. 1999.

174. Hansard, House of Commons, 2 July 1952.

175. Hansard, House of Commons, 2 July 1952. For Driberg's activities at the end of the 1940s, on Vietnam see George Rosie, *The British in Vietnam: How the Twenty-Five Year War Began* (London: Panther, 1970); on Malaya, Howe, *Anticolonialism in British Politics*, 154–6; and Christopher Bayly and Tim Harper, *Forgotten Wars: The End of Britain's Asian Empire* (London: Penguin, 2008).

176. Hansard, House of Commons, 2 July 1952. As MP for Brixton, on 25 June 1948 Lipton had been at the Astoria publicly to welcome forty West Indians who had sailed on the *Windrush*: Vivienne Francis, *With Hope in their Eyes* (London: Nia, 1998), 40.

177. Hansard, House of Commons, 2 July 1952.

178. Hansard, House of Commons, 2 July 1952.

179. Hansard, House of Commons, 13 Dec. 1955. Harlech, as William Ormsby-Gore, had been a protégé of Milner, and thereafter devoted his public life to the colonies and to the arts.

180. Martin Gilbert, *Never Despair: Winston S. Churchill,* viii. *1945–1965* (London: Heinemann, 1988), 1095.

181. Virginia Woolf, *The Crowded Dance of Modern Life: Selected Essays,* ii (Harmondsworth: Penguin, 1993), 127.

182. It wasn't only racial susceptibilities which caused him trouble. In 1942 his Jacob and Angel were exiled to Blackpool pier, for 'adults only'. Visitors were charged 3d to see 'Epstein's latest sensation', Edward Lucie-Smith, 'Forbidden Culture', *Index on Censorship,* 28/6 (1999).

183. Jacob Epstein, *An Autobiography* (London: Art Treasures Book Club, 1963; 1955), 150. And see Alain Locke's favourable estimation of Epstein from 1925, 'The New Negro Digs up his Past', in Locke, *The New Negro.*

184. Epstein, *Autobiography.*

185. Cited ibid. 44.

186. An early scandal arose from Epstein's figures for the offices of the British Medical Association on Agar Street, off the Strand, in 1908. In 1935 Southern Rhodesia took over the property and named it Rhodesia House. The new owners wanted the sculptures removed and prevailed upon the architectural firm responsible—Sir Herbert Baker's company—to get this done.

187. There has been a move in recent times to render a more positive reading of Epstein than the one I offer here. In the incomparable exhibition devoted to the Harlem renaissance—*Rhapsodies in Black*—held at the Hayward Gallery in London in 1997, Epstein was presented as a pivotal figure, 'powerfully influenced by the commanding aesthetic of the Harlem renaissance'. The purpose of seeing him in this light was to emphasize the cosmopolitan dimensions of Harlem in the 1920s, and to indicate the reach of Harlem, activating not only black but white as well. I am sympathetic to this endeavour, but unsure whether Epstein can carry the weight of this representation. I am sceptical about the degree of transaction between his own Jewish culture and black cultures on the lower east side in the 1880s and 1890s. I am sceptical too about his positioning in Harlem in 1927. Like many other whites—and like many others escorted by Van Vechten—he was essentially a tourist. I think he gets it about right himself, in his autobiography: 'I went with Paul Robeson and a party to Harlem, and made the round of negro dance places, but I saw nothing to wonder at beyond the usual stamina of the negro when dancing.' *Autobiography,* 129. For the view emanating from the Hayward exhibition, see Bill Schwarz, 'Rhapsodising Black: Harlem in London, 1997. An Interview with David A. Bailey', *New Formations,* 33 (1998), 86. I am grateful for discussions with Alex Potts on this issue, and esp. to David Bailey and Phil Cohen.

188. See Richard Buckle, *Jacob Epstein. Sculptor* (London: Faber & Faber, 1963); and Stephen Gardiner, *Epstein: Artist Against the Establishment* (London: Michael Joseph, 1992).

189. *The Times*, 23 Mar. 1956.

190. *The Times*, 18 July 1956. One can also see the degree to which *The Times* functioned as the house journal of the political classes: on 5 Oct. it addressed all MPs, announcing that two tickets per MP were available for all those who informed the Speaker's Secretary's Office.

191. *The Times*, 29 and 30 Oct. 1956. For Smuts's family, other intimations of mortality were active at this time. At the end of Aug. six of his forebears were exhumed from the family cemetery on the farm where Smuts himself had been born, and buried in an adjacent town. The farm had been taken over by a cement works which was extending its operations: *The Times*, 1 Sept. 1956.

192. Moran, *Churchill: Struggle for Survival*, 741.

193. Selwyn Lloyd, *Suez 1956: A Personal Account* (London: Cape, 1978), 206–7.

194. For the events of 7 Nov., David Carlton, *Britain and the Suez Crisis* (Oxford: Blackwell, 1988), 82–3.

195. I have relied on the Pathé and Movietone newsreels; Powell can be clearly seen in the former.

196. Cited in Gilbert, *Never Despair*, 1221. The implication of Gilbert's account seems to be that Churchill was present, which is not the case.

197. *The Times*, 8 Nov. 1956.

198. *Poems of C. Day Lewis, 1925–1972* (London: Cape, 1977), 106. The poem— *Newsreel*—was written in 1938, and in it Day Lewis suggests that the distinctiveness of the newsreel lay in its combination of the heroic and the trivial. The best exploration of these themes is Philip Noyce's 1978 film, *Newsfront*.

199. I borrow this phrase from Dick Hebdige, *Subculture: The Meaning of Style* (London: Methuen, 1979), 45.

200. For an early hint, Stuart Hall and Paddy Whannel, *The Popular Arts* (London: Hutchinson, 1964); and for the same themes developed, Stuart Hall, 'What is This "Black" in Black Popular Culture?', in Gina Dent and Michele Wallace (eds.), *Black Popular Culture* (Seattle: Bay Press, 1992).

201. *Melody Maker*, 12 May 1956. These comments followed the beating of Nat King Cole in Birmingham, Alabama, on 10 Apr.

202. See Dan T. Carter, *The Politics of Rage: George Wallace, the Origins of the New Conservatism, and the Transformation of American Politics* (Baton Rouge, La.: Louisiana State UP, 1995).

203. Lipton's views can be consulted in *Melody Maker*, 30 June 1956.

204. Margery Perham, *The Colonial Reckoning* (London: Collins, 1962), 155.

205. *The Times*, 4 Sept. 1956. This phenomenon was not restricted to east London. Three youths in Twickenham were bound over for singing rock and roll songs. 'It was said that people opened their windows and told them to be quiet, but they refused.' The *Daily Mail* provided its thoughts on the African influences

on rock'n'roll on 4 and 5 Sept., arriving at the same conclusion as Perham, though with all irony effaced. According to *Melody Maker,* 15 Sept. 1956, there were also riots in Manchester, Blackburn, Croydon, and Preston.

206. For indications: Stephen Ellis, 'The ANC in Exile', *African Affairs,* 90/3 (1991); and for a moving memoir, amongst a number, from the later period, AnneMarie Wolpe, *A Long Way from Home* (London: Virago, 1996). Ronald Segal is an interesting example. He was editor of *Africa South*—or *Africa South in Exile* as it became from July 1960; he edited the influential Penguin Africa Library; he was the author of *The Race War* (New York: Bantam, 1967; 1966); and—in expanding the purview of race for the British—he publ. in the UK the Student Nonviolent Coordinating Committee photographic essay, *A Matter of Colour: Documentary of the Struggle for Racial Equality in the USA* (Harmondsworth: Penguin, 1965). The story of the cohering of popular British opposition to South Africa after 1948 has yet to be told: it comprises a surprisingly minor key in Howe, *Anticolonialism in British Politics.* An early intervention of significance came from the inimitable Basil Davidson, *Report on Southern Africa* (London: Jonathan Cape, 1952).

207. The BBC found itself having to tread a delicate line, recognizing but not giving too much credence to dissident opinion: Smith, 'Apartheid, Sharpeville and "Impartiality"'. Smith argues that the Sharpeville massacre of 21 Mar. 1960 marked the critical break in terms of the coverage of South Africa by the British media. Ian Berry's photographs of the massacre—prevented from appearing in *Drum* in South Africa—appeared in the London *Observer.* The evidence from Howe, *Anticolonialism in British Politics,* seems to suggest that for the labour movement this too was the key moment.

208. Trevor Huddleston, *Naught for your Comfort* (London: Fontana, 1976), 13; it was republ. in 1976 as 'the book that foretold the Soweto uprising'. In 1990, it was Huddleston, in full bishop's regalia, who opened the televised concert in Wembley to celebrate the release of Nelson Mandela—a vindication of another history. On many occasions Desmond Tutu has written how shocking it was, as a child, to see Huddleston doffing his hat to Tutu's own mother— a white man respectfully greeting an uneducated black woman. An overview can be found in Robin Denniston, *Trevor Huddleston: A Life* (London: Macmillan, 1999), and in the obituary in the *Guardian,* 21 Apr. 1998.

209. For a revealing fictional discussion of a Briton arriving in South Africa at this time, and having to negotiate the racial divide, Nadine Gordimer, *A World of Strangers* (Harmondsworth; Penguin, 1962; 1958).

210. During Suez, the connection between decolonization and immigration did enter the popular imagination. At a pro-war demonstration in Oxford on 4 Nov. placards were seen declaring: 'We want war'; 'Wogs go home'; and 'Shoot the wogs': letter from the indefatigable Nicolas Walter, and others, to the *Manchester Guardian,* 5 Nov. 1956.

211. Dan Jacobson, 'After Notting Hill', *Encounter* (Dec. 1958). Just down the road from the gleaming new studio complex of the BBC, the pub used to be singularly depressing, and for a long while was an empty wreck. Most of it is now given over to an Arab-Mediterranean fast-food joint, Zizinia, with just a remnant functioning as a pub. It still remains home to the unrelieved economic dispossession of poor local whites.

212. Nelson Mandela, *Long Walk to Freedom* (London: Little, Brown, 1994), 291; Mary Benson, *Nelson Mandela: The Man and the Movement* (New York: Norton, 1986), 114. In 1985 Zenani Mandela and Oliver Tambo unveiled a bust of Mandela on the South Bank. Early in 2001, a public subscription was launched to create a likeness outside South Africa House in Trafalgar Square: the controversies which followed—the exact location, the qualities of the final figure—were almost as long-running as those which dogged the unveiling of Smuts. In the event Mandela ended up in some proximity to, though not in the line of vision of, Lincoln in Westminster Square: and alongside, but not in place of, Smuts. The unveiling took place on 29 Aug. 2007, and was for the most part attractively multicultural, reminiscent more of past Greater London Council local events than of formal state occasions. Mandela recalled his earlier visit with Tambo and went on to ask when there would be a black man 'within the eyes of Smuts?' Mandela had become the first honorary president of a students' union in the UK in 1964, and first had a road named after him, in Brent, in 1981. Thereafter housing blocks, parks, sports centres, and more streets were given his name: an echo of the memorialization of Smuts in a different time. Indeed, on 11 July 1996 Mandela addressed both houses of parliament to applause as rapturous as Smuts had received some half century before: Anthony Sampson, *Mandela: The Authorised Biography* (London: HarperCollins, 1999), recounts these late visits to London, though the press reports of Mandela in Brixton on 12 July provide a vivid, and very different, cameo.

CHAPTER 6

1. See Ch. 1.

2. Interview with the author, House of Lords, 27 July 1988. This was said—a quarter of a century on—with laughter. Home indicated on the same occasion that the cause of the political difficulties was that no white politician was prepared to allow sufficient black representation. Yet not much earlier he had told Brian Lapping that 'There was a strong case for dominion status for [Southern] Rhodesia. They had over the years made the grade in many ways. I think their relations with Africans were pretty friendly, totally unlike South Africa.' Brian Lapping, *End of Empire* (London: Grafton, 1989; 1985), 572.

3. Simon Ball, *The Guardsmen: Harold Macmillan, Three Friends, and the World they Made* (London: Harper Perennial, 2005), 366.

4. In his diary of 14 Dec. 1960 Harold Macmillan noted: 'Central Africa is really our Algeria, on a smaller scale', cited in Alistair Horne, *Macmillan,* ii. *1957–1986* (London: Macmillan, 1988), 211. And see Miles Kahler, *Decolonization in Britain and France: The Domestic Consequences of International Relations* (Princeton: Princeton UP, 1984).

5. Stephen Howe notes the 'gradual abandonment' of Labour's commitment to African paramountcy in the aftermath of Lord Passfield's declaration, made in 1930 during Labour's second administration. Its complete abandonment may simply have come about as a result of an accumulation of smaller, pragmatic decisions, with partnership representing the symbolic end-point of this longer process. Stephen Howe, *Anticolonialism in British Politics: The Left and the End of Empire, 1918–1964* (Oxford: Clarendon Press, 1993), 51. For an alternative view, which argues for greater ideological intervention, Suke Wolton, *Lord Hailey, the Colonial Office and the Politics of Race and Empire in the Second World War: The Loss of White Prestige* (Houndmills: Macmillan, 2000).

6. Kenneth D. Kaunda, *Zambia Shall be Free: An Autobiography* (London: Heinemann, 1962), and Joshua Nkomo, *Nkomo: The Story of my Life* (London: Methuen, 1984). Even through British eyes the extent of the opposition is well described in the memoirs of one official, Cyril Greenall: E. Cyril Greenall and David G. Coe, *Kaunda's Gaoler: Memoirs of a District Officer in Northern Rhodesia and Zambia* (London: Radcliffe Press, 2003). This should be read alongside Henry Phillips, *From Obscurity to Bright Dawn: How Nyasaland Became Malawi. An Insider's Account* (London: Radcliffe Press, 1998), though it is less conclusive. The extent of black militancy in Northern Rhodesia should not be underestimated. C. L. R. James ended two studies on Pan-Africanism, both 1st publ. in 1938, with a discussion of the strike of miners in the territory in 1935: *The Black Jacobins: Toussaint L'Ouverture and the San Domingo Revolution* (London: Allison & Busby, 1989), and *A History of Negro Revolt* (London: Race Today, 1985). James saw the black workers of Northern Rhodesia as *the future.*

7. R. A. Butler, minute of 6 Mar. 1963 in Philip Murphy (ed.), *British Documents on the End of Empire,* B/9. *Central Africa,* part II. *Crisis and Dissolution, 1959–1965* (London: Stationery Office, 2005), 362. Butler was aggrieved not only by the complexity of the negotiations but by the obstructions of the Federal government, seeing in them a parallel to the machinations of Winston Churchill and his allies as they tried to wreck the India Bill.

8. It remains unacknowledged in his history of the empire: Simon Schama, *A History of Britain,* iii. *The Fate of Empire, 1776–2000* (London: BBC Books, 2003).

9. Lord Alport, *The Sudden Assignment: Central Africa, 1961–63* (London: Hodder & Stoughton, 1965), 74.

10. For an early manifestation, from within Britain, see Basil Davidson, *Report on Southern Africa* (London: Jonathan Cape, 1952), which also predicted that Welensky's scheme for federation would become a political 'volcano', 269.

11. Robin Palmer, 'European Resistance to African Majority Rule: The Settlers' and Residents' Association of Nyasaland, 1960–63', *African Affairs*, 72/288 (1973), 265: this was in a communication dated 16 Dec. 1972.

12. In the view of the distinguished foreign correspondent, James Cameron, the Labour party was entirely culpable in refusing to challenge the Conservative imperial record in the 1959 election: 'Africa and the British Electorate', *Africa South*, 4/4 (1960). I am grateful to Ken Parker for lending me his old copies of the journal, and of it successor, *Africa South in Exile*. Even so 60% of Labour candidates mentioned central Africa in their manifestos, and a third the Hola atrocity in Kenya: J. D. Hargreaves, *Decolonization in Africa* (Harlow: Longman, 1988), 187.

13. Cub Alport, Britain's high commissioner in the Federation, noted that Welensky often complained that the British engaged in 'double-talk', which Alport judged to be unfair, as one might expect. He was considerably more sympathetic to Sir Edgar Whitehead, the Rhodesian prime minister, who 'speaking with much greater sophistication, said that in dealing with the British it was necessary to listen to the undertones of what they said and to read between the lines of what was written', Alport, *Sudden Assignment*, 15. Harold Macmillan concurred, finding Whitehead 'a cultivated and broadminded man with sound political instincts', *Pointing the Way, 1959–1961* (London: Macmillan, 1972), 144. In other words, Whitehead was of a recognizable social caste and was not deemed to be a colonial.

14. In the final days of the Federation, in Nov. 1963, Welensky was in London for a further round of discussions with Rab Butler. Welensky—referring to the task assigned to the Duke of Edinburgh of lowering the Union Jack in Kenya as British rule came to an end—asked Butler if 'there is no limit to the extent to which you people are prepared to degrade yourselves'. It appears that Butler's only answer was a shrug of the shoulders: J. R. T. Wood, *The Welensky Papers: A History of the Federation of Rhodesia and Nyasaland* (Durban: Graham Publishing, 1983), 1224–5.

15. Rhodes House Oxford. Welensky Papers, 665/5, Welensky to Salisbury, 25 Feb. 1962.

16. When he left London for the Gold Coast in 1953 Banda was an unknown figure to the British public. Patrick Keatley, *The Politics of Partnership* (Harmondsworth: Penguin, 1963), 424, offers an interesting account.

17. Todd was a New Zealander missionary who had migrated to Rhodesia in 1934, supervising the mission school at Dadaya (where a young Robert Mugabe taught). In 1953, in order to represent African interests, he entered politics and five years later became prime minister. He came to be known as a liberal; he had been ordained into the church, espousing a radical humanitarianism, though he distrusted organized African nationalism; and he was perhaps one of the last public figures to justify racial separation on classically liberal grounds. As later events were to prove he was also a man of courage. From the middle of 1957 public opinion began to turn against him. He introduced a bill to promote

multiracial trade unions. He opposed a private member's bill to regulate further interracial sexual relations. When he attempted to open the franchise to Africans educationally qualified to vote, but who lacked the requisite income, a populist storm broke and by Feb. 1958 he was politically destroyed. The United Federal Party's justifications for his ousting disguised the lethal antagonisms unleashed in private, and there was widespread suspicion that Welensky had been responsible: see the correspondence of 6 May 1958 from the UK high commissioner, M. R. Metcalf, to Home, in Philip Murphy (ed.), *British Documents on the End of Empire*, B/9. *Central Africa,* part I. *Closer Association, 1945–1958* (London: Stationery Office, 2005), 409. From then until his death in 2002 he was a lone figure, opposing his white successors and thence Mugabe as well.

18. Guy Clutton-Brock, arrested in the clamp-down, offers a sober account: 'The 1959 "Emergency" in Southern Rhodesia', in Colin Leys and Cranford Pratt (eds.), *A New Deal in Central Africa* (London: Heinemann, 1963). Clutton-Brock was a missionary who in 1957 had drafted the manifesto of the Rhodesian African National Congress and who was finally deported to the UK in 1971. When he died in 1995 Mugabe named him a hero of Zimbabwe.

19. For which he was taken to task by the *Daily Express*: Colin Baker, *State of Emergency: Crisis in Central Africa, Nyasaland, 1959–60* (London: I. B. Tauris, 1977), 31.

20. Philip Murphy, *Alan Lennox-Boyd: A Biography* (London: I. B. Tauris, 1999), 206; and see Murphy's 'A Police State? The Nyasaland Emergency and Colonial Intelligence', *Journal of Southern African Studies*, 36/4 (2010).

21. Cited ibid. 207.

22. Ibid.; Baker, *State of Emergency*, 38.

23. John Darwin, *Britain and Decolonisation: The Retreat from Empire in the Post-War World* (Houndmills: Macmillan, 1988), 270–1.

24. Ibid. 271.

25. John Darwin, 'The Central African Emergency, 1959', *Journal of Imperial and Commonwealth History*, 21/3 (1993), 220. This was part of a special issue of great interest devoted to the theme of 'Emergencies and Disorder in the European Empires after 1945', ed. Robert Holland.

26. *Report of the Nyasaland Commission of Inquiry* (Cmnd. 814, 1959), para. 2. This is a gripping if terrifying document. It charts the movement from the everyday disorders of colonial life in which white authority was mocked—'jeering' and 'disrespect' (para. 33); 'insults' (para. 62); being 'cheeky' (para. 237)—to the violent reaction designed to put the colonial order back in place. For a sharp contemporary account of the response to Devlin in Southern Rhodesia— arguing that in the territory 'African nationalism means Mau Mau' and that the settlers *needed* to believe in the massacre plot— see Terence Ranger, 'Devlin in Southern Rhodesia', *Africa South*, 4/2 (1960), 69–70.

27. Horne, *Macmillan,* ii. 181. In the end Macmillan thought the fallout from Devlin was not as bad as he had feared, believing it was only the usual suspects within

the Tory ranks who had caused difficulty, amongst whom he included Enoch Powell, described by Macmillan as 'a sort of Fakir'.

28. On 20 July 1959 the cabinet discussed whether the events in Nyasaland equated more to Mau Mau or to the Sepoy Rebellion of 1857: Darwin, 'Central African Emergency', 20.

29. *Report of the Advisory Commission on the Review of the Constitution of Rhodesia and Nyasaland* (Cmnd. 1148, 1960), 27: 'The dislike of Federation amongst Africans in the two Northern Territories is widespread, sincere, and of long standing. It is almost pathological. It is associated almost everywhere with a picture of Southern Rhodesia as a white man's country.'

30. Philip Murphy, '"An Intricate and Distasteful Subject": British Planning for the Use of Force against the European Settlers of Central Africa, 1952–65', *English Historical Review*, 121/492 (2006).

31. Welensky had known Butler since they spent time together on a private holiday in the eastern highlands in 1958: Anthony Howard, *Rab: The Life of R. A. Butler* (London: Macmillan, 1988), 289.

32. Even political insiders confessed their inability to understand the details of the various constitutional proposals for Northern Rhodesia: Mark Garnett, *Alport: A Study in Loyalty* (Teddington: Acumen, 1999), 164.

33. Here I concur with Dan Horowitz, 'Attitudes of British Conservatives towards Decolonization in Africa', *African Affairs*, 69/1 (1970), 22–3. In using the term 'ideological crisis of the state' I am drawing from the neo-Gramscian perspectives of Nicos Poulantzas, *Fascism and Dictatorship: The Third International and the Problem of Fascism* (London: New Left Books, 1977), and his *The Crisis of the Dictatorships: Portugal, Greece, Spain* (London: New Left Books, 1976); and from Stuart Hall, *The Hard Road to Renewal: Thatcherism and the Crisis of the British Left* (London: Verso, 1988); and see Stuart Hall and Bill Schwarz, 'State and Society, 1880–1930', in Mary Langan and Bill Schwarz (eds.), *Crises in the British State, 1880–1930* (London: Hutchinson, 1985).

34. In terms of economic management this critique became significant slightly earlier, but in my view it only began to cohere politically when it was articulated to a more general apprehension of prevailing social dissolution: Bill Schwarz, 'Conservatives and Corporatism', *New Left Review*, 166 (1987).

35. Murphy, *Central Africa*, part II. 184–9, for the Chiefs of Staff Committee discussions.

36. Alport, *Sudden Assignment*, 59–60.

37. See C. J. M. Alport, *Kingdoms in Partnership: A Study of Political Change in the British Commonwealth* (London: Lovat Dickson, 1937), a publication distributed by the Right Book Club. And his *Hope in Africa* (London: Herbert Jenkins, 1952): the 'hope' of the title rested, Alport argued, only with Britain's enlightened intervention in the continent. This should be contrasted to Davidson's *Report on Southern Africa* published in the same year, a passionate justification for black self-activity.

38. For most of the time Alport was in the House of Commons Haileybury ranked third (after Eton and Westminster) in its tally of MPs. This included Clement Attlee who, when Alport became an MP, invited him for a drink, as one old boy to another: Garnett, *Alport*, 98.

39. Fenner Brockway, the anti-colonial agitator, found him 'ill-tempered, snobbish, patronising and unhelpful', cited in Andrew Roth's obituary, 'Lord Alport: A Rebel Upstairs', *Guardian*, 2 Nov. 1998.

40. Quoted in Garnett, *Alport*, 117.

41. Roth, 'Lord Alport'. Alport's attachment to a politics of consensus was matched in his private life: after his wife died he embarked upon a discreet cross-party romance with Lady (Pat) Llewellyn-Davies, Labour's first female chief whip in the Lords and one-time Bevanite.

42. Alport, *Sudden Assignment*, 20.

43. Ibid. 21.

44. Ibid. 29.

45. In a television interview, on 3 Jan. 1969, Powell was asked by David Frost if he had a single regret, to which he responded that he hadn't spoken out against the formation of the Federation in 1953. He noted that he had four other rebellions on the go at the time, and that this had hampered his room for manœuvre: Enoch Powell, *Reflections of a Statesman* (London: Bellew, 1991), 230–1.

46. Alport, *Sudden Assignment*, 23.

47. Ibid. 42, 45–6.

48. Ibid. 185 and 186.

49. Robert Walsh, 'The One Nation Group: A Tory Approach to Backbench Politics and Organization, 1950–55', *Twentieth Century British History*, 11/2 (2000), and his 'The One Nation Group and One Nation Conservatism, 1950–2002', *Contemporary British History*, 17/2 (2003).

50. Alport, *Kingdoms in Partnership*; Garnett, *Alport*, 62 and 129; Alport, *Sudden Assignment*, 21, 22, 77 and 186. Garnett also notes that while awaiting the results of the 1945 election Alport tried his hand at writing a novel 'in the style of John Buchan', *Alport*, 65.

51. Garnett, *Alport*, 185.

52. This encounter he treated with a levity which never arose when black men took to the streets: Alport, *Sudden Assignment*, 157; and Garnett, *Alport*, 175–6. There were in fact two demonstrations at the high commission, one on 6 Dec. 1961 and one on the following day. When on the second of these occasions Alport refused to meet with the demonstrators, hundreds of arrests were made and fourteen Africans were wounded by police gunfire: J. R. T. Wood, *'So Far and No Further!': Rhodesia's Bid for Independence during the Retreat from Empire, 1959–1965* (Crewe: Trafford, 2005), 95. For the social and political conditions of this militancy, invisible to Alport, Teresa A. Barnes, *'We Women Worked So Hard': Gender, Urbanization, and Social Reproduction in Colonial Harare, Zimbabwe, 1930–1956* (Oxford: James Currey, 1999).

53. Cited in Garnett, *Alport*, 168.

54. Cited ibid. 175–6.

55. Alport, *Sudden Assignment*, 239.

56. Garnett, *Alport*, 65.

57. Cited ibid. 63.

58. Cited ibid. 66.

59. Cited ibid. 219 and 232. The first quote comes from his diary of 28 and 30 Apr.; the second from a speech in the House of Lords on 21 Nov.

60. For this tradition see G. R. Searle, *Country Before Party: Coalition and the Idea of 'National Government' in Britain, 1885–1987* (London: Longman, 1995).

61. The unexpected influence of an older proconsular imperialism on Tory moderates of the 1970s was not restricted to Alport. Testimony to the continuing significance of Milner can be found in Peter Walker, *The Ascent of Britain* (London: Sidgwick & Jackson, 1977).

62. *The Times*, 8 Jan. 1968.

63. Cited in Garnett, *Alport*, 245; 12 Oct. 1972.

64. Murphy, *Central Africa*, part I, 214–16.

65. Cited in Garry Allighan, *The Welensky Story* (Cape Town: Purnell, 1962), 130. Allighan never claimed his book was a 'formal biography', preferring to see it as 'the authenticated life-story of a Statesman'. It was, he says, written with 'every possible assistance' from Welensky, based on private documents which he passed to him, and 'with his knowledge'. Allighan had once been a Labour MP but in 1947 he condemned fellow MPs for accepting back-handers from the press. It turned out that as an MP he himself, an experienced journalist and former news editor of the *Daily Mirror*, had been accepting weekly payments from the *Evening Standard*, earning him the sobriquet of Glass-House Garry. He was expelled from the Commons and resigned from the Labour party. The year after *The Welensky Story* was published Allighan was appointed principal of the Premier School of Journalism in Johannesburg.

66. Sir Roy Welensky, *Welensky's 4000 Days: The Life and Death of the Federation of Rhodesia and Nyasaland* (London: Collins, 1964), 110.

67. Robert Blake, 'Foreword', to Wood, *Welensky Papers,* 22.

68. *Face to Face*, BBC television, 29 May 1960. In fact this was a reply to a question from Freeman asking whether Welensky carried a 'chip on his shoulder'. Welensky retorted: 'If your question really means: do I know the African…?'

69. Allighan, *Welensky Story*, 111 and 113. The extent of segregation in Broken Hill during Welensky's time there is described by his neighbour, Cyril Greenall: Greenall and Coe, *Kaunda's Gaoler*.

70. Allighan, *Welensky Story*, 106.

71. Or almost so: it appears that he was buried in a Reform Jewish section of an Anglican cemetery.

72. Cited ibid. 259.

73. Welensky, *4000 Days*, 38–9. For an equally emphatic rejection of democracy for Africans, Oliver Lyttleton, Viscount Chandos, *The Memoirs of Lord Chandos*

(London: Bodley Head, 1962), 388–9: Lyttleton, along with Lords Salisbury and Swinton, had been one of the architects of the Central African Federation. See J. A. Cross, *Lord Swinton* (Oxford: Clarendon Press, 1982).

74. Greenall and Coe, *Kaunda's Gaoler*, 97.

75. Colonial Office memorandum, 17 July 1951, reproduced in Murphy, *Central Africa*, part I. 166–7.

76. Welensky publicly declared himself an admirer of Smuts: *4000 Days*, 56 and 78. Blake claims that it was hearing Smuts speak, when Welensky was 14, that first awakened his interest in politics, 'Foreword', 69. It seems though that as he was growing up his family was hostile. In 1913 an elder brother was arrested during the miners' uprising on the Rand, when Smuts restored order; and in the 1922 referendum in Rhodesia—offering the choice between association with South Africa or internal self-government with crown colony status—his father voted against the former due to his conviction that Smuts was an opponent of the working class: Allighan, *Welensky Story*, 53 and 68.

77. Allighan, *Welensky Story*, 274.

78. Quoted in Keatley, *Politics of Partnership*, 491–2. Compare this to Charles Pearson's fears of 1893 that the white man was about to be 'elbowed and hustled, and perhaps even thrust aside', *National Life and Character: A Forecast* (London: Macmillan, 1893), 85.

79. Cited in Allighan, *Welensky Story*, 258–9.

80. Thus Lord Molson, a member of the Monckton inquiry, wrote in a letter to *The Times* on 14 Feb. 1961 that multi-racialism as used in the Federation 'covers the plain desire to retain the domination of the white inhabitants', an interpretation echoed by the *Sunday Telegraph* shortly after: cited in Dan Horowitz, 'The British Conservatives and the Racial Issue in the Debate on Decolonization', *Race*, 12/2 (1970), 171–2. For the vagaries of the idea of partnership, and for its competing usages, Anthony King's examination of the press is illuminating: 'The *Central African Examiner*, 1957–1965', *Zambezia*, 13/2 (1996).

81. And see Palmer, 'European Resistance to African Majority Rule'.

82. Allighan, *Welensky Story*, 224–5.

83. In Feb. 1953 Movietone, in 'Partnership in Central Africa', had Welensky enthusing direct to camera about 'inter-racial partnership'. The narrator added a touch of caution: 'The British people, who always believe in moderation, will watch with something more than interest the efforts of such men as Mr Welensky'. But as the whole narrative of the clip had turned on the benefits of 'Western civilization'—'hospitals and hygiene'—the cautious qualification was little more than gestural. The report closed with an image of Rhodes. This is included in the compilation *Visions of Change: Empire*, written by Nicholas Pronay and produced by Harold Smith, BBC1, 1983. I am most grateful to Harold Smith for giving me a copy of the video. Basil Davidson quotes a migrant from the UK who had arrived in Southern Rhodesia in the mid-1940s, who stated that Rhodesians were 'trying to steer a middle course'

between the South African Nationalists and the Labour government's colonial liberalism, *Report on Southern Africa*, 14.

84. Welensky, *4000 Days*, 326; and Allighan, *Welensky Story*, 256.

85. See e.g. the correspondence between Welensky and Menzies in the summer of 1963. Welensky suggested that conceding majority rule in central Africa would be the equivalent of giving Australia to the Aborigines, Wood, *Welensky Papers*, 1216–17.

86. Nor should we underestimate the degree to which the Federal government sought to manage the images of life in central Africa relayed back to Britain: Andrew Cohen, '"Voice and Vision"—the Federation of Rhodesia and Nyasaland's Public Relations Campaign in Britain: 1960–1963', *Historia*, 54/2 (2009); Ian Waller, 'Pressure Politics', *Encounter* (Aug. 1962); and Philip Murphy, *Party Politics and Decolonization: The Conservative Party and British Colonial Policy in Tropical Africa, 1951–1964* (Oxford: Clarendon Press, 1995), 73–85.

87. In his biography of Alport, Mark Garnett—in a rare moment when he distances himself from his subject—declares that 'He should have realised that Welensky himself had been struggling to sustain a middle position between white supremacists and those who demanded immediate majority rule', and claims that Welensky's 'popular appeal meant that no one else could have brought about true partnership within the Federation', *Alport*, 151 and 158. With whom did his 'popular appeal' lie? With Kaunda, Banda, and Nkomo who were all jailed during his term of office? With the women of the Harare township? In the 1990s Garnett was a political researcher for Edward Heath and, later, co-author with Ian Gilmour of *Whatever Happened to the Tories? The Conservative Party since 1945* (London: Fourth Estate, 1997).

88. *Daily Express*, 11 Nov. 1961; reproduced in Allighan, *Welensky Story*, 294–303.

89. Cited in Cohen, 'Voice and Vision', 121, a view corroborated by *The Economist*. Cohen explains that it was his public relations advisers who insisted that Welensky should make the speech.

90. Allighan, *Welensky Story*, 298.

91. Welensky, *4000 Days*, 319. Alport denied the vomiting but admitted to having been angry. 'I realised that quite inadvertently Sandys had given to the Rhodesian critics of British policy an apparent justification for the myth which they were so busy concocting to the effect that Britain was played out and spineless, while they were continuing to face their problems with manly determination.' *Sudden Assignment*, 168. There had been an enmity between Alport and Sandys since the One Nation days: Garnett, *Alport*, 150.

92. More than 200 mercenaries signed up in offices in Salisbury and Bulawayo: Matthew Hughes, 'Diary', *London Review of Books*, 9 Aug. 2001. Welensky's overtures to Katanga need to be seen in the wider regional geopolitics: Movement for Colonial Freedom, *The Unholy Alliance: Salazar, Verwoerd, Welensky* (London: Movement for Colonial Freedom, n.d. [1962]).

93. Colin Legum, *Congo Disaster* (Harmondsworth: Penguin, 1961), 57.

94. Simon Ball offers a worthless, cold war travesty: Lumumba 'was a prima donna, in the pay of the Russians, and often high on drugs'. *The Guardsmen*, 359.

95. Ludo De Wit, *The Assassination of Lumumba* (London:Verso, 2001), 1–3: this, originally publ. in 1999, opened to public scrutiny the participation of the Belgian authorities in Lumumba's murder. On 5 Feb. 2002 the Belgian parliament accepted the nation's moral responsibility in failing to prevent his death, while refusing to concede the presence of official intervention. In 2001 the Haitian director, Raoul Peck, made a movie based on De Wit's chronicle, *Lumumba*.

96. For the complicity of the British—Home and Macmillan—in the US plans to assassinate Lumumba: De Wit, *Assassination of Lumumba*, pp. xv–xvi.

97. 'When Patrice Lumumba was murdered on 17 January 1961, white women all over Western Europe, North America and the "settler" countries of Africa began to see him in their dreams. I have met women in London and Cape Town, Berlin and Los Angeles, who talked about this haunting. Sometimes he was a black priapic bogeyman; more often he was a dark and reproachful presence who inspired unbelievable guilt and terror. It seemed not to matter whether the dreamer was a "liberal" who by day marched in the streets to protest against his death, or a right-winger who regarded him as a Communist agitator who had got much what he deserved. Something about Lumumba penetrated the skin of rationality and released chaotic, repressed emotions about "the other". His spirit began to walk at night, climbing into the bedrooms of double-locked bungalows.' Neal Ascherson, 'The Crocodiles Gathered' *London Review of Books*, 4 Oct. 2001. Rachel Alport's nightmare, cited above, should be seen in this context: and for the significance of colonial dreams, David Macey, *Frantz Fanon: A Life* (London: Granta, 2000), 136–7.

98. A riveting account by a controversial participant, who was decisive in turning the military power of the UN against Katanga, is Conor Cruise O'Brien, *To Katanga and Back: A UN Case History* (London: Hutchinson, 1962). Alport, *Sudden Assignment*, 108, and Welensky, *4000 Days*, 221, were both convinced that O'Brien's hostility to British interests was spurred by Irish recidivism. In Sept. 1961, in the course of the UN campaign to reconcile Katanga with the remainder of the Congo, the secretary general, Dag Hammarskjöld, flew to Northern Rhodesia for a meeting with Tshombe, but his aircraft went missing and all aboard were killed. The meeting was to have been held in great secrecy. Alport was at the airfield with Tshombe awaiting Hammarskjöld's arrival. Many rumours surrounded this episode, some of which identified Welensky's responsibility for the downing of the plane. O'Brien in *To Katanga* believed it to be the work of 'fascists', with 'Algeria, Suez, Tunisia' on their minds, 286–7; while in his *Memoir: My Life and Themes* (London: Profile, 1998), he was more specific, citing OAS irregulars, 230–4. Hughes pretty much concurs, concluding that Katangan and Belgian irregulars were responsible, fearful that Tshombe was about to strike a deal with Hammarskjöld.

99. Keatley, *Politics of Partnership*, 454. Alport thought it merely 'fortuitous' that Katanga was under Belgian sovereignty, implying it should more naturally be a part of Northern Rhodesia· *Sudden Assignment*, 97.

100. In Aug. 1960 the Ugandan special branch reported that forty-two Congolese (out of 14 million) had Communist contacts, nine of whom had been to the USSR and five of whom were perceived to be hard-core: Alan James, *Britain and the Congo Crisis, 1960–63* (London: Macmillan, 1996), 61.

101. According to Philip Murphy, senior MI6 figures were sympathetic to the settlers, particularly over Katanga: 'Intelligence and Decolonization: The Life and Death of the Federal Intelligence and Security Bureau, 1954–63', *Journal of Imperial and Commonwealth History*, 29/2 (2001), 117.

102. Welensky, *4000 Days*, 45. Iain Macleod responded to this exercise in autobiography: 'Welensky's World, or the Cops and Robbers Theory of History', *Spectator*, 29 May 1964.

103. James Barber, *Rhodesia: The Road to Rebellion* (Oxford: Oxford UP and the Institute of Race Relations, 1967), 260.

104. Inscribed on a banner greeting Iain Macleod when he arrived in Salisbury in Mar. 1960, protesting against his putative sell-out of Kenya: Barber, *Rhodesia*, 25.

105. Murphy, *Party Politics and Decolonization*, 2 and 168. For the events of early 1961 I am indebted to Murphy's careful account and to Robert Shepherd, *Iain Macleod: A Biography* (London: Hutchinson, 1994).

106. And—slightly, if significantly—a different generation. This was also apparent in his relations with Welensky. During the Commonwealth Prime Ministers' Conference in May 1960, which Welensky was permitted to attend, Macleod invited him to his Chelsea home where he played him Tom Lehrer. This was hardly likely to have endeared his guest to him, especially as Welensky's own tastes were for the light classics: Shepherd, *Macleod*, 204.

107. Particularly for Julian Amery, who had inherited his father's dedication to empire: ibid. 154.

108. Murphy, *Party Politics and Decolonization*, 174. See too David Goldsworthy, *Colonial Issues in British Politics, 1945–1961: From 'Colonial Development' to 'Wind of Change'* (Oxford: Clarendon Press, 1971); and D.Horowitz, 'Attitudes of British Conservatives Towards Decolonization in Africa during the Macmillan Government, 1957–1963', unpublished D.Phil., Oxford University, 1967.

109. In a memorandum of 16 Apr. 1951: Ronald Hyman, 'The Geopolitical Origins of the Central African Federation: Britain, Rhodesia and South Africa, 1948–1953', *Historical Journal*, 30/1 (1987), 145–5.

110. Philip Murphy, ' "Government by Blackmail": The Origins of the Central African Federation Reconsidered', in Martin Lynn (ed.), *The British Empire in the 1950s: Retreat or Revival?* (Basingstoke: Macmillan, Palgrave, 2005).

111. Ibid. 66.

112. Macleod to Macmillan, 3 Dec. 1959 in Murphy, *Central Africa*, part II. 94; initially the 'hard core' numbered fifty; three weeks later they had declined to twenty, ibid. 100.

113. Frank Furedi, 'Creating a Breathing Space: The Political Management of Colonial Emergencies', *Journal of Imperial and Commonwealth History*, 21/3 (1993); and Darwin, 'Central African Emergency', 227.

114. This was exactly the course of action recommended by a number of Tory progressives: see Lord Altrincham (John Grigg), 'Tories and the Commonwealth', *Africa South*, 4/2 (1960). Altrincham was the son of the Milnerite governor of Kenya, Edward Grigg; in 1982 he left the Conservatives for the SDP.

115. Cited in Shepherd, *Macleod*, 188.

116. Cited ibid. 215. Although according to Keith Kyle he felt differently—or had to act differently—in relation to Kenyatta: 'The Politics of the Independence of Kenya', *Contemporary British History*, 11/4 (1997). In Apr. 1961 Swinton was telling Home that if Kenyatta were released there would be a Conservative rebellion, and he would be joining it, 50.

117. Wood, *Welensky Papers*, 201–2; Welensky Papers, 665/3, Welensky to Salisbury, 27 Jan. 1961.

118. Anthony Fell, a future votary of the Monday Club, had spent his early teenage years in New Zealand, where his naval officer father had emigrated, and carried into Westminster politics something of the sensibilities of colonial populism. He visited Welensky in Salisbury in 1960, courtesy of *Voice and Vision*, returning to announce that he believed him to be one of the three greatest men in the world. The others were de Gaulle and Krushchev: *Guardian*, 25 Mar. 1998.

119. Wood, *Welensky Papers*, 868.

120. Philip Murphy, *Tory Reactions to Rapid Decolonisation in East and Central Africa* (London: Institute for Commonwealth Studies, 1993), 5.

121. Quoted from his diary of 22 Feb. 1961, Horne, *Macmillan*, ii. 389.

122. This was the occasion when Macmillan arranged to have Welensky's suite in the Savoy bugged: Horne, *Macmillan*, ii. 396. In Jan. the previous year the Security Branch of the British South African Police had bugged Hastings Banda's discussions with his legal representative, Dingle Foot, the Labour MP, and the transcripts were then passed to Welensky and Whitehead. It subsequently became clear that at least one of Welensky's allies in London, Lord Lambton, had read them: Murphy, *Central Africa*, part II. 249.

123. Shepherd, *Macleod*, 228.

124. Quoted in Ball, *The Guardsmen*, 344.

125. Robert Gordon Menzies, *Speech is of Time: Selected Speeches and Writings* (London: Cassell, 1958), 71–2.

126. Cited by David Goldsworthy, 'Lord Salisbury, Third Marquess', in Colin Matthew and Brian Harrison (eds.), *Oxford Dictionary of National Biography*, x (Oxford: Oxford UP, 2004), 760.

127. Roy Jenkins, *Portraits and Miniatures* (London: Macmillan, 1993), 44.

128. Ball, *The Guardsmen*: his story includes Oliver Lyttleton and Harry Crookshank, who also shared exactly this historical formation. In the following paragraphs I draw closely on Ball.

129. Quoted in Horne, *Macmillan*, ii. 37.

130. Ball, *The Guardsmen*, 329.

131. John Barnes, 'From Eden to Macmillan, 1955–1959', in Peter Hennessy and Anthony Seldon (eds.), *Ruling Performance: British Governments from Attlee to Thatcher* (Oxford: Blackwell, 1987), 110–11; and Ball, *The Guardsmen*, 313.

132. Lord Salisbury, 'Trouble in Africa' (letter), *Spectator*, 7 Feb. 1964, a riposte to Macleod.

133. A position then passed to his son, the sixth Marquess, who was also president of the Anglo-Rhodesian Society.

134. I have pursued this argument in 'Ancestral Citizens: Reflections on British Conservatism', *New Formations*, 28 (1996); on Salisbury, Peter Marsh is particularly good: *The Discipline of Popular Government: Lord Salisbury's Domestic Statecraft, 1881–1902* (Hassocks: Harvester, 1978).

135. Welensky Papers, 665/1–5, Welensky–Salisbury correspondence, 1957–63. The Welensky–Salisbury connection was not only a matter of high politics. During the collapse of Rhodesia, soldiers smuggled out of the Rhodesian Light Infantry barracks a life-size statue of a trooper, which has now been resurrected in the grounds of Hatfield House. As a result Hatfield House has become a place of pilgrimage for Rhodesian ex-servicemen. I am most grateful to Donal Lowry for this information.

136. Welensky Papers, 665/2, Welensky to Salisbury, 18 Aug. 1960.

137. Welensky Papers, 665/5, Welensky to Salisbury, 9 May 1963.

138. Welensky Papers, 665/5, Salisbury to Welensky, 16 May 1963.

139. Welensky Papers, 665/5, Welensky to Salisbury, 28 May 1963.

140. Welensky Papers, 665/2, Welensky to Salisbury, 4 Oct. 1960.

141. Welensky Papers, 665/2, Welensky to Salisbury, 21 Oct. 1960.

142. Welensky Papers, 665/4, Welensky to Salisbury, 1 Aug. 1962.

143. Welensky Papers, 665/5, Welensky to Salisbury, 23 Dec. 1963.

144. Welensky Papers, 665/4, Salisbury to Welensky, 3 Feb. 1962.

145. Welensky Papers, 665/4, Salisbury to Welensky, n.d. (Aug. 1962); 24 Oct. 1962.

146. Welensky Papers, 665/5, Salisbury to Welensky, 21 July 1963, and Welensky to Salisbury, 27 July 1963.

147. Ball, *The Guardsmen*, 344.

148. Cited ibid. 350.

149. Cited ibid. 351.

150. Hinchingbrooke was an old Suez militant, and Lambton (along with Enoch Powell) had been antagonists of Macmillan since Hola: Murphy, *Lennox-Boyd*, 216; Macmillan, cited in Ball, *The Guardsmen*, 357.

151. House of Lords Debates, 7 Mar. 1961, cols. 307–12. He described Rhodesia as 'the most British, in the fullest sense of that word, of any of the realms and territories of the British Crown', charging the British government with showing it only 'suspicion', 'contempt', and 'almost...hatred', col. 306. He was backed by Swinton and attacked from his own side by Molson, Lucan, and Kilmuir, who declared it the 'bitterest' invective he had ever heard in parliament, col. 349.

152. *The Times*, 11, 14, and 20 Mar. 1961.

153. Ball, *The Guardsmen*, 362.

154. Macmillan's diary, 18 Dec. 1961, quoted in Ball, *The Guardsmen*, 364.

155. Through the 1960s Sandys became an anti-immigration, pro-Rhodesia tyro, his sympathies close to the Monday Club: shortly after he left the Commonwealth Office in 1962 he was linked to a sex scandal involving the Duchess of Argyle and Douglas Fairbanks Jnr, recorded on what was reputed to have been the only Polaroid camera in the UK, the property of the Ministry of Defence.

156. Cited in Murphy, *Party Politics and Decolonization*, 194; and for Wall's future investments in the region, John Major, 'Patrick Wall and South Africa', *South African Historical Journal,* 52/1 (2005).

157. Macmillan's diary, 10 Jan. 1962, quoted in Horne, *Macmillan,* ii. 408.

158. Butler's habit, when confronted by awkward questions about his political integrity, of remaining silent and shrugging his shoulders may offer a clue: see n. 14.

159. Shepherd, *Macleod*, 245.

160. It now functions as the government wine cellar.

161. Murphy, *Party Politics and Decolonization*, 23.

162. Ibid. 141.

163. It is commonly claimed that the Club was named after the day when Macmillan delivered his 'Wind of change' speech. In fact it was so called because the Club met on Mondays. Macmillan made his speech on a Wednesday.

164. Ball, *The Guardsmen*, 353. Cedric Gunnery, interview with the author, 28 Oct. 1986. Gunnery, a graduate of Oxford University, was one of the founders of the Monday Club.

165. Murphy, *Party Politics and Decolonization*, 205.

166. Ball, *The Guardsmen*, 354.

167. See Paul Gilroy, *'There Ain't No Black in the Union Jack': The Cultural Politics of Race and Nation* (London: Hutchinson, 1987); and Centre for Contemporary Cultural Studies, *The Empire Strikes Back: Race and Racism in 70s Britain* (London: Hutchinson, 1982). For the argument, which has influenced me greatly, that race functioned as the means for articulating the perceptions of the many disorders which stalked the metropole, see Stuart Hall, Chas Critcher, Tony Jefferson, John Clarke, and Brian Roberts, *Policing the Crisis: Mugging, the State and Law and Order* (London: Macmillan, 1978).

168. Andrew Gamble, *The Conservative Nation* (London: Routledge & Kegan Paul, 1974), 81–6; and John Ramsden, *The Winds of Change: Macmillan to Heath, 1957–1975. A History of the Conservative Party,* vi (Harlow: Longman, 1996), 129. I am conscious that more should be said about the role of the popular press as an impetus for these developments. In Jan. 1961 e.g. the *Daily Express* was condemning Macleod as 'the most calamitous Colonial Secretary in history', cited in Shepherd, *Macleod*, 218—a view echoed by the press in the Federation: Palmer, 'European Resistance to African Majority Rule', 265.

169. Murphy, *Central Africa*, Part II, 367.

170. Here I depart from Murphy, who contends that Welensky's allies in Britain did not 'adopt an explicit defence of "white" interests', but that had they done so they 'might have generated greater support from "grass-roots" Conservatives', *Party Politics and Decolonization*, 237–8. Perhaps too much is made to rest on 'explicit'. As I have argued throughout, whatever the rhetorics of partnership and multiracialism, both friends and foes would have had no difficulty in discerning the commitment of Welensky's supporters, and of Welensky himself, to the essentials of white civilization. Murphy goes on to say that after the collapse of the Federation, the Monday Club and its sympathizers could more wholeheartedly pursue a populist racial politics, 238.

171. Ramsden, *The Winds of Change*, 6.

172. The committee was composed of Lord Kilmuir, Rab Butler, Iain Macleod, Duncan Sandys, John Hare, Enoch Powell, and Henry Brooke. Butler, the home secretary, admitted that it was not possible to legislate 'openly on grounds of colour' though later noted that the 'great merit' of the 1962 Act was that 'its restrictive effect is intended to, and would in fact, operate on coloured people almost exclusively', cited in Kathleen Paul, *Whitewashing Britain: Race and Citizenship in the Postwar Era* (Ithaca, NY: Cornell UP, 1997), 164 and 166. This was the Rab Butler who could later claim that multiracialism was representative of 'British tradition', *The Art of the Possible: The Memoirs of Lord Butler* (London: Hamish Hamilton, 1971), 226.

173. See e.g. Stanley Cohen, *Folk Devils and Moral Panics: The Creation of the Mods and Rockers* (St Albans: Paladin, 1972); and Michael Tracey and David Morrison, *Whitehouse* (London: Macmillan, 1979). I have made an initial exploration of these developments in 'Disorderly Politics', in Brian Meeks (ed.), *Stuart Hall: Culture, Politics, Race and Diaspora* (Kingston, Jamaica and London: Ian Randle and Lawrence & Wishart, 2007).

174. 8 Feb. 1960, cited in Shepherd, *Macleod*, 179.

CHAPTER 7

1. Agatha Christie, *The Man in the Brown Suit* (London: Granada, 1981; 1924), 11. The action takes place against the backdrop of the 1922 uprising on the Rand, and includes the figure of Smuts.

2. Quoted in Alice Ritscherle, 'Opting Out of Utopia: Race and Working-Class Political Culture in Britain during the Age of Decolonization, 1948–1968', unpublished Ph.D., University of Michigan, 2005, 262.

3. This was added to her reply to Churchill's letter of resignation, in which she effusively thanked him for his services, Margaret Thatcher Foundation, www.margaretthatcher.org/document/103498, accessed 26 Sept. 2010.

4. Tsitsi Dangarembga, *Nervous Conditions* (London: Women's Press, 2001; 1988), 18.

5. Ian Smith, *The Great Betrayal: The Memoirs of Ian Douglas Smith* (London: Blake, 1997), 198; the same volume also appears under the title *Bitter Harvest: The Great Betrayal*.

6. Strictly, although founded in 1890, the territory which became Southern Rhodesia (British South Africa Company) wasn't officially named as such until 1898. From 1923–53 it became the Colony of Southern Rhodesia. During the years of the Federation, from 1953 to 1963, it was a component part of the new polity. In 1964 it took the name Rhodesia, altered again in 1970–9 to the Republic of Rhodesia. In the moment of transition to majority rule it was renamed, in 1979, the Republic of Zimbabwe-Rhodesia, before its brief and only period of direct rule from London as, again, the Colony of Southern Rhodesia (1979–80). Since 1980 the territory has been the Republic of Zimbabwe.

7. This was known as the Nyadzonya Raid, conducted by the Selous Scouts and led by Major Ron Reid-Daly. The Selous Scouts were named after Frederick Courteney Selous, who served as guide to the Pioneer Column in 1890, and Reid-Daly had learnt his skills as a member of the SAS in the Malaya emergency. Film of the carnage is available on the web, carrying the warning that it contains 'adult themes'. Four days before the ceremony in Cecil Square, Smith had moved the putative instigator of the raid, P. K. van der Byl, the menacing svengali of the UDI regime, from his post as defence minister—notwithstanding the fact that Smith himself had given his approval for the expedition: Peter Godwin and Ian Hancock, *'Rhodesians Never Die': The Impact of War and Political Change in White Rhodesia, c1970–1980* (Oxford: Oxford UP, 1993), 157. In Smith's final days as prime minister he recounted how he 'went out to pay my respects to the Selous Scouts and reassure them over the future of our country . . . At the conclusion they sang their tremendous song—nothing could be more stirring.' *Great Betrayal*, 298.

8. *Rebellion*, BBC2, 14 Mar. 1998. At the same time he also announced that he would consider co-opting individual blacks into the government, a 'major concession' for his Rhodesian Front party; Godwin and Hancock, *'Rhodesians Never Die'*, 153.

9. When Smith unilaterally declared Rhodesia independent from Britain in 1965 South Africa's prime minister, Hendrik Verwoerd, did not welcome the move, nor did he want the Union drawn into the imbroglio: Alexander Hepple, *Verwoerd* (Harmondsworth: Penguin, 1969), 196–7. Smith had met with Henry Kissinger in Pretoria on 18 Sept.—another decisive encounter.

10. From the middle years of the 1950s, when a simple racial supremacism became awkward to assert publicly, the idea of the differing 'standards' of European and African became a favoured means for those who advocated the continuation of white rule. See Colin Leys, *European Politics in Southern Rhodesia* (Oxford: Clarendon Press, 1959), 249, 274–7, and 284–5; Richard West, *The White Tribes of Africa* (London: Jonathan Cape, 1965), 76: 'Standards means white supremacy'.

11. Martin Rubin, *Sarah Gertrude Millin: A South African Life* (Johannesburg: A. D. Donker, 1977); by 1964 Millin was claiming a direct lineage from Rhodes, through Smuts, to the Nationalists in South Africa (ibid. 265–6). She had earlier written an enthusiastic account of Rhodes: Sarah Gertrude Millin, *Rhodes* (London: Chatto & Windus, 1937; 1933).

12. In June 1961 she stated in the *Natal Mercury* that 'The greatest man in Africa today is Sir Roy Welensky and his fight to hold the Federation together is the key to Africa's future', quoted in Garry Allighan, *The Welensky Story* (Cape Town: Purnell, 1962), 263. Millin shared with Welensky her Jewish background, and her consequent experience of feeling herself an outsider.

13. In the novel the young white protagonist, John, comments: 'If we had Churchill now, he wouldn't be pouring England through his fingers', to which his sister, Allison, replies: 'Pouring is the word. Everything is running in Africa now. People. Blood.' Sarah Gertrude Millin, *The Wizard Bird* (London: Heinemann, 1962), 168.

14. Sarah Gertrude Millin (ed.), *White Africans are Also People* (Cape Town: Howard Timmins, 1966). I am grateful to John Noyes for acquiring a copy of this for me.

15. Quoted in Rubin, *Millin*, 271. She went on to say: 'If you do not want Arab majority rule in Palestine, you should not require white men to endure black savage rule in Rhodesia.'

16. Quoted in Donal Lowry, '"White Women's Country": Ethel Tawse Jollie and the Making of White Rhodesia', *Journal of Southern African Studies*, 23/2 (1997), 260. Kipling spent a lifetime turning empire-builders into heroes; and of the many whom he heroized it was Cecil Rhodes he most admired. Kipling was with Rhodes in Cape Town during his final days in Mar. 1902. He marched through the city with the coffin, and was moved by the extent of the public manifestations of grief. He wrote a poem in memory of his lost friend ('The Burial') which was read at the internment in the Matopo Hills in Rhodesia. For Kipling, Rhodes personified more than any the majesty of empire: he operated not as a statesman but as a buccaneer, free from the common obligations to government and public opinion. He was, in this vision, uncompromising, driven only by his desire to extend to new lands the sovereignty of the mother country; and indeed two new colonies took his name. There was much that was legendary about Rhodes, though Kipling's role in orchestrating the legend, and making it live after Rhodes had died, was decisive. The parallels between the loyalist rebellions of Ulster and Southern Rhodesia have been made both by the historical actors involved in the various events and by historians: Donal Lowry, 'Ulster Resistance and Loyalist Rebellion in the Empire', in Keith Jeffery (ed.), *An Irish Empire? Aspects of Ireland the British Empire* (Manchester: Manchester UP, 1996).

17. Ernest Renan, 'What is a Nation?', reproduced in Homi Bhabha (ed.), *Nation and Narration* (London: Routledge, 1990), 11.

18. In Mar. 1889, on a visit to London to meet Queen Victoria, Lobengula's *indunas*, Mshete and Babayane, were shown the effectiveness of the maxim gun without, it seems, apprehending the fact that the guns would soon be turned on them: John Flint, *Ceil Rhodes* (London: Hutchinson, 1976), 100. Reporting back to Lobengula they were reticent in revealing all they saw. They did inform him, however, that 'The hands of the Europeans never tire of making things. It is for this reason that white men's faces are often so fatigued and sad. They wage war with one another not for virile glory or to test their strength, but for things.' Cited in Neil Parsons, 'British Press and Public Responses to the Visits of Southern African Royalty and Envoys to London, 1882–1894', British World Conference, Cape Town, 2001.

19. T. O. Ranger, *Revolt in Southern Rhodesia, 1896–7: A Study in African Resistance* (London: Heinemann, 1967), 46 and 89.

20. Patrick Keatley, *The Politics of Partnership* (Harmondsworth: Penguin, 1963), 284.

21. Frederick Courteney Selous, *Sunshine and Storm in Rhodesia* (London: Rowland Ward, 1896), 86–7. Ranger, *Revolt in Southern Rhodesia*, 129–31 and 393.

22. See Jock McCulloch, *Black Peril, White Virtue: Sexual Crime in Southern Rhodesia, 1902–1935* (Bloomington, Ind.: Indiana UP, 2000); and John Pape, 'Black and White: The "Perils of Sex" in Colonial Zimbabwe', *Journal of Southern African Studies*, 16/4 (1990).

23. Robert Baden-Powell, *The Matabele Campaign, 1896: Being a Narrative of the Native Rising in Matabeleland and Mashonaland* (London: Methuen, 1897); Dane Kennedy, *Islands of White: Settler Society and Culture in Kenya and Southern Rhodesia, 1890–1939* (Durham, NC: Duke UP, 1987), 130–1.

24. Selous, *Sunshine and Storm* 31; Kennedy, *Islands of White*, 131; and Robert Blake, *A History of Rhodesia* (London: Eyre Methuen, 1977), 125.

25. Kennedy, *Islands of White*, 137.

26. Ranger, *Revolt in Southern Rhodesia*, 131–2; Kennedy, *Islands of White*, 130; Blake, *Rhodesia*, 125. Such ideas are coolly discussed by Selous in *Sunshine and Storm*, which recounts 'all the horrors of a native rebellion' (p. xix), and in doing so produces a narrative which in structure is close to John Buchan's *Prester John*.

27. Cited in Cyril Dunn, *Central African Witness* (London: Victor Gollancz, 1959), 176. On two occasions before the First World War Charles Coghlan, who in 1923 was to become Rhodesia's first premier, argued that if the British South Africa Company failed to protect white women from the depredations of black men, then vigilante action would have to come into force. He was practising law at the time. J. P. R. Wallis, *One Man's Hand: The Story of Sir Charles Coghlan and the Liberation of Southern Rhodesia* (London: Longmans, Green, 1950), 67–8 and 112–13.

28. Robert H. MacDonald, *The Language of Empire: Myths and Metaphors of Popular Imperialism, 1880–1918* (Manchester: Manchester UP, 1994), 134 and 131–5.

29. See Donal Lowry, '"The Granite of the Ancient North": Race, Empire and Nation at Cecil Rhodes's Mountain Mausoleum', in Matthew Craske and

RichardWrigley (eds.), *Pantheons:Transformations of a Monumental Idea* (Aldershot: Ashgate, 2004).

30. But other forms of remembering occurred. When the Central African Federation was dissolved Joshua Nkomo, the leader of ZAPU (the Zimbabwe African People's Union), was handed an assegai by an old man who had fought for Lobengula, and urged to continue the struggle: Keatley, *Politics of Partnership*, 480; and see the photo in Joshua Nkomo, *Nkomo:The Story of my Life* (London: Methuen, 1984), opposite 51.This longer story is reconstructed in Joceyln Alexander, JoAnn McGregor, and Terence Ranger, *Violence and Memory: One Hundred Years in the 'Dark Forests' of Matabeleland* (Oxford: James Currey, 2000).

31. Ranger, *Revolt in Southern Rhodesia*, 323.

32. Ibid. 336.

33. A leading ideologue of the Responsible Government Association was Ethel Tawse Jollie, who had been a prominent figure in the National Efficiency, anti-women's suffrage milieu of prewar England, presenting her views, under her first married name, in Mrs Archibald Colquhoun, *The Vocation of Woman* (London: Macmillan, 1913). But she was a tireless advocate for women's emigration, and on conservative, pro-empire grounds she supported women's vote in the colonies: Lowry, 'White Woman's Country'.

34. Through the 1920s Leo Amery was an important figure in London promoting settler power in the region. After journeying to southern Africa in 1927 he thought that Rhodesia would only ever enter the Union on its own terms, safeguarding its 'British character'. Failing that, he imagined Rhodesians wanting to build 'an independent Central South African Dominion to check and counterbalance the parochial South African Union', cited in Martin Channock, *Unconsummated Union: Britain, Rhodesia and South Africa, 1900–45* (Manchester: Manchester UP, 1977), 194.

35. See Donal Lowry, '"Shame upon 'Little England' While Greater England Stands!" Southern Rhodesia and the Imperial Idea', in Andrea Bosco and Alex May (eds.), *The Round Table:The Empire/Commonwealth and British Foreign Policy* (London: Lothian Foundation Press, 1997).

36. Sir Ian Hamilton, inspector-general of overseas forces, argued in a 1911 report that 'for years to come it is by the sword and the rifle alone that the white man must retain his hold on the country', quoted in Channock, *Unconsummated Union*, 21.

37. See Kenneth Good, 'Settler Colonialism in Rhodesia', *African Affairs*, 73/1 (1974).

38. Lowry, 'Shame upon "Little England"', 321.

39. Peter Joyce, *Anatomy of a Rebel: Smith of Rhodesia. A Biography* (Salisbury: Graham Publishing, 1974), 44. During the 1937 coronation, three of the Shangani survivors, eleven Pioneer Column veterans, and assorted girl guides composed the major part of the Southern Rhodesia contingent in the London celebrations: Humphrey Jennings *et al., May the Twelfth: Mass-Observation Day-Surveys 1937* (London: Faber & Faber, 1937), 23–4.

40. Charles van Onselen, *Chibaro: African Mine Labour in Southern Rhodesia, 1900–1933* (London: Pluto Press, 1980), 142–53.

41. Alan Megahey, *Humphrey Gibbs: Beleaguered Governor. Southern Rhodesia, 1929–69* (Houndmills: Macmillan, 1998), 73. The volume carries an introduction by Mugabe and a foreword by Blake.

42. See Ian Henderson, 'White Populism in Southern Rhodesia', *Comparative Studies in Society and History*, 14 (1972).

43. Blake, *Rhodesia*, 111.

44. *Rebellion.*

45. Blake, *Rhodesia*, 155.

46. J. R. T. Wood, *'So Far and No Further!': Rhodesia's Bid for Independence during the Retreat from Empire, 1959–1965* (Crewe: Trafford, 2005), 211.

47. Martin Meredith, *The Past is Another Country: Rhodesia, 1890–1979* (London: André Deutsch, 1979), 23; Leys, *European Politics in Rhodesia*, 73.

48. Good, 'Settler Colonialism in Rhodesia', 13. And see Donal Lowry, 'Rhodesia 1890–1980: "The Lost Dominion"', in Robert Bickers (ed.), *Settlers and Expatriates: Britain over the Seas: Oxford History of the British Empire, Companion Volume* (Oxford: Oxford UP, 2010).

49. West, *White Tribes of Africa*, 71.

50. Martin Loney, *Rhodesia: White Racism and Imperial Response* (Harmondsworth: Penguin, 1975), 114; and Leys, *European Politics in Rhodesia*, ch. 1.

51. Cited in West, *White Tribes*, 70. The Surbiton tag was an old one: see Ethel Tawse Jollie, *The Real Rhodesia* (London: Hutchinson, 1924), 3.

52. Cited in West, *White Tribes*, 65–6; and David Caute, *Under the Skin: The Death of White Rhodesia* (London: Allen Lane, 1983), 115. The Whitehead government caused a scandal by upholding the judicial decision to integrate public swimming pools. Maybe the increase in private pools made this less of an issue than it had been once; or perhaps their popularity was a consequence of the legal ruling? Welensky's Salisbury home had a decent-sized pool, and he was happy to have visiting journalists film him fooling around in it with his grandchildren: Pathé News, 25 Nov. 1965.

53. Soon after UDI Smith laid the foundation stone for Rhodesia's first casino, located by Victoria Falls: Pathé News, 25 Nov. 1965; for Disneyland: *Great Betrayal*, 276.

54. Leys, *European Politics in Rhodesia*, 88.

55. Ibid. 90.

56. The co-author of 'Rhodesians Never Die', Clem Tholet, was Smith's son-in-law, who first launched the song to accompany UDI, though it only took off later during the war years. Identification with white Rhodesia could take heterodox forms and be at odds with the protocols of official society: e.g. Alexandra Fuller, *Don' Let's Go to the Dogs Tonight: An African Childhood* (London: Picador, 2003).

57. Leys, *European Politics in Rhodesia*, 242–3.

58. Ibid. 36.

59. Ibid. 174. For a critique of this viewpoint, from a position sympathetic to the settlers, which argues that this system was the only way that parliamentary government could be preserved, see L. H. Gann and P. Duigan, *White Settlers in Tropical Africa* (Harmondsworth: Penguin, 1962), 127.

60. Leys, *European Politics in Rhodesia*, 293.

61. Cited in L. H. Gann and Michael Gelfand, *Huggins of Rhodesia: The Man and his Country* (London: Allen & Unwin, 1964), 70. In Jan. 1953 Movietone produced a newsreel, 'The heritage of Cecil Rhodes', which had Huggins placed in front of a portrait of Rhodes declaring that he was looking forward to the opportunity to build 'a strong, virile, progressive British state' in central Africa, which would prove 'a great and stimulating adventure'. This is included in *Visions of Change: Empire*, written by Nicholas Pronay and produced by Harold Smith, BBC1, 1983.

62. Gann and Gelfand, *Huggins*, 208. Though in 1953 and again in 1956 Huggins did threaten a repetition of the Boston Tea Party were the Federation not offered independence.

63. Colin Legum, 'Commentary', in Michael D. Kandiah (ed.), *Rhodesian UDI* (London: Institute for Contemporary British History, 2001), 57. I am grateful to Michael Kandiah for passing this to me.

64. Terence Ranger, *Crisis in Southern Rhodesia* (London: Fabian Commonwealth Bureau, 1960), comes directly out of these events, dated 25 July 1960. Ranger himself was amongst the 430 people arrested on 25 Feb.

65. In the early 1940s Huggins began to have doubts about the efficacy of the Act, just at the time when Smuts, in South Africa, was drawing parallel conclusions: Gann and Gelfand, *Huggins*, 172–3; and James Barber, *Rhodesia: The Road to Rebellion* (Oxford: Oxford UP and the Institute for Race Relations, 1967), 11.

66. Reproduced in Barber, *Rhodesia*, 160–1.

67. Ibid. 168.

68. During the final collapse of the Federation the Conservative government in London, in opposition to the UN, ensured that the bulk of the Federation's military equipment, its aircraft in particular, passed to Rhodesia: Elaine Windrich, *Britain and the Politics of Rhodesian Independence* (London: Croom Helm, 1978), 16. According to Philip Murphy, in Sept. 1963 'at a point when the threat of a unilateral declaration of independence by Southern Rhodesia was becoming ever more real, Britain appears to have handed the RRAF [Royal Rhodesian Air Force] to the Southern Rhodesians almost in its entirety': '"An Intricate and Distasteful Subject": British Planning for the Use of Force Against the European Settlers of Central Africa, 1952–65', *English Historical Review*, 121/492 (2006), 764. At the time of UDI the Rhodesian land forces comprised 3,400 on active duty with a further 8,400 white reservists. There were 1,000 airmen. In addition the state could call on 6,000 police (of whom 2,000 were white) and 28,000 volunteers (of whom 21,000 were white): *Daily Telegraph*, 13 Nov. 1965. Murphy seeks to explain why Harold Wilson, on 30

Oct. 1965, publicly declared that he would not resort to military intervention, a statement which even those close to him, including his defence secretary, Denis Healey, believed ill-judged. He suggests that, since the mobilization of Feb. 1961, the British military were convinced that any intervention in the region would result in a full-scale war and that the commanders had no faith in the government's political will for such a venture.

69. Megahey, *Humphrey Gibbs*, 106. This gives a good account of Gibbs's family background in the City and Conservatism, and is informative too on his long friendship (from prep school) with Lord Home. According to Patrick Keatley on the morning of UDI four senior soldiers informed Gibbs that they were prepared to arrest Smith: there followed 'the fatal moment of hesitation', cited in Carl Watts, 'Killing Kith and Kin: The Viability of British Military Intervention in Rhodesia, 1964–5', *Twentieth Century British History*, 16/4 (2005), 394.

70. The document is reproduced in Joyce, *Anatomy of a Rebel*, 231–3.

71. For one 'unofficial' childhood memory: 'All we saw was some boring adult [Ian Smith] speaking in words of far too many syllables for us to understand. After his speech, a teacher asked us who he was and what he said. A lot of us didn't know, and were caned for our ignorance!' This comes from 'Neil, Ireland' on a BBC webpage, accessed 20 June 2008: http://news.bbc.co.uk/onthisday/hi/witness/march/2/newsid_3497000/3497239.stm.

72. *Rebellion.*

73. *Daily Mirror*, 12 Nov. 1965. In the words of Howard Johnson, the *Mirror*'s journalist, this was a 'typical reaction'.

74. Cited in Barber, *Rhodesia*, 290.

75. Smith worked on these memoirs with the historian J. R. T. Wood, who had compiled the Welensky papers and who, from his base in Durban, publishes vast works on the history of Rhodesia. During the crisis in Nyasaland in Mar. 1959, when fifty-one Africans were killed by the security forces, Wood was serving as a young rifleman at Nkata Bay, where the greatest outrage occurred: J. R. T. Wood, *The Welensky Papers: A History of the Federation of Rhodesia and Nyasaland* (Durban: Graham Publishing, 1983), ch. 22. At the end of the guerrilla war in Rhodesia he served in military intelligence. His webpages indicate that he is a member of the Cleveland Pistol Club, Macintosh Users Durban, the Special Air Services Regimental Association of Southern Africa, and the Colonials' Café (Superbru 2004 Champion).

76. Peter Godwin, *Mukiwa: A White Boy in Africa* (London: Picador, 1996), 326.

77. See Tony King, 'Rhodesians in Hyperspace', in Karim H. Karim (ed.), *The Media of Diaspora* (London: Routledge, 2003). Godwin and Hancock suggest that through the 1970s three-quarters of the electorate supported Smith and a majority of the white population 'revered' him. For the same period they follow what appears to be the conventional calculation that some third of Rhodesian whites were diehard supremacists, noting too that 'a sizeable section of his [Smith's] own party regarded him as a dangerous liberal', '*Rhodesians*

Never Die', 46 and 8. Their analysis emphasizes the degree to which Rhodesian identity was improvised after UDI, although insisting that a common racial identity produced no uniformity in political behaviour.

78. Stephen Glover, 'Badly Flawed, Yes, But Ian Smith's Sins Pale Beside Mugabe's'; and Richard Pendlebury, 'Ian Smith, the Defiant Leader of Rhodesia for 15 Years, Dies Aged 88', *Daily Mail*, 21 Nov. 2007. The same day as the obituaries were published reports appeared announcing that the BBC was planning a 'white season' of television programmes.

79. Smith, *Great Betrayal*, 3; and for the Thatcher version: *What's Wrong with Politics?* (London: Conservative Political Centre, 1968), and her *The Path to Power* (London: HarperCollins, 1995).

80. Joyce, *Anatomy of a Rebel*, 44. This volume contains much direct interview material with Ian Smith.

81. A fine sense of this world is conveyed in Diana Jeater, 'No Place for a Woman: Gwelo, 1894–1920', *Journal of Southern African Studies*, 26/1 (2000).

82. Smith, *Great Betrayal*, 200.

83. Ibid. 314.

84. Ibid. 31.

85. Ibid. 200 and 45.

86. Ibid. 269.

87. Ibid. 272, 63, and 86.

88. The words are Doris Lessing's, recalling in the postwar moment the mythic quality which accrued to the young Rhodesian flyers: *A Proper Marriage* (London: Flamingo, 1993; 1954), 216 and 215. Daphne Anderson notes that when RAF personnel arrived from Britain the Rhodesians could barely understand their accents: *The Toe-Rags* (London: Cardinal, 1990), 340. More generally on the emotional politics of wartime airmen, Martin Francis, *The Flyer: British Culture and the Royal Air Force, 1939–1945* (Oxford: Oxford UP, 2008); and the unpublished paper by Bill Nasson, 'A Flying Springbok of Wartime British Skies: A. G. "Sailor" Malan': I'm grateful to Bill Nasson for passing this to me.

89. Quoted in Caute, *Under the Skin*, 90. Nor was Smith alone in drawing from his wartime memories: at the time of UDI twelve out of the thirteen Rhodesian cabinet ministers had served in the war. 15,000 Southern Rhodesian blacks had also served, though for the Rhodesian Front this was never the issue.

90. Smith, *Great Betrayal*, 185. As this was articulated by an Australian contemporary in the RAF, in a celebrated account, the stress fell on the transcendental manliness of the pilot: 'only in the air' does he know 'suddenly he is a man in a world of men'. Richard Hillary, *The Last Enemy* (London: Pimlico, 1997; 1942), 43.

91. To which even his innermost emotions conformed. He confessed to experiencing what he called 'the "welling up" sensation' on hearing the regimental song of the Rhodesian Light Infantry: Smith, *Great Betrayal*, 362.

92. Ibid. 191.

93. Ibid. 23–4 and 187.

94. ibid. 25 and 24.
95. The Smiths had one further child of their own, Alec. None of the children receives more than cursory recognition in their father's memoirs. Until his early twenties Alec led a life of anarchic hedonism which only came to an end in 1972 when driving through Salisbury—maybe as the result of too many hallucinogens—he heard a voice instructing him to go home and read the Bible. His conversion allowed him to give up drugs and liquor, and persuaded him of the justice of black majority rule which, it seems, had not concerned him for the years he had been stoned. Becoming a friend of black leaders he was later to serve as a channel of communication between Ian Smith and the nationalists. In the final years, in a nice denouement, father and son became very close. Obituaries of Alec Smith appeared in the *Independent*, 2 Feb. 2006, and in *The Times*, 12 Apr. 2006.
96. Smith, *Great Betrayal*, 28–9.
97. Ibid. 4–6.
98. He came to believe that the 1922 referendum decision that Rhodesia should not join the Union had been an error.
99. Cited in Joyce, *Anatomy of a Rebel*, 78–9.
100. Smith, *Great Betrayal*, 31.
101. Ibid. 272 and 166.
102. Ibid. 309. That the issue of black emancipation was posed in terms of timing was all-important for it provided a significant point of convergence between the Rhodesian Front and the Labour government in Britain. In 1964–70, while Wilson himself may well have experienced a genuine revulsion towards Smith's racism, he did not accept the desirability of an immediate transfer to black nationalist rule. At the very moment when Smith as prime minister first began to negotiate with the British government, using the need to move slowly as his political alibi, Martin Luther King, in jail in Birmingham, Alabama, drafted his devastating critique of such racial thinking: 'Letter from Birmingham Jail' (1963) in *Why We Can't Wait* (New York: Signet, 2000).
103. Smith, *Great Betrayal*, 25 and 409.
104. Ibid. 2–3.
105. In 1907 Lord Cromer, shortly after his return to Britain from Egypt, addressed the boys of the Leys school. 'Love your country', he instructed them. 'Tell the truth, and don't dawdle': quoted in Brian Harrison, *Separate Spheres: The Opposition to Women's Suffrage in Britain* (London: Croom Helm, 1978), 143.
106. Smith makes much of his regard for Josiah Tongogara, who had been commander of ZANLA (the Zimbabwe African National Liberation Army) and who was an important presence at the final Lancaster House negotiations. He died in suspicious circumstances a few days after the conference ended in Dec. 1979. His parents had worked on Smith's farm. Smith's own insistence on Tongogara's character is an unlikely reconstruction but not impossible, though easier to maintain after he had died.

107. Diana Jeater notes this paradox: 'The authors of the official ideology of the British Empire were never particularly concerned with the ordinary lives of women, yet colonial agents—colonial administrators as well as British missionaries—spent a great deal of time and effort attempting to regulate and control their lives.' 'The British Empire and African Women in the Twentieth Century', in Philip D. Morgan and Sean Hawkins (eds.), *Black Experience and the Empire: Oxford History of the British Empire, Companion Volume* (Oxford: Oxford UP, 2004), 228.

108. Smith, *Great Betrayal*, 210.

109. Ibid. 353, 411, and 329.

110. Ibid. 224. At Churchill's funeral Smith notes that he received a nod from General de Gaulle. But I don't think this counts.

111. Ibid. 72–3.

112. Ibid. 224.

113. Ibid. 251.

114. Ibid. 207.

115. Ibid.186.

116. Ibid. 319–20.

117. Ibid. 125.

118. In 1979 Smith was granted immunity from arrest and thus able to set foot in Britain for the first time since UDI, and he was invited by Douglas Bader to be his personal guest at the Battle of Britain Association Annual Dinner. He also attended a rugby match at Twickenham, appearing that evening on ITV's *The Big Match*: Caute, *Under the Skin*, 378. In 1976 the British comedian, Jimmy Edwards, another RAF veteran of decidedly right-wing disposition, defied the metropolitan government and, with Eric Sykes, embarked upon a tour of Rhodesia.

119. See esp. Stuart Hall, *A Hard Road to Renewal: Thatcherism and the Crisis of the Left* (London: Verso, 1988); Stuart Hall and Martin Jacques (eds.), *The Politics of Thatcherism* (London: Lawrence & Wishart, 1983); Beatrix Campbell, *The Iron Ladies: Why do Women Vote Tory?* (London: Virago, 1987); and Andrew Gamble, *The Free Economy and the Strong State. The Politics of Thatcherism* (Houndmills: Macmillan, 1994), esp. 'Enemies within', 65–8.

120. Donal Lowry argues that Ethel Tawse Jollie was 'steeped in the philosophy of the Edwardian "Radical Right"', "White Woman's Country"', 259. Although she died in 1950 her writings, according to Lowry, 'came to be appropriated by advocates of UDI to justify their actions' (279)—particularly her, *The Real Rhodesia*. This indicates the existence of one direct link between older radical right traditions, in the metropole, and the philosophies of Rhodesian Front sympathizers in the 1960s. If, as I suggest here, these ideas from Rhodesia influenced a 'new' right in Britain in the 1960s, then they can be understood, in one sense, as having come home.

121. Evelyn Waugh to Graham Greene, in a letter in the 1960s, contrasting *Brideshead Revisited* to *A Burnt-Out Case*, quoted in Martin Green, *Dreams of Adventure,*

Deeds of Empire (London: Routledge & Kegan Paul, 1980), 109; and Bill Schwarz, 'The Tide of History: The Reconstruction of Conservatism, 1945–51', in Nick Tiratsoo (ed.), *The Attlee Years* (London: Pinter, 1991), 147.

122. Dunn, *Central African Witness*, 206. See too Keatley's reconstruction of the fictional Smiths' migration from Birmingham, *Politics of Partnership*, 238–43. Dunn, the *Observer* correspondent in central Africa, 1954–8, was an astute witness to the drama of the time. Under the editorship of David Astor the *Observer* in these years was an influential anti-colonial voice, particularly in relation to Africa. Keatley, a Canadian, was the *Manchester Guardian's* correspondent in central Africa.

123. Basil Davidson, *Report on Southern Africa* (London: Jonathan Cape, 1952), 224. One of these postwar migrants was Tiny Rowland who, as the tycoon who created the Lonrho mining conglomerate, certainly made it big: unacceptably so, in Edward Heath's famous denunciation.

124. Dunn, *Central African Witness*, 210. Thus an advert aimed at encouraging migrants from Britain published in the *Daily Express* on 21 June 1965 called for 'go-getters', quoted in Ritscherle, 'Opting Out of Utopia', 237.

125. Quoted in Kathleen Paul, *Whitewashing Britain: Race and Citizenship in the Postwar Era* (Ithaca, NY: Cornell UP, 1997), 31 and 59.

126. Caute, *Under the Skin*, 88; and Dunn, *Central African Witness*, 207.

127. Cited in Barber, *Rhodesia*, 291–2. Brigadier Dunlop had been born in India in 1907, attended Wellington College and Sandhurst, and migrated to Rhodesia after the war; he was close to many Tory MPs. As a junior member of the Rhodesian Front cabinet in 1965 he was present at the signing of UDI, but not himself a signatory. Frank Clements, Salisbury's mayor, 'a pleasant and liberal man', was also proud that 'There have been no race riots here, even in the sense that you have them in London. We haven't got any "Mods and Rockers" ', West, *White Tribes of Africa*, 70. And more generally, see Donal Lowry, 'The Impact of Anti-Communism on White Rhodesian Political Culture, c.1920s–1980', in Sue Onslow (ed.), *Cold War in Southern Africa: White Power, Black Liberation* (New York: Routledge, 2009).

128. Smith, *Great Betrayal*, 106, 227, 411, and 39.

129. Ian Smith broadcast, June 1964: quoted in Barber, *Rhodesia*, 255–6.

130. There was an early, direct connection between the politics of Rhodesia and the beginnings of student militancy. When it was announced in 1966 that the LSE was to appoint Walter Adams, from University College in Salisbury, as its new director, the students were appalled and a sit-in ensued, one of the first student occupations of the period. Crucial in mobilizing the student response was Basker Vashee, a native of Salisbury and once a student at University College under Adams.

131. See the full-page leader in the *Mirror*, 15 Nov. 1965. This had not prevented the *Mirror*, two days earlier, reporting that 'honey-blonde' Miss Rhodesia (22-year-old Lesley Bunting, originating from Bury) was determined to go

on with the Miss World competition at the Lyceum Ballroom despite the presence of demonstrations and counter-demonstrations—and this five years before the contest became the focus for feminist agitation. For the *Mirror's* radical past, A. C. H. Smith with Elizabeth Immirzi and Trevor Blackwell, *Paper Voices: The Popular Press and Social Change 1935–1965* (London: Chatto & Windus, 1975).

132. Hansard, House of Commons, 15 Nov. 1965, col. 782. Biggs-Davison was to play a prominent part in the Monday Club. In the Second World War he had served in the Indian civil service, during the transfer of power in 1947 with the Border Military Police, and in the founding years of Pakistan with the new nation's administrative service. In the upper chamber Lord Coleraine—Andrew Bonar Law's son, and himself a member of the Monday Club—expressed deep sympathy for Ian Smith, unperturbed by the legalities. His father, after all, had pursued a similar course in Ulster a generation earlier: Lowry, 'Ulster Resistance and Loyalist Rebellion', 204.

133. See Sue Onslow, 'The Conservative Party and Rhodesian UDI', in Kandiah, *Rhodesian UDI*.

134. See Philip Norton (ed.), *Dissension in the House of Commons: Intra-Party Dissent in the House of Commons Division Lobbies, 1945–74* (London: Macmillan, 1975), 256.

135. In his letter of resignation to Mrs Thatcher, Winston Churchill explained: 'While a British Government is leading the pack in holding down the people of Rhodesia so that surrogates of the Soviets may more steadfastly slit their throats—unquestionably the most ignominious act of any British Government this century—I cannot in all honesty pretend that I do not know which way to vote.' Cited in Caute, *Under the Skin*, 292.

136. On the tactic of exploiting Trafalgar Square, Robert Copping, *The Story of the Monday Club: The First Decade* (n.pl.: Current Affairs Information Service, 1972), 11.

137. Some of Worsthorne's more extreme prejudices have softened over the years, but for most of his professional life as a journalist he was, somewhat like Powell, supremely conscious of the finality of empire, but could never quite let go. In this his identifications with Rhodesia played a large part. Even as late as 1977, when Smith was engaged in a catastrophic war, Worsthorne accompanied a Rhodesian unit on a mission. 'What can one do but take their side? As they chug off in the petrol boat after dinner I shout "good luck." It is impossible under such circumstances not to feel the pulls of kith and kinship.' Quoted by Caute, *Under the Skin*, 169.

138. Ritscherle, 'Opting Out of Utopia', 270, quoting from the *Birmingham Post*, 31 Dec. 1965.

139. Ritscherle, 'Opting Out of Utopia', 275, from *Panorama*, BBC 15 Nov. 1965.

140. Interview with the author, 28 Oct. 1986. Membership statistics appear to be approximate, and Gunnery had no figures to hand.

141. It is not· at all clear what these tenets comprised, other than a distrust of Macmillan. Cedric Gunnery, for one, was not knowledgeable about the history of Conservatism, and I suspect that much was improvised.

142. Interview with Gunnery; and Copping, *The Story of the Monday Club*. Copping's business ventures included the introduction of saunas to Britain.

143. See Monday Club, *Wind of Change or Whirlwind?* (London: Monday Club, n.d. [1962?]); and Monday Club, *Bury the Hatchet* (London: Monday Club, 1962).

144. In Oct. 2001 Iain Duncan Smith severed the official links between the party and the Monday Club, due to its policy on race and immigration.

145. Philip Murphy, *Party Politics and Decolonization: The Conservative Party and British Colonial Policy in Tropical Africa, 1951–1964* (Oxford: Clarendon Press, 1995), 207 and 204.

146. Patrick Seyd, 'Factionalism within the Conservative Party: The Monday Club', *Government and Opposition*, 7/4 (1972), 469–85; on Home, interview with Gunnery; and see John Biggs-Davison, 'The Current Situation in Portuguese Guinea', *African Affairs*, 70/4 (1971), where he extolled Portugal as a model colonizer.

147. John Biggs-Davison, *Facing the Facts on Rhodesia* (London: Monday Club, n.d.); and Monday Club, *Rhodesia: A Minority View?* (London: Monday Club, 1966), 7. The latter comprised the speeches delivered at the Central Hall, London, on 3 Feb. 1966, including those by Salisbury, Julian Amery, Patrick Wall, and Biggs-Davison—and where a member of the audience urged Amery to 'Speak for England, like your father did, Mr Amery' (ibid. 7). Throughout the meeting it was emphasized that the Monday Club was not right-wing, or fascist, but merely a movement of the British people, won by the values of traditional Conservatism. Employing his own 17th-cent. allusion Amery had earlier referred to the 'Cromwellian' virtues of Rhodesians: Hansard, House of Commons, 15 Nov. 1965, col. 716.

148. Copping, *Story of the Monday Club*, 22.

149. Cited in Murphy, *Party Politics and Decolonization*, 30.

150. Quoted by Caute, *Under the Skin*, 90. Soref had been a delegate to the first All-British Africa conference in Bulawayo in 1937.

151. Harold Soref and Ian Grieg, *The Puppeteers: An Examination of Those Organizations and Bodies Concerned with the Elimination of the White Man in Africa* (London: Tandem Books, 1965); and see John Biggs-Davison, *The New Scramble for Africa* (London: Monday Club, 1966).

152. John Biggs-Davison, *The Centre Cannot Hold: Or, Mao, Marcuse and All That Marx* (London: Monday Club, 1969), 8 and 10. As an Oxford student Biggs-Davison had been a member of the Communist party. And see Patrick Wall, *Student Power* (London: Monday Club, 1968).

153. See Peter Griffiths, *A Question of Colour?* (London: Frewin, 1966).

154. 'Monday Club memorandum on immigration to the UK', unpublished typescript, undated (1965), London School of Economics Library, paras. 11 and 18; and Murphy, *Party Politics and Decolonization*, 225.

155. Copping, *Story of the Monday Club*, 17.
156. Interview with Gunnery.
157. Copping, *Story of the Monday Club*, 26.
158. Biggs-Davison, *Centre Cannot Hold*, 10.
159. Copping, *Story of the Monday Club*, 13.
160. George K. Young, *Who Goes Home?* (London: Monday Club, 1969).
161. Seyd, 'Factionalism within the Conservative Party', 471. Seyd calculated that national individual membership was between 1,600 and 2,500. Gunnery estimated a figure of about 2,000: interview with Gunnery.
162. On occasion the Club seemed not to worry over much about the expertise of its authors. The sole booklet on education was written by a road maintenance consultant: Seyd, 'Factionalism within the Conservative Party', 471–2 and 479–80. A full roster of the organization's publications, up until 1970, is listed by Seyd, ibid. 479.
163. Comdr. Anthony T. Courtney, OBE, RN, the managing director of New English Typewriting School, rehearses the usual litany of anxieties in his *The Enemies within* (London: Monday Club, 1974), detecting 'a common thread' binding subversion in schools to terror in Northern Ireland, and locating the source of these evils in Moscow (p. 5). The booklet carries a foreword by Jonathan Guinness, the Club's chairman.
164. Martin Walker, *The National Front* (London: Fontana, 1977), ch. 5, 'The Respectability of Racialism: the National Front and the Conservative Party', dates the infiltration from 1967.
165. Robert Copping, *The Monday Club: Crisis and After* (London: Monday Club, 1975). In May 1973 Scotland Yard was called in. John Biggs-Davison, Harold Soref, and Patrick Wall counter-attacked in defence of the elected chairman, Jonathan Guinness, and against those—supporting George K. Young, who had close ties to British intelligence—whom Copping called the 'political freaks', 8. A further bout of blood-letting occurred at the beginning of 1991, resulting in the resignations of, amongst others, Sir George Gardiner and Julian Amery: *Guardian*, 29 Jan. 1991. It is difficult to untangle the connections between the various factions of the Monday Club and the security services, though they certainly existed. For a post-imperial perspective on this larger issue, Philip Murphy, 'South African Intelligence, the Wilson Plot and Post-Imperial Trauma', in Patrick Major and Christopher R. Moran (eds.), *Spooked: Britain, Empire and Intelligence since 1945* (Newcastle: Cambridge Scholars Press, 2010).
166. Interview with Gunnery.
167. The beguiling observation comes from S. S. Prawer, commenting on Marx's reading of Eugène Sue: *Karl Marx and World Literature* (Oxford: Oxford UP, 1978), 98. In this context see David Cannadine's valuable investigations: *The Decline and Fall of the British Aristocracy* (London: Yale UP, 1990); and *Aspects of Aristocracy: Grandeur and Decline in Modern Britain* (London: Penguin, 1995).

168. Cited in Philip Murphy, *Lennox-Boyd: A Biography* (London: I. B. Tauris, 1999), p. viii.
169. Ibid., 13–14 and 22.
170. Ibid., 13, 17, and 57.
171. Ibid. 210.
172. Cited ibid. 162.
173. Cited ibid. 207.
174. Ibid. 89–90, and cited 249.
175. Ibid., 106–7.
176. Murphy, *Party Politics and Decolonization*, 225.
177. These arguments need more elaboration. I have in mind the studies of Ross McKibbin, for the preceding period: *The Ideologies of Class: Social Relations in Britain, 1880–1950* (Oxford: Clarendon Press, 1990); and *Classes and Cultures: England, 1918–1951* (Oxford: Oxford UP, 2000).
178. See ch. 4.
179. Where to go? The answer, for a time at least was Iceland. And Thailand and Japan. For a short period at the beginning of the new century, long after Rhodesia had disappeared, each accommodated a Rhodesian embassy. Google Rhodesia and up would come a bilingual paean to the old nation—God's own country, as it was known—in English and Icelandic. What could be more telling about the mobility of racial memories?

Index